Fred K

D1095422

THE MODERN LIBRARY
OF THE WORLD'S BEST BOOKS

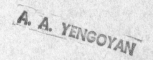

THE MAKING OF SOCIETY

The publishers will be pleased to send, upon request, an illustrated folder setting forth the purpose and scope of THE MODERN LIBRARY, *and listing each volume in the series. Every reader of books will find titles he has been looking for, handsomely printed, in unabridged editions, and at an unusually low price.*

THE MAKING OF SOCIETY

THE MAKING
OF SOCIETY

An Outline of Sociology

Edited by V. F. CALVERTON

THE
MODERN LIBRARY
NEW YORK

Random House IS THE PUBLISHER OF

THE MODERN LIBRARY

BENNETT A. CERF · DONALD S. KLOPFER · ROBERT K. HAAS

Manufactured in the United States of America

Printed by Parkway Printing Company   Bound by H. Wolff

To

HARRY ELMER BARNES

WHO HAS DONE SO MUCH TO SYNTHESIZE SOCIAL
THOUGHT AND HELP MAKE SOCIOLOGY A SCIENCE.

PREFACE

INNUMERABLE anthologies of social thought have been published within the last decade, but none of them, so far as I have discovered, has attempted to include the social thought of our day within its scope. The vast majority of them have been concerned only with the social thought of the past, as if the social thought of the present were something to be eschewed, or something that did not exist. That weakness, to be sure, is not confined only to anthologies of sociology. It is a weakness peculiar to American sociology in general, which has been in a conspiracy against contemporaneity.

At a time when the crucial sociological issues in the modern world are revolving about the conflicting philosophies of liberalism, fascism, socialism and communism, American sociologists, with but few exceptions, dodge such issues on principle. No doubt that tendency can be traced to the fact that such issues have not become dominant on the American scene. But sociology as a science should not be concerned solely with America. As a science it should be concerned with society as a whole; its scope should be international, not national; its interests should be universal, not local.

American sociology, I am convinced, should be concerned primarily, in these parlous years, with what forms such social philosophies will take in this country when conditions similar to those in Europe overtake us, as in all likelihood they eventually will. Without such concern, American sociology cannot orient itself as a science and cannot function as a progressive technique. Few people today are so brash as to make a defense of "the art for art's sake" conception of esthetics; yet such a defense, with all its weaknesses and lack of cogency, has far more tenability and plausibility than a defense of "sociology for sociology's sake," which is a contradiction in itself.

Sociology can have meaning only insofar as it leads us to understand societal phenomena and provides us with ways and means of controlling them. With that objective in mind, I have tried so far as possible to choose articles, essays and excerpts for this book which best serve that purpose. Without doing an injustice to the sociological work of the past, I have intentionally devoted a disproportionately large section of the volume to contemporary sociology, and to those writers whose work has most bearing upon contemporary sociology, because it is with the social thought of today that we should be most concerned if sociology is to serve as a science of prediction and control as well as one of analysis.

Since sociology is so elastic a science, it is difficult to determine just where its boundaries begin and end. Where sociology becomes social psychology and where social psychology becomes sociology, or where economic theory becomes sociological doctrine, or biological doctrine becomes sociological theory, is something which is impossible to decide. The confusion results from the fact that all four sciences converge so markedly in their generalizations, however much they differ in their specificities, that any attempt to narrow them down to their immediate confines is but to destroy their social value. Ultimately, the only way out of the dilemma is to make sociology into the kind of science which Comte, its founder, envisioned it as being, namely, a synthesis of all the other sciences, in which all the contributions of all the other sciences, or at least of all the life-sciences, are combined in a new amalgam, to make a super-science, *a science of the sciences,* as it were, in which the whole is more than the sum of its parts.

Society, like the human organism, can be studied only as a whole and not in terms of its parts, for its parts have no meaning except in relationship to the whole. What is needed in sociology is a corrective such as the Gestalt method introduced into psychology. Sociology needs to develop the concept of the configuration, and, hazardous though it is, in our present state of scientific ignorance and confusion, to leap from one science to another and argue by analogy, I shall go even further and contend, exploiting the nomenclature of the Gestaltists, that in the study of society more than in the study of the individual it is important that we focus our attention upon the *total process* in an attempt to come to grips with what is the *dynamics* of the social situation rather than with what is merely an angle or an aspect of it. Just as the human body reveals an order, a structure and a functional topography, which condition the nature of its responses and determine the character of its reaction, so likewise we can observe in society a structural arc, an interactive dynamic, a compulsive pattern of behavior, which make for order, no matter what kind of society is regnant.

During periods of economic crisis and revolutionary turbulence, that social affinity of impulse, finding expression in the fantastic marriage of opposites of which society for ages has been constituted, breaks down, collapses, crumbles and, like the human body at the point of disintegration and decay, surrenders itself to a chaos in which all that held it together before—its structural tensions, its cohesive compulsions, its cultural imperatives—disappear in the fire and smoke of strife. But once the strife is over, no matter what kind of social order arises from the ashes of the struggle, the human-all-too-human compulsion to cohesion returns, just as a body once sick acquires the rhythm of health after convalescence has begun.

In Europe today, we are witnessing various aspects of that process. It is almost as if Europe had offered itself as a vast social laboratory in which the sociologist can test out his hypotheses and discover the principles and laws underlying social phenomena. In Spain, as this preface is being written, the breakdown has already occurred, and the strife begun. In France the conflicts indicative of decay have already begun, although the strife is still a matter of the future. In England the decay has set in, although the cohesive compulsions are still in the ascendant. In Soviet Russia the cohesive compulsions are dominant, as they also are in the Fascist regimes of Germany and Italy, where the decay which preceded has been superseded by the regimented disciplines and social cohesives of totalitarian states. In Poland and all through Central Europe and the Balkan areas cohesion and chaos are at a stalemate; in some territories breakdown has already occurred, in others it is imminent, and in still others it is a matter of the more distant future. In the Scandivanian countries, where the contradictions in capitalist economics have resulted in less disastrous consequences, the cohesive forces remain relatively unchallenged and unthreatened.

It is because in these days the disequilibrium created by the conflicting forces leading to cohesion and chaos are predominantly economic, I have devoted a considerable portion of this anthology to considerations in that realm of what is to be done to control those forces, if we are not eventually to be plunged into a similar situation, in which the choices will be not between two possibilities, one good and one evil, but between two evils, one little better than the other.

At this point, I wish to express my gratitude to various persons who have helped me in the way of suggestions and advice in editing this volume. My greatest thanks are to Max Nomad and Harry Elmer Barnes, whose suggestions and aid have proved unfailingly fruitful.

As in the case of a previous anthology I edited, *The Making of Man,* I want to warn the reader against the danger of viewing my Introduction as representative of the spirit of the volume as a whole. I have expressed in the Introduction a point of view that is specifically my own and which should be considered as such, and not construed as representing that of the other contributors to the book.

Special note should also be made of the fact that this is the first book in which the work of Vico appears in English. Thanks to the aid of Dr. Elio Gianturco, who has just translated Vico's *Scienza Nuova,* one of the most original and memorable of modern sociological studies, it has been possible to include in this volume selected passages from Vico which are best representative of his work.

It should also be added that the selection from Proudhon was translated from the French by S. L. Solon, and the selections from Machajski were translated from Polish by Max Nomad.

V.F.C.

construed as representing that of the other contributors to the book.

Special note should also be made of the fact that this is the first book in which the work of Vico appears in English. Thanks to the aid of Dr. Elio Gianturco, who has just translated Vico's *Scienza Nuova*, one of the most original and memorable of modern sociological studies, it has been possible to include in this volume selected passages from Vico which are best representative of his work. It should also be added that the selection from Proudhon was translated from the French by S. L. Solon, and the selections from Machiajski were translated from Polish by Max Nomad.

V.F.C.

PAGE

Of the Natural Con-
dition of Mankind . *Thomas Hobbes* 114
Selections from *The
Social Contract* . . *Jean Jacques Rousseau* 149
Of Monarchy and
Hereditary Succes-
sion . . . . *Thomas Paine* 168
Of Laws in Relation
to the Nature of the
Climate . . . . *Baron de Montesquieu* 178
Division of Labor . *Adam Smith* 194

V. SOCIOLOGY COMES OF AGE

An Essay on the
Principle of Popula-
tion . . . . *T. R. Malthus* 221
The Authority of So-
ciety Over the Indi-
vidual . . . . *John Stuart Mill* 237
The Action of Posi-
tivism upon the
Working Classes . *Auguste Comte* 259
Political Economy
and Utopian Social-
ism . . . . *Pierre-Joseph Proudhon* 274
Selections from *The
State* . . . . *Michael Bakunin* 281
Natural Selection; or
the Survival of the
Fittest . . . . *Charles Darwin* 284
Influence of Physical
Laws . . . . *Henry Thomas Buckle* 307
The Communist
Manifesto . . . *Karl Marx and Friederich
Engels* 339

VI. SOCIOLOGY AND SOCIAL CONFLICT

Division of Labor
and Social Solidar-
ity . . . . . *Emile Durkheim* 381

CONTENTS

		PAGE
PREFACE		vii
INTRODUCTION. The American Pattern .	V. F. Calverton	1

I. RELIGIOUS AND ETHICAL CONTRIBUTIONS

The Ten Commandments . . .		15
The Sermon on the Mount . . .		17
The Code of Hammurabi . . .		25
Selections from the Koran		27
On Government . .	Confucius	33
On Co-operation . .	Lao Tse	38

II. GREEK THEORIES

| Philosophers as Kings and Kings as Philosophers . . . . | Plato | 41 |
| On Property . . . | Aristotle | 47 |

III. MEDIEVAL CONCEPTIONS

| On the Law of Heaven and Earth . | St. Augustine | 63 |

IV. THE ADVANCE OF MODERN SOCIOLOGICAL THOUGHT

Selections from Scienza Nuova . .	Giambattista Vico	73
The Art of War .	Niccolo Machiavelli	94
Selections from Two Treatises on Civil Government . . .	John Locke	100

Selections from *The Outline of Sociology* . . . . . Ludwig Gumplowicz 386

The Tendency of the Development of the State . . . . . Franz Oppenheimer 395

Class Society and the State . . . . . Nicolai Lenin 404

What Is the Permanent Revolution? . Leon Trotsky 421

On the Expropriation of the Capitalists . . Waclaw Machajaski 427

The Collectivist Wages System . . . Peter Kropotkin 437

Personality and the Conception of the State . . . . . Adolph Hitler 454

The Fascist State and the Future . . Benito Mussolini 458

VII. SOCIOLOGY AND CULTURE

The Sociological View of Ethics . . Herbert Spencer 489

The Spirit of Capitalism . . . . . Max Weber 506

Proletariat and Religion and Nationalism . . . . . Werner Sombart 532

Sociology as a Science . . . . . Vilfredo Pareto 538

Intellectual Egalitarianism . . . . . Lester Ward 546

Selections from *Folkways* . . . . . William Graham Sumner 568

Conspicuous Consumption . . . . . Thorsten Veblen 584

The Scientific Scrutiny of Societal Facts F. H. Giddings 610

The Economics of Genius . . . . . J. M. Robertson 624

PAGE

VIII. Contemporary Sociological Reflections

    Liberal

      The Development of Sociology . . . . *Harry Elmer Barnes*   661

      Classes of Social Interest . . . . *R. M. MacIver*   681

      The Cultural Approach to Sociology *Malcom M. Willey and Melville S. Herskovits*   692

      The Mitigation of Class Struggle . . *Edward A. Ross*   702

      The Hypothesis of Cultural Lag . . *William Fielding Ogburn*   719

      Art, Science, and Sociology . . . . *C. H. Cooley*   725

      Mental Patterns in Relation to Culture . *Wilson D. Wallis*   730

      Renascent Liberalism *John Dewey*   735

      Law as a Social Science . . . . *Huntington Cairns*   748

      The Idol of the Laboratory . . *Graham Wallas*   764

      Anglo-Saxonism and Nordicism in America . . . . *F. H. Hankins*   775

    Radical

      A Planned Society— Communist Version . *John Strachey*   785

      Technocracy . . . *Stuart Chase*   807

      Marxian Philosophy *Max Eastman*   833

      The Scope of Marxian Theory . . . *Sidney Hook*   851

      Sociological Criticism of Literature . . . *V. F. Calverton*   861

      Masters — Old and New . . . . *Max Nomad*   882

      The Applications of Engineering Methods to Finance . . . *C. H. Douglas*   894

Biographies 905

only philosophic thought which has ever made any head
talism of John De...

seems to lack that total view which is necessary for the development ... ... in Edison and
Americans are more ... ... doing than thinking

INTRODUCTION

THE AMERICAN PATTERN

By V. F. CALVERTON

THE UNITED STATES is the least creative and yet the most
inventive of modern countries. No nation has been so barren of scientific originality or theoretical insight and yet at
the same time so productive of inventive genius, engineering
efficiency, and mechanical skill.

And therein lies part of the essential contradiction which
besets us as a nation. We are a practical but not a theoretical
people. We like to press buttons, shift gears, release brakes
whirr dynamos, and are most interested in observing and
utilizing what the buttons, gears, brakes, and dynamos do,
*but are very little interested in the why and wherefore of
what they do.* We are content to accept things for what they
are without worrying ourselves about why they are that way
or how they got that way.

American scientists and philosophers are just as guilty of
that form of intellectual indolence as is the American populace. Nothing illustrates that better than the nature of
American scientific and philosophic thought. Our scientists
are first rate technicians, experts of a high order, who are
internationally respected for their experimental genius, but
little more. With the exception of an occasional Michelson,
or Burbank, they have been very little interested in, and
have contributed very little to, scientific theory. A record of
the great scientists of the last fifty years who have been distinguished for their revolutionary contributions to scientific
theory would include but few Americans in it.

In philosophy our poverty is even more conspicuous. The

only philosophic thought which has ever made any head-way in this country has been the canny, opportunistic prag-matism of William James and the commonsense instrumen-talism of John Dewey.

The American mind, with its *enterpreneur* perspective, seems to lack that *total view* which is necessary for the de-velopment of theory. We are content with an Edison and feel no need for an Einstein. Still intellectual frontiersmen, Americans are more concerned with doing than thinking, and with thinking only in terms of doing.

Nowhere is this more apparent than in our work in the social sciences, especially economics and sociology, where we have written more and contributed less in the form of theory than almost any European country. We have excellent syn-thesizers but poor theorizers. The science of criminology will illustrate precisely what I mean. We have published thousands of books on crime and various aspects of crimin-ality but have yet to develop one theorist in the field who has advanced a single hypothesis about the nature of crime or its control which has commanded national or interna-tional attention. We do develop special reformatories, insti-tutions, asylums, and what not, which attempt to deal with crime as a practical problem. We even gave birth to the Elmira system of reform. But that is where we stop. The best we have produced in the field is a man like Maurice Parme-lee who wrote one of the soundest books on the subject pub-lished in this country; but what kind of book was it? In a word, a synthesis, a most intelligent and satisfactory synthe-sis, but a synthesis nonetheless, of the works of the various European criminologists. Italy has given us a Beccaria, a Lombroso, a Garofalo, a Ferri; Holland has given us a Bonger; Spain has given us a De Quiros; France has given us a Tarde; Austria has given us a Gross. But America has produced no one to match them, no one even to compare with them.

Our criminologists are concerned with ways and means of dealing with crime, with reform measures, therapeutic devices, schemes of detecting and suppressing it, but not with the underlying causes which create and condition it.

The same holds true of all our work in the social sciences. The only persons we have produced of any theoretic originality or profundity in those fields are Thorstein Veblen and Lester F. Ward. Of course men like John Dewey and George Mead deserve mention, but only in a secondary sense; after all, their contributions to sociological thought have been more critical than creative. Which doesn't mean that we have not produced men of high calibre in most if not all the social sciences, but simply that they were not, and still are not, men interested in theory. Their interest is in the parts, not the whole. Their studies have been confined in the main to aspects of society but not to society as a total entity. The search for laws underlying social phenomena and the development of society, such as absorbed the energies and gripped the imaginations of Vico, Montesquieu, Helvetius, Condorcet, Buckle, Marx, Darwin, Spencer, Gumplowicz, Freud, Oppenheimer, Spengler, Pareto, and a score of lesser minds, has seldom arrested the interest of American sociologists. The same is true in large part of American anthropologists, who have been exceedingly adept in puncturing the theories of others but not in creating any of their own.

And yet without theory, as the most elementary scientist is aware, we can get nowhere. Theory without fact is worthless; but fact without theory is even more worthless. How deep-rooted that anti-theoretic tendency is can be seen in the history of American radical thought, where one might expect a more ambitious and adventurous approach. Most American radicals, like most European radicals, have adopted Marxism as their credo, and Marxism, as is well-known, is a highly theoretical system of thought. But what have American radicals done with the Marxism they have adopted? Have they added to Marxian theory? Not at all. Whereas in Europe Marxism as a theory has been expanded and extended, and has produced such outstanding theorists as Lenin, Trotsky, Plechanov, LaSalle, Kautsky, Dietzgen,

Hilferding, Grossman, Bonger, Bukharin, and many others; in America it has given birth to no one of comparable significance.

American Marxists in general tend to use Marxism as a substitute instead of an inspiration for thought. In too many cases, they have adopted Marxism for subjective instead of objective reasons. Their allegiance, consequently, has been a liability rather than an asset. And Marxism, in this country, as a result, has proved to be unfecund of originality or vision.

The great desideratum from which American sociology has always suffered has not only been its indifference to theory, but its indifference to theory in terms of the American social fact. One of the most important sociological problems of our day is to understand America, the American mind, American society, the American people. There is no greater need than for a sound sociological analysis of the factors and forces which have produced what, for lack of a better phrase, we must call the *American pattern*. In Europe, despite the differences between countries, the sociological pattern is reasonably similar and obvious. In the United States, on the other hand, the pattern is not only dissimilar but to date is scarcely discernible. In democratic countries such as France and England as well as in fascist countries such as Germany and Italy, the sociological pattern is more or less formed, crystallized. In the United States the pattern is still amorphous. What will happen here is not only difficult to determine, but, at the present time at least, unpredictable.

It should be obvious that sociological theory takes on character in terms of the environment out of which it is born. Marxism, for example, evolved in the mind of Marx, as well as in the minds of his followers, out of the throes of European society. It was a product of the European fact, of European economic conditions, and as such functioned as a dynamic social force. In the United States, on the contrary, Marxism has never made any headway for three reasons: first, because its general proposition of the class struggle and the increasing misery of the proletariat do not apply in the sense that they do in Europe; secondly, because the meta-physical nature of its dialectic, with its pyramidal triads, are alien to the empiricistic, pragmatic, matter-of-fact type of American mind; and thirdly, because what Marxians we have had, with but a scant handful of exceptions, have been either unable to, or uninterested in, *Americanizing* the Marxian approach.

Although within the last five years many American intel-lectuals in and out of the universities have become Marxians, they have done little to reconcile Marxian propositions with American facts. The result has been that Marxism has con-tributed little to American sociology. In general it has been a tangential, peripheral influence rather than a central one. In Germany, prior to the triumph of Hitler, in France to-day, and in the majority of the central European countries, and most actively of all in Spain, and, of course, in the So-viet Union, where it is the dominant philosophy of the state, Marxism has been the spearhead of social theory and con-flict. Only in England and the United States has Marxism failed to progress in theory as well as in practice. In Eng-land, to be sure, Marxism has made much greater advance than in the United States, because the English situation is a closer approximation to the European than is the American. In neither country, however, will it make marked advance until its exponents learn to adapt its propositions to the specific conditions of the environments in question and to the specific psychologies which have been produced by those respective environments.

It is very doubtful whether Marxism will ever be able to make much progress in the United States unless it disembar-rasses itself of its metaphysical trappings, with its Hegelian absolutes, however inverted, and adjusts itself in simple, forthright terms to the type of mind constitutionally charac-teristic of this country as a whole.

The American mind, born of the frontier, of the pioneer-ing spirit of multiplying generations and centuries, of a country disparate from every other, is a different mind from the European. It is not different in the sense that it functions differently, or adopts different postulates or categories; it is different only in the sense that it has worked with different materials, has been shaped by a different environment, and has been driven to different illations because of the different social forces which have conditioned it. The difference, to be sure, is functional and not organic. It has to do mainly with difference of stimuli, not difference of response. But that difference in stimuli has produced a difference in response, which, for the time being at least, must be considered part of the American equation. It is with those differences that we must be concerned in trying to understand the American phenomenon, which means understanding the American mind.

The anti-theoretical nature of the American mind is not difficult to understand. It can be accounted for easily enough in terms of the necessity of the country; in its virginal and later its constructive phase, its energies were largely consumed in a struggle to find itself, to develop order out of chaos. And finally, at the very time when order began to evolve, it found itself plunged into another struggle, the struggle of the machine. To convert inert metals into moving mechanisms, to resolve stubborn resources into dynamic structures, absorbed its energies for another century and still continue to drain them. In Europe, that struggle for order was over at the time when America was bending all its strength to establish it, forge it out of the wilderness. In Europe that struggle, and all the memories of it, were already congealed in tradition. In America tradition had still to form. And what form it did assume was foreign, an extension of the traditions of European *milieus* instead of our own.

In one sense, America, compared with Europe, is a traditionless country. Our major traditions, as the history of our culture attests, have been derivative rather than original. For centuries we suffered from a colonial complex from which we began to achieve an escape only at the beginning of this century. No matter what doctrines, what theories, what standards, what manners, we adopted, they were inevitably imitative. They were taken over, spiritually wholesale, from the countries from which America derived. There was a time in our history, as every sociologist knows, when German traditions in part of the country at least, competed with English. Considerably before the end of the nineteenth century, however, the English tradition had won out, and the country was indubitably Anglicized, in language as well as in social philosophy.

The twentieth century marked our coming of age. Able to stand on our own legs, as it were, having changed from an agrarian into a predominantly industrial country, we began to develop, spiritually speaking, our native resources, and work out our own philosophy of life. The first expressions of that development were in cultural fields; in literature, painting, music, sculpture, architecture, and finally even in dancing. Already, within the span of a few decades, we have begun to evolve a tradition in those fields.

In economics and politics on the other hand, we have evolved nothing—at least nothing of any consequence. We are still, in those realms, a shapeless, haphazard nation. We have no moral standards, no political criteria, no spiritual shibboleths. The party which promises "a chicken in every pot" is the party that wins, whether it is headed by Andrew Jackson, Tippecanoe-Harrison, Cal Coolidge, Franklin D. Roosevelt. If the party before didn't produce the chicken, the other party might—in that way America, however crudely and stumblingly and wrong-headedly, gives life to logic. Politically and economically speaking it has no other logic.

Now what is behind that fact is a sociologic conclusion of great consequence. In a word, it is that this country, with all its limitations of spirit and dream, is the only country in the world which has given its populace, not all of it but a large part of it, a chance to think of itself as individuals, and to view whatever comes within its ken from an individualistic point of view. To turn to politics and economics, what is at once obvious is that it has produced the most amazing, bewildering, and contradictory set-up of interests which the world has ever seen. Of all countries, the United States is the only one which is philosophically, politically, and sociologically classless—notwithstanding the fact that economically it has its classes and its class categories, like every European country, demarcated by occupation as well as income. The difference, however, is more than paradoxical; it is profound. Despite the economic fact, the country is psychologically classless. When an election occurs, even the most recent, many of the *big guys,* multimillionaires, millionaires, and what not, often get behind a man whom they think they can mold into their own pattern, but once that man is defeated, as in the case of Landon, in 1936, they shift their position, like the wind in summer, and rally, as Rockefeller and Hearst have already done, to the support of the man who is elected. The same thing is true at the bottom of the economic scale, of the American working class, which shifts from one extreme to another, without any pivot about which to revolve.

The basis for such indetermination and indecision is fundamentally economic. There has been no need in the United States to date to formulate doctrine or platform which has a class bias, in the economic sense of the word. Millionaires in this country are eager to pass off as workers (take the declarations of Henry Ford and Charles Schwab that they are workers and nothing more), whereas workers are eager to pass off as potential millionaires. This, of course, has nothing to do with the fact that the millionaires never become workers or the workers never become millionaires.

These are simple facts, hard as stone and lucid as light, which are the necessary prerequisites to an understanding of the American problem, with all its sociological peculiarities and psychological contradictions. Radicals in this country have adopted the false assumption, and continue to do so today, that Americans are like Europeans, and can be allocated and divided in the same manner, and fitted into the same categories. But they can't. Reduced to a biological level, all peoples are the same. But in psychological terms they are not.

Psychologically, people are what their respective environments have made them and the American people are the strange amalgam they are, different from every other people, because their economic background and cultural heritage are different from those of Europe. That, of course, does not mean completely different, but sufficiently different to be significant.

With all peoples there are both resemblances and differences, and sociology must be concerned with the relatively greater importance of one or the other in the cultural complex. The English are different from the French, the French from the Germans, the Spaniards from the Italians, and yet their differences in respective cultural patterns are less significant, from a sociological point of view, than their resemblances. All European countries, which have advanced industrially, have developed economic similarities, class likenesses, and cultural affinities, which are greater than the differences which exist between them. The French workers, the German workers before Hitler's seizure of power, the Italian workers before Mussolini's victory, the Spanish workers of today, all developed a similarity of class outlook, of class philosophy. It was not always Marxism which dominated that class philosophy, but it was always a specifically working class philosophy, Syndicalist, Anarchist, Anarcho-syndicalist, or Marxist, which did. In short, the resemblances in working class philosophy in all European countries were far greater than the differences between them. The same is more or less true of the social outlooks and economic philosophies of the European middle classes, upper as well as lower, industrial as well as commercial, and the same has been equally true of European aristocracies wherever they have lingered on in the national scheme. There have been differences between them all, to be sure, owing to the differences in the particular developments of the respective countries, but the differences have been inconspicuous compared with the resemblances.

What are even more striking are the similarities in political and philosophic patterns that have developed in those countries which have gone Fascist in the last ten or fifteen years. In each of those countries the middle classes have adopted approximately the same stand and made the same allies and alliances. Face to face with a working class which threatens to seize and socialize its property, the middle classes in Europe tend to take the Fascist road as their best means of protection from such an eventuality.

In the United States, where, as I have tried to show, the pattern is different, no such development has occurred. That does not mean that it will never occur, but it does mean that until it does occur it cannot be considered part of the American pattern. The working class here has never given birth to a proletarian philosophy in the widespread sense that it has done in Europe; fragmentary sections of it have adopted at different times Marxian and Syndicalist points of view, but by far the larger sections of it have adhered in the main to a philosophy of populism (which is a philosophy of the lower middle class) rather than to one of proletarianism. At the same time, the vested interests in this country have never developed a consistent Tory philosophy. In a word, to date, we have no class philosophies in this country, which approximate or suggest resemblances to the European pattern. On the contrary, what we have is a situation in which underdogs and Tories vote on the same ticket, and middle-dogs and middle-middle dogs get together for reasons economically disadvantageous to both. In short, Americans, regardless of class, have not yet acquired a class perspective. They have no conception of the economic organization of society and depend more upon ethical ideas than economic facts for the determination of their decisions.

What we need in America today is an analysis of the whole composite of factors which constitute the American complex.

Either the United States is going to develop the same sociological pattern which Europe has, or it is not. If, in time, it is going to develop the same pattern, as I am inclined to believe it will, analysis is necessary to show just *how* and *when* such development will occur; if it is not, analysis is equally necessary to show what pattern will emerge and how it will differ from the European.

Either the United States is going to develop the same sociological pattern which Europe has, or it is not. If, in time, it is going to develop the same pattern, as I am inclined to believe it will, analysis is necessary to show just how and when such development will occur; that is to say, analysis is equally necessary to show what pattern will emerge and how it will differ from the European.

I

RELIGIOUS AND ETHICAL CONTRIBUTIONS

COMMENTARY

The history of social thought dates back to ancient times, and the selections made here record man's earliest struggles to give literate form to his social conceptions. Long before the Ten Commandments were written, however. and long before the ancient world emerges from the obscurity of primitive legend, man works out codes and mores which he lives by and without which human society can never evolve. But those codes and mores are never written down; they develop before man learns to write. Whatever we know about th...., ...rned from anthropologists who have studied primitive life in person, living with the natives to discover what semblances of law and morality exist among them. By the time man acquires the ability to write, however, his social intelligence is already developed to the point where he is able to frame his social concepts and moral ideals in forms which even to this day remain a testament to his advancing social vision. The fact that in practice he never realizes what he proclaims in theory, or in maxim, does not invalidate the more important fact that he has begun to develop an outlook on life which is becoming more and more impregnated with a sense of social responsibility and aspiration.

The Ten Commandments and the Sermon on the Mount are the best illustrations of the evolution of a social outlook among ancient peoples, as also, although in a more secondary sense, are the Koran and Hammurabi's Code. In the latter particularly we find the class aspects of ancient society stressed more conspicuously than in the other documents.

As we advance from religious lore to philosophic, especially as evinced in the case of Oriental contributions, we realize that their social idealism is in no sense backward compared to that of Asiatic nations.

13

On the part of all peoples in these days, there is the same struggling, stumbling effort to find some scheme by which man's urgency to become a social animal can be reconciled with his anti-social, individualistic tendencies which always play havoc with his social behavior. Although class differences determine in good part the respective values of the period, as evidenced in religion as well as in politics, there is always, in the case of the teachers and prophets at least, who are the intellectuals of their time, a classless point of view, an ethical ideal, which, however much it fails of its purpose, is more concerned with society than class, and which finds its aspiration, as do the majority of these selections, in a social outlook upon the destiny of the race.

THE TEN COMMANDMENTS

CHAPTER 20. Exodus

And God spake all these words, saying,

2 I *am* the LORD thy God, which have brought thee out of the land of Egypt, out of the house of bondage.

3 Thou shalt have no other gods before me.

4 Thou shalt not make unto thee any graven image, or any likeness *of any thing* that *is* in heaven above, or that *is* in the earth beneath, or that *is* in the water under the earth:

5 Thou shalt not bow down thyself to them, nor serve them: for I the LORD thy God *am* a jealous God, visiting the iniquity of the fathers upon the children unto the third and fourth *generation* of them that hate me;

6 And shewing mercy unto thousands of them that love me, and keep my commandments.

7 Thou shalt not take the name of the LORD thy God in vain; for the LORD will not hold him guiltless that taketh his name in vain.

8 Remember the sabbath day, to keep it holy.

9 Six days shalt thou labour, and do all thy work:

10 But the seventh day *is* the sabbath of the LORD thy God; *in it* thou shalt not do any work, thou nor thy son, nor thy daughter, thy manservant, nor thy maidservant, nor thy cattle, nor thy stranger that *is* within thy gates:

11 For *in* six days the LORD made heaven and earth, the sea, and all that in them *is,* and rested the seventh day: wherefore the LORD blessed the sabbath day, and hallowed it.

12 Honour thy father and thy mother; that thy days may be long upon the land which the LORD thy God giveth thee.

13 Thou shalt not kill.

14 Thou shalt not commit adultery.

15 Thou shalt not steal.

16 Thou shalt not bear false witness against thy neighbor.

17 Thou shalt not covet thy neighbour's house, thou shalt not covet thy neighbour's wife, nor his manservant, nor his maidservant, nor his ox, nor his ass, nor any thing that *is* thy neighbour's.

18 And all the people saw the thunderings, and the lightnings, and the noise of the trumpet, and the mountain smoking: and when the people saw *it,* they removed and stood far off.

19 And they said unto Moses, Speak thou with us, and we will hear: but let not God speak with us, lest we die.

THE SERMON ON THE MOUNT

THE SERMON ON THE MOUNT

And seeing the multitudes, he went up into a mountain: and when he was set, his disciples came unto him:

And he opened his mouth, and taught them, saying,

Blessed are the poor in spirit: for their's is the kingdom of heaven.

Blessed are they that mourn: for they shall be comforted.

Blessed are the meek: for they shall inherit the earth.

Blessed are they which do hunger and thirst after righteousness: for they shall be filled.

Blessed are the merciful: for they shall obtain mercy.

Blessed are the pure in heart: for they shall see God.

Blessed are the peacemakers: for they shall be called the children of God.

Blessed are they which are persecuted for righteousness' sake: for their's is the kingdom of heaven.

Blessed are ye, when men shall revile you, and persecute you, and shall say all manner of evil against you falsely, for my sake.

Rejoice, and be exceeding glad: for great is your reward in heaven: for so persecuted they the prophets which were before you.

Ye are the salt of the earth: but if the salt have lost his savour, wherewith shall it be salted? It is thenceforth good for nothing, but to be cast out, and to be trodden under foot of men.

Ye are the light of the world. A city that is set on an hill cannot be hid.

Neither do men light a candle, and put it under a bushel, but on a candlestick; and it giveth light unto all that are in the house.

Let your light so shine before men, that they may see your good works, and glorify your Father which is in heaven.

Think not that I am come to destroy the law, or the prophets: I am not come to destroy, but to fulfil.

For verily I say unto you, Till heaven and earth pass, one jot or one tittle shall in no wise pass from the law, till all be fulfilled.

Whosoever therefore shall break one of these least commandments, and shall teach men so, he shall be called the least in the kingdom of heaven: but whosoever shall do and teach them, the same shall be called great in the kingdom of heaven.

For I say unto you, That except your righteousness shall exceed the righteousness of the scribes and the Pharisees, ye shall in no case enter into the kingdom of heaven.

Ye have heard that it was said by them of old time, Thou shalt not kill: and whosoever shall kill shall be in danger of the judgment:

But I say unto you, That whosoever is angry with his brother without a cause, shall be in danger of the judgment: and whosoever shall say to his brother, Raca, shall be in danger of the council: but whosoever shall say, Thou fool, shall be in danger of hell fire.

Therefore, if thou bring thy gift to the altar, and there rememberest that thy brother hath aught against thee,

Leave there thy gift before the altar, and go thy way; first be reconciled to thy brother, and then come and offer thy gift.

Agree with thine adversary quickly, whiles thou art in the way with him; lest at any time the adversary deliver thee to the judge, and the judge deliver thee to the officer, and thou be cast into prison.

Verily I say unto thee, Thou shalt by no means come out thence, till thou hast paid the uttermost farthing.

Ye have heard that it was said by them of old time, Thou shalt not commit adultery:

But I say unto you, That whosoever looketh on a woman to lust after her, hath committed adultery with her already in his heart.

And if thy right eye offend thee, pluck it out, and cast it from thee: for it is profitable for thee that one of thy members should perish, and not that thy whole body should be cast into hell.

And if thy right hand offend thee, cut it off, and cast it from thee: for it is profitable for thee that one of thy members should perish, and not that thy whole body should be cast into hell.

It hath been said, Whosoever shall put away his wife, let him give her a writing of divorcement:

But I say unto you, That whosoever shall put away his wife, saving for the cause of fornication, causeth her to commit adultery: and whosoever shall marry her that is divorced, committeth adultery.

Again, ye have heard that it hath been said by them of old time, Thou shalt not forswear thyself, but shalt perform unto the LORD thine oaths:

But I say unto you, Swear not at all: neither by heaven; for it is God's throne:

Nor by the earth; for it is his footstool: neither by Je-ru-sa-lem; for it is the city of the great King.

Neither shalt thou swear by thy head, because thou canst not make one hair white or black.

But let your communication be, Yea, yea; Nay, nay: for whatsoever is more than these, cometh of evil.

Ye have heard that it hath been said, An eye for an eye, and a tooth for a tooth:

But I say unto you, That ye resist not evil: but whosoever shall smite thee on thy right cheek, turn to him the other also.

And if any man will sue thee at the law, and take away thy coat, let him have thy cloke also.

And whosoever shall compel thee to go a mile, go with him twain.

Give to him that asketh thee, and from him that would borrow of thee turn not thou away.

Ye have heard that it hath been said, Thou shalt love thy neighbour, and hate thine enemy:

But I say unto you, Love your enemies, bless them that curse you, do good to them that hate you, and pray for them which despitefully use you, and persecute you:

That ye may be the children of your Father which is in heaven: for he maketh his sun to rise on the evil and on the good, and sendeth rain on the just and on the unjust.

For if ye love them which loved you, what reward have ye? do not even the publicans the same?

And if ye salute your brethren only, what do ye more than others? do not even the publicans so?

Be ye therefore perfect, even as your Father which is in heaven is perfect.

Take heed that ye do not your alms before men, to be seen of them: otherwise ye have no reward of your Father which is in heaven.

Therefore when thou doest thine alms, do not sound a trumpet, before thee, as the hypocrites do in the synagogues and in the streets, that they may have the glory of men. Verily I say unto you, They have their reward.

But when thou doest alms, let not thy left hand know what thy right hand doeth:

That thine alms may be in secret: and thy Father, which seeth in secret, himself shall reward thee openly.

And when thou prayest, thou shalt not be as the hypocrites are: for they love to pray standing in the synagogues and in the corners of the streets, that they may be seen of men. Verily I say unto you, They have their reward.

But thou, when thou prayest, enter into thy closet, and when thou hast shut thy door, pray to thy Father which is in secret; and thy Father, which seeth in secret, shall reward thee openly.

But when ye pray, use not vain repetitions, as the heathen do: for they think that they shall be heard for their much speaking.

Be not ye therefore like unto them: for your Father knoweth what things ye have need of before ye ask him.

After this manner therefore pray ye: Our Father which art in heaven, Hallowed be thy name:

Thy kingdom come. Thy will be done in earth, as it is in heaven.

Give us this day our daily bread:

And forgive us our debts, as we forgive our debtors.

And lead us not into temptation, but deliver us from evil: For thine is the kingdom, and the power, and the glory, for ever. Amen.

For if ye forgive men their trespasses, your heavenly Father will also forgive you.

But if ye forgive not men their trespasses, neither will your Father forgive your trespasses.

Moreover, when ye fast, be not, as the hypocrites, of a sad countenance; for they disfigure their faces, that they may appear unto men to fast. Verily I say unto you, They have their reward.

But thou, when thou fastest, anoint thine head, and wash thy face;

That thou appear not unto men to fast, but unto thy Father which is in secret: and thy Father, which seeth in secret, shall reward thee openly.

Lay not up for yourselves treasures upon earth, where moth and rust doth corrupt, and where thieves break through and steal:

But lay up for yourselves treasures in heaven, where neither moth nor rust doth corrupt, and where thieves do not break through nor steal:

For where your treasure is, there will your heart be also.

The light of the body is the eye: if therefore thine eye be single, thy whole body shall be full of light:

But if thine eye be evil, thy whole body shall be full of darkness. If therefore the light that is in thee be darkness, how great is that darkness!

No man can serve two masters: for either he will hate the one, and love the other; or else he will hold to the one, and despise the other. Ye cannot serve God and mammon.

Therefore I say unto you, Take no thought for your life, what ye shall eat, or what ye shall drink; nor yet for your body, what ye shall put on. Is not the life more than meat, and the body than raiment?

Behold the fowls of the air; for they sow not, neither do they reap, nor gather into barns; yet your heavenly Father feedeth them. Are ye not much better than they?

Which of you by taking thought can add one cubit unto his stature?

And why take ye thought for raiment? Consider the lilies of the field, how they grow; they toil not, neither do they spin: And yet I say unto you, That even Sol-o-mon in all his glory was not arrayed like one of these.

Wherefore, if God so clothe the grass of the field, which to day is, and to morrow is cast into the oven, shall he not much more clothe you, O ye of little faith?

Therefore take no thought, saying, What shall we eat? or, What shall we drink? or, Wherewithal shall we be clothed?

(For after all these things do the Gentiles seek:) for your heavenly Father knoweth that ye have need of all these things.

But seek ye first the kingdom of God, and his righteousness; and all these things shall be added unto you.

Take therefore no thought for the morrow: for the morrow shall take thought for the things of itself. Sufficient unto the day is the evil thereof.

Judge not, that ye be not judged.

For with what judgment ye judge, ye shall be judged: and with what measure ye mete, it shall be measured to you again.

And why beholdest thou the mote that is in thy brother's eye, but considerest not the beam that is in thine own eye? Or how wilt thou say to thy brother, Let me pull out the mote out of thine eye; and behold, a beam is in thine own eye?

Thou hypocrite, first cast out the beam out of thine own eye; and then shalt thou see clearly to cast out the mote out of thy brother's eye.

Give not that which is holy unto the dogs, neither cast ye your pearls before swine, lest they trample them under their feet, and turn again and rend you.

Ask, and it shall be given you; seek, and ye shall find; knock, and it shall be opened unto you:

For every one that asketh receiveth; and he that seeketh findeth; and to him that knocketh it shall be opened.

Or what man is there of you, whom if his son ask bread, will he give him a stone?

Or if he ask a fish, will he give him a serpent?

If ye then, being evil, know how to give good gifts unto your children, how much more shall your Father which is in heaven give good things to them that ask him?

Therefore all things whatsoever ye would that men should do to you, do ye even so to them: for this is the law and the prophets.

Enter ye in at the strait gate: for wide is the gate, and broad is the way that leadeth to destruction, and many there be which go in thereat:

Because strait is the gate, and narrow is the way, which leadeth unto life; and few there be that find it.

Beware of false prophets, which come to you in sheep's clothing, but inwardly they are ravening wolves.

Ye shall know them by their fruits. Do men gather grapes of thorns, or figs of thistles?

Even so every good tree bringeth forth good fruit; but a corrupt tree bringeth forth evil fruit.

A good tree cannot bring forth evil fruit, neither can a corrupt tree bring forth good fruit.

Every tree that bringeth not forth good fruit is hewn down, and cast into the fire.

Wherefore by their fruits ye shall know them.

Not every one that saith unto me, Lord, Lord, shall enter into the kingdom of heaven; but he that doeth the will of my Father which is in heaven.

Many will say to me in that day, Lord, Lord, have we not prophesied in thy name? and in thy name have cast out devils? and in thy name done many wonderful works?

And then will I profess unto them, I never knew you; depart from me, ye that work iniquity.

Therefore whosoever heareth these sayings of mine, and doeth them, I will liken him unto a wise man, which built his house upon a rock:

And the rain descended, and the floods came, and the winds blew, and beat upon that house; and it fell not; for it was founded upon a rock.

And every one that heareth these sayings of mine, and doeth them not, shall be likened unto a foolish man, which built his house upon the sand:

And the rain descended, and the floods came, and the winds blew, and beat upon that house; and it fell: and great was the fall of it.

And it came to pass, when Jesus had ended these sayings, the people were astonished at his doctrine:

For he taught them as one having authority, and not as the scribes.

THE CODE OF HAMMURABI

If a man has caused the loss of a gentleman's eye, his eye one shall cause to be lost.

If he has shattered a gentleman's limb, one shall shatter his limb.

If has caused a poor man to lose his eye or shattered a poor man's limb, he shall pay one mina of silver.

If a man has made the tooth of a man that is his equal to fall out, one shall make his tooth fall out.

If he has made the tooth of a poor man to fall out, he shall pay one-third of a mina of silver.

If a man has struck the strength of a man who is great above him, he shall be struck in the assembly with sixty strokes of a cow-hide whip.

If a man of gentle birth has struck the strength of a man of gentle birth who is like himself, he shall pay one mina of silver.

If a poor man has struck the strength of a poor man, he shall pay ten shekels of silver.

If a gentleman's servant has struck the strength of a free-man, one shall cut off his ear.

If a man has struck a man in a quarrel, and has caused him a wound, that man shall swear "I do not strike him knowing" and shall answer for the doctor.

If he has died of his blows, he shall swear, and if he be of gentle birth he shall pay half a mina of silver.

If he be the son of a poor man, he shall pay one-third of a mina of silver.

If a man has struck a gentleman's daughter and caused her to drop what is in her womb, he shall pay ten shekels of silver for what was in her womb.

If that woman has died, one shall put to death his daughter.

If the daughter of a poor man through his blows he has

caused to drop that which is in her womb, he shall pay five shekels of silver.

If that woman has died, he shall pay half a mina of silver.

If he has struck a gentleman's maidservant and caused her to drop that which is in her womb, he shall pay two shekels of silver.

If that maidservant has died, he shall pay one-third of a mina of silver.

If a doctor has treated a gentleman for a severe wound with a bronze lancet and has cured the man, or has opened an abscess of the eye for a gentleman with the bronze lancet and has cured the eye of the gentleman, he shall take ten shekels of silver.

If he (the patient) be the son of a poor man, he shall take five shekels of silver.

If he be a gentleman's servant, the master of the servant shall give two shekels of silver to the doctor.

If the doctor has treated a gentleman for a severe wound with a lancet of bronze and has caused the gentleman to die, or has opened an abscess of the eye for a gentleman with the bronze lancet and has caused the loss of the gentleman's eye, one shall cut off his hands.

If a doctor has treated the severe wound of a slave of a poor man with a bronze lancet and has caused his death, he shall render slave for slave.

If he has opened his abscess with a bronze lancet and has made him lose his eye, he shall pay money, half his price.

If a doctor has cured the shattered limb of a gentleman, or has cured the diseased bowel, the patient shall give five shekels of silver to the doctor.

If it is a poor man, he shall give three shekels of silver.

If a gentleman's servant, the master of the slave shall give two shekels of silver to the doctor.

If a cow doctor or a sheep doctor has treated a cow or a sheep for a severe wound and cured it, the owner of the cow or sheep shall give one-sixth of a shekel of silver to the doctor as his fee.

SELECTIONS FROM THE KORAN

Those Who Give Short Measure or Weight; Revealed at Mecca.

In the name of the most merciful God.

Woe be unto those who give short measure or weight, who, when they receive by measure from *other* men, take the full; but when measure unto them, or weigh unto them, defraud! Do not these think they shall be raised again, at the great day, the day whereon mankind shall stand before the Lord of all creatures? By no means. Verily the register of *the actions* of the wicked *is* surely in Sejjin. And what shall make thee to understand what Sejjin is? It is a book distinctly written. Woe be on that day, unto those who accused *the prophets* of imposture; who denied the day of judgment as a falsehood! And none denieth the same as a falsehood, except every unjust *and* flagitious person: who, when our signs are rehearsed unto him, saith, *They* are fables of the ancients. By no means; but rather their lusts have cast a veil over their hearts. By no means. Verily they *shall* be shut out from their Lord on that day; and they shall be sent into hell to be burned; then shall it be said *unto them by the infernal guards,* This *is* what ye denied as a falsehood. Assuredly. But the register of *the actions* of the righteous is Illiyyun; and what shall cause thee to understand what Illiyyun is? It is a book distinctly written: those who approach near *unto God* are witnesses there to. Verily the righteous *shall dwell* among delights; seated on couches they shall behold *objects of pleasure;* thou shalt see in their faces the brightness of joy. They shall be given to drink of pure wine, sealed; the seal whereof *shall be* musk; and to this let those aspire who aspire to *happiness:* and the *water* mixed therewith *shall be* of Tasnim, a fountain whereof those shall drink who approach near *unto the divine presence*. They who act wickedly laugh the true believers to scorn: and when they pass by them, they wink at one another: and when they turn aside to their people, they turn aside making scurrilous jests; and when they see them, they say, Verily these *are* mistaken men. But they are not sent to be keepers over them. Wherefore one day the true believers, *in their turn,* shall laugh the infidels to scorn; *lying* in couches they shall look down *upon them in hell*. Shall not the infidels be rewarded for that which they have done?

Intitled, the Rending in Sunder; Revealed at Mecca.
In the name of the most merciful God.

When the heaven shall be rent in sunder, and shall obey its Lord, and shall be capable *thereof;* and when the earth shall be stretched out, and shall cast forth that which *is* therein, and shall remain empty, and shall obey its Lord, and shall be capable *thereof;* O man, verily laboring thou laborest to *meet* thy Lord, and thou shalt meet him. And he who shall have his book given into his right hand shall be called to an easy account, and shall turn unto his family with joy: but he who shall have his book given him behind his back shall invoke destruction *to fall upon him,* and he shall be sent into hell to be burned; because he rejoiced insolently amidst his family *on earth*. Verily he thought he should never return *unto God:* yea verily, but his Lord beheld him. Wherefore I swear by the redness of the sky after sunset, and by the night, and the *animals* which it driveth together, and by the moon when she is in the full; ye shall surely be transferred *successively* from state to state. What *aileth* them, therefore, that they believe not *the resurrection;* and that, when the Koran is read unto them, they worship not? Yea: the unbelievers accuse *the same* of imposture: but God well knoweth the *malice* which they keep hidden *in their* breasts. Wherefore denounce unto them a grievous punishment, except those who believe and do good works: for them *is prepared* a never-failing reward.

Intitled, the Celestial Signs; Revealed at Mecca.
In the name of the most merciful God.

By the heaven *adorned* with signs; by the promised day *of judgment;* by the witness, and the witnessed; cursed were the contrivers of the pit, of fire supplied with fuel when they sat around the same, and were witnesses of what they did against the true believers, and they afflicted them for no other reason, but because they believed in the mighty the glorious God, unto whom *belongeth* the kingdom of heaven and earth: and God is witness of all things. Verily for those who persecute the true believers of either sex, and afterwards repent not, *is prepared* the torment of hell; and they *shall suffer* the pain of burning. But for those who believe, and do that which is right, *are destined* gardens beneath which rivers flow: this *shall be* great felicity. Verily the vengeance of thy Lord is severe. He createth, and he restoreth *to life:* he is inclined to forgive, and gracious; the possessor of the glorious throne, who effecteth that which he pleaseth. Hath not the story of the hosts of Pharaoh and of Thamud reached thee? Yet the unbelievers cease not to accuse *the divine revelations* of falsehood: but God encompasseth them behind, *that they cannot escape.* Verily *that which they reject* is a glorious Koran; the *original whereof is written* in a table kept *in heaven.*

Intitled, the Star which Appeared by Night: Revealed at Mecca.
In the name of the most merciful God.

By the heaven, and that which appeareth by night: but what shall cause thee to understand what that which appeareth by night *is? it is* the star of piercing brightness!

every soul hath a guardian *set* over it. Let a man consider, therefore, of what he is created. He is created of seed poured forth, issuing from the loins, and the breastbones. Verily *God is* able to restore him *to life,* the day whereon *all* secret thoughts and actions shall be examined into; and he shall have no power *to defend himself,* nor any protector. By the heaven which returneth *the rain;* and by the earth which openeth *to let forth vegetables and springs;* verily this is a discourse distinguishing *good from evil;* and it is not *composed* with lightness. Verily *the infidels* are laying a plot *to frustrate my designs:* but I will lay a plot *for their ruin.* Wherefore, *O prophet,* bear with the unbelievers: let them alone a while.

Intitled, the Most High; Revealed at Mecca.
In the name of the most merciful God.

Praise the name of thy Lord, the most high; who hath created, and completely formed *his creatures:* and who determineth *them to various ends,* and directeth *them to attain the same;* and who produceth the pasture *for cattle,* and *afterwards* rendereth the same dry stubble of a dusky hue. We will enable thee to rehearse *our revelations;* and thou shalt not forget *any part thereof,* except what God shall please; for he knoweth that which is manifest, and that which is hidden. And we will facilitate unto thee the most easy *way.* Wherefore admonish *thy people,* if *thy* admonition shall be profitable *unto them.* Whoso feareth *God,* he will be admonished: but the most wretched *unbeliever* will turn away therefrom; who shall be cast to be broiled in the greater fire *of hell,* wherein he shall not die, neither shall he live. Now hath he attained felicity, who is purified *by faith,* and who remembereth the name of his Lord, and prayeth. But ye prefer this present life: yet the life to come *is* better, and more durable. Verily this *is written* in the ancient books, the books of Abraham and Moses.

Intitled, the Overwhelming; Revealed at Mecca.
In the name of the most merciful God.

Hath news of the overwhelming *day of judgment* reached thee? The countenances *of some,* on that day, *shall be* cast down; laboring *and* toiling: they shall be cast into scorching fire to be broiled: they shall be given to drink of a boiling fountain: they shall have no food, but of dry thorns and thistles: which shall not fatten, neither shall they satisfy hunger. *But* the countenances *of others,* on that day, *shall be* joyful; well pleased with their *past* endeavor: they *shall be placed* in a lofty garden, wherein thou shalt hear no vain discourse; therein *shall be a* running fountain; therein shall be raised beds, and goblets placed *before them,* and cushions laid in order, and carpets ready spread. Do they not consider the camels, how they are created; and the heaven, how it is raised; and the mountains, how they are fixed; and the earth, how it is extended? Wherefore warn *thy people;* foɪ thou *art* a warner only: thou art not impowered to act with authority over them. But whoever shall turn back, and disbelieve, God shall punish him with the greater punishment *of the life to come.* Verily unto us shall they return: then shall it be our part to bring them to account.

Intitled, The Daybreak; Revealed at Mecca.
In the name of the most merciful God.

By the daybreak, and ten nights; by that which is double, and that which is single; and by the night when it cometh on: *is there* not in this an oath formed with understanding? Hast thou not considered how thy Lord dealt with Ad, *the people* of Irem, adorned with lofty buildings, the like whereof hath not been erected in the land; and with Thamud, who hewed the rocks in the valley *into houses;* and with Pharaoh, the contriver of the stakes: who had behaved insolently in the earth, and multiplied corruption therein? Wherefore thy Lord poured on them various kinds of chastisement; for thy Lord *is* surely in a watch-tower, *whence he observeth the actions of men.* Moreover man, when his Lord trieth him *by prosperity,* and honoreth him, and is bounteous unto him, saith, My Lord honoreth me; but when he proveth him *by afflictions,* and withholdeth his provisions from him, he saith, My Lord despiseth me. By no means: but ye honor not the orphan, neither do ye excite *one another* to feed the poor; and ye devour the inheritance *of the weak,* with undistinguishing greediness, and ye love riches with much affection. By no means *should ye do thus.* When the earth shall be minutely ground to dust; and thy Lord shall come, and the angels rank by rank; and hell, on that day, shall be brought nigh: on that day shall man call to remembrance *his evil deeds;* but how *shall* remembrance *avail* him? He shall say, Would to God that I had heretofore done *good works* in my lifetime!

ON GOVERNMENT

By *CONFUCIUS*

ACCORDING to the nature of man, government is the greatest thing for him.

When right principles prevail in the empire, there will be no discussion among the common people.

To govern means to make right. If you lead the people uprightly, who will dare not to be upright?

Employ the upright and put aside all the crooked; in this way the crooked can be made to be upright.

Go before the people with your example, and spare yourself not in their affairs.

There is good government when those who are near are made happy, and when those who are afar are attracted.

The art of government is to keep its affairs before the mind without weariness, and to attend to them with undeviating consistency.

There is government when the prince is prince, the minister is minister; when the father is father, and the son is son.

In hearing litigations I am like any other body. What is necessary is to have no litigations.

The rude tribes of the East and North have their princes, and are not like the States of our great land, which are without them. What is called a great minister is one who serves his ruler according to what is right, and when he finds he cannot do so retires.

He who exercises government by means of his virtue may be compared to the polar star, which keeps its place, and all the stars turn toward it.

It is necessary that there should be sufficiency of good, sufficiency of military equipment, and the confidence of the people in their ruler.

With the right men the growth of government is rapid, just as the growth of vegetation is rapid. Government is like an easily growing rush.

Dignities should not be conferred on men of evil practices. If they be, how can the people set themselves to correct their ways?

When a country is well governed, poverty and a mean condition are something to be ashamed of. When a country is ill governed, riches and honors are something to be ashamed of.

In the service of a ruler, a minister should not condescend to subjects beneath him, nor set a high value on speeches, nor accept an introduction from improper individuals.

Truly straightforward was the historiographer Yu. When good government prevailed in his State, he was like an arrow. When bad government prevailed, he was like an arrow.

If a minister is correct in his own conduct, what difficulty will he have in aiding the government? If he cannot make himself upright, what has he to do with making others upright?

Ke K'ang, distressed about the number of thieves, asked advice of Confucius. Confucius said, "If you, sir, were not covetous, although you should reward them to do it, they would not steal."

A minister, in serving his prince, reverently discharges his duties, and makes his emolument a secondary consideration.

When a prince's personal conduct is correct, his government is effective without the issuing of orders. If his personal conduct is not correct, he may issue orders, but they will not be obeyed.

When those who are in high stations perform all their duties to their relations, the people are aroused to virtue. When old ministers and friends are not neglected by them, the people are preserved from meanness.

When good government prevails in a State, language may

be lofty and bold, and actions the same. When bad government prevails, the actions may be lofty and bold, but the language should be with some reserve.

A superior man, indeed, is Keu Pihyuh. When good government prevails in his State, he is to be found in office. When bad government prevails, he can roll his principles up and keep them in his breast.

Chung-Kung, being chief minister to the head of the Ke family, asked about government. The Master said, "Employ first the services of your various officers, pardon small faults, and raise to office men of virtue and talents."

If good men were to govern a country a hundred years, they would be able to transform the violently bad, and dispense with capital punishments.

Tsze-Kung asked, "What qualities must a man possess to entitle him to become an officer?"

The Master said, "He who in his conduct preserves a sense of shame, and when sent to any quarter will not disgrace his prince's commission, deserves to be called an officer."

To see men of worth and not be able to raise them to office; to raise them to office and not be able to do so quickly, —this is treating them with disrespect. To see bad men and not be able to remove them, but not to send them far away; —this is weakness.

Though a man be able to recite the three hundred odes, yet if, when intrusted with governmental commission, he knows not how to act, or if, when sent to any quarter on a mission, he cannot give of himself the proper replies, notwithstanding his attainments, of what practical use are they?

Tsze-Haw, being governor of Keufou, asked about government. The Master said, "Do you not be desirous to have things done quickly; do not look at small advantages. Desire to have things done quickly prevents their being done thoroughly. Looking at small advantages prevents great affairs from being accomplished."

To be fond of learning is near to wisdom; to practise with

vigor is near to benevolence; to be conscious of shame is near to fortitude. He who knows these three things knows how to cultivate his own character. Knowing how to cultivate his own character, he knows how to govern other men. Knowing how to govern other men, he knows how to govern the kingdom, with its States and families.

A minister in the service of his ruler will first offer words of counsel, and when they are accepted, he will bow and voluntarily offer his person to make good his sincerity. Hence, whatever services a ruler requires from his minister, the minister will die in support of his words. In this way the salary he receives is not obtained on false pretenses, and the things for which he may be blamed will be fewer and fewer.

The exemption of nobles and high dignitaries from the application of the penal laws was based upon the assumption that men destined to occupy such honorable and prominent positions would be found superior to the faults and failings of those who had not enjoyed the advantages of fortune. That exemption has been from a desire to place the ruling classes before the public in such a light as would cause them to be regarded with special veneration.

The king's words are at first as threads of silk; but when sent forth they become as cords. Or, they are at first as cords, but when sent forth they become as ropes. Therefore, the great man does not lead in idle speaking. The superior man does not speak words which may not be embodied in deeds, nor does he actions which may not be expressed in words. When this is the case, the words of the people may be carried into action without risk, and their actions can be spoken of without risk.

In passing by the side of Mount Thai, Confucius came on a woman who was weeping bitterly by a grave. The Master pressed forward and drove quickly to her; then he sent Tze-lu to question her. "Your wailing," said he, "is that of one who has suffered sorrow on sorrow." She replied, "That is so. Once my husband's father was killed here by a tiger.

My husband was also killed, and now my son has died in the same way." The Master said, "Why do you not leave the place?" The answer was, "There is no oppressive government here," The Master then said, "Remember this, my children: oppressive government is more terrible than tigers."

The kings of three dynasties, in taking care of the old, always had the ages of those connected with them brought to their notice. At eighty a son was free from all government service. At ninety all the members of the family were released from government duty. In the case of those who were disabled or ill, and required attendance, one man was discharged from those duties. Those mourning for their parents had a discharge for three years. Those mourning for a year or nine months had a discharge for three months.

Orphans, an old man without sons, an old man who has lost his wife, and an old woman who has lost her husband; these four were considered as the most forlorn of heaven's people, for they had none to whom they could tell their wants. These all received regular allowances.

. . . The feast on grain-fed animals accompanied by drinking was not intended to have bad effects; yet cases of litigation are more numerous in consequence of it. It is the excessive drinking with produces the evil. Therefore the old kings framed rules to regulate drinking. Where there is but one presentation of the cup at one time, guest and host may bow to each other a hundred times without getting drunk. This was the way in which those kings guarded against this evil.

There were five things by which the ancient kings secured the good government of the whole kingdom,—the honor which they paid to the virtuous, to the noble and to the old, the reverence they paid to the aged, and their kindness to the young. It was by these five things that they maintained the stability of the kingdom.

ON COOPERATION *

By LAO TSE

Pu-tse, in the Cheng State, was rich in wise men, and Tung-li in men of administrative talent. Among the vassals of Pu-tse was a certain Po Feng Tzu, who happened to travel through Tungli and had a meeting with Teng Hsi.

The latter cast a glance at his followers, and asked them, with a smile: "Would you like to see me have some sport with this stranger?" They understood what he would be at, and assented. Teng Hsi then turned to Po Feng Tzu. "Are you acquainted with the true theory of Sustentation?" he inquired. "To receive sustenance from others, through inability to support oneself, places one in the category of dogs and swine. It is man's prerogative to give sustenance to other creatures, and to use them for his own purposes. That you and your fellows are provided with abundant food and comfortable clothing is due to the Government. Young and old, you herd together, and are penned up like cattle destined for the shambles: in what respect are you to be distinguished from dogs and swine?"

Po Feng Tzu made no reply, but one of his company, disregarding the rules of precedence, stepped forward and said: "Has your Excellency never heard of the variety of craftsmen in Ch'i and Lu? Some are skilled potters and carpenters, others are clever workers in metal and leather; there are good musicians, trained scribes and accountants, military experts and men learned in the ritual of ancestor-worship. All kinds of craftsmanship are there fully represented. Now, if there were no division of ranks and duties, mutual co-operation would be impossible. Those of higher social standing are lacking in technical knowledge, those who are employed by them are lacking in power. Only

* Translated by Lionel Giles, London, 1912

38

when there is a combination of technical knowledge and power can co-operative service exist.

It is really *we* who may be said to employ the Government authorities. Why then should you pity us?"

Teng Hsi could think of nothing to say in reply. He made a sign to his disciples and retreated.

ON CAUSE AND EFFECT

In the course of Lieh Tzu's instruction by Huch'iu Tzu-lin, the latter said to him: "You must familiarise yourself with the theory of consequents." "Look at your shadow," said his Master, "and then you will know." Lieh turned and looked at his shadow. When his body was bent, the shadow was crooked; when his body was upright, the shadow was straight. Thus it appeared that the attributes of straightness and crookedness were not inherent in the shadow, but corresponded to certain positions of the body. Likewise, contraction and extension are not inherent in the subject, but take place in obedience to external causes. Holding this theory of consequents is to be at home in the antecedent.

Kuan Yin spoke to the Master Lieh Tzu, saying: "If speech is sweet, the echo will be sweet; if speech is harsh, the echo will be harsh. If the body is long, the shadow will be long; if the body is short, the shadow will be short. Reputation is only an echo, external conduct only a shadow.

"Hence the saying: 'Heed your words, and they will meet with harmonious response; heed your actions, and they will find agreeable accord.' Therefore, the Sage observes the issue in order to know the origin, scrutinises the past in order to know the future. Such is the principle whereby he attains foreknowledge.

"The standard of conduct lies with one's own self; the testing of it lies with other men. We are impelled to love those who love us, and to hate those who hate us. T'ang and Wu loved the Empire, and therefore each became King. Chieh and Chou hated the Empire, and therefore they perished. Here we have the test applied. He who does not follow Tao when standard and test are both clear may be likened to one who, when leaving a house, does not go by the door, or, when travelling abroad, does not keep to the straight road. To seek profit in this way, is it not a thing that is impossible?

"You may consider the virtues of Shen Nung and Yu Yen, you may examine the books of Yu, Hsia, Shang and Chou, you may weigh the utterances of great teachers and sages, but you will find no instances of preservation or destruction, fullness or decay, which has not obeyed this supreme Law."

LAO TSE IN POVERTY

The Master Lieh Tzu was very poor, and his face wore a hungry look. A certain stranger spoke about it to Tzu Yang, Prince of Cheng, "Lieh Yu-k'ou," said he, "is a scholar in possession of Tao. Yet here he is, living in destitution, within your Highness's dominion. It surely cannot be that you have no liking for scholars?" Tzu Yang forthwith directed that an official allowance of grain should be sent to him. Lieh Tzu came out to receive the messengers, made two low bows and declined the gift, whereupon the messengers went away, and Lieh Tzu reentered the house. There he was confronted by his wife, who beat her breast and cried aloud: "I have always understood that the wife and family of a man of Tao live a life of ease and pleasure. Yet now, when your Prince sends you a present of food, on account of your starved appearance, you refuse to accept it! I suppose you will call that 'destiny'!" The Master Lieh Tzu smiled and replied: "The Prince did not know about me himself. His present of grain was made on the suggestion of another. If it had been a question of punishing me, that too would have been done at some one else's prompting. That is the reason why I did not accept the gift."

Later on, the masses rose in actual rebellion against Tzu Yang, and slew him.

II

GREEK THEORIES

COMMENTARY

The first people to give social thought a philosophic character are the Greeks. The Jews and all the other ancient races conceive of social thought mainly in moral or ethical terms, of which the selections in the preceding section of this volume are a conclusive testimony. With the Greeks, social thought becomes an intellectual consideration, to be weighed and measured by rational conceptions and shibboleths.

Plato and Aristotle are the thinkers who give most convincing and eloquent form to Greek ideas on the subject. In The Republic, Plato, with a vision almost clairvoyant, anticipates so many of the ideas which have become accepted fact in modern times, and Aristotle, with his essay on Politics, sets the pace for political argumentation for centuries afterward.

The few people to give social thought a philosophic character were the Greeks. The Jews and all the other ancient views conceive of social thought mainly in moral or ethical terms, of which the selections in the preceding section of this volume are a conclusive testimony. With the Greeks social thought becomes an intellectual consideration to be weighed and measured by rational conceptions and subtleties.

Plato and Aristotle are the thinkers who give most continuity and eloquent form to Greek ideas on the subject. In The Republic, Plato, with a vision almost clairvoyant, anticipates so many of the ideas which have become accepted fact in modern times; and Aristotle, with his essay on Politics, sets the pace for political organization for centuries afterward.

PHILOSOPHERS AS KINGS AND KINGS AS PHILOSOPHERS

PLATO *

THUS, Glaucon, I said, after pursuing a lengthened inquiry we have, not without difficulty, discovered who are true philosophers and who are not.

Yes, he replied; probably it was not easy to abridge the inquiry.

Apparently not, I said. However that may be, I think, for my part, that the result would have been brought out still more clearly, if we had to speak of this only, without discussing the many points that still await our notice, if we wish to ascertain wherein the superiority of a righteous over an unrighteous life consists.

Then what are we to do next?

We have only to take the step next on order. Since those who are able to apprehend the eternal and immutable, are philosophers, while those who are incapable of this and who wander in the region of change and multiformity, are not philosophers, which of the two, tell me, ought to be governors of a state?

What must I reply, if I am to do justice to the question?

Ask yourself which of the two are to be thought capable of guarding the laws and customs of states, and let these be appointed guardians.

You are right.

Can there be any question as to whether a blind man, or one with quick sight, is the right person to guard and keep any thing?

There can be no question about it.

Then do you think that there is a particle of difference be-

* From *The REPUBLIC* Book VI.

tween the condition of blind persons, and the state of those
who are absolutely destitute of the knowledge of things as
they really are, and who possess in their soul no distinct
exemplar, and cannot, like painters, fix their eyes on perfect
truth as a perpetual standard of reference, to be contemplated with the minutest care, before they proceed to deal
with earthly canons about things beautiful and just and
good, laying them down where they are required, and
where they already exist watching over their preservation?

No, indeed, there is not much difference.

Shall we then appoint such persons to the office of guardians, in preference to those who not only have gained a
knowledge of each thing in its reality, but in practical skill
are not inferior to the former, and come behind them in no
other department of excellence?

Why, if these latter are not wanting in the other qualifications, it would be perfectly absurd to choose any others.
For just the point in which they are superior may be said
to be the most important of all.

Then shall we proceed to explain how the same persons
will be enabled to possess both qualifications?

By all means.

If so, we must begin by gaining a thorough insight into
their proper character, as we said at the outset of this discussion. And I think, if we agree tolerably on that point, we
shall also agree that the two qualifications may be united
in the same persons, and that such characters, and no others,
are the proper governors of states.

How so?

With regard to the philosophic nature, let us take for
granted that its possessors are ever enamoured of all learning, that will reveal to them somewhat of that real and permanent existence, which is exempt from the vicissitudes of
generation and decay.

Let it be granted.

Again, I said, let us also assume that they are enamoured
of the whole of that real existence, and willingly resign no

part of it, be it small or great, honoured or slighted; as we shewed on a previous occasion, in speaking of the ambitious and the amorous.

You are right.

Now then proceed to consider, whether we ought not to find a third feature in the character of those who are to realize our description.

What feature do you mean?

I mean truthfulness, that is, a determination never to admit falsehood in any shape, if it can be helped, but to abhor it, and love the truth.

Yes, it is probable we shall find it.

Nay, my friend, it is not only probable, but absolutely inevitable, that one who is by nature prone to any passion, should be well pleased with everything that is bound by the closest ties to the beloved object.

True, he said

And can you find any thing allied to wisdom more closely than truth?

Certainly not.

And is it possible for the same nature to love wisdom, and at the same time love falsehood?

Unquestionably it is not.

Consequently, the genuine lover of knowledge must, from his youth up, strive intensely after all truth.

Yes, he must thoroughly.

Well, but we cannot doubt that when a person's desires set strongly in one direction, they run with corresponding feebleness in every other channel, like a stream whose waters have been diverted into another bed.

Undoubtedly they do.

So that when the current has set towards science, and all its branches, a man's desires will, I fancy, hover around pleasures that are purely mental, abandoning those in which the body is instrumental,—provided that the man's love of wisdom is real, not artificial.

It cannot be otherwise.

Again, such a person will be temperate and thoroughly uncovetous; for he is the last person in the world to value those objects, which make men anxious for money at any cost.

True.

Once more, there is another point which you ought to take into consideration, when you are endeavouring to distinguish a philosophic from an unphilosophic character.

What is that?

You must take care not to overlook any taint of meanness. For surely little-mindedness thwarts above everything the soul that is destined ever to aspire to grasp truth, both divine and human, in its integrity and universality.

That is most true.

And do you think that a spirit full of lofty thoughts, and privileged to contemplate all time, and all existence, can possibly attach any great importance to this life?

No, it is impossible.

Then such a person will not regard death as a formidable thing, will he?

Certainly not.

So that a mean and cowardly character can have no part, as it seems, in true philosophy.

I think it cannot.

What then? Can the man whose mind is well-regulated, and free from covetousness, meanness, pretentiousness, and cowardice, be by any possibility hard to deal with or unjust?

No; it is impossible.

Therefore, when you are noticing the indications of a philosophical or unphilosophical temper, you must also observe in early youth whether the mind is just and gentle, or unsociable and fierce.

Quite so.

There is still another point, which I think you must certainly not omit.

What is that?

Whether the mind in question is quick or slow at learning. For you can never expect a person to take a decent delight in an occupation which he goes through with pain, and in which he makes small progress with great exertion?

No, it would be impossible.

Again, if he can remember nothing of what he has learned, can he fail, being thus full of forgetfulness, to be void of knowledge?

No, he cannot.

Then, will not his fruitless toil, think you, compel him at last to hate both himself and such employment?

Doubtless it will.

Let us never, then, admit a forgetful mind into the ranks of those that are counted worthy of philosophy; but let us look out for a good memory as a requisite for such admission.

Yes, by all means.

Again, we should certainly say that the tendency of an unrefined and awkward nature is wholly towards disproportion.

Certainly.

And do you think that truth is akin to disproportion, or to proportion?

To proportion.

In addition, then, to our other acquirements, let us search for a mind naturally well-proportioned and graceful, whose native instincts will permit it to be easily led to apprehend the Forms of things as they really are.

By all means.

What then? Do you think that the qualities which we have enumerated are in any way unnecessary or inconsistent with one another, provided the soul is to attain unto full and satisfactory possession of real existence?

On the contrary, they are most strictly necessary.

Then can you find any fault with an employment which requires of a man who would pursue it satisfactorily, that nature shall have given him a retentive memory, and made him quick at learning, lofty-minded and graceful, the friend and brother of truth, justice, fortitude, and temperance?

No, he replied; the very Genius of criticism could find no fault with such an employment.

Well, can you hesitate to entrust such characters with the sole management of state affairs, when time and education have made them ripe for the task?

ON PROPERTY

By ARISTOTLE

As a slave is a particular species of property, let us by all means inquire into the nature of property in general, and the acquisition of money, according to the manner we have proposed. In the first place, then, some one may doubt whether the getting of money is the same thing as economy, or whether it is a part of it, or something subservient to it; and if so, whether it is as the art of making shuttles is to the art of weaving, or the art of making brass to that of statue-founding, for they are not of the same service, for the one supplies the tools, the other the matter; by the matter I mean the subject out of which the work is finished, as wool for the cloth and brass for the statue. It is evident then that the getting of money is not the same thing as economy, for the business of the one is to furnish the means, of the other to use them; and what art is there employed in the management of a family but economy, but whether this is a part of it, or something of a different species, is a doubt; for if it is the business of him who is to get money to find out how riches and possessions may be procured, and both these arise from various causes, we must first inquire whether the art of husbandry is part of money-getting or something different, and in general whether the same is not true of every acquisition, and every attention which relates to provision. But as there are many sorts of provision, so are the methods of living, both of man and the brute creation, very various; and as it is impossible to live without food, the difference in that particular makes the lives of animals so different from each other. Of beasts, some live in herds, others separate, as is most convenient for procuring themselves food; as some of them live upon flesh, others on fruit, and others on what-

47

soever they light on, Nature having so distinguished their
course of life that they can very easily procure themselves
subsistence; and as the same things are not agreeable to all,
but one animal likes one thing and another another, it
follows that the lives of those beasts who live upon flesh must
be different from the lives of those who live on fruits; so is
it with men, their lives differ greatly from each other; and
of all these, the shepherds' is the idlest, for they live upon
the flesh of tame animals, without any trouble, while they
are obliged to change their habitations on account of their
flocks, which they are compelled to follow, cultivating, as it
were, a living farm. Others live exercising violence over
living creatures, one pursuing this thing, another that, these
preying upon men; those who live near lakes and marshes
and rivers, or the sea itself, on fishing, while others are
fowlers, or hunters of wild beasts; but the greater part of
mankind live upon the produce of the earth, and its cultivated fruits; and the manner in which all those live who
follow the direction of Nature, and labour for their own subsistence, is nearly the same, without ever thinking to procure any provision by way of exchange or merchandise, such
are shepherds, husbandmen, robbers, fishermen, and hunters; some join different employments together, and thus live
very agreeably, supplying those deficiencies which were
wanting to make their subsistence depend upon themselves
only; thus, for instance, the same person shall be a shepherd
and a robber, or a husbandman and a hunter, and so with
respect to the rest, they pursue that mode of life which
necessity points out. This provision then Nature herself
seems to have furnished all animals with, as well immediately upon their first origin, as also when they are arrived
at a state of maturity; for at the first of these periods, some
of them are provided in the womb with proper nourishment,
which continues till that which is born can get food for itself,
as is the case with worms and birds; and as to those which
bring forth their young alive, they have the means for their
subsistence for a certain time within themselves—namely,

milk. It is evident then that we may conclude of those things that are, that plants are created for the sake of animals, and animals for the sake of men; the tame for our use and provision; the wild, at least the greater part, for our provision also, or for some other advantageous purpose, as furnishing us with clothes, and the like. As Nature therefore makes nothing either imperfect or in vain, it necessarily follows that she has made all these things for men; for which reason what we gain in war is, in a certain degree, a natural acquisition; for hunting is a part of it, which it is necessary for us to employ against wild beasts; and those men, who being intended by Nature for slavery are unwilling to submit to it, on which occasion, such a war is by Nature just; that species of acquisition then only which is according to Nature, is part of economy; and this ought to be at hand, or if not, immediately procured—namely, what is necessary to be kept in store to live upon and which are useful as well for the State as the family. And true riches seem to consist in these; and the acquisition or those possessions which are necessary for a happy life is not infinite, though Solon says otherwise in this verse,

No bounds to riches can be fixed for man;

for they may be fixed as in other arts; for the instruments of an art whatsoever are infinite, either in their number or their magnitude; but riches are a number of instruments in domestic and civil economy; it is therefore evident that the acquisition of certain things according to Nature is a part both of domestic and civil economy, and for what reason.

SHOULD PROPERTY BE COMMON

We proceed next to consider in what manner property should be regulated in a State which is formed after the most perfect mode of government, whether it should be common or not; for this may be considered as a separate question from what had been determined concerning wives and children; I mean whether it is better that these should be held separate, as they now everywhere are, or that not only possessions but also the usufruct of them should be in common, or that the soil should have a particular owner, but that the produce should be brought together and used as one common stock as some nations at present do; or, on the contrary, should the soil be common, and should it also be cultivated in common, while the produce is divided amongst the individuals for their particular use, which is said to be practised by some barbarians; or shall both the soil and the fruit be common? When the business of the husbandman devolves not on the citizen, the matter is much easier settled, but when those labour together, who have a common right of possession, this may occasion several difficulties; for there may not be an equal proportion between their labour and what they consume; and those who labour hard, and have but a small proportion of the produce, will certainly complain of those who take a large share of it, and do but little for that. Upon the whole, as a community between man and man so entire as to include everything possible, and thus to have all things that man can possess in common, is very difficult, so is it particularly so with respect to property; and this is evident from that community which takes place between those who go out to settle a colony; for they frequently have disputes with each other upon the most common occasions, and come to blows upon trifles; we find, too, that we oftenest correct those slaves who are generally employed in the common offices of the family; a community of property then has these and other inconveniences attending it. But the manner of life which is now established, more particularly when embellished with good morals and a system of equal laws, is far superior to it, for it will have the advantage of both; by both I mean properties being common and divided also: for in some respects it ought to be in a manner common, but upon the whole private; for every man's attention being employed on his own particular concerns, will prevent mutual complaints against each other; nay, by this means industry will be increased, as each person will labour to improve his own private property; and it will then be that, from a principle of virtue, they will mutually perform good offices to each other, according to the proverb, "All things are common amongst friends;" and in some cities there are traces of this custom to be seen, so that is not impracticable, and particularly in those which are best governed; some things are by this means in a manner common, and others might be so; for there, every person enjoying his own private property, some things he assists his friend with, others are considered as in common; as in Lacedaemon, where they use each other's slaves as if they were, so to speak, their own, as they do their horses and dogs, or even any provision they may want in a journey. It is evident then that it is best to have property private, but to make the use of it common; but how the citizens are to be brought to it is the particular business of the legislator. And also with respect to pleasure, it is unspeakable how advantageous it is that a man should think he has something which he may call his own; for it is by no means to no purpose that each person should have an affection for himself, for that is natural, and yet to be a self-lover is justly censured; for we mean by that, not one that simply loves himself, but one that loves himself more than he ought; in like manner we blame a money-lover, and yet both money and self is what all men love. Besides, it is very pleasing to us to oblige and assist our friends and companions, as well as those whom we are connected with by the rights of hospitality; and this cannot be done without the establishment of private property, which cannot take place with those who make a city too much one; besides, they prevent every opportunity of exercising two principal virtues, modesty and liberality. Modesty, with respect to the female sex, for this virtue requires you to abstain from her who is another's; liberality, which depends upon private property, for without that no one can appear liberal, or do any generous action; for liberality consists in imparting to others what is our own. This system of polity does indeed recommend itself by its good appearance and specious pretences to humanity, and when first proposed to any one must give him great pleasure, as he will conclude it to be a wonderful bond of friendship, connecting all to all; particularly when any one censures the evils which are now to be found in society, as arising from properties not being common; I mean the disputes which happen between man and man upon their different contracts with each other; those judgments which are passed in court in consequence of fraud and perjury, and flattering the rich, none of which arise from properties being private, but from the vices of mankind. Besides, those who live in one general community, and have all things in common, oftener dispute with each other than those who have their property separate; from the very small number indeed of those who have their property in common compared with those where it is appropriated, the instances of their quarrels are but few. It is also but right to mention not only the inconveniences they are preserved from who live in a communion of goods, but also the advantages they are deprived of; for when the whole comes to be considered, this manner of life will be found impracticable. We must suppose, then, that Socrates' mistake arose from the principle he set out with being false; we admit, indeed, that both a family and a city ought to be one in some particulars, but not entirely; for there is a point beyond which if a city proceeds in reducing itself to one, it will be no longer a city. There is also another point at which it will still continue to be a city, but it will approach so near to not being one that it will be worse than none; as if any one should reduce the voices of those who sing in concert to one, or a verse to a foot. But the people ought to be made one and a community, as I have already said, by education; as property at Lacedaemon and their public tables at Crete were made common by their legislators. But yet whosoever shall introduce any education and think thereby to make his city excellent and respectable will be absurd, while he expects to form it by that means and not by manners, philosophy, and laws. And whoever would establish a government upon a community of goods ought to know that he should consult the experience of many years, which would plainly enough inform him whether such a scheme is useful; for almost all things have already been found out, but some have been neglected, and others which have been known have not been put in practice. But this would be most evident if any one could see such a government really established; for it would be impossible to frame such a city without dividing and separating it into its distinct parts, as public tables, wards, and tribes; so that here the laws will do nothing more than forbid the military to engage in agriculture, which is what the Lacedaemonians are at present endeavouring to do. Nor has Socrates told us (nor is it easy to say) what plan of government should be pursued with respect to the individuals in the State where there is a community of goods established; for though the majority of his citizens will in general consist of a multitude of persons of different occupations, of those he has determined nothing; whether the property of the husbandman ought to be in common, or whether each person should have his share to himself, and also whether their wives and children ought to be in common; for if all things are to be alike common to all, where will be the difference between them and the military, or what would they get by submitting to their government? and upon what principles would they do it unless they should establish the wise practice of the Cretans? for they, allowing everything else to their slaves, forbid them only gymnastic exercises and the use of arms. And if they are not, but these should be in the same situation with respect to their property which they are in other cities, what sort of a community will there be? In one city there must of necessity be two, and those contrary to each other; for he makes the military the guardians of the State, and the husbandman, artisans, and other citizens; and all those quarrels, accusations, and things of the like sort, which he says are the bane of other cities, will be found in his also; notwithstanding Socrates says they will not want many laws in consequence of their education, but such only as may be necessary for regulating the streets, the markets, and the like, while at the same time it is the education of the military only that he has taken any care of. Besides, he makes the husbandmen masters of property upon paying a tribute, but this would be likely to make them far more troublesome and high-spirited than the helots, the penestiae, or the slaves which others employ; nor has he ever determined whether it is necessary to give any attention to them in these particulars, nor thought of what is connected therewith, their polity, their education, their laws; besides, it is of no little consequence, nor is it easy to determine, how these should be framed so as to preserve the community of the military. Besides, if he makes the wives common while the property continues separate, who shall manage the domestic concerns with the same care which the man bestows upon his fields? Nor will the inconvenience be remedied by making property as well as wives common; and it is absurd to draw a comparison from the brute creation, and say that the same principle should regulate the connection of a man and a woman which regulates theirs amongst whom there is no family association. It is also very hazardous to settle the magistracy as Socrates has done, for he would have persons of the same rank always in office, which becomes the cause of sedition even amongst those who are of no account, but more particularly amongst those who are of a courageous and warlike disposition; it is indeed evidently necessary that he should frame his community in this manner; for that golden particle which God has mixed up in the soul of man flies not from one to the other, but always continues with the same; for he says that some of our species have gold and others silver blended in their composition from the moment of their birth; but those who are to be husbandmen and artists, brass and iron; besides, though he deprives the military of happiness, he says that the legislator ought to make all the citizens happy; but it is impossible that the whole city can be happy, without all, or the greater, or some part of it be happy. For happiness is not like that numerical equality which arises from certain numbers when added together, although neither of them may separately contain it; for happiness cannot be thus added together, but must exist in every individual, as some properties belong to every integral; and if the military are not happy, who else are so? for the artisans are not, nor the multitude of those who are employed in inferior offices. The State which Socrates has described has all these defects, and others which are not of less consequence.

SKETCH OF THE IDEAL STATE

He who proposes to make that inquiry which is necessary concerning what government is best, ought first to determine what manner of living is most eligible, for while this remains uncertain it will also be equally uncertain what government is best; for, provided no unexpected accidents interfere, it is highly probable that those who enjoy the best government will live the most happily according to their circumstances. He ought, therefore, first to know what manner of life is most desirable for all, and afterwards whether this life is the same to the man and the citizen, or different. As I imagine that I have already sufficiently shown what sort of life is best, in my popular discourses on the subject, I think I may very properly repeat the same here, as most certainly no one ever called in question the propriety of one of the divisions—namely, that as what is good relative to man may be divided into three sorts, what is external, what appertains to the body, and what to the soul—it is evident that all these must conspire to make a man happy; for no one would say that a man was happy who had no fortitude, no temperance, no justice, no prudence, but was afraid of the flies that flew round him; nor would abstain from the meanest theft, if he was either hungry or dry, or would murder his dearest friend for a farthing; and also was in every particular as wanting in his understanding as an infant or an idiot. These truths are so evident that all must agree to them, though some may dispute about the quantity and the degree; for they may think that a very little virtue is sufficient for happiness, but for riches, property, power, honour, and all such things they endeavour to increase them without bounds; but to such we reply, that it is easy to prove from what experience teaches us in these cases that these external goods produce not virtue, but virtue them. As to a happy life, whether it is to be found in pleasure or virtue, or both, certain it is that those whose morals are most pure, and whose understandings are best cultivated, will enjoy more of it, although their fortune is but moderate, than those do who own an exuberance of wealth, are deficient in those, and this utility any one who reflects may easily convince himself of; for whatsoever is external has its boundary, as a machine, and whatsoever is useful in its excess is either necessarily hurtful, or at best useless to the possessor, but every good quality of the soul, the higher it is in degree, so much the more useful it is, if it is permitted on this subject to use the word useful as well as noble. It is also very evident that the accidents of each subject take place of each other, as the subjects themselves, of which we allow they are accidents, differ from each other in value, so that if the soul is more noble than any outward possession, as the body, both in itself and with respect to us, it must be admitted of course that the best accidents of each must follow the same analogy. Besides, it is for the sake of the soul that these things are desirable, and it is on this account that wise men should desire them, not the soul for them. Let us therefore be well assured that every one enjoys as much happiness as he possesses virtue and wisdom, and acts according to their dictates, since for this we have the example of God Himself, who is completely happy, not from any external good, but in Himself, and because such is His nature. For good fortune is something different from happiness, as every good which depends not on the mind is owing to chance or fortune; but it is not from fortune that any one is wise and just, hence it follows that that city is happiest which is the best and acts best; for no one can do well who acts not well, nor can the deeds either of man or city be praiseworthy without virtue and wisdom, for whatsoever is just or wise or prudent in a man, the same things are just, wise, and prudent in a city.

Thus much by way of introduction, for I could not but just touch upon this subject, though I could not go through a complete investigation of it, as it properly belongs to another question; let us at present suppose so much, that a man's happiest life, both as an individual and as a citizen, is a life of virtue, accompanied with those enjoyments which virtue usually procures. If there are any who are not convinced by what I have said, their doubts shall be answered hereafter; at present we shall proceed according to our intended method

ON EDUCATION

When a child is born it must be supposed that the strength of its body will depend greatly upon the quality of its food. Now whoever will examine into the nature of animals, and also observe those people who are very desirous their children should acquire a warlike habit, will find that they feed them chiefly with milk, as being best accommodated to their bodies, but without wine, to prevent any distempers; those notions also which are natural to their age are very serviceable; and to prevent any of their limbs from being crooked, on account of their extreme ductility, some people even now use particular machines that their bodies may not be distorted. It is also useful to inure them to the cold when they are very little, for this is very serviceable for their health; and also to inure them to the business of war; for which reason it is customary with many of the barbarians to dip their children in rivers when the water is cold, with others to clothe them very slightly, as among the Celts; for whatever it is possible to accustom children to, it is best to accustom them to it at first, but to do it by degrees; besides boys have naturally a habit of loving the cold, on account of the heat. These, then, and such-like things ought to be the first object of our attention; the next age to this continues till the child is five years old, during which time it is best to teach him nothing at all, not even necessary labour, lest it should hinder his growth; but he should be accustomed to use so much motion as not to acquire a lazy habit of body, which he will get by various means and by play also; his play also ought to be neither illiberal nor too laborious, nor lazy. Their governors and preceptors also should take care what sort of tales and stories it may be proper for them to hear, for all these ought to pave the way for their future instruction: for which reason the generality of their play should be imitations of what they are afterwards to do seriously. They, too, do wrong who forbid by laws the disputes between boys and their quarrels, for they contribute to increase their growth, as they are a sort of exercise to the body; for the struggles of the heart and the compression of the spirits give strength to those who labour, which happens to boys in their disputes. The preceptors also ought to have an eye upon their manner of life, and those with whom they converse; and to take care that they are never in the company of slaves. At this time and till they are seven years old it is necessary that they should be educated at home. It is also very proper to banish, both from their hearing and sight, everything which is illiberal, and the like. Indeed it is as much the business of the legislator, as anything else, to banish every indecent expression out of the State; for, from a permission to speak whatever is shameful, very quickly arises the doing it, and this particularly with young people; for which reason let them never speak nor hear any such things; but if it appears that any freeman has done or said anything that is forbidden, before he is of age to be thought fit to partake of the common meals, let him be punished by disgrace and stripes; but if a person above that age does so, let him be treated as you would a slave, on account of his being infamous. Since we forbid his speaking everything which is forbid, it is necessary that he neither sees obscene stories or pictures; the magistrates therefore are to take care that there are no statues or pictures of anything of this nature, except only to those gods to whom the law permits them, and to which the law allows persons of certain age to pay their devotions for themselves, their wives, and children. It should also be illegal for young persons to be present either at iambics or comedies before they are arrived at that age when they are allowed to partake of the pleasures of the table; indeed a good education will preserve them from all the evils which attend on these things. We have at present just touched upon this subject; it will be our business hereafter, when we properly come to it, to determine whether this care of children is unnecessary, or, if necessary, in what manner it must be done; at present we have only mentioned it as necessary. Probably the saying of Theodorus, the tragic actor, was not a bad one —that he would permit no one, not even the meanest actor, to go upon the stage before him, that he might first engage the ear of the audience. The same thing happens both in our connections with men and things: what we meet with first pleases best; for which reason children should be kept strangers to everything which is bad, more particularly whatsoever is loose and offensive to good manners. When five years are accomplished, the two next may be very properly employed in being spectators of those exercises they will afterwards have to learn. There are two periods into which education ought to be divided, according to the age of the child; the one is, from his being seven years of age to the time of puberty; the other, from the thence till he is one-and-twenty; for those who divide ages by the number seven are in general wrong; it is much better to follow the division of Nature; for every art and every instruction is intended to complete what Nature has left defective; we must first consider, if any regulation whatsoever is requisite for children; in the next place, if it is advantageous to make it a common care, or that every one should act therein as he pleases, which is the general practice in most cities; in the third place, what it ought to be.

III
MEDIEVAL CONCEPTIONS

COMMENTARY

In Saint Augustine's City of God, *we are confronted with the best picture of what the Middle Ages conceived of as a social ideal. Thomas Aquinas might write of logic and ethics and religion as a theological fact, but it is Saint Augustine who catches the spirit of the epoch, and translates it into sociological form in his* City of God. *Saint Augustine realizes better than any of his contemporaries that Catholicism is not just an other-worldly conception, but a this-worldly one, which can assume meaning only when men and women decide to give body to its dream. In* The City of God, *he comes closest to realizing that dream.*

Although Saint Augustine represents the medieval mind in one of its most interesting aspects, it is the medieval mind before any of the stirrings of modernity begin to sprout in it.

OF THE LAW OF HEAVEN AND EARTH WHICH SWAYS HUMAN SOCIETY BY COUNSEL AND UNTO WHICH COUNSEL HUMAN SOCIETY IS OBEDIENT*

By ST. AUGUSTINE

Now God, our good Master, teaching us in the two great commandments the love of Him, and the love of our neighbour, to love three things, God, our neighbour, and ourselves, and seeing he that loves God, offends not in loving himself; it follows that he ought to counsel his neighbour to love God, and to provide for him in the love of God, sure he is commanded to love him, as his own self. So must he do for his wife, children, family, and all men besides: and wish likewise that his neighbour would do as much for him, in his need: thus shall he be settled in peace and orderly concord with all the world. The order whereof is, first, to do no man hurt, and secondly, to help all that he can. So that his own have the first place in his care, and those, his place and order in human society affords him more conveniency to benefit. Whereupon St. Paul says, "He that provideth not for his own, and, namely, for them that be of his household, denieth the faith, and is worse than an infidel." For this is the foundation of domestic peace, which is, an orderly rule, and subjection in the parts of the family, wherein the provisors are the commanders, as the husband over his wife; parents over their children, and masters over their servants: and they that are provided for, obey, as the wives do their husbands, children their parents, and servants their masters. But in the family of the faithful man, the heavenly pilgrim, there the commanders are indeed the servants of those they seem to command: ruling not in ambition, but being bound

* From The City of God.

by careful duty: not in proud sovereignty, but in nourishing pity.

NATURE'S FREEDOM, AND BONDAGE, CAUSED BY SIN: IN WHICH MAN IS A SLAVE TO HIS OWN PASSIONS, THOUGH HE BE NOT BONDSMAN TO ANY ONE BESIDES

Thus has nature's order prescribed, and man by God was thus created. "Let them rule," saith He, "over the fishes of the sea, and the fowls of the air, and over every thing that creepeth upon the earth." He made him reasonable, and lord only over the unreasonable, not over man, but over beasts. Whereupon the first holy men were rather shepherds than kings, God shewing herein what both the order of the creation desired, and what the merit of sin exacted. For justly was the burden of servitude laid upon the back of transgression. And therefore in all the Scriptures we never read the word servant, until such time as that just man Noah laid it as a curse upon his offending son. So that it was guilt, and not nature that gave original unto that name. The Latin word *servus,* had the first derivation from hence: those that were taken in the wars, being in the hands of the conquerors to massacre or to preserve, if they saved them, then were they called *servi,* or *servo,* "to save." Nor was this effected beyond the desert of sin. For in the justest war, the sin upon one side causes it; and if the victory fall to the wicked (as sometimes it may) it is God's decree to humble the conquered, either reforming their sins herein, or punishing them. Witness that holy man of God, Daniel, who, being in captivity, confessed unto his Creator that his sins, and the sins of the people were the real causes of that captivity.

Sin therefore is the mother of servitude, and first cause of man's subjection to man: which notwithstanding comes not to pass but by the direction of the highest, in whom is no injustice, and who alone knows best how to proportionate his punishment unto man's offences: and he himself says: "Whosoever committeth sin is the servant of sin," and therefore many religious Christians are servants unto wicked masters, yet not unto freemen, for that which a man is addicted unto, the same is he slave unto. And it is a happier servitude to serve man than lust: for lust (to omit all the other passions) practises extreme tyranny upon the hearts of those that serve it, be it lust after sovereignty or fleshly lust. But in the peaceful orders of states, wherein one man is under another, as humility does benefit the servant, so does pride endamage the superior. But take a man as God created him at first, and so he is neither slave to man nor to sin. But penal servitude had the institution from that law which commands the conservation, and forbids the disturbance of nature's order: for if that law had not first been transgressed, penal servitude had never been enjoined.

Therefore the apostle warns servants to obey their masters and to serve them with cheerfulness, and good will: to the end that if they cannot be made free by their masters, they make their servitude a freedom to themselves, by serving them, not in deceitful fear, but in faithful love, until iniquity be overpassed, and all man's power and principality disannulled, and God only be all in all.

OF THE JUST LAW OF SOVEREIGNTY

Wherefore although our righteous forefathers had servants in their families, and according to their temporal estates, made a distinction between their servants and their children, yet in matter of religion (the fountain whence all eternal good flows), they provided for all their household with an equal respect unto each member thereof. This, nature's order prescribed, and hence came the name of, "The Father of the family," a name which even the worst masters love to be called by. But such as merit that name truly, do care that all their families should continue in the service of God, as if they were all their own children, desiring that they should all be placed in the household of heaven, where command is wholly unnecessary, because then they are past their

charge, having attained immortality, which until they be installed in, the masters are to endure more labour in their
government, than the servants in their service. If any be dis-
obedient, and offend this just peace, he is forthwith to be
corrected, with strokes, or some other convenient punishment, whereby he may be reingraffed into the peaceful
stock from whence his disobedience has torn him. For as it
is no good turn to help a man unto a smaller good by the
loss of a greater: no more is it the part of innocence by par-
doning a small offence, to let it grow unto a fouler. It is the
duty of an innocent to hurt no man, but, withal, to curb sin
in all he can, and to correct sin in whom he can, that the
sinner's correction may be profitable to himself, and his
example a terror unto others. Every family then being part
of the city, every beginning having relation unto some end,
and every part tending to the integrity of the whole, it follows apparently, that the family's peace adheres unto the
city's, that is, the orderly command, and obedience in the
family, has real reference to the orderly rule and subjection
in the city. So that "the father of the family" may fetch his
instructions from the city's government, whereby he may
proportionate the peace of his private estate, by that of the
common.

THE GROUNDS OF THE CONCORD AND DISCORD BETWEEN THE CITIES OF HEAVEN AND EARTH

But they that live not according to faith, angle for all
their peace in the sea of temporal profits: whereas the
righteous live in full expectation of the glories to come, using the occurrences of this world, but as pilgrims, not to
abandon their course towards God for mortal respects, but
thereby to assist the infirmity of the corruptible flesh, and
make it more able to encounter with toil and trouble. Wherefore the necessaries of this life are common, both to the
faithful and the infidel, and to both their families: but the
ends of their two usages thereof are far different.

The faithless, "worldly city" aims at earthly peace, and settles the self therein, only to have an uniformity of the citizens' wills in matters only pertaining to mortality. And the "Heavenly City," or rather that part thereof, which is as yet a pilgrim on earth and lives by faith, uses this peace also: as it should, it leaves this mortal life, wherein such a peace is requisite, and therefore lives (while it is here on earth) as if it were in captivity, and having received the promise of redemption and divers spiritual gifts as seals thereof, it willingly obeys such laws of the "temporal city" as order the things pertaining to the sustenance of this mortal life, to the end that both the cities might observe a peace in such things as are pertinent hereunto. But because that the "earthly city" has some members whom the Holy Scriptures utterly disallow, and who standing either too well affected to the devils, or being deluded by them, believed that each thing had a peculiar deity over it, and belonged to the charge of a several god: as the body to one, the soul to another, and in the body itself the head to one, the neck to another, and so of every member: as likewise of the soul, one had the wit, another the learning, a third the wrath, a fourth the desire: as also in other necessaries or accidents belonging to man's life, the cattle, the corn, the wine, the oil, the woods, the monies, the navigation, the wars, the marriages, the generations, each being a several charge unto a particular power, whereas the citizens of the "Heavenly State" acknowledged but one only God, to whom that worship, which is called λατρεία was peculiarly and solely due; hence came it that the "two hierarchies" could not be combined in one religion, but must needs dissent herein, so that the good part was fain to bear the pride and persecution of the bad, had not their own multitude sometimes, and the providence of God continually stood for their protection.

This "celestial society" while it is here on earth, increases itself out of all languages, never respecting the temporal laws that are made against so good and religious a practice: yet not breaking, but observing their diversity in divers nations, all which do tend unto the preservation of earthly peace, if they oppose not the adoration of one only God. So that you see, the "Heavenly City" observes and respects this temporal peace here on earth, and the coherence of men's wills in honest morality, as far as it may with a safe conscience; yea, and so far desires it, making use of it for the attainment of the peace eternal: which is so truly worthy of that name, as that the orderly and uniform combination of men in the fruition of God, and of one another in God, is to be accounted the reasonable creature's only peace, which being once attained, mortality is banished, and life then is the true life indeed, nor is the carnal body any more an encumbrance to the soul, by corruptibility, but is now become spiritual, perfected and entirely subject unto the sovereignty of the will.

This peace is that unto which the pilgrim in faith refers the other which he has here in his pilgrimage, and then lives he according to faith, when all that he does for the obtaining hereof is by himself referred unto God, and his neighbour withal, because being a citizen, he must not be all for himself, but sociable in his life and actions.

IV

THE ADVANCE OF MODERN SOCIOLOGICAL THOUGHT

COMMENTARY

At the end of the Middle Ages, modernity supersedes medievalism, which means that unity of vision is supplanted by diversity of outlook, and into the field of social theory a number of new figures now appear, each contributing, from his special angle, a new insight or intuition as to what society is or should be. In the Middle Ages one concept of society was dominant, whereas now, at the beginning of the modern age, several concepts emerge, to be followed, not much later, by a multiplying variety of concepts, most of which are centrifugal rather than centripetal in direction.

At this time, as the selections in this section of the book illustrate, the tendency toward diversity has only just begun.

Vico's Scienza Nuova is one of the first treatises in the sociological realm which gives dynamic life to the modern approach. Vico is a brilliant forerunner of the scientific sociology, to be developed later, of such indubitably modern thinkers as Montesquieu, Locke, Rousseau, Comte, Buckle, and Marx.

The great battle at this time is between the landed class and the rising middle class, and sociological theory revolves about that conflict. Machiavelli leads the way from a strategic point of view in outlining the tactics necessary for a Prince to rule in the parlous days which overtake the world at this time, but it is Hobbes, somewhat later, who gives the best theoretical defense of the monarchical conception of society. Having lived through the chaos of civil war and the brief dictatorship of the middle class (Puritans) in England, Hobbes, who declared that "he and terror were twins," makes it clear in The Leviathan that only rulership by a King is an acceptable state for mankind. His logic, impeccably clear if not always cogent, is an unadulterated ration-

alization of the rights of aristocratic sovereignty. When the people, in order to escape the inexorable cruelty of nature, surrender their liberty into the hands of a monarch, the action, Hobbes declares, is irrevocable. The most intolerable oppression, he maintains, cannot justify their revolt, for the state of nature, to which they revert when they revolt, is far worse than the most arrant despotism.

In the case of Locke and Rousseau, and later of Thomas Paine, we are face to face with a new conception, which is completely antagonistic to that of Hobbes. All of these men, however unconsciously, voice the social philosophy of the rising middle class. For Locke the state of Nature is no savage chaos, as Hobbes envisioned it; consequently, men do not sign away their rights when they accepted a king as ruler. No political manifesto or royal decree can rob the people of rights that are sacred and inalienable. Kings, Locke contends, do not inherit their prerogatives from God but from the people.

Locke attacks kings and defends representative government because the social conflict of his day, between the aristocracy and the middle class, leads him, as a proponent of middle-class ideas, to such conclusions, and in his Treatises on Government, *he defends regicide and the right to revolution.*

In France, Rousseau, many decades later, writes The Social Contract, *in which he propounds, in his own unique individualistic way, ideas of an astonishingly similar character. Rousseau, in his defense of "the people against the monarch," goes much further than Locke, and makes a fetish of "the state of nature." For Rousseau the artificial becomes anathema and the natural sacred. It was his stress upon the fact that sovereignty inheres in the people and not in the monarch, as Hobbes had argued, which gives to his* Social Contract *the spiritual dynamite which set off the French Revolution. By the time the French Revolution bursts into flame, Rousseau's ideas have become the accepted social logic of the time—or sociology, of the time, and the inspiration not only of French intellectuals and revolutionaries but also of their English cousins.*

In Thomas Paine, Rousseau's revolutionary ideas find a dynamic English counterpart. Paine, to be sure, is more of a soap-boxing mentality than Rousseau, and, consequently, declaims as well as reasons, but his declamations, in influencing the American Revolution, are heard round the world.

On the more purely intellectual and non-political side, the work of Montesquieu and Adam Smith foreshadow sociological conceptions which are to take root the next century. Monestquieu with his stress upon climate is the forerunner of Buckle, and Adam Smith with his advocacy of laissez-faire is the father of the whole school of capitalist economics and sociology which is to develop with such melodramatic rapidity in the nineteenth century.

SELECTIONS FROM *SCIENZA NUOVA*

By GIAMBATTISTA VICO

I

THE human mind, by nature unlimited, when plunged into ignorance, patterns the universe after itself.

This axiom is the cause of two common human habits: one, that renown is magnified as it spreads, the other that presence detracts from fame. Fame has been the perennial source of all the overstatements that have been made concerning the remotest antiquity of the world.

Tacitus, in his life of Agricola, says: "Whatever is unknown is held to be unusually great."

II

Men judge remote and unknown things, of which they cannot form any idea, by the things they see and know.

This axiom bares the inexhaustible source of all the errors committed by entire nations and by all scholars concerning the beginnings of mankind. It is only when nations have reached an enlightened, cultivated, extremely civilized stage of development, that they turn their attention to their origins. It is likewise at this stage that scholars start studying the origins of nations. They judge such origins according to the standards of their own time. But in reality they must have been inconspicuous, uncouth, and very obscure.

This may be blamed on two kinds of conceit; that of nations and that of scholars.

73

III

There is a golden saying of Diodorus Siculus on the conceit of nations: "Nations, Greek as well as barbarian, showed such conceit. Each boasted of having preceded the others in inventing the conveniences of human life and of having preserved records of their accomplishments from the beginning of the world."

This destroys the claims of the Chaldeans, Scythians, Egyptians, and Chinese of having founded the civilization of the ancient world.

IV

To this conceit of nations is to be added the conceit of scholars. They claim that their knowledge is coeval with the beginnings of the world.

This axiom destroys all the opinions of scholars concerning the incomparable wisdom of the ancients: it convicts of imposture the oracles of Zoroaster and Chaldean, those of Anacharsis the Scythian, the Pimander of Mercurius Trismegistus, the verses of Orpheus, the *Carmen aureum* of Pythagoras. Moreover it convicts of falsity all the mystical meanings which scholars have read into Egyptian hieroglyphics and the philosophical allegories attributed to Greek fables.

V

Philosophy, in order to be useful to mankind, must raise and support weak and fallen man, not pervert his nature or abandon him to his corruption.

This axiom excludes the Stoics from the system of doctrines set forth in this science, since they advocate the mortification of the senses. It also excludes the Epicureans who make the senses a standard of life. Both deny the existence of Providence. On the other hand this axiom admits political philosophers into this science, especially the Platonists, who are agreed with all legislators on these three points: that Divine Providence exists, that human passions must be moderated and transformed into human virtues, and that human souls are immortal.

VI

Philosophy considers man *such as he must be*. Thus it can be of benefit only to a very few people, those who desire to live in the republic of Plato, not among the scum of Romulus.

VII

Legislation considers man *such as he is,* in order to make good use of him in human society. Legislation transforms three vices, greed, ambition, ferocity, into courtly life, art of war, commerce. Thus wisdom, fortitude, wealth, spring into being; and out of greed, ambition, ferocity, which, if left to themselves, would destroy the human race, legislation compounds the happiness of society.

VIII

Things out of their natural state have neither temporary nor long duration.

IX

Men ignorant of the truth of things stick to certainty. Not being able to satisfy their intelligence with knowledge, they are content to have their will supported by the consciousness of certainty.

X

Philosophy deals with reason, from which the knowledge of truth derives; philology with the authority of the human will whence springs the consciousness of certainty.

I term 'philologists' all grammarians, historians, and critics, whose labours are employed in the study of languages and the events of history: events both internal (customs and laws) and external (war, peace, alliances, travel, and trade).

This axiom shows that both philosophers and philologists have accomplished only half their task: the philosophers not having buttressed their reasons with the authority of the philologists, and the philologists not having cared to give truth to their authority by means of philosophical demonstrations.

XII

Common sense is judgment without reflection, held by a whole people, by a whole nation, or by all mankind.

This axiom with the definition following it, gives us a new critical method for judging the traditions which have been handed down concerning the founders of nations. Nations in fact do not show written documents until over a thousand years after their foundation. Critics have been thus far exclusively occupied with these written documents.

XIII

Identical ideas born among nations which have had no contact with each other must have a common basis of truth.

This axiom establishes the fact that the common sense of the human race is a providential criterion wherewith nations arrive at certainty in respect to the dictates of the natural law. Nations form a firm conviction of certainty in respect to the dictates of natural law by grasping the substantial unities of natural law in which they all agree—with some differences. In view of this common agreement of nations, it is possible to compile a mental dictionary, showing the origins of the various languages, and containing an eternal history of ideas, out of which the temporal histories of all nations derive. It is a shocking error to suppose that culture sprang from a single nation which afterwards transmitted it to others. This error was committed by Egyptians and Greeks who boasted of having spread civilization throughout the world. It was because of this error that it was believed that the Law of XII Tables was carried from Athens to Rome. But, if this were so, it would be a civil law communicated to other nations through human agency, *not* a law naturally established by Providence through the instrumentality of human customs.

Each nation evolved its own political and legal institutions separately and in complete ignorance of the others.

XIV

The "nature" of things is nothing but the fact of their being born at certain times and in certain manners. These times and manners being such, things are born such, and not otherwise.

XV

Qualities inseparable from their subjects must be produced by the special manner in which things are born; therefore, they truthfully inform us that such, and no other, is the nature, or *nascence,* of things.

XVI

No tradition is wholly false. Traditions persisting among whole nations for long intervals of time must have had

public motives of truth. The goal of this work is the discovery of the elements of truth which, with the passing of
the centuries and the changes in language and custom, have
come down to us overgrown with falsity.

XVII

Popular languages are the most important testimonies of
the customs which were practised at the time when these
languages were formed.

XVIII

A language of an ancient nation, which has been in use
up to its point of perfection, must be considered as a great
repository of the culture of the early epochs.

This axiom assures us that the philological proofs of the
cultural development of nations, drawn from Latin words,
have great weight. The same may be said of the words of
the German language, which possesses the same quality as
the ancient Roman.

XIX

Since the Law of the XII Tables consists of customs of
the peoples of Latium, practised by them as far back as the
age of Saturn, always changing elsewhere but fixed in
bronze by the Romans and religiously guarded by jurisprudence of Rome, such a law is a great testimony of the
ancient natural law of the peoples of Latium.

XX

If the poems of Homer are civil histories containing the
ancient customs of the Greeks, they are two great treasures
of the natural law of the peoples of Greece.

XXI

Greek philosophers hastened the natural course which their nation had to run. They appeared in Greece when it was still in a state of barbarity, and caused it to pass at once into a state of extreme refinement, while simultaneously the nation preserved its divine and heroic legends intact. On the other hand, the Romans, who, in the development of their national life marched at a moderate pace, completely lost sight of the history of their gods. Therefore the period which the Egyptians called "the age of the gods" Varro terms "the obscure age of the Romans." The Romans preserved in their vulgar language the heroic history which extends from Romulus to the *lex Publilia* and the *lex Poetelia*. I shall show that the heroic history of Rome is a perpetual parallel of the heroic age of Greece.

France ran the same course in the development of her civilization as did Greece. In France, in the midst of the barbarism of the XIIth century, was founded the University of Paris, where the celebrated Pietro Lombardo taught very subtle scholastic philosophy. Like an Homeric poem, the history of Turpin, Bishop of Paris, full of all the legends of the French paladins, which later filled so many novels and poems, was still extant at this time in France. And through this precocious passage from barbarism to the subtlest sciences, the French language acquired an extreme refinement, so that, of all the living languages, it seems to have reproduced in our time the atticism of the Greeks, and like Greek it is superior to all other languages in dealing with scientific matters. And, even as did Greek, French has preserved many diphthongs, which is a characteristic of a barbaric language, still unplastic and experiencing difficulty in combining consonants with vowels.

Romulus founded Rome in the midst of older cities of Latium as a place of refuge. This, Livy defines in general terms as the manner in which cities were founded in ancient times. Violence was still rife, so he naturally founded Rome in the manner in which the primitive cities had their inception. Therefore, after Roman customs had progressed along the lines set down by the establishment of the asylum, in an age in which the vulgar languages of Latium had also made many advances, it must have happened that the events occurring in the Roman community (similar to those which the Greeks expressed in the *heroic* language) were expressed by the Romans in the *vulgar* language. Ancient Roman history is, as it were, a perpetual symbolic mythology of the heroic history of the Greeks. It must have been for this reason that the Romans were the heroes of the world: Rome subjugated the other cities of Latium, then all of Italy, and lastly the world, when heroism was still young among the Romans. Among the other peoples of Latium, instead, from whose subjugation derived the greatness of Rome, heroism must have begun to grow old.

XXII

There is a mental language common to all nations, whereby they uniformly grasp the substance of the actions of associated life, and express this substance with as many different modifications as there are different aspects of such actions.

This mental language is peculiar to this work. Philologists who approach their studies in the light of its principles will be enabled to form a mental vocabulary common to all various articulated languages, past or present. In the first edition of this *Scienza Nuova* I have listed in a great number of dead and living languages the names of the first patriarchal rulers; names referring to the several functions which they exerted in the patriarchal stage, i. e. that stage in which languages were formed.

XXVIII

The Egyptians divided all time preceding their own into three ages: the age of gods, of heroes and of men. In these three ages, three languages were spoken: hieroglyphic or sacred, symbolic or language by similitudes; and "vulgar," consisting of conventional signs, expressing the everyday needs of life.

XXIX

Homer, in five places in both of his poems, mentions a language more ancient than his own, which must undoubtedly have been in the heroic, and calls it "language of the Gods."

XXX

Varro diligently collected no less than twenty thousand names of Gods known to the Greeks. These names indicated the needs of life, natural, moral, economic or civil, from the primeval age onward.

Nations everywhere began with religion.

XXXI

When nations have become savage through warfare, so that human laws no longer command respect among them, the only powerful means of controlling them is religion.

This axiom established the fact that, in the lawless state, Divine Providence made it possible for wild and violent people to take the first steps towards civilization and the founding of nations. It awakened in them a confused idea of deity, so that they, in their ignorance, incongruously attributed divinity to unworthy objects. Thus, through the fear of such an imagined deity, some semblance of order was established.

XXXII

Men, ignorant of the natural causes of things, whenever they cannot explain them by similarities, attribute to things their own nature, as the common people, for example, say that the magnet is *in love* with iron.

XXXIV

A true quality of human nature is noted by Tacitus when he says "mobiles ad superstitiones perculsae semel mentes;" meaning that once haunted by a frightful superstition, men attribute to it whatever they imagine, see, or do.

XXXVII

The sublimity of poetry consists in giving sense and passion to inanimate objects. It is a characteristic of children to take inanimate objects in their hands and, playing with them, talk to them as if they were living persons.

This philologic-philosophic axiom proves that in the beginning of the world, when races were very young, men were by nature sublime poets.

XL

Sacrifices arose out of superstitious religions, which caused cruel, fierce primitive man to make votive offerings and to slay human victims. These victims, as Plautus says, were called by the Latins *Saturni hostiae,* and were the sacrifices to Moloch among the Phoenicians, who flung into the flames babies consecrated to that false god. Some of these consecrations are preserved in the Law of the XII Tables. These things, just as they give the correct meaning to that saying: *"Primus in orbe deos fecit timor,"*—i. e. that false religions were born not out of imposture, but out of credulity—likewise prove that the cruel vow and sacrifice, which Agamemnon made of his pious daughter Iphigenia, impiously commented on by Lucretius when he says that so many ills were caused by religion, was inspired by providence. Nothing less than these cruelties was needed in order that the offspring of primeval man might become human, and that a later civilization might produce such men as Aristides, Socrates, Laelius, and Scipio Africanus.

XLIII

Every heathen nation had its Hercules, who was the son of Jupiter. Varro was able to count forty of them.

This axiom is the principle of the heroism of the first nations, born from a false opinion which they had that heroes stemmed from a divine progenitor.

This axiom also demonstrates that nations could not be founded without religion, nor be enlarged without virtue. Nations were, at the beginning, savage and impenetrable, not knowing, consequently, of each other's existence. The first fables must have contained truths relating to man's life in the social state; they, therefore, must have been the earliest histories of nations.

XLIV

The first sages of the Greek world were the theological poets, who undoubtedly flourished before the heroic ones, just as Jupiter was the father of Hercules.

Heathen nations, since they all had their Jupiters and their Hercules, were, in the beginning, poetic; and among them the first type of poetry to arise was divine, followed by heroic.

XLVII

The human mind tends to take pleasure in uniformity.

This axiom is confirmed by the custom that common people have of devising fables about famous men, placing them in imaginary situations and making them act in conformity with the character attributed to them. These fables are ideal truths corresponding to the type of the men whose deeds they relate. On close inspection, poetic truth is a metaphysical truth. If physical truth is not in conformity with it, then physical truth must be reputed false.

XLIX

Primitive man was a child, incapable of conceiving abstract ideas. He was obliged by his nature to imagine certain *poetic types* which constitute the essence of fables and which are general categories under which all concrete species can be subsumed. Thus the Egyptians attributed to Mercurius Trismegistus, for them the symbolic type of ruler, intent on the welfare of society and anxious to further it by useful discoveries, all the inventions useful or necessary to the human race. They did so because they did not know how to grasp the abstract idea of "the socially minded ruler," and even less the idea of "social wisdom." This shows how little the Egyptians were philosophers.

LI

All pagan civilization had its inception in poetry, from which all other arts derive. The earliest poets were poets not by art but by nature.

LII

All arts pertaining to necessary, useful, convenient and

most of the pleasurable human things, were invented in the poetic centuries, before the coming of the philosophers.

LIII

At first men simply feel without consciousness of feeling, then they become conscious of the passionate turmoil of their souls, and finally they reflect with pure intellect.

This axiom is the principle of poetry, which is created from passion and feeling, unlike philosophy which results from reason and reflection. Therefore philosophical truth is best expressed in abstractions and poetic truth in concrete terms.

LIV

Man naturally is influenced in his interpretation of doubtful or obscure things by his nature, passions, and customs.

This axiom is a great canon of our mythology. It explains the strict severity of primitive fables, devised by early men who had just left behind them the stage of a fierce beast-like liberty. The fables arose after a long interval of years and many changes in customs; they were altered to fit a new stage of civilization, obscured in the dissolute, corrupt times preceding Homer. The Greeks set great store by religion, hence, fearing that the gods might be as contrary to their wishes as their customs were contrary to their gods, they attributed their customs to their gods, and gave indecent, scandalous, obscene meaning to their fables.

LV

There is a passage in Eusebius which is truly golden when applied, not only to its particular object, Egyptian wisdom, but to all Pagan wisdom. He says: "The earliest theology of the Egyptians was merely history intermixed with fables.

Later generations, being ashamed of such fables, started af-
fixing to them mystical meanings." Maneton, Egyptian high
priest, did this when he transformed all Egyptian history
into a sublime natural theology.

This axiom and the preceding one prove our historic
mythology. They destroy the assumption of the incomparable wisdom of the ancients.

LXIII

The human mind is naturally inclined, through the instrumentality of the senses, to describe its own operations in
terms of physical objects, and it is only through many efforts that, by means of reflection, it can grasp its own substance.

This axiom gives us the universal principle of etymology
of all languages, in which words are transposed from bodies
and from qualities of bodies to signify mental and spiritual
things.

LXIV

The order of ideas must proceed according to the order of
things.

LXV

The order of human things proceeded thus: there were
first forests, then hovels, then villages, then cities, finally
academies.

This axiom is a great principle of etymology: it warns us
that it is according to this order of human things that histories of the words of native languages must be told; we observe,
accordingly, that almost the whole body of words of Latin
is composed of rustic, peasant vocables. For instance: *lex*
meant at first "acorn gathering," from which, we believe,

derives *ilex* (probably a reduction from *illex*) meaning holm-oak (just as, undoubtedly, *aquilex* means "the water gatherer"), since the holm-oak produces the acorn. Afterwards, *lex* meant "pulse gathering," hence pulse was called *legumina*. Later, at the time when vulgar characters with which to write laws had not yet been invented, through a necessity of social nature, *lex* must have meant "citizens' gathering," namely, a public assembly; therefore, the presence of the people was the law which gave solemnity to the wills that were made in public assembly. Finally, picking up letters, and making out of them, as it were, a mental bundle, in the operation of reading, was called *legere* (to read).

LXII

Presumably ideas and languages developed simultaneously.

Verse-speech, among all nations, preceded prose-speech.

LXVII

The nature of nations is at first crude, then severe, then benign, then refined, and finally dissolute.

LXVIII

In mankind there arise first enormous, dull-witted beings, such as Polyphemes; then magnanimous and haughty men like Achilles; then men of worth and of justice, such as Aristides, Scipio Africanus; in times closer to us, showy personages, with great appearance of virtue joined with great vice, such as Alexander, Caesar, men whom the rabble noisily crown with tinselled glory; later on, wicked, reflective natures such as Tiberius; finally shameless and debauched madmen, such as Caligula, Nero and Domitian.

This axiom demonstrates that the first were needed in

order that man might be forced to obey man in the patriarchal state, and in order to dispose him to obey laws in
the state of the cities, which was coming; the second, who
naturally did not yield to their peers, in order to establish,
on the foundation of the family, the aristocratic states; the
third, to open the way for democratic liberty; the fourth, to
introduce monarchies; the fifth, to stabilize them; the
sixth, to overthrow them.

This is the pattern of the eternal history of ideas on the
foundation of which runs the course of all nations, with
their rise, progress, political forms, decline, and end.

LXX

In the primeval, lawless world, some few, stronger human
beings—the patriarchs—deserted the wild pack of their fellows and founded families and tilled the fields; and after a
long lapse of time, other human beings deserted the pack,
taking refuge in the lands cultivated by the patriarchs.

LXXV

The tradition that the first kings were sages is false. In
the persons of the patriarchs were joined wisdom, priesthood, and kingship; kingship and priesthood were dependencies of their wisdom, which was *not* the recondite wisdom of philosophy, but the vulgar, practical wisdom of law
givers.

LXXVI

The tradition that monarchy was the first form of government is false.

The patriarchs must have exerted a monarchic rule, subject only to God, over the persons as well as the acquisitions
of their sons, and a stronger rule over the serfs who had

taken shelter on their lands, and their possessions. Consequently they were the first monarchs of the world.

LXXVIII

If the word family has any etymological appropriateness it must derive from *famuli,* the serfs of the patriarchs in the state of nature.

LXXIX

It is impossible to imagine or conceive that before the time when the *famuli*—serfs—took shelter on the lands of the patriarchs, there might have existed other men associated with the patriarchs. The serfs bonded themselves to the patriarchs, and were obliged, in order to maintain themselves, to cultivate the fields of their masters. These serfs turn out to be the *true* associates of the heroes, who later were the plebeians of the heroic cities, and finally the provincial subjects of ruling peoples.

LXXXII

All ancient nations offer abundant examples of clients and clienteles, which can very aptly be interpreted as vassals and fiefs; nor are the scholars who have studied feudal law able to find any more apposite Roman words to designate vassals and fiefs, than *clientes* and *clientelae.* It is impossible that the state should have arisen from the family, if it had been composed exclusively of sons, and not of slaves as well.

LXXXIII

The law pertaining to the distribution of lands was the first agrarian law established in the world, nor can it be imagined that there ever was a more restricted one.

This agrarian law distinguished the three kinds of land-ownership which can exist naturally in society, and which are held by three kinds of persons: the *dominium bonita-rium,* held by the plebeians; the *dominium quiritarium,* preserved with arms and, consequently, aristocratic, among the patriarchs; and the *dominium eminens,* held by the patriarchal caste. This last, collectively, is the sovereignty, namely the sovereign power, in the aristocratic states.

XCII

The weak clamour for laws, the powerful refuse them, the ambitious, in order to gain a following, promote them, the kings, in order to equalize the powerful with the weak, protect the laws.

This axiom, in its first and second parts, is a torch illuminating the darkness of history enfolding the heroic rivalries of aristocratic states, in which the patricians strive with all their might to keep the laws secret to their caste in order that the laws may depend on their arbitrary will alone and so that they may administer them with kinglike power.

XCV

Men at first strive to free themselves from subjection and desire equality: these are the plebeians of the aristocratic states which are finally changed into democracies. Then men strive to overcome their equals: this is the case of the plebeians in democratic states which by corruption are changed into oligarchies. Finally men want to tread the laws underfoot: these are the anarchies or unrestrained democratic states: there is no worse tyranny than this. Thereupon the plebeian multitudes, having become aware of their own evils, in order to remedy them, seek their salvation in monarchy. This is the natural *lex regia* with which Tacitus legitimizes the Roman monarchy under Augustus, "who brought the state, torn by internecine strife, under his rule, assuming the name of *princeps*."

XCVI

From native, lawless liberty the patricians, when the first cities were established on the foundation of the family, were reduced in spite of their reluctance, to restraints and burdens. These are the aristocratic states in which patricians rule. Afterward they were forced by the plebeians, who had grown to a great number and had become strengthened by war, to submit to laws and burdens equally with the plebeians. These are the noblemen in the democratic states. Finally, in order to lead a comfortable life, they became naturally inclined to be ruled by a single man. These are the noblemen under monarchy.

CVII

Races began before cities, and they are those which the Latins called *gentes majores,* i. e. noble ancient families, like the families of the patriarchs with whom Romulus composed the Senate, and, with the Senate, the city of Rome. On the other hand *gentes minores* was the name given to the new noble families, founded after the establishment of the cities, like the families of the patriarchs with whom Junius Brutus, after the expulsion of the kings, filled the Senate, almost exhausted by the death of the senators whom Tarquinius the Proud had had killed.

CVIII

The gods were divided into two classes: those of the *gentes majores* and those of the *gentes minores.* The gods of the *gentes majores* were the gods worshipped in the epoch

preceding the foundation of the cities. These gods were undoubtedly eleven in number, among the Greeks and Latins
as well as among the Chaldeans, Phoenicians, and Egyptians. They were Jupiter, Diana, Apollo; Vulcan, Saturn,
Vesta; Mars, Venus; Minerva, Mercury; Neptune.

The gods of the *minores gentes* are instead the gods worshipped by the peoples at a later date; for example Romulus,
whom the Roman people called Deus Quirinus after his
death.

The systems of Grotius, Selden and Pufendorf are wanting in firm basic principles, since they begin by considering
the nations at an epoch in which they had already been
founded, and were already a part of the general society of
mankind; whereas the history of all primeval nations began
with the patriarchal epoch, under the rule of the gods, so-
called, of the *majores gentes*.

CIX

Dull-witted people think that whatever is expressed in
legal formulas of a fixed character is just law.

CXI

The "certain" in laws is an obscurity of legal right, supported solely by authority, which makes us feel that laws
are severe, but forces us to observe them on account of the
certainty they give us in dubious cases. "Certum" in Latin
means "singularized," established to cover a particular case,
or, as the Scholastics say, "individuated;" in which regard
certum and *commune* have exactly the opposite signification, by an elegance of the Latin language.

This axiom constitutes the principle of *strict law,* of which
civil equity is the rule; with whose *certum,* i. e. with the
literal signification of whose verbal formulae the barbarians,
whose minds are incapable of rising to abstract ideas, are

satisfied, and according to whose formulae they judge the justice due them. Therefore Ulpian says, in this connection, "harsh is the law, but it is written;" whereas we, with more Latin beauty and greater legal elegance, would phrase it thus: "harsh is the law but it is certain."

CXIV

Natural equity of fully unfolded human reason is a practice of wisdom in matters pertaining to self-advantage, since wisdom, in the amplitude of its meaning, is nothing but the science of putting things to such use as their nature demands.

This axiom with the two following definitions, constitutes the principle of mild law, regulated by natural equity, which is second-nature in civilized nations. It is from civilization that philosophy arises.

It was Providence which instituted the natural law of nations. Providence permitted nations, since they had to live during long centuries incapable of grasping truth and natural equity (on which it was the role of the philosophers later to throw light) to cling to the *certum* and to civil equity, which scrupulously guards the letter of institutions and of laws; and, in order that their existence might be ensured, provided that they should observe their laws and institutions even in cases in which they proved to be too harsh.

The three great theorists of the doctrine of the natural law of nations (Grotius, Selden, and Pufendorf) unanimously went astray in establishing their systems. They thought that natural equity in its perfect idea must have been grasped by the Heathen nations as far back as their beginnings, without noticing the fact that almost two thousand years were needed in order that philosophers might arise in one or the other nation.

SELECTIONS FROM SCIENZA NUOVA

THE ART OF WAR*

By NICCOLO MACHIAVELLI

A PRINCE ought to have no other aim or thought, nor select anything else for his study, than war and its rules and
discipline; for this is the sole art that belongs to him who
rules, and it is of such force that it not only upholds those
who are born princes, but it often enables men to rise from
a private station to that rank. And, on the contrary, it is
seen that when princes have thought more of ease than of
arms they have lost their states. And the first cause of your
losing it is to neglect this art; and what enables you to acquire a state is to be master of the art. Francesco Sforza,
through being martial, from a private person became Duke
of Milan; and the sons, through avoiding the hardships and
troubles of arms, from dukes became private persons. For
among other evils which being unarmed brings you, it
causes you to be despised, and this is one of those ignominies
against which a prince ought to guard himself, as is shown
later on. Because there is nothing proportionate between
the armed and the unarmed; and it is not reasonable that
he who is armed should yield obedience willingly to him
who is unarmed, or that the unarmed man should be secure among armed servants. Because, there being in the one
disdain and in the other suspicion, it is not possible for them
to work well together. And therefore a prince who does not
understand the art of war, over and above the other misfortunes already mentioned cannot be respected by his soldiers,
nor can he rely on them. He ought never, therefore, to
have out of his thoughts this subject of war, and in peace
he should addict himself more to its exercise than in war;

* From *The Prince*

this he can do in two ways, the one by action, the other by study.

As regards action, he ought above all things to keep his men well organised and drilled, to follow incessantly the chase, by which he accustoms his body to hardships, and learns something of the nature of localities, and gets to find out how the mountains rise, how the valleys open out, how the plains lie, and to understand the nature of rivers and marshes, and in all this to take the greatest care. Which knowledge is useful in two ways. Firstly, he learns to know his country, and is better able to undertake its defence; afterwards, by means of the knowledge and observation of that locality, he understands with ease any other which it may be necessary for him to study hereafter; because the hills, valleys, and plains, and rivers and marshes that are, for instance, in Tuscany, have a certain resemblance to those of other countries, so that with a knowledge of the aspect of one country one can easily arrive at a knowledge of others. And the prince that lacks this skill lacks the essential which it is desirable that a captain should possess, for it teaches him to surprise his enemy, to select quarters, to lead armies, to array the battle, to besiege towns to advantage.

Philopoemen, Prince of the Acheans, among other praises which writers have bestowed on him, is commended because in time of peace he never had anything in his mind but the rules of war; and when he was in the country with friends, he often stopped and reasoned with them: "If the enemy should be upon that hill, and we should find ourselves here with our army, with whom would be the advantage? How should one best advance to meet him, keeping the ranks? If we should wish to retreat, how ought we to set about it? If they should retreat, how ought we to pursue?" And he would set forth to them, as he went, all the chances that could befall an army; he would listen to their opinion and state his, confirming it with reasons, so that these continual discussions there could never arise, in time of war, or any unexpected circumstances that he could not deal with.

But to exercise the intellect the prince should read histories, and study there the actions of illustrious men, to see how they have borne themselves in war, to examine the causes of their victories and defeat, so as to avoid the latter and imitate the former; and above all do as an illustrious man did, who took as an exemplar one who had been praised and famous before him, and whose achievements and deeds he always kept in his mind, as it is said Alexander the Great imitated Achilles, Caesar Alexander, Scipio Cyrus. And whoever reads the life of Cyrus, written by Xenophon, will recognise afterwards in the life of Scipio how that imitation was his glory, and how in chastity, affability, humanity, and liberality Scipio conformed to those things which have been written of Cyrus by Xenophon. A wise prince ought to observe some such rules, and never in peaceful times stand idle, but increase his resources with industry in such a way that they may be available to him in adversity, so that if fortune changes it may find him prepared to resist her blows.

THE WAY PRINCES KEEP FAITH

Every one admits how praiseworthy it is in a prince to keep faith, and to live with integrity and not with craft. Nevertheless our experience has been that those princes who have done great things have held good faith of little account, and have known how to circumvent the intellect of men by craft, and in the end have overcome those who have relied on their word. You must know there are two ways of contesting, the one by the law, the other by force; the first method is proper to men, the second to beasts; but because the first is frequently not sufficient, it is necessary to have recourse to the second. Therefore it is necessary for a prince to understand how to avail himself of the beast and the man. This has been figuratively taught to princes by ancient writers, who describe how Achilles and many other princes of old were given to the Centaur Chiron to nurse, who brought them up in his discipline; which means solely that, as they had for a teacher one who was half beast and half man, so it is necessary for a prince to know how to make use of both natures, and that one without the other is not durable. A prince, therefore, being compelled knowingly to adopt the beast, ought to choose the fox and the lion; because the lion cannot defend himself against snares and the fox cannot defend himself against wolves. Therefore, it is necessary to be a fox to discover the snares and a lion to terrify the wolves. Those who rely simply on the lion do not understand what they are about. Therefore a wise lord cannot, nor ought he, to keep faith when such observance may be turned against him, and when the reasons that caused him to pledge it exist no longer. If men were entirely good this precept would not hold, but because they are bad, and will not keep faith with you, you too are not bound to observe it with them. Nor will there ever be wanting to a prince legitimate reasons to excuse this non-observance. Of this endless modern examples could be given, showing how many treaties and engagements have been made void and of no effect through the faithlessness of princes; and he who has known best how to employ the fix has succeeded best.

But it is necessary to know well how to disguise this characteristic, and to be a great pretender and dissembler; and men are so simple, and so subject to present necessities, that he who seeks to deceive will always find some one who will allow himself to be deceived. One recent example I cannot pass over in silence. Alexander the Sixth did nothing else but deceive men, nor ever thought of doing otherwise and he always found victims; for there never was a man who had greater power in asserting, or who with greater oaths would affirm a thing, yet would observe it less; nevertheless his deceits always succeeded according to his wishes, because he well understood this side of mankind.

Therefore it is unnecessary for a prince to have all the

good qualities I have enumerated, but it is very necessary to appear to have them. And I shall dare to say this also, that to have them and always to observe them is injurious, and that to appear to have them is useful; to appear merciful, faithful, humane, religious, upright, and to be so, but with a mind so framed that should you require not to be so, you may be able and know how to change to the opposite.

And you have to understand this, that a prince, especially a new one, cannot observe all those things for which men are esteemed, being often forced, in order to maintain the state, to act contrary to fidelity, friendship, humanity, and religion. Therefore it is necessary for him to have a mind ready to turn itself accordingly as the winds and variations of fortune force it, yet, as I have said above, not to diverge from the good if he can avoid doing so, but, if compelled, then to know how to set about it.

For this reason a prince ought to take care that he never lets anything slip from his lips that is not replete with the above-named five qualities, that he may appear to him who sees and hears him altogether merciful, faithful, humane, upright, and religious. There is nothing more necessary to appear to have than this last quality, inasmuch as men judge generally more by the eye than by the hand, because it belongs to everybody to see you, to few to come in touch with you. Every one sees what you appear to be, few really know what you are, and those few dare not oppose themselves to the opinion of the many, who have the majesty of the state to defend them; and in the actions of all men, and especially of princes, which it is not prudent to challenge, one judges by the result.

For that reason, let a prince have the credit of conquering and holding his state, the means will always be considered honest, and he will be praised by everybody; because the vulgar are always taken by what a thing seems to be and by what comes of it; and in the world there are only the vulgar, for the few find a place there only when the many have no ground to rest on.

One prince of the present time, whom it is not well to name, never preaches anything else but peace and good faith, and to both he is most hostile, and either, if he had kept it, would have deprived him of reputation and kingdom many a time.

SELECTIONS FROM TWO TREATISES ON CIVIL GOVERNMENT

By JOHN LOCKE

OF SLAVERY

The natural liberty of man is to be free from any supe-rior power on earth, and not to be under the will or legis-lative authority of man, but to have only the law of Nature for his rule. The liberty of man in society is to be under no other legislative power but that established by consent in the commonwealth, nor under the dominion of any will, or restraint of any law, but what that legislative shall enact ac-cording to the trust put in it. Freedom, then, is not what Sir Robert Filmer tells us (O. A., 55): "A liberty for every one to do what he lists, to live as he pleases, and not to be tied by any laws;" but freedom of men under government is to have a standing rule to live by, common to every one of that society, and made by the legislative power erected in it. A liberty to follow my own will in all things where that rule prescribes not, not to be subject to the inconstant, uncertain, unknown, arbitrary will of another man, as free-dom of nature is to be under no other restraint but the law of Nature.

OF PROPERTY

Whether we consider natural reason, which tells us that men, being once born, have a right to their preservation, and consequently to meat and drink and such other things as Nature affords for their subsistence, or "revelation," which gives us an account of those grants God made of the world to Adam, and to Noah and his sons, it is very clear that

God, as King David says (Psalm cav. 16), "has given the earth to the children of men," given it to mankind in common. But, this being supposed, it seems to some a very great difficulty how any one should ever come to have a property in anything, I will not content myself to answer, that, if it be difficult to make out "property" upon a supposition that God gave the world to Adam and his posterity in common, it is impossible that any man but one universal monarch should have any "property" upon a supposition that God gave the world to Adam and his heirs in succession, exclusive of all the rest of his posterity; but I shall endeavour to show how men might come to have a property in several parts of that which God gave to mankind in common and that without any express compact of all the commoners.

God, who hath given the world to men in common, hath also given them reason to make use of it to the best advantage of life and convenience. The earth and all that is therein is given to men for the support and comfort of their being. And though all the fruits it naturally produces, and beasts it feeds, belong to mankind in common, as they are produced by the spontaneous hand of Nature, and nobody has originally a private dominion exclusive of the rest of mankind in any of them, as they are thus in their natural state, yet being given for the use of men, there must of necessity be a means to appropriate them some way or other before they can be of any use, or at all beneficial, to any particular men. The fruit or venison which nourishes the wild Indian, who knows no enclosure, and is still a tenant in common, must be his, and so his—i. e., a part of him, that another can no longer have any right to it before it can do him any good for the support of his life.

Though the earth and all inferior creatures be common to all men, yet every man has a "property" in his own "person." This nobody has any right to but himself. The "labour" of his body and the "work" of his hands, we may say, are properly his. Whatsoever, then, he removes out of the state that Nature hath provided and left it in, he hath mixed his labour with it, and joined to it something that is his own, and thereby makes it his property. It being by him removed from the common state Nature placed it in, it hath by this labour something annexed to it that excludes the common right of other men. For this "labour" being the unquestionable property of the labourer, no man but he can have a right to what that is once joined to, at least where there is enough, and as good left in common for others.

He that is nourished by the acorns he picked up under an oak, or the apples he gathered from the trees in the wood, has certainly appropriated them to himself. Nobody can deny but the nourishment is his. I ask, then, when did they begin to be his? when he digested? or when he ate? or when he boiled? or when he brought them home? or when he picked them up? And it is plain, if the first gathering made them not his, nothing else could. That labour put a distinction between them and common. That added something to them more than Nature, the common mother of all, had done, and so they became his private right. And will any one say he had no right to those acorns or apples he thus appropriated because he had not the consent of all mankind to make them his? Was it a robbery thus to assume to himself what belonged to all in common? If such a consent as that was necessary, man had starved, notwithstanding the plenty God had given him. We see in commons, which remain so by compact, that it is the taking any part of what is common and removing it out of the state Nature leaves it in, which begins the property, without which the common is of no use. And the taking of this or that part does not depend on the express consent of all the commoners. Thus, the grass my horse has bit, the turfs my servant has cut, and the ore I have digged in any place, where I have a right to them in common with others, become my property without the assignation or consent of anybody. The labour that was mine, removing them out of that common state they were in, hath fixed my property in them.

By making an explicit consent of every commoner necessary to any one's appropriating to himself any part of what is given in common, children or servants could not cut the meat which their father or master had provided for them in common without assigning to every one his peculiar part. Though the water running in the fountain be every one's, yet who can doubt but that in the pitcher is his only who drew it out? His labour hath taken it out of the hands of Nature where it was common, and belonged equally to all her children, and hath thereby appropriated it to himself.

Thus this law of reason makes the deer that Indian's who hath killed it; it is allowed to be his goods who hath bestowed his labour upon it, though, before, it was the common right of every one. And amongst those who are counted the civilized part of mankind, who have made and multiplied positive laws to determine property, this original law of Nature for the beginning of property, in what was before common, still takes place, and by virtue thereof, what fish any one catches in the ocean, that great and still remaining common of mankind; or what ambergris any one takes up here is by the labour that removes it out of that common state Nature left it in, made his property who takes that pains about it. And even amongst us, the hare that any one is hunting is thought his who pursues her during the chase. For being a beast that is still looked upon as common, and no man's private possession, whoever has employed so much labour about any of that kind as to find and pursue her has thereby removed her from the state of Nature wherein she was common, and hath began a property.

It will, perhaps, be objected to this, that if gathering the acorns or other fruits of the earth, &c., makes a right to them, then any one may engross as much as he will. To which I answer, Not so. The same law of Nature that does by this means give us property, does also bound that property too. "God has given us all things richly" (1 Tim. vi. 12). Is the voice of reason confirmed by inspiration? But how far has He given it us—"to enjoy?" As much as any one can make use of to any advantage of life before it spoils, so much he may by his labour fix a property in. Whatever is beyond this is more than his share, and belongs to others. Nothing was made by God for man to spoil or destroy. And thus considering the plenty of natural provisions there was a long time in the world, and the few spenders, and to how small a part of that provision the industry of one man could extend itself and engross it to the prejudice of others, especially keeping within the bounds set by reason of what might serve for his use, there could be then little room for quarrels or contentions about property so established.

But the chief matter of property being now not the fruits of the earth and the beasts that subsist on it, but the earth itself, as that which takes in and carries with it all the rest; I think it is plain that property in that too is acquired as the former. As much land as a man tills, plants, improves, cultivates, and can use the product of, so much is his property. He by his labour does, as it were, enclose it from the common. Nor will it invalidate his right to say everybody else has an equal title to it, and therefore he cannot appropriate, he cannot enclose, without the consent of all his fellow-commoners, all mankind. God, when He gave the world in common to all mankind, commanded man also to labour, and the penury of his condition required it of him. God and his reason commanded him to subdue, till, and sow any part of it, thereby annexing to it something that was his property, which another had no title to, nor could without injury take from him.

Nor was this appropriation of any parcel of land, by improving it, any prejudice to any other man, since there was still enough and as good left, and more than the yet unprovided could use. So that, in effect, there was never the less left for others because of his enclosure for himself. For he that leaves as much as another can make use of does as good as take nothing at all. Nobody could think himself injured by the drinking of another man, though he took a good draught, who had a whole river of the same water left him to quench his thirst. And the case of land and water, where there is enough of both, is perfectly the same.

God gave the world to men in common, but since He gave it them for their benefit and the greatest conveniences of life they were capable to draw from it, it cannot be supposed he meant it should always remain common and uncultivated. He gave it to the use of the industrious and rational (and labour was to be his title to it); not to the fancy or covetousness of the quarrelsome and contentious. He that had as good left for his improvement as was already taken up needed not complain, ought not to meddle with what was already improved by another's labour; if he did it is plain he desired the benefit of another's pains, which he had no right to, and not the ground which God had given him, in common with others, to labour on, and whereof there was as good left as that already possessed; and more than he knew what to do with, or his industry could reach to.

And thus, I think, it is very easy to conceive, without any difficulty, how labour could at first begin a title of property in the common things of Nature, and how the spending it upon our uses bounded it; so that there could then be no reason of quarreling about title, nor any doubt about the largeness of possession it gave. Right and conveniency went together. For as a man had a right to all he could employ his labour upon, so he had no temptation to labour for more than he could make use of. This left no room for controversy about the title, nor for encroachment on the right of others. What portion a man carved to himself was easily seen; and it was useless, as well as dishonest, to carve himself too much, or take more than he needed.

OF THE DISSOLUION OF GOVERNMENTS

He that will, with any clearness, speak of the dissolution of government, ought in the first place to distinguish between the dissolution of the society and the dissolution of the government. That which makes the community, and brings men out of the loose state of Nature into one politic society, is the agreement which every one has with the rest to incorporate and act as one body, and so be one distinct commonwealth. The usual, and almost only way whereby this union is dissolved, is the inroad of foreign force making a conquest upon them. For in that case (not being able to maintain and support themselves as one entire and independent body) the union belonging to that body, which consisted therein, must necessarily cease, and so every one return to the state he was in before, with a liberty to shift for himself and provide for his own safety, as he thinks fit, in some other society. Whenever the society is dissolved, it is certain the government of that society cannot remain. Thus conquerors' swords often cut up governments by the roots, and mangle societies to pieces, separating the subdued or scattered multitude from the protection of and dependence on that society which ought to have preserved them from violence. The world is too well instructed in, and too forward to allow of this way of dissolving of governments, to need any more to be said of it; and there wants not much argument to prove that where the society is dissolved, the government cannot remain; that being is impossible as for the frame of a house to subsist when the materials of it are scattered and displaced by a whirlwind, or jumbled into a confused heap by an earthquake.

Besides this overturning from without, governments are dissolved from within:

First. When the legislative is altered, civil society being a state of peace amongst those who are of it, from whom the state of war is excluded by the umpirage which they have provided in their legislative for the ending all differences that may arise amongst any of them; it is in their legislative that the members of a commonwealth are united and combined together into one coherent living body. This is the soul that gives form, life, and unity to the commonwealth; from hence the several members have their mutual influence, sympathy, and connection; and therefore when the legislative is broken, or dissolved, dissolution and death follows. For the essence and union of the society consisting in having one will, the legislative, when once established by the majority, has the declaring and, as it were, keeping of that will. The constitution of the legislative is the first and fundamental act of society, whereby provision is made for the continuation of their union under the direction of persons and bonds of laws, made by persons authorized thereunto, by the consent and appointment of the people, without which no one man, or number of men, amongst them can have authority of making laws that shall be binding to the rest. When any one, or more, shall take upon them to make laws whom the people have not appointed so to do they make laws without authority, which the people are, not therefore bound to obey; by which means they come again to be out of subjection, and may constitute to themselves a new legislative, as they think best, being in full liberty to resist the force of those who, without authority, would impose anything upon them. Every one is at the disposure of his own will, when those who had, by the delegation of the society, the declaring of the public will, are excluded from it, and others usurp the place, who have no such authority or delegation.

The reasons why men enter into society is the preservation of their property; and the end while they choose and authorize a legislative is that there may be laws made, and rules set, as guards and fences to the properties of all the society, to limit the power, and moderate the dominion of every part and member of the society. For since it can never be supposed to be the will of the society that the legislative should have a power to destroy that which every one designs to secure by entering into society, and for which the people submitted themselves to legislators of their own making; whenever the legislators endeavour to take away and destroy the property of the people, or to reduce them to slavery under arbitrary power, they put themselves into a state of war with the people, who are thereupon absolved

from any farther obedience, and are left to the common
refuge which God hath provided for all men against force
and violence. Whensoever, therefore, the legislative shall
transgress this fundamental rule of society, and either by
ambition, fear, folly, or corruption, endeavour to grasp
themselves, or put into the hands of any other, an absolute
power over the lives, liberties, and estates of the people;
by this breach of trust they forfeit the power the people had
put into their hands for quite contrary ends, and it devolves to the people, who have a right to resume their original liberty, and by the establishment of a new legislative
(such as they shall think fit), provide for their own safety
and security, which is the end for which they are in society.
What I have said here concerning the legislative in general
holds true also concerning the supreme executor, who having a double trust put in him, both to have a part in the
legislative and the supreme execution of the law, acts against
both, when he goes about to set up his own arbitrary will as
the law of the society. He acts also contrary to his trust
when he employs the force, treasure, and offices of the society to corrupt the representatives, and gain them to his
purposes, when he openly pre-engages the electors, and prescribes, to their choice, such whom he has, by solicitation,
threats, promises, or otherwise, won to his designs, and employs them to bring in such who have promised beforehand
what to vote and what to enact. Thus to regulate candidates
and electors, and new model the ways of election, what is
it but to cut up the government by the roots, and poison the
very fountain of public security? For the people having reserved to themselves the choice of their representatives as
the fence to their properties, could do it for no other end
but that they might always be freely chosen, and so chosen,
freely act and advise as the necessity of the commonwealth
and the public good should, upon examination and mature
debate, be judged to require. This, those who give their votes
before they hear the debate, and have weighed the reasons on
all sides, are not capable of doing. To prepare such an as-

SELECTIONS ON CIVIL GOVERNMENT 109

sembly as this, and endeavour to set up the declared abettors of his own will, for the true representatives of the people, and the lawmakers of the society, is certainly as great a breach of trust, and as perfect a declaration of a design to subvert the government, as is possible to be met with. To which, if one shall add rewards and punishments visibly employed to the same end, and all the arts of perverted law made use of to take off and destroy all that stand in the way of such a design, and will not comply and consent to betray the liberties of their country, it will be past doubt what is doing. What power they ought to have in the society who thus employ it contrary to the trust went along with it in its first institution, is easy to determine; and one cannot but see that he who has once attempted any such thing as this cannot any longer be trusted.

To this, perhaps, it will be said that the people being ignorant and always discontented, to lay the foundation of government in the unsteady opinion and uncertain humour of the people, is to expose it to certain ruin; and no government will be able long to subsist if the people may set up a new legislative whenever they take offence at the old one. To this I answer, quite the contrary. People are not so easily got out of their old forms as some are apt to suggest. They are hardly to be prevailed with to amend the acknowledged faults in the frame they have been accustomed to. And if there be any original defects, or adventitious ones introduced by time or corruption, it is not an easy thing to get them changed, even when all the world sees there is an opportunity for it. This slowness and aversion in the people to quit their old constitutions has in the many revolutions that have been seen in this kingdom, in this and former ages, still kept us to, or after some interval of fruitless attempts, still brought us back again to our old legislative of king, lords and commons; and whatever provocations have made the crown be taken from some of our princes' heads, they never carried the people so far as to place it in another line.

But it will be said this hypothesis lays a ferment for frequent rebellion. To which I answer:

First: no more than any other hypothesis. For when the people are made miserable, and find themselves exposed to the ill usage of arbitrary power, cry up their governors as much as you will for sons of Jupiter, let them be sacred and divine, descended or authorized from Heaven; give them out for whom or what you please, the same will happen. The people generally ill treated, and contrary to right, will be ready upon any occasion to ease themselves of a burden that sits heavy upon them. They will wish and seek for the opportunity, which in the change, weakness, and accidents of human affairs, seldom delays long to offer itself. He must have lived but a little while in the world, who has not seen examples of this in his time; and he must have read very little who cannot produce examples of it in all sorts of governments in the world. Secondly: I answer, such revolutions happen not upon every little mismanagement in public affairs. Great mistakes in the ruling part, many wrong and inconvenient laws, and all the slips of human frailty will be borne by the people without mutiny or murmur. But if a long train of abuses, prevarications, and artifices, all tending the same way, make the design visible to the people, and they cannot but feel what they lie under, and see whither they are going, it is not to be wondered that they should then rouse themselves, and endeavour to put the rule into such hands which may secure to them the ends for which government was at first erected, and without which, ancient names and specious forms are so far from being better, that they are much worse than the state of Nature or pure anarchy; the inconveniencies being all as great and as near, but the remedy farther off and more difficult. Thirdly: I answer, that this power in the people of providing for their safety anew by a new legislative when their legislators have acted contrary to their trust by invading their property, is the best fence against rebellion, and the probablest means to hinder it. For rebellion being an opposition, not to persons, but authority, which is founded only in the constitutions and laws of the government; those, whoever they be, who, by force, break through, and, by force, justify their violation of them, are truly and properly rebels. For when men, by entering into society and civil government, have excluded force, and introduced laws for the preservation of property, peace, and unity amongst themselves, those who set up force again in a position to the laws, do rebellare—that is, bring back again the state of war, and are properly rebels, which they who are in power, by the pretence they have to authority, the temptation of force they have in their hands, and the flattery of those about them being likeliest to do, the properest way to prevent the evil is to show them the danger and injustice of it who are under the greatest temptation to run into it.

In both the forementioned cases, when either the legislative is changed, or the legislators act contrary to the end for which they were constituted, those who are guilty are guilty of rebellion. For if any one by force takes away the established legislative of any society, and the laws by them made, pursuant to their trust, he thereby takes away the umpirage which every one had consented to for a peaceable decision of all their controversies, and a bar to the state of war amongst them. They who remove or change the legislative take away this decisive power, which nobody can have but by the appointment and consent of the people, and so destroying the authority which the people did, and nobody else can set up, and introducing a power which the people hath not authorized, actually introduce a state of war, which is that of force without authority; and thus by removing the legislative established by the society in whose decisions the people acquiesced and united as to that of their own will, they untie the knot, and expose the people anew to the state of war. And if those, who by force take away the legislative, are rebels, the legislators themselves, as had been shown, can be no less esteemed so, when they who were set up for the protection and preservation of the people, their liberties and properties shall by force invade and endeavour to take them away; and so they putting themselves into a state of war with those who made them the protectors and guardians of their peace, are properly, and with the greatest aggravation, rebellants, rebels.

But if they who say it lays a foundation for rebellion mean that it may occasion civil wars or intestine broils to tell the people they are absolved from obedience when illegal attempts are made upon their liberties or properties, and may oppose the unlawful violence of those who were their magistrates when they invade their properties, contrary to the trust put in them, and that, therefore, this doctrine is not to be allowed, being so destructive to the peace of the world; they may as well say, upon the same ground, that honest men may not oppose robbers or pirates, because this may occasion disorder or bloodshed. If any mischief come in such cases, it is not to be charged upon him who defends his own right, but on him that invades his neighbour's. If the innocent honest man must quietly quit all he has for peace sake to him who will lay violent hands upon it, I desire it may be considered what a kind of peace there will be in the world which consists only in violence and rapine, and which is to be maintained only for the benefit of robbers and oppressors. Who would not think it an admirable peace betwixt the mighty and the mean, when the lamb, without resistance, yielded his throat to be torn by the imperious wolf? Polyphemus's den gives us a perfect pattern of such a peace. Such a government wherein Ulysses and his companions had nothing to do but quietly to suffer themselves to be devoured. And no doubt Ulysses, who was a prudent man, preached up passive obedience, and exhorted them to a quiet submission by representing to them of what concernment peace was to mankind, and by showing the inconveniencies might happen if they should offer to resist Polyphemus, who had now the power over them.

The end of government is the good of mankind; and which is best for mankind, that the people should be always exposed to the boundless will of tyranny, or that the rulers should be sometimes liable to be opposed when they grow exorbitant in the use of their power, and employ it for the destruction, and not the preservation, of the properties of their people?

OF THE NATURALL CONDITION OF MANKIND, AS CONCERNING THEIR FELICITY, AND MISERY*

By THOMAS HOBBES

NATURE hath made men so equall, in the faculties of body, and mind; as that though there bee found one man some-times manifestly stronger in body, or of quicker mind than another; yet when all is reckoned together, the difference between man, and man, is not so considerable, as that one man can thereupon claim to himselfe any benefit, to which another may not pretend, as well as he. For as to the strength of body, the weakest has strength enough to kill the strong-est, either by secret machination, or by confederacy with others, that are in the same danger with himselfe.

And as to the faculties of the mind, (setting aside the arts grounded upon words, and especially that skill of proceeding upon generall, and infallible rules, called Science; which very few have, and but in few things; as being not a native fac-ulty, born with us; nor attained, as Prudence,) while we look after somewhat els,) I find yet a greater equality amongst men, than that of strength. For Prudence, is but Experience which equall time, equally bestowes on all men, in those things they equally apply themselves unto. That which may perhaps make such equality incredible, is but a vain conceit of ones owne wisdome, which almost all men think they have in a greater degree, than the Vulgar; that is, than all men but themselves, and a few others, whom by Fame, or for concurring with themselves, they approve. For such is the nature of men, that howsoever they may acknow-ledge many others to be more witty, or more eloquent, or

* From *Leviathan*

more learned; Yet they will hardly believe there be many so wise as themselves: For they see their own wit at hand, and other mens at a distance. But this proveth rather that men are in that point equall, than unequall. For there is not ordinarily a greater signe of the equall distribution of any thing, than that every man is contented with his share.

From this equality of ability, ariseth equality of hope in the attaining of our Ends. And therefore if any two men desire the same thing, which neverthelesse they cannot both enjoy, they become enemies; and in the way to their End, (which is principally their owne conservation, and sometimes their delectation only,) endeavour to destroy, or subdue one an other. And from hence it comes to passe, that where an Invader hath more to feare, than an other mans single power; if one plant, sow, build, or possesse a convenient Seat, others may probely be expected to come prepared with forces united, to dispossesse, and deprive him, not only of the fruit of his labour, but also of his life, or liberty. And the Invader again is in the like danger of another.

And from this diffidence of one another, there is no way for any man to secure himselfe, so reasonable, as Anticipation; that is, by force, or wiles, to master the persons of all men he can, so long, till he see no other power great enough to endanger him: And this is no more than his own conservation requireth, and is generally allowed. Also because there be some, that taking pleasure in contemplating their own power in the acts of conquest, which they pursue farther than their security requires; if others, that otherwise would be glad to be at ease within modest bounds, should not by invasion increase their power, they would not be able, long time, by standing only on their defences, to subsist. And by consequence, such augmentation of dominion over men, being necessary to a man's conservation, it ought to be allowed him.

Againe, men have no pleasure, (but on the contrary a great deale of griefe) in keeping company, where there is no power able to overawe them all. For every man looketh that his companion should value him, at the same rate he sets upon himselfe: And upon all signes of contempt, or undervaluing, naturally endeavours, as far as he dares (which amongst them that have no common power to keep them in quiet, is far enough to make them destroy each other,) to extort a greater value from his contemners, by dommage; and from others, by the example.

So that in the nature of man, we find three principall causes of quarrell. First, Competition; Secondly, Diffidence; Thirdly, Glory.

The first, maketh men invade for Gain; the second, for Safety; and the third, for Reputation. The first use Violence, to make themselves Masters of other mens persons, wives, children, and cattell; the second, to defend them; the third, for trifles, as a word, a smile, a different opinion, and any other signe of undervalue, either direct in their Persons, or by reflexion in their Kindred, their Friends, their Nation, their Profession, or their Name.

Hereby it is manifest, that during the time men live without a common Power to keep them all in awe, they are in that condition which is called Warre; and such a warre, as is of every man, against every man. For Warre, consisteth not in Battell onely, or the act of fighting; but in a tract of time, wherein the Will to contend by Battell is sufficiently known: and therefore the notion of Time, is to be considered in the nature of Warre, as it is in the nature of Weather. For as the nature of Foule weather, lyeth not in a showre or two of rain; but in an inclination thereto of many dayes together; So the nature of War, consisteth not in actuall fighting; but in the known disposition thereto, during all the time there is no assurance to the contrary. All other time is Peace.

Whatsoever therefore is consequent to a time of Warre, where every man is Enemy to every man; the same is consequent to the time, wherein men live without other security, than what their own strength, and their own invention shall furnish them withall. In such condition, there is no place for Industry; because the fruit thereof is uncertain: and consequently no Culture of the Earth, no Navigation, nor use of the commodious Building; no Instruments of moving, and removing such things as require much force; no Knowledge of the face of the Earth; no account of Time; no Arts; no Letters; no Society; and which is worst of all, continuall feare, and danger of violent death; And the life of man, solitary, poore, nasty, brutish, and short.

It may seem strange to some man, that has not well weighed these things; that Nature should thus dissociate, and render men apt to invade, and destroy one another: and he may therefore, not trusting to this Inference, made from the Passions, desire perhaps to have the same confirmed by Experience. Let him therefore consider with himselfe, when taking a journey, he armes himselfe, and seeks to go well accompanied; when going to sleep, he locks his dores; when even in his house he locks his chests; and this when he knowes there bee Lawes, and publike Officers, armed, to revenge all injuries shall bee done him; what opinion he has of his fellow subjects, when he rides armed; of his fellow Citizens, when he locks his dores; and of his children, and servants, when he locks his chests. Does he not there as much accuse mankind by his actions, as I do my words? But neither of us accuse man's nature in it. The Desires, and other Passions of man, are in themselves no Sin. No more are the Actions, that proceed from those Passions, till they know a Law that forbids them: which till Lawes be made they cannot know: nor can any Law be made, till they have agreed upon the Person that shall make it.

It may peradventure be thought, there was never such a time, nor condition of warre as this; and I believe it was never generally so, over all the world; but there are many places, where they live so now. For the savage people in many places of America, except the government of small Families, the concord whereof dependeth on naturall lust, have no government at all; and live this day in that brutish manner, as I said before. Howsoever, it may be perceived

what manner of life there would be, where there were no
common Power to feare; by the manner of life, which men
that have formerly lived under a peacefull government, use
to degenerate into, in a civill Warre.

But though there had never been any time, wherein particular men were in a condition of warre one against another; yet in all times, Kings, and Persons of Soveraigne
authority, because of their Independency, are in continuall
jealousies, and in the state and posture of Gladiators; having
their weapons pointing, and their eyes fixed on one another;
that is, their Forts, Garrisons, and Guns, upon the Frontiers
of their Kingdomes; and continuall Spyes upon their neighbours; which is a posture of War. But because they uphold
thereby, the Industry of their Subjects; there does not follow from it, that misery, which accompanies the Liberty of
particular men.

To this warre of every man against every man, this also
is consequent; that nothing can be Unjust. The notions of
Right and Wrong, Justice and Injustice have there no place.
Where ther is no common Power, there is no Law: where no
Law, no Injustice. Force, and Fraud, are in warre the two
Cardinall vertues. Justice, and Injustice are none of the Faculties neither of the Body, nor Mind. If they were, they
might be in a man that were alone in the world, as well as
his Senses, and Passions. They are Qualities, that relate to
men in Society, not in Solitude. It is consequent also to the
same condition, that there be no Propriety, no Dominion, no
Mine and Thine distinct; but onely that to be every mans,
that he can get; and for so long, as he can keep it. And thus
much for the ill condition, which man by meer Nature is
actually placed in; though with a possibility to come out of
it, consisting partly in the Passions, partly in his Reason.

The Passions that encline men to Peace, are Feare of
Death; Desire of such things as are necessary to commodious living; and a Hope by their Industry to obtain them.
And Reason suggesteth convenient Articles of Peace, upon
which men may be drawn to agreement. These Articles,

are they, which otherwise are called the Lawes of Nature: whereof I shall speak more particularly, in the two following Chapters.

OF THE FIRST AND SECOND NATURALL LAWES, AND OF CONTRACTS

The Right of Nature, which Writers commonly call Jus Naturale, is the Liberty each man hath, to use his own power, as he will himselfe, for the preservation of his own Nature; that is to say, of his own Life; and consequently, of doing any thing, which in his own Judgment, and Reason, hee shall conceive to be the aptest means thereunto.

By Liberty, is understood, according to the proper signification of the word, the absence of externall Impediments: which Impediments, may oft take away part of a mans power to do what hee would; but cannot hinder him from using the power left him, according as his judgement, and reason shall dictate to him.

A LAW OF NATURE, (Lex Naturalis,) is a Precept, or generall Rule, found out by Reason, by which a man is forbidden to do, that, which is destructive of his life, or taketh away the means of preserving the same; and to omit, that, by which he thinketh it may be best preserved. For though they that speak of this subject, use to confound Jus, and Lex, Right and Law; yet they ought to be distinguished; because RIGHT, consisteth in Liberty to do, or to forbeare; Whereas Law, determineth, and bindeth to one of them: so that Law, and Right, differ as much, as Obligation, and Liberty; which in one and the same matter are inconsistent.

And because the condition of Man, (as hath been declared in the precedent Chapter) is a condition of Warre of every one against every one; in which case every one is governed by his own Reason; and there is nothing he can make us of, that may not be a help unto him, in preserving his life against his enemyes; It followeth, that in such a condition, every man has a Right to every thing; even to one anothers body. And therefore, as long as this naturall Right of every

man to every thing endureth, there can be no security to
any man, (how strong or wise soever he be,) of living out the
time, which Nature ordinarily alloweth men to live. And
consequently it is a precept, or generall rule of Reason, That
every man, ought to endeavour Peace, as farre as he has
hope of obtaining it; and when he cannot obtain it, that he
may seek, and use, all helps and advantages of Warre. The
first branch of which Rule, containeth the first, and Fundamentall Law of Nature; which is, to seek Peace, and follow
it. The Second, the summe of the Right of Nature; which is
By all means we can, to defend our selves.

From this Fundamentall Law of Nature, by which men
are commanded to endeavour Peace, is derived this second
Law; That a man be willing, when others are so too, as
farre-forth, as for Peace, and defence of himselfe he shall
think it necessary, to lay down this right to all things; and
be contented with so much liberty against other men, as he
would allow other men against himselfe. For as long as every
man holdeth this Right, of doing any thing he liketh; so
long are all men in the condition of Warre. But if other
men will not lay down their Right, as well as he; then there
is no Reason for any one, to devest himselfe of his; For that
were to expose himselfe to Peace. This is that Law of the
Gospell; Whatsoever you require that others should do to
you, that do ye to them. And that Law of all men, Qued
tibi fieri non vis, alteri ne feceris.

To lay downe a mans Right to any thing, is to devest himselfe of the Liberty of hindring another of the benefit of his
own Right to the same. For he that renounceth, or passeth
away his Right, giveth not to any other man a Right which
he had not before; because there is nothing to which every
man had not Right by Nature: but onely standeth out of
his way, that he may enjoy his own originall Right, without
hindrance from him; not without hindrance from another.
So that the effect which redoundeth to one man, by another
mans defect of Right, is but so much diminution of impediments to the use of his own Right originall.

Right is layd aside, either by simply Renouncing it; or by Transferring it to another. By Simply Renouncing; when he cares not to whom the benefit thereof redoundeth. By Transferring; when he intendeth the benefit thereof to some certain person, or persons. And when a man hath in either manner abandoned, or granted away his Right; then is he said to be OBLIGED, or BOUND, not to hinder those, to whom such Right is granted, or abandoned, from the benefit of it: and that he OUGHT, and it is his DUTY, not to make voyd that voluntary act of his own: and that such hindrance is INJUSTICE, and INJURY, as being Sine Jure; the Right being before renounced, or transferred. So that Injury, of Injustice, in the controversies of the world, is somewhat like to that, which in the disputations of Scholers is called Absurdity. For as it is there called an Absurdity, to contradict what one maintained in the Beginning: so in the world, it is called Injustice, and Injury, voluntarily to undo that, which from the beginning he had voluntarily done. The way by which a man either simply Renounceth, or Transferreth his Right, is a Declaration, or Signification, by some voluntary and sufficient signe, or signes, that he doth so Renounce, or Transferre; or hath so Renounced, or Transferred the same, to him that accepteth it. And these Signes are either Words onely, or Actions onely; or (as it happeneth most often) both Words, and Actions. And the same are the Bonds, by which men are bound, and obliged: Bonds, that have their strength, not from their own Nature, (for nothing is more easily broken then a man's word,) but from Feare of some evill consequence upon the rupture.

Whensoever a man Transferreth his Right, or Renounceth it; it is either in consideration of some Right reciprocally transferred to himselfe; or for some other good he hopeth for thereby. For it is a voluntary act: and of the voluntary acts of every man, the object is some Good to himselfe. And therefore there be some Rights, which no man can be understood by any words, or other signes, to have abandoned, or transferred. As first a man cannot lay down the right of resisting them, that assault him by force, to take away his life; because he cannot be understood to ayme thereby, at any Good to himselfe. The same may be sayd of Wounds, and Chayns, and Imprisonment; both because there is no benefit consequent to such patience; as there is to the patience of suffering another to be wounded, or imprisoned: as also because a man cannot tell, when he seeth men proceed against him by violence, whether they intend his death or not. And lastly the motive, and end for which this renouncing, and transferring of Right is introduced, is nothing else but the security of a mans person, in his life, and in the means of so preserving life, as not to be weary of it. And therefore if a man by words, or other signes, seem to despoyle himselfe of the End, for which those signes were intended; he is not to be understood as if he meant it, or that it was his will; but that he was ignorant of how such words and actions were to be interpreted.

The mutuall transferring of Right, is that which men call CONTRACT.

There is difference, between transferring of Right to the Thing; and transferring, or tradition, that is, delivery of the Thing it selfe. For the Thing may be delivered together with the Translation of the Right; as in buying and selling with ready mony: or exchange of goods, or lands: and it may be delivered some time after.

Again, one of the Contractors, may deliver the Thing contracted for on his part, and leave the other to perform his part at some determinate time after, and in the mean time be trusted; and then the Contract on his part, is called PACT, or COVENANT: Or both parts may contract now, to performe hereafter: in which cases, he that is to performe in time to come, being trusted, his performance is called Keeping of Promise, or Faith; and the fayling of performance (if it be voluntary) Violation of Faith.

When the transferring of Right, is put mutuall; but one of the parties transferreth, in hope to gain thereby friendship, or service from another, or from his friends; or in hope to gain the reputation of Charity, or Magnanimity; or to deliver his mind from the pain of compassion; or in hope of reward in heaven; This is not Contract, but GIFT, FREE-GIFT, GRACE: which words signifie one and the same thing.

Signes of Contract, are either Expresse (or by Inference. Expresse, are words spoken with understanding of what they signifie; And such words are either of the time Present, or Past; as, I Give, I Grant, I have Given, I have Granted, I will that this be yours: Or of the future; as, I will Give, I will Grant: which words of the future, are called PROMISE.

Signes by Inference, are sometimes the consequence of Words; sometimes the consequence of Silence; sometimes the consequence of Actions; sometimes the consequence of Forbearing an Action: and generally a signe by Inference, of any Contract, is whatsoever sufficiently argues the will of the Contractor.

Words alone, if they be of the time to come, and contain a bare promise, are an insufficient signe of a Free-gift and therefore not obligatory. For if they be of the time to Come, as, To morrow I will Give, they are a signe I have not given yet, and consequently that my right is not transferred, but remaineth till I transferre it by some other Act. But if the words be of the time Present, or Past, as, I have given, or do give to be delivered to morrow, then is my to morrows Right given away to day; and that by the vertue of the words, though there were no other argument of my will. And there is a great difference in the signification of these words, Volo hoc tuum esse cras, and Cras dobo; that is, between I will that this be thine to morrow, and, I will give it thee to morrow: For the word I will, in the former manner of speech, signifies an act of the will Present; but in the later, it signifies a promise of an act of the will to Come: and therefore the former words, being of the Present, transferre a future right; the later, that be of the Future, transferre nothing. But if there be other signes of the Will to transferre a Right, besides Words; then, though the gift be Free, yet may the Right be understood to passe by words of the future: as if a man propound a Prize to him that comes first to the end of a race. The gift is Free; and though the words be of the Future, yet the Right passeth: for if he would not have his words so be understood, he should not have let them runne.

In Contracts, the right passeth, not onely where the words are of the time Present, or Past; but also where they are of the Future: because all Contract is mutuall translation, or change of Right; and therefore he that promiseth onely, because he hath already received the benefit for which he promiseth, is to be understood as if he intended the Right should passe: for unlesse he had been content to have his words so understood, the other would not have performed his part first. And for that cause, in buying, and selling, and other acts of Contract, a Promise is equivalent to a Covenant; and therefore obligatory.

He that performeth first in the case of a Contract, is said to MERIT that which he is to receive by the performance of the other; and he hath it as Due. Also when a Prize is propounded to many, which is to be given to him onely that winneth; or mony is thrown amongst many, to be enjoyed by them that catch it; though this be a Free gift; yet so to Win, or so to Catch, is to Merit, and to have it as DUE. For the Right is transferred in the Propounding of the Prize, and in throwing down the mony; though it be not determined to whom, but by the Event of the contention. But there is between these two sorts of Merit, this difference, that In Contract, I Merit by vertue of my own power, and the Contractors need; but in this case of Free gift, I am enabled to Merit onely by the benignity of the Giver: In Contract, I merit at the Contractors hand that he should depart with his right; In this case of Gift, I Merit not that the giver should part with his right; but that when he has parted with it, it should be mine, rather than an others. And this I think to be the meaning of that distinction of the Schooles, between *Meritum congrui*, and *Meritum condigni*. For God Almighty, having promised Paradise to those men (hoodwinkt with carnall desires,) that can walk through this world according to the Precepts, and Limits prescribed by him; they say, he that shall so walk, shall Merit Paradise *Ex congruo*. But because no man can demand a right to it, by his own Righteousnesse, or any other power in himselfe, but by the Free Grace of God onely; they say, no man can Merit Paradise *ex condigno*. This I say, I think is the meaning of that distinction; but because Disputers do not agree upon the signification of their own termes of Art, longer than it serves their turn; I will not affirme any thing of their meaning: onely this I say; when a gift is given indefinitely, as a prize to be contended for, he that winneth Meriteth, and may claime the Prize as Due.

If a Covenant be made, wherein neither of the parties performe presently, but trust one another; in the condition of meer Nature, (which is a condition of Warre of every man against every man,) upon any reasonable suspicion, it is Voyd: But if there be a common Power set over them both, with right and force sufficient to compell performance; it is not Voyd. For he that performeth first, has no assurance the other will performe after; because the bonds of words are too weak to bridle men's ambition, avarice, anger, and other Passions, without the feare of some coerceive Power; which in the condition of meer Nature, where all men are equall, and judges of the justnesse of their own fears, cannot possibly be supposed. And therefore he which performeth first, does but betray himselfe to his enemy; contrary to the Right (he can never abandon) of defending his life, and means of living.

But in a civill estate, where there is a Power set up to constrain those that would otherwise violate their faith, that feare is no more reasonable; and for that cause, he which by the Covenant is to perform first, is obliged so to do.

The cause of feare, which maketh such a Covenant invalid, must be always something arising after the Covenant made; as some new fact, or other signe of the Will not to performe: else it cannot make the Covenant voyd. For that which could not hinder a man from promising, ought not to be admitted as a hindrance of performing.

He that transferreth any Right, transferreth the Means of enjoying it, as farre as lyeth in his power. As he that selleth Land, is understood to transferre the Herbage, and whatsoever growes upon it; Nor can he that sells a Mill turn away the Stream that drives it. And they that give to a man the Right of government in Soveraignty, are understood to give him the right of levying mony to maintain Souldiers; and of appointing Magistrates for the administration of Justice.

To make Covenants with bruit Beasts, is impossible; because not understanding our speech, they understand not, nor accept of any translation of Right; nor can translate any Right to another: and without mutuall acceptation, there is no Covenant.

To make Covenant with God, is impossible, but by Mediation of such as God speaketh to, either by Revelation supernaturall, or by his Lieutenants that govern under him, and in his Name: For otherwise we know not whether our Covenants be accepted, or not. And therefore they that Vow any thing contrary to any law of Nature, Vow in vain; as being a thing unjust to pay such Vow. And if it be a thing commanded by the Law of Nature, it is not the Vow, but the Law that binds them.

The matter, or subject of a Covenant, is always something that falleth under deliberation; (For to Covenant, is an act of the Will; that is to say an act, and the last act, of deliberation;) and is therefore alwayes understood to be something to come; and which is judged Possible for him that Covenanteth, to performe.

And therefore, to promise that which is known to be Impossible, is no Covenant. But if that prove impossible afterwards, which before was thought possible, the Covenant is valid, and bindeth, (though not to the thing it selfe,) yet to the value; or, if that also be impossible, to the unfeigned endeavour of performing as much as is possible: for to more no man can be obliged.

Men are freed of their Covenants two wayes; by Performing; or by being Forgiven. For Performance, is the naturall end of obligation; and Forgivenesse, the restitution of liberty; as being a re-transferring of that Right, in which the obligation consisted.

Covenants entred into by fear, in the condition of meer Nature, are obligatory. For example, if I Covenant to pay a ransome, or service for my life, to an enemy; I am bound by it. For it is a Contract, wherein one receiveth the benefit of life; the other is to receive mony, or service for it; and consequently, where no other Law (as in the condition, of meer nature) forbiddeth the performance, the Covenant is valid. Therefore Prisoners of warre, if trusted with the payment of their Ransome, are obliged to pay it: And if a weaker Prince, make a disadvantageous peace with a stronger, for feare; he is bound to keep it; unless (as hath been sayd before) there ariseth some new, and just cause of feare, to renew the war. And even in Common-wealths, if I be forced to redeem my selfe from a Theefe by promising him mony, I am bound to pay it, till the Civill Law discharge me. For whatsoever I may lawfully do without Obligation, the same I may lawfully Covenant to do through feare: and what I lawfully Covenant, I cannot lawfully break.

A former Covenant makes voyd a later. For a man that hath passed away his Right to one man to day, hath it not to passe to morrow to another: and therefore the later promise passeth no Right, but is null.

A Covenant not to defend my selfe from force, by force, is alwayes voyd. For (as I have shewed before) no man can transferre, or lay down his Right to save himselfe from Death, Wounds, and Imprisonment, (the avoyding whereof is the onely End of laying down any Right, and therefore the promise of not resisting force, in no Covenant transferreth any right; nor is obliging. For though a man may

Covenant thus, *Unlesse I do so, or so, kill me*; he cannot Covenant thus, *Unlesse I do so, or so, I will not resist you, when you come to kill me*. For man by nature chooseth the lesser evill, which is danger of death in resisting; rather than the greater, which is certain and present death in not resisting. And this is granted to be true by all men, in that they lead Criminals to Execution, and Prison, with armed men, notwithstanding that such Criminals have consented to the Law, by which they are condemned.

A Covenant to accuse ones selfe, without assurance of pardon, is likewise invalid. For in the condition of Nature, where every man is Judge, there is no place for Accusation: and in the Civill State, the Accusation is followed with Punishment; which being Force, a man is not obliged not to resist. The same is also true of the Accusation of those, by whose Condemnation a man falls into misery; as of a Father, Wife, or Benefactor.

For the Testimony of such an Accuser, if it be not willingly given, is praesumed to be corrupted by Nature; and therefore not to be received: and where a man's Testimony is not to be credited, he is not bound to give it. Also Accusations upon Torture, are not to be reputed as Testimonies. For Torture is to be used but as means of conjecture, and light, in the further examination, and search of truth: and what is in that case confessed, tendeth to the ease of him that is Tortured; not to the informing of the Tortures: and therefore ought not to have the credit of a sufficient Testimony: for whether he deliver himselfe by true, or false Accusation, he does it by the Right of preserving his own life.

The force of Words, being (as I have formerly noted) too weak to hold men to the performance of their Covenants; there are in man's nature, but two imaginable helps to strengthen it. And those are either a *Feare* of the consequence of breaking their word; or a *Glory*, or *Pride* in appearing not to need to breake it. This later is a Generosity too rarely found to be presumed on, especially in the pursuers of Wealth, Command, or sensuall Pleasure; which are the greatest part of Mankind. The Passion to be reckoned upon, is Fear; whereof there be two very generall Objects: one, The Power of Spirits Invisible; the other, The Power of those men they shall therein Offend. Of these two, though the former be the greater Power, yet the feare of the later is commonly the greater Feare. The Feare of the former is in every man, his own Religion, which hath place in the nature of man before Civill Society. The later hath not so; at least not place enough, to keep men to their promises; because in the condition of meer Nature, the inequality of Power is not discerned, but by the event of Battell. So that before the time of Civill Society, or in the interruption thereof by Warre, there is nothing can strengthen a Covenant of Peace agreed on, against the temptations of Avarice, Ambition, Lust, or other strong desire, but the feare of that Invisible Power, which they every one Worship as God; and Feare as a Revenger of their perfidy. All therefore that can be done between two men not subject to Civill Power, is to put one another to swear by the God he feareth: Which Swearing, or OATH, is a Forme of Speech, added to a Promise; by which he that promiseth, signifieth, that unlesse he performe, he renounceth the mercy of his God, or calleth to him for vengeance on himselfe. Such was the Heathen Forme, Let Jupiter kill me else, as I kill this Beast. So is our Forme, I shall do thus, and thus, so help me God. And this, with the Rites and Ceremonies, which every one useth in his own Religion, that the feare of breaking faith might be the greater.

By this it appears, that an Oath taken according to any other Forme, or Rite, then his, that sweareth, is in vain; and no Oath: And that there is no Swearing by any thing which the Swearer thinks not God. For though men have sometimes used to swear by their Kings, for feare, or flattery; yet they would have it thereby understood, they attributed to them Divine honour. And that Swearing unnecessarily by God, is but prophaning of his name: and Swearing by other things, as men do in common discourse, is not Swearing but

an impious Custome, gotten by too much vehemence of talking.

It appears also, that the Oath addes nothing to the Obligation. For a Covenant, if lawfull, binds in the sight of God,
without the Oath, as much as with it; if unlawfull, bindeth
not at all; though it be confirmed with an Oath.

OF OTHER LAWES OF NATURE

From that law of Nature, by which we are obliged to
transferre to another, such Rights, as being retained, hinder
the peace of Mankind, there followeth a Third; which is
this, That men performe their Covenants made: without
which, Covenants are in vain, and but Empty words; and
the Right of all men to all things remaining, wee are still
in the condition of Warre.

And in this law of Nature, consisteth the Fountain and
Originall of JUSTICE. For where no Covenant hath pre-
ceeded, there hath no Right been transferred, and every
man has right to every thing and consequently, no action
can be Unjust. But when a Covenant is made, then to break
it is Unjust: And the definition of INJUSTICE, is no other
than the not Performance of Covenant. And whatsoever
is not Unjust, is Just.

But because Covenants of mutuall trust, where there is
a feare of not performance on either part, (as hath been
said in the former Chapter,) are invalid; though the
Originall of Justice be the making of Covenants; yet Injustice actually there can be none, till the cause of such feare
be taken away; which while men are in the naturall condition of Warre, cannot be done. Therefore before the names
of Just, and Unjust can have place, there must be some coercive Power, to compell men equally to the performance of
their Covenants, by the terrour of some punishment, greater than the benefit they expect by the breach of their Covenant; and to make good that Propriety, which by mutuall
Contract men acquire, in recompence of the universall Right

they abandon: and such power there is none before the errection of a Common-wealth. And this is also to be gathered out of the ordinary definition of Justice in the Schooles: For they say, that Justice is the constant Will of giving to every man his own. And therefore where there is no Own, that is, no Propriety, there is no Injustice; and where there is no coerceive Power erected, that is, where there is no Common-wealth, there is no Propriety; all men having Right to all things: Therefore where there is no Common-wealth, there nothing is Unjust. So that the nature of Justice, consisteth in keeping of valid Covenants: but the Validity of Covenants begins not but with the Constitution of a Civill Power, sufficient to compell men to keep them: And then it is also that Propriety begins.

The Foole hath sayd in his heart, there is no such thing as Justice; and sometimes also with his tongue; seriously alleaging, that every man's conservation, and contentment, being committed to his own care, there could be no reason, why every man might not do what he thought conduced thereunto: and therefore also to make, or not make; keep, or not keep Covenants, was not against Reason, when it conduced to ones benefit. He does not therein deny, that there be Covenants; and that they are sometimes broken, sometimes kept; and that such breach of them may be called Injustice, and the observance of them Justice: but he questioneth, whether Injustice, taking away the feare of God (for the same Foole hath said in his heart there is no God.) may not sometimes stand with that Reason, which dictateth to every man his own good; and particularly then, when it conduceth to such a benefit, as shall put a man in a condition, to neglect not onely the dispraise, and revilings, but also the power of other men. The Kingdome of God is gotten by violence: but what if it could be gotten by unjust violence? were it against Reason so to get it, when it is impossible to receive hurt by it? and if it be not against Reason, it is not against Justice: or else Justice is not to be approved for good. From such reasoning as this, Successfull wickednesse hath obtained the name of Vertue: and some that in all other things have disallowed the violation of Faith; yet have allowed it, when it is for the getting of a Kingdome. And the Heathen that believed, that Saturn was deposed by his son Jupiter, believed nevertheless the same Jupiter to be the avenger of Injustice: Somewhat like to a piece of Law in Cokes Commentaries on Litleton; where he sayes, If the right Heire of the Crown be attained of Treason; yet the Crown shall descend to him, and *eo instante* the Atteynder be voyd: From which instances a man will be very prone to inferre; that when the Heire apparent of a Kingdome, shall kill him that is in possession, though his father; you may call it Injustice, or by what other name you will; yet it can never be against Reason, seeing all the voluntary actions of men tend to the benefit of themselves; and those actions are most Reasonable, that conduce most to their ends. This specious reasoning is neverthelesse false.

For the question is not of promises mutuall, where there is no security of performance on either side; as when there is no Civill Power erected over the parties promising; for such promises are no Covenants: But either where one of the parties has performed already; or where there is a Power to make him performe; there is the question whether it be against reason, that is, against the benefit of the other to performe, or not. And I say it is not against reason. For the manifestation whereof, we are to consider; First, that when a man doth do thing, which notwithstanding any thing can be forseen, and reckoned on, tendeth to his own destruction, howsoever some accident which he could not expect, arriving may turne it to his benefit; yet such events do not make it reasonably or wisely done. Secondly, that in a condition of Warre, wherein every man to every man, for want of a common Power to keep them all in awe, is an Enemy, there is no man can hope by his own strength, or wit, to defend himselfe from destruction, without the help of Confederates; where every one expects the same defence by the Confederation, that any one else does: and therefore he

which declares he thinks it reason to deceive those that
help him, can in reason expect no other means of safety,
than what can be had from his own single Power. He therefore that breaketh his Covenant, and consequently declareth
that he thinks he may with reason do so cannot be received
into any Society, that unite themselves for Peace and Defence, but by the error of them that receive him; nor when
he is received, be retayned in it, without seeing the danger
of their error; which errours a man cannot reasonably
reckon upon as the means of his security; and therefore if
he be left, or cast out of Society, he perisheth; and if he
live in Society, it is by the errours of other men, which he
could not foresee, nor reckon upon; and consequently
against the reason of his preservation; and so, as all men
that contribute not to his destruction, forbear him onely out
of ignorance of what is good for themselves.

As for the Instance of gaining the secure and perpetual
felicity of Heaven, by any way; it is frivolous: there being
but one way imaginable; and that is not breaking, but keeping of Covenant.

And for the other Instance of attaining Soveraignty by
Rebellion; it is manifest, that though the event follow, yet
because it cannot reasonably be expected, but rather the contrary; and because by gaining it so, others are taught to gain
the same in like manner, the attempt thereof is against
reason. Justice therefore, that is to say, Keeping of Covenant, is a Rule of Reason, by which we are forbidden to do
any thing destructive to our life; and consequently a Law of
Nature.

There be some that proceed further; and will not have
the Law of Nature, to be those Rules which conduce to the
preservation of mans life on earth; but to the attaining of
an eternall felicity after death; to which they think the
breach of Covenant may conduce; and consequently be just
and reasonable; (such are they that think it a work of merit
to kill, or depose, or rebell against, the Soveraigne Power
constituted over them by their own consent.) But because

there is no naturall knowledge of mans estate after death; much lesse of the reward that is then to be given to breach of Faith; but onely a beliefe grounded upon other mens saying that they know it supernaturally, or that they know those that knew them, that knew others, that knew it supernaturally; Breach of Faith cannot be called a Precept of Reason, or Nature.

Others, that allow for a Law of Nature, the keeping of Faith, do neverthelesse make exception of certain persons; as Heretiques, and such as use not to performe their Covenant to others: And this also is against reason. For if any fault of a man, be sufficient to discharge our Covenant made; the same ought in reason to have been sufficient to have hindred the making of it.

The names of Just and Injust, when they are attributed to Men, signifie one thing; and when they are attributed to Actions, another. When they are attributed to Men, they signifie Conformity, or Inconformity of Manners, to Reason. But when they are attributed to Actions, they signifie the Conformity or Inconformity to Reason, not of Manners, or manner of life, but of particular Actions. A Just man therefore, is he that taketh all the care he can, that his Actions may be all Just: and an Unjust man, is he that neglecteth it. And such men are more often in our Language stiled by the names of Righteous, and Unrighteous; then Just, and Unjust; though the meaning be the same. Therefore a Righteous man, does not lose that Title, by one, or a few unjust Actions, that proceed from sudden Passion, or mistake of Things, or Persons: nor does an Unrighteous man, lose his character, for such Actions, as he does, or forbeares to do, for feare; because his Will is not framed by the Justice, but by the apparent benefit of what he is to do. That which gives to humane Actions the relish of Justice, is a certain Noblenesse of Gallantnesse of courage, (rarely found,) by which a man scorns to be beholding for the contentment of his life, to fraud, or breach of promise. This

Justice of the Manners, is that which is meant, where Justice is called a Vertue; and Injustice a Vice.

But the Justice of Actions dominates men, not Just, Guiltlesse: and the Injustice of the same, (which is also called Injury,) gives them but the name of Guilty.

Again, the Injustice of Manners, is the disposition, or aptitude to do Injurie; and is Injustice before it proceed to Act; and without supposing any individuall person injured. But the Injustice of an Action, (that is to say Injury,) supposeth an individuall person Injured; namely him, to whom the Covenant was made; And therefore many times the injury is received by one man, when the dammage redoundeth to another. As when the Master commandeth his servant to give mony to a stranger; if it be not done, the Injury is done to the Master, whom he had before Covenanted to obey; but the dammage redoundeth to the stranger, to whom he had no Obligation; and therefore could not Injure him. And so also in Common-wealths, private men may remit to one another their debts; but not robberies or other violences, whereby they are endammaged; because the detaining of Debt, is an Injury to themselves; but Robbery and Violence, are Injuries to the Person of the Common-wealth.

Whatsoever is done to a man, conformable to his own Will signified to the doer, is no Injury to him. For if he that doeth it, hath not passed away his originall right to do what he please, by some Antecedent Covenant, there is no breach of Covenant; and therefore no Injury done him. And if he have; then his Will to have it done being signified, is a release of that Covenant: and so again there is no Injury done him.

Justice of Actions, is by Writers divided into Commutative, and Distributive: and the former they say consisteth in proportion Arithmeticall; the later in proportion Geometricall. Commutative therefore, they place in the equality of value of the things contracted for; And Distributive, in the distribution of equall benefit, to men of equall merit As if it were Injustice to sell dearer than we buy; or to give more to a man than he merits. The value of all things contracted for, is measured by the Appetite of the Contractors: and therefore the just value, is that which they be contented to give. And Merit (besides that which is by Covenant, where the performance on one part, meriteth the performance of the other part, and falls under Justice Commutative, not Distributive,) is not due by Justice; but is rewarded of Grace onely. And therefore this distinction, in the sense wherein it useth to be expounded, is not right. To speak properly, Commutative Justice, is the Justice of a Contractor; that is, a Performance of Covenant, in Buying, and Selling; Hiring, and Letting to Hire; Leading, and Borrowing; Exchanging, Batering, and other acts of Contract.

And Distributive Justice, the Justice of an Arbitrator; that is to say, the act of defining what is Just. Wherein, (being trusted by them that make him Arbitrator,) if he performe his Trust, he is said to distribute to every man his own: and this is indeed Just Distribution, and may be called (though improperly) Distributive Justice; but more properly Equity; which also is a Law of Nature, as shall be shown in due place.

As Justice dependeth on Antecedent Covenant; so does GRATITUDE depend on Antecedent Grace; that is to say, Antecedent-Free-Gift: and is the fourth Law of Nature; which may be conceived in this Forme, That a man which receiveth Benefit from another of meer Grace Endeavour that he which giveth it, have no reasonable cause to repent him of his good will. For no man giveth, but with intention of Good to himselfe; because Gift is Voluntary; and of all Voluntary Acts, the Object is to every man his own Good; of which if men see they shall be frustrated, there will be no beginning of benevolence, or trust; nor consequently of mutuall help; nor of reconciliation of one man to another; and therefore they are to remain still in the condition of War; which is contrary to the first and Fundamentall Law of Nature, which commandeth men to Seek Peace. The breach of this Law, is called Ingratitude; and hath the same relation to Grace, that Injustice hath to Obligation by Covenant.

A fifth Law of Nature, is COMPLEASANCE; that is to say, That every man strive to accommodate himselfe to the rest. For the understanding whereof, we may consider, that there is in mens aptnesse to Society, a diversity of Nature, rising from their diversity of Affections; not unlike to that we see in stones brought together for building of an Edifice. For as that stone which by the asperity, and irregularity of Figure, takes more room from others, than it selfe fills; and for the hardnesse, cannot be easily made plain, and thereby hindereth the building, is by the builders cast away as unprofitable, and troublesome: so also, a man that by asperity of Nature, will strive to retain those things which to himselfe are superfluous, and to others necessary; and for the stubbornness of his Passions, cannot be corrected is to be left, or cast out of Society, as combersome thereunto. For seeing every man, not onely by Right, but also by necessity of Nature, is supposed to endeavour all he can, to obtain that which is necessary for his conservation; He that shall oppose himselfe against it, for things superflous, is guilty of the warre that thereupon is to follow; and therefore doth that, which is contrary to the fundamentall Law of Nature, which commandeth to seek Peace. The observers of this Law, may be called SOCIABLE, (the Latines call them Commodi;) The contrary, Stubborn, Insociable, Forward, Intractable.

A sixth Law of Nature, is this, That upon caution of the Future time, a man ought to pardon the offences past of them that repenting, desire it. For PARDON, is nothing but granting of Peace; which though granted to them that persevere in their hostility, be not Peace, but Feare; yet not granted to them that give caution of the Future time, a signe of an aversion to Peace; and therefore contrary to the Law of Nature.

A seventh is, That in Revenges, (that is, retribution of Evil for Evil,) Men look not at the greatnesse of the evill past, but the greatnesse of the good to follow. Whereby we are forbidden to inflict punishment with any other designe, than for correction of the offender, or direction of others. For this Law is consequent to the next before it, that commandeth Pardon, upon security of the Future time. Besides, Revenge without respect to the Example, and profit to come, is a triumph, or glorying in the hurt of another, tending to no end; (for the End is alwayes somewhat to Come;) and glorying to no end, is vain-glory, and contrary to reason; and to hurt without reason, tendeth to the introduction of Warre; which is against the Law of Nature; and is commonly stiled by the name of Cruelty.

And because all signes of hatred, or contempt, provoke to fight; insomuch as most men choose rather to hazard their life, than not to be revenged; we may in the eighth place, for a Law of Nature, set down this Precept, That no man by deed, word, contenance, or gesture, declare Hatred, or Contempt of another. The breach of which Law, is commonly called Contumely.

The question who is the better man, has no place in the condition of meer Nature; where, (as has been shewn before,) all men are equall. The inequallity that now is, has been introduced by the Lawes civill. I know that Aristotle in the first booke of his Politiques, for a foundation of his doctrine, maketh men by Nature, some more worthy to Command, meaning the wiser sort (such as he thought himselfe to be for his Philosophy;) others to Serve, (meaning those that had strong bodies, but were not Philosophers as he;) as if Master and Servant were not introduced by consent of men, but by difference of Wit; which is not only against reason; but also against experience. For there are very few so foolish, that had not rather governe themselves, than be governed by others: Nor when the wise in their own conceit, contend by force, with them who distrust their owne wisdome, do they alwaies, or often, or almost at any time, get the Victory. If Nature therefore have made men equall, that equalitie is to be acknowledged: or if Nature have made men unequall; yet because men that think themselves equall, will not enter into conditions of Peace, but upon Equall termes, such equalitie must be admitted. And therefore for the ninth law of Nature, I put this, That every man acknowledge other for his Equall by Nature. The breach of this Precept is Pride.

On this law, dependeth another, That at the entrance into conditions of Peace, no man require to reserve to himselfe any Right, which he is not content should be reserved to every one of the rest. As it is necessary for all men that seek peace, to lay down certaine Rights of Nature; that is to say, not to have libertie to do all they list: so is it necessarie for man life, to retaine some; as right to governe their owne bodies; enjoy aire, water, motion, waies to go from place to place; and all things else without which a man cannot live, or not live well. If in this case, at the making of Peace, men require for themselves, that which they would not have to be granted to others, they do contrary to the precedent law, that commandeth the acknowledgment of naturall equalitie, and therefore also against the law of Nature. The observers of this law, are those we call Modest, and the breakers Arrogant men. The Greeks call the violation of this law πλεονεξια; that is, a desire of more than their share.

Also if a man be trusted to judge between man and man, it is a precept of the Law of Nature, that he deale Equally between them. For without that, the Controversies of men cannot be determined but by Warre. He therefore that is partiall in judgement, doth what in him lies, to deterre men from the use of Judges, and Arbitrators; and consequently, (against the fundamentall Lawe of Nature) is the cause of Warre.

The observance of this law, from the equall distribution to each man, of that which in reason belongeth to him, is called EQUITY, and (as I have sayd before) distributive Justice: the violation, Acception of persons, προσωποληψια.

And from this followeth another law, That such things as

cannot be divided, be enjoyed in Common, if it can be; and if the quantity of the thing permit, without Stint; otherwise Propertionably to the number of them that have Right. For otherwise the distribution is Unequall, and contrary to Equitie.

But some things there be, that can neither be divided, nor enjoyed in common. Then, the Entire Right; or else, (making the use alternate,) the First Possession, be determined by Lot. For equall distribution, is of the Law of Nature; and other means of equall distribution cannot be imagined.

Of Lots there be two sorts, Arbitrary, and Naturall. Arbitrary, is that which is agreed on by the Competitors: Naturall, is either Primogeniture, (which the Greek calls Κληρονομια which signifies, Given by Lot;) or First Seisure.

And therefore those things which cannot be enjoyed in common, nor divided, ought to be adjudged to the First Possessor; and in some cases to the First-Borne, as acquired by Lot.

It is also a Law of Nature, That all men that mediate Peace, be allowed safe Conduct. For the Law that commandeth Peace, as the End, commandeth Intercession, as the Means; and to Intercession the Means is safe Conduct.

And because, though men be never so willing to observe these Lawes, there may nevertheless arise questions concerning a mans action; First, whether it were done, or not done; Secondly (if done) whether against the Law, or not against the Law; the former whereof, is called a question Of Fact; the later a question Of Right; therefore unlesse the parties to the question, Covenant mutually to stand to the sentence of another, they are as farre from Peace as ever. This other, to whose Sentence they submit, is called an ARBITRATOR. And therefore it is of the Law of Nature, That they that are at controversie, submit their Right to the judgement of an Arbitrator.

And seeing every man is presumed to do all things in order to his own benefit, no man is a fit Arbitrator in his own cause: and if he were never so fit; yet Equity allowing to each party equall benefit, if one be admitted to be Judge, the other is to be admitted also; and so the controversie, that is, the cause of War, remains, against the Law of Nature.

For the same reason no man in any Cause ought to be received for Arbitrator, to whom greater profit, or honour, or pleasure apparently ariseth out of the victory of one party, than of the other: for hee hath taken (though an unavoydable bribe, yet) a bribe; and no man can be obliged to trust him. And thus also the controversie, and the condition of War remaineth, contrary to the Law of Nature.

And in a controversie of Fact, the Judge being to give no more credit to one, than to the other, (if there be no other Arguments) must give credit to a third; or to a third and fourth; or more: For else the question is undecided, and left to force, contrary to the Law of Nature.

These are the Lawes of Nature, dictating Peace, for a means of the conservation of men in multitudes; and which onely concern the doctrine of Civill Society. There be other things tending to the destruction of particular men; as Drunkenness, and all other parts of Intemperance; which may therefore also be reckoned amongst those things which the Law of Nature hath forbidden; but are not necessary to be mentioned, nor are pertiment enough to this place.

And though this may seem too subtile a deduction of the Lawes of Nature, to be taken notice of by all men; whereof the most part are too busie in getting food, and the rest too negligent to understand; yet to leave all men unexcusable, they have been contracted into one easie sum, intelligible, even to the meanest capacity; and that is, Do not that to another, which thou wouldest not have done to thy selfe; which sheweth him, that he has no more to do in learning the Lawes of Nature, but, when weighing the actions of other men with his own, they seem too heavy, to put them into the other part of the ballance, and his own into their place, that his own passions, and selfe-love, may adde nothing to the weight; and then there is none of these Lawes of Nature that will not appear unto him very reasonable.

The Lawes of Nature oblige in foro interno; that is to say, they bind to a desire they should take place: but in foro externo; that is, to the putting them in act, not alwayes. For he that should be modest, and tractable, and performe all he promises, in such time, and place, where no man els should do so, should but make himselfe a prey to others, and procure his own certain ruine, contrary to the ground of all Lawes of Nature, which tend to Natures preservation. And again, he that having sufficient Security, that others shall observe the same Lawes towards him, observes them not himselfe, seeking not Peace, but War; & consequently the destruction of his Nature by Violence.

And whatsoever Lawes bind in foro interno, may be broken, not onely by a fact contrary to the Law, but also by a fact according to it, in case a man think it contrary. For though his Action in this case, be according to the Law; yet his Purpose was against the Law; which where the Obligation is in foro interno, is a breach.

The Lawes of Nature are Immutable and Eternall, for Injustice, Ingratitude, Arrogance, Pride, Iniquity, Acception of persons, and the rest, can never be made lawfull. For it can never be that Warre shall preserve life, and Peace destroy it.

The (same) Lawes, because they oblige onely to a desire, and endeavour, I mean an unfeigned and constant endeavour are easie to be observed. For in that they require nothing but endeavour; he that endeavoureth their performance, fulfilleth them; and he that fulfilleth the Law, is Just.

And the Science of them, is the true and onely Moral Philosophy. For Morall Philosophy is nothing else but the Science of what is Good, and Evill, in the conversation, and Society of man-kind. Good, and Evill, are names that signifie our Appetites, and Aversions; which in different tempers, customes, and doctrines of men, are different: And divers men, differ not onely in their Judgement, on the senses of what is pleasant, and unpleasant to the taste, smell, hearing, touch, and sight; but also of what is conformable, or disagreeable to Reason, in the actions of common life. Nay, the same man, in divers times, differs from himselfe; and one time praiseth, that is, calleth Good, what another time he dispraiseth, and calleth Evil: From whence arise Disputes, Controversies, and at last War. And therefore so long a man is in the condition of meer Nature, (which is a condition of War,) as private Appetite is the measure of Good, and Evill: And consequently all men agree on this, that Peace is Good, and therefore also the way, or means of Peace, which (as I have shewed before) are Justice, Gratitude, Modesty, Equity, Mercy, & the rest of the Laws of Nature, are good; that is to say, Morall Vertues; and their contrarie Vices, Evill. Now the science of Vertue and Vice, is Morall Philosophie; and therefore the true Doctrine of the Lawes of Nature, is the true Morall Philosophie. But the Writers of Morall Philosophie, though they acknowledge the same Vertues and Vices; Yet not seeing wherein consisted their Goodnesse; not that they come to be praised, as the meanes of peaceable, sociable, and comfortable living; place them in a mediocrity of passions: as if not the Cause, but the Degree of daring, made Fortitude; or not the Cause, but the Quantity of a gift, made Liberality.

These dictates of Reason, men use to call by the name of Lawes; but improperly; for they are but Conclusions, or Theoremes concerning what conduceth to the conservation and defence of themselves; whereas Law, properly is the word of him, that by right hath command over others. But yet if we consider the same Theoremes, as delivered in the word of God, that by right commandeth all things; then are they properly called Lawes.

OF COMMON-WEALTH

OF THE CAUSES, GENERATION, AND DEFINITION OF A COMMON-WEALTH

The finall Cause, End or Designe of men, (who naturally love Liberty, and Dominion over others,) in the introduction of that restraint upon themselves, (in which wee see them live in Common-wealths,) is the foresight of their own preservation, and of a more contented life thereby; that is to say, of getting themselves out from that miserable condition of Warre, which is necessarily consequent (as hath benn shewn) to the naturall Passions of men, when there is no visible Power to keep them in awe, and tye them by feare of punishment to the performance of their Cove-nants, and observation of those Lawes of Nature set down in the fourteenth and fifteenth Chapters.

For the Lawes of Nature (as Justice, Equity, Modesty, Mercy, and (in summe) doing to others, as wee would be done to,) of themselves, without the terror of some Power, to cause them to be observed, are contrary to our naturall Passions, that carry us to Partiality, Pride, Revenge, and the like. And Covenants, without the Sword, are but Words, and of no strength to secure a man at all. Therefore notwith-standing the Lawes of Nature, (which every one hath then kept, when he has the will to keep them, when he can do it safely,) if there be no Power erected, or not great enough for our security; every man will, and may lawfully rely on his own strength and art, for caution against all other men. And in all places, where men have lived by small Families, to robbe and spoyle one another, has been a Trade, and so farre from being reputed against the Law of Nature, that the greater spoyles they gained, the greater was their hon-our; and men observed no other Lawes therein, but the Lawes of Honour; that is, to abstain from cruelty, leaving to men their lives, and instruments of husbandry. And as small Familyes did then; so now do Cities and Kingdomes, which are but greater Families (for their own security) en-large their Dominions, upon all pretences of danger, and fear of Invasion, or assistance that may be given to Invaders, endeavour as much as they can, to subdue, or weaken their neighbours, by open force, and secret arts, for want of other Caution, justly; and are remembred for it in after ages with honour.

Nor is it the joyning together of a small number of men, that gives them this security; because in small numbers, small additions on the one side or the other, make the advantage of strength so great, as is sufficient to carry the Victory; and therefore gives encouragement to an Invasion. The Multitude sufficient to confide in for our Security, is not determined by any certain number, but by comparison with the Enemy we feare; and is then sufficient, when the odds of the Enemy is not of so visible and conspicuous moment, to determine the event of warre, as to move him to attempt.

And be there never so great a Multitude; yet if their actions be directed, according to their particular judgements, and particular appetites, they can expect thereby no defence, nor protection neither against a common enemy, nor against the injuries of one another. For being distracted in opinions concerning the best use and application of their strength, they do not help, but hinder one another; and reduce their strength by mutuall opposition to nothing whereby they are easily, not onely subdued by a very few that agree together; but also when there is no common enemy, they make warre upon each other, for their particular interests. For if we could suppose a great Multitude of men to consent in the observation of Justice, and other Lawes of Nature, without a common Power to keep them all in awe; we might as well suppose all Man-kind to do the same; and then there neither would be, nor need to be any Civill Government, or Common-wealth at all; because there would be Peace without subjection.

Nor is it enough for the security, which men desire should last all the time of their life, that they be governed, and directed by one judgement, for a limited time; as in one Battel, or one Warre. For though they obtain a Victory by their unanimous endeavour against a forraign enemy; yet afterwards, when either they have no common enemy, or he that by one part is held for an enemy, is by another part held for a friend, they must needs by the difference of their interests dissolve, and fall again into a Warre amongst themselves.

It is true, that certain living creatures, as Bess, and Ants, live sociably one with another, (which are therefore by Aristotle numbred amongst Politicall creatures;) and yet have no other direction, than their particular judgements and appetites; nor speech, whereby one of them can signifie to another, what he thinks expedient for the common benefit: and therefore some man may perhaps desire to know, why Man-kind cannot do the same. To which I answer,

First, that men are continually in competition for Honour and Dignity, which these creatures are not; and consequently amongst men there ariseth on that ground, Envy and Hatred, and finally Warre; but amongst these not so.

Secondly, that amongst these creatures, the Common good differeth not from the Private; and being by nature enclined to their private, they procure thereby the common benefit. But man, whose Joy consisteth in comparing himselfe with other men, can relish nothing but what is eminent.

Thirdly, that these creatures, having not (as man) the use of reason, do not see, nor think they see any fault, in the administration of their common businesse; whereas amongst men, there are very many, that thinke themselves wiser, and abler to govern the Publique, better than the rest; and these strive to reforme and innovate, one this way, another that way; and thereby bring it into Distraction and Civill warre.

Fourthly, that these creatures, though they have some use of voice, in making knowne to one another their desires, and other affections; yet they want that art of words, by which some men can represent to others, that which is Good, in the likenesse of Evill; an Evill, in the likenesse of Good; and augument, or diminish the apparent greatnesse of Good and Evill; discontenting men, and troubling their Peace at their pleasure.

Fifthly, irrationall creatures cannot distinguish betweene Injury, and Dammage; and therefore as long as they be at ease, they are not offended with their fellowes; whereas Man is then most troublesome, when he is most at ease; for then it is that he loves to shew his Wisdome, and controule the Actions of them that governe the Common-wealth.

Lastly, the agreement of these creatures is Naturall; that of men, is by Covenant only, which is Artificiall: and therefore it is no wonder if there be somewhat else required (besides Covenant) to make their Agreement constant and lasting; which is a Common Power, to keep them in awe, and to direct their actions to the Common Benefit.

The only way to erect such a Common Power, as may be able to defend them from the invasion of Forraigners, and the injuries of one another, and thereby to secure them in such sort, as that by their owne industrie, and by the fruites of the Earth, they may nourish themselves and live contentedly; is, to conferre all their power and strength upon one Man, or upon one Assembly of men, that may reduce all their Wills, by plurality of voices, unto one Will: which is as much as to say, to appoint one Man, or Assembly of men, to beare their Person; and every one to owne, and acknowledge himselfe to be Author of whatsoever he that so beareth their Person, shall Act, or cause to be Acted, in those things which concerne the Common Peace and Safetie; and therein to submit their Wills, every one to his Will, and their Judgements, to his Judgement. This is more than Consent, or Concord; it is a reall Unitie of them all, in one and the same Person, made by Covenant of every man with every man, in such manner, as if every man should· say to every man, I Authorise and give up my Right of Governing my selfe, to this Man, or to this Assembly of men, on this condition, that thou give up thy Right to him, and Authorise all his Actions in like manner. This done, the Multitude so united in one Person, is called a COMMON-WEALTH, in latine CIVITAS. This is the Generation of the great LEVIATHAN, or rather (to speake more reverently) of that Mortall God, to which wee owe under the Immortall God, our peace and defence. For by this Authoritie, given him by every particular man in the Common-Wealth, he hath the use of so much Power and Strength conferred on him, that by terror thereof, he is inabled to forme the wills of them all, to Peace at home, and mutuall ayd against their enemies abroad. And in him consisteth the Essence of the Common-wealth; which (to define it,) is One Person, of whose Acts a great Multitude, by mutuall Covenante one with another, have made themselves every one the Author, to the end he may use the strength and means of them all, as he shall think expedient, for their Peace and Common Defence.

And he that carryeth this Person, is called SOVER-AIGNE, and said to have Soveraigne Power; and every one besides, his SUBJECT.

The attaining to this Soveraigne Power, is by two wayes. One, by Naturall force; as when a man maketh his children, to submit themselves, and their children to his government, as being able to destroy them if they refuse; or by Warre subdueth his enemies to his will, giving them their lives on that condition. The other, is when men agree amongst themselves, to submit to some Man, or Assembly of men, voluntarily, on confidence to be protected by him against all others. This later, may be called a Politicall Common-wealth, or Common-wealth by Institution; and the former, a Common-wealth by Acquisition.

SELECTIONS FROM THE SOCIAL CONTRACT

By JEAN JACQUES ROUSSEAU

I MEAN to inquire if, in the civil order, there can be any sure and legitimate rule of administration, men being taken as they are and laws as they might be. In this inquiry I shall endeavour always to unite what right sanctions with what is prescribed by interest, in order that justice and utility may in no case be divided.

I enter upon my task without proving the importance of the subject. I shall be asked if I am a prince or a legislator, to write on politics. I answer that I am neither, and that is why I do so. If I were a prince or a legislator, I should not waste time in saying what wants doing; I should do it, or hold my peace.

As I was born a citizen of a free State, and a member of the Sovereign, I feel that, however feeble the influence my voice can have on public affairs, the right of voting on them makes it my duty to study them: and I am happy, when I reflect upon governments, to find my inquiries always furnish me with new reasons for loving that of my own country.

SUBJECT OF THE FIRST BOOK

Man is born free; and everywhere he is in chains. One thinks himself the master of others, and still remains a greater slave than they. How did this change come about? I do not know. What can make it legitimate? That question I think I can answer.

If I took into account only force, and the effects derived from it, I should say: "As long as a people is compelled to obey, and obeys, it does well; as soon as it can shake off the

yoke, and shakes it off, it does still better; for, regaining its
liberty by the same right as took it away, either it is justified in resuming it, or there was no justification for those
who took it away." But the social order is a sacred right
which is the basis of all other rights. Nevertheless, this right
does not come from nature, and must therefore be founded
on conventions. Before coming to that, I have to prove what
I have just asserted.

THE RIGHT OF THE STRONGEST

The strongest is never strong enough to be always the
master, unless he transforms strength into right, and obedience into duty. Hence the right of the strongest, which,
though to all seeming meant ironically, is really laid down
as a fundamental principle. But are we never to have an
explanation of this phrase? Force is a physical power, and
I fail to see what moral effect it can have. To yield to force
is an act of necessity, not of will—at the most, an act of
prudence. In what sense can it be a duty?

Suppose for a moment that this so-called "right" exists.
I maintain that the sole result is a mass of inexplicable nonsense. For, if force creates right, the effect changes with the
cause: every force that is greater than the first succeeds to
its right. As soon as it is possible to disobey with impunity,
disobedience is legitimate; and, the strongest being always
in the right, the only thing that matters is to act so as to
become the strongest. But what kind of right is that which
perishes when force fails? If we must obey perforce, there
is no need to obey because we ought; and if we are not forced
to obey, we are under no obligation to do so. Clearly, the
word "right" adds nothing to force: in this connection, it
means absolutely nothing.

Obey the powers that be. If this means yield to force, it is
a good precept, but superfluous: I can answer for its never
being violated. All power comes from God, I admit; but so
does all sickness: does that mean that we are forbidden to

call in the doctor? A brigand surprises me at the edge of
a wood: must I not merely surrender my purse on compulsion; but, even If I could withhold it, am I in conscience
bound to give it up? For certainly the pistol he holds is also
a power.

Let us then admit that force does not create right, and that
we are obliged to obey only legitimate powers. In that case,
my original question recurs.

SLAVERY

Since no man has a natural authority over his fellow,
and force creates no right, we must conclude that conventions form the basis of all legitimate authority among men.

If an individual, says Grotius, can alienate his liberty and
make himself the slave of a master, why could not a whole
people do the same and make itself subject to a king? There
are in this passage plenty of ambiguous words which would
need explaining; but let us confine ourselves to the word
alienate. To alienate is to give or to sell. Now, a man who
becomes the slave of another does not give himself; he sells
himself, at the least for his subsistence: but for what does a
people sell itself? A king is so far from furnishing his subjects with their subsistence that he gets his own only from
them; and, according to Rabelais, kings do not live on
nothing. Do subjects then give their persons on condition
that the king takes their goods also? I fail to see what they
have left to preserve.

It will be said that the despot assures his subjects civil
tranquillity. Granted; but what do they gain, if the wars
his ambition brings down upon them, his insatiable avidity,
and the vexatious conduct of his ministers press harder on
them than their own dissensions would have done? What do
they gain, if the very tranquillity they enjoy is one of their
miseries? Tranquillity is found also in dungeons; but is that
enough to make them desirable places to live in? The Greeks
imprisoned in the cave of the Cyclops lived there very tran-

quilly, while they were awaiting their turn to be devoured.

To say that a man gives himself gratuitously, is to say what is absurd and inconceivable; such an act is null and illegitimate, from the mere fact that he who does it is out of his mind. To say the same of a whole people is to suppose a people of madmen; and madness creates no right.

Even if each man could alienate himself, he could not alienate his children: they are born men and free; their liberty belongs to them, and no one but they has the right to dispose of it. Before they come to years of discretion, the father can, in their name, lay down conditions for their preservation and well-being, but he cannot give them irrevocably and without conditions; such a gift is contrary to the ends of nature, and exceeds the rights of paternity. It would therefore be necessary, in order to legitimise an arbitrary government, that in every generation the people should be in a position to accept or reject it; but, were this so, the government would be no longer arbitrary.

To renounce liberty is to renounce being a man, to surrender the rights of humanity and even its duties. For him who renounces everything no indemnity is possible. Such a renunciation is incompatible with man's nature; to remove all liberty from his will is to remove all morality from his acts. Finally, it is an empty and contradictory convention that sets up, on the one side, absolute authority, and, on the other, unlimited obedience. Is it not clear that we can be under no obligation to a person from whom we have the right to exact everything? Does not this condition alone, in the absence of equivalence or exchange, in itself involve the nullity of the act? For what right can my slave have against me, when all that he has belongs to me, and, his right being mine, this right of mine against myself is a phrase devoid of meaning?

Grotius and the rest find in war another origin for the so-called right of slavery. The victor having, as they hold, the right of killing the vanquished, the latter can buy back his life at the price of his liberty; and this convention is the more legitimate because it is to the advantage of both parties.

But it is clear that this supposed right to kill the conquered is by no means deducible from the state of war. Men, from the mere fact that, while they are living in their primitive independence, they have no mutual relations stable enough to constitute either the state of peace or the state of war, cannot be naturally enemies. War is constituted by a relation between things, and not between persons; and, as the state of war cannot arise out of simple personal relations, but only out of real relations, private war, or war of man with man, can exist neither in the state of nature, where there is no constant property, nor in the social state, where everything is under the authority of the laws.

Individual combats, duels and encounters, are acts which cannot constitute a state; while the private wars, authorised by the Establishments of Louis IX, King of France, and suspended by the Peace of God, are abuses of feudalism, in itself an absurd system if ever there was one, and contrary to the principles of natural right and to all good polity.

War then is a relation, not between man and man, but between State and State; and individuals are enemies only accidentally, not as men, nor even as citizens, but as soldiers; not as members of their country, but as its defenders. Finally, each State can have for enemies only other States, and not men; for between things disparate in nature there can be no real relation.

Furthermore, this principle is in conformity with the established rules of all times and the constant practice of all civilised peoples. Declarations of war are intimations less to powers than to their subjects. The foreigner, whether king, individual, or people, who robs, kills or detains the subjects, without declaring war on the prince, is not an enemy, but a brigand. Even in real war, a just prince, while laying hands, in the enemy's country, on all that belongs to the public, respects the lives and goods of individuals; he respects rights on which his own are founded. The object of the war being the destruction of the hostile State, the other side has a right to kill its defenders, while they are bearing arms; but as soon as they lay them down and surrender, they cease to be enemies or instruments of the enemy, and become once more merely men, whose life no one has any right to take. Sometimes it is possible to kill the State without killing a single one of its members; and war gives no right which is not necessary to the gaining of its object. These principles are not those of Grotius: they are not based on the authority of poets, but derived from the nature of reality and based on reason.

The right of conquest has no foundation other than the right of the strongest. If war does not give the conqueror the right to massacre the conquered peoples, the right to enslave them cannot be based upon a right which does not exist. No one has a right to kill an enemy except when he cannot make him a slave, and the right to enslave him cannot therefore be derived from the right to kill him. It is accordingly an unfair exchange to make him buy at the price of his liberty his life, over which the victor holds no right. Is it not clear that there is a vicious circle in founding the right of life and death on the right of slavery, and the right of slavery on the right of life and death?

Even if we assume this terrible right to kill everybody, I maintain that a slave made in war, or a conquered people, is under no obligation to a master, except to obey him as far as he is compelled to do so. By taking an equivalent for his life, the victor has not done him a favour; instead of killing him without profit, he has killed him usefully. So far then is he from acquiring over him any authority in addition to that of force, that the state of war continues to subsist between them: their mutual relation is the effect of it, and the usage of the right of war does not imply a treaty of peace. A convention has indeed been made; but this convention, so far from destroying the state of war, presupposes its continuance.

So, from whatever aspect we regard the question, the right of slavery is null and void, not only as being illegitimate, but also because it is absurd and meaningless. The words slave and right contradict each other, and are mutually exclusive. It will always be equally foolish for a man to say to a man or to a people: "I make with you a convention wholly at your expense and wholly to my advantage; I shall keep it as long as I like, and you will keep it as long as I like."

THAT WE MUST ALWAYS GO BACK TO A FIRST CONVENTION

Even if I granted all that I have been refuting, the friends of despotism would be no better off. There will always be a great difference between subduing a multitude and ruling a society. Even if scattered individuals were successively enslaved by one man, however numerous they might be, I still see no more than a master and his slaves, and certainly not a people and its ruler; I see what may be termed an aggregation, but not an association; there is as yet neither public good nor body politic. The man in question, even if he has enslaved half the world, is still only an individual; his interest, apart from that of others, is still a purely private interest. If this same man comes to die, his empire, after him, remains scattered and without unity, as an oak falls and dissolves into a heap of ashes when the fire has consumed it.

A people, says Grotius, can give itself to a king. Then, according to Grotius, a people is a people before it gives itself. The gift is itself a civil act, and implies public deliberation. It would be better, before examining the act by which a people gives itself to a king, to examine that by which it has become a people; for this act, being necessarily prior to the other, is the true foundation of society.

Indeed, if there were no prior convention, where, unless the election were unanimous, would be the obligation on the minority to submit to the choice of the majority? How have a hundred men who wish for a master the right to vote on behalf of ten who do not? The law of majority voting is it-self something established by convention, and presupposes unanimity, on one occasion at least.

THE SOCIAL COMPACT

I suppose men to have reached the point at which the obstacles in the way of their preservation in the state of nature show their power of resistance to be greater than the resources at the disposal of each individual for his main-tenance in that state. That primitive condition can then subsist no longer; and the human race would perish un-less it changed its manner of existence.

But, as men cannot engender new forces, but only unite and direct existing ones, they have no other means of pre-serving themselves than the formation, by aggregation, of a sum of forces great enough to overcome the resistance. These they have to bring into play by means of a single motive power, and cause to act in concert.

This sum of forces can arise only where several persons come together; but, as the force and liberty of each man are the chief instruments of his self-preservation, how can he pledge them without harming his own interests, and neglecting the care he owes to himself? This difficulty, in its bearing on my present subject, may be stated in the following terms—

"The problem is to find a form of association which will defend and protect with the whole common force the per-son and goods of each associate, and in which each, while uniting himself with all, may still obey himself alone, and remain as free as before." This is the fundamental problem of which the Social Contract provides the solution.

The clauses of this contract are so determined by the nature of the act that the slightest modification would make them vain and ineffective; so that, although they have perhaps never been formally set forth, they are everywhere the same and everywhere tacitly admitted and recognised, until, on the violation of the social compact, each regains his original rights and resumes his natural liberty, while losing the conventional liberty in favour of which he renounced it.

These clauses, properly understood, may be reduced to one—the total alienation of each associate, together with all his rights, to the whole community; for, in the first place, as each gives himself absolutely, the conditions are the same for all; and, this being so, no one has any interest in making them burdensome to others.

Moreover, the alienation being without reserve, the union is as perfect as it can be, and no associate has anything more to demand: for, if the individuals retained certain rights, as there would be no common superior to decide between them and the public, each, being on one point his own judge, would ask to be so on all; the state of nature would thus continue, and the association would necessarily become inoperative or tyrannical.

Finally, each man, in giving himself to all, gives himself to nobody; and as there is no associate over whom he does not acquire the same right as he yields others over himself, he gains an equivalent for everything he loses, and an increase of force for the preservation of what he has.

If then we discard from the social compact what is not of its essence, we shall find that it reduces itself to the following terms—

"Each of us puts his person and all his power in common under the supreme direction of the general will, and, in our corporate capacity, we receive each member as an indivisible part of the whole."

At once, in place of the individual personality of each contracting party, this act of association creates a moral and collective body, composed of as many members as the assembly contains votes, and receiving from this act its unity, its common identity, its life and its will. This public person, so formed by the union of all other persons, formerly took the name of city, and now takes that of Republic or body politic; it is called by its members State when passive, Sovereign when active, and Power when compared with others like itself. Those who are associated in it take collectively the name of people, and severally are called citizens, as sharing in the sovereign power, and subjects, as being under the laws of the State. But these terms are often confused and taken one for another; it is enough to know how to distinguish them when they are being used with precision.

HOW TO CHECK THE USURPATIONS OF GOVERNMENT

What we have just said confirms Chapter XVI, and makes it clear that the institution of government is not a contract, but a law; that the depositaries of the executive power are not the people's masters, but its officers; that it can set them up and pull them down when it likes; that for them there is no question of contract, but of obedience; and that in taking charge of the functions the State imposes on them they are doing no more than fulfilling their duty as citizens, without having the remotest right to argue about the conditions.

When therefore the people sets up an hereditary government, whether it be monarchial and confined to one family, or aristocratic and confined to a class, what it enters into is not an undertaking; the administration is given a provisional form, until the people chooses to order it otherwise.

It is true that such changes are always dangerous, and that the established government should never be touched except when it comes to be incompatible with the public good; but the circumspection this involves is a maxim of policy and not a rule of right, and the State is no more bound to leave civil authority in the hands of its rulers than military authority in the hands of its generals.

It is also true that it is impossible to be too careful to observe, in such cases, all the formalities necessary to distinguish a regular and legitimate act from a seditious tumult, and the will of a whole people from the clamour of a faction. Here above all no further concession should be made to the untoward possibility than cannot, in the strictest logic, be refused it. From this obligation the prince derives a great advantage in preserving his power despite the people, without it being possible to say he has usurped it; for, seeming to avail himself only of his rights, he finds it very easy to extend them, and to prevent, under the pretext of keeping the peace, assemblies that are destined to the re-establishment of order; with the result that he takes advantage of a silence he does not allow to be broken, or of irregularities he causes to be committed, to assume that he has the support of those whom fear prevents from speaking, and to punish those who dare to speak. Thus it was that the decemvirs, first elected for one year and then kept on in office for a second, tried to perpetuate their power by forbidding the comitia to assemble; and by this easy method every government in the world, once clothed with the public power, sooner or later usurps the sovereign authority.

The periodical assemblies of which I have already spoken are designed to prevent or postpone this calamity, above all when they need no formal summoning; for in that case, the prince cannot stop them without openly declaring himself a law-breaker and an enemy of the State.

The opening of these assemblies, whose sole object is the maintenance of the social treaty, should always take the form of putting two propositions that may not be suppressed, which should be voted on separately.

The first is: "Does it please the Sovereign to preserve the present form of government?"

The second is: "Does it please the people to leave its administration in the hands of those who are actually in charge of it?"

I am here assuming what I think I have shown; that there is in the State no fundamental law that cannot be revoked, not excluding the social compact itself; for if all the citizens assembled of one accord to break the compact, it is impos-

sible to doubt that it would be very legitimately broken.
Grotius even thinks that each man can renounce his membership of his own State, and recover his natural liberty and
his goods on leaving the country. It would be indeed absurd
if all the citizens in assembly could not do what each can do
by himself.

THAT THE GENERAL WILL IS INDESTRUCTIBLE

As long as several men in assembly regard themselves as
a single body, they have only a single will which is concerned with their common preservation and general well-
being. In this case, all the springs of the State are vigorous
and simple and its rules clear and luminous; there are no
embroilments or conflicts of interests; the common good is
everywhere clearly apparent, and only good sense is needed
to perceive it. Peace, unity and equality are the enemies of
political subtleties. Men who are upright and simple are difficult to deceive because of their simplicity; lures and ingenious pretexts fail to impose upon them, and they are not
even subtle enough in the world, bands of peasants are seen
regulating affairs of State under an oak, and always acting
wisely, can we help scorning the ingenious methods of other
nations, which make themselves illustrious and wretched
with so much art and mystery?

A State so governed needs very few laws; and, as it becomes necessary to issue new ones, the necessity is universally seen. The first man to propose them merely says what all
have already felt, and there is no question of factions or intrigues or eloquence in order to secure the passage into law
of what every one has already decided to do, as soon as he is
sure that the rest will act with him.

Theorists are led into error because, seeing only States that
have been from the beginning wrongly constituted, they
are struck by the impossibility of applying such a policy to
them. They make great game of all the absurdities a clever
rascal or an insinuating speaker might get the people of

Paris or London to believe. They do not know that Cromwell would have been put to "the bells" by the people of Berne, and the Duc de Beaufort on the treadmill by the Genevese.

But when the social bond begins to be relaxed and the State to grow weak, when particular interests begin to make themselves felt and the smaller societies to exercise an influence over the larger, the common interest changes and finds opponents: opinion is no longer unanimous; the general will ceases to be the will of all; contradictory views and debates arise; and the best advice is not taken without question.

Finally, when the State, on the eve of ruin, maintains only a vain, illusory and formal existence, when in every heart the social bond is broken, and the meanest interest brazenly lays hold of the sacred name of "public good," the general will becomes mute; all men, guided by secret motives, no more give their views as citizens than if the State had never been; and iniquitous decrees directed solely to private interest get passed under the name of laws.

Does it follow from this that the general will is exterminated or corrupted? Not at all: it is always constant, unalterable and pure; but it is subordinated to other wills which encroach upon its sphere. Each man, in detaching his interest from the common interest, sees clearly that he cannot entirely separate them; but his share in the public mishaps seems to him negligible beside the exclusive good he aims at making his own. Apart from this particular good, he wills the general good in his own interest, as strongly as any one else. Even in selling his vote for money, he does not extinguish in himself the general will, but only eludes it. The fault he commits is that of changing the state of the question, and answering something different from what he is asked. Instead of saying, by his vote, "It is to the advantage of the State," he says, "It is of advantage to this or that man or party that this or that view should prevail." Thus the law of public order in assemblies is not so much to maintain in them the general will as to secure that the question be always put to it, and the answer always given by it.

I could here set down many reflections on the simple right of voting in every act of Sovereignty—a right which no-one can take from the citizens—and also on the right of stating views, making proposals, dividing and discussing, which the government is always most careful to leave solely to its members; but this important subject would need a treatise on itself, and it is impossible to say everything in a single work.

VOTING

It may be seen, from the last chapter, that the way in which general business is managed may give a clear enough indication of the actual state of morals and the health of the body politic. The more concert reigns in the assemblies, that is, the nearer opinion approaches unanimity, the greater is the dominance of the general will. On the other hand, long debates, dissensions and tumult proclaim the ascendancy of particular interests and the decline of the State.

This seems less clear when two or more orders enter into the constitution, as patricians and plebeians did at Rome; for quarrels between these two orders often disturbed the comitia, even in the best days of the Republic. But the exception is rather apparent than real; for then, through the defect that is inherent in the body politic, there were, so to speak, two States in one, and what is not true of the two together is true of either separately. Indeed, even in the most stormy times, the plebiscite of the people, when the Senate did not interfere with them, always went through quietly and by large majorities. The citizens having but one interest, the people had but a single will.

At the other extremity of the circle, unanimity recurs; this is the case when the citizens, having fallen into servitude, have lost both liberty and will. Fear and flattery then change votes into acclamation; deliberation ceases, and only worship or malediction is left. Such was the vile manner in which the senate expressed its views under the Emperors. It did so sometimes with absurd precautions. Tacitus observes that, under Otho, the senators, while they heaped curses on Vitellius, contrived at the same time to make a deafening noise, in order that, should he ever become their master, he might not know what each of them had said.

On these various considerations depend the rules by which the methods of counting votes and comparing opinions should be regulated, according as the general will is more or less easy to discover, and the State more or less in its decline.

There is but one law which, from its nature, needs unanimous consent. This is the social compact; for civil association is the most voluntary of all acts. Every man being born free and his own master, no-one, under any pretext whatsoever, can make any man subject without his consent. To decide that the son of a slave is born a slave is to decide that he is not born a man.

If then there are opponents when the social compact is made, their opposition does not invalidate the contract, but merely prevents them from being included in it. They are foreigners among citizens. When the State is instituted, residence constitutes consent; to dwell within its territory is to submit to the Sovereign.

Apart from this primitive contract, the vote of the majority always binds all the rest. This follows from the contract itself. But it is asked how a man can be both free and forced to conform to wills that are not his own. How are the opponents at once free and subject to laws they have not agreed to?

I retort that the question is wrongly put. The citizen gives his consent to all the laws, including those which are passed in spite of his opposition, and even those which punish him when he dares to break any of them. The constant will of all the members of the State is the general will; by virtue of it they are citizens and free. When in the popular assem bly a law is proposed, what the people is asked is not exactly whether it approves or rejects the proposal, but whether it is in conformity with the general will, which is their will. Each man, in giving his vote, states his opinion on that point; and the general will is found by counting votes. When therefore the opinion that is contrary to my own prevails, this proves neither more nor less than that I was mistaken, and that what I thought to be the general will was not so. If my particular opinion had carried the day I should have achieved the opposite of what was my will; and it is in that case that I should not have been free.

This presupposes, indeed, that all the qualities of the general will still reside in the majority; when they cease to do so, whatever side a man may take, liberty is no longer possible.

In my earlier demonstration of how particular wills are substituted for the general will in public deliberation, I have adequately pointed out the practicable methods of them later on. I have also given the principles for determining the proportional number of votes for declaring that will. A difference of one vote destroys equality; a single opponent destroys unanimity; but between equality and unanimity, there are several grades of unequal division, at each of which this proportion may be fixed in accordance with the condition and the needs of the body politic.

There are two general rules that may serve to regulate this relation. First, the more grave and important the questions discussed, the nearer should the opinion that is to prevail approach unanimity. Secondly, the more the matter in hand calls for speed, the smaller the prescribed difference in the numbers of votes may be allowed to become: where an instant decision has to be reached, a majority of one vote should be enough. The first of these two rules seems more in harmony with the laws, and the second with practical affairs. In any case, it is the combination of them, that gives the best proportions for determining the majority necessary.

THE DICTATORSHIP

The inflexibility of the laws, which prevents them from adapting themselves to circumstances, may, in certain cases, render them disastrous, and make them bring about, at a time of crisis, the ruin of the State. The order and slowness of the forms they enjoin require a space of time which circumstances sometimes withhold. A thousand cases against which the legislator has made no provision may present themselves and it is a highly necessary part of foresight to be conscious that everything cannot be foreseen.

It is wrong therefore to wish to make political institutions so strong as to render it impossible to suspend their operation. Even Sparta allowed its laws to lapse.

However, none but the greatest dangers can counterbalance that of changing the public order, and the sacred power of the laws should never be arrested save when the existence of the country is at stake. In these rare and obvious cases, provision is made for the public security by a particular act entrusting it to him who is most worthy. This commitment may be carried out in either of two ways, according to the nature of the danger.

If increasing the activity of the government is a sufficient remedy, power is concentrated in the hands of one or two of its members: in this case the change is not in the authority of the laws, but only in the form of administering them. If, on the other hand, the peril is of such a kind that the paraphernalia of the laws are an obstacle to their preservation, the method is to nominate a supreme ruler, who shall silence all the laws and suspend for a moment the sovereign authority. In such a case, there is no doubt about the general will, and it is clear that the people's first intention is that the State shall not perish. Thus the suspension of the legislative authority is in no sense its abolition; the magistrate who silences it cannot make it speak; he dominates it, but cannot represent it. He can do anything, except make laws.

The first method was used by the Roman senate when

in a consecrated formula, it charged the consuls to provide for the safety of the Republic. The second was employed when one of the two consuls nominated a dictator: a custom Rome borrowed from Alba.

During the first period of the Republic, recourse was very often had to the dictatorship, because the State had not yet a firm enough basis to be able to maintain itself by the strength of its constitution alone. As the state of morality then made superfluous many of the precautions which would have been necessary at other times, there was no fear that a dictator would abuse his authority, or try to keep it beyond his term of office. On the contrary, so much power appeared to be burdensome to him who was clothed with it, and he made all speed to lay it down, as if taking the place of the laws had been too troublesome and too perilous a position to retain.

It is therefore the danger not of its abuse, but of its cheapening, that makes me attack the indiscreet use of this supreme magistracy in the earliest times. For as long as it was freely employed at elections, dedications and purely formal functions, there was danger of its becoming less formidable in time of need, and of men growing accustomed to regarding as empty a title that was used only on occasions of empty ceremonial.

Towards the end of the Republic, the Romans, having grown more circumspect, were as unreasonably sparing in the use of the dictatorship as they had formerly been lavish. It is easy to see that their fears were without foundation, that the weakness of the capital secured it against the magistrates who were in its midst; that a dictator might, in certain cases, defend the public liberty, but could never endanger it; and that the chains of Rome would be forged, not in Rome itself, but in her armies. The weak resistance offered by Marius to Sulla, and by Pompey to Caesar, clearly showed what was to be expected from authority at home against force from abroad.

This misconception led the Romans to make great mistakes; such, for example, as the failure to nominate a dictator in the Catilinarian conspiracy. For, as only the city itself, with at most some province in Italy, was concerned, the unlimited authority the laws gave to the dictator would have enabled him to make short work of the conspiracy, which was, in fact, stifled only by a combination of lucky chances human prudence had no right to expect.

Instead, the senate contented itself with entrusting its whole power to the consuls, so that Cicero, in order to take effective action, was compelled on a capital point to exceed his powers; and if, in the first transports of joy, his conduct was approved, he was justly called, later on, to account for the blood of citizens spilt in violation of the laws. Such a reproach could never have been levelled at a dictator. But the consul's eloquence carried the day; and he himself, Roman though he was, loved his own glory better than his country, and sought, not so much the most lawful and secure means of saving the State, as to get for himself the whole honour of having done so. He was therefore justly honoured as the liberator of Rome, and also justly punished as a law-breaker. However brilliant his recall may have been, it was undoubtedly an act of pardon.

However this important trust be conferred, it is important that its duration should be fixed at a very brief period, incapable of being ever prolonged. In the crises which lead to its adoption, the State is either soon lost, or soon saved; and, the present need passed, the dictatorship becomes either tyrannical or idle. At Rome, where dictators held office for six months only, most of them abdicated before their time was up. If their term had been longer, they might well have tried to prolong it still further, as the decemvirs did when chosen for a year. The dictator had only time to provide against the need that had caused him to be chosen; he had none to think of further projects.

OF MONARCHY AND HEREDITARY
SUCCESSION*

By THOMAS PAINE

MANKIND being originally equals in the order of creation, the equality could only be destroyed by some subsequent circumstance: the distinctions of rich and poor may in a great measure be accounted for, and that without having recourse to the harsh ill-sounding names of oppression and avarice. Oppression is often the consequence, but seldom or never the means of riches; and tho' avarice will preserve a man from being necessitously poor, it generally makes him too timorous to be wealthy.

But there is another and greater distinction for which no truly natural or religious reason can be assigned, and that is the distinction of men into KINGS and SUBJECTS. Male and female are the distinctions of nature, good and bad the distinctions of Heaven; but how a race of men came into the world so exalted above the rest, and distinguished like some new species, is worth inquiring into, and whether they are the means of happiness or of misery to mankind.

In the early ages of the world, according to the scripture chronology there were no kings; the consequence of which was, there were no wars; it is the pride of kings which throws mankind into confusion. Holland, without a king hath enjoyed more peace for this last century than any of the monarchical governments in Europe. Antiquity favours the same remark; for the quiet and rural lives of the first Patriarchs have a happy something in them, which vanishes when we come to the history of Jewish royalty.

Government by kings was first introduced into the world by the Heathens, from whom the children of Israel copied

* From *Common Sense*

the custom. It was the most prosperous invention the Devil ever set on foot for the promotion of idolatry. The Heathens paid divine honours to their deceased kings, and the Christian World hath improved on the plan by doing the same to their living ones. How impious is the title of sacred Majesty applied to a worm, who in the midst of his splendor is crumbling into dust!

As the exalting one man so greatly above the rest cannot be justified on the equal rights of nature, so neither can it be defended on the authority of scripture; for the will of the Almighty as declared by Gideon, and the prophet Samuel, expressly disapproves of government by Kings. All anti-monarchical parts of scripture, have been very smoothly glossed over in monarchical governments, but they undoubtedly merit the attention of countries which have their governments yet to form. Render unto Caesar the things which are Caesar's, is the scripture doctrine of courts, yet it is no support of monarchical government, for the Jews at that time were without a king, and in a state of vassalage to the Romans.

Near three thousand years passed away, from the Mosaic account of the creation, till the Jews under a national delusion requested a king. Till then their form of government (except in extraordinary cases where the Almighty interposed) was a kind of Republic, administered by a judge and the elders of the tribes. Kings they had none, and it was held sinful to acknowledge any being under that title but the Lord of Hosts. And when a man seriously reflects on the idolatrous homage which is paid to the persons of kings, he need not wonder that the Almighty, ever jealous of his honour, should disapprove a form of government which so impiously invades the prerogative of Heaven.

Monarchy is ranked in scripture as one of the sins of the Jews, for which a curse in reserve is denounced against them. The history of that transaction is worth attending to.

The children of Israel being oppressed by the Midianites, Gideon marched against them with a small army, and vic-

tory thro' the divine interposition decided in his favour. The
Jews, elate with success, and attributing it to the generalship
of Gideon, proposed making him a king, saying, Rule thou
over us, thou and thy son, and thy son's son. Here was
temptation in its fullest extent; not a kingdom only, but an
hereditary one; but Gideon in the piety of his soul replied,
I will not rule over you, neither shall my son rule over you.
THE LORD SHALL RULE OVER YOU. Words need
not be more explicit; Gideon doth not decline the honour,
but denieth their right to give it; neither doth he compli-
ment them with invented declarations of his thanks, but in
the positive stile of a prophet charges them with disaffection
to their proper Sovereign, the King of Heaven.

About one hundred and thirty years after this, they fell
again into the same error. The hankering which the Jews
had for the idolatrous customs of the Heathens, is something
exceedingly unaccountable; but so it was, that laying hold of
the misconduct of Samuel's two sons, who were intrusted
with some secular concerns, they came in an abrupt and
clamorous manner to Samuel, saying, Behold thou art old,
and thy sons walk not in thy ways, now make us a king to
judge us like all the other nations. And here we cannot but
observe that their motives were bad, viz. that they might be
like unto other nations, i. e. the Heathens, whereas their
true glory lay in being as much unlike them as possible. But
the thing displeased Samuel when they said, give us a King
to judge us; and Samuel prayed unto the Lord, and the
Lord said unto Samuel, hearken unto the voice of the people
in all that they say unto thee, for they have not rejected
thee, but they have rejected me, THAT I SHOULD NOT
REIGN OVER THEM. According to all the works which
they have done since the day that I brought them up out
of Egypt even unto this day, wherewith they have forsaken
me, and served other Gods: so do they also unto thee. Now
therefore hearken unto their voice, howbeit, protest solemnly unto them and show them the manner of the King that
shall reign over them, i. e., not of any particular King, but

the general manner of the Kings of the earth whom Israel was so eagerly copying after. And notwithstanding the great distance of time and difference of manners, the character is still in fashion. And Samuel told all the words of the Lord unto the people, that asked of him a King. And he said, This shall be the manner of the King that shall reign over you. He will take your sons and appoint them for himself for his chariots and to be his horsemen, and some shall run before his chariots (this description agrees with the present mode of impressing men) and he will appoint him captains over thousands and captains over fifties, will set them to ear his ground and to reap his harvest, and to make his instruments of war, and instruments of his chariots. And he will take your daughters to be confectionaries, and to be cooks, and to be bakers (this describes the expense and luxury as well as the oppression of Kings) and he will take your fields and your vineyards, and your olive years, even the best of them and give them to his servants. And he will take the tenth of your seed, and of your vineyards, and give them to his officers and to his servants (by which we see that bribery, corruption, and favouritism, are the outstanding vices of Kings) and he will take the tenth of your men servants, and your maid servants, and your goodliest young men, and your asses, and put them to his work; and he will take the tenth of your sheep, and ye shall be his servants and ye shall cry out in that day because of your king which ye shall have chosen, AND THE LORD WILL NOT HEAR YOU IN THAT DAY. This accounts for the continuation of Monarchy; neither do the characters of the few good kings which have lived since, either sanctify the title, or blot out the sinfulness of the origin; the high encomium given of David takes no notice of him officially as a King, but only as a Man after God's own heart. Nevertheless the people refused to obey the voice of Samuel, and they said, Nay but we will have a king over us, that we may be like all the nations, and that our king may judge us, and go out before us and fight our battles. Samuel continued to reason with them but to no purpose; he set before them their in-gratitude, but all would not avail; and seeing them fully bent on their folly, he cried out, I will call unto the Lord, and he shall send thunder and rain (which was then a punishment, being in the time of wheat harvest) that ye may perceive and see that your wickedness is great which ye have done in the sight of the Lord, IN ASKING YOU A KING. So Samuel called unto the Lord, and the Lord sent thunder and rain that day, and all the people greatly feared the Lord and Samuel. And all the people said unto Samuel, Pray for thy servants unto the Lord thy God that we die not, for WE HAVE ADDED UNTO OUR SINS THIS EVIL, TO ASK A KING. These portions of scrip-ture are direct and positive. They admit of no equivocal construction. That the Almighty hath here entered his pro-test against monarchical government is true, or the scripture is false. And a man hath good reason to believe that there is as much of kingcraft as priestcraft in withholding the scrip-ture from the public in popish countries. For monarchy in every instance is the popery of government.

To the evil of monarchy we have added that of hereditary succession; and as the first is a degradation and lessening of ourselves, so the second, claimed as a matter of right, is an insult and imposition on posterity. For all men being origin-ally equals, no one by birth could have a right to set up his own family in perpetual preference to all others for ever, and tho' himself might deserve some decent degree of hon-ours of his contemporaries, yet his descendants might be far too unworthy to inherit them. One of the strongest nat-ural proofs of the folly of hereditary right in Kings, is that nature disapproves it, otherwise she would not so frequently turn it into ridicule, by giving mankind an Ass for a Lion.

Secondly as no man at first could possess any other public honors than were bestowed upon him, so the givers of those honors could have no power to give away the right of pos-terity, and though they might say "We choose you for our head," they could not without manifest injustice to their children say "that your children and your children's children shall reign over ours forever." Because such an unwise, unjust, unnatural compact might (perhaps) in the next succession put them under the government of a rogue or a fool. Most wise men in their private sentiments have ever treated hereditary right with contempt; yet it is one of those evils which when once established is not easily removed: many submit from fear, others from superstition, and more powerful part shares with the king the plunder of the rest.

This is supposing the present race of kings in the world to have had an honourable origin: whereas it is more than probable, that, could we take off the dark covering of antiquity and trace them to their first rise, we should find the first of them nothing better than the principal ruffian of some restless gang, whose savage manners or pre-eminence in subtilty obtained him the title of chief among plunderers: and who by increasing in power and extending his depredations, overawed the quiet and defenceless to purchase their safety by frequent contributions. Yet his electors could have no idea of giving hereditary right to his descendants, because such a perpetual exclusion of themselves was incompatible with the free and unrestrained principles they professed to live by. Wherefore, hereditary succession in the early ages of monarchy could not take place as a matter of claim, but as something casual or complemental; but as few or no records were extant in those days, and traditionary history stuff'd with fables, it was very easy, after the lapse of a few generations, to trump up some superstitious tale conveniently timed, Mahomet-like, to cram hereditary right down the throats of the vulgar. Perhaps the disorders which threatened, or seemed to threaten, on the decease of a leader and the choice of a new one (for elections among ruffians could not be very orderly) induced many at first to favour hereditary pretensions; by which means it happened, as it hath happened since, that what at first was submitted to as a convenience was afterwards claimed as a right.

England since the conquest hath known some few good monarchs, but groaned beneath a much larger number of bad ones: yet no man in his senses can say that their claim under William the Conqueror is a very honourable one. A French bastard landing with an armed Banditti and establishing himself king of England against the consent of the natives, is in plain terms a very paltry rascally original. It certainly hath no divinity in it. However it is needless to spend much time in exposing the folly of hereditary right: if there are any so weak as to believe it, let them promiscuously worship the Ass and the Lion, and welcome. I shall neither copy their humility, nor disturb their devotion.

Yet I should be glad to ask how they suppose kings came at first? The question admits but of three answers, viz. either by lot, by election, or by usurpation. If the first king was taken by lot, it establishes a precedent for the next, which excludes hereditary succession. Saul was by lot, yet the succession was not hereditary, neither does it appear from that transaction that there was any intention it ever should. If the first king of any country was by election, that likewise establishes a precedent for the next: for to say, that the right of all future generations is taken away, by the act of the first electors, in their choice not only of a king but of a family of kings for ever, hath no parallel in or out of scripture but the doctrine of original sin, which supposes the free will of all men lost in Adam; and from such comparison, and it will admit of no other, hereditary succession can derive no glory. For as in Adam all sinned, and as in the first electors all men obeyed; as in the one all mankind were subjected to Satan, and in the other to sovereignty; as our innocence was lost in the first, and our authority in the last; and as both disable us from re-assuming some former state and privilege, it unanswerably follows that original sin and hereditary succession are parallels. Dishonourable rank! inglorious connection! yet the most subtle sophist cannot produce a juster simile.

As to usurpation, no man will be so hardy as to defend

it; and that William the Conqueror was an usurper is a fact not to be contradicted. The plain truth is, that the antiquity of English monarchy will not bear looking into.

But it is not so much the absurdity as the evil of hereditary succession which concerns mankind. Did it ensure a race of good and wise men it would have the seal of divine authority, but as it opens a door to the foolish, the wicked, and the improper, it hath in it the nature of oppression. Men who look upon themselves born to reign, and others to obey, soon grow insolent. Selected from the rest of mankind, their minds are early poisoned by importance; and the world they act in differs so materially from the world at large, that they have but little opportunity of knowing its true interests, and when they succeed to the government are frequently the most ignorant and unfit of any throughout the dominions.

Another evil which attends hereditary succession is, that the throne is subject to be possessed by a minor at any age; all which time the regency acting under the cover of a king have every opportunity and inducement to betray their trust. The same national misfortune happens when a king worn out with age and infirmity enters the last stage of human weakness. In both these cases the public becomes a prey to every miscreant who can temper successfully with the follies either of age or infancy.

The most plausible plea which hath ever been offered in favour of hereditary succession is, that it preserves a nation from civil wars; and were this true, it would be weighty; whereas it is the most bare-faced falsity ever imposed upon mankind. The whole history of England disowns the fact. Thirty kings and two minors have reigned in that distracted kingdom since the conquest, in which time there has been (including the revolution) no less than eight civil wars and nineteen Rebellions. Wherefore instead of making for peace, it makes against it, and destroys the very foundation it seems to stand upon.

The contest for monarchy and succession, between the

houses of York and Lancaster, laid England in a scene of blood for many years. Twelve pitched battles besides skirmishes and sieges were fought between Henry and Edward. Twice was Henry prisoner to Edward, who in his turn was prisoner to Henry. And so uncertain is the fate of war and the temper of a nation, when nothing but personal matters are the ground of a quarrel, that Henry was taken in triumph from a prison to a palace, and Edward obliged to fly from a palace to a foreign land; yet, as sudden transitions of temper are seldom lasting, Henry in his turn was driven from the throne, and Edward re-called to succeed him. The parliament always following the strongest side.

This contest began in the reign of Henry the Sixth, and was not entirely extinguished till Henry the Seventh, in whom the families were united. Including a period of 67 years, viz. from 1422 to 1489.

In short, monarchy and succession have laid (not this or that kingdom only) but the world in blood and ashes. 'Tis a form of government which the word of God bears testimony against, and blood will attend it.

If we enquire into the business of a King, we shall find that in some countries they may have none; and after sauntering away their lives without pleasure to themselves or advantage to the nation, withdraw from the scene, and leave their successors to tread the same idle round. In absolute monarchies the whole weight of business civil and military lies on the King; the children of Israel in their request for a king urged this plea, "that he may judge us, and go out before us and fight our battles." But in countries where he is neither a Judge nor a General, as in England, a man would be puzzled to know what is his business.

The nearer any government approaches to a Republic, the less business there is for a King. It is somewhat difficult to find a proper name for the government of England. Sir William Meredith calls it a Republic; but in its present state it is unworthy of the name, because the corrupt influence of the Crown, by having all the places in its disposal, hath so effectually swallowed up the power, and eaten out the virtue of the House of Commons (the Republican part in the constitution) that the government of England is nearly as monarchical as that of France or Spain. Men fall out with names without understanding them. For 'tis the Republican and not the Monarchical part of the constitution of England which Englishmen glory in, viz. the liberty of choosing an House of Commons from out of their own body—and it is easy to see that when Republican virtues fail, slavery ensues. Why is constitution of England sickly, but because monarchy hath poisoned the Republic; the Crown hath engrossed the Commons.

In England a King hath little more to do than to make war and give away places; which, in plain terms, is to empoverish the nation and set it together by the ears. A pretty business indeed for a man to be allowed eight hundred thousand sterling a year for, and worshipped into the bargain! Of more worth is one honest man to society, and in the sight of God, than all the crowned ruffians that ever lived.

OF LAWS IN RELATION TO THE NATURE OF THE CLIMATE*

By BARON DE MONTESQUIEU

GENERAL IDEA

If it be true that the temper of the mind and the passions of the heart are extremely different in different climates, the laws ought to be in relation both to the variety of those tempers.

OF THE DIFFERENCE OF MEN IN DIFFERENT CLIMATES

Cold air constringes the extremities of the external fibres of the body;[1] this increases their elasticity, and favors the return of the blood from the extreme parts to the heart. It contracts[2] those very fibres; consequently it increases also their force. On the contrary warm air relaxes and lengthens the extremes of the fibres; of course it diminishes their force and elasticity.

People are, therefore, more vigorous in cold climates. Here the action of the heart and the reaction of the extremities of the fibres are better performed, the temperature of the humors is greater, the blood moves more freely towards the heart, and reciprocally the heart has more power. This superiority of strength must produce various effects; for instance, a greater boldness, that is, more courage; a greater sense of superiority, that is, less desire of revenge; a greater opinion of security, that is, more frankness, less suspicion, policy, and cunning. In short, this must be productive of very different tempers. Put a man into a close, warm place, and for the reasons above given he will feel a great faintness. If under this circumstance you propose a bold enterprise to him,

* From *Of Laws in Relation to the Nature of the Climate*

I believe you will find him very little disposed towards it; his present weakness will throw him into despondency; he will be afraid of everything, being in a state of total incapacity. The inhabitants of warm countries are, like old men, timorous; the people in cold countries are, like young men, brace. If we reflect on the late wars,[3] which are more recent in our memory, and in which we can better distinguish some particular effects that escape us at a greater distance of time, we shall find that the northern people, transplanted into southern regions,[4] did not perform such exploits as their countrymen, who, fighting in their own climate, possessed their full vigor and courage.

This strength of the fibres in northern nations is the cause that the coarser juices are extracted from their ailments. Hence two things result; one, that the parts of the chyle or lymph are more proper, by reason of their large surface, to be applied to and to nourish the fibres; the other, that they are less proper, from their coarseness, to give a certain subtility to the nervous juice. Those people have, therefore, large bodies and but little vivacity.

The nerves that terminate from all parts in the cutis form each a nervous bundle; generally speaking, the whole nerve is not moved, but a very minute part. In warm climates, where the cutis is relaxed, the ends of the nerves are expanded and laid open to the weakest action of the smallest objects. In cold countries the cutis is constringed and the papillae compressed: the miliary glands are in some measure paralytic; and the sensation does not reach the brain, except when it is very strong and proceeds from the whole nerve at once. Now, imagination, taste, sensibility, and vivacity depend on an infinite number of small sensations.

I have observed the outermost part of a sheep's tongue, where, to the naked eye, it seems covered with papillae. On these papillae I have discerned through a microscope small hairs, or a kind of down; between the papillae were pyramids shaped towards the ends like pincers. Very likely these pyramids are the principal organ of taste.

I caused the half of this tongue to be frozen, and observing it with the naked eye I found the papillae considerably diminished: even some rows of them were sunk into their sheath. The outermost part I examined with the microscope, and perceived no pyramids. In proportion as the frost went off, the papillae seemed to the naked eye to rise, and with the microscope the miliary glands began to appear.

This observation confirms what I have been saying, that in cold countries the nervous glands are less expanded: they sink deeper into their sheaths, or they are sheltered from the action of external objects; consequently they have not such lively sensations.

In cold countries they have very little sensibility for pleasure; In temperate countries, they have more; in warm countries, their sensibility is exquisite. As climates are distinguished by degrees of latitude, we might distinguish them also in some measure by those of sensibility. I have been at the opera in England and in Italy, where I have seen the same pieces and the same performers; and yet the same music produces such different effects on the two nations: one is so cold and phlegmatic, and the other so lively and enraptured, that it seems almost inconceivable.

It is the same with regard to pain, which is excited by the laceration of some fibre of the body. The Author of nature has made it an established rule that this pain should be more acute in proportion as laceration is greater: now it is evident that the large bodies and course fibres of the people of the North are less capable of laceration than the delicate fibres of the inhabitants of warm countries; consequently the soul is there less sensible of pain. You must flay a Muscovite alive to make him feel.

From this delicacy of organs peculiar to warm climates it follows that the soul is most sensibly moved by whatever relates to the union of the two sexes: here everything leads to this object.

In northern climates scarcely has the animal part of love a power of making itself felt. In temperate climates, love, attended by a thousand appendages, endeavors to please by things that have at first the appearance, though not the reality, of this passion. In warmer climates it is like for its own sake, it is the only cause of happiness, it is life itself.

In southern countries a machine of a delicate frame but strong sensibility resigns itself either to a love which rises and is incessantly laid in a seraglio, or to a passion which leaves women in a greater independence, and is consequently exposed to a thousand inquietudes. In northern regions a machine robust and heavy finds pleasure in whatever is apt to throw the spirits into motion, such as hunting, travelling, war, and wine. If we travel towards the North, we meet with people who have few vices, many virtues, and a great share of frankness and sincereity. If we draw near the South, we fancy ourselves entirely removed from the verge of morality; here the strongest passions are productive of all manner of crimes, each man endeavouring, let the means be what they will, to indulge his inordinate desires. In temperate climates we find the inhabitants inconstant in their manners, as well as in their vices and virtues: the climate has not a quality determinate enough to fix them.

The heat of the climate may be so excessive as to deprive the body of all vigor and strength. Then the faintness is communicated to the mind; there is no curiosity, no enterprise, no generosity of sentiment; the inclinations are all passive; indolence constitutes the utmost happiness; scarcely any punishment is so severe as mental employment; and slavery is more supportable than the force and vigor of mind necessary for human conduct.

CONTRADICTION IN THE TEMPERS OF SOME SOUTHERN NATIONS

The Indians[5] are naturally a pusillanimous people; even the children[6] of Europeans born in India lose the courage peculiar to their own climate. But how shall we reconcile this with their customs and penances so full of barbarity? The men voluntarily undergo the greatest hardships, and the women burn themselves: here we find a very odd compound of fortitude and weakness.

Nature, having framed those people of a texture so weak as to fill them with timidity, has formed them at the same time of an imagination so lively that every object makes the strongest impression upon them. That delicacy of organs which renders them apprehensive of death contributes likewise to make them dread a thousand things more than death: the very same sensibility induces them to fly and dare all dangers.

As a good education is more necessary to children than to such as have arrived at maturity of understanding, so the inhabitants of those countries have much greater need than the European nations of a wiser legislator. The greater their sensibility, the more it behooves them to receive proper impressions, to imbibe no prejudices, and to let themselves be directed by reason.

At the time of the Romans the inhabitants of the north of Europe were destitute of arts, education, and almost of laws; and yet the good sense annexed to the gross fibres of those climates enabled them to make an admirable stand against the power of Rome, till the memorable period in which they quitted their woods to subvert that great empire.

CAUSE OF THE IMMUTABILITY OF RELIGION, MANNERS, CUSTOMS, AND LAWS IN THE EASTERN COUNTRIES

If to that delicacy of organs which renders the eastern nations so susceptible of every impression you add likewise a sort of indolence of mind, naturally connected with that of the body, by means of which they grow incapable of any exertion or effort, it is easy to comprehend that when once the soul has received an impression it cannot change it. This is the reason that the laws, manners, and customs,[7] even those which seem quite indifferent, such as their mode of dress, are the same to this very day in eastern countries as they were a thousand years ago.

THAT THOSE ARE BAD LEGISLATORS WHO FAVOR THE VICES OF THE
CLIMATE, AND GOOD LEGISLATORS WHO OPPOSE THOSE VICES

The Indians believe that repose and non-existence are the
foundation of all things, and the end in which they terminate. Hence they consider entire inaction as the most perfect
of all states, and the object of their desires. To the Supreme
Being they give the title of immovable.[8] The inhabitants of
Siam believe that their utmost happiness[9] consists in not
being obliged to animate a machine or to give motion to a
body.

In those countries where the excess of heat enervates and
exhausts the body, rest is so delicious, and motion so painful,
that this system of metaphysics seems natural; and Foe,[10]
the legislator of the Indies, was directed by his own sensations when he placed mankind in a state extremely passive;
but his doctrine arising from the laziness of the climate
favored it also in its turn; which has been the source of an
infinite deal of mischief.

The legislators of China were more rational when, considering men not in the peaceful state which they are to
enjoy hereafter, but in the situation proper for discharging
the several duties of life, they made their religion, philosophy, and laws all practical. The more the physical causes
incline mankind to inaction, the more the moral causes
should estrange them from it.

OF AGRICULTURE IN WARM CLIMATES

Agriculture is the principal labor of man. The more the
climate inclines him to shun this labor, the more the religion
and laws of the country ought to incite him to it. Thus the
Indian laws, which give the lands to the prince, and destroy
the spirit of property among the subjects, increase the bad
effects of the climate, that is, their natural indolence.

OF MONKERY

The very same mischiefs result from monkery: it had its rise in the warm countries of the East, where they are less inclined to action than to speculation.

In Asia the number of dervishes or monks seems to increase together with the warmth of the climate. The Indies, where the heat is excessive, are full of them; and the same difference is found in Europe.

In order to surmount the laziness of the climate, the laws ought to endeavor to remove all means of subsisting without labor: but in the southern parts of Europe they act quite the reverse. To those who want to live in a state of indolence, they afford retreats the most proper for a speculative life, and endow them with immense revenues. These men who live in the midst of plenty which they know not how to enjoy, are in the right to give their superfluities away to the common people. The poor are bereft of property; and these men indemnify them by supporting them in idleness, so as to make them even grow fond of their misery.

AN EXCELLENT CUSTOM OF CHINA

The historical relations[11] of China mention a ceremony[12] of opening the ground which the emperor performs every year. The design of this public and solemn act is to excite the people to tillage.[13]

Further, the emperor is every year informed of the husbandman who has distinguished himself most in his profession; and he makes him a mandarin of the eighth order.

Among the ancient Persians[14] the kings quitted their grandeur and pomp on the eighth day of the month, called Charrem-ruz, to eat with the husbandmen. These institutions were admirably calculated for the encouragement of agriculture.

MEANS OF ENCOURAGING INDUSTRY

We shall show, in the nineteenth book, that lazy nations are generally proud. Now the effect might well be turned against the cause, and laziness be destroyed by pride. In the south of Europe, where people have such a high notion of the point of honor, it would be right to give prizes to husbandmen who had excelled in agriculture; or to artists who had made the greatest improvements in their several professions. This practice has succeeded in our days in Ireland, where it has established one of the most considerable linen manufactures in Europe.

OF THE LAWS IN RELATION TO THE SOBRIETY OF THE PEOPLE

In warm countries the aqueous part of the blood loses itself greatly by perspiration[15] it must, therefore, be supplied by a like liquid. Water is there of admirable use; strong liquors would congeal the globules[16] of blood that remain after the transuding of the aqueous humor.

In cold countries the aqueous part of the blood is very little evacuated by perspiration. They may, therefore, make use of spirituous liquors, without which the blood would congeal. They are full of humors; consequently strong liquors, which give a motion to the blood, are proper for those countries.

The law of Mahomet, which prohibits the drinking of wine, is, therefore, fitted to the climate of Arabia; and, indeed, before Mahomet's time, water was the common drink of the Arabs. The law[1] which forbade the Carthaginians to drink wine was a law of the climate; and, indeed, the climate of those two countries is pretty nearly the same.

Such a law would be improper for cold countries, where the climate seems to force them to a kind of national intemperance, very different from personal ebriety. Drunkennes‹

predominates throughout the world, in proportion to the coldness and humidity of the climate. Go from the equator to the North Pole, and you will find this vice increasing together with the degree of latitude. Go from the equator again to the South Pole, and you will find the same vice travelling south[2] exactly in the same proportion.

It is very natural that where wine is contrary to the climate, and consequently to health, the excess of it should be more severely punished than in countries where intoxication produces very bad effects to the person, fewer to the society, and where it does not make people frantic and wild, but one stupid and heavy. Hence those laws[3] which inflicted a double punishment for crimes committed in drunkenness were applicable only to a personal, and not to a national, ebriety. A German drinks through custom, and a Spaniard by choice.

In warm countries the relaxing of the fibres produces a great evacuation of the liquids, but the solid parts are less transpired. The fibres, which act but faintly, and have very little elasticity, are not much impaired; and a small quantity of nutritious juice is sufficient to repair them; for which reason they eat very little.

It is the variety of wants in different climates that first occasioned a difference in the manner of living, and this gave rise to a variety of laws. Where people are very communicative there must be particular laws, and others where there is but little communication.

OF THE LAWS IN RELATION TO THE DISTEMPERS OF THE CLIMATE

Herodotus[4] informs us that the Jewish laws concerning the Leprosy were borrowed from the practice of the Egyptians. And, indeed, the same distemper required the same remedies. The Greeks and the primitive Romans were strangers to these laws, as well as to the disease. The climate of Egypt and Palestine rendered them necessary; and the facility with which this disease is spread is sufficient to make us sensible of the wisdom and sagacity of those laws.

Even we ourselves have felt the effects of them. The Crusades brought the leprosy amongst us; but the wise regulations made at that time hindered it from infecting the mass of the people.

We find by the law of the Lombards[5] that this disease was spread in Italy before the Crusades, and merited the attention of the legislature. Rotharis ordained that a leper should be exepelled from his house, banished to a particular place, and rendered incapable of disposing of his property; because from the very moment he had been turned out of his house he was reckoned dead in the eye of the law. In order to prevent all communication with lepers, they were rendered incapable of civil acts.

I am apt to think that this disease was brought into Italy by the conquests of the Greek emperors, in whose armies there might be some soldiers from Palestine or Egypt. Be that as it may, the progress of it was stopped till the time of the Crusades.

It is related that Pompey's soldiers returning from Syria brought a distemper home with them not unlike the leprosy. We have no account of any regulation made at that time; but it is highly probable that some such step was taken, since the distemper was checked till the time of the Lombards.

It is now two centuries since a disease unknown to our ancestors was first transplanted from the new world to ours, and came to attack human nature even in the very source of life and pleasure. Most of the principal families in the south of Europe were seen to perish by a distemper that had grown too common to be ignominious, and was considered in no other light than in that of its being fatal. It was the thirst of gold that propagated this disease; the Europeans went continually to America, and always brought back a new leaven of it.[6]

Reasons drawn from religion seemed to require that this punishment of guilt should be permitted to continue; but the infection had reached the bosom of matrimony, and given the vicious taint even to guiltless infants.

As it is the business of legislators to watch over the health of the citizens, it would have been a wise part in them to have stopped this communication by laws made on the plan of those of Moses.

The plague is a disease whose infectious progress is much more rapid. Egypt is its principal seat, whence it spreads over the whole globe. Most countries in Europe have made exceedingly good regulations to prevent this infection, and in our times an admirable method has been contrived to stop it; this is by forming a line of troops round the infected country, which cuts off all manner of communication.

The Turks[7] who have no such regulations, see the Christians escape this infection in the same town, and none but themselves perish; they buy the clothes of the infected, wear them, and proceed in their old way, as if nothing had happened. The doctrine of a rigid fate, which directs their whole conduct, renders the magistrate a quiet spectator; he thinks that everything comes from the hand of God, and that man has nothing more to do than to submit.

OF THE LAWS AGAINST SUICIDES

We do not find in history that the Romans ever killed themselves without a cause; but the English are apt to commit suicide most unaccountably; they destroy themselves even in the bosom of happiness. This action among the Romans was the effect of education, being connected with their principles and customs; among the English it is the consequence of a distemper[8] being connected with the physical state of the machine, and independent of every other cause.

In all probability it is a defect of the filtration of the nervous juice: the machine, whose motive faculties are often unexerted, is weary of itself; the soul feels no pain, but a certain uneasiness in existing. Pain is a local sensation, which leads us to the desire of seeing an end of it; the burden of life, which prompts us to the desire of ceasing to exist, is an evil confined to no particular part.

It is evident that the civil laws of some countries may have reasons for branding suicide with infamy: but in England it cannot be punished without punishing the effects of madness.

EFFECTS ARISING FROM THE CLIMATE OF ENGLAND

In a nation so distempered by the climate as to have a disrelish of everything, nay, even of life, it is plain that the government most suitable to the inhabitants is that in which they cannot lay their uneasiness to any single person's charge, and in which, being under the direction rather of the laws than of the prince, it is impossible for them to change the government without subverting the laws themselves.

And if this nation has likewise derived from the climate a certain impatience of temper, which renders them incapable of bearing the same train of things for any long continuance, it is obvious that the government above mentioned is the fittest for them.

This impatience of temper is not very considerable of itself; but it may become so when joined with courage.

It is quite a different thing from levity, which makes people undertake or drop a project without cause; it borders more upon obstinacy, because it proceeds from so lively a sense of misery that it is not weakened even by the habit of suffering.

This temper in a free nation is extremely proper for disconcerting the projects of tyranny[9] which is always slow and feeble in its commencement, as in the end it is active and lively; which at first only stretches out a hand to assist, and exerts afterwards a multitude of arms to oppress.

Slavery is ever preceded by sleep. But a people who find no rest in any situation, who continually explore every part, and feel nothing but pain, can hardly be lulled to sleep.

Politics are a smooth file, which cuts gradually, and attains its end by a slow progression. Now the people of whom we have been speaking are incapable of hearing the delays, the details, and the coolness of negotiations: in these they are more unlikely to succeed than any other nation; hence they are apt to lose by treaties what they obtain by their arms.

OTHER EFFECTS OF THE CLIMATE

Our ancestors, the ancient Germans, lived in a climate where the passions were extremely calm. Their laws decided only in such cases where the injury was visible to the eye, and went no farther. And as they judged of the outrages done to men from the greatness of the wound, they acted with no other delicacy in respect to the injuries done to women. The law of the Alemans[10] on this subject is very extraordinary. If a person uncovers a woman's head, he pays a fine of fifty sous; if he uncovers her leg up to the knee, he pays the same; and double from the knee upwards. One would think that the law measured the insults offered to women as we measure a figure in geometry; it did not punish the crime of the imagination, but that of the eye. But upon the migration of a German nation into Spain, the climate soon found a necessity for different laws. The law of the Visigoths inhibited the surgeons to bleed a free woman, except either her father, mother, brother, son, or uncle was present. As the imagination of the people grew warm, so did that of the legislators; the law suspected everything when the people had become suspicious.

These laws had, therefore, a particular regard for the two sexes. But in their punishments they seem rather to humor the revengeful temper of private persons than to administer public justice. Thus, in most cases, they reduced both the criminals to be slaves to the offended relatives or to the injured husband; a free-born woman[11] who had yielded to the embraces of a married man was delivered up to his wife to dispose of her as she pleased. They obliged the slaves[12] if they found their master's wife in adultery, to bind her and carry her to her husband; they even permitted her children[13] to be her accusers, and her slaves to be tortured in order to convict her. Thus their laws were far better adapted to refine, even to excess, a certain point of honor than to form a good civil administration. We must not, therefore, be surprised if Count Julian was of opinion that an affront of that kind ought to be expiated by the ruin of his king and country: we must not be surprised if the Moors, with such a conformity of manners, found it so easy to settle and to maintain themselves in Spain, and to retard the fall of their empire.

OF THE DIFFERENT CONFIDENCE WHICH THE LAWS HAVE IN THE PEOPLE, ACCORDING TO THE DIFFERENCE OF CLIMATES

The people of Japan are of so stubborn and perverse a temper that neither their legislators nor magistrates can put any confidence in them; they set nothing before their eyes but judgments, menaces, and chastisements; every step they take is subject to the inquisition of the civil magistrate. Those laws which out of five heads of families establish one as a magistrate over the other four; those laws which punish a family or a whole ward for a single crime; those laws, in fine, which find nobody innocent where one may happen to be guilty, are made with a design to implant in the people a mutual distrust, and to make every man the inspector, witness, and judge of his neighbor's conduct.

On the contrary, the people of India are mild,[14] tender, and compassionate. Hence their legislators repose great confidence in them. They have established[15] very few punishments; these are not severe, nor are they rigorously executed. They have subjected nephews to their uncles, and orphans to their guardians, as in other countries they are subjected to their fathers; they have regulated the succession by the acknowledged merit of the successor. They seem to think that every individual ought to place entire confidence in the good nature of his fellow-subjects.[16]

They enfranchise their slaves without difficulty, they marry them, they treat them as their children.[17] Happy climate which gives birth to innocence, and produces a lenity in the laws!

NOTES

[1] This appears even in the countenance: in cold weather people look thinner.

[2] We know that it shortens iron.

[3] Those for the succession to the Spanish monarchy.

[4] For instance, in Spain.

[5] "One hundred European soldiers," says Tavernier, "would without any great difficulty beat a thousand Indian soldiers."

[6] Even the Persians who settle in the Indies contract in the third generation the indolence and cowardice of the Indians. See Bernier on the "mogal," tom. i. p. 182.

[7] We find by a fragment of Nicolaus Damascenue, collected by Constantine Porphyrogenitus, that it was an ancient custom in the East to send to strangle a Governor who had given any displeasure; it was in the time of the Medes. Vol. 1.-15.

[8] Panamanack: See Kircher.

[9] La Loubiere, "Relation of Siam," p. 446.

[10] Foe endeavored to reduce the heart to a mere vacuum: "We have eyes and ears, but perfection consists in neither seeing nor hearing; a mouth, hands, etc., but perfection requires that these members should be inactive." This is taken from the dialogue of a Chinese philosopher, quoted by Father Du Halde, tom. iii.

[11] Father Du Halde, "History of China," tom. i., p. 72.

[12] Several of the kings of India do the same. "Relation of the Kingdom of Siam," by La Loubiere, p. 69.

[13] Venty, the third Emperor of the third dynasty, tilled the lands himself, and made the Empress and his wives employ their time in the silkworks in his palace. "History of China."

[14] Hyde, "Religion of the Persians."

[15] Monsieur Bernier, travelling from Lahore to Cashmere, wrote thus: "My body is a sieve; scarcely have I swallowed a pint of water, but I see it transude like dew out of all my limbs, even to my fingers' ends. I drink ten pints a day, and it does me no manner of harm."—Bernier's "Travels," tom. ii. p. 261.

[16] In the blood there are red globules, fibrous parts, white globules, and water, in which the whole swims.

NOTES

[1] Plato, book II. of "Laws"; Aristotle, of the care of domestic affairs; Eusebius's "Evangelical Preparation," book XII. chap. xvii.

[2] This is seen in the Hottentots, and the inhabitants of the most southern part of Chili.

[3] As Pittacus did, according to Aristotle, "Polit." lib. I. cap. iii. He lived in a climate where drunkenness is not a national vice.

[4] Book II.

[5] Book II. tit. 1, sec. 3, and tit. 18, sec. 1.

[6] It has been thought that this malady has a still more ancient origin, and that it is probable the Spaniards carried it to America at the start.—Ed.

[7] Ricaut on the "Ottoman Empire," p. 284.

[8] It may be complicated with the scurvy, which, in some countries especially, renders a man whimsical and unsupportable to himself. See Pirad's "Voyages," part II. chap. xxi.

[9] Here I take this word for the design of subverting the established power, and especially that of democracy; this is the signification in which it was understood by the Greeks and Romans.

[10] Chap. lviii. secs. 1 and 2.

[11] "Law of the Visigoths," book III. tit. 4, sec. 9.

[12] Ibid. book III. tit. 4, sec. 6.

[13] Ibid. book III. tit. 4, sec. 13.

[14] See Bernier, tom. ii. p. 140.

[15] "Edifying Letters," p. 403, the principal laws or customs of the inhabitants of the peninsula on this side the Ganges.

[16] See "Edifying Letters," LX. 378. Great exception has been taken to Montesquieu's abuse upon the effects of climate physically; it is Servan who avers that the weakness attributed to organisms under the equator is erroneous.—Ed.

[17] I had once thought that the lenity of slavery in India had made Diodorus say that there was neither master nor slave in that country; but Diodorus has attributed to the whole continent of India what, according to Strabo, lib. XV., belonged only to a particular nation.

DIVISION OF LABOR *

By ADAM SMITH

OF THE DIVISION OF LABOUR

THE greatest improvement in the productive powers of labour, and the greater part of the skill, dexterity, and judgment with which it is anywhere directed, or applied, seem to have been the effects of the division of labour.

The effects of the division of labour, in the general business of society, will be more easily understood by considering in what manner it operates in some particular manufactures. It is commonly supposed to be carried furthest in some very trifling ones; not perhaps that it really is carried further in them than in others of more importance: but in those trifling manufactures which are destined to supply the small wants of but a small number of people, the whole number of workmen must necessarily be small; and those employed in every different branch of the work can often be collected into the same workhouse, and placed at once under the view of the spectator. In those great manufactures, on the contrary, which are destined to supply the great wants of the great body of the people, every different branch of the work employs so great a number of workmen that it is impossible to collect them all into the same workhouse. We can seldom see more, at one time, than those employed in one single branch. Though in such manufactures, therefore, the work may really be divided into a much greater number of parts than in those of a more trifling nature, the division is not near so obvious, and has accordingly been much less observed.

* From *The Wealth of Nations*

To take an example, therefore, from a very trifling manufacture; but one in which the division of labour has been
very often taken notice of, the trade of the pin-maker; a
workman not educated to this business (which the division
of labour has rendered a distinct trade), nor acquainted with
the use of the machinery employed in it (to the invention
of which the same division of labour has probably given
occasion), could scarce, perhaps, with his utmost industry,
make one pin in a day, and certainly could not make twenty.
But in the way in which this business is now carried on, not
only the whole work is a peculiar trade, but it is divided
into a number of branches, of which the greater part are
likewise peculiar trades. One man draws out the wire, another straights it, a third cuts it, a fourth points it, a fifth
grinds it at the top for receiving the head; to make the head
requires two or three distinct operations; to put it on is a
peculiar business, to whiten the pins is another; it is even
a trade by itself to put them into the paper; and the important business of making a pin is, in this manner, divided
into about eighteen distinct operations, which, in some
manufactories, are all performed by distinct hands, though
in others the same man will sometimes perform two or three
of them. I have seen a small manufactory of this kind where
ten men only were employed, and where some of them consequently performed two or three distinct operations. But
though they were very poor, and therefore but indifferently
accommodated with the necessary machinery, they could,
when they exerted themselves, make among them about
twelve pounds of pins in a day. There are in a pound upwards of four thousand pins of a middling size. Those ten
persons, therefore, could make among them upwards of
forty-eight thousand pins in a day. Each person, therefore,
making a tenth part of forty-eight thousand pins, might be
considered as making four thousand eight hundred pins in
a day. But if they had all wrought separately and independently, and without any of them having been educated to
this peculiar business, they certainly could not each of them

have made twenty, perhaps not one pin in a day; that is, certainly, not the two hundred and fortieth, perhaps not the four thousand eight hundredth part of what they are at present capable of performing, in consequence of a proper division and combination of their different operations.

In every other art and manufacture, the effects of the division of labour are similar to what they are in this very trifling one; though, in many of them, the labour can neither be so much subdivided, nor reduced to so great a simplicity of operation. The division of labour, however, so far as it can be introduced, occasions, in every art, a proportionable increase of the productive powers of labour. The separation of different trades and employments from one another seems to have taken place in consequence of this advantage. This separation, too, is generally carried furthest in those countries which enjoy the highest degree of industry and improvement; what is the work of one man in a rude state of society being generally that of several in an improved one. In every improved society, the farmer is generally nothing but a farmer; the manufacturer, nothing but a manufacturer. The labour, too, which is necessary to produce any one complete manufacture is almost always divided among a great number of hands. How many different trades are employed in each branch of the linen and woollen manufactures from the growers of the flax and the wool, to the bleachers and smoothers of the linen, or to the dyers and dressers of the cloth! The nature of agriculture, indeed, does not admit of so many subdivisions of labour, nor of so complete a separation of one business from another, as manufactures. It is impossible to separate so entirely the business of the grazier from that of the corn-farmer as the trade of the carpenter is commonly separated from that of the smith. The spinner is almost always a distinct person from the weaver; but the ploughman, the harrower, the sower of the seed, and the reaper of the corn, are often the same. The occasions for those different sorts of labour returning with the different seasons of the year, it is impossible that one man should be constantly employed in any one of them. This impossibility of making so complete and entire a separation of all the different branches of labour employed in agriculture is perhaps the reason why the improvement of the productive powers of labour in this art does not always keep pace with their improvement in manufactures. The most opulent nations, indeed, generally excel all their neighbours in agriculture as well as in manufactures; but they are commonly more distinguished by their superiority in the latter than in the former. Their lands are in general better cultivated, and having more labour and expense bestowed upon them, produce more in proportion to the extent and natural fertility of the ground. But this superiority of produce is seldom much more than in proportion to the superiority of labour and expense. In agriculture, the labour of the rich country is not always much more productive than that of the poor; or, at least, it is never so much more productive as it commonly is in manufactures. The corn of the rich country, therefore, will not always, in the same degree of goodness, come cheaper to market than that of the poor. The corn of Poland, in the same degree of goodness, is as cheap as that of France, notwithstanding the superior opulence and improvement of the latter country. The corn of France is, in the corn provinces, fully as good, and in most years nearly about the same price with the corn of England, though, in opulence and improvement, France is perhaps inferior to England. The corn-lands of England, however, are better cultivated than those of France, and the corn-lands of France are said to be much better cultivated than those of Poland. But though the poor country, notwithstanding the inferiority of its cultivation, can, in some measure, rival the rich in the cheapness and goodness of its corn, it can pretend to no such competition in its manufactures; at least if those manufactures suit the soil, climate, and situation of the rich country. The silks of France are better and cheaper than those of England, be cause the silk manufacture, at least under the present high duties upon the importation of raw silk, does not so well suit the climate of England as that of France. But the hardware and the coarse woollens of England are beyond all comparison superior to those of France, and much cheaper too in the same degree of goodness. In Poland there are said to be scarce any manufactures of any kind, a few of those coarser household manufactures excepted, without which no country can well subsist.

This great increase of the quantity of work which, in consequence of the division of labour, the same number of people are capable of performing, is owing to three different circumstances; first, to the increase of dexterity in every particular workman; secondly, to the saving of the time which is commonly lost in passing from one species of work to another; and lastly, to the invention of a great number of machines which facilitate and abridge labour, and enable one man to do the work of many.

First, the improvement of the dexterity of the workman necessarily increases the quantity of the work he can perform; and the division of labour, by reducing every man's business to some one simple operation, and by making this operation the sole employment of his life, necessarily increases very much the dexterity of the workman. A common smith, who, though accustomed to handle the hammer, has never been used to make nails, if upon some particular occasion he is obliged to attempt it, will scarce, I am assured, be able to make above two or three hundred nails in a day, and those too very bad ones. A smith who has been accustomed to make nails, but whose sole or principal business has not been that of a nailer, can seldom with his utmost diligence make more than eight hundred or a thousand nails in a day. I have seen several boys under twenty years of age who had never exercised any other trade but that of making nails, and who, when they exerted themselves, could make, each of them, upwards of two thousand three hundred nails in a day. The making of a nail, however, is by no means one of the simplest operations. The same person blows the bellows, stirs or mends the fire as there is occasion, heats the iron, and forges every part of the nail: in forging the head too he is obliged to change his tools. The different operations into which the making of a pin, or of a metal button, is subdivided, are all of them much more simple, and the dexterity of the person, of whose life it has been the sole business to perform them, is usually much greater. The rapidity with which some of the operations of those manufactures are performed, exceeds what the human hand could, by those who had never seen them, be supposed capable of acquiring.

Secondly, the advantage which is gained by saving the time commonly lost in passing from one sort of work to another is much greater than we should at first view be apt to imagine it. It is impossible to pass very quickly from one kind of work to another that is carried on in a different place and with quite different tools. A country weaver, who cultivates a small farm, must lose a good deal of time in passing from his loom to the field, and from the field to his loom. When the two trades can be carried on in the same workhouse, the loss of time is no doubt much less. It is even in this case, however, very considerable. A man commonly saunters a little in turning his hand from one sort of employment to another. When he first begins the new work he is seldom very keen and hearty; his mind, as they say, does not go to it, and for some time he rather trifles than applies to good purpose. The habit of sauntering and of indolent careless application, which is naturally, or rather necessarily acquired by every country workman who is obliged to change his work and his tools every half hour, and to apply his hand in twenty different ways almost every day of his life, renders him almost always slothful and lazy, and incapable of any vigorous application even on the most pressing occasions. Independent, therefore, of his deficiency in point of dexterity, this cause alone must always reduce considerably the quantity of work which he is capable of performing.

Thirdly, and lastly, everybody must be sensible how much labour is facilitated and abridged by the application of proper machinery. It is unnecessary to give any example. I shall only observe, therefore, that the invention of all those machines by which labour is so much facilitated and abridged seems to have been originally owing to the division of labour. Men are much more likely to discover easier and readier methods of attaining any object when the whole attention of their minds is directed towards that single object than when it is dissipated among a great variety of things. But in consequence of the division of labour, the whole of every man's attention comes naturally to be directed towards some one very simple object. It is naturally to be expected, therefore, that some one or other of those who are employed in each particular branch of labour should soon find out easier and readier methods of performing their own particular work, wherever the nature of it admits of such improvement. A great part of the machines made use of in those manufactures in which labour is most subdivided, were originally the inventions of common workmen, who, being each of them employed in some very simple operation, naturally turned their thoughts towards finding out easier and readier methods of performing it. Whoever has been much accustomed to visit such manufactures must frequently have been shown very pretty machines, which were the inventions of such workmen in order to facilitate and quicken their own particular part of the work. In the first fire-engines, a boy was constantly employed to open and shut alternately the communication between the boiler and the cylinder, according as the piston either ascended or descended. One of those boys, who loved to play with his companions, observed that, by tying a string from the handle of the valve which opened this communication to another part of the machine, the valve would open and shut without his assistance, and leave him at liberty to divert himself with his play-fellows. One of the greatest improvements that has been made upon this machine, since it was first invented, was in this manner the discovery of a boy who wanted to save his own labour.

All the improvements in machinery, however, have by no means been the inventions of those who had occasion to use the machines. Many improvements have been made by the ingenuity of the makers of the machines, when to make them became the business of a peculiar trade; and some by that of those who are called philosophers or men of speculation, whose trade it is not to do anything, but to observe everything; and who, upon that account, are often capable of combining together the powers of the most distant and dissimilar objects. In the progress of society, philosophy or speculation becomes, like every other employment, the principal or sole trade and occupation of a particular class of citizens. Like every other employment too, it is subdivided into a great number of different branches, each of which affords occupation to a peculiar tribe or class of philosophers; and this subdivision of employment in philosophy, as well as in every other business, improves dexterity, and saves time. Each individual becomes more expert in his own peculiar branch, more work is done upon the whole, and the quantity of science is considerably increased by it.

It is the great multiplication of the productions of all the different arts, in consequence of the division of labour, which occasions, in a well-governed society, that universal opulence which extends itself to the lowest ranks of the people. Every workman has a great quantity of his own work to dispose of beyond what he himself has occasion for; and every other workman being exactly in the same situation, he is enabled to exchange a great quantity of his own goods for a great quantity, or, what comes to the same thing, for the price of a great quantity of theirs. He supplies them abundantly with what they have occasion for, and they accommodate him as amply with what he has occasion for, and a general plenty diffuses itself through all the different ranks of the society.

Observe the accommodation of the most common artificer or day-labourer in a civilised and thriving country, and you will perceive that the number of people of whose industry a part, though but a small part, has been employed in procuring him this accommodation, exceeds all computation. The woollen coat, for example, which covers the day-labourer, as coarse and rough as it may appear, is the produce of the joint labour of a great multitude of workmen. The shepherd, the sorter of the wool, the wool-comber or carder, the dyer, the scribbler, the spinner, the weaver, the fuller, the dresser, with many others, must all join their different arts in order to complete even this homely production. How many merchants and carriers, besides, must have been employed in transporting the materials from some of those workmen to others who often live in a very distant part of the country! how much commerce and navigation in particular, how many ship-builders, sailors, sail-makers, rope-makers, must have been employed in order to bring together the different drugs made use of by the dyer, which often come from the remotest corners of the world! What a variety of labour, too, is necessary in order to produce the tools of the meanest of those workmen! To say nothing of such complicated machines as the ship of the sailor, the mill of the fuller, or even the loom of the weaver, let us consider only what a variety of labour is requisite in order to form that very simple machine, the shears with which the shepherd clips the wool. The miner, the builder of the furnace for smelting the ore, the seller of the timber, the burner of the charcoal to be made use of in the smelting-house, the brick-maker, the brick-layer, the workmen who attend the furnace, the mill-wright, the forger, the smith, must all of them join their different arts in order to produce them. Were we to examine, in the same manner, all the different parts of his dress and household furniture, the coarse linen shirt which he wears next his skin, the shoes which cover his feet, the bed which he lies on, and all the different parts which compose it, the kitchen-grate at which he prepares his victuals, the coals which he makes use of for that purpose, dug from the bowels of the earth, and brought to him perhaps by a long sea and a long land carriage, all the other utensils of his kitchen, all the furniture of his table, the knives and forks, the earthen or pewter plates upon which he serves up and divides his victuals, the different hands employed in preparing his bread and his beer, the glass window which lets in the heat and the light, and keeps out the wind and the rain, with all the knowledge and art requisite for preparing that beautiful and happy invention, without which these northern parts of the world could scarce have afforded a very comfortable habitation, together with the tools of all the different workmen employed in producing those different conveniences; if we examine, I say, all these things, and consider what a variety of labour is employed about each of them, we shall be sensible that, without the assistance and co-operation of many thousands, the very meanest person in a civilised country could not be provided, even according to what we very falsely imagine the easy and simple manner in which he is commonly accommodated. Compared, indeed, with the more extravagant luxury of the great, his accommodation must no doubt appear extremely simple and easy; and yet it may be true, perhaps, that the accommodation of a European prince does not always so much exceed that of an industrious and frugal peasant as the accommodation of the latter exceeds that of many an African king, the absolute master of the lives and liberties of ten thousand naked savages.

OF THE PRINCIPLE WHICH GIVES OCCASION TO THE DIVISION OF LABOUR

This division of labour, from which so many advantages are derived, is not originally the effect of any human wisdom, which foresees and intends that general opulence to which it gives occasion. It is the necessary, though very slow and gradual consequence of a certain propensity in human nature which has in view no such extensive utility; the propensity to truck, barter, and exchange one thing for another.

Whether this propensity be one of those original principles in human nature of which no further account can be given; or whether, as seems more probable, it be the necessary consequence of the faculties of reason and speech, it belongs not to our present subject to inquire. It is common to all men, and to be found in no other race of animals, which seem to know neither this nor any other species of contracts. Two greyhounds, in running down the same hare, have sometimes the appearance of acting in some sort of concert. Each turns her towards his companion, or endeavours to intercept her when his companion turns her towards himself. This, however, is not the effect of any contract, but of the accidental concurrence of their passions in the same object at that particular time. Nobody ever saw a dog make a fair and deliberate exchange of one bone for another with another dog. Nobody ever saw one animal by its gestures and natural cries signify to another, this is mine, that yours; I am willing to give this for that. When an animal wants to obtain something either of a man or of another animal, it has no other means of persuasion but to gain the favour of those whose service it requires. A puppy fawns upon its dam, and a spaniel endeavours by a thousand attractions to engage the attention of its master who is at dinner, when it wants to be fed by him. Man sometimes uses the same arts with his brethren, and when he has no other means of engaging them to act according to his inclinations, endeavours by every servile and fawning attention to obtain their good will. He has not time, however, to do this upon every occasion. In civilised society he stands at all times in need of the co-operation and assistance of great multitudes, while his whole life is scarce sufficient to gain the friendship of a few persons. In almost every other race of animals each individual, when it is grown up to maturity, is entirely independent, and in its natural state has occasion for the assistance of no other living creature. But man has almost constant occasion for the help of his brethren, and it is in vain for him to expect it from their benevolence only. He will be more likely to prevail if he can interest their self-love in his favour, and show them that it is for their own advantage to do for him what he requires of them. Whoever offers to another a bargain of any kind, proposes to do this. Give me that which I want, and you shall have this which you want, is the meaning of every such offer; and it is in this manner that we obtain from one another the far greater part of those good offices which we stand in need of. It is not from the benevolence of the butcher, the brewer, or the baker that we expect our dinner, but from their regard to their own interest. We address ourselves, not to their humanity but to their self-love, and never talk to them of our own necessities but of their advantages. Nobody but a beggar chooses to depend chiefly upon the benevolence of his fellow-citizens. Even a beggar does not depend upon it entirely. The charity of well-disposed people, indeed, supplies him with the whole fund of his subsistence. But though this principle ultimately provides him with all the necessaries of life which he has occasion for, it neither does nor can provide him with them as he has occasion for them. The greater part of his occasional wants are supplied in the same manner as those of other people, by treaty, by barter, and by purchase. With the money which one man gives him he purchases food. The old clothes which another bestows upon him he exchanges for other old clothes which suit him better, or for lodging, or for food, or for money, with which he can buy either food, clothes, or lodging, as he has occasion.

As it is by treaty, by barter, and by purchase that we obtain from one another the greater part of those mutual good offices which we stand in need of, so it is this same trucking disposition which originally gives occasion to the division of labour. In a tribe of hunters or shepherds a particular person makes bows and arrows, for example, with more readiness and dexterity than any other. He frequently exchanges them for cattle or for venison with his companions; and he finds at last that he can in this manner get more cattle and venison than if he himself went to the field to catch them. From a regard to his own interest, therefore, the making of bows and arrows grows to be his chief business, and he becomes a sort of armourer. Another excels in making the frames and covers of their little huts or movable houses. He is accustomed to be of use in this way to his neighbours, who reward him in the same manner with cattle and with venison, till at last he finds it his interest to dedicate himself entirely to this employment, and to become a sort of house-carpenter. In the same manner a third becomes a smith or a brazier, a fourth a tanner or dresser of hides or skins, the principal part of the clothing of savages. And thus the certainty of being able to exchange all that surplus part of the produce of his own labour, which is over and above his own consumption, for such parts of the produce of other men's labour as he may have occasion for, encourages every man to apply himself to a particular occupation, and to cultivate and bring to perfection whatever talent or genius he may possess for that particular species of business.

The difference of natural talents in different men is, in reality, much less than we are aware of; and the very different genius which appears to distinguish men of different professions, when grown up to maturity, is not upon many occasions so much the cause as the effect of the division of labour. The difference between the most dissimilar characters, between a philosopher and a common street porter, for example, seems to arise not so much from nature as from habit, custom, and education. When they came into the world, and for the first six or eight years of their existence, they were perhaps very much alike, and neither their parents nor play-fellows could perceive any remarkable difference. About that age, or soon after, they come to be employed in very different occupations. The difference of talents comes then to be taken notice of, and widens by degrees, till at last the vanity of the philosopher is willing to acknowledge scarce any resemblance. But without the disposition to truck, barter, and exchange, every man must have procured to himself every necessary and conveniency of life which he wanted. All must have had the same duties to perform, and the same work to do, and there could have been no such difference of employment as could alone give occasion to any great difference of talents.

As it is this disposition which forms that difference of talents, so remarkable among men of different professions, so it is this same disposition which renders that difference useful. Many tribes of animals acknowledged to be all of the same species derive from nature a much more remarkable distinction of genius, than what, antecedent to custom and education, appears to take place among men. By nature a philosopher is not in genius and disposition half so different from a street porter, as a mastiff is from a greyhound, or a greyhound from a spaniel, or this last from a shepherd's dog. Those different tribes of animals, however, though all of the same species, are of scarce any use to one another. The strength of the mastiff is not, in the least, supported either by the swiftness of the greyhound, or by the sagacity of the spaniel, or by the docility of the shepherd's dog. The effects of those different geniuses and talents, for want of the power or disposition to barter and exchange, cannot be brought into a common stock, and do not in the least contribute to the better accommodation and conveniency of the species. Each animal is still obliged to support and defend itself, separately and independently, and derives no sort of advantage from that variety of talents with which nature has distinguished its fellows. Among men, on the contrary, the most dissimilar geniuses are of use to one another; the different produces of their respective talents, by the general disposition to truck, barter, and exchange, being brought, as

it were, into a common stock, where every man may purchase whatever part of the produce of other men's talents he
has occasion for.

THAT THE DIVISION OF LABOUR IS LIMITED BY THE
EXTENT OF THE MARKET

As it is the power of exchanging that gives occasion to the
division of labour, so the extent of this division must always
be limited by the extent of that power, or, in other word, by
the extent of the market. When the market is very small, no
person can have any encouragement to dedicate himself
entirely to one employment, for want of the power to exchange all that surplus part of the produce of his own labour,
which is over and above his own consumption, for such
parts of the produce of other men's labour as he has occasion for.

There are some sorts of industry, even of the lowest kind,
which can be carried on nowhere but in a great town. A
porter, for example, can find employment and subsistence in
no other place. A village is by much too narrow a sphere
for him; even an ordinary market town is scarce large
enough to afford him constant occupation. In the lone
houses and very small villages which are scattered about in
so desert a country as the Highlands of Scotland, every
farmer must be butcher, baker and brewer for his own
family. In such situations we can scarce expect to find even a
smith, a carpenter, or a mason, within less than twenty
miles of another of the same trade. The scattered families
that live at eight or ten miles distance from the nearest of
them must learn to perform themselves a great number of
little pieces of work, for which, in more populous countries,
they would call in the assistance of those workmen. Country
workmen are almost everywhere obliged to apply themselves to all the different branches of industry that have so
much affinity to one another as to be employed about the
same sort of materials. A country carpenter deals in every

sort of work that is made of wood: a country smith in every
sort of work that is made of iron. The former is not only
a carpenter, but a joiner, a cabinet-maker, and even a
carver in wood, as well as a wheel-wright, a plough-wright,
a cart and waggon maker. The employments of the latter
are still more various. It is impossible there should be such
a trade as even that of a nailer in the remote and inland
parts of the Highlands of Scotland. Such a workman at the
rate of a thousand nails a day, and three hundred working
days in the year, will make three hundred thousand nails
in the year. But in such a situation it would be impossible
to dispose of one thousand, that is, of one day's work in the
year.

As by means of water-carriage a more extensive market
is opened to every sort of industry than what land-carriage
alone can afford it, so it is upon the sea-coast, and along
the banks of navigable rivers, that industry of every kind
naturally begins to subdivide and improve itself, and it is
frequently not till a long time after that those improvements
extend themselves to the inland parts of the country. A
broad-wheeled waggon, attended by two men, and drawn
by eight horses, in about six weeks' time carries and brings
back between London and Edinburgh near four ton weight
of goods. In about the same time a ship navigated by six or
eight men, and sailing between the ports of London and
Leith, frequently carries and brings back two hundred ton
weight of goods. Six or eight men, therefore, by the help of
water-carriage, can carry and bring back in the same time
the same quantity of goods between London and Edinburgh, as fifty broad-wheeled waggons, attended by a hundred men, and drawn by four hundred horses. Upon two
hundred tons of goods, therefore, carried by the cheapest
land-carriage from London to Edinburgh, there must be
charged the maintenance of a hundred men for three weeks,
and both the maintenance, and, what is nearly equal to the
maintenance, the wear and tear of four hundred horses as
well as of fifty great waggons. Whereas, upon the same

quantity of goods carried by water, there is to be charged only the maintenance of six or eight men, and the wear and tear of a ship of two hundred tons burden, together with the value of the superior risk, or the difference of the insurance between land and water-carriage. Were there no other communication between those two places, therefore, but by land-carriage, as no goods could be transported from the one to the other, except such whose price was very considerable in proportion to their weight, they could carry on but a small part of that commerce which at present subsists between them, and consequently could give but a small part of that encouragement which they at present mutually afford to each other's industry. There could be little or no commerce of any kind between the distant parts of the world. What goods could bear the expense of land-carriage between London and Calcutta? Or if there were any so precious as to be able to support this expense, with what safety could they be transported through the territories of so many barbarous nations? Those two cities, however, at present carry on a very considerable commerce with each other, and by mutually affording a market, give a good deal of encouragement to each other's industry.

Since such, therefore, are the advantages of water-carriage, it is natural that the first improvements of art and industry should be made where this conveniency opens the whole world for a market to the produce of every sort of labour, and that they should always be much later in extending themselves into the inland parts of the country. The inland parts of the country can for a long time have no other market for the greater part of their goods, but the country which lies round about them, and separates them from the sea-coast, and the great navigable rivers. The extent of their market, therefore, must for a long time be in proportion to the riches and populousness of that country, and consequently their improvement must always be posterior to the improvement of that country. In our North American colonies the plantations have constantly followed either the sea-coast or the banks of the navigable rivers, and have scarce anywhere extended themselves to any considerable distance from both.

The nations that, according to the best authenticated history, appear to have been first civilised, were those that dwelt round the coast of the Mediterranean Sea. That sea, by far the greatest inlet that is known in the world, having no tides, nor consequently any waves except such as are caused by the wind only, was, by the smoothness of its surface, as well as by the multitude of its islands, and the proximity of its neighbouring shores, extremely favourable to the infant navigation of the world; when, from their ignorance of the compass, men were afraid to quit the view of the coast, and from the imperfection of the art of ship-building, to abandon themselves to the boisterous waves of the ocean. To pass beyond the pillars of Hercules, that is, to sail out of the Straits of Gibraltar, was, in the ancient world, long considered as a most wonderful and dangerous exploit of navigation. It was late before even the Phœnicians and Carthaginians, the most skilful navigators and ship-builders of those old times, attempted it, and they were for a long time the only nations that did attempt it.

Of all the countries on the coast of the Mediterranean Sea, Egypt seems to have been the first in which either agriculture or manufactures were cultivated and improved to any considerable degree. Upper Egypt extends itself nowhere above a few miles from the Nile, and in Lower Egypt that great river breaks itself into many different canals, which, with the assistance of a little art, seem to have afforded a communication by water-carriage, not only between all the great towns, but between all the considerable villages, and even to many farm-houses in the country; nearly in the same manner as the Rhine and the Maese do in Holland at present. The extent and easiness of this inland navigation was probably one of the principal causes of the early improvement of Egypt.

The improvements in agriculture and manufactures seem

likewise to have been of very great antiquity in the provinces of Bengal, in the East Indies, and in some of the eastern provinces of China; though the great extent of this antiquity is not authenticated by any histories of whose authority we, in this part of the world, are well assured. In Bengal the Ganges and several other great rivers form a great number of navigable canals in the same manner as the Nile does in Egypt. In the Eastern provinces of China too, several great rivers form, by their different branches, a multitude of canals, and by communicating with one another afford an inland navigation much more extensive than that either of the Nile or the Ganges, or perhaps than both of them put together. It is remarkable that neither the ancient Egyptians, nor the Indians, nor the Chinese, encouraged foreign commerce, but seem all to have derived their great opulence from this inland navigation.

All the inland parts of Africa, and all that part of Asia which lies any considerable way north of the Euxine and Caspian seas, the ancient Scythia, the modern Tartary and Siberia, seem in all ages of the world to have been in the same barbarous and uncivilised state in which we find them at present. The Sea of Tartary is the frozen ocean which admits of no navigation, and though some of the greatest rivers in the world run through that country, they are at too great a distance from one another to carry commerce and communication through the greater part of it. There are in Africa none of those great inlets, such as the Baltic and Adriatic seas in Europe, the Mediterranean and Euxine seas in both Europe and Asia, and the gulfs of Arabia, Persia, India, Bengal, and Siam, in Asia, to carry maritime commerce into the interior parts of that great continent: and the great rivers of Africa are at too great a distance from one another to give occasion to any considerable inland navigation. The commerce besides which any nation can carry on by means of a river which does not break itself into any great number of branches or canals, and which runs into another territory before it reaches the sea, can never be very considerable; because it is always in the power of the nations who possess that other territory to obstruct the communication between the upper country and the sea. The navigation of the Danube is of very little use to the different states of Bavaria, Austria and Hungary, in comparison of what it would be if any of them possessed the whole of its course till it falls into the Black Sea.

very considerable; because it is always in the power of the nations who possess that other territory to obstruct the communication between the upper country and the sea. The navigation of the Danube is of very little use to the different states of Bavaria, Austria and Hungary, in comparison of what it would be if any of them possessed the whole of its course till it falls into the Black Sea.

V

SOCIOLOGY COMES OF AGE

V

SOCIOLOGY COMES OF AGE

COMMENTARY

Malthus and John Stuart Mill carry on, in a different way, the work of Adam Smith. Smith's advocacy of laissez-faire as an economic principle becomes the economic dogma of the century. About it cluster a multiplying variety of theories which soon become the ideology of the new epoch.

Malthus' theory that population growth always exceeds food supply, springing out of the same ideological strata as Smith's doctrine, soon becomes the accepted theory of the day. The populational factor becomes a bugaboo. There is not enough to go around for all, and never can be, which soon provides the background for the "survival of the species" theory of Darwin, which overtakes the century not many decades afterward.

John Stuart Mill, with his Utilitarian doctrine, derived from the lucubrations of Jeremy Bentham, is one of the first to challenge the old dogmas. In his essay on Liberty as well as in his defense of the women and his advocacy of economic justice, he paves the way for many of the progressive doctrines of his generation. Without becoming a communist, in the sense that Karl Marx does, he, nevertheless, does not hesitate to declare that "between communism with all its chances, and the present state of society with all its sufferings and injustices, all the difficulties great and small of communism would be but as dust in the balance."

August Comte, familiarly known as the father of sociology, aims to study society in the same scientific manner that physicists and chemists do inorganic materials. He is eager to disencumber the study of society from the theological and metaphysical conceptions which have marred the vision of social thinkers in the past, and raise such study to a scientific level where subjective prejudice is supplanted by objective reason. His hope, which is soon to become the hope of all nineteenth century sociologists, is to discover social laws which operate with the same inevitability and finality as physical and chemical laws. Like most of his contemporaries, he adds a moral element to his science, to give it human justification, and urges that revealed religion be replaced by a religion of humanity, with the concept of God superseded by that of Humanity.

Following Comte is a long line of thinkers, many of whom scarcely can be classified as sociologists in the precise sense of the term but whose ideas have had such a profound influence upon social thought that no volume dealing with the history of social thought could possibly be worthwhile without them. Most notable among these are Marx, Buckle, Darwin, Proudhon, Bakunin, John Stuart Mill, and Henry George.

Marx adds to Comte's desire for scientific objectivity an even greater moral element. Whereas Comte is content with substituting Humanity for God and science for metaphysics, Marx gives to science an ethical drive which becomes the source of his great influence over so large a section of society. Rousseau has a revolution (French Revolution) waged in his name, but Marx not only has a revolution undertaken in his name, (Bolshevik Revolution) but his name becomes the watchword of a new state, the Soviet State (USSR), which occupies one-sixth of the entire globe. Employing a different approach, and envisioning society through different philosophic lenses, Marx, nevertheless, conceives of society in the same "stage-sense" as Comte. Comte sees man evolving from the theological stage to the metaphysical and then to the scientific; Marx sees him evolving from the feudal stage to the capitalistic and then to the communistic. Marx's classic analysis of capitalism, in Das Kapital, purports to show that capitalism can no more endure than feudalism did years ago, and that it will be superseded by a communist regime, such as, in embryonic form, is to be seen in Soviet Russia today. In The Communist Manifesto, Marx lays down his general principles of sociological anal-

ysis, and it is that Manifesto, more than anything else Marx
ever wrote, which outlines the historical position of Marxism
as sociological doctrine and dogma.

In the case of Buckle, we are face to face with a different
type of mind. Buckle believed in the society in which he
lived, and was not concerned with changing it in any fundamental, revolutionary way. He was concerned exclusively
with discovering the nature and behavior of social phenomena, and intruded very little moralistic judgment into
his analysis. Whereas Marx stressed the economic factor, or
rather the mode of production, as the most important determinant in society, Buckle saw the climatic factor as the
key to civilization. Later, to be sure, in his analysis of advanced civilizations, Buckle shifted his emphasis from climate to ideas as the preponderant factor in conditioning
social change. At all times, however, Buckle was predominantly concerned with causes rather than ends, which was
true, in a somewhat different sense, of Darwin, whose investigations into biologic phenomena effected such a revolution in western thought.

Darwin, by virtue of his theory of evolution, succeeded
better than anyone else in shifting man's concern from whys
and wherefores to nows, from concern with origins to concern with relations, from concern with purpose to concern
with behavior. Many people before Darwin had been concerned with the same thing, but Darwin's work, appearing
when it did, impacted with the mind of the time in such a
way that it helped shift the entire intellectual interest of the
century.

Proudhon and Bakunin are more interested in changing
society than in analyzing it, although both are concerned
with analyses of the social process. In his work on Property
he attempts to show how the property fact is bound up with
the nature of our society, and that only when man learns to
eliminate property from society will he be able to live in
peace and harmony with himself. He is the first to proclaim the anarchist ideal, and to use the word anarchy as

symbolic of progress. "The highest perfection of society is found in the union of order and anarchy" he declares, and like Bakunin who subscribes to the same ideal, dedicates his life to struggling for that perfection. Bakunin is more of a leader than a thinker, and his writings consequently are scattered, disjointed, and fragmentary, although always shot through with brilliant insights and intuitions. The work of Proudhon and Bakunin take on more significance today than ever, because it is in the Anarchist and Anarcho-Syndicalist movements in Spain, where they have proved so powerful in the Spanish Civil War, that their ideas are bearing social fruit.

AN ESSAY ON THE PRINCIPLE OF POPULATION

By T. R. MALTHUS

In an inquiry concerning the improvement of society, the mode of conducting the subject which naturally presents itself, is,

1. To investigate the causes that have hitherto impeded the progress of mankind towards happiness; and,

2. To examine the probability of the total or partial removal of these causes in future.

To enter fully into this question, and to enumerate all the causes that have hitherto influenced human improvement, would be much beyond the power of an individual. The principal object of the present essay is to examine the effects of one great cause intimately united with the very nature of man; which, though it has been constantly and powerfully operating since the commencement of society, has been little noticed by the writers who have treated this subject. The facts which establish the existence of this cause have, indeed, been repeatedly stated and acknowledged; but its natural and necessary effects have been almost totally overlooked; though probably among these effects may be reckoned a very considerable portion of that vice and misery, and of that unequal distribution of the bounties of nature, which it has been the unceasing object of the enlightened philanthropist in all ages to correct.

The cause to which I allude is the constant tendency in all animated life to increase beyond the nourishment prepared for it.

It is observed by Dr. Franklin that there is no bound to the prolific nature of plants or animals but what is made by their crowding and interfering with each other's means of subsistence. Were the face of the earth, he says, vacant of other plants, it might be gradually sowed and overspread with one kind only, as for instance with fennel: and were it empty of other inhabitants, it might in a few ages be replenished from one nation only, as for instance with Englishmen.[1]

This is incontrovertibly true. Through the animal and vegetable kingdoms Nature has scattered the seeds of life abroad with the most profuse and liberal hand; but has been comparatively sparing in the room and the nourishment necessary to rear them. The germs of existence contained in this earth, if they could freely develop themselves, would fill millions of worlds in the course of a few thousand years. Necessity, that imperious, all pervading law of nature, restrains them within the prescribed bounds. The race of plants and the race of animals shrink under this great restrictive law; and man cannot by any efforts of reason escape from it.

In plants and irrational animals, the view of the subject is simple. They are all impelled by a powerful instinct to the increase of their species; and this instinct is interrupted by no doubts about providing for their offspring. Wherever therefore there is liberty, the power of increase is exerted; and the superabundant effects are repressed afterwards by want of room and nourishment.

The effects of this check on man are more complicated. Impelled to the increase of his species by an equally powerful instinct, reason interrupts his career, and asks him whether he may not bring beings into the world for whom he cannot provide the means of support. If he attend to this natural suggestion, the restriction too frequently produces vice. If he hear it not, the human race will be constantly endeavouring to increase beyond the means of subsistence. But as, by that law of our nature which makes food necessary to the life of man, population can never actually increase beyond the lowest nourishment capable of supporting it, a strong check on population, from the difficulty of ac-

[1] Franklin's Miscell. p. 9.

quiring food, must be constantly in operation. This difficulty must fall somewhere, and must necessarily be severely felt in some or other of the various forms of misery, or the fear of misery, by a large portion of mankind.

That population has this constant tendency to increase beyond the means of subsistence, and that it is kept to its necessary level by these causes, will sufficiently appear from a review of the different states of society in which man has existed. But, before we proceed to this review, the subject will, perhaps, be seen in a clearer light if we endeavour to ascertain what would be the natural increase of population if left to exert itself with perfect freedom; and what might be expected to be the rate of increase in the productions of the earth under the most favourable circumstances of human industry.

It will be allowed that no country has hitherto been known where the manners were so pure and simple, and the means of subsistence so abundant, that no check whatever has existed to early marriages from the difficulty of providing for a family, and that no waste of the human species has been occasioned by vicious customs, by towns, by unhealthy occupations, or too severe labour. Consequently in no state that we have yet known has the power of population been left to exert itself with perfect freedom.

Whether the law of marriage be instituted, or not, the dictate of nature and virtue seems to be an early attachment to one woman; and where there were no impediments of any kind in the way of an union to which such an attachment would lead, and no causes of depopulation afterwards, the increase of the human species would be evidently much greater than any increase which has been hitherto known.

In the northern states of America, where the means of subsistence have been more ample, the manners of the people more pure, and the checks to early marriages fewer than in any of the modern states of Europe, the population has been found to double itself, for above a century and a half successively, in less than twenty-five years.[1] Yet, even

during these periods, in some of the towns, the deaths exceeded the births,[2] a circumstance which cleary proves that,
in those parts of the country which supplied this deficiency,
the increase must have been much more rapid than the
general average.

In the back settlements, where the sole employment is
agriculture, and vicious customs and unwholesome occupations are little known, the population has been found to
double itself in fifteen years. Even this extraordinary rate
of increase is probably short of the utmost power of population. Very severe labour is requisite to clear a fresh country; such situations are not in general considered as particularly healthy; and the inhabitants, probably, are occasionally subject to the incursions of the Indians, which may
destroy some lives, or at any rate diminish the fruits of
industry.

According to a table of Euler, calculated on a mortality of
1 in 36, if the births be to the deaths in the proportion of
3 to 1, the period of doubling will be only 12 years and 4-5ths.
And this proportion is not only a possible supposition, but
has actually occurred for short periods in more countries
than one.

Sir William Petty supposes a doubling possible in so
short a time as ten years.

But, to be perfectly sure that we are far within the truth,
we will take the slowest of these rates of increase, a rate in
which all concurring testimonies agree, and which has
been repeatedly ascertained to be from procreation only.

It may safely be pronounced, therefore, that population,
when unchecked, goes on doubling itself every twenty-five
years, or increases in a geometrical ratio.

The rate according to which the productions of the earth
may be supposed to increase, it will not be so easy to determine. Of this, however, we may be perfectly certain, that the
ratio of their increase in a limited territory must be of a
totally different nature from the ratio of the increase of
population. A thousand millions are just as easily doubled

every twenty-five years by the power of population as a thousand. But the food to support the increase from the greater number will by no means be obtained with the same facility. Man is necessarily confined in room. When acre has been added to acre till all the fertile land is occupied, the yearly increase of food must depend upon the melioration of the land already in possession. This is a fund, which, from the nature of all soils, instead of increasing, must be gradually diminishing. But population, could it be supplied with food, would go on with unexhausted vigour; and the increase of one period would furnish the power of a greater increase the next, and this without any limit.

From the accounts we have of China and Japan, it may be fairly doubted whether the best-directed efforts of human industry could double the produce of these countries even once in any number of years. There are many parts of the globe indeed, hitherto uncultivated, and almost unoccupied; but the right of exterminating, or driving into a corner where they must starve, even the inhabitants of these thinly-peopled regions, will be questioned in a moral view. The process of improving their minds and directing their industry would necessarily be slow; and during this time, as population would regularly keep pace with the increasing produce, it would rarely happen that a great degree of knowledge and industry would have to operate at once upon rich unappropriated soil. Even where this might take place, as it does sometimes in new colonies, a geometrical ratio increases with such extraordinary rapidity, that the advantage could not last long. If the United States of America continue increasing, which they certainly will do, though not with the same rapidity as formerly, the Indians will be driven further and further back into the country, till the whole race is ultimately exterminated, and the territory is incapable of further extension.

These observations are, in a degree, applicable to all the parts of the earth where the soil is imperfectly cultivated. To exterminate the inhabitants of the greatest part of Asia and Africa is a thought that could not be admitted for a moment. To civilise and direct the industry of the various tribes of Tartars and Negroes would certainly be a work of considerable time and of variable and uncertain success.

Europe is by no means so fully peopled as it might be. In Europe there is the fairest chance that human industry may receive its best direction. The science of agriculture has been much studied in England and Scotland; and there is still a great portion of uncultivated land in these countries. Let us consider at what rate the produce of this island might be supposed to increase under circumstances the most favourable to improvement.

If it be allowed that by the best possible policy, and great encouragements to agriculture, the average produce of the island could be doubled in the first twenty-five years, it will be allowing, probably, a greater increase than could with reason be expected.

In the next twenty-five years, it is impossible to suppose that the produce could be quadrupled. It would be contrary to all our knowledge of the properties of land. The improvement of the barren parts would be a work of time and labour; and it must be evident to those who have the slightest acquaintance with agricultural subjects that, in proportion as cultivation extended, the additions that could yearly be made to the former average produce must be gradually and regularly diminishing. That we may be the better able to compare the increase of population and food, let us make a supposition, which, without pretending to accuracy, is clearly more favourable to the power of production in the earth than any experience we have had of its qualities will warrant.

Let us suppose that the yearly additions which might be made to the former average produce, instead of decreasing, which they certainly would do, were to remain the same; and that the produce of this island might be increased every twenty-five years by a quantity equal to what it at present produces. The most enthusiastic speculator cannot suppose a greater increase than this. In a few centuries it would make every acre of land in the island like a garden.

If this supposition be applied to the whole earth, and if it be allowed that the subsistence for man which the earth affords might be increased every twenty-five years by a quantity equal to what it at present produces, this will be supposing a rate of increase much greater than we can imagine that any possible exertions of mankind could make it.

It may be fairly pronounced, therefore, that, considering the present average state of the earth, the means of subsistence, under circumstances the most favourable to human industry, could not possibly be made to increase faster than in an arithmetical ratio.

The necessary effects of these two different rates of increase, when brought together, will be very striking. Let us call the population of this island eleven millions; and suppose the present produce equal to the easy support of such a number. In the first twenty-five years the population would be twenty-two millions, and the food being also doubled, the means of subsistence would be equal to this increase. In the next twenty-five years, the population would be forty-four millions, and the means of subsistence only equal to the support of thirty-three millions. In the next period the population would be eighty-eight millions, and the means of subsistence just equal to the support of half that number. And, at the conclusion of the first century, the population would be a hundred and seventy-six millions, and the means of subsistence only equal to the support of fifty-five millions, leaving a population of a hundred and twenty-one millions totally unprovided for.

Taking the whole earth, instead of this island, emigration would of course be excluded; and, supposing the present population equal to a thousand millions, the human species would increase as the numbers, 1, 2, 4, 8, 16, 32, 64, 128, 256, and subsistence as 1, 2, 3, 4, 5, 6, 7, 8, 9. In two centuries the population would be to the means of subsistence as 256 to 9;

in three centuries as 4096 to 13, and in two thousand years the difference would be almost incalculable.

In this supposition no limits whatever are placed to the produce of the earth. It may increase for ever and be greater than any assignable quantity; yet still the power of population being in every period so much superior, the increase of the human species can only be kept down to the level of the means of subsistence by the constant operation of the strong law of necessity, acting as a check upon the greater power.

II

OF THE GENERAL CHECKS TO POPULATION, AND THE MODE OF THEIR OPERATION

The ultimate check to population appears then to be a want of food, arising necessarily from the different ratios according to which population and food increase. But this ultimate check is never the immediate check, except in cases of actual famine.

The immediate check may be stated to consist in all those customs, and all those diseases, which seem to be generated by a scarcity of the means of subsistence; and all those causes, independent of this scarcity, whether of a moral or physical nature, which tend prematurely to weaken and destroy the human frame.

These checks to population, which are constantly operating with more or less force in every society, and keep down the number to the level of the means of subsistence, may be classed under two general heads—the preventive and the positive checks.

The preventive check, as far as it is voluntary, is peculiar to man, and arises from that distinctive superiority in his reasoning faculties which enables him to calculate distant consequences. The checks to the indefinite increase of plants and irrational animals are all either positive, or, if preventive, involuntary. But man cannot look around him and see the distress which frequently presses upon those who have large families; he cannot contemplate his present possessions or earnings, which he now nearly consumes himself, and calculate the amount of each share, when with very little addition they must be divided, perhaps, among seven or eight, without feeling a doubt whether, if he follow the bent of his inclinations, he may be able to support the offspring which he will probably bring into the world. In a state of equality, if such can exist, this would be the simple question. In the present state of society other considerations occur. Will he not lower his rank in life, and be obliged to give up in great measure his former habits? Does any mode of employment present itself by which he may reasonably hope to maintain family? Will he not at any rate subject himself to greater difficulties, and more severe labour, than in his single state? Will he not be unable to transmit to his children the same advantages of education and improvement that he had himself possessed? Does he even feel secure that, should he have a large family, his utmost exertions can save them from rags and squalid poverty, and their consequent degradation in the community? And may he not be reduced to the grating necessity of forfeiting his independence, and of being obliged to the sparing hand of Charity for support?

These considerations are calculated to prevent, and certainly do prevent, a great number of persons in all civilised nations from pursuing the dictate of nature in an early attachment to one woman.

If this restraint do not produce vice, it is undoubtedly the least evil that can arise from the principle of population. Considered as a restraint on a strong natural inclination, it must be allowed to produce a certain degree of temporary unhappiness; but evidently slight, compared with the evils which result from any of the other checks to population; and merely of the same nature as many other sacrifices of temporary to permanent gratification, which it is the business of a moral agent continually to make.

When this restraint produces vice, the evils which follow are but too conspicuous. A promiscuous intercourse to such a degree as to prevent the birth of children seems to lower, in the most marked manner, the dignity of human nature. It cannot be without its effect on men, and nothing can be more obvious than its tendency to degrade the female character, and to destroy all its most amiable and distinguishing characteristics. Add to which, that among those unfortunate females, with which all great towns abound, more real distress and aggravated misery are, perhaps, to be found than in any other department of human life.

When a general corruption of morals, with regard to the sex, pervades all the classes of society, its effects must necessarily be to poison the springs of domestic happiness, to weaken conjugal and parental affection, and to lessen the united exertions and ardour of parents in the care and education of their children—effects which cannot take place without a decided diminution of the general happiness and virtue of the society; particularly as the necessity of art in the accomplishment and conduct of intrigues, and in the concealment of their consequences, necessarily leads to many other vices.

The positive checks to population are extremely various, and include every cause, whether arising from vice or misery, which in any degree contributes to shorten the natural duration of human life. Under this head, therefore, may be enumerated all unwholesome occupations, severe labour and exposure to the seasons, extreme poverty, bad nursing of children, great towns, excesses of all kinds, the whole train of common diseases and epidemics, wars, plague, and famine.

On examining these obstacles to the increase of population which I have classed under the heads of preventive and positive checks, it will appear that they are all resolvable into moral restraint, vice, and misery.

Of the preventive checks, the restraint from marriage which is not followed by irregular gratifications may properly be termed moral restraint.[1]

Promiscuous intercourse, unnatural passions, violations of the marriage bed, and improper arts to conceal the consequences of irregular connections, are preventive checks that clearly come under the head of vice.

Of the positive checks, those which appear to arise unavoidably from the laws of nature, may be called exclusively misery; and those which we obviously bring upon ourselves, such as wars, excesses, and many others which it would be in our power to avoid, are of a mixed nature. They are brought upon us by vice, and their consequences are misery.

The sum of all these preventive and positive checks, taken together, forms the immediate check to population; and it is evident that, in every country where the whole of the procreative power cannot be called into action, the preventive and the positive checks must vary inversely as each other; that is, in countries either naturally unhealthy, or subject to a great mortality, from whatever cause it may arise, the preventive check will prevail very little. In those countries, on the contrary, which are naturally healthy, and where the preventive check is found to prevail with considerable force, the positive check will prevail very little, or the mortality be very small.

In every country some of these checks are, with more or less force, in constant operation; yet, notwithstanding their general prevalence, there are few states in which there is not a constant effort in the population to increase beyond the means of subsistence. This constant effort as constantly tends to subject the lower classes of society to distress, and to prevent any great permanent melioration of their condition.

These effects, in the present state of society, seem to be produced in the following manner. We will suppose the means of subsistence in any country just equal to the easy support of its inhabitants. The constant effort towards population, which is found to act even in the most vicious societies, increases the number of people before the means of subsistence are increased. The food, therefore, which before supported eleven millions, must now be divided among eleven millions and a half. The poor consequently must live much worse, and many of them be reduced to severe distress. The number of labourers also being above the proportion of work in the market, the price of labour must tend to fall, while the price of provisions would at the same time tend to rise. The labourer therefore must do more work to earn the same as he did before. During this season of distress, the discouragements to marriage and the difficulty of rearing a family are so great that the progress of population is retarded. In the meantime, the cheapness of labour, the plenty of labourers, and the necessity of an increased industry among them, encourage cultivators to employ more labour upon their land, to turn up fresh soil, and to manure and improve more completely what is already in tillage, till ultimately the means of subsistence may become in the same proportion to the population as at the period from which we set out. The situation of the labourer being then again tolerably comfortable, the restraints to population are in some degree loosened; and, after a short period, the same retrograde and progressive movements, with respect to happiness, are repeated.

This sort of oscillation will not probably be obvious to common view; and it may be difficult even for the most attentive observer to calculate its periods. Yet that, in the generality of old states, some alternation of this kind does exist though in a much less marked, and in a much more irregular manner, than I have described it, no reflecting man, who considers the subject deeply, can well doubt.

One principal reason why this oscillation has been less remarked, and less decidedly confirmed by experience than might naturally be expected, is, that the histories of mankind which we possess are, in general, histories only of the higher classes. We have not many accounts that can be depended upon of the manners and customs of that part of mankind where these retrograde and progressive movements chiefly take place. A satisfactory history of this kind, of one people and of one period, would require the constant and minute attention of many observing minds in local and general remarks on the state of the lower classes of society, and the causes that influenced it; and to draw accurate inferences upon this subject, a succession of such historians for some centuries would be necessary. This branch of statistical knowledge has, of late years, been attended to in some countries, and we may promise ourselves a clearer insight into the internal structure of human society from the progress of these inquiries. But the science may be said yet to be in its infancy, and many of the objects, on which it would be desirable to have information, have been either omitted or not stated with sufficient accuracy. Among these, perhaps, may be reckoned the proportion of the number of adults to the number of marriages; the extent to which vicious customs have prevailed in consequence of the restraints upon matrimony; the comparative mortality among the children of the most distressed part of the community and of those who live rather more at their ease; the variations in the real price of labour; the observable differences in the state of the lower classes of society, with respect to ease and happiness, at different times during a certain period; and very accurate registers of births, deaths, and marriages, which are of the utmost importance in this subject.

A faithful history, including such particulars, would tend greatly to elucidate the manner in which the constant check upon population acts; and would probably prove the existence of the retrograde and progressive movements that have been mentioned; though the times of their vibration must necessarily be rendered irregular from the operation of many interrupting causes; such as, the introduction or failure of certain manufactures; a greater or less prevalent spirit of agricultural enterprise; years of plenty or years of scarcity; wars, sickly seasons, poor laws, emigrations, and other causes of a similar nature.

A circumstance which has, perhaps, more than any other, contributed to conceal this oscillation from common view is the difference between the nominal and real price of labour. It very rarely happens that the nominal price of labour universally falls; but we well know that it frequently remains the same while the nominal price of provisions has been gradually rising. This, indeed, will generally be the case if the increase of manufactures and commerce be sufficient to employ the new labourers that are thrown into the market, and to prevent the increased supply from lowering the money-price. But an increased number of labourers receiving the same money-wages will necessarily, by their competition, increase the money-price of corn. This is, in fact, a real fall in the price of labour; and, during this period, the condition of the lower classes of the community must be gradually growing worse. But the farmers and capitalists are growing rich from the real cheapness of labour. Their increasing capitals enable them to employ a greater number of men; and, as the population had probably suffered some check from the greater difficulty of supporting a family, the demand for labour, after a certain period, would be great in proportion to the supply, and its price would of course rise, if left to find its natural level; and thus the wages of labour, and consequently the condition of the lower classes of society, might have progressive and retrograde movements, though the price of labour might never nominally fall.

In savage life, where there is no regular price of labour, it is little to be doubted that similar oscillations took place. When population has increased nearly to the utmost limits of the food, all the preventive and the positive checks will naturally operate with increased force. Vicious habits with respect to the sex will be more general, the exposing of children more frequent, and both the probability and fatality of wars and epidemics will be considerably greater; and these causes will probably continue their operation till the population is sunk below the level of the food; and then the return to comparative plenty will again produce an increase, and, after a certain period, its further progress will again be checked by the same causes.

But without attempting to establish these progressive and retrograde movements in different countries, which would evidently require more minute histories than we possess, and which the progress of civilisation naturally tends to counteract, the following propositions are intended to be proved:—

1. Population is necessarily limited by the means of subsistence.

2. Population invariably increases where the means of subsistence increase, unless prevented by some very powerful and obvious checks.

3. These checks, and the checks which repress the superior power of population, and keep its effects on a level with the means of subsistence, are all resolvable into moral restraint, vice, and misery.

III

OF THE CHECKS TO POPULATION IN THE LOWEST STAGE OF HUMAN SOCIETY

THE wretched inhabitants of Tierra del Fuego have been placed, by the general consent of voyagers, at the bottom of the scale of human beings.[1] Of their domestic habits and manners, however, we have few accounts. Their barren country, and the miserable state in which they live, have prevented any intercourse with them that might give such information; but we cannot be at a loss to conceive the checks to population among a race of savages, whose very appearance indicates them to be half starved, and who, shivering with cold and covered with filth and vermin, live in one of the most inhospitable climates in the world, without having sagacity enough to provide themselves with such conveniences as might mitigate its severities, and render life in some measure more comfortable.[2]

Next to these, and almost as low in genius and resources,

[1] Cook's First Voy. vol. ii. p. 59.
[2] Cook's Second Voy. vol. ii. p. 187.

have been placed the natives of Van Diemen's land;[3] but some late accounts have represented the islands of Andaman in the East as inhabited by a race of savages still lower in wretchedness even than these. Everything that voyagers have related of savage life is said to fall short of the barbarism of this people. Their whole time is spent in search of food: and as their woods yield them few or no supplies of animals, and but little vegetable diet, their principal occupation is that of climbing the rocks, or roving along the margin of the sea, in search of a precarious meal of fish, which, during the tempestuous season, they often seek for in vain. Their stature seldom exceeds five feet; their bellies are protuberant, with high shoulders, large heads, and limbs disproportionably slender. Their countenances exhibit the extreme of wretchedness, a horrid mixture of famine and ferocity; and their extenuated and diseased figures plainly indicate the want of wholesome nourishment. Some of these unhappy beings have been found on the shores in the last stage of famine.[4]

[3] Vancouver's Voy. vol. ii. b. iii. c. i. p. 13.
[4] Symes's Embassy to Ava, ch. i. p. 129, and Asiatic Researches, vol. iv. p. 401.

THE AUTHORITY OF SOCIETY OVER
THE INDIVIDUAL*

By JOHN STUART MILL

WHAT, then, is the rightful limit to the sovereignty of the individual over himself? Where does the authority of society begin? How much of human life should be assigned to individuality, and how much to society?

Each will receive its proper share, if each has that which more particularly concerns it. To individuality should belong the part of life in which it is chiefly the individual that is interested; to society, the part which chiefly interests society.

Though society is not founded on a contract, and though no good purpose is answered by inventing a contract in order to deduce social obligations from it, every one who receives the protection of society owes a return for the benefit, and the fact of living in society renders it indispensable that each should be bound to observe a certain line of conduct towards the rest. This conduct consists, first, in not injuring the interests of one another; or rather certain interests, which, either by express legal provision or by tacit understanding, ought to be considered as rights; and secondly, in each person's bearing his share (to be fixed on some equitable principle) of the labours and sacrifices incurred for defending the society or its members from injury and molestation. These conditions society is justified in enforcing at all costs to those who endeavour to withhold fulfilment. Nor is this all that society may do. The acts of an individual may be hurtful to others, or wanting in due consideration for their welfare, without going the length of violating any of their constituted rights. The offender may then be justly

* From *On Liberty*

punished by opinion, though not by law. As soon as any part of a person's conduct affects prejudically the interests of others, society has jurisdiction over it, and the question whether the general welfare will or will not be promoted by interfering with it, becomes open to discussion. But there is no room for entertaining any such question when a person's conduct affects the interests of no persons besides himself, or needs not affect them unless they like (all the persons concerned being of full age, and the ordinary amount of understanding). In all such cases there should be perfect freedom, legal and social, to do the action and stand the consequences.

It would be a great misunderstanding of this doctrine to suppose that it is one of selfish indifference, which pretends that human beings have no business with each other's conduct in life, and that they should not concern themselves about the well-doing or well-being of one another, unless their own interest is involved. Instead of any diminution, there is need of a great increase of disinterested exertion to promote the good of others. But disinterested benevolence can find other instruments to persuade people to their good, than whips and scourges, either of the literal or the metaphorical sort. I am the last person to under-value the self-regarding virtues; they are only second in importance, if even second, to the social. It is equally the business of education to cultivate both. But even education works by conviction and persuasion as well as by compulsion, and it is by the former only that, when the period of education is past, the self-regarding virtues should be inculcated. Human beings owe to each other help to distinguish the better from the worse, and encouragement to choose the former and avoid the latter. They should be for ever stimulating each other to increased exercise of their higher faculties, and increased direction of their feelings and aims towards wise instead of foolish, elevating instead of degrading, objects and contemplations. But neither one person, nor any number of persons, is warranted in saying to another human creature of ripe years, that he shall not do with his life for his own benefit what he chooses to do with it. He is the person most interested in his own well-being: the interest which any other person, except in cases of strong personal attachment, can have in it, is trifling, compared with that which he himself has; the interest which society has in him individually (except as to his conduct to others) is fractional, and altogether indirect: while, with respect to his own feelings and circumstances, the most ordinary man or woman has means of knowledge immeasurably surpassing those that can be possessed by any one else. The interference of society to overrule his judgement and purposes in what only regards himself, must be grounded on general presumptions; which may be altogether wrong, and even if right, are as likely as not to be misapplied to individual cases, by persons no better acquainted with the circumstances of such cases than those are who look at them merely from without. In this department, therefore, of human affairs, Individuality has its proper field of action. In the conduct of human beings towards one another, it is necessary that general rules should for the most part be observed, in order that people may know what they have to expect; but in each person's own concerns, his individual spontaneity is entitled to free exercise. Considerations to aid his judgment, exhortations to strengthen his will, may be offered to him, even obtruded on him, by others; but he himself is the final judge. All errors which he is likely to commit against advice and warning, are far outweighed by the evil of allowing others to constrain him to what they deem his good.

I do not mean that the feelings with which a person is regarded by others, ought not to be in any way affected by his self-regarding qualities or deficiencies. This is neither possible nor desirable. If he is eminent in any of the qualities which conduce to his own good, he is, so far, a proper object of admiration. He is so much the nearer to the ideal perfection of human nature. If he is grossly deficient in those qualities, a sentiment the opposite of admiration will follow. There is a degree of folly, and a degree of what may be called (though the phrase is not unobjectionable) lowness or depravation of taste, which, though it cannot justify doing harm to the person who manifests it, renders him necessarily and properly a subject of distaste, or, in extreme cases, even of contempt: a person could not have the opposite qualities in due strength without entertaining these feelings. Though doing no wrong to any one, a person may so act as to compel us to judge him, and feel to him, as a fool, or as a being of an inferior order: and since this judgement and feeling are a fact which he would prefer to avoid, it is doing him a service to warn him of it beforehand, as of any other disagreeable consequence to which he exposes himself. It would be well, indeed, if this good office were much more freely rendered than the common notions of politeness at present permit, and if one person could honestly point out to another that he thinks him in fault, without being considered unmannerly or presuming. We have a right, also, in various ways, to act upon our unfavourable opinion of any one, not to the oppression of his individuality, but in the exercise of ours. We are not bound, for example, to seek his society; we have a right to avoid it (though not to parade the avoidance), for we have a right to choose the society most acceptable to us. We have a right, and it may be our duty, to caution others against him, if we think his example or conversation likely to have a pernicious effect on those with whom he associates. We may give others a preference over him in optional good offices, except those which tend to his improvement. In these various modes a person may suffer very severe penalties at the hands of others, for faults which directly concern only himself; but he suffers these penalties only in so far as they are the natural, and, as it were, the spontaneous consequences of the faults themselves, not because they are purposely inflicted on him for the sake of punishment. A person who shows rashness, obstinacy, self-conceit—who cannot live within moderate means—who cannot restrain himself from hurtful indulgences—who pursues animal pleasures at the expense of those of feeling and intellect—must expect to be lowered in the opinion of others, and to have a less share of their favourable sentiments; but of this he has no right to complain, unless he has merited their favour by special excellence in his social relations, and has thus established a title to their good offices, which is not affected by his demerits towards himself.

What I contend for is, that the inconveniences which are strictly inseparable from the unfavourable judgement of others, are the only ones to which a person should ever be subjected for that portion of his conduct and character which concerns his own good, but which does not affect the interests of others in their relations with him. Acts injurious to others require a totally different treatment. Encroachment on their rights; infliction on them of any loss or damage not justified by his own rights; falsehood or duplicity in dealing with them; unfair or ungenerous use of advantages over them; even selfish abstinence from defending them against injury—these are fit objects of moral reprobation, and, in grave cases, of moral retribution and punishment. And not only these acts, but the dispositions which lead to them, are properly immoral, and fit subjects of disapprobation which may rise to abhorrence. Cruelty of disposition; malice and ill nature; that most anti-social and odious of all passions, envy; dissimulation and insincerity; irascibility on insufficient cause, and resentment disproportioned to the provocation; the love of domineering over others; the desire to engross more than one's share of advantages; the pride which derives gratification from the abasement of others; the egotism which thinks self and its concerns more important than everything else, and decides all doubtful questions in its own favour;—these are moral vices, and constitute a bad and odious moral character: unlike the self-regarding faults previously mentioned, which are not properly immoralities, and to whatever pitch they may be carried, do not constitute wickedness. They may be proofs of any amount of folly, or want of personal dignity and self-respect but they are only a subject of moral reprobation when they involve a breach of duty to others, for whose sake the individual is bound to have care for himself. What are called duties to ourselves are not socially obligatory, unless circumstances render them at the same time duties to others. The term duty to oneself, when it means anything more than prudence, means self-respect or self-development; and for none of these is any one accountable to his fellow creatures, because for none of them is it for the good of mankind that he be held accountable to them.

The distinction between the loss of consideration which a person may rightly incur by defect of prudence or of personal dignity, and the reprobation which is due to him for an offence against the rights of others, is not a merely nominal distinction. It makes a vast difference both in our feelings and in our conduct towards him, whether he displeases us in things in which we think we have a right to control him, or in things in which we know that we have not. If he displeases us, we may express our distaste, and we may stand aloof from a person as well as from a thing that displeases us; but we shall not therefore feel called on to make his life uncomfortable. We shall reflect that he already bears, or will bear, the whole penalty of his errors; if he spoils his life by mismanagement, we shall not, for that reason, desire to spoil it still further: instead of wishing to punish him, we shall rather endeavour to alleviate his punishment, by showing him how he may avoid or cure the evils his conduct tends to bring upon him. He may be to us an object of pity, perhaps of dislike, but not of anger or resentment; we shall not treat him like an enemy of society; the worst we shall think ourselves justified in doing is leaving him to himself, if we do not interfere benevolently by showing interest or concern for him. It is far otherwise if he has infringed the rules necessary for the protection of his fellow creatures, individually or collectively. The evil consequences of his acts do not then fall on himself, but on others; and society, as the protector of all its members, must retaliate on him; must inflict pain on him for the express purpose of punishment, and must take care that it be sufficiently severe. In the one case, he is an offender at our bar, and we are called on not only to sit in judgement on him, but, in one shape or another, to execute our own sentence; in the other case, it is not our part to inflict any suffering on him, except what may incidentally follow from our using the same liberty in the regulation of our own affairs, which we allow to him in his.

The distinction here pointed out between the part of a person's life which concerns only himself, and that which concerns others, many persons will refuse to admit. How (it may be asked) can any part of the conduct of a member of society be a matter of indifference to the other members? No person is an entirely isolated being; it is impossible for a person to do anything seriously or permanently hurtful to himself, without mischief reaching at least to his near connexions, and often far beyond them. If he injures his property, he does harm to those who directly or indirectly derived support from it, and usually diminishes, by a greater or less amount, the general resources of the community. If he deteriorates his bodily or mental faculties, he not only brings evil upon all who depended on him for any portion of their happiness, but disqualifies himself for rendering the services which he owes to his fellow creatures generally; perhaps becomes a burthen on their affection or benevolence; and if such conduct were very frequent, hardly any offence that is committed would detract more from the general sum of good. Finally, if by his vices or follies a person does no direct harm to others, he is nevertheless (it may be said) injurious by his example: and ought to be compelled to control himself, for the sake of those whom the sight or knowledge of his conduct might corrupt or mislead.

And even (it will be added) if the consequence of misconduct could be confined to the vicious or thoughtless individual, ought society to abandon to their own guidance those who are manifestly unfit for it? If protection against themselves is confessedly due to children and persons under age, is not society equally bound to afford it to persons of mature years who are equally incapable of self-government? If gambling, or drunkeness, or incontinence, or idleness, or uncleanliness, are as injurious to happiness, and as great a hindrance to improvement, as many or most of the acts prohibited by law, why (it may be asked) should not law, so far as is consistent with practicability and social convenience, endeavour to repress these also? And as a supplement to the unavoidable imperfections of law, ought not opinion at least to organize a powerful police against these vices, and visit rigidly with social penalties those who are known to practise them? There is no question here (it may be said) about restricting individuality, or impeding the trial of new and original experiments in living. The only things it is sought to prevent are things which have been tried and condemned from the beginning of the world until now; things which experience has shown not to be useful or suitable to any person's individuality. There must be some length of time and amount of experience, after which a moral or prudential truth may be regarded as established: and it is merely desired to prevent generation after generation from falling over the same precipice which has been fatal to their predecessors.

I fully admit that the mischief which a person does to himself may seriously affect, both through their sympathies and their interests, those nearly connected with him, and in a minor degree, society at large. When, by conduct of this sort, a person is led to violate a distinct and assignable obligation to any other person or persons, the case is taken out of the self-regarding class, and becomes amenable to moral disapprobation in the proper sense of the term. If, for example, a man, through intemperance or extravagance, becomes unable to pay his debts, or, having undertaken the moral responsibility of a family, becomes from the same cause incapable of supporting or educating them, he is deservedly reprobated, and might be justly punished; but it is for the breach of duty to his family or creditors, not for the extravagance. If the resources which ought to have been devoted to them, had been diverted from them for the most prudent investment, the moral culpability would have been the same. George Barnwell murdered his uncle to get money for his mistress, but if he had done it to set himself up in business, he would equally have been hanged. Again, in the frequent case of a man who causes grief to his family by addiction to bad habits, he deserves reproach for his unkindness or ingratitude; but so he may for cultivating habits not in themselves vicious, if they are painful to those with whom he passes his life, or who from personal ties are dependent on him for their comfort. Whoever fails in the consideration generally due to the interests and feelings of others, not being compelled by some more imperative duty, or justified by allowable self-preference, is a subject of moral disapprobation for that failure, but not for the cause of it, nor for the errors, merely personal to himself, which may have remotely led to it. In like manner, when a person disables himself, by conduct purely self-regarding, from the performance of some definite duty incumbent on him to the public, he is guilty of a social offence. No person ought to be punished simply for being drunk; but a soldier or a policeman should be punished for being drunk on duty. Whenever, in short, there is a definite damage, or a definite risk of damage, either to an individual or to the public, the case is taken out of the province of liberty, and placed in that of morality or law.

But with regard to the merely contingent, or, as it may be called, constructive injury which a person causes to society, by conduct which neither violates any specific duty to the public, nor occasions perceptible hurt to any assignable individual except himself; the inconvenience is one which society can afford to bear, for the sake of the greater good of human freedom. If grown persons are to be punished for not taking proper care of themselves, I would rather it were for their own sake, than under pretence of preventing them from impairing their capacity of rendering to society benefits which society does not pretend it has a right to exact. But I cannot consent to argue the point as if society had no means of bringing its weaker members up to its ordinary standard of rational conduct, except waiting till they do something irrational, and then punishing them, legally or morally, for it. Society has had absolute power over them during all the early portion of their existence: it has had the whole period of childhood and nonage in which to try whether it could make them capable of rational conduct in life. The existing generation is master both of the training and the entire circumstances of the generation to come; it cannot indeed make them perfectly wise and good, because it is itself so lamentably deficient in goodness and wisdom; and its best efforts are not always, in individual cases, its most successful ones; but it is perfectly well able to make the rising generation, as a whole, as good as, and a little better than, itself. If society lets any considerable number of its members grow up mere children, incapable of being acted on by rational consideration of distant motives, society has itself to blame for the consequences. Armed not only with all the powers of education, but with the ascendancy which the authority of a received opinion always exercises over the minds who are least fitted to judge for themselves; and aided by the natural penalties which cannot be prevented from falling on those who incur the distaste or the contempt of those who know them; let not society pretend that it needs, besides all this, the power to issue commands and enforce obedience in the personal concerns of individuals, in which, on all principles of justice and policy, the decision ought to rest with those who are to abide the consequences. Nor is there anything which tends more to discredit and frustrate the better means of influencing conduct, than a resort to the worse. If there be among those whom it is attempted to coerce into prudence or temperance, any of the material of which vigorous and independent characters are made, they will infallibly rebel against the yoke. No such person will ever feel that others have a right to control him in his concerns, such as they have to prevent him from injuring them in theirs; and it easily comes to be considered a mark of spirit and courage to fly in the face of such usurped authority, and do with ostentation the exact opposite of what it enjoins; as in the fashion of grossness which succeeded, in the time of Charles II, to the fanatical moral intolerance of the Puritans. With respect to what is said of the necessity of protecting society from the bad example set to others by the vicious or the self-indulgent; it is true that bad example may have a pernicious effect, especially the example of doing wrong to others with impunity to the wrong-doer. But we are now speaking of conduct which, while it does no wrong to others, is supposed to do great harm to the agent himself: and I do not see how those who believe this, can think otherwise than that the example, on the whole, must be more salutary than hurtful, since, if it displays the misconduct, it displays also the painful or degrading consequences which, if the conduct is justly censured, must be supposed to be in all or most cases attendant on it.

But the strongest of all the arguments against the interference of the public with purely personal conduct, is that when it does interfere, the odds are that it interferes wrongly, and in the wrong place. On questions of social morality, of duty to others, the opinion of the public, that is, of an overruling majority, though often wrong, is likely to be still oftener right; because on such questions they are only required to judge of their own interests; of the manner in which some mode of conduct, if allowed to be practised, would affect themselves. But the opinion of a similar majority, imposed as a law on the minority, on questions of self-regarding conduct, is quite as likely to be wrong as right; for in these cases public opinion means, at the best, some people's opinion of what is good or bad for other people; while very often it does not even mean that; the public, with the most perfect indifference, passing over the pleasure or convenience of those whose conduct they censure, and considering only their own preference. There are many who consider as an injury to themselves any conduct which they have a distaste for, and resent it as an outrage to their feelings; as a religious bigot, when charged with disregarding the religious feelings of others, has been known to retort that they disregard his feelings, by persisting in their abominable worship or creed. But there is no parity between the feeling of a person for his own opinion, and the feeling of another who is offended at his holding it; no more than between the desire of a thief to take a purse, and the desire of the right owner to keep it. And a person's taste is as much his own peculiar concern as his opinion or his purse. It is easy for any one to imagine an ideal public, which leaves the freedom and choice of individuals in all uncertain matters undisturbed, and only requires them to abstain from modes of conduct which universal experience has condemned. But where has there been seen a public which set any such limit to its censorship? or when does the public trouble itself about universal experience? In its interferences with personal conduct it is seldom thinking of anything but the enormity of acting or feeling differently from itself; and this standard of judgement, thinly disguised, is held up to mankind as the dictate of religion and philosophy, by nine-tenths of all moralists and speculative writers. These teach that things are right because they are right; because we feel them to be so. They tell us to search in our own minds and hearts for laws of conduct binding on ourselves and on all others. What can the poor public do but apply these instructions, and make their own personal feelings of good and evil, if they are tolerably unanimous in them, obligatory on all the world?

The evil here pointed out is not one which exists only in theory; and it may perhaps be expected that I should specify the instances in which the public of this age and country improperly invests its own preferences with the character of moral laws. I am not writing an essay on the aberrations of existing moral feeling. That is too weighty a subject to be discussed parenthetically, and by way of illustration. Yet examples are necessary, to show that the principle I maintain is of serious and practical moment, and that I am not endeavouring to erect a barrier against imaginary evils. And it is not difficult to show, by abundant instances, that to extend the bounds of what may be called moral police, until it encroaches on the most unquestionably legitimate liberty of the individual, is one of the most universal of all human propensities.

As a first instance, consider the antipathies which men cherish on no better grounds than that persons whose religious opinions are different from theirs, do not practise their religious observances, especially their religious abstinences. To cite a rather trivial example, nothing in the creed or practice of Christians does more to envenom the hatred of Mohammedans against them, than the fact of their eating pork. There are few acts which Christians and Europeans regard with more unaffected disgust, than Musselmans regard this particular mode of satisfying hunger. It is, in the first place, an offence against their religion; but this circumstance by no means explains either the degree or the kind of their repugnance; for wine also is forbidden by their religion, and to partake of it is by all Musselmans accounted wrong, but not disgusting. Their aversion to the flesh of the 'unclean beast' is, on the contrary, of that peculiar character, resembling an instinctive antipathy, which the idea of uncleanness, when once it thoroughly sinks into the feelings, seems always to excite even in those whose personal habits are anything but scrupulously cleanly, and of which the sentiment of religious impurity, so intense in the Hindoos, is a remarkable example. Suppose now that in a people, of whom the majority were Musselmans, that majority should insist upon not permitting pork to be eaten within the limits of the country. This would be nothing new in Mohammedan countries. Would it be a legitimate exercise of the moral authority of public opinion? and if not, why not? The practice is really revolting to such a public. They also sincerely think that it is forbidden and abhorred by the Deity. Neither could the prohibition be censured as religious persecution. It might be religious in its origin, but it would not be persecution for religion, since nobody's religion makes it a duty to eat pork. The only tenable ground of condemnation would be, that with the personal tastes and self-regarding concerns of individuals the public has no business to interfere.

To come somewhat nearer home: the majority of Spaniards consider it a gross impiety, offensive in the highest degree to the Supreme Being, to worship him in any other manner than the Roman Catholic; and no other public worship is lawful on Spanish soil. The people of all Southern Europe look upon a married clergy as not only irreligious, but unchaste, indecent, gross, disgusting. What do Protestants think of these perfectly sincere feelings, and of the attempt to enforce them against non-Catholics? Yet, if mankind are justified in interfering with each other's liberty in things which do not concern the interests of others, on what principle is it possible consistently to exclude these cases? or who can blame people for desiring to suppress what they regard as a scandal in the sight of God and man? No stronger case can be shown for prohibiting anything which is regarded as a personal immorality, than is made out for suppressing these practices in the eyes of those who regard them as impieties; and unless we are willing to adopt the logic of persecutors, and to say that we may persecute others because we are right, and that they must not persecute us because they are wrong, we must beware of admitting a principle of which we should resent as a gross injustice the application to ourselves.

The preceding instances may be objected to, although unreasonably, as drawn from contingencies impossible among us: opinion, in this country, not being likely to enforce abstinence from meats, or to interfere with people for worshipping, and for either marrying or not marrying, according to their creed or inclination. The next example, however, shall be taken from an interference with liberty which we have by no means passed all danger of. Wherever the Puritans have been sufficiently powerful, as in New England, and in Great Britain at the time of the Commonwealth, they have endeavoured, with considerable success, to put down all public, and nearly all private, amusements: especially music, dancing, public games, or other assemblages for purposes of diversion, and the theatre. There are still in this country large bodies of persons by whose notions of morality and religion these recreations are condemned; and those persons belonging chiefly to the middle class, who are the ascendant power in the present social and political condition of the kingdom, it is by no means impossible that persons of these sentiments may at some time or other command a majority in Parliament. How will the remaining portion of the community like to have the amusements that shall be permitted to them regulated by the religious and moral sentiments of the stricter Calvinists and Methodists? Would they not, with considerable peremptoriness, desire these intrusively pious members of society to mind their own business? This is precisely what should be said to every government and every public, who have the pretension that no person shall enjoy any pleasure which they think wrong. But if the principle of the pretension be admitted, no one can reasonably object to its being acted on in the sense of the majority, or other preponderating power in the country; and all persons must be ready to conform to the idea of a Christian commonwealth, as understood by the early settlers in New England, if a religious profession similar to theirs should ever succeed in regaining its lost ground, as religions supposed to be declining have so often been known to do.

To imagine another contingency, perhaps more likely to be realized than the one last mentioned. There is confessedly a strong tendency in the modern world towards a democratic constitution of society, accompanied or not by popular political institutions. It is affirmed that in the country where this tendency is most completely realized—where both society and the government are most democratic—the United States—the feeling of the majority, to whom any appearance of a more showy or costly style of living than they can hope to rival is disagreeable, operates as a tolerably effectual sumptuary law, and that in many parts of the Union it is really difficult for a person possessing a very large income, to find any mode of spending it, which will not incur popular disapprobation. Though such statements as these are doubtless much exaggerated as a representation of existing facts, the state of things they describe is not only a conceivable and possible, but a probable result of democratic feeling, combined with the notion that the public has a right to a veto on the manner in which individuals shall spend their incomes. We have only further to suppose a considerable diffusion of Socialist opinions, and it may become infamous in the eyes of the majority to possess more property than some very small amount, or any income not earned by manual labour. Opinions similar in principle to these, already prevail widely among the artisan class, and weigh oppressively on those who are amenable to the opinion chiefly of that class, namely, its own members. It is known that the bad workmen who form the majority of the operatives in many branches of industry are decidedly of opinion that bad workmen ought to receive the same wages as good, and that no one ought to be allowed, through piecework or otherwise, to earn by superior skill or industry more than others can without it. And they employ a moral police, which occasionally becomes a physical one, to deter skilful workmen from receiving, and employers from giving, a larger remuneration for a more useful service. If the public have any jurisdiction over private concerns, I cannot see that these people are in fault, or that any individual's particular public can be blamed for asserting the same authority over his individual conduct, which the general public asserts over people in general.

But, without dwelling upon supposititious cases, there are,

in our own day, gross usurpations upon the liberty of private life actually practised, and still greater ones threatened with some expectations of success, and opinions propounded which assert an unlimited right in the public not only to prohibit by law everything which it thinks wrong, but in order to get at what it thinks wrong, to prohibit any number of things which it admits to be innocent.

Under the name of preventing intemperance, the people of one English colony, and of nearly half the United States, have been interdicted by law from making any use whatever of fermented drinks, except for medical purposes: for prohibition of their sale is in fact, as it is to be, prohibition of their use. And though the impracticability of executing the law has caused its repeal in several of the States which had adopted it, including the one from which it derives its name, an attempt has notwithstanding been commenced, and is prosecuted with considerable zeal by many of the professed philanthropists, to agitate for a similar law in this country. The association, or 'Alliance' as it terms itself, which has been formed for this purpose, has acquired some notoriety through the publicity given to a correspondence between its Secretary and one of the very few English public men who hold that a politician's opinions ought to be founded on principles. Lord Stanley's share in this correspondence is calculated to strengthen the hopes already built on him, by those who know how rare such qualities as are manifested in some of his public appearances, unhappily are among those who figure in political life. The organ of the Alliance, who would 'deeply deplore the recognition of any principle which could be wrested to justify bigotry and persecution' undertakes to point out the 'broad and impassable barrier' which divides such principles from those of the association. 'All matters relating to thought, opinion, conscience, appear to me,' he says 'to be without the sphere of legislation; all pertaining to social act, habit, relation, subject only to a discretionary power vested in the State itself, and not in the individual, to be within it.' No mention is made of a third class, different from either of these, viz. acts and habits which are not social, but individual; although it is to this class, surely, that the act of drinking fermented liquors belongs. Selling fermented liquors, however, is trading, and trading is a social act. But the infringement complained of is not on the liberty of the seller, but on that of the buyer and consumer; since the State might just as well forbid him to drink wine, as purposely make it impossible for him to obtain it. The Secretary, however, says, 'I claim, as a citizen, a right to legislate whenever my social rights are invaded by the social act of another.' And now for the definition of these 'social rights.' 'If anything invades my social rights, certainly the traffic in strong drink does. It destroys my primary right of security, by constantly creating and stimulating social disorder. It invades my right of equality, by deriving a profit from the creation of a misery I am taxed to support. It impedes my right to free moral and intellectual development, by surrounding my path with dangers, and by weakening and demoralizing society, from which I have a right to claim mutual aid and intercourse.' A theory of 'social rights,' the like of which probably never before found its way into distinct language: being nothing short of this—that it is the absolute social right of every individual, that every other individual shall act in every respect exactly as he ought; that whosoever fails thereof in the smallest particular, violates my social right, and entitles me to demand from the legislature the removal of the grievance. So monstrous a principle is far more dangerous than any single interference with liberty; there is no violation of liberty which it would not justify; it acknowledges no right to any freedom whatever, except perhaps to that of holding opinions in secret, without ever disclosing them: for, the moment an opinion which I consider noxious passes any one's lips, it invades all the 'social rights' attributed to me by the Alliance. The doctrine ascribes to all mankind a vested interest in each other's moral, intellectual, and even physical perfection, to be defined by each claimant according to his own standard.

Another important example of illegitimate interference with the rightful liberty of the individual, not simply threatened, but long since carried into triumphant effect, is Sabbatarian legislation. Without doubt, abstinence on one day in the week, so far as the exigencies of life permit, from the usual daily occupation, though in no respect religiously binding on any except Jews, is a highly beneficial custom. And inasmuch as this custom cannot be observed without a general consent to that effect among the industrious classes, therefore, in so far as some persons by working may impose the same necessity on others, it may be allowable and right that the law should guarantee to each the observance by others of the custom, by suspending the greater operations of industry on a particular day. But this justification, grounded on the direct interest which others have in each individual's observance of the practice, does not apply to the self-chosen occupations in which a person may think it to employ his leisure; nor does it hold good, in the smallest degree, for legal restrictions on amusements. It is true that the amusement of some is the day's work of others; but the pleasure, not to say the useful recreation, of many, is worth the labour of a few, provided the occupation is freely chosen, and can be freely resigned. The operatives are perfectly right in thinking that if all worked on Sunday, seven days' work would have to be given for six days' wages: but so long as the great mass of employments are suspended, the small number who for the enjoyment of others must still work, obtain a proportional increase of earnings; and they are not obliged to follow those occupations, if they prefer leisure to emolument. If a further remedy is sought, it might be found in the establishment by custom of a holiday on some other day of the week for those particular classes of persons. The only ground, therefore, on which restrictions on Sunday amusements can be defended, must be that they are religiously wrong; a motive of legislation which never can be too earnestly protested against. 'Deorum injuriae Diis curae.' It remains to be proved that society or any of its officers holds a commission from on high to avenge any supposed offense to Omnipotence, which is not also a wrong to our fellow creatures. The notion that it is one man's duty that another should be religious, was the foundation of all the religious persecutions ever perpetrated, and if admitted, would fully justify them. Though the feeling which breaks out in the repeated attempts to stop railway travelling on Sunday, in the resistance to the opening of Museums, and the like, has not the cruelty of the old persecutors, the state of mind indicated by it is fundamentally the same. It is a determination not to tolerate others in doing what is permitted by their religion, because it is not permitted by the persecutor's religion. It is a belief that God not only abominates the act of the misbeliever, but will not hold us guiltless if we leave him unmolested.

I cannot refrain from adding to these examples of the little account commonly made of human liberty, the language of downright persecution which breaks out from the press of this country, whenever it feels called on to notice the remarkable phenomenon of Mormonism. Much might be said on the unexpected and instructive fact, that an alleged new revelation, and a religion founded on it, the product of palpable imposture, not even supported by the prestige of extraordinary qualities in its founder, is believed by hundreds of thousands, and has been made the foundation of a society, in the age of newspapers, railways, and the electric telegraph. What here concerns us is, that this religion, like other and better religions, has its martyrs; that its prophet and founder was, for his teaching, put to death by a mob; that others of its adherents lost their lives by the same lawless violence; that they were forcibly expelled, in a body, from the country in which they first grew up; while, now that they have been chased into a solitary recess in the midst of a desert, many in this country openly declare that it would be right (only that it is not convenient) to send an expedition against them, and compel them by force to conform to the opinions of other people. The article of the Mormonite doctrine which is the chief provocative to the antipathy which thus breaks through the ordinary restraints of religious tolerance, is its sanction of polygamy; which, though permitted to Mohammedans, and Hindoos, and Chinese, seems to excite unquenchable animosity when practised by persons who speak English, and profess to be a kind of Christians. No one has a deeper disapprobation than I have of this Mormon institution; both for other reasons, and because, far from being in any way countenanced by the principle of liberty, it is a direct infraction of that principle, being a mere riveting of the chains of one-half of the community, and an emancipation of the other from reciprocity of obligation towards them. Still, it must be remembered that this relation is as much voluntary on the part of the women concerned in it, and who may be deemed the sufferers by it, as is the case with any other form of the marriage institution; and however surprising this fact may appear, it has its explanation in the common ideas and customs of the world, which teaching women to think marriage the one thing needful, make it intelligible that many a woman should prefer being one of several wives, to not being a wife at all. Other countries are not asked to recognize such unions, or release any portion of their inhabitants from their own laws on the score of Mormonite opinions. But when the dissentients have conceded to the hostile sentiments of others, far more than could justly be demanded; when they have left the countries to which their doctrines were unacceptable, and established themselves in a remote corner of the earth, which they have been the first to render habitable to human beings; it is difficult to see on what principles but those of tyranny they can be prevented from living there under what laws they please, provided they commit no aggression on other nations, and allow perfect freedom of departure to those who are dissatisfied with their ways. A recent writer, in some respects of considerable merit, proposes (to use his own words) not a crusade, but a civilizade, against this polygamous community, to put an end to what seems to him a retrograde step in civilization. It also appears so to me, but I am not aware that any community has a right to force another to be civilized. So long as the sufferers by the bad law do not invoke assistance from other communities, I cannot admit that persons entirely unconnected with them ought to step in and require that a condition of things with which all who are directly interested appear to be satisfied, should be put an end to because it is a scandal to persons some thousands of miles distant, who have no part or concern in it. Let them send missionaries, if they please, to preach against it; and let them, by any fair means (of which silencing the teachers is not one), oppose the progress of similar doctrines among their own people. If civilization has got the better of barbarism when barbarism had the world to itself, it is too much to profess to be afraid lest barbarism, after having been fairly got under, should revive and conquer civilization. A civilization that can thus succumb to its vanquished enemy, must first have become so degenerate, that neither its appointed priests and teachers, nor anybody else, has the capacity, or will take the trouble to stand up for it. If this be so the sooner such a civilization receives notice to quit, the better. It can only go on from bad to worse, until destroyed and regenerated (like the Western Empire) by energetic barbarians.

THE ACTION OF POSITIVISM UPON THE WORKING CLASSES*

By AUGUSTE COMTE

Positivism whether looked at as a philosophical system or as an instrument of social renovation, cannot count upon much support from any kind of the classes, whether in Church or State, by whom the government of mankind has hitherto been conducted. There will be isolated exceptions of great value, and these will soon become more numerous; but the prejudices and passions of these classes will present serious obstacles to the work of moral and mental reorganisation which constitutes the second phase of the great Western revolution. Their faulty education and their repugnance to system prejudice them against a philosophy which subordinates specialities to general principles. Their aristocratic instincts make it very difficult for them to recognise the supremacy of Social Feeling; that doctrine which lies at the root of social regeneration, as conceived by Positivism. That no support can be expected from the classes who were in the ascendant before the Revolution, is of course obvious; and we shall probably meet with opposition, quite as real though more carefully concealed, from the middle classes, to whom that revolution transferred the authority and social influence which they had long been coveting. Their thoughts are entirely engrossed with the acquisition of power; and they concern themselves but little with the mode in which it is used, or the objects to which it is directed. They were quite convinced that the Revolution had found a satisfactory issue in the parliamentary system instituted during the recent period of political oscillation. They will long continue to regret that stationary period, because it was peculiarly

* From *System of Positive Polity*

favourable to their restless ambition. A movement tending to the complete regeneration of society is almost as much dreaded now by the middle classes as it was formerly by the higher. And both would at all events agree in prolonging, so far as republican institutions admitted, the system of theological hypocrisy, the only effective instrument of retrogression now left to them. This ignoble system offers the double attraction of securing respect and submission on the part of the masses, while imposing no unpleasant duties on their governors. All their critical and metaphysical prejudices indispose them to terminate the state of spiritual anarchy which is the greatest obstacle, to social regeneration; while at the same time their ambition dreads the establishment of a new moral authority, the restrictive influence of which would of course press most heavily upon themselves. In the eighteenth century, men of rank, and even kings, accepted the purely negative philosophy that was then in vogue: it removed many obstacles, it was an easy path to reputation, and it imposed no great sacrifice. But we can hardly hope from this precedent that the wealthy and literary classes of our own time will be equally willing to accept Positive philosophy; the declared purpose of which is to discipline our intellectual powers, in order to reorganize our modes of life.

The avowal of such a purpose is quite sufficient to prevent Positivism from gaining the sympathies of any one of the governing classes. The classes to which it must appeal are those who have been left untrained in the present worthless methods of instruction by words and entities, who are animated with strong social instincts, and who consequently have the largest stock of good sense and good feeling. In a word it is among the working classes that the new philosophers will find their most energetic allies. The force necessary for social regeneration depends essentially on the combined action of those two extreme terms of the ultimate social order. Notwithstanding their difference of position, a difference which indeed is more apparent than real, there are strong affinities between them, both morally and intellectually. Both have the same sense of the real, the same preference for the useful, and the same tendency to subordinate special points to general principles. Morally they resemble each other in generosity of feeling, in wise unconcern for material prospects, and in indifference to worldly grandeur. This at least will be the case as soon as philosophers in the true sense of that word have mixed sufficiently with the nobler members of the working classes to raise their own character to its proper level. When the sympathies which unite them upon these essential points have had time to show themselves, it will be felt that the philosopher is, under certain aspects, a member of the working class fully trained; while the working man is in many respects a philosopher without the training. Both too will look with similar feelings upon the intermediate or capitalist class. As that class is necessarily the possessor of material power, the pecuniary existence of both will as a rule be dependent upon it.

These affinities follow as a natural result from their respective position and functions. The reason of their not having been recognised more distinctly is, that at present we have nothing that can be called a philosophic class, or at least it is only represented by a few isolated types. Workmen worthy of their position are happily far less rare; but hitherto it is only in France, or rather in Paris, that they have shown themselves in their true light, as men emancipated from chimerical beliefs, and careless of the empty prestige of social position. It is, then, only in Paris, that the truth of the preceding remarks can be fully verified.

The occupations of working men are evidently far more conducive to philosophical views than those of the middle classes; since they are not so absorbing as to prevent continuous thought, even during the hours of labour. And besides having more time for thinking, they have a moral advantage in the absence of any responsibility when their work is over. The workman is preserved by his position from the schemes of aggrandisement which are constantly harassing the capitalist. Their difference in this respect causes a cor responding difference in their modes of thought; the one cares more for general principles, the other more for details. To a sensible workman, the system of dispersive speciality now so much in vogue shows itself in its true light. He sees it, that is, to be brutalising, because it would condemn his intellect to the most paltry mode of culture, such as will never be accepted in France in spite of the irrational endeavours of our Anglomaniac economists. To the capitalist on the contrary and even to the man of science that system, however rigidly and consistently carried out, will seem far less degrading; or rather it will be looked upon as most desirable, unless his education has been such as to counteract these tendencies, and to give him the desire and the ability for abstract and general thought.

Morally, the contrast between the position of the workman and the capitalist is even more striking. Proud as most men are of worldly success, the degree of moral or mental excellence implied in the acquisition of wealth or power, even when the means used have been strictly legitimate, is hardly such as to justify that pride. Looking at intrinsic qualities rather than at visible results, it is obvious that practical success, whether in industry or in war, depends far more on character than on intellect or affection. The principal condition for it is the combination of a certain amount of energy with great caution, and a fair share of perseverance. When a man has these qualities, mediocrity of intellect and moral deficiency will not prevent his taking advantage of favourable chances; chance being usually a very important element in worldly success. Indeed it would hardly be an exaggeration to say that poverty of thought and feeling has often something to do with forming and maintaining the disposition requisite for the purpose. Vigorous exertion of the active powers is more frequently induced by the personal propensities of avarice, ambition, or vanity, than by the higher instincts. Superiority of position, when legitimately obtained, deserves respect; but the philosopher, like the religionist, and with still better grounds, refuses to regard it as a proof of moral superiority, a conclusion which would be wholly at variance with the true theory of human nature.

The life of the workman, on the other hand, is far more favourable to the development of the nobler instincts. In practical qualities he is usually not wanting, except in caution, a deficiency which makes his energy and perseverance less useful to himself, though fully available for society. But it is in the exercise of the higher feelings that the moral superiority of the working class is most observable. When our habits and opinions have been brought under the influence of systematic principles, the true character of this class, which forms the basis of modern society, will become more distinct; and we shall see that home affections are naturally stronger with them than with the middle classes, who are too much engrossed with personal interests for the full enjoyment of domestic ties. Still more evident is their superiority in social feelings strictly so called, for these with them are called into daily exercise from earliest childhood. Here it is that we find the highest and most genuine types of friendship, and this even amongst those who are placed in a dependent position, aggravated often by the aristocratic prejudices of those above them, and whom we might imagine on that account condemned to a lower moral standard. We find sincere and simple respect for superiors, untainted by servility, not vitiated by the pride of learning, not disturbed by the jealousies of competition. Their personal experience of the miseries of life is a constant stimulus to the nobler sympathies. In no class is there so strong an incentive to social feeling, at least to the feeling of Solidarity between contemporaries; for all are conscious of the support that they derive from union, support which is not at all incompatible with strong individuality of character. The sense of Continuity with the past has not, it is true, been sufficiently developed; but this is a want which can only be supplied by systematic culture. It will hardly be disputed that there are more remarkable instances of prompt and unostentatious self-sacrifice at the call of a great public necessity in this class than in any other. Note too that, in the utter absence of any systematic education, all these moral excellences must be looked upon as inherent in the class. It is impossible to attribute them to theological influence, now that they have so entirely shaken off the old faith. And although it is only in Paris that this hitherto unrecognised type can be seen in its perfection, yet the fact of its existence in the centre of Western Europe is enough for all rational observers. A type so fully in accordance with what we know of human nature cannot fail ultimately to spread everywhere, especially when these spontaneous tendencies are placed under the systematic guidance of Positivism.

These remarks will prepare us to appreciate the wise and generous instincts of the Convention in looking to the Proletariat as the mainspring of its policy; and this not merely on account of the incidental danger of foreign invasion, but in dealing with the larger question of social regeneration, which it pursued so ardently, though in such ignorance of its true principles. Owing however to the want of a satisfactory system, and the disorder produced by the metaphysical theories of the time, the spirit in which this alliance with the people was framed was incompatible with the real object in view. It was considered that government ought as a rule to be in the hands of the people. Now under the special circumstances of the time popular government was undoubtedly very useful. The existence of the republic depended almost entirely upon the proletariate, the only class that stood unshaken and true to its principles. But in the absolute spirit of the received political theories, this state of things was regarded as normal, a view which is incompatible with the most important conditions of modern society. It is of course always right for the people to assist government in carrying out the law, even to the extent of physical force, should the case require it. Interference of this subordinate kind, whether in foreign or internal questions, so far from leading to anarchy, is obviously a guarantee for order which ought to exist in every properly constituted society. Indeed in this respect our habits in France are still very defective; men are too often content to remain mere lookers on, while the police to whom they owe their daily protection is doing its duty. But for the people to take a direct part in government, and to have the final decision of political measures, is a state of things which in modern society is only adapted to times of revolution. To recognise it as final would lead at once to anarchy, were it not so utterly impossible to realise.

Positivism rejects the metaphysical doctrine of the Sovereignty of the people. But it appropriates all that is really sound in the doctrine, and this with reference not merely to exceptional cases but to the normal state; while at the same time it guards against the danger involved in its application as an absolute truth. In the hands of the revolutionary party the doctrine is generally used to justify the right of insurrection. Now in Positive Polity this right is looked upon as an ultimate resource with which no society should allow itself to dispense. Absolute submission, which is too strongly inculcated by modern Catholicism, would expose us to the danger of tyranny. Insurrection may be regarded scientifically as a sort of reparative crisis of which societies stand in more need than individuals, in accordance with the well-known biological law, that the higher and the more complicated the organism, the more frequent and also the more dangerous is the pathological state. Therefore the fear that Positivism when generally accepted will encourage passive obedience, is perfectly groundless; although it is certainly not favourable to the pure revolutionary spirit, which would fain take the disease for the normal type of health. Its whole character is so essentially relative, that it finds no difficulty in accepting subordination as the rule, and yet in allowing for exceptional cases of revolt; a course by which good sense and human dignity are alike satisfied. Positivism looks upon insurrection as a dangerous remedy that should be reserved for extreme cases; but it would never scruple to sanction and even to encourage it when it was really indispensable. This is quite compatible with refusing, as a rule, to submit the decision of political questions and the choice of rulers to judges who are obviously incompetent; and who, under the influence of Positivism, will be induced voluntarily to abdicate rights subversive of order.

The metaphysical doctrine of the Sovereignty of the people contains, however, a truth of permanent value, though in a very confused form. This truth Positivism separates very distinctly from its dangerous alloy, yet without weakening, on the contrary, with the effect of enforcing its social import. There are two distinct conceptions in this doctrine, which have hitherto been confounded; a political conception applicable to certain special cases; a moral conception applicable to all.

In the first place the name of the whole body politic ought to be invoked in the announcement of any special measure of which the motives are sufficiently intelligible, and which directly concern the practical interests of the whole community. Under this head would be included decisions of law courts, declarations of war, etc. When society has reached the Positive state, and the sense of universal solidarity is more generally diffused, there will be even more significance and dignity in such expressions than there is now, because the name invoked will no longer be that of a special nation, but that of Humanity as a whole. It would be absurd however to extend this practice to those still more numerous cases where the people is incompetent to express any opinion, and has merely to adopt the opinion of superior officers who have obtained its confidence. This may be owing either to the difficulty of the question or to the fact of its application being indirect or limited. Such, for instance, would be enactments, very often of great importance, which deal with scientific principles; or again most questions relating to special professions or branches of industry. In all these cases popular good sense would under Positivist influence easily be kept clear from political illusions. It is only under the stimulus of metaphysical pride that such illusions become dangerous;

and the untaught masses have but little experience of this feeling.

There is, however, another truth implied in the expression, Sovereignty of the people. It implies that it is the first of duties to concentrate all the efforts of society upon the common good. And in this there is a more direct reference to the working class than to any other; first, on account of their immense numerical superiority, and, secondly, because the difficulties by which their life is surrounded require special interference to a degree which for other classes would be unnecessary. From this point of view it is a principle which all true republicans may accept. It is, in fact, identical with what we have laid down as the universal basis of morality, the direct and permanent preponderance of social feeling over all personal interests. Not merely, then, is it incorporated by Positivism, but, as was shown in the first chapter, it forms the primary principle of the system, even under the intellectual aspect. Since the decline of Catholicism the metaphysical spirit has been provisionally the guardian of this great social precept. Positivism now finally appropriates it, and purifies it for the future from all taint of anarchy. Revolutionists, as we should expect from their characteristic dislike to the separation of the two powers, had treated the question politically. Positivism avoids all danger by shifting it to the region of morality. I shall show presently that this very salutary change, so far from weakening the force of the principle, increases its permanent value, and at the same time removes the deceptive and subversive tendencies which are always involved in the metaphysical mode of regarding it.

What, then, it will be asked, is the part assigned to the Proletariat in the final constitution of society? The similarity of position which I pointed out between themselves and the philosophic class suggests the answer. They will be of the most essential service to the spiritual power in each of its three social functions, judgment, counsel, and even education. All the intellectual and moral qualities that we have just indicated in this class concur in fitting them for this service. If we except the philosophic body, which is the recognised organ of general principles, there is no class which is so habitually inclined to take comprehensive views of any subject. Their superiority in Social Feeling is still more obvious. In this even the best philosophers are rarely their equals; and it would be a most beneficial corrective of the tendency of the latter to over-abstraction to come into daily contact with the noble and spontaneous instincts of the people. The working class, then, is better qualified than any other for understanding, and still, more for sympathising with the highest truths of morality, though it may not be able to give them a systematic form. And as we have seen it is in social morality, the most important and the highest of the three branches of Ethics, that their superiority is most observable. Besides, independently of their intrinsic merits, whether intellectual or moral, the necessities of their daily life serve to impress them with respect for the great rules of morality, which in most cases were framed for their own protection. To secure the application of these rules in daily life, is a function of the spiritual power in the performance of which it will receive but slight assistance from the middle classes; for as it is with them that temporal power naturally resides, it is their own misuse of power that has to be controlled and set right. The working classes are the chief sufferers from the selfishness and domineering of men of wealth and power. For this reason they are the likeliest to come forward in defence of public morality. And they will be all the more disposed to give it their hearty support, if they have nothing to do directly with political administration. Habitual participation in temporal power, to say nothing of its unsettling influence, would lead them away from the best remedy for their sufferings of which the constitution of society admits. Popular sagacity will soon detect the utter hollowness of the off-hand solutions that are now being obtruded upon us. The people will rapidly become convinced that the surest method of satisfying all legitimate claims lies in the moral agencies which Positivism offers, though it appeals to them at the same time to abdicate a political function which is either illusory or subversive.

One step in this direction they have already taken of their own accord, though its importance has not been duly appreciated. The well-known scheme of Communism, which has found such rapid acceptance with them, serves, in the absence of sounder doctrine, to express the way in which they are now looking at the great social problem. The experience of the first part of the Revolution has not yet wholly disabused them of political illusions, but it has at least brought them to feel that Property is of more importance than Power in the ordinary sense of the word. So far communism has given a wider meaning to the great social problem, and has thereby rendered an essential service, which is not neutralised by the temporary dangers involved in the metaphysical forms in which it comes before us. Communism should therefore be carefully distinguished from the numerous extravagant schemes brought forward in this time of spiritual anarchy; a time which stimulates incompetent and ill-trained minds to the most difficult subjects of thought. The foolish schemes referred to have so few definite features, that we have to distinguish them by the names of their authors. But communism bears the name of no single author, and is something more than an accidental product of anomalous circumstances. We should look upon it as the natural progress in the right direction of the revolutionary spirit; progress of a moral rather than intellectual kind. It is a proof that revolutionary tendencies are now concentrating themselves upon moral questions, leaving all purely political questions in the background. It is quite true that the solution of the problem which Communists are now putting forward, is still as essentially political as that of their predecessors; since the only mode by which they propose to regulate the employment of property, is by a change in the mode of its tenure. Still it is owing to them that the question of property is at last brought forward for discussion: and it is a question which so evidently needs a moral solution, the solution of it by political means, is at once so inadequate and so destructive, that it cannot long continue to be debated without leading to the more satisfactory result offered by positivism. Men will see that it forms a part of the final regeneration of opinion and of life, which positivism is now inaugurating.

To do justice to communism, we must look at the generous sympathies by which it is inspired, not at the shallow theories in which those sympathies find expression provisionally, until circumstances enable them to take some other shape. The workmen connected with the Communist utopia, caring but very little for metaphysical principles, do not attach nearly the same importance to these theories as is done by men of literary education. As soon as they see a better way of bringing forward the points on which they have such legitimate claims, they will very soon adopt the clear and practical conceptions of positivism, which can be carried out peaceably and permanently, in preference to these vague and confused chimeras, which, as they will instinctively feel, lead only to anarchy. Till then they will naturally abide by communism, as the only method of bringing forward the most fundamental of social problems in a way which there shall be no evading. The very alarm aroused by these proposed solutions of the problem helps to stir public attention, and fix it on this great subject. But for this constant appeal to their fears, the metaphysical delusions and aristocratic self-seeking of the governing classes would shelve the question altogether, or pass it by with indifference. And even when the mistakes of Communists have been rectified, it does not follow that they should give up the name, which is a simple assertion of the paramount importance of Social Feeling. However, now that we have happily passed from monarchy to republicanism, the name of Communist is no longer indispensable; the word Republican expresses the meaning as well, and without the same danger. Positivism, then, has nothing to fear from communism; on the contrary, it will probably be accepted by most of the Communist workmen, especially in France, where abstractions have but little influence on minds thoroughly emancipated from theology. The people will gradually find that the solution of the great social problem which positivism offers is better than the Communistic solution.

A tendency in this direction has already shown itself since the first edition of this work was published. French workmen have now adopted a new expression, socialism, thus indicating that they accept the problem of the Communists while rejecting their solution. Indeed that solution would seem to be finally disposed of by the voluntary exile of their leader. Yet, if the Socialists at present keep clear of communism, it is only because their position is one of criticism or inaction. If they were to succeed to power, with principles so far below the level of their sympathies, they would inevitably fall into the same errors and extravagances which they now instinctively feel to be wrong. Consequently the rapid spread of socialism very naturally alarms the upper classes; and their resistance, blind though it be, is at present the only legal guarantee for material order. In fact, the problem brought forward by the Communists admits of no solution but their own, so long as the revolutionary confusion of temporal and spiritual power continues. Therefore the universal blame that is lavished on these utopian schemes cannot fail to lead men towards positivism, as the only doctrine which can preserve Western Europe from some serious attempt to bring communism into practical operation. Positivists stand forward now as the party of construction, with a definite basis for political action; namely, systematic prosecution of the wise attempt of mediaeval statesmen to separate the two social powers. On this basis they are enabled to satisfy the poor, and at the same time to restore the confidence of the rich. It is a final solution of our difficulties which will make the titles of which we have been speaking unnecessary. Stripping the old word Republican of any false meaning at present attached to it, we may retain it as the best expression of the social sympathies on which the regeneration of society depends. For the opinions, manners, and even institutions of future society, Positivist is the only word suitable. Positivists accept, and indeed very much enlarge, the programme of communism; but we reject its practical solution on the ground that it is at once inadequate and subversive. The chief difference between our own solution and theirs is that we substitute moral agencies for political. Thus we come to our leading principle of separating spiritual from temporal power; a principle which, disregarded as it has hitherto been in the system of modern renovators, will be found in every one of the important problems of our time to be the sole possible issue. In the present case, while throwing such light on the fallacy of communism, it should lead us to excuse the fallacy, by reminding us that politicians of every accredited school are equally guilty of it. At a time when there are so very few, even of cultivated minds, who have a clear conception of this the primary principle of modern polities, it would be harsh to blame the people for still accepting a result of revolutionary empiricism, which is so universally adopted by other classes.

Such, then, is the nature of the compact into which all true philosophers should enter with the leading members of the proletary class. Their object is to direct the organic and final phase through which the Great Revolution is now passing, by a wise prolongation of the provisional system of the Convention; ignoring as far as possible the traditions of all succeeding governments, whether stationary or retrograde. Comprehensiveness of view and social sympathy predominate alike in both members of this great alliance; and it is thus a guarantee for our present state of transition, and a sure earnest of the normal future. The people are the spontaneous representatives of this alliance; philosophers should become its systematic organ. The intellectual deficiencies of the former will easily be remedied by philosophers, who will show them how essential it is on social grounds that they should understand the true meaning of history; since otherwise their conception of the union of mankind must be limited to the present generation, ignoring the more important truth of the continuity of the Present with the Past and the Future. A far greater obstacle is the moral deficiency of most philosophers of our time. But the wholesome influence of the people upon them, combined with a deep philosophic conviction of the preponderance of Feeling in every subject of thought, will do much to overcome the ambitious instincts which weaken and distract their energies in the common cause of social renovation.

POLITICAL ECONOMY AND UTOPIAN
SOCIALISM*

By PIERRE-JOSEPH PROUDHON

POLITICAL economy is the natural history of the customs, traditions, usages and origins which have been adopted by mankind relating to the production and distribution of wealth. Thus, political economy regards itself to be realistically and naturally based; the phenomena which it studies are certainly necessary and universal manifestations of human activity. Socialism declares that the present social system and thereby all former systems are contradictions. It asserts and proves that the present civilized state is shot through with miserable contradictions; the alleged aims of this society are negated by the general prevalence of oppression, poverty and crime. Socialism declares that classical political economy is essentially false, a sophistry perpetrated against the majority by the oppressive minority.

Socialism regards political economy as the organized theory of thievery and poverty just as jurisprudence is, according to socialism the collection of rubrics approving lawful robbery symbolized in the single word, possession. Against the principle of ownership socialism opposes the principle of associationism and self-confidently affirms that it will change society at its very roots, introducing a new law, new politics, new adjustments and customs which will be diametrically opposed to the old order. In the place of egoism, deified by the classical economists, the socialist offers the spirit of communism. The classical economists preach the holiness of the status quo—real optimists they! On the other hand the socialists more hopeful for the future are less optimistic about the present.

* From *Political Economy and Utopian Socialism*

The classical economists are defenders of religion, state power and all the other institutions which safeguard private property; the socialists discard authority and religious faith and appeal entirely to reason. To the workman who complains about low wages and insecurity political economy replies with the slogan "freedom of trade," which is the freedom of the propertied citizen. Thus, society has always been divided into two groups: one group adheres closely to tradition and is essentially hierarchical sometimes utilizing monarchy and sometimes working through democracy. The other group which flares up in every social crisis is opposed to authority and stands for socialism. But now modern criticism indicates that in such a crisis truth is not wholly on one or another side. The solution rather is to be found in a reconciliation of the opposites.

The most controversial question is undoubtedly the problem of work organization. The classical economists solve the problem glibly enough with the assertion that work is already organized. This is however entirely untenable because it is notorious that no aspect of work—neither supply nor demand, nor distribution, nor abundance, nor price—in short, nothing is organized: on the contrary everything is left to chance. We declare, contrary to the economists and socialists not that work must be organized, not that work is organized, but that it must and will organize itself. Political economy teaches the first, elementary steps of organization; socialism correctly points out, however, that in its present form this organization is inadequate and transitory. Socialism thus is an extension, continually developing, of political economy.

An equally controversial question is the problem of usury, the interest paid on loans. Usury may be called the return which the owner of capital receives for its use. The ancient philosophers and the church fathers allowed the lending of money but prohibited the payment of interest, holding that money is unproductive. They distinguished between the loan of things which were used up in production, among which they included money, and the loan of goods which brought their owner profit without being consumed. It was easy for the economists, basing themselves on the concept of rent, to insist that the productivity and effect of capital was the same regardless of whether it was consumed in loans or used to keep tools working; therefore, they said, either rent paid for the use of land should also be condemned or interest on borrowed money should be permitted. Both land and capital they held, were similar in character and both or neither should therefore be entitled to payment for use.

The interest paid on capital, was then, merely an illustration of the aphorism: All work must create a surplus. But in opposition to this theory which insisted on the productivity of capital there arises an equally reasonable hypothesis. Every value comes from work and is estimated in money; in other words, no value is originally created by privilege. How can the theory that capital is productive, that rent is a return for value created by land, a theory apparently confirmed thru universal application, be reconciled with concept that value is created by wage-labor. The socialists questioned the origins of the first surpluses accumulated by the owners of land and capital and urged the higher validity of the principle that all such surpluses were first created by labor. It is a well known principle of our society that the rights of private property cannot be abridged or violated except in the interests of the common welfare and after due compensation. This principle is in thorough accord with economics. It recognizes the property right of the individual citizen who is paid for the expropriated property what it is worth according to the universal laws of barter. The expropriation of the individual in the interests of society may be compared to a domestic transaction where the consent of all parties concerned is required for the final consummation of the bargain. The indemnity to the individual owner is the seal to the social right of the community. The railroad laws have confirmed the payments made for road-bed property. Apparently, however, it has occured to no one that the workmen who have been thrown out of work by the destruction of factories in the way of the railroad is similarly entitled to compensation. No one, of course, has questioned the right of the industrialist to payment for his appropriated property. The system of justice approved by the State thus acts against the interests of certain social classes.

Now the socialists appear and accuse political economy of all the existing evils. In the law of eminent domain they find the germ of agrarian law and they suddenly conclude in favor of universal expropriation to be followed by common production and consumption. But at this point socialism leaps from criticism into utopianism. If the logical outcome of universal expropriation is a complete change of society then it is necessary to analyze the new organization.

It will be necessary to guarantee, if not actually pay, to the expropriated citizens for the property they have lost; in a word, they must be guaranteed security in exchange for their property losses. Where does socialism expect to find the substance wherewith to guarantee security to the expropriated if not from the public wealth? But what do the querulous parties reply? It may almost be said that they do not understand the questions asked of them. What for instance do they propose in relation to the division of profits and wages?

What is profit? Profit is that which remains to the capitalist after costs have been deducted. The costs are measured in work-days and finally in wages. How high are the workman's wages? They are as little as the capitalist can get away with paying, what exactly cannot be generally determined. And what is the value of the goods which the merchant brings to market? It is as much as he can get—what exactly cannot be theoretically determined. Political economy refuses even to assume that prices or wages can be fixed in advance although it is admitted that these may be attached since the process of evaluation is subject to natural laws.

How, then, is it possible to estimate the extent of two unknown quantities while, according to political economy, can in no way be determined.

Thus, economy presents insoluble problems which, however, must find solution before the end of the century.

The relation of profit to wages must be accepted in an absolute sense and not from the limited point of view of exchange and the separation of interests. The value of the goods produced may be divided into two parts. First, that which repays the capitalist for his production costs and second, that which represents his profit according to the quoted axiom: all work creates a surplus. Let us now decide the relationship of the two quantities. We begin with the two human operators in production: the businessman who undertakes the enterprise and hopes to make a profit and the workman who works for wages. In order that this relationship exist there must be present an internal and external law explaining the fixing of wages and the fluctuation of prices.

Among the socialists one group disdains to analyze this problem. The other holds forth with a demand for universal suffrage as a solution to the problem.

Personal liberty and property rights find their expression in political economy but equality and soldiarity must seek elsewhere. Under the present system each one takes what he can and the devil get the hindmost. Labor, like other commodities, is subject to the basic mistake which political economy makes as to regard the present division of society into patricians and proletarians as an eternal and natural state as fixed and predetermined as the stars in the sky. It should be understood that it is no longer possible to accept the theory of the *contrat social*. As Montesquieu has indicated the character of society should be studied on the basis of existing reality. Already a "left" movement has arisen with a decided social outlook to replace the antiquated judgments of the parliamentarians with sharper and more revealing analyses of the economic facts. Political science, denying real science, can advance no further.

Without the division of labor production would still be at the medieval level; the demoralized worker would be incapable of efficient work. But besides cheap products the use of machinery brings with it overproduction and loss of work. Competition is increasingly superceded by monopolization and taxation becomes a plague which one fears as fire or hell. The bedmate of credit is bankruptcy; property becomes a combine of misuse and oppression; trade is subject to chance and chicanery and corruption rule the roost. In short, the order of the day is disorder. The economists sit comfortably, hands folded over paunches and pontifically assert in reply to each suggestion which may improve the situation that this system of disorder is organised according to natural and immutable law.

It is generally believed that since mythological times to the present fifty-seventh year of the great revolution universal well-being has increased. Christianity claims for itself the chief honor for this progress but at present their claim is contested by the economists who assert, "Christianity could have had little influence on society. Utopian in the beginning it could grow and develop only in so far as it adopted economic categories: work, tenure of property, capital, payment and interest, trade, property, in short, as it accepted the Roman law." Christianity to which the theories of production and consumption were alien is to European civilization what the Masonic Order and the guilds were for the wandering mechanics of the past. It affords a means allowing for mutual assistance and co-operation.

It is not to self-sacrifice and humanity that we must look for social betterment; the happiness of society can be increased only through the organization of work and justice. In order to do full credit to the institution of property I am ready to admit that it has certain favorable aspects. But I must emphasize that these few good points are more than counterbalanced by the host of evils that have followed in the wake of property rights. We are prepared to prove that in our society the growth of misery and oppression for the many keeps pace with the accumulation of wealth and luxury for the few. It has been the function of political economy to explain and justify this. But in justifying misery political economy ceases to have a higher justification for its own existence. The unique service rendered by socialism is that it has succeeded in indicating the bankruptcy of economy.

SELECTIONS FROM *THE STATE*

By *MICHAEL BAKUNIN*

PROPOSALS placed before the Committee of Peace and League of Freedom, Bern, 1867.

We must proclaim:

1. That the only path of freedom, justice, and peace in the international relationships in Europe, the only means of preventing civil war among the various peoples of the European families is the establishment of the United States of Europe.

2. That these states can never be formed from the states as they now exist on account of their great dissimilarities in size and power.

3. That the example of the present German Confederation preemptorily proves that a federation of monarchies is an irony as it is powerless to guarantee peace and freedom to its subjects.

4. That no centralized, bureaucratic and therefore militaristic state, even though it calls itself a republic, can enter sincerely and earnestly upon an international confederation. Its constitution, which means negation of internal freedom, would of necessity be a permanent declaration of war. It would be a threat at the existence of neighboring counties. Such a state is formed primarily upon an act of violence, of conquest, or of theft, blessed by all forms of religion and consecrated by custom. Upon this divine consecration of triumphant force the centralized state stands as the negation of the rights of all other states, which it recognizes only from political interest.

5. That all the participants of the League must therefore seek to change the lands to which they belong in order to replace the old organization founded upon force and the principles of authority into a new organization whose only

foundations are the interests, needs, and natural power of attraction of those nations whose principles are the free federation of the individual into the community, of the community into the province, of the province into the nation, and finally of the nation into the United States of Europe and of the whole world.

6. Consequently there must be an absolute rejection of all that is called the historical right of the states; all questions concerning natural, political, strategic, commercial boundaries must from now on be viewed as belonging to the history of the past, and must be rejected with energy by all the participants of the league.

7. Recognition of the absolute right of the complete autonomy of each large or small nation, each weak or strong people, each province and community provided that its internal constitution is not a threat and danger for the autonomy and freedom of neighboring countries.

8. The fact that a country has once entered the League does not force upon it the obligation always to remain a member. Human justice, the only authority we recognize, cannot accept eternal obligations; and we shall never recognize other rights and duties than those founded upon liberty. The right of voluntary union and the right of voluntary separation are the most important of all political rights. Without these fundamental rights our confederation would be merely a mask for a centralized state.

9. All this proves that the league must cast aside the alliance of any national fraction of European democracy with the monarchical states even though it should have as its aim the rewinning of the independence or liberty of a suppressed country, since such an alliance could only lead to deception and would be a betrayal of the Revolution.

10. For this reason, the League must fight against nationalistic instincts, and must support each insurrection based on our principles and the political and economic interests of the masses.

11. The League will fight to the utmost everything that

may be called the renown, greatness, and power of the states. For all those false and harmful idols for whom millions of human beings were sacrificed, we shall substitute the glory of the human spirit as it manifests itself in science and the glory of a common well-being founded upon work, justice, and freedom.

12. The League will recognize nationality as a natural fact possessing the right of existence and development. But the League will not recognize nationality as a principle. The so-called Principle of Nationalism proclaimed recently by French, Russian, Prussian, and even by German, Polish, Italian, and Hungarian patriots is only a means of diversion set up by reaction to offset the growing spirit of Revolution. It is eminently aristocratic, despising the dialects of uncultured people, and denying real autonomy to national groups. This "nationality" is nowhere supported by the masses of the people whose real interest is constantly sacrificed for a so-called public weal, which signifies only the weal of the privileged classes.

13. Unity is the goal toward which humanity unresistingly strives. But unity becomes a menace destroying reason, dignity, and well-being if it is achieved through the authority of a theological, metaphysical, political, or even economic idea. A unity so achieved is harmful to the real interests of the people it seeks to elevate and serve. Such a unity is a friend of reaction and an enemy of revolution. The League can recognize only one unity; it is a unity which grows freely through the development of autonomous parts into a whole which is not the negation of the special rights and interests of a part, is not the burial place of each local prosperity, but which is, on the contrary, the confirmation and source of all these autonomies. The League will therefore attack each religious, political, economic, and social organization which is not completely permeated with this great principle of freedom. Without this principle of freedom there is no intelligence, no justice, no well-being, no humanity ...

NATURAL SELECTION; OR THE SURVIVAL OF THE FITTEST*

By CHARLES DARWIN

Natural Selection—its power compared with man's selection—its power
on characters of trifling importance—its power at all ages and on
both sexes—Sexual Selection—On the generality of intercrosses between individuals of the same species—Circumstances favourable and
unfavourable to the results of Natural Selection, namely, intercrossing,
isolation, number of individuals—Slow action—Extinction caused by
Natural Selection—Divergence of Character, related to the diversity
of inhabitants of any small area, and to naturalisation—Action of
Natural Selection, through Divergence of Character, and Extinction,
on the descendants from a common parent—Explains the grouping of
all organic beings—Advance in organisation—Low forms preserved—
Convergence of character—Indefinite multiplication of species—Summary.

How will the struggle for existence act in regard to variation? Can the principle of selection, which we have seen is
so potent in the hands of man, apply under nature? I think
we shall see that it can act most efficiently. Let the endless
number of slight variations and individual differences occurring in our domestic productions, and, in a lesser degree,
in those under nature, be borne in mind; as well as the
strength of the hereditary tendency. Under domestication, it
may be truly said that the whole organisation becomes in
some degree plastic. But the variability, which we almost
universally meet with in our domestic productions, is not
directly produced, as Hooker and Asa Gray have well remarked, by man; he can neither originate varieties, nor
prevent their occurrence; he can only preserve and accumulate such as do occur. Unintentionally he exposes organic
beings to new and changing conditions of life, and variability ensues; but similar changes of conditions might and do

* From *The Origin of Species*

occur under nature. Let it also be borne in mind how infinitely complex and close-fitting are the mutual relations of all organic beings to each other and to their physical conditions of life; and consequently what infinitely varied diversities of structure might be of use to each being under changing conditions of life. Can it, then, be thought improbable, seeing that variations useful to man have undoubtedly occurred, that other variations useful in some way to each being in the great and complex battle of life should occur in the course of many successive generations? If such do occur, can we doubt (remembering that many more individuals are born than can possibly survive) that individuals having any advantage, however slight, over others, would have the best chance of surviving and of procreating their kind? On the other hand, we may feel sure that any variation in the least degree injurious would be rigidly destroyed. This preservation of favourable individual differences and variations, and the destruction of those which are injurious, I have called Natural Selection, or the Survival of the Fittest. Variations neither useful nor injurious would not be affected by natural selection, and would be left either a fluctuating element, as perhaps we see in certain polymorphic species, or would ultimately become fixed, owing to the nature of the organism and the nature of the conditions.

Several writers have misapprehended or objected to the term Natural Selection. Some have even imagined that natural selection induces variability, whereas it implies only the preservation of such variations as arise and are beneficial to the being under its conditions of life. No one objects to agriculturists speaking of the potent effects of man's selection; and in this case the individual differences given by nature, which man for some object selects, must of necessity first occur. Others have objected that the term selection implies conscious choice in the animals which become modified; and it has even been urged that, as plants have no volition, natural selection is not applicable to them! In the literal sense of the word, no doubt, natural selection is a false term; but who ever objected to chemists speaking of the elective affinities of the various elements?—and yet an acid cannot strictly be said to elect the base with which it in preference combines. It has been said that I speak of natural selection as an active power or Deity; but who objects to an author speaking of the attraction of gravity as ruling the movements of the planets? Everyone knows what is meant and is implied by such metaphorical expressions; and they are almost necessary for brevity. So again it is difficult to avoid personifying the word Nature; but I mean by Nature, only the aggregate action and product of many natural laws, and by laws the sequence of events as ascertained by us. With a little familiarity such superficial objections will be forgotten.

We shall best understand the probable course of natural selection by taking the case of a country undergoing some slight physical change, for instance, of climate. The proportional numbers of its inhabitants will almost immediately undergo a change, and some species will probably become extinct. We may conclude, from what we have seen of the intimate and complex manner in which the inhabitants of each country are bound together, that any change in the numerical proportions of the inhabitants, independently of the change of climate itself, would seriously affect the others. If the country were open on its borders, new forms would certainly immigrate, and this would likewise seriously disturb the relations of some of the former inhabitants. Let it be remembered how powerful the influence of a single introduced tree or mammal has been shown to be. But in the case of an island, or of a country partly surrounded by barriers, into which new and better adapted forms could not freely enter, we should then have places in the economy of nature which would assuredly be better filled up, if some of the original inhabitants were in some manner modified; for, had the area been open to immigration, these same places would have been seized on by intruders. In such cases, slight modifications, which in any way favoured the individuals of any species, by better adapting them to their altered conditions, would tend to be preserved; and natural selection would have free scope for the work of improvement.

We have good reason to believe that changes in the conditions of life give a tendency to increased variability; and in the foregoing cases the conditions have changed, and this would manifestly be favourable to natural selection, by affording a better chance of the occurrence of profitable variations. Unless such occur, natural selection can do nothing. Under the term of "variations," it must never be forgotten that mere individual differences are included. As man can produce a great result with his domestic animals and plants by adding up in any given direction individual differences, so could natural selection, but far more easily, from having incomparably longer time for action. Nor do I believe that any great physical change, as of climate, or any unusual degree of isolation to check immigration, is necessary in order that new and unoccupied places should be left, for natural selection to fill up by improving some of the varying inhabitants. For as all the inhabitants of each country are struggling together with nicely balanced forces, extremely slight modifications in the structure or habits of one species would often give it an advantage over others; and still further modifications of the same kind would often still further increase the advantage, as long as the species continued under the same conditions of life and profited by similar means of subsistence and defence. No country can be named in which all the native inhabitants are now so perfectly adapted to each other and to the physical conditions under which they live, that none of them could be still better adapted or improved; for in all countries the natives have been so far conquered by naturalised productions, that they have allowed some foreigners to take firm possession of the land. And as foreigners have thus in every country beaten some of the natives, we may safely conclude that the natives might have been modified with advantage, so as to have better resisted the intruders.

As man can produce, and certainly has produced, a great result by his methodical and unconscious means of selection, what may not natural selection effect? Man can act only on external and visible characters: Nature, if I may be allowed to personify the natural preservation or survival of the fittest, cares nothing for appearances, except in so far as they are useful to any being. She can act on every internal organ, on every shade of constitutional difference, on the whole machinery of life. Man selects only for his own good: Nature only for that of the being which she tends. Every selected character is fully exercised by her, as is implied by the fact of their selection. Man keeps the natives of many climates in the same country; he seldom exercises each selected character in some peculiar and fitting manner; he feeds a long- and a short-beaked pigeon on the same food; he does not exercise a long-backed or long-legged quadruped in any peculiar manner; he exposes sheep with long and short wool to the same climate. He does not allow the most vigorous males to struggle for the females. He does not rigidly destroy all inferior animals, but protects during each varying season, as far as lies in his power, all his productions. He often begins his selection by some half-monstrous form; or at least by some modification prominent enough to catch the eye or to be plainly useful to him. Under nature, the slightest differences of structure or constitution may well turn the nicely balanced scale in the struggle for life, and so be preserved. How fleeting are the wishes and efforts of man! how short his time! and consequently how poor will be his results, compared with those accumulated by Nature during whole geological periods! Can we wonder, then, that Nature's productions should be far "truer" in character than man's productions; that they should be infinitely better adapted to the most complex conditions of life, and should plainly bear the stamp of far higher workmanship?

It may metaphorically be said that natural selection is daily and hourly scrutinising, throughout the world, the slightest variations; rejecting those that are bad, preserving and adding up all that are good; silently and insensibly working, *whenever and wherever opportunity offers,* at the improvement of each organic being in relation to its organic and inorganic conditions of life. We see nothing of these slow changes in progress, until the hand of time has marked the lapse of ages, and then so imperfect is our view into long-past geological ages, that we see only that the forms of life are now different from what they formerly were.

In order that any great amount of modification should be effected in a species, a variety when once formed must again, perhaps after a long interval of time, vary or present individual differences of the same favourable nature as before; and these must be again preserved, and so onwards step by step. Seeing that individual differences of the same kind perpetually recur, this can hardly be considered as an unwarrantable assumption. But whether it is true, we can judge only by seeing how far the hypothesis accords with and explains the general phenomena of nature. On the other hand, the ordinary belief that the amount of possible variation is a strictly limited quantity is likewise a simple assumption.

Although natural selection can act only through and for the good of each being, yet characters and structures, which we are apt to consider as of very trifling importance, may thus be acted on. When we see leaf-eating insects green, and bark-feeders mottled-grey; the alpine ptarmigan white in winter, the red grouse the colour of heather, we must believe that these tints are of service to these birds and insects in preserving them from danger. Grouse, if not destroyed at some period of their lives, would increase in countless numbers; they are known to suffer largely from birds of prey; and hawks are guided by eyesight to their prey—so much so, that on parts of the Continent persons are warned not to keep white pigeons, as being the most liable to destruction. Hence natural selection might be effective in giving the proper colour to each kind of grouse, and in keeping that colour, when once acquired, true and constant. Nor ought we to think that the occasional destruction of an animal of any particular colour would produce little effect: we should remember how essential it is in a flock of white sheep to destroy a lamb with the faintest trace of black. We have seen how the colour of the hogs, which feed on the "paint-root" in Virginia, determines whether they shall live or die. In plants, the down on the fruit and the colour of the flesh are considered by botanists as characters of the most trifling importance: yet we hear from an excellent horticulturist, Downing, that in the United States smooth-skinned fruits suffer far more from a beetle, a *Curculio,* than those with down; that purple plums suffer far more from a certain disease than yellow plums; whereas another disease attacks yellow-fleshed peaches far more than those with other coloured flesh. If, with all the aids of art, these slight differences make a great difference in cultivating the several varieties, assuredly, in a state of nature, where the trees would have to struggle with other trees and with a host of enemies, such differences would effectually settle which variety, whether a smooth or downy, a yellow or purple fleshed fruit, should succeed.

In looking at many small points of difference between species, which, as far as our ignorance permits us to judge, seem quite unimportant, we must not forget that climate, food, etc., have no doubt produced some direct effect. It is also necessary to bear in mind that, owing to the law of correlation, when one part varies, and the variations are accumulated through natural selection, other modifications, often of the most unexpected nature, will ensue.

As we see that those variations which, under domestication, appear at any particular period of life, tend to reappear in the offspring at the same period;—for instance, in the shape, size, and flavour of the seeds of the many varieties of our culinary and agricultural plants; in the caterpillar and cocoon stages of the varieties of the silkworm; in the eggs of poultry, and in the colour of the down of their chickens; in the horns of our sheep and cattle when nearly adult;—so in a state of nature, natural selection will be enabled to act on and modify organic beings at any age, by the accumulation of variations profitable at that age, and by their inheritance at a corresponding age. If it profit a plant to have its seeds more and more widely disseminated by the wind, I can see no greater difficulty in this being effected through natural selection, than in the cotton-planter increasing and improving by selection the down in the pods on his cottontrees. Natural selection may modify and adapt the larva of an insect to a score of contingencies, wholly different from those which concern the mature insect; and these modifications may affect, through correlation, the structure of the adult. So, conversely, modifications in the adult may affect the structure of the larva; but in all cases natural selection will ensure that they shall not be injurious: for if they were so, the species would become extinct.

Natural selection will modify the structure of the young in relation to the parent, and of the parent in relation to the young. In social animals it will adapt the structure of each individual for the benefit of the whole community, if the community profits by the selected change. What natural selection cannot do, is to modify the structure of one species, without giving it any advantage, for the good of another species; and though statements to this effect may be found in works of natural history, I cannot find one case which will bear investigation. A structure used only once in an animal's life, if of high importance to it, might be modified to any extent by natural selection; for instance, the great jaws possessed by certain insects, used exclusively for opening the cocoon,—or the hard tip to the beak of unhatched birds, used for breaking the egg. It has been asserted, that of the best short-beaked tumbler-pigeons a greater number perish in the egg than are able to get out of it; so that fanciers assist in the act of hatching. Now if nature had to make the beak of a full-grown pigeon very short for the bird's own advantage, the process of modification would be very slow, and there would be simultaneously the most rigorous selection of all the young birds within the egg, which had the most power ful and hardest beaks, for all with weak beaks would in·

evitably perish; or, more delicate and more easily broken shells might be selected, the thickness of the shell being known to vary like every other structure.

It may be well here to remark that with all beings there must be much fortuitous destruction, which can have little or no influence on the course of natural selection. For instance a vast number of eggs or seeds are annually devoured, and these could be modified through natural selection only if they varied in some manner which protected them from their enemies. Yet many of these eggs or seeds would perhaps, if not destroyed, have yielded individuals better adapted to their conditions of life than any of those which happened to survive. So again a vast number of mature animals and plants, whether or not they be the best adapted to their conditions, must be annually destroyed by accidental causes, which would not be in the least degree mitigated by certain changes of structure or constitution which would in other ways be beneficial to the species. But let the destruction of the adults be ever so heavy, if the number which can exist in any district be not wholly kept down by such causes,—or again let the destruction of eggs or seeds be so great that only a hundredth or a thousandth part are developed,—yet of those which do survive, the best adapted individuals, supposing that there is any variability in a favourable direction, will tend to propagate their kind in larger numbers than the less well adapted. If the numbers be wholly kept down by the causes just indicated, as will often have been the case, natural selection will be powerless in certain beneficial directions; but this is no valid objection to its efficiency at other times and in other ways; for we are far from having any reason to suppose that many species ever undergo modification and improvement at the same time in the same area.

SEXUAL SELECTION

Inasmuch as peculiarities often appear under domestication in one sex and become hereditarily attached to that sex, so no doubt it will be under nature. Thus it is rendered possible for the two sexes to be modified through natural selection in relation to different habits of life, as is sometimes the case; or for one sex to be modified in relation to the other sex, as commonly occurs. This leads me to say a few words on what I have called Sexual Selection. This form of selection depends, not on a struggle for existence in relation to other organic beings or to external conditions, but on a struggle between the individuals of one sex, generally the males, for the possession of the other sex. The result is not death to the unsuccessful competitor, but few or no offspring. Sexual selection is, therefore, less rigorous than natural selection. Generally, the most vigorous males, those which are best fitted for their places in nature, will leave most progeny. But in many cases, victory depends not so much on general vigour, as on having special weapons, confined to the male sex. A hornless stag or spurless cock would have a poor chance of leaving numerous offspring. Sexual selection, by always allowing the victor to breed, might surely give indomitable courage, length to the spur, and strength to the wing to strike with the spurred leg, in nearly the same manner as does the brutal cock-fighter by the careful selection of his best cocks. How low in the scale of nature the law of battle descends, I know not; male alligators have been described as fighting, bellowing, and whirling round, like Indians in a war-dance, for the possession of the females; male salmons have been observed fighting all day long; male stag-beetles sometimes bear wounds from the huge mandibles of other males; the males of certain hymenopterous insects have been frequently seen by that inimitable observer, M. Fabre, fighting for a particular female who sits by, an apparently unconcerned beholder of the struggle, and then retires with the conqueror. The war is, perhaps, severest between the males of polygamous animals, and these seem oftenest provided with special weapons. The males of carnivorous animals are already well armed; though to them and to others, special means of defence may be given through means of sexual selection, as the mane to the lion, and the hooked jaw to the male salmon; for the shield may be as important for victory as the sword or spear.

Amongst birds, the contest is often of a more peaceful character. All those who have attended to the subject, believe that there is the severest rivalry between the males of many species to attract, by singing, the females. The rock-thrush of Guiana, birds of paradise, and some others, congregate; and successive males display with the most elaborate care, and show off in the best manner, their gorgeous plumage; they likewise perform strange antics before the females, which, standing by as spectators, at last choose the most attractive partner. Those who have closely attended to birds in confinement well know that they often take individual preferences and dislikes: thus Sir R. Heron has described how a pied peacock was eminently attractive to all his hen birds. I cannot here enter on the necessary details; but if man can in a short time give beauty and an elegant carriage to his bantams, according to his standard of beauty, I can see no good reason to doubt that female birds, by selecting, during thousands of generations, the most melodious or beautiful males, according to their standard of beauty, might produce a marked effect. Some well-known laws, with respect to the plumage of male and female birds, in comparison with the plumage of the young, can partly be explained through the action of sexual selection on variations occurring at different ages, and transmitted to the males alone or to both sexes at corresponding ages; but I have not space here to enter on this subject.

Thus it is, as I believe, that when the males and females of any animal have the same general habits of life, but differ in structure, colour, or ornament, such differences have been mainly caused by sexual selection: that is, by individual males having had, in successive generations, some slight advantage over other males, in their weapons, means of defence, or charms, which they have transmitted to their male offspring alone. Yet, I would not wish to attribute all sexual differences to this agency: for we see in our domestic animals peculiarities arising and becoming attached to the male sex, which apparently have not been augmented through selection by man. The tuft of hair on the breast of the wild turkey-cock cannot be of any use, and it is doubtful whether it can be ornamental in the eyes of the female bird; —indeed, had the tuft appeared under domestication, it would have been called a monstrosity.

ILLUSTRATIONS OF THE ACTION OF NATURAL SELECTION, OR THE
SURVIVAL OF THE FITTEST

In order to make it clear how, as I believe, natural selection acts, I must beg permission to give one or two imaginary illustrations. Let us take the case of a wolf, which preys on various animals, securing some by craft, some by strength, and some by fleetness; and let us suppose that the fleetest prey, a deer for instance, had from any change in the country increased in numbers, or that other prey had decreased in numbers, during that season of the year when the wolf was hardest pressed for food. Under such circumstances the swiftest and slimmest wolves would have the best chance of surviving, and so be preserved or selected,—provided always that they retained strength to master their prey at this or some other period of the year, when they were compelled to prey on other animals. I can see no more reason to doubt that this would be the result, than that man should be able to improve the fleetness of his greyhounds by careful and methodical selection, or by that kind of unconscious selection which follows from each man trying to keep the best dogs without any thought of modifying the breed. I may add, that, according to Mr. Pierce, there are two varieties of the wolf inhabiting the Catskill Mountains in the United States, one with a light greyhound-like form, which pursues deer, and the other more bulky, with shorter legs, which more frequently attacks the shepherd's flocks.

It should be observed that, in the above illustration, I speak of the slimmest individual wolves, and not of any single strongly marked variation having been preserved. In former editions of this work I sometimes spoke as if this latter alternative had frequently occurred. I saw the great importance of individual differences, and this led me fully to discuss the results of unconscious selection by man, which depends on the preservation of all the more or less valuable individuals, and on the destruction of the worst. I saw, also, that the preservation in a state of nature of any occasional deviation of structure, such as a monstrosity, would be a rare event; and that, if at first preserved, it would generally be lost by subsequent intercrossing with ordinary individuals. Nevertheless, until reading an able and valuable article in the *North British Review* (1867), I did not appreciate how rarely single variations, whether slight or strongly marked, could be perpetuated. The author takes the case of a pair of animals, producing during their lifetime two hundred offspring, of which, from various causes of destruction, only two on an average survive to procreate their kind. This is rather an extreme estimate for most of the higher animals, but by no means so for many of the lower organisms. He then shows that if a single individual were born, which varied in some manner, giving it twice as good a chance of life as that of the other individuals, yet the chances would be strongly against its survival. Supposing it to survive and to breed, and that half its young inherited the favourable variation; still, as the Reviewer goes on to show, the young would have only a slightly better chance of surviving and breeding; and this chance would go on decreasing in the succeeding generations. The justice of these remarks cannot, I think, be disputed. If, for instance, a bird of some kind could procure its food more easily by having its beak curved, and if one were born with its beak strongly curved, and which consequently flourished, nevertheless there would be a very poor chance of this one individual perpetuating its kind to the exclusion of the common form; but there can hardly be a doubt, judging by what we see taking place under domestication, that this result would follow from the preservation during many generations of a large number of individuals with more or less strongly curved beaks, and from the destruction of a still larger number with the straightest beaks.

It should not, however, be overlooked that certain rather strongly marked variations, which no one would rank as mere individual differences, frequently recur owing to a similar organisation being similarly acted on,—of which fact numerous instances could be given with our domestic productions. In such cases, if the varying individual did not actually transmit to its offspring its newly acquired character, it would undoubtedly transmit to them, as long as the existing conditions remained the same, a still stronger tendency to vary in the same manner. There can also be little doubt that the tendency to vary in the same manner has often been so strong that all the individuals of the same species have been similarly modified without the aid of any form of selection. Or only a third, fifth, or tenth part of the individuals may have been thus affected, of which fact several instances could be given. Thus Graba estimates that about one-fifth of the guillemots in the Faroe Islands consist of a variety so well marked, that it was formerly ranked as a distinct species under the name of *Uria lacrymans*. In cases of this kind, if the variation were of a beneficial nature, the original form would soon be supplanted by the modified form, through the survival of the fittest.

To the effects of intercrossing in eliminating variations of all kinds, I shall have to recur; but it may be here remarked that most animals and plants keep to their proper homes, and do not needlessly wander about; we see this even with migratory birds, which almost always return to the same spot. Consequently each newly formed variety would generally be at first local, as seems to be the common rule with varieties in a state of nature; so that similarly modified individuals would soon exist in a small body together, and would often breed together. If the new variety were successful in its battle for life, it would slowly spread from a central district, competing with and conquering the unchanged individuals on the margins of an ever-increasing circle.

It may be worth while to give another and more complex illustration of the action of natural selection. Certain plants excrete sweet juice, apparently for the sake of eliminating something injurious from the sap: this is effected, for instance, by glands at the base of the stipules in some Leguminosæ, and at the backs of the leaves of the common laurel. This juice, though small in quantity, is greedily sought by insects; but their visits do not in any way benefit the plant. Now, let us suppose that the juice or nectar was excreted from the inside of the flowers of a certain number of plants of any species. Insects in seeking the nectar would get dusted with pollen, and would often transport it from one flower to another. The flowers of two distinct individuals of the same species would thus get crossed; and the act of crossing, as can be fully proved, gives rise to vigorous seedlings, which consequently would have the best chance of flourishing and surviving. The plants which produced flowers with the largest glands or nectaries, excreting most nectar, would oftenest be visited by insects, and would oftenest be crossed; and so in the long-run would gain the upper hand and form a local variety. The flowers, also, which had their stamens and pistils placed in relation to the size and habits of the particular insect which visited them, so as to favour in any degree the transportal of the pollen, would likewise be favoured. We might have taken the case of insects visiting flowers for the sake of collecting pollen instead of nectar; and as pollen is formed for the sole purpose of fertilisation, its destruction appears to be a simple loss to the plant; yet if a little pollen were carried, at first occasionally and then habitually, by the pollen-devouring insects from flower to flower, and a cross thus effected, although ninetenths of the pollen were destroyed, it might still be a great gain to the plant to be thus robbed; and the individuals which produced more and more pollen, and had larger anthers, would be selected.

When our plant, by the above process long continued, had been rendered highly attractive to insects, they would, unintentionally on their part, regularly carry pollen from flower to flower; and that they do this effectually, I could easily show by many striking facts. I will give only one, as likewise illustrating one step in the separation of the sexes of plants. Some holly-trees bear only male flowers, which have four stamens producing a rather small quantity of pollen, and a rudimentary pistil; other holly-trees bear only female flowers; these have a full-sized pistil, and four stamens with shrivelled anthers, in which not a grain of pollen can be detected. Having found a female tree exactly sixty yards from a male tree, I put the stigmas of twenty flowers, taken from different branches, under the microscope, and on all, without exception, there were a few pollen-grains, and on some a profusion. As the wind had set for several days from the female to the male tree, the pollen could not thus have been carried. The weather had been cold and boisterous, and therefore not favourable to bees, nevertheless every female flower which I examined had been effectually fertilised by the bees, which had flown from tree to tree in search of nectar. But to return to our imaginary case: as soon as the plant had been rendered so highly attractive to insects that pollen was regularly carried from flower to flower, another process might commence. No naturalist doubts the advantage of what has been called the "physiological division of labour"; hence we may believe that it would be advantageous to a plant to produce stamens alone in one flower or on one whole plant, and pistils alone in another flower or on another plant. In plants under culture and placed under new conditions of life, sometimes the male organs and sometimes the female organs become more or less impotent; now if we suppose this to occur in ever so slight a degree under nature, then, as pollen is already carried regularly from flower to flower, and as a more complete separation of the sexes of our plant would be advantageous on the principle of the division of labour, individuals with this tendency more and more increased would be continually favoured or selected, until at last a complete separation of the sexes might be effected. It would take up too much space to show the various steps, through dimorphism and other means, by which the separation of the sexes in plants of various kinds is apparently now in progress; but I may add that some of the species of holly in North America are, according to Asa Gray, in an exactly intermediate condition, or, as he expresses it, are more or less diœciously polygamous.

Let us now turn to the nectar-feeding insects; we may suppose the plant, of which we have been slowly increasing the nectar by continued selection, to be a common plant; and that certain insects depended in main part on its nectar for food. I could give many facts showing how anxious bees are to save time: for instance, their habit of cutting holes and sucking the nectar at the bases of certain flowers, which, with a very little more trouble, they can enter by the mouth. Bearing such facts in mind, it may be believed that under certain circumstances individual differences in the curvature or length of the proboscis, etc., too slight to be appreciated by us, might profit a bee or other insect, so that certain individuals would be able to obtain their food more quickly than others; and thus the communities to which they belonged would flourish and throw off many swarms inheriting the same peculiarities. The tubes of the corolla of the common red and incarnate clovers (*Trifolium pratense* and *incarnatum*) do not on a hasty glance appear to differ in length; yet the hive-bee can easily suck the nectar out of the incarnate clover, but not out of the common red clover, which is visited by humble-bees alone; so that whole fields of the red clover offer in vain an abundant supply of precious nectar to the hive-bee. That this nectar is much liked by the hive-bee is certain; for I have repeatedly seen, but only in the autumn, many hive-bees sucking the flowers through holes bitten in the base of the tube by humble-bees. The difference in the length of the corolla in the two kinds of clover, which determines the visits of the hive-bee, must be very trifling; for

I have been assured that when red clover has been mown, the flowers of the second crop are somewhat smaller, and that these are visited by many hive-bees. I do not know whether this statement is accurate; nor whether another published statement can be trusted, namely, that the Ligurian bee, which is generally considered a mere variety of the common hive-bee, and which freely crosses with it, is able to reach and suck the nectar of the red clover. Thus, in a country where this kind of clover abounded, it might be a great advantage to the hive-bee to have a slightly longer or differently constructed proboscis. On the other hand, as the fertility of this clover absolutely depends on bees visiting the flowers, if humble-bees were to become rare in any country, it might be a great advantage to the plant to have a shorter or more deeply divided corolla, so that the hive-bees should be enabled to suck its flowers. Thus I can understand how a flower and a bee might slowly become, either simultaneously or one after the other, modified and adapted to each other in the most perfect manner, by the continued preservation of all the individuals which presented slight deviations of structure mutually favourable to each other.

I am well aware that this doctrine of natural selection, exemplified in the above imaginary instances, is open to the same objections which were first urged against Sir Charles Lyell's noble views on "the modern changes of the earth, as illustrative of geology"; but we now seldom hear the agencies which we see still at work, spoken of as trifling or insignificant, when used in explaining the excavation of the deepest valleys or the formation of long lines of inland cliffs. Natural selection acts only by the preservation and accumulation of small inherited modifications, each profitable to the preserved being; and as modern geology has almost banished such views as the excavation of a great valley by a single diluvial wave, so will natural selection banish the belief of the continued creation of new organic beings, or of any great and sudden modification in their structure.

EXTINCTION CAUSED BY NATURAL SELECTION

This subject will be more fully discussed in our chapter on Geology; but it must here be alluded to from being intimately connected with natural selection. Natural selection acts solely through the preservation of variations in some way advantageous, which consequently endure. Owing to the high geometrical rate of increase of all organic beings, each area is already fully stocked with inhabitants; and it follows from this, that as the favoured forms increase in number, so, generally, will the less favoured decrease and become rare. Rarity, as geology tells us, is the precursor to extinction. We can see that any form which is represented by few individuals will run a good chance of utter extinction, during great fluctuations in the nature of the seasons, or from a temporary increase in the number of its enemies. But we may go farther than this; for, as new forms are produced, unless we admit that specific forms can go on indefinitely increasing in number, many old forms must become extinct. That the number of specific forms has not indefinitely increased, geology plainly tells us; and we shall presently attempt to show why it is that the number of species throughout the world has not become immeasurably great.

We have seen that the species which are most numerous in individuals have the best chance of producing favourable variations within any given period. We have evidence of this in the facts stated in the second chapter, showing that it is the common and diffused or dominant species which offer the greatest number of recorded varieties. Hence, rare species will be less quickly modified or improved within any given period; they will consequently be beaten in the race for life by the modified and improved descendants of the commoner species.

From these several considerations I think it inevitably follows, that as new species in the course of time are formed through natural selection, others will become rarer and rarer, and finally extinct. The forms which stand in closest competition with those undergoing modification and improvement, will naturally suffer most. And we have seen in the chapter on the Struggle for Existence that it is the most closely allied forms,—varieties of the same species, and species of the same genus or of related genera,—which, from having nearly the same structure, constitution, and habits, generally come into the severest competition with each other; consequently, each new variety or species, during the progress of its formation, will generally press hardest on its nearest kindred, and tend to exterminate them. We see the same process of extermination amongst our domesticated productions, through the selection of improved forms by man. Many curious instances could be given showing how quickly new breeds of cattle, sheep, and other animals, and varieties of flowers, take the place of older and inferior kinds. In Yorkshire, it is historically known that the ancient black cattle were displaced by the long-horns, and that these "were swept away by the short-horns" (I quote the words of an agricultural writer) "as if by some murderous pestilence."

SUMMARY

If under changing conditions of life organic beings present individual differences in almost every part of their structure, and this cannot be disputed; if there be, owing to their geometrical rate of increase, a severe struggle for life at some age, season, or year, and this certainly cannot be disputed; then, considering the infinite complexity of the relations of all organic beings to each other and to their conditions of life, causing an infinite diversity in structure, constitution, and habits, to be advantageous to them, it would be a most extraordinary fact if no variations had ever occurred useful to each being's own welfare, in the same manner as so many variations have occurred useful to man. But if variations useful to any organic being ever do occur, assuredly individuals thus characterised will have the best chance of being preserved in the struggle for life; and from the strong principle of inheritance, these will tend to produce offspring similarly characterised. This principle of preservation, or the survival of the fittest, I have called Natural Selection. It leads to the improvement of each creature in relation to its organic and inorganic conditions of life; and consequently, in most cases, to what must be regarded as an advance in organisation. Nevertheless, low and simple forms will long endure if well fitted for their simple conditions of life.

Natural selection, on the principle of qualities being inherited at corresponding ages, can modify the egg, seed, or young, as easily as the adult. Amongst many animals, sexual selection will have given its aid to ordinary selection, by assuring to the most vigorous and best adapted males the greatest number of offspring. Sexual selection will also give characters useful to the males alone, in their struggles or rivalry with other males; and these characters will be transmitted to one sex or to both sexes, according to the form of inheritance which prevails.

Whether natural selection has really thus acted in adapting the various forms of life to their several conditions and stations, must be judged by the general tenor and balance of evidence given in the following chapters. But we have already seen how it entails extinction; and how largely extinction has acted in the world's history, geology plainly declares. Natural selection, also, leads to divergence of character; for the more organic beings diverge in structure, habits, and constitution, by so much the more can a large number be supported on the same area,—of which we see proof by looking to the inhabitants of any small spot, and to the productions naturalised in foreign lands. Therefore, during the modification of the descendants of any one species, and during the incessant struggle of all species to increase in numbers, the more diversified the descendants become, the better will be their chance of success in the battle for life. Thus the small differences distinguishing varieties of the same species steadily tend to increase, till they equal the greater differences between species of the same genus, or even of distinct genera.

We have seen that it is the common, the widely diffused, and widely ranging species, belonging to the larger genera within each class, which vary most; and these tend to transmit to their modified offspring that superiority which now makes them dominant in their own countries. Natural selection, as has just been remarked, leads to divergence of character and to much extinction of the less improved and intermediate forms of life. On these principles, the nature of the affinities, and the generally well-defined distinctions between the innumerable organic beings in each class throughout the world, may be explained. It is a truly wonderful fact—the wonder of which we are apt to overlook from familiarity—that all animals and all plants throughout all time and space should be related to each other in groups subordinate to groups, in the manner which we everywhere behold—namely, varieties of the same species most closely related, species of the same genus less closely and unequally related, forming sections and sub-genera, species of distinct genera much less closely related, and genera related in different degrees, forming sub-families, families, orders, sub-classes, and classes. The several subordinate groups in any class cannot be ranked in a single file, but seem clustered round points, and these round other points, and so on in almost endless cycles. If species had been independently created, no explanation would have been possible of this kind of classification; but it is explained through inheritance and the complex action of natural selection, entailing extinction and divergence of character, as we have seen illustrated in the diagram.

The affinities of all the beings of the same class have sometimes been represented by a great tree. I believe this simile largely speaks the truth. The green and budding twigs may represent existing species; and those produced during former years may represent the long succession of extinct species. At each period of growth all the growing twigs have tried to branch out on all sides, and to overtop and kill the surrounding twigs and branches, in the same manner as species and groups of species have at all times overmastered other species in the great battle for life. The limbs divided into great branches, and these into lesser and lesser branches, were themselves once, when the tree was young, budding twigs; and this connection of the former and present buds by ramifying branches may well represent the classification of all extinct and living species in groups subordinate to groups. Of the many twigs which flourished when the tree was a mere bush, only two or three, now grown into great branches, yet survive and bear the other branches; so with the species which lived during long-past geological periods, very few have left living and modified descendants. From the first growth of the tree, many a limb and branch has decayed and dropped off; and these fallen branches of various sizes may represent those whole orders, families, and genera which have now no living representatives, and which are known to us only in a fossil state. As we here and there see a thin straggling branch springing from a fork low down in a tree, and which by some chance has been favoured and is still alive on its summit, so we occasionally see an animal like the Ornithorhynchus or Lepidosiren, which in some small degree connects by its affinities two large branches of life, and which has apparently been saved from fatal competition by having inhabited a protected station. As buds give rise by growth to fresh buds, and these, if vigorous, branch out and overtop on all sides many a feebler branch, so by generation I believe it has been with the great Tree of Life, which fills with its dead and broken branches the crust of the earth, and covers the surface with its ever-branching and beautiful ramifications.

INFLUENCE OF PHYSICAL LAWS*

By HENRY THOMAS BUCKLE

CHAPTER II

INFLUENCE EXERCISED BY PHYSICAL LAWS OVER THE ORGANIZA-
TION OF SOCIETY AND OVER THE CHARACTER OF INDIVIDUALS

IF we inquire what those physical agents are by which the human race is most powerfully influenced, we shall find that they may be classed under four heads: namely, *Climate, Food, Soil, and the General Aspect of Nature;* by which last, I mean those appearances which, though presented chiefly to the sight, have, through the medium of that or other senses, directed the association of ideas, and hence in different countries have given rise to different habits of national thought. To one of these four classes may be referred all the external phenomena by which Man has been permanently affected. The last of these classes, or what I call the General Aspect of Nature, produces its principal results by exciting the imagination, and by suggesting those innumerable superstitions which are the great obstacles to advancing knowledge. And as, in the infancy of a people, the power of such superstitions is supreme, it has happened that the various Aspects of Nature have caused corresponding varieties in the popular character, and have imparted to the national religion peculiarities which, under certain circumstances, it is impossible to efface. The other three agents, namely, Climate, Food, and Soil, have, so far as we are aware, had no direct influence of this sort; but they have, as I am about to prove, originated the most important consequences in regard to the general organization of society, and from them there have followed

* From *History of Civilization in England*

307

many of those large and conspicuous differences between nations, which are often ascribed to some fundamental differences in the various races into which mankind is divided. But while such original distinctions of race are altogether hypothetical, the discrepancies which are caused by difference of climate, food, and soil, are capable of a satisfactory explanation, and, when understood, will be found to clear up many of the difficulties which still obscure the study of history. I purpose, therefore, in the first place, to examine the laws of these three vast agents in so far as they are connected with Man in his social condition; and having traced the working of those laws with as much precision as the present state of physical knowledge will allow, I shall then examine the remaining agent, namely, the General Aspect of Nature, and shall endeavour to point out the most important divergencies to which its variations have, in different countries, naturally given rise.

Beginning, then, with climate, food, and soil, it is evident that these three physical powers are in no small degree dependent on each other: that is to say, there is a very close connection between the climate of a country and the food which will ordinarily be grown in that country; while at the same time the food is itself influenced by the soil which produces it, as also by the elevation or depression of the land, by the state of the atmosphere, and, in a word, by all those conditions to the assemblage of which the name of Physical Geography is, in its largest sense, commonly given.

The union between these physical agents being thus intimate, it seems advisable to consider them not under their own separate heads, but rather under the separate heads of the effects produced by their united action. In this way we shall rise at once to a more comprehensive view of the whole question; we shall avoid the confusion that would be caused by artificially separating phenomena which are in themselves inseparable; and we shall be able to see more clearly the extent of that remarkable influence which, in an early stage of society, the powers of Nature exercise over the fortunes of Man.

Of all the results which are produced among a people by their climate, food, and soil, the accumulation of wealth is the earliest, and in many respects the most important. For although the progress of knowledge eventually accelerates the increase of wealth, it is nevertheless certain that, in the first formation of society, the wealth must accumulate before the knowledge can begin. As long as every man is engaged in collecting the materials necessary for his own subsistence, there will be neither leisure nor taste for higher pursuits; no science can possibly be created, and the utmost that can be effected will be an attempt to economize labour by the contrivance of such rude and imperfect instruments as even the most barbarous people are able to invent.

In a state of society like this, the accumulation of wealth is the first great step that can be taken, because without wealth there can be no leisure, and without leisure there can be no knowledge. If what a people consume is always exactly equal to what they possess, there will be no residue, and therefore, no capital being accumulated, there will be no means by which the unemployed classes may be maintained. But if the produce is greater than the consumption, an overplus arises, which, according to well-known principles, increases itself, and eventually becomes a fund out of which, immediately or remotely, every one is supported who does not create the wealth upon which he lives. And now it is that the existence of an intellectual class first becomes possible, because for the first time there exists a previous accumulation, by means of which men can use what they did not produce, and are thus enabled to devote themselves to subjects for which at an earlier period the pressure of their daily wants would have left them no time.

Thus it is that of all the great social improvements the accumulation of wealth must be the first, because without it there can be neither taste nor leisure for that acquisition of knowledge on which, as I shall hereafter prove, the progress of civilization depends. Now, it is evident that among an entirely ignorant people, the rapidity with which wealth is created will be solely regulated by the physical peculiarities of their country. At a later period, and when the wealth has been capitalized, other causes come into play; but until this occurs, the progress can only depend on two circumstances: first on the energy and regularity with which labour is conducted, and secondly on the returns made to that labour by the bounty of nature. And these two causes are themselves the result of physical antecedents. The returns made to labour are governed by the fertility of the soil, which is itself regulated partly by the admixture of its chemical components, partly by the extent to which, from rivers or from other natural causes, the soil is irrigated, and partly by the heat and humidity of the atmosphere. On the other hand, the energy and regularity with which labour is conducted, will be entirely dependent on the influence of climate. This will display itself in two different ways. The first, which is a very obvious consideration, is, that if the heat is intense, men will be indisposed, and in some degree unfitted, for that active industry which in a milder climate they might willingly have exerted. The other consideration, which has been less noticed, but is equally important, is, that climate influences labour not only by enervating the labourer or by invigorating him, but also by the effect it produces on the regularity of his habits. Thus we find that no people living in a very northern latitude have ever possessed that steady and unflinching industry for which the inhabitants of temperate regions are remarkable. The reason of this becomes clear, when we remember that in the more northern countries the severity of the weather, and, at some seasons, the deficiency of light, render it impossible for the people to continue their usual out-of-door employments. The result is, that the working-classes, being compelled to cease from their ordinary pursuits, are rendered more prone to desultory habits; the chain of their industry is as it were broken, and they lose that impetus which long-continued and uninterrupted practice never fails to give. Hence there arises a national character more fitful and capricious than that possessed by a people whose climate permits the regular exercise of their ordinary industry. Indeed, so powerful is this principle, that we may perceive its operation even under the most opposite circumstances. It would be difficult to conceive a greater difference in government, laws, religion, and manners, than that which distinguishes Sweden and Norway on the one hand, from Spain and Portugal on the other. But these four countries have one great point in common. In all of them, continued agricultural industry is impracticable. In the two southern countries, labour is interrupted by the heat, by the dryness of the weather, and by the consequent state of the soil. In the two northern countries, the same effect is produced by the severity of the winter and the shortness of the days. The consequence is, that these four nations, though so different in other respects, are all remarkable for a certain instability and fickleness of character; presenting a striking contrast to the more regular and settled habits which are established in countries whose climate subjects the working-classes to fewer interruptions, and imposes on them the necessity of a more constant and unremitting employment.

These are the great physical causes by which the creation of wealth is governed. There are, no doubt, other circumstances which operate with considerable force, and which, in a more advanced state of society, possess an equal, and sometimes a superior, influence. But this is at a later period; and looking at the history of wealth in its earliest stage, it will be found to depend entirely on soil regulating the returns made to any given amount of labour; the climate regulating the energy and constancy of the labour itself. It requires but a hasty glance at past events to prove the immense power of these two great physical conditions. *For there is no instance in history of any country being civilized by its own efforts, unless it has possessed one of these conditions in a very favourable form.* In Asia, civilization has always been confined to that vast tract where a rich and alluvial soil has secured to man that wealth without some share of which no intellectual progress can begin. This great region extends, with a few interruptions, from the east of Southern China to the western coasts of Asia Minor, of Phoenicia, and of Palestine. To the north of this immense belt, there is a long line of barren country which has invariably been peopled by rude and wandering tribes, who are kept in poverty by the ungenial nature of the soil, and who, as long as they remained on it, have never emerged from their uncivilized state. How entirely this depends on physical causes, is evident from the fact that these same Mongolian and Tartarian hordes have, at different periods, founded great monarchies in China, in India, and in Persia, and have, on all such occasions, attained a civilization nowise inferior to that possessed by the most flourishing of the ancient kingdoms. For in the fertile plains of Southern Asia, nature has supplied all the materials of wealth; and there it was that these barbarous tribes acquired for the first time some degree of refinement, produced a national literature, and organized a national polity; none of which things they, in their native land, had been able to effect. In the same way, the Arabs in their own country have, owing to the extreme aridity of their soil, always been a rude and uncultivated people; for in their case, as in all others, great ignorance is the fruit of great poverty. But in the seventh century they conquered Persia; in the eighth century they conquered the best part of Spain; in the ninth century they conquered the Punjaub, and eventually nearly the whole of India. Scarcely were they established in their fresh settlements, when their character seemed to undergo a great change. They, who in their original land were little else than roving savages, were now for the first time able to accumulate wealth, and, therefore, for the first time did they make some progress in the arts of civilization. In Arabia they had been a mere race of wandering shepherds; in their new abodes they became the founders of mighty empires,—they built cities, endowed schools, collected libraries; and the traces of their power are still to be seen at Cordova, at Bagdad, and at Delhi. Precisely in the same manner, there is adjoining Arabia at the north, and only separated from it elsewhere by the narrow waters of the Red Sea, an immense sandy plain, which, covering the whole of Africa in the same latitude, extends westward until it reaches the shores of the Atlantic. This enormous tract is, like Arabia, a barren waste; and therefore, as in Arabia, the inhabitants have always been entirely uncivilized, acquiring no knowledge, simply because they have accumulated no wealth. But this great desert is, in its eastern part, irrigated by the waters of the Nile, the overflowing of which covers the sand with a rich alluvial deposit, that yields to labour the most abundant, and indeed the most extraordinary, returns. The consequence is, that in that spot, wealth was rapidly accumulated, the cultivation of knowledge quickly followed, and this narrow strip of land became the seat of Egyptian civilization; a civilization which, though grossly exaggerated, forms a striking contrast to the barbarism of the other nations of Africa, none of which have been able to work out their own progress, or emerge, in any degree, from the ignorance to which the penury of nature has doomed them.

These considerations clearly prove that of the two, primary causes of civilization, the fertility of the soil is the one which in the ancient world exercised most influence. But in European civilization, the other great cause, that is to say, climate, has been the most powerful; and this, as we have seen, produces an effect partly on the capacity of the labourer for work, partly on the regularity or irregularity of his habits. The difference in the result has curiously corresponded with the difference in the cause. For although all civilization must have for its antecedent the accumulation of wealth, still what subsequently occurs will be in no small degree determined by the conditions under which the accumulation took place. In Asia, and in Africa, the condition was a fertile soil, causing an abundant return; in Europe, it was a happier climate, causing more successful labour. In the former case, the effect depends on the relation between the soil and its produce; in other words, the mere operation of one part of external nature upon another. In the latter case, the effect depends on the relation between the climate and the labourer; that is, the operation of external nature not upon itself, but upon man. Of these two classes of relations, the first, being the less complicated, is the less liable to disturbance, and therefore came sooner into play. Hence it is, that, in the march of civilization, the priority is unquestionably due to the most fertile parts of Asia and Africa. But although their civilization was the earliest, it was very far, indeed, from being the best or most permanent. Owing to circumstances which I shall presently state, the only progress which is really effective depends, not upon the bounty of nature, but upon the energy of man. *Therefore, it is, that the civilization of Europe, which, in its earliest stage, was governed by climate, has shown a capacity of development unknown to those civilizations which were originated by soil.* For the powers of nature, notwithstanding their apparent magnitude, are limited and stationary; at all events, we have not the slightest proof that they have ever increased, or that they will ever be able to increase. But the powers of man, so far as experience and analogy can guide us, are unlimited; nor are we possessed of any evidence which authorizes us to assign even an imaginary boundary at which the human intellect will, of necessity be brought to a stand. And as this power which the mind possesses of increasing its own resources, is a peculiarity confined to man, and one eminently distinguishing him from what is commonly called external nature, it becomes evident that the agency of climate, which gives him wealth by stimulating his labour, is more favourable to his ultimate progress than the agency of soil, which likewise gives him wealth, but which does so, not by exciting his energies, but by virtue of a mere physical relation between the character of the soil and the quantity or value of the produce that it almost spontaneously affords.

Thus far as to the different ways in which climate and soil

affect the creation of wealth. But another point of equal, or perhaps of superior, importance remains behind. After the wealth has been created, a question arises as to how it is to be distributed; that is to say, what proportion is to go to the up-per classes, and what to the lower. In an advanced stage of society, this depends upon several circumstances of great complexity, and which it is not necessary here to examine. But in a very early stage of society, and before its later and refined complications have begun, it may, I think, be proved that the distribution of wealth is, like its creation, governed entirely by physical laws; and that those laws are moreover so active as to have invariably kept a vast majority of the in-habitants of the fairest portion of the globe in a condition of constant and inextricable poverty. If this can be demonstrat-ed, the immense importance of such laws is manifest. For since wealth is an undoubted source of power, it is evident that, supposing other things equal, an enquiry into the dis-tribution of wealth is an inquiry into the distribution of power, and, as such, will throw great light on the origin of those social and political inequalities, the play and opposi-tion of which form a considerable part of the history of every civilized country.

If we take a general view of this subject, we may say that after the creation and accumulation of wealth have once fairly begun, it will be distributed among two classes, those who labour, and those who do not labour; the latter being, as a class, the more able, the former the more numerous. The fund by which both classes are supported is immediately cre-ated by the lower class, whose physical energies are directed, combined, and as it were economized, by the superior skill of the upper class. The reward of the workmen is called their wages; the reward of the contrivers is called their profits. At a later period, there will arise what may be called the saving class; that is, a body of men who neither contrive nor work, but lend their accumulations to those who contrive, and in return for the loan, receive a part of that reward which be-longs to the contriving class. In this case, the members of the saving class are rewarded for their abstinence in refraining from spending their accumulations, and this reward is termed the interest of their money; so that there is made a threefold division,—Interest, Profits, and Wages. But this is a subsequent arrangement, which can only take place to any extent when wealth has been considerably accumulated; and in the stage of society we are now considering, this third, or saving class, can hardly be said to have a separate existence. For our present purpose, therefore, it is enough to ascertain what those natural laws are, which, as soon as wealth is accumulated, regulate the proportion in which it is distributed to the two classes of labourers and employers.

Now, it is evident that wages being the price paid for labour, the rate of wages must, like the price of all other commodities, vary according to the changes in the market. If the supply of labourers outstrips the demand, wages will fall; if the demand exceeds the supply, they will rise. Supposing, therefore, that in any country there is a given amount of wealth to be divided between employers and workmen, every increase in the number of the workmen will tend to lessen the average reward each can receive. And if we set aside those disturbing causes by which all general views are affected, it will be found that, in the long-run, the question of wages is a question of population; for although the total sum of the wages actually paid, depends upon the largeness of the fund from which they are drawn, still the amount of wages received by each man must diminish as the claimants increase, unless, owing to other circumstances, the fund itself should so advance as to keep pace with the greater demands made upon it.

To know the circumstances most favourable to the increase of what may be termed the wages-fund is a matter of great moment, but is one with which we are not immediately concerned. The question we have now before us, regards not the accumulation of wealth, but its distribution; and the object is, to ascertain what those physical conditions are, which, by encouraging a rapid growth of population, over-supply the labour-market, and thus keep the average rate of wages at a very low point.

Of all the physical agents by which the increase of the labouring classes is affected, that of food is the most active and universal. If two countries, equal in all other respects, differ solely in this,—that in one the national food is cheap and abundant, and in the other scarce and dear, the population of the former country will inevitably increase more rapidly than the population of the latter. And, by a parity of reasoning, the average rate of wages will be lower in the former than in the latter, simply because the labour-market will be more amply stocked. An inquiry, therefore, into the physical laws on which the food of different countries depends, is, for our present purpose, of the greatest importance; and fortunately it is one respecting which we are able, in the present state of chemistry and physiology, to arrive at some precise and definite conclusions.

The food consumed by man produces two, and only two, effects necessary to his existence. These are, first to supply him with that animal heat without which the functions of life would stop; and secondly, to repair the waste constantly taking place in his tissues, that is, in the mechanism of his frame. For each of these separate purposes there is a separate food. The temperature of our body is kept up by substances which contain no nitrogen, and are called non-azotized; the incessant decay in our organism is repaired by what are known as azotized substances, in which nitrogen is always found. In the former case, the carbon of non-azotized food combines with the oxygen we take in, and gives rise to that internal combustion by which our animal heat is renewed. In the latter case, nitrogen having little affinity for oxygen, the nitrogenous or azotized food is, as it were, guarded against combustion; and being thus preserved, is able to perform its duty of repairing the tissues, and supplying those losses which the human organism constantly suffers in the wear and tear of daily life.

These are the two great divisions of food; and if we inquire into the laws which regulate the relation they bear to man, we shall find that in each division the most important agent is climate. When men live in a hot country, their animal heat is more easily kept up than when they live in a cold one; therefore they require a smaller amount of that non-azotized food, the sole business of which is to maintain at a certain point the temperature of the body. In the same way, they, in the hot country, require a smaller amount of azotized food, because on the whole their bodily exertions are less frequent, and on that account the decay of their tissues is less rapid.

Since, therefore, the inhabitants of hot climates do, in their natural and ordinary state, consume less food than the inhabitants of cold ones, it inevitably follows that, provided other things remain equal, the growth of population will be more rapid in countries which are hot than in those which are cold. For practical purposes it is immaterial whether the greater plenty of a substance by which the people are fed arises from a larger supply, or whether it arises from a smaller consumption. When men eat less, the result will be just the same as if they had more; because the same amount of nutriment will go further, and thus population will gain a power of increasing more quickly than it could do in a colder country, where, even if provisions were equally abundant, they, owing to the climate, would be sooner exhausted.

This is the first point of view in which the laws of climate are, through the medium of food, connected with the laws of population, and therefore with the laws of the distribution of wealth. But there is also another point of view, which follows the same line of thought, and will be found to strengthen the argument just stated. This is, that in cold countries, not only are men compelled to eat more than in hot ones, but their food is dearer, that is to say, to get it is more difficult, and requires a greater expenditure of labour. The reason of this I will state as briefly as possible, without entering into any details beyond those which are absolutely necessary for a right understanding of this interesting subject.

The objects of food are, as we have seen, only two; namely, to keep up the warmth of the body, and repair the waste in the tissues. Of these two objects, the former is effected by the oxygen of the air entering our lungs, and, as it travels through the system, combining with the carbon which we take in our food. This combination of oxygen and carbon never can occur without producing a considerable amount of heat, and it is in this way that the human frame is maintained at its necessary temperature. By virtue of a law familiar to chemists, carbon and oxygen, like all other elements, will only unite in certain definite proportions; so that to keep up a healthy balance, it is needful that the food which contains the carbon should vary according to the amount of oxygen taken in: while it is equally needful that we should increase the quantity of both of these constituents whenever a greater external cold lowers the temperature of the body. Now it is obvious that in a very cold climate, this necessity of providing a nutriment more highly carbonized will arise in two distinct ways. In the first place, the air being denser, men imbibe at each inspiration a greater volume of oxygen than they would do in a climate where the air is rarefied by heat. In the second place, cold accelerates their respiration, and thus obliging them to inhale more frequently than the inhabitants of hot countries, increases the amount of oxygen which they on an average take in. On both these grounds the consumption of oxygen becomes greater: it is therefore requisite that the consumption of carbon should also be greater; since by the union of these two elements in certain definite proportions, the temperature of the body and the balance of the human frame can alone be maintained.

Proceeding from these chemical and physiological principles, we arrive at the conclusion, that the colder the country is in which a people live, the more highly carbonized will be their food. And this, which is a purely scientific inference, has been verified by actual experiment. The inhabitants of the polar regions consume large quantities of whale-oil and blubber; while within the tropics such food would soon put an end to life, and therefore the ordinary diet consists almost entirely of fruit, rice, and other vegetables. Now it has been ascertained by careful analysis, that in the polar food there is an excess of carbon; in the tropical food an excess of oxygen. Without entering into details, which to the majority of readers would be distasteful, it may be said generally, that the oils contain about six times as much carbon as the fruits, and that they have in them very little oxygen; while starch, which is the most universal, and, in reference to nutrition, the most important constituent in the vegetable world, is nearly half oxygen.

The connexion between this circumstance and the subject before us is highly curious; for it is a most remarkable fact, and one to which I would call particular attention, that owing to some more general law, of which we are ignorant, highly carbonized food is more costly than food in which comparatively little carbon is found. The fruits of the earth, of which oxygen is the most active principle, are very abundant; they may be obtained without danger, and almost without trouble. But that highly carbonized food which in a very cold climate is absolutely necessary to life, is not produced in so facile and spontaneous a manner. It is not, like vegetables, thrown up by the soil; but it consists of the fat, the blubber, and the oil, of powerful and ferocious animals. To procure it, man must incur great risk, and expend great labour. And although this is undoubtedly a contrast of extreme cases, still it is evident that the nearer a people approach to either extremity, the more subject will they be to the conditions by which that extremity is governed. It is evident that, as a general rule, the colder a country is, the more its food will be carbonized; the warmer it is, the more its food will be oxidized. At the same time, carbonized food, being chiefly drawn from the animal world, is more difficult to obtain than oxidized food, which is drawn from the vegetable world. The result has been, that among nations where the coldness of the climate renders a highly carbonized diet essential, there is for the most part displayed, even in the infancy of society, *a bolder and more adventurous character than we find among those other nations* whose ordinary nutriment, being highly oxidized, is easily obtained, and indeed is supplied to them, by the bounty of nature, gratuitously and without a struggle. From this original divergence there follow many other consequences, which, however, I am not now concerned to trace; my present object being merely to point out how this difference of food affects the proportion in which wealth is distributed to the different classes.

The way in which this proportion is actually altered has, I hope, been made clear by the preceding argument. But it may be useful to recapitulate the facts on which the argument is based. The facts, then, are simply these. The rate of wages fluctuates with the population; increasing when the labour-market is under-supplied, diminishing when it is over-supplied. The population itself, though affected by many other circumstances, does undoubtedly fluctuate with the supply of food; advancing when the supply is plentiful, halting or receding when the supply is scanty. The food essential to life, is scarcer in cold countries than in hot ones; and not only is it scarcer, but more of it is required; so that on both grounds smaller encouragement is given to the growth of that population from whose ranks the labour-market is stocked. *To express therefore, the conclusion in its simplest form, we may say, that there is a strong and constant tendency in hot countries for wages to be low, in cold countries for them to be high.*

Applying now this great principle to the general course of history, we shall find proofs of its accuracy in every direction. Indeed, there is not a single instance to the contrary. In Asia, in Africa, and in America, all the ancient civilizations were seated in hot climates; and in all of them the rate of wages was very low, and therefore the condition of the labouring classes very depressed. In Europe for the first time, civilization arose in a colder climate: hence the reward of labour was increased, and the distribution of wealth rendered more equal than was possible in countries where an excessive abundance of food stimulated the growth of population. This difference produced, as we shall presently see, many social and political consequences of immense importance. But before discussing them, it may be remarked, that the only apparent exception to what has been stated, is one which strikingly verifies the general law. There is one instance, and only one, of a great European people possessing a very cheap national food. This people, I need hardly say, are the Irish. In Ireland the labouring classes have for more than two hundred years been principally fed by potatoes, which were introduced into their country late in the sixteenth, or early in the seventeenth, century. Now, the peculiarity of the potato is, that until the appearance of the late disease, it was, and perhaps still is, cheaper than any other food equally wholesome. If we compare its reproductive power with the amount of nutriment contained in it, we find that one acre of average land sown with potatoes will support twice as many persons as the same quantity of land sown with wheat. The consequence is, that in a country where men live on potatoes, the population will, if other things are tolerably equal, increase twice as fast as in a country where they live on wheat. And so it has actually occurred. Until a very few years ago, when the face of affairs was entirely altered by pestilence and emigration, the population of Ireland was, in round numbers, increasing annually three per cent; the population of England during the same period increasing one and a half per cent. The result was, that in these two countries the distribution of wealth was altogether different. Even in England the growth of population is somewhat too rapid; and the labour market being overstocked, the working classes are not sufficiently paid for their labour. But their condition is one of sumptuous splendour, compared to that in which only a few years ago the Irish were forced to live. The misery in which they were plunged has no doubt always been aggravated by the ignorance of their rulers, and by that scandalous mis-government which, *until very recently,* formed one of the darkest blots on the glory of England. The most active cause, however, was, that their wages were so low as to debar them, not only from the comforts, but from the common decencies of civilized life; and this evil condition was the natural result of that cheap and abundant food, which encouraged the people to so rapid increase, that the labour market was constantly gorged. So far was this carried, that an intelligent observer who travelled through Ireland twenty years ago, mentions that at that time the average wages were fourpence a day; and that even this wretched pittance could not always be relied upon for regular employment.

Such have been the consequences of cheap food in a country which, on the whole, possesses greater natural resources than any other in Europe. And if we investigate on a larger scale the social and economical condition of nations, we shall see the same principle every where at work. *We shall see that, other things remaining equal, the food of a people determines the increase of their numbers, and the increase of their numbers determines the rate of their wages.* We shall moreover find, that when the wages are invariably low, the distribution of wealth being thus very unequal, the distribution of political power and social influence will also be very unequal; in other words, it will appear that the normal and average relation between the upper and lower classes will, in its origin, depend upon those peculiarities of nature, the operations of which I have endeavoured to indicate. After putting all these things together, we shall, I trust, be able to discern, with a clearness hitherto unknown, the intimate connexion between the physical and moral world; the laws by which that connexion is governed; and the reasons why so many ancient civilizations reached a certain stage of development, and then fell away, unable to resist the pressure of nature, or make head against those external obstacles by which their progress was effectually retarded.

If passing from the history of Asia and Africa, we now turn to the New World, we shall meet with fresh proof of the accuracy of the preceding views. The only parts of America which before the arrival of the Europeans were in some degree civilized were Mexico and Peru; to which may probably be added that long and narrow tract which stretches from the south of Mexico to the Isthmus of Panama. In this latter country, which is now known as Central America, the inhabitants, aided by the fertility of the soil, seem to have worked out for themselves a certain amount of knowledge; since the ruins still extant, prove the possession of a mechanical and architectural skill too considerable to be acquired by any nation entirely barbarous. Beyond this, nothing is known of their history; but the accounts we have of such buildings as Copan, Palenque, and Uxmal, make it highly probable that Central America was the ancient seat of a civilization, in all essential points similar to those of India and Egypt; that is to say, similar to them in respect to the unequal distribution of wealth and power, and the thraldom in which the great body of the people consequently remained.

But although the evidence from which we might estimate the former condition of Central America is almost entirely lost, we are more fortunate in regard to the histories of Mexico and Peru. There are still existing considerable and authentic materials, from which we may form an opinion on the ancient state of those two countries, and on the nature and extent of their civilization. Before, however, entering upon this subject, it will be convenient to point out what those physical laws were which determined the localities of American civilization; or in other words, why it was that in these countries alone, society should have been organized into a fixed and settled system, while the rest of the New World was peopled by wild and ignorant barbarians. Such an inquiry will be found highly interesting, as affording further proof of the extraordinary, and indeed irresistible, force with which the powers of Nature have controlled the fortunes of Man.

The first circumstance by which we must be struck, is that in America, as in Asia and Africa, all the original civilizations were seated in hot countries; the whole of Peru proper being within the southern tropic, the whole of Central America and Mexico within the northern tropic. How the heat of the climate operated on the social and political arrangements of India and Egypt, I have attempted to examine; and it has, I trust, been proved that the result was brought about by diminishing the wants and requirements of the people, and thus producing a very unequal distribution of wealth and power. But, besides this, there is another way in which the average temperature of a country affects its civilization, and the discussion of which I have reserved for the present moment, because it may be more clearly illustrated in America than elsewhere. Indeed, in the New World, the scale on which Nature works, being much larger than in the Old, and her forces being more overpowering, it is evident that her operations on mankind may be studied with greater advantage than in countries where she is weaker, and where, therefore, the consequences of her movements are less conspicuous.

If the reader will bear in mind the immense influence which an abundant national food has been shown to exercise, he will easily understand how, owing to the pressure of physical phenomena, the civilization of America was, of necessity, confined to those parts where alone it was found by the discoverers of the New World. For, setting aside the chemical and geognostic varieties of soil, it may be said that the two causes which regulate the fertility of every country are heat and moisture. Where these are abundant, the land will be exuberant; where they are deficient, it will be sterile. This rule is of course, in its application subject to exceptions, arising from physical conditions which are independent of it; but if other things are equal, the rule is invariable. And the vast additions which, since the construction of isothermal lines, have been made to our knowledge of geographical botany, enable us to lay this down as a law of nature, proved not only by arguments drawn from vegetable physiology, but also by a careful study of the proportions in which plants are actually distributed in different countries.

A general survey of the continent of America will illustrate the connexion between this law and the subject now before us. In the first place, as regards moisture, all the great rivers in the New World are on the eastern coast, none of them on the western. The causes of this remarkable fact are unknown, but it is certain that neither in North, nor in South America, does one considerable river empty itself into the Pacific; while on the opposite side there are numerous rivers, some of enormous magnitude, all of great importance, as the Negro, the LaPlata, the San Francisco, the Amazon, the Orinoco, the Mississippi, the Alabama, the Saint John, the Potomac, the Susquehannah, the Delaware, the Hudson, and the Saint Lawrence. By this vast water-system the soil is towards the east constantly irrigated: but towards the west there is in North America only one river of value, the Oregon; while in South America, from the Isthmus of Panama to the Straits of Magellan, there is no great river at all.

But as to the other main cause of fertility, namely heat, we find in North America a state of things precisely the reverse. There we find that while the irrigation is on the east, the heat is on the west. This difference of temperature between the two coasts, is probably connected with some great meteorological law; for in the whole of the northern hemisphere, the eastern part of continents and of islands is colder than the western. Whether, however, this is owing to some large and comprehensive cause, or whether each instance has a cause peculiar to itself, is an alternative, in the present state of knowledge, impossible to decide; but the fact is unquestionable, and its influence upon the early history of America is extremely curious. In consequence of it, the two great conditions of fertility have not been united in any part of the continent north of Mexico. The countries on the one side have wanted heat; those on the other side have wanted irrigation. The accumulation of wealth being thus impeded, the progress of society was stopped; and until, in the six-teenth century, the knowledge of Europe was brought to bear upon America, there is no instance of any people north of the twentieth parallel, reaching even that imperfect civilization to which the inhabitants of India and Egypt easily attained. On the other hand, south of the twentieth parallel, the continent suddenly changes its form, and, rapid-ly contracting, becomes a small strip of land, until it reaches the Isthmus of Panama. This narrow tract was the centre of Mexican civilization; and a comparison of the proceeding arguments will easily show why such was the case; for the peculiar configuration of the land secured a very large amount of coast, and thus gave to the southern part of North America the character of an island. Hence there arose one of the characteristics of an insular climate, namely, an in-crease of moisture caused by the watery vapour which springs from the sea. While, therefore, the position of Mexico near the equator gave it heat, the shape of the land gave it humidity; and this being the only part of North America in which these two conditions were united, it was likewise the only part which was at all civilized. There can be no doubt that if the sandy plains of California and southern Columbia, instead of being scorched into sterility, had been irrigated by the rivers of the east, or if the rivers of the east had been accompanied by the heat of the west, the result of either combination would have been that exuberance of soil by which, as the history of the world decisively proves, every early civilization was preceded. But inasmuch as, of the two elements of fertility, one was deficient in every part of America north of the twentieth parallel, it followed that, until that line was passed, civilization could gain no resting-place; and there never has been found, and we may con-fidently assert never will be found, any evidence that even a single ancient nation, in the whole of that enormous con-tinent, was able to make much progress in the arts of life, or organize itself into a fixed and permanent society.

Thus far as to the physical agents which controlled the

early destinies of North America. But in reference to South America, a different train of circumstances came into play; for the law by virtue of which the eastern coasts are colder than the western, is not only inapplicable to the southern hemisphere, but is replaced by another law precisely the reverse. North of the equator, the east is colder than the west; south of the equator, the east is hotter than the west. If now, we connect this fact with what has been noticed respecting the vast river-system which distinguishes the east of America from the west, it becomes evident that South America is remarkable for its exuberance, not only within the tropic, but considerably beyond it; the south of Brazil, and even part of Uruguay, possessing a fertility not to be found in any country of North America situated under a corresponding latitude.

On a hasty view of the preceding generalizations, it might be expected that the eastern side of South America, being thus richly endowed by nature, would have been the seat of one of those civilizations, which, in other parts of the world, similar causes produced. But if we look a little further, we shall find that what has just been pointed out, by no means exhausts even the physical bearings of this subject, and that we must take into consideration a third great agent, which has sufficed to neutralize the natural results of the other two, and to retain in barbarism the inhabitants of what otherwise would have been the most flourishing of all the countries of the New World.

The *agent to which I allude is the trade-wind;* a striking phenomenon, by which, as we shall hereafter see, all the civilizations anterior to those of Europe were greatly and injuriously influenced. This wind covers no less than 56° of latitude; 28° north of the equator, and 28° south of it. In this large tract, which comprises some of the most fertile countries in the world, the trade-wind blows, during the whole year, either from the north-east or from the south-east. The causes of this regularity are now well understood, and are known to depend partly on the displacement of air at

the equator, and partly on the motion of the earth; for the
cold air from the poles is constantly flowing towards the
equator, and thus producing northerly winds in the northern
hemisphere, and southerly winds in the southern. These
winds are, however, deflected from their natural course by
the movement of the earth, as it revolves on its axis from
west to east. And as the rotation of the earth is, of course,
more rapid at the equator than elsewhere, it happens that in
the neighbourhood of the equator the speed is so great as to
outstrip the movements of the atmosphere from the poles,
and forcing them into another direction, gives rise to those
easterly currents which are called trade-winds. What, however, we are now rather concerned with, is not so much an
explanation of the trade-winds, as an account of the way in
which this great physical phenomenon is connected with the
history of South America.

The trade-wind, blowing on the eastern coast of South
America, and proceeding from the east, crosses the Atlantic
ocean, and therefore reaches the land surcharged with the
vapours accumulated in its passage. These vapours, on
touching the shore, are, at periodical intervals, condensed
into rain; and as their progress westward is checked by that
gigantic claim of the Andes, which they are unable to pass,
they pour the whole of their moisture on Brazil, which, in
consequence, is often deluged by the most destructive tor-
rents. This abundant supply, being aided by that vast river-
system peculiar to the eastern part of America, and being
also accompanied by heat, has stimulated the soil into an
activity unequalled in any other part of the world. Brazil,
which is nearly as large as the whole of Europe, is covered
with a vegetation of incredible profusion. Indeed, so rank
and luxuriant is the growth, that Nature seems to riot in
the very wantonness of power. A great part of this immense
country is filled with dense and tangled forests, whose noble
trees, blossoming in unrivalled beauty, and exquisite with a
thousand hues, throw out their produce in endless prodigality. On their summit are perched birds of gorgeous plum-

age, which nestle in their dark and lofty recesses. Below, their base and trunks are crowded with brushwood, creeping plants, innumerable parasites, all swarming with life. There, too, are myriads of insects of every variety; reptiles of strange and singular form; serpents and lizards, spotted with deadly beauty; all of which find means of existence in this vast workshop and repository of Nature. And that nothing may be wanting to this land of marvels, the forests are skirted by enormous meadows, which, reeking with heat and moisture, supply nourishment to countless herds of wild cattle, that browse and fatten on their herbage; while the adjoining plains, rich in another form of life, are the chosen abode of the subtlest and most ferocious animals, which prey on each other, but which it might almost seem no human power can hope to extirpate.

Such is the flow and abundance of life by which Brazil is marked above all other countries of the earth. But, amid this pomp and splendour of Nature, no place is left for Man. He is reduced to insignificance by the majesty with which he is surrounded. The forces that oppose him are so formidable, that he has never been able to make head against them, never able to rally against their accumulated pressure. The whole of Brazil, notwithstanding its immense apparent advantages, has always remained entirely uncivilized; its inhabitants wandering savages, incompetent to resist those obstacles which the very bounty of Nature had put in their way. For the natives, like every people in the infancy of society, are averse to enterprise; and being unacquainted with the arts by which physical impediments are removed, they have never attempted to grapple with the difficulties that stopped their social progress. Indeed, those difficulties are so serious, that during more than three hundred years the resources of European knowledge have been vainly employed in endeavouring to get rid of them. Along the coast of Brazil, there has been introduced from Europe a certain amount of that civilization, which the natives by their own efforts could never have reached. But such civilization, in itself very imperfect, has never penetrated the recesses of the country; and in the interior there is still found a state of things similar to that which has always existed. The people, ignorant, and therefore brutal, practising no restraint, and recognizing no law, continue to live on in their old and inveterate barbarism. In their country, the physical causes are so active, and do their work on a scale of such unrivalled magnitude, that it has hitherto been found impossible to escape from the effects of their united action. The progress of agriculture is stopped by impassable forests, and the harvests are destroyed by innumerable insects. The mountains are too high to scale, the rivers are too wide to bridge; every thing is contrived to keep back the human mind, and repress its rising ambition. It is thus that the energies of Nature have hampered the spirit of Man. Nowhere else is there so painful a contrast between the grandeur of the external world and the littleness of the internal. And the mind, cowed by this unequal struggle, has not only been unable to advance, but without foreign aid it would undoubtedly have receded. For even at present, with all the improvements constantly introduced from Europe, there are no signs of real progress; while notwithstanding the frequency of colonial settlements, less than one-fiftieth of the land is cultivated. The habits of the people are as barbarous as ever; and as to their numbers, it is well worthy of remark, that Brazil, the country where, of all others, physical resources are most powerful, where both vegetables and animals are most abundant, where the soil is watered by the noblest rivers, and the coast studded by the finest harbours,—this immense territory, which is more than twelve times the size of France, contains a population not exceeding six millions of people.

These considerations sufficiently explain why it is, that in the whole of Brazil there are no monuments even of the most imperfect civilization: no evidence that the people had, at any period, raised themselves above the state in which they were found when their country was first discovered. But immediately opposite to Brazil there is another country. which, though situated in the same continent, and lying under the same latitude, is subjected to different physical conditions, and therefore was the scene of different social results. This is the celebrated kingdom of Peru, which included the whole of the southern tropic, and which, from the circumstances just stated, was naturally the only part of South America where anything approaching to civilization could be attained. In Brazil, the heat of the climate was accompanied by a twofold irrigation, arising first from the immense river-system incidental to the eastern coast; and secondly, from the abundant moisture deposited by the trade-winds. From this combination there resulted that unequalled fertility, which, so far as Man was concerned, defeated its own ends, stopping his progress by an exuberance, which, had it been less excessive, it would have aided. For, as we have clearly seen, when the productive powers of Nature are carried beyond a certain point, the imperfect knowledge of uncivilized men is unable to cope with them, or in any way turn them to their own advantage. If, however, those powers, being very active, are nevertheless confined within manageable limits, there arises a state of things similar to that noticed in Asia and Africa; where the profusion of Nature, instead of hindering social progress, favoured it, by encouraging that accumulation of wealth, without some share of which, progress is impossible.

In estimating, therefore, the physical conditions by which civilization was originally determined, we have to look, not merely at the exhuberance, but also at what may be called the *manageability of Nature;* that is, we have to consider the ease with which the resources may be used, as well as the number of the resources themselves. Applying this to Mexico and Peru, we find that they were the countries of America where this combination most happily occurred. For though their resources were much less numerous than those of Brazil, they were far more easy to control; while at the same time the heat of the climate brought into play those other laws by which, as I have attempted to show, all the early civilizations were greatly influenced. It is a very remarkable fact, which, I believe, has never been observed, that even in reference to latitude, the present limit of Peru to the south corresponds with the ancient limit of Mexico to the north; while, by a striking, but to me perfectly natural coincidence, both these boundaries are reached before the tropical line is passed; the boundary of Mexico being 21° N. lat., that of Peru 21½° S. lat.

Such is the wonderful regularity which history, when comprehensively studied, presents to our view. And if we compare Mexico and Peru with those countries of the Old World which have been already noticed, we shall find, as in all the civilizations anterior to those of Europe, that their social phenomena were subordinate to their physical laws. In the first place, the characteristics of their national food were precisely those met with in the most flourishing parts of Asia and Africa. For although few of the nutritious vegetables belonging to the Old World were found in the New, their place was supplied by others exactly analogous to rice and dates; that is to say, marked by the same abundance, by the same facility of growth, and by the same exuberant returns; therefore, followed by the same social results. In Mexico and Peru, one of the most important articles of food has always been maize, which we have every reason to believe, was peculiar to the American continent. This, like rice and dates, is eminently the product of a hot climate; and although it is said to grow at an elevation of upwards of 7,000 feet, it is rarely seen beyond the fortieth parallel, and its exuberance rapidly diminishes with the diminution of temperature. Thus, for example, in New California its average yield is seventy or eighty fold; but in Mexico proper the same grain yields three or four hundred fold, and, under very favourable circumstances, even eight hundred fold.

A people who derived their sustenance from a plant of such extraordinary fecundity, had little need to exercise their industrious energies; while at the same time they had every opportunity of increasing their numbers, and thus producing a train of social and political consequences smiilar to those which I have noticed in India and in Egypt. Besides this, there were, in addition to maize, other kinds of food to which the same remarks are applicable. The potato, which, in Ireland, has brought about such injurious effects by stimulating the growth of population is said to be indigenous to Peru; and although this is denied by a very high authority, there is, at all events, no doubt that it was found there in great abundance when the country was first discovered by the Europeans. In Mexico, potatoes were unknown till the arrival of the Spaniards; but both Mexicans and Peruvians lived to a great extent on the produce of the banana; a vegetable whose reproductive powers are so extraordinary, that nothing but the precise and unimpeachable testimony of which we are possessed could make them at all credible. This remarkable plant is, in America, intimately connected with the physical laws of climate; since it is an article of primary importance for the subsistence of man whenever the temperature passes a certain point. Of its nutritive powers, it is enough to say, that an acre sown with it will support more than fifty persons; whereas the same amount of land sown with wheat in Europe will only support two persons. As to the exuberance of its growth, it is calculated that, other circumstances remaining the same, its produce is forty-four times greater than that of potatoes and a hundred and thirty-three times greater than that of wheat.

It will now be easily understood why it was that, in all important respects, the civilizations of Mexico and Peru were strictly analogous to those of India and Egypt. In these four countries, as well as in a few others in Southern Asia and Central America, there existed an amount of knowledge, despicable indeed if tried by an European standard, but most remarkable if contrasted with the gross ignorance which prevailed among the adjoining and contemporary nations. But in all of them there was the same inability to diffuse even that scanty civilization which they really possessed; there was the same utter absence of any thing approaching to the democratic spirit; there was the same despotic power on the part of the upper classes, and the same contemptible subservience on the part of the lower. For, as we have clearly seen, all these civilizations were affected by certain physical causes, which, though favourable to the accumulation of wealth, were unfavourable to a just subdivision of it. And as the knowledge of men was still in its infancy, it was found impossible to struggle against these physical agents or prevent them from producing these effects on the social organization which I have attempted to trace. Both in Mexico and in Peru, the arts, and particularly those branches of them which minister in the luxury of the wealthy classes, were cultivated with great success. The houses of the higher ranks were filled with ornaments and utensils of admirable workmanship; their chambers were hung with splendid tapestries; their dresses and their personal decorations betrayed an almost incredible expense; their jewels of exquisite and varied form; their rich and flowing robes embroidered with the rarest feathers, collected from the most distant parts of the empire; all supplying evidence of the possession of unlimited wealth, and of the ostentatious prodigality with which that wealth was wasted. Immediately below this class came the people; and what their condition was, may be easily imagined. In Peru the whole of the taxes were paid by them; the nobles and the clergy being altogether exempt. But as, in such a state of society, it was impossible for the people to accumulate property, they were obliged to defray the expenses of government by their personal labour, which was placed under the entire command of the state. At the same time, the rulers of the country were well aware that, with a system like this, feelings of personal independence were incompatible; they therefore contrived laws by which, even in the most minute matters, freedom of action was controlled. The people were so shackled, that they could neither change their residence, nor alter their clothes without permission from the governing powers. To each man the law prescribed the trade he was to follow, the dress he was to wear, the wife he was to marry, and the amusements he was to enjoy. Among the Mexicans the course of affairs was similar; the same physical conditions being followed by the same social results. In the most essential particular for which history can be studied, namely, the state of the people, Mexico and Peru are the counterpart of each other. For though there were many minor points of difference, both were agreed in this, that there were only two classes—the upper class being tyrants, and the lower class being slaves. This was the state in which Mexico was found when it was discovered by the Europeans, and towards which it must have been tending from the earliest period. And so insupportable had all this become, that we know from the most decisive evidence, that the general disaffection it produced among the people was one of the causes which, by facilitating the progress of the Spanish invaders, hastened the downfall of the Mexican empire.

The further this examination is carried, the more striking becomes the similarity between those civilizations which flourished anterior to what may be called the European epoch of the human mind. The division of a nation into castes would be impossible in the great European countries; but it existed from a remote antiquity in Egypt, in India, and apparently in Persia. The very same institution was rigidly enforced in Peru; and what proves how consonant it was to that stage of society, is, that in Mexico, where castes were not established by law, it was nevertheless a recognised custom that the son should follow the occupation of his father. This was the political symptom of that stationary and conservative spirit, which, as we shall hereafter see, has marked every country in which the upper classes have monopolized power. The religious symptom of the same spirit was displayed in that inordinate reverence for antiquity, and in that hatred of change, which the greatest of all the writers on America has well pointed out as an analogy between the natives of Mexico and those of Hindostan. To this may be added, that those who have studied the history of the ancient Egyptians, have observed among that people a similar tendency. Wilkinson, who is well known to have paid great attention to their monuments, says, that they were more unwilling than any other nation to alter their religious worship; and Herodotus, who travelled in their country two thousand three hundred years ago, assures us that, while they preserved old customs, they never acquired new ones. In another point of view, the similarity between these distant countries is equally interesting, since it evidently arises from the causes already noticed as common to both. In Mexico and Peru, the lower classes being at the disposal of the upper, there followed that frivolous waste of labour which we have observed in Egypt, and evidence of which may also be seen in the remains of those temples and palaces that are still found in several parts of Asia. Both Mexicans and Peruvians erected immense buildings, which were as useless as those of Egypt, and which no country could produce, unless the labour of the people were ill-paid and ill-directed. The cost of these monuments of vanity is unknown; but it must have been enormous; since the Americans, being ignorant of the use of iron, were unable to employ a resource by which, in the construction of large works, labour is greatly abridged. Some particulars, however, have been preserved, from which an idea may be formed on this subject. To take, for instance, the palaces of their kings: we find that in Peru the erection of the royal residence occupied, during fifty years, 20,000 men; while that of Mexico cost the labour of no less than 200,000: striking facts, which, if all other testimonies had perished, would enable us to appreciate the condition of countries in which, for such insignificant purposes, such vast power was expended.

The preceding evidence, collected from sources of unquestioned credibility, proves the force of those great physical laws, which, in the most flourishing countries out of Europe, encouraged the accumulation of wealth, but prevented its dispersion; and thus secured to the upper classes a monopoly of one of the most important elements of social and political power. The result was, that in all those civilizations the great body of the people derived no benefit from the national improvement; hence, the basis of the progress being very narrow, the progress itself was very insecure. When, therefore unfavourable circumstances arose from without, it was but natural that the whole system should fall to the ground. In such countries, society, being divided against itself, was unable to stand. And there can be no doubt that long before the crisis of their actual destruction, these one-sided and irregular civilizations had begun to decay; so that their own degeneracy aided the progress of foreign invaders, and secured the overthrow of those ancient kingdoms, which, under a sounder system, might have been easily saved.

THE COMMUNIST MANIFESTO

By KARL MARX AND FRIEDRICH ENGELS

A SPECTRE is haunting Europe—the spectre of Communism. All the powers of old Europe have entered into a holy alliance to exorcise this spectre: Pope and Czar, Metternich and Guizot, French Radicals and German police-spies.

Where is the party in opposition that has not been decried as communistic by its opponents in power? Where the Opposition that has not hurled back the branding reproach of Communism, against the more advanced opposition parties, as well as against its reactionary adversaries?

Two things result from this fact:

I. Communism is already acknowledged by all European powers to be itself a power.

II. It is high time that Communists should openly, in the face of the whole world, publish their views, their aims, their tendencies, and meet this nursery tale of the spectre of Communism with a manifesto of the party itself.

To this end, Communists of various nationalities have assembled in London, and sketched the following manifesto, to be published in the English, French, German, Italian, Flemish and Danish languages.

I

BOURGEOIS AND PROLETARIANS

The history of all hitherto existing society is the history of class struggles.

Freeman and slave, patrician and plebeian, lord and serf, guildmaster and journeyman, in a word, oppressor and oppressed, stood in constant opposition to one another, carried on an uninterrupted, now hidden, now open fight, a fight that each time ended, either in a revolutionary reconstitution of society at large, or in the common ruin of the contending classes.

In the earlier epochs of history, we find almost everywhere a complicated arrangement of society into various orders, a manifold gradation of social rank. In ancient Rome we have patricians, knights, plebeians, slaves; in the Middle Ages, feudal lords, vassals, guild-masters, journeymen, apprentices, serfs; in almost all of these classes, again, subordinate gradations.

The modern bourgeois society that has sprouted from the ruins of feudal society, has not done away with class antagonisms. It has but established new classes, new conditions of oppression, new forms of struggle in place of the old ones.

Our epoch, the epoch of the bourgeoisie, possesses, however, this distinctive feature: It has simplified the class antagonisms. Society as a whole is more and more splitting up into two great hostile camps, into two great classes directly facing each other—bourgeoisie and proletariat.

From the serfs of the Middle Ages sprang the chartered burghers of the earliest towns. From these burgesses the first elements of the bourgeoisie were developed.

The discovery of America, the rounding of the Cape, opened up fresh ground for the rising bourgeoisie. The East-Indian and Chinese markets, the colonisation of America, trade with the colonies, the increase in the means of exchange and in commodities generally, gave to commerce, to navigation, to industry, an impulse never before known, and thereby, to the revolutionary element in the tottering feudal society, a rapid development.

The feudal system of industry, in which industrial production was monopolised by closed guilds, now no longer sufficed for the growing wants of the new markets. The manufacturing system took its place. The guild-masters were pushed aside by the manufacturing middle class; division of labour between the different corporate guilds vanished in the face of division of labour in each single workshop.

Meantime the markets kept ever growing, the demand ever rising. Even manufacture no longer sufficed. Thereupon, steam and machinery revolutionised industrial production. The place of manufacture was taken by the giant, modern industry, the place of the industrial middle class, by industrial millionaires—the leaders of whole industrial armies, the modern bourgeois.

Modern industry has established the world market, for which the discovery of America paved the way. This market has given an immense development to commerce, to navigation, to communication by land. This development has, in its turn, reacted on the extension of industry; and in proportion as industry, commerce, navigation, railways extended, in the same proportion the bourgeoisie developed, increased its capital, and pushed into the background every class handed down from the Middle Ages.

We see, therefore, how the modern bourgeoisie is itself the product of a long course of development, of a series of revolutions in the modes of production and of exchange.

Each step in the development of the bourgeoisie was accompanied by a corresponding political advance of that class. An oppressed class under the sway of the feudal nobility, it became an armed and self-governing association in the mediæval commune; here independent urban republic (as in Italy and Germany), there taxable "third estate" of the monarchy (as in France); afterwards, in the period of manufacture proper, serving either the semi-feudal or the absolute monarchy as a counterpoise against the nobility, and, in fact, corner-stone of the great monarchies in general—the bourgeoisie has at last, since the establishment of modern industry and of the world market, conquered for itself, in the modern representative state, exclusive political sway. The executive of the modern state is but a committee for managing the common affairs of the whole bourgeoisie.

The bourgeoisie has played a most revolutionary rôle in history.

The bourgeoisie, wherever it has got the upper hand, has put an end to all feudal, patriarchal, idyllic relations. It has pitilessly torn asunder the motley feudal ties that bound man to his "natural superiors," and has left no other bond between man and man than naked self-interest, than callous "cash payment." It has drowned the most heavenly ecstasies of religious fervour, of chivalrous enthusiasm, of philistine sentimentalism, in the icy water of egotistical calculation. It has resolved personal worth into exchange value, and in place of the numberless indefeasible chartered freedoms, has set up that single, unconscionable freedom—Free Trade. In one word, for exploitation, veiled by religious and political illusions, it has substituted naked, shameless, direct, brutal exploitation.

The bourgeoisie has stripped of its halo every occupation hitherto honoured and looked up to with reverent awe. It has converted the physician, the lawyer, the priest, the poet, the man of science, into its paid wage-labourers.

The bourgeoisie has torn away from the family its sentimental veil, and has reduced the family relation to a mere money relation.

The bourgeoisie has disclosed how it came to pass that the brutal display of vigour in the Middle Ages, which reactionaries so much admire, found its fitting complement in the most slothful indolence. It has been the first to show what man's activity can bring about. It has accomplished wonders far surpassing Egyptian pyramids, Roman aqueducts, and Gothic cathedrals; it has conducted expeditions that put in the shade all former migrations of nations and crusades.

The bourgeoisie cannot exist without constantly revolutionising the instruments of production, and thereby the relations of production, and with them the whole relations of society. Conservation of the old modes of production in unaltered form, was, on the contrary, the first condition of existence for all earlier industrial classes. Constant revolutionising of production, uninterrupted disturbance of all social conditions, everlasting uncertainty and agitation distinguish the bourgeois epoch from all earlier ones. All fixed, fast-frozen relations, with their train of ancient and venerable prejudices and opinions, are swept away, all new-formed ones become antiquated before they can ossify. All that is solid melts into air, all that is holy is profaned, and man is at last compelled to face with sober senses his real conditions of life and his relations with his kind.

The need of a constantly expanding market for its products chases the bourgeoisie over the whole surface of the globe. It must nestle everywhere, settle everywhere, establish connections everywhere.

The bourgeoisie has through its exploitation of the world market given a cosmopolitan character to production and consumption in every country. To the great chagrin of re-actionaries, it has drawn from under the feet of industry the national ground on which it stood. All old-established national industries have been destroyed or are daily being destroyed. They are dislodged by new industries, whose introduction becomes a life and death question for all civilised nations, by industries that no longer work up indigenous raw material, but raw material drawn from the remotest zones; industries whose products are consumed, not only at home, but in every quarter of the globe. In place of the old wants, satisfied by the production of the country, we find new wants, requiring for their satisfaction the products of distant lands and climes. In place of the old local and national seclusion and self-sufficiency, we have intercourse in every direction, universal inter-dependence of nations. And as in material, so also in intellectual production. The intellectual creations of individual nations become common property. National one-sidedness and narrow-mindedness become more and more impossible, and from the numerous national and local literatures there arises a world literature.

The bourgeoisie, by the rapid improvement of all instruments of production, by the immensely facilitated means of communications, draws all nations, even the most barbarian, into civilisation. The cheap prices of its commodities are the heavy artillery with which it batters down all Chinese walls, with which it forces the barbarians' intensely obstinate hatred of foreigners to capitulate. It compels all nations, on pain of extinction, to adopt the bourgeois mode of production; it compels them to introduce what it calls civilisation into their midst, *i. e.,* to become bourgeois themselves. In a word, it creates a world after its own image.

The bourgeoisie has subjected the country to the rule of the towns. It has created enormous cities, has greatly increased the urban population as compared with the rural, and has thus rescued a considerable part of the population from the idiocy of rural life. Just as it has made the country dependent on the towns, so it has made barbarian and semi-barbarian countries dependent on the civilised ones, nations of peasants on nations of bourgeois, the East on the West.

More and more the bourgeoisie keeps doing away with the scattered state of the population, of the means of production, and of property. It has agglomerated population, centralised means of production, and has concentrated property in a few hands. The necessary consequence of this was political centralization. Independent, or but loosely connected provinces, with separate interests, laws, governments and systems of taxation, became lumped together into one nation, with one government, one code of laws, one national class interest, one frontier and one customs tariff.

The bourgeoisie, during its rule of scarce one hundred years, has created more massive and more colossal productive forces than have all preceding generations together. Subjection of nature's forces to man, machinery, application of chemistry to industry and agriculture, steam-navigation, railways, electric telegraphs, clearing of whole continents for cultivation, canalisation of rivers, whole populations conjured out of the ground—what earlier century had even a presentiment that such productive forces slumbered in the lap of social labour?

We see then that the means of production and of exchange, which served as the foundation for the growth of the bourgeoisie, were generated in feudal society. At a certain stage in the development of these means of production and of exchange, the conditions under which feudal society produced and exchanged, the feudal organisation of agriculture and manufacturing industry, in a word, the feudal relations of property became no longer compatible with the already developed productive forces; they became so many fetters. They had to be burst asunder; they were burst asunder.

Into their place stepped free competition, accompanied by a social and political constitution adapted to it, and by the economic and political sway of the bourgeois class.

A similar movement is going on before our own eyes. Modern bourgeois society with its relations of production, of exchange and of property, a society that has conjured up such gigantic means of production and of exchange, is like the sorcerer who is no longer able to control the powers of the nether world whom he has called up by his spells. For many a decade past the history of industry and commerce is but the history of the revolt of modern productive forces against modern conditions of production, against the property relations that are the conditions for the existence of the bourgeoisie and of its rule. It is enough to mention the commercial crises that by their periodical return put the existence of the entire bourgeois society on trial, each time more threateningly. In these crises a great part not only of the existing products, but also of the previously created productive forces, are periodically destroyed. In these crises there breaks out an epidemic that, in all earlier epochs, would have seemed an absurdity—the epidemic of over-production. Society suddenly finds itself put back into a state of momentary barbarism; it appears as if a famine, a universal war of devastation had cut off the supply of every means of subsistence; industry and commerce seem to be destroyed. And why? Because there is too much civilisation, too much means of subsistence, too much industry, too much commerce. The productive forces at the disposal of society no longer tend to further the development of the conditions of bourgeois property; on the contrary, they have become too powerful for these conditions, by which they are fettered, and no sooner do they overcome these fetters than they bring disorder into the whole of bourgeois society, endanger the existence of bourgeois property. The conditions of bourgeois society are too narrow to comprise the wealth created by them. And how does the bourgeoisie get over these crises? On the one hand by enforced destruction of a mass of productive forces; on the other, by the conquest of new markets, and by the more thorough exploitation of the old ones. That is to say, by paving the way for more extensive and more destructive crises, and by diminishing the means whereby crises are prevented.

The weapons with which the bourgeoisie felled feudalism to the ground are now turned against the bourgeoisie itself.

But not only has the bourgeoisie forged the weapons that bring death to itself; it has also called into existence the men who are to wield those weapons—the modern working class —the proletarians.

In proportion as the bourgeoisie, *i. e.,* capital, is developed, in the same proportion is the proletariat, the modern working class, developed—a class of labourers, who live only so long as they find work, and who find work only so long as their labour increases capital. These labourers, who must sell themselves piecemeal, are a commodity, like every other article of commerce, and are consequently exposed to all the vicissitudes of competition, to all the fluctuations of the market.

Owing to the extensive use of machinery and to division of labour, the work of the proletarians has lost all individual character, and, consequently, all charm for the workman. He becomes an appendage of the machine, and it is only the most simple, most monotonous, and most easily acquired knack, that is required of him. Hence, the cost of production of a workman is restricted, almost entirely, to the means of subsistence that he requires for his maintenance, and for the propagation of his race. But the price of a commodity, and therefore also of labour, is equal to its cost of production. In proportion, therefore, as the repulsiveness of the work increases, the wage decreases. Nay more, in proportion as the use of machinery and division of labour increases, in the same proportion the burden of toil also increases, whether by prolongation of the working hours, by increase of the work exacted in a given time, or by increased speed of the machinery, etc.

Modern industry has converted the little workshop of the patriarchal master into the great factory of the industrial capitalist. Masses of labourers, crowded into the factory, are organised like soldiers. As privates of the industrial army they are placed under the command of a perfect hierarchy of officers and sergeants. Not only are they slaves of the bourgeois class, and of the bourgeois state; they are daily and hourly enslaved by the machine, by the over-looker, and, above all, by the individual bourgeois manufacturer himself. The more openly this despotism proclaims gain to be its end and aim, the more petty, the more hateful and the more embittering it is.

The less the skill and exertion of strength implied in manual labour, in other words, the more modern industry develops, the more is the labour of men superseded by that of women. Differences of age and sex have no longer any distinctive social validity for the working class. All are instruments of labour, more or less expensive to use, according to their age and sex.

No sooner has the labourer received his wages in cash, for the moment escaping exploitation by the manufacturer, than he is set upon by the other portions of the bourgeoisie, the landlord, the shopkeeper, the pawnbroker, etc.

The lower strata of the middle class—the small tradespeople, shopkeepers, and retired tradesmen generally, the handicraftsmen and peasants—all these sink gradually into the proletariat, partly because their diminutive capital does not suffice for the scale on which modern industry is carried on, and is swamped in the competition with the large capitalists, partly because their specialised skill is rendered worthless by new methods of production. Thus the proletariat is recruited from all classes of the population.

The proletariat goes through various stages of development. With its birth begins its struggle with the bourgeoisie. At first the contest is carried on by individual labourers, then by the work people of a factory, then by the operatives of one trade, in one locality, against the individual bourgeois who directly exploits them. They direct their attacks not against the bourgeois conditions of production, but against the instruments of production themselves; they destroy imported wares that compete with their labour, they smash machinery to pieces, they set factories ablaze, they seek to restore by force the vanished status of the workman of the Middle Ages.

At this stage the labourers still form an incoherent mass scattered over the whole country, and broken up by their mutual competition. If anywhere they unite to form more compact bodies, this is not yet the consequence of their own active union, but of the union of the bourgeoisie, which class, in order to attain its own political ends, is compelled to set the whole proletariat in motion, and is moreover still able to do so for a time. At this stage, therefore, the proletarians do not fight their enemies, but the enemies of their enemies, the remnants of absolute monarchy, the landowners, the non-industrial bourgeois, the petty bourgeoisie. Thus the whole historical movement is concentrated in the hands of the bourgeoisie; every victory so obtained is a victory for the bourgeoisie.

But with the development of industry the proletariat not only increases in number; it becomes concentrated in greater masses, its strength grows, and it feels that strength more. The various interests and conditions of life within the ranks of the proletariat are more and more equalised, in proportion as machinery obliterates all distinctions of labour and nearly everywhere reduces wages to the same low level. The growing competition among the bourgeois, and the resulting commercial crises, make the wages of the workers ever more fluctuating. The unceasing improvement of machinery, ever more rapidly developing, makes their livelihood more and more precarious; the collisions between individual workmen and individual bourgeois take more and more the character of collisions between two classes. Thereupon the workers begin to form combinations (trade unions) against the bourgeoisie; they club together in order to keep up the rate of wages; they found permanent associations in order to make provision beforehand for these occasional revolts. Here and there the contest breaks out into riots.

Now and then the workers are victorious, but only for a time. The real fruit of their battles lies, not in the immediate result, but in the ever expanding union of the workers. This union is furthered by the improved means of communication which are created by modern industry, and which place the workers of different localities in contact with one another. It was just this contact that was needed to centralise the numerous local struggles, all of the same character, into one national struggle between classes. But every class struggle is a political struggle. And that union, to attain which the burghers of the Middle Ages, with their miserable highways, required centuries, the modern proletarians, thanks to railways, achieve in a few years.

This organisation of the proletarians into a class, and consequently into a political party, is continually being upset again by the competition between the workers themselves. But it ever rises up again, stronger, firmer, mightier. It compels legislative recognition of particular interests of the workers, by taking advantage of the divisions among the bourgeoisie itself. Thus the ten-hour bill in England was carried.

Altogether, collisions between the classes of the old society further the course of development of the proletariat in many ways. The bourgeoisie finds itself involved in a constant battle. At first with the aristocracy; later on, with those portions of the bourgeoisie itself whose interests have become antagonistic to the progress of industry; at all times with the bourgeoisie of foreign countries. In all these battles it sees itself compelled to appeal to the proletariat, to ask for its help, and thus, to drag it into the political arena. The bourgeoisie itself, therefore, supplies the proletariat with its own elements of political and general education, in other words, it furnishes the proletariat with weapons for fighting the bourgeoisie.

Further, as we have already seen, entire sections of the ruling classes are, by the advance of industry, precipitated into the proletariat, or are at least threatened in their conditions of existence. These also supply the proletariat with fresh elements of enlightenment and progress.

Finally, in times when the class struggle nears the decisive hour, the process of dissolution going on within the ruling class, in fact within the whole range of old society, assumes such a violent, glaring character, that a small section of the ruling class cuts itself adrift, and joins the revolutionary class, the class that holds the future in its hands. Just as, therefore, at an earlier period, a section of the nobility went over to the bourgeoisie, so now a portion of the bourgeoisie goes over to the proletariat, and in particular, a portion of the bourgeois ideologists, who have raised themselves to the level of comprehending theoretically the historical movement as a whole.

Of all the classes that stand face to face with the bourgeoisie today, the proletariat alone is a really revolutionary class. The other classes decay and finally disappear in the face of modern industry; the proletariat is its special and essential product.

The lower middle class, the small manufacturer, the shopkeeper, the artisan, the peasant, all these fight against the bourgeoisie, to save from extinction their existence as fractions of the middle class. They are therefore not revolutionary, but conservative. Nay more, they are reactionary, for they try to roll back the wheel of history. If by chance they are revolutionary, they are so only in view of their impending transfer into the proletariat; they thus defend not their present, but their future interests; they desert their own standpoint to adopt that of the proletariat.

The "dangerous class," the social scum (*Lumpenproletariat*), that passively rotting mass thrown off by the lower layers of old society, may, here and there, be swept into the movement by a proletarian revolution; its conditions of life, however, prepare it far more for the part of a bribed tool of reactionary intrigue.

The social conditions of the old society no longer exist for the proletariat. The proletarian is without property; his relation to his wife and children has no longer anything in common with bourgeois family relations; modern industrial labour, modern subjection to capital, the same in England as in France, in America as in Germany, has stripped him of every trace of national character. Law, morality, religion, are to him so many bourgeois prejudices, behind which lurk in ambush just as many bourgeois interests.

All the preceding classes that got the upper hand, sought to fortify their already acquired status by subjecting society at large to their conditions of appropriation. The proletarians cannot become masters of the productive forces of society, except by abolishing their own previous mode of appropriation, and thereby also every other previous mode of appropriation. They have nothing of their own to secure and to fortify; their mission is to destroy all previous securities for, and insurances of, individual property.

All previous historical movements were movements of minorities, or in the interest of minorities. The proletarian movement is the self-conscious, independent movement of the immense majority, in the interest of the immense majority. The proletariat, the lowest stratum of our present society, cannot stir, cannot raise itself up, without the whole superincumbent strata of official society being sprung into the air.

Though not in substance, yet in form, the struggle of the

proletariat with the bourgeoisie is at first a national struggle. The proletariat of each country must, of course, first of all settle matters with its own bourgeoisie.

In depicting the most general phases of the development of the proletariat, we traced the more or less veiled civil war, raging within existing society, up to the point where that war breaks out into open revolution, and where the violent overthrow of the bourgeoisie lays the foundation for the sway of the proletariat.

Hitherto, every form of society has been based, as we have already seen, on the antagonism of oppressing and oppressed classes. But in order to oppress a class, certain conditions must be assured to it under which it can, at least, continue its slavish existence. The serf, in the period of serfdom, raised himself to membership in the commune, just as the petty bourgeois, under the yoke of feudal absolutism, managed to develop into a bourgeois. The modern labourer, on the contrary, instead of rising with the progress of industry, sinks deeper and deeper below the conditions of existence of his own class. He becomes a pauper, and pauperism develops more rapidly than population and wealth. And here it becomes evident, that the bourgeoisie is unfit any longer to be the ruling class in society, and to impose its conditions of existence upon society as an over-riding law. It is unfit to rule because it is incompetent to assure an existence to its slave within his slavery, because it cannot help letting him sink into such a state, that it has to feed him, instead of being fed by him. Society can no longer live under this bourgeoisie, in other words, its existence is no longer compatible with society.

The essential condition for the existence and sway of the bourgeois class, is the formation and augmentation of capital; the condition for capital is wage-labour. Wage-labour rests exclusively on competition between the labourers. The advance of industry, whose involuntary promoter is the bourgeoisie, replaces the isolation of the labourers, due to competition, by their revoluntionary combination, due to association. The development of modern industry, therefore, cuts from under its feet the very foundation on which the bourgeoisie produces and appropriates products. What the bourgeoisie therefore produces, above all, are its own gravediggers. Its fall and the victory of the proletariat are equally inevitable.

II

PROLETARIANS AND COMMUNISTS

In what relation do the communists stand to the proletarians as a whole?

The communists do not form a separate party opposed to other working class parties.

They have no interests separate and apart from those of the proletariat as a whole.

They do not set up any sectarian principles of their own, by which to shape and mould the proletarian movement.

The communists are distinguished from the other working class parties by this only: 1. In the national struggles of the proletarians of the different countries, they point out and bring to the front the common interests of the entire proletariat, independently of all nationality. 2. In the various stages of development which the struggle of the working class against the bourgeoisie has to pass through, they always and everywhere represent the interests of the movement as a whole.

The communists, therefore, are on the one hand, practically, the most advanced and resolute section of the working class parties of every country, that section which pushes forward all others; on the other hand, theoretically, they have over the great mass of the proletariat the advantage of clearly understanding the line of march, the conditions, and the ultimate general results of the proletarian movement.

The immediate aim of the communists is the same as that

of all the other proletarian parties: Formation of the proletariat into a class, overthrow of bourgeois supremacy, conquest of political power by the proletariat.

The theoretical conclusions of the communists are in no way based on ideas or principles that have been invented, or discovered, by this or that would-be universal reformer.

They merely express, in general terms, actual relations springing from an existing class struggle, from a historical movement going on under our very eyes. The abolition of existing property relations is not at all a distinctive feature of communism.

All property relations in the past have continually been subject to historical change consequent upon the change in historical conditions.

The French Revolution, for example, abolished feudal property in favour of bourgeois property.

The distinguishing feature of communism is not the abolition of property generally, but the abolition of bourgeois property. But modern bourgeois private property is the final and most complete expression of the system of producing and appropriating products that is based on class antagonisms, on the exploitation of the many by the few.

In this sense, the theory of the communists may be summed up in the single sentence: Abolition of private property.

We communists have been reproached with the desire of abolishing the right of personally acquiring property as the fruit of a man's own labour, which property is alleged to be the groundwork of all personal freedom, activity, and independence.

Hard-won, self-acquired, self-earned property! Do you mean the property of the petty artisan and of the small peasant, a form of property that preceded the bourgeois form? There is no need to abolish that; the development of industry has to a great extent already destroyed it, and is still destroying it daily.

Or do you mean modern bourgeois private property?

But does wage-labour create any property for the labourer? Not a bit. It creates capital, *i. e.,* that kind of property which exploits wage-labour, and which cannot increase except upon condition of begetting a new supply of wage-labour for fresh exploitation. Property in its present form, is based on the antagonism of capital and wage-labour. Let us examine both sides of this antagonism.

To be a capitalist, is to have not only a purely personal, but a social *status* in production. Capital is a collective product, and only by the united action of many members, nay, in the last restort, only by the united action of all members of society, can it be set in motion.

Capital is therefore not a personal, it is a social, power.

When, therefore, capital is converted into common property, into the property of all members of society, personal property is not thereby transformed into social property. It is only the social character of the property that is changed. It loses its class character.

Let us now take wage-labour.

The average price of wage-labour is the minimum wage, *i. e.,* that quantum of the means of subsistence which is absolutely requisite to keep the labourer in bare existence as a labourer. What, therefore, the wage-labourer appropriates by means of his labour, merely suffices to prolong and reproduce a bare existence. We by no means intend to abolish this personal appropriation of the products of labour, an appropriation that is made for the maintenance and reproduction of human life, and that leaves no surplus wherewith to command the labour of others. All that we want to do away with is the miserable character of this appropriation, under which the labourer lives merely to increase capital, and is allowed to live only insofar as the interest of the ruling class requires it.

In bourgeois society, living labour is but a means to increase accumulated labour. In communist society, accumulated labour is but a means to widen, to enrich, to promote the existence of the labourer.

In bourgeois society, therefore, the past dominates the present; in communist society, the present dominates the past. In bourgeois society capital is independent and has individuality, while the living person is dependent and has no individuality.

And the abolition of this state of things is called by the bourgeois, abolition of individuality and freedom! And rightly so. The abolition of bourgeois individuality, bourgeois independence, and bourgeois freedom is undoubtedly aimed at.

By freedom is meant, under the present bourgeois conditions of production, free trade, free selling and buying.

But if selling and buying disappears, free selling and buying disappears also. This talk about free selling and buying, and all the other "brave words" of our bourgeoisie about freedom in general, have a meaning, if any, only in contrast with restricted selling and buying, with the fettered traders of the Middle Ages, but have no meaning when opposed to the communist abolition of buying and selling, of the bourgeois conditions of production, and of the bourgeoisie itself.

You are horrified at our intending to do away with private property. But in your existing society, private property is already done away with for nine-tenths of the population; its existence for the few is solely due to its non-existence in the hands of those nine-tenths. You reproach us, therefore, with intending to do away with a form of property, the necessary condition for whose existence is the non-existence of any property for the immense majority of society.

In a word, you reproach us with intending to do away with your property. Precisely so; that is just what we intend.

From the moment when labour can no longer be converted into capital, money, or rent, into a social power capable of being monopolised, *i. e.,* from the moment when individual property can no longer be transformed into bourgeois property, into capital, from that moment, you say, individuality vanishes.

You must, therefore, confess that by "individual" you

mean no other person than the bourgeois, than the middle class owner of property. This person must, indeed, be swept out of the way, and made impossible.

Communism deprives no man of the power to appropriate the products of society; all that it does is to deprive him of the power to subjugate the labour of others by means of such appropriation.

It has been objected, that upon the abolition of private property all work will cease, and universal laziness will overtake us.

According to this, bourgeois society ought long ago to have gone to the dogs through sheer idleness; for those of its members who work, acquire nothing, and those who acquire anything, do not work. The whole of this objection is but another expression of the tautology: There can no longer be any wage-labour when there is no longer any capital.

All objections urged against the communist mode of producing and appropriating material products, have, in the same way, been urged against the communist modes of producing and appropriating intellectual products. Just as, to the bourgeois, the disappearance of class property is the disappearance of production itself, so the disapearance of class culture is to him identical with the disappearance of all culture.

That culture, the loss of which he laments, is, for the enormous majority, a mere training to act as a machine.

But don't wrangle with us so long as you apply, to our intended abolition of bourgeois property, the standard of your bourgeois notions of freedom, culture, law, etc. Your very ideas are but the outgrowth of the conditions of your bourgeois production and bourgeois property, just as your jurisprudence is but the will of your class made into a law for all, a will whose essential character and direction are determined by the economic conditions of existence of your class.

The selfish misconception that induces you to transform into eternal laws of nature and of reason, the social forms springing from your present mode of production and form of property—historical relations that rise and disappear in the progress of production—this misconception you share with every ruling class that has preceded you. What you see clearly in the case of ancient property, what you admit in the case of feudal property, you are of course forbidden to admit in the case of your own bourgeois form of property.

Abolition of the family! Even the most radical flare up at this infamous proposal of the communists.

On what foundation is the present family, the bourgeois family, based? On capital, on private gain. In its completely developed form this family exists only among the bourgeoisie. But this state of things finds its complement in the practical absence of the family among the proletarians, and in public prostitution.

The bourgeois family will vanish as a matter of course when its complement vanishes, and both will vanish with the vanishing of capital.

Do you charge us with wanting to stop the exploitation of children by their parents? To this crime we plead guilty.

But, you will say, we destroy the most hallowed of relations, when we replace home education by social.

And your education! Is not that also social, and determined by the social conditions under which you educate, by the intervention of society, direct or indirect, by means of schools, etc? The communists have not invented the intervention of society in education; they do but seek to alter the character of that intervention, and to rescue education from the influence of the ruling class.

The bourgeois claptrap about the family and education, about the hallowed co-relation of parent and child, becomes all the more disgusting, the more, by the action of modern industry, all family ties among the proletarians are torn asunder, and their children transformed into simple articles of commerce and instruments of labour.

But you communists would introduce community of women, screams the whole bourgeoisie in chorus.

The bourgeois sees in his wife a mere instrument of production. He hears that the instruments of production are to be exploited in common, and, naturally, can come to no other conclusion than that the lot of being common to all will likewise fall to the women.

He has not even a suspicion that the real point aimed at is to do away with the status of women as mere instruments of production.

For the rest, nothing is more ridiculous than the virtuous indignation of our bourgeois at the community of women which, they pretend, is to be openly and officially established by the communists. The communists have no need to introduce community of women; it has existed almost from time immemorial.

Our bourgeois, not content with having the wives and daughters of their proletarians at their disposal, not to speak of common prostitutes, take the greatest pleasure in seducing each other's wives.

Bourgeois marriage is in reality a system of wives in common and thus, at the most, what the communists might possibly be reproached with is that they desire to introduce, in substitution for a hypocritically concealed, an openly legalised community of women. For the rest, it is self-evident, that the abolition of the present system of production must bring with it the abolition of the community of women springing from that system, *i. e.,* of prostitution both public and private.

The communists are further reproached with desiring to abolish countries and nationality.

The workingmen have no country. We cannot take from them what they have not got. Since the proletariat must first of all acquire political supremacy, must rise to be the leading class of the nation, must constitute itself *the* nation, it is, so far, itself national, though not in the bourgeois sense of the word.

National differences and antagonisms between peoples are vanishing gradually from day to day, owing to the development of the bourgeoisie, to freedom of commerce, to the world market, to uniformity in the mode of production and in the conditions of life corresponding thereto.

The supremacy of the proletariat will cause them to vanish still faster. United action, of the leading civilised countries at least, is one of the first conditions for the emancipation of the proletariat.

In proportion as the exploitation of one individual by another is put an end to, the exploitation of one nation by another will also be put an end to. In proportion as the antagonism between classes within the nation vanishes, the hostility of one nation to another will come to an end.

The charges against communism made from a religious, a philosophical, and, generally, from an ideological standpoint, are not deserving of serious examination.

Does it require deep intuition to comprehend that man's ideas, views, and conceptions, in one word, man's consciousness, changes with every change in the conditions of his material existence, in his social relations and in his social life?

What else does the history of ideas prove, than that intellectual production changes its character in proportion as material production is changed? The ruling ideas of each age have ever been the ideas of its ruling class.

When people speak of ideas that revolutionise society, they do but express the fact that within the old society the elements of a new one have been created, and that the dissolution of the old ideas keeps even pace with the dissolution of the old conditions of existence.

When the ancient world was in its last throes, the ancient religions were overcome by Christianity. When Christian ideas succumbed in the 18th century to rationalist ideas, feudal society fought its death-battle with the then revolutionary bourgeoisie. The ideas of religious liberty and freedom of conscience, merely gave expression to the sway of free competition within the domain of knowledge.

"Undoubtedly," it will be said, "religion, moral, philosophical and juridical ideas have been modified in the course of historical development. But religion, morality, philosophy, political science, and law, constantly survived this change."

"There are, besides, eternal truths, such as Freedom, Justice, etc., that are common to all states of society. But communism abolishes eternal truths, it abolishes all religion, and all morality, instead of constituting them on a new basis; it therefore acts in contradiction to all past historical experience."

What does this accusation reduce itself to? The history of all past society has consisted in the development of class antagonisms, antagonisms that assumed different forms at different epochs.

But whatever form they may have taken, one fact is common to all past ages, *viz.*, the exploitation of one part of society by the other. No wonder, then, that the social consciousness of past ages, despite all the multiplicity and variety it displays, moves within certain common forms, or general ideas, which cannot completely vanish except with the total disappearance of class antagonisms.

The communist revolution is the most radical rupture with traditional property relations; no wonder that its development involves the most radical rupture with traditional ideas.

But let us have done with the bourgeois objections to communism.

We have seen above, that the first step in the revolution by the working class, is to raise the proletariat to the position of ruling class, to establish democracy.

The proletariat will use its political supremacy to wrest, by degrees, all capital from the bourgeoisie, to centralise all instruments of production in the hands of the state, *i.e.*, of the proletariat organised as the ruling class; and to increase the total of productive forces as rapidly as possible.

Of course, in the beginning, this cannot be effected except by means of despotic inroads on the rights of property, and on the conditions of bourgeois production; by means of measures, therefore, which appear economically insufficient and untenable, but which, in the course of the movement, outstrip themselves, necessitate further inroads upon the old social order, and are unavoidable as a means of entirely revolutionising the mode of production.

These measures will of course be different in different countries.

Nevertheless in the most advanced countries, the following will be pretty generally applicable.

1. Abolition of property in land and application of all rents of land to public purposes.

2. A heavy progressive or graduated income tax.

3. Abolition of all right of inheritance.

4. Confiscation of the property of all emigrants and rebels.

5. Centralisation of credit in the hands of the state, by means of a national bank with state capital and an exclusive monopoly.

6. Centralisation of the means of communication and transport in the hands of the state.

7. Extension of factories and instruments of production owned by the state; the bringing into cultivation of waste lands, and the improvement of the soil generally in accordance with a common plan.

8. Equal obligation of all to work. Establishment of industrial armies, especially for agriculture.

9. Combination of agriculture with manufacturing industries; gradual abolition of the distinction between town and country, by a more equable distribution of the population over the country.

10. Free education for all children in public schools. Abolition of child factory labour in its present form. Combination of education with industrial production, etc.

When, in the course of development, class distinctions have disappeared, and all production has been concentrated in the hands of a vast association of the whole nation, the public power will lose its political character. Political power, properly so called, is merely the organised power of one class for oppressing another. If the proletariat during its contest with the bourgeoisie is compelled, by the force of circumstances, to organise itself as a class; if, by means of a revolution, it makes itself the ruling class, and, as such sweeps away by force the old conditions of production, then it will, along with these conditions, have swept away the conditions for the existence of class antagonisms, and of classes generally, and will thereby have abolished its own supremacy as a class.

In place of the old bourgeois society, with its classes and class antagonisms, we shall have an association, in which the free development of each is the condition for the free development of all.

III

SOCIALIST AND COMMUNIST LITERATURE

1. Reactionary Socialism

a. Feudal Socialism

OWING to their historical position, it became the vocation of the aristocracies of France and England to write pamphlets against modern bourgeois society. In the French revolution of July, 1830, and in the English reform agitation, these aristocracies again succumbed to the hateful upstart. Thenceforth, a serious political struggle was altogether out of the question. A literary battle alone remained possible. But even in the domain of literature the old cries of the restoration period had become impossible.

In order to arouse sympathy, the aristocracy was obliged to lose sight, apparently, of its own interests, and to formulate its indictment against the bourgeoisie in the interest of the exploited working class alone. Thus the aristocracy took its revenge by singing lampoons against its new master, and whispering in his ears sinister prophecies of coming catastrophe.

In this way arose feudal socialism: Half lamentation, half lampoon; half echo of the past, half menace of the future; at times, by its bitter, witty and incisive criticism, striking the bourgeoisie to the very heart's core, but always ludicrous in its effect through total incapacity to comprehend the march of modern history.

The aristocracy, in order to rally the people to them, waved the proletarian alms-bag in front for a banner. But the people, as often as it joined them, saw on their hind-quarters the old feudal coats of arms, and deserted with loud and irreverent laughter.

One section of the French legitimists, and "Young England," exhibited this spectacle.

In pointing out that their mode of exploitation was different from that of the bourgeoisie, the feudalists forget that they exploited under circumstances and conditions that were quite different, and that are now antiquated. In showing that, under their rule, the modern proletariat never existed, they forget that the modern bourgeoisie is the necessary offspring of their own form of society.

For the rest, so little do they conceal the reactionary character of their criticism, that their chief accusation against the bourgeoisie amounts to this, that under the bourgeois regime a class is being developed, which is destined to cut up root and branch the old order of society.

What they upbraid the bourgeoisie with is not so much that it creates a proletariat, as that it creates a *revolutionary* proletariat.

In political practice, therefore, they join in all coercive measures against the working class; and in ordinary life, despite their high-falutin phrases, they stoop to pick up the golden apples dropped from the tree of industry, and to barter truth, love, and honour for traffic in wool, beetroot-sugar, and potato spirits.

As the parson has ever gone hand in hand with the landlord, so has clerical socialism with feudal socialism.

Nothing is easier than to give Christian asceticism a socialist tinge. Has not Christianity declaimed against private property, against marriage, against the state? Has it not preached in the place of these, charity and poverty, celibacy and mortification of the flesh, monastic life and Mother Church? Christian socialism is but the holy water with which the priest consecrates the heart-burnings of the aristocrat.

b. Petty Bourgeois Socialism

The feudal aristocracy was not the only class that was ruined by the bourgeoisie, not the only class whose conditions of existence pined and perished in the atmosphere of modern bourgeois society. The mediæval burgesses and the small peasant proprietors were the precursors of the modern bourgeoisie. In those countries which are but little developed, industrially and commercially these two classes still vegetate side by side with the rising bourgeoisie.

In countries where modern civilisation has become fully developed, a new class of petty bourgeois has been formed, fluctuating between proletariat and bourgeoisie, and ever renewing itself as a supplementary part of bourgeois society. The individual members of this class, however, are being constantly hurled down into the proletariat by the action of competition, and, as modern industry develops, they even see the moment approaching when they will completely disappear as an independent section of modern society, to be replaced, in manufactures, agriculture and commerce, by overlookers, bailiffs and shopmen.

In countries, like France, where the peasants constitute far more than half of the population, it was natural that writers who sided with the proletariat against the bourgeoisie, should use, in their criticism of the bourgeois regime, the standard of the peasant and petty bourgeois, and from the standpoint of these intermediate classes should take up the cudgels for the working class. Thus arose petty bourgeois socialism. Sismondi was the head of this school, not only in France but also in England.

This school of socialism dissected with great acuteness the contradictions in the conditions of modern production. It laid bare the hypocritical apologies of economists. It proved, incontrovertibly, the disastrous effects of machinery and division of labour; the concentration of capital and land in a few hands; overproduction and crises; it pointed out the inevitable ruin of the petty bourgeois and peasant, the misery of the proletariat, the anarchy in production, the crying inequalities in the distribution of wealth, the industrial war of extermination between nations, the dissolution of old moral bonds, of the old family relations, of the old nationalities.

In its positive aims, however, this form of socialism aspires either to restoring the old means of production and of exchange, and with them the old property relations, and the old society, or to cramping the modern means of production and of exchange within the framework of the old property relations that have been, and were bound to be, exploded by those means. In either case, it is both reactionary and utopian.

Its last words are: Corporate guilds for manufacture; patriarchal relations in agriculture.

Ultimately, when stubborn historical facts had dispersed all intoxicating effects of self-deception, this form of socialism ended in a miserable fit of the blues.

c. German or "True" Socialism

The socialist and communist literature of France, a literature that originated under the pressure of a bourgeoisie in power, and that was the expression of the struggle against this power, was introduced into Germany at a time when the bourgeoisie, in that country, had just begun its contest with feudal absolutism.

German philosophers, would-be philosophers, and men of letters eagerly seized on this literature, only forgetting that when these writings immigrated from France into Germany, French social conditions had not immigrated along with them. In contact with German social conditions, this French literature lost all its immediate practical significance, and assumed a purely literary aspect. Thus, to the German philosophers of the 18th century, the demands of the first French Revolution were nothing more than the demands of "Practical Reason" in general, and the utterance of the will of the revolutionary French bourgeoisie signified in their eyes the laws of pure will, of will as it was bound to be, of true human will generally.

The work of the German *literati* consisted solely in bringing the new French ideas into harmony with their ancient philosophical conscience, or rather, in annexing the French ideas without deserting their own philosophic point of view.

This annexation took place in the same way in which a foreign language is appropriated, namely by translation.

It is well known how the monks wrote silly lives of Catholic saints *over* the manuscripts on which the classical works of ancient heathendom had been written. The German *literati* reversed this process with the profane French literature. They wrote their philosophical nonsense beneath the French original. For instance, beneath the French criticism of the economic functions of money, they wrote "alienation of humanity," and beneath the French criticism of the bourgeois state, they wrote, "dethronement of the category of the general," and so forth.

The introduction of these philosophical phrases at the back of the French historical criticisms they dubbed "Philosophy of Action," "True Socialism," "German Science of Socialism," "Philosophical Foundation of Socialism," and so on.

The French socialist and communist literature was thus completely emasculated. And, since it ceased in the hands of the German to express the struggle of one class with the other, he felt conscious of having overcome "French onesidedness" and of representing, not true requirements, but the requirements of truth; not the interests of the proletariat, but the interests of human nature, of man in general, who belongs to no class, has no reality, who exists only in the misty realm of philosophical phantasy.

This German socialism, which took its school-boy task so seriously and solemnly, and extolled its poor stock-in-trade in such mountebank fashion, meanwhile gradually lost its pedantic innocence.

The fight of the German and especially of the Prussian bourgeoisie against feudal aristocracy and absolute monarchy, in other words, the liberal movement, became more earnest.

By this, the long-wished-for opportunity was offered to "True" socialism of confronting the political movement with the socialist demands, of hurling the traditional anathemas against liberalism, against representative government, against bourgeois competition, bourgeois freedom of the press, bourgeois legislation, bourgeois liberty and equality, and of preaching to the masses that they had nothing to gain, and everything to lose, by this bourgeois movement. German socialism forgot, in the nick of time, that the French criticism, whose silly echo it was, presupposed the existence of modern bourgeois society, with its corresponding economic conditions of existence, and the political constitution adapted thereto, the very things whose attainment was the object of the pending struggle in Germany.

To the absolute governments, with their following of parsons, professors, country squires and officials, it served as a welcome scarecrow against the threatening bourgeoisie.

It was a sweet finish after the bitter pills of floggings and bullets, with which these same governments, just at that time, dosed the risings of the German working class.

While this "True" socialism thus served the governments as a weapon for fighting the German bourgeoisie, it, at the same time, directly represented a reactionary interest, the interest of the German philistines. In Germany the petty bourgeois class, a relic of the 16th century, and since then constantly cropping up again under various forms, is the real social basis of the existing state of things.

To preserve this class, is to preserve the existing state of things in Germany. The industrial and political supremacy of the bourgeoisie threatens it with certain destruction—on the one hand, from the concentration of capital; on the other, from the rise of a revolutionary proletariat. "True" socialism appeared to kill these two birds with one stone. It spread like an epidemic.

The robe of speculative cobwebs, embroidered with flowers of rhetoric, steeped in the dew of sickly sentiment, this transcendental robe in which the German socialists wrapped their sorry "eternal truths," all skin and bone, served to increase wonderfully the sale of their goods amongst such a public.

And on its part, German socialism recognised, more and more, its own calling as the bombastic representative of the petty bourgeois philistine.

It proclaimed the German nation to be the model nation, and the German petty philistine to he the typical man. To every villainous meanness of this model man it gave a hidden, higher, socialistic interpretation, the exact contrary of his real character. It went to the extreme length of directly opposing the "brutally destructive" tendency of communism, and of proclaiming its supreme and impartial contempt of all class struggles. With very few exceptions, all the so-called socialist and communist publications that now (1847) circulate in Germany belong to the domain of this foul and enervating literature.

2. CONSERVATIVE OR BOURGEOIS SOCIALISM

A part of the bourgeoisie is desirous of redressing social grievances, in order to secure the continued existence of bourgeois society.

To this section belong economists, philanthropists, humanitarians, improvers of the condition of the working class, organisers of charity, members of societies for the prevention of cruelty to animals, temperance fanatics, hole-and-corner reformers of every imaginable kind. This form of socialism has, moreover, been worked out into complete systems.

We may cite Proudhon's *Philosophy of Poverty* as an example of this form.

The socialistic bourgeois want all the advantages of modern social conditions without the struggles and dangers necessarily resulting therefrom. They desire the existing state of society minus its revolutionary and disintegrating elements. They wish for a bourgeoisie without a proletariat. The bourgeoisie naturally conceives the world in which it is supreme to be the best; and bourgeois socialism develops this comfortable conception into various more or less complete systems. In requiring the proletariat to carry out such a system, and thereby to march straightway into the social New Jerusalem, it but requires in reality, that the proletariat should remain within the bounds of existing society, but should cast away all its hateful ideas concerning the bourgeoisie.

A second and more practical, but less systematic, form of this socialism sought to depreciate every revolutionary movement in the eyes of the working class, by showing that no mere political reform, but only a change in the material conditions of existence, in economic relations, could be of any advantage to them. By changes in the material conditions of existence, this form of socialism, however, by no means understands abolition of the bourgeois relations of production, an abolition that can be effected only by a revolution, but administrative reforms, based on the continued existence of these relations; reforms, therefore, that in no respect affect the relations between capital and labour, but, at the best, lessen the cost, and simplify the administrative work of bourgeois government.

Bourgeois socialism attains adequate expression, when, and only when, it becomes a mere figure of speech.

Free trade: For the benefit of the working class. Protective duties: For the benefit of the working class. Prison reform: For the benefit of the working class. These are the last words and the only seriously meant words of bourgeois socialism.

It is summed up in the phrase: the bourgeois are bourgeois —for the benefit of the working class.

3. CRITICAL-UTOPIAN SOCIALISM AND COMMUNISM

We do not here refer to that literature which, in every great modern revolution, has always given voice to the demands of the proletariat, such as the writings of Babeuf and others.

The first direct attempts of the proletariat to attain its own ends—made in times of universal excitement, when feudal society was being overthrown—necessarily failed, owing to the then undeveloped state of the proletariat, as well as to the absence of the economic conditions for its emancipation, conditions that had yet to be produced, and could be produced by the impending bourgeois epoch alone. The revolutionary literature that accompanied these first movements of the proletariat had necessarily a reactionary character. It inculcated universal asceticism and social levelling in its crudest form.

The socialist and communist systems properly so called, those of St. Simon, Fourier, Owen and others, spring into existence in the early undeveloped period, described above of the struggle between proletariat and bourgeoisie (see Section 1. Bourgeois and Proletarians).

The founders of these systems see, indeed, the class antagonisms, as well as the action of the decomposing elements in the prevailing form of society. But the proletariat, as yet in its infancy, offers to them the spectacle of a class without any historical initiative or any independent political movement.

Since the development of class antagonism keeps even pace with the development of industry, the economic situation, as such socialists find it, does not as yet offer to them

the material conditions for the emancipation of the proletariat. They therefore search after a new social science, after
new social laws, that are to create these conditions.

Historical action is to yield to their personal inventive action; historically created conditions of emancipation to phantastic ones; and the gradual, spontaneous class organisation
of the proletariat to an organisation of society specially contrived by these inventors. Future history, resolves itself, in
their eyes, into the propaganda and the practical carrying
out of their social plans.

In the formation of their plans they are conscious of caring
chiefly for the interests of the working class, as being the
most suffering class. Only from the point of view of being
the most suffering class does the proletariat exist for them.

The undeveloped state of the class struggle, as well as their
own surroundings, causes socialists of this kind to consider
themselves far superior to all class antagonisms. They want
to improve the condition of every member of society, even
that of the most favoured. Hence, they habitually appeal to
society at large, without distinction of class; nay, by preference, to the ruling class. For how can people, when once they
understand their system, fail to see in it the best possible plan
of the best possible state of society?

Hence, they reject all political, and especially all revolutionary action; they wish to attain their ends by peaceful
means, and endeavour, by small experiments, necessarily
doomed to failure, and by the force of example, to pave the
way for the new social gospel.

Such phantastic pictures of future society, painted at a
time when the proletariat is still in a very undeveloped state
and has but a phantastic conception of its own position, correspond with the first instinctive yearnings of that class for a
general reconstruction of society.

But these socialist and communist writings contain also a
critical element. They attack every principle of existing society. Hence they are full of the most valuable materials for
the enlightenment of the working class. The practical meas-

ures proposed in them—such as the abolition of the distinction between town and country; abolition of the family, of
private gain and of the wage-system; the proclamation of
social harmony; the conversion of the functions of the state
into a mere superintendence of production—all these proposals point solely to the disappearance of class antagonisms
which were, at that time, only just cropping up, and which,
in these publications, are recognised in their earliest, indis-
tinct and undefined forms only. These proposals, therefore,
are of a purely utopian character.

The significance of critical-utopian socialism and communism bears an inverse relation to historical development.
In proportion as the modern class struggle develops and
takes definite shape, this phantastic standing apart from the
contest, these phantastic attacks on it, lose all practical value
and all theoretical justification. Therefore, although the orig-
inators of these systems were, in many respects, revolutionary, their disciples have, in every case, formed mere reactionary sects. They hold fast by the original views of their
masters, in opposition to the progressive historical development of the proletariat. They, therefore, endeavour, and that
consistently, to deaden the class struggle and to reconcile the
class antagonisms. They still dream of experimental realisation of their social utopias, of founding isolated *phalanstères,*
of establishing "Home Colonies," or setting up a "Little
Icaria"—pocket editions of the New Jerusalem—and to
realise all these castles in the air, they are compelled to appeal to the feelings and purses of the bourgeois. By degrees
they sink into the category of the reactionary conservative
socialists depicted above, differing from these only by more
systematic pedantry, and by their fanatical and superstitious
belief in the miraculous effects of their social science.

They, therefore, violently oppose all political action on the
part of the working class; such action, according to them,
can only result from blind unbelief in the new gospel.

The Owenites in England, and the Fourierists in France,
respectively, oppose the Chartists and the *Réformistes.*

IV

POSITION OF THE COMMUNISTS IN RELATION TO THE VARIOUS EXISTING OPPOSITION PARTIES

SECTION II has made clear the relations of the communists to the existing working class parties, such as the chartists in England and the agrarian reformers in America.

The communists fight for the attainment of the immediate aims, for the enforcement of the momentary interests of the working class; but in the movement of the present, they also represent and take care of the future of that movement. In France the communists ally themselves with the social-democrats, against the conservative and radical bourgeoisie, reserving, however, the right to take up a critical position in regard to phrases and illusions traditionally handed down from the great Revolution.

In Switzerland they support the radicals, without losing sight of the fact that this party consists of antagonistic elements, partly of democratic socialists, in the French sense, partly of radical bourgeois.

In Poland they support the party that insists on an agrarian revolution as the prime condition for national emancipation, that party which fomented the insurrection of Cracow in 1846.

In Germany they fight with the bourgeoisie whenever it acts in a revolutionary way, against the absolute monarchy, the feudal squirearchy, and the petty bourgeoisie.

But they never cease, for a single instant, to instil into the working class the clearest possible recognition of the hostile antagonism between bourgeoisie and proletariat, in order that the German workers may straightway use, as so many weapons against the bourgeoisie, the social and political conditions that the bourgeoisie must necessarily introduce along with its supremacy, and in order that, after the fall of the reactionary class in Germany, the fight against the bourgeoisie itself may immediately begin.

The communists turn their attention chiefly to Germany, because that country is on the eve of a bourgeois revolution that is bound to be carried out under more advanced conditions of European civilisation and with a much more developed proletariat than what existed in England in the 17th and in France in the 18th century, and because the bourgeois revolution in Germany will be but the prelude to an immediately following proletarian revolution.

In short, the communists everywhere support every revolutionary movement against the existing social and political order of things.

In all these movements they bring to the front, as the leading question in each case, the property question, no matter what its degree of development at the time.

Finally, they labour everywhere for the union and agreement of the democratic parties of all countries.

The communists disdain to conceal their views and aims. They openly declare that their ends can be attained only by the forcible overthrow of all existing social conditions. Let the ruling classes tremble at a communist revolution. The proletarians have nothing to lose but their chains. They have a world to win.

Workingmen of all countries, unite!

reactionary class in Germany, the fight against the bourgeoisie itself may immediately begin.

The Communists turn their attention chiefly to Germany, because that country is on the eve of a bourgeois revolution that is bound to be carried out under more advanced conditions of European civilisation and with a much more developed proletariat than what existed in England in the 17th, and in France in the 18th century, and because the bourgeois revolution in Germany will be but the prelude to an immediately following proletarian revolution.

In short, the Communists everywhere support every revolutionary movement against the existing social and political order of things.

In all these movements they bring to the front, as the leading question in each case, the property question, no matter what its degree of development at the time.

Finally, they labour everywhere for the union and agreement of the democratic parties of all countries.

The Communists disdain to conceal their views and aims. They openly declare that their ends can be attained only by the forcible overthrow of all existing social conditions. Let the ruling classes tremble at a communist revolution. The proletarians have nothing to lose but their chains. They have a world to win.

Workingmen of all countries, unite!

VI

SOCIOLOGY AND SOCIAL CONFLICT

COMMENTARY

After sociology comes of age, it begins to develop new outlooks and attitudes, and the problem which soon arises, as the Industrial Revolution advances and overturns the old way of life, is that of social justice and economic equality. The Industrial Revolution brings with it an awakening sense of individualism, which creates new difficulties in the organization of society.

Durkheim is the first of the new social thinkers to give sociological form to the problem. Marx had described it in economic terms, but Durkheim gives it sociological and psychological formulation. He realizes, better than any of his contemporaries, the real difficulty involved in the conflict between collective and individualistic culture. Gumplowicz goes even further in translating that difficulty into class terms, and, despite his social cynicism, in giving what might be loosely described as a semi-Marxian interpretation of the social process, except that he does not envision the proletariat in the sublime sense that Marx does. Oppenheimer then does for the State what Marx and Gumplowicz had foreshadowed in their reflections upon social phenomena, and instead of interpreting it as a source of order, as most thinkers of his time did, he views it as a form of group or class domination.

Lenin, Trotsky, Machajski, and Kropotkin all construe the state as it is in somewhat similar terms: namely, as a device by means of which the ruling class is able to keep all other classes in subjection. In their eyes the state is fundamentally an instrument of oppression, not of order. Like Marx and Engels, Lenin and Trotsky view the state as a necessary evil in class-ridden societies. Once classes are destroyed, however, and a classless society is created, the state,

*Lenin and Trotsky both contend, will gradually but even-
tually "wither away." Kropotkin, of course, "goes them one
better" in that he contends that the state is not something
which we must wait to wither away, but something which,
following the anarchist philosophy of Proudhon and Bakunin, should be done away with now, once and for all. Lenin
and Trotsky, despite the fact that they are revolutionists
rather than evolutionists in their social philosophy, believe
in the evolutionary disappearance of the state under a proletarian dictatorship. Kropotkin, however, will not accept such
a compromise with the temporal process. He believes that it
is possible to re-organize society today, not fifty years from
now, about such a state-less basis, and that the delays in that
realization which Lenin, Trotsky, and now Stalin, accept as
inevitable are but subterfuges and compromises which are
unnecessary in the light of the economics of plenty which is
the economics of the present-day world. Kropotkin, it is important to note, like Sorel and the whole anarcho-syndicalist
school, is eager to preserve individualistic rights amid a social or collective economy. Lenin and Trotsky are less concerned with such individualistic rights—not that they would
deny their value ultimately. They believe the basic task is to
collectivize the economy and establish a proletarian state,
which in time, when the dictatorship of the proletariat disappears and is replaced by a classless society, will provide
these rights and fortify these freedoms.*

*In the Soviet Union, to be sure, since the death of Lenin,
a great struggle is taking place, in which the attitudes of
Stalin and Trotsky are in conflict. Stalin contends that it is
possible that a socialist society can be built in one country;
Trotsky argues that that is impossible, and in his theory of
"permanent revolution," he maintains that socialism is possible only when several countries at least, industrial ones as
well as agrarian, have gone socialist and united in a joint
enterprise.*

*In the case of Mussolini and Hitler, we are faced with the
antipodes of such radical conceptions. Mussolini and Hitler*

believe that capitalism must be preserved, and that the great struggle facing western civilization today is that of defeating socialist and communist doctrines. Their conception of national socialism, *in essence, represents an attempt to save capitalist economics by harnessing it behind a* totalitarian *state. The labor movement, in the fascist economics of Mussolini and Hitler, is suppressed in order to effect a harmony between classes in which the state will be the arbiter of all differences and disagreements. The state in fascist countries is exalted into the great social force of all time. Individualism of every variety is discouraged as inimical to the fascist ideal. Anything or anyone hostile to the fascist conception is outlawed and persecuted. In Germany, Jews, Catholics, and dissident Protestants as well as socialists and communists are persecuted.*

DIVISION OF LABOR AND SOCIAL SOLIDARITY

By EMILE DURKHEIM

THE most striking effect of the division of labor is that instead of emphasizing the distinction of functions, it rather makes them interdependent. Its role is not merely to polish or perfect existing societies, but to make possible societies which without it could not exist. If the division of labor between the sexes were diminished beyond a certain point, the family would no longer exist and relations between the sexes would be only temporary. If the sexes had never been separated, no kind of social life would ever have developed. Very likely the economic force of the division of labor has been an element in the development of the existing form of marriage. The society that has developed, however, is not merely the product of economic influences. It is a unique social and moral order. Individuals who otherwise would lead individual existences, are bound to each other. They unite their efforts instead of developing separately. They are interdependent parts of a unity that is permanent. The monogamous marriage of existing society exerts its influence on all phases of life. In contrast, societies that are created by division of labor, inevitably bear the mark of their origin. Thus they cannot resemble those societies which have their origin in the attraction of like for like. These latter have a different composition, rest on different foundations, and appeal to other sentiments.

The belief that the social relations resulting from the division of labor consist of an exchange of services is a misconception of what such exchange implies and of the effects it produces. It assumes that two people depend upon each other because the one is incomplete without the other. It thinks of this mutual dependence as a purely external rela-

381

tion. In reality, this is merely the outward expression of a complicated internal state. Just because this state is constant, it provokes a series of mental images that function with a continuity independent of the external relations. The image of that which completes us is inseparable from the image of ourselves, not only because it is associated with us but also because it is our own natural complement. It therefore becomes a permanent and integral part of the conciousness of self; not only can we not do without it, but we try in every way to emphasize and intensify it. We like the society of the one whose image haunts us because the actual presence of the object strengthens the perception and gives reassurance and confidence. We suffer from every circumstance which, like death or separation, is likely to decrease the vitality of the idea which we have come to identify with our idea of ourselves.

This analysis, brief though it is, suffices to show that this complex is not to be identified with that which is based on sentiments of sympathy arising from mere likeness. A sense of solidarity between ourselves and others can exist only when we conceive of others as united with ourselves. When the union results from a perception of likeness, it is a cohesion. The two elements become united because they are mingled and are no more than one, and are united only to the extent that they are mingled. In contrast, in the case of division of labor, each is outside the other, and their union is possible only because they are distinct. Very naturally, both the sentiments and the social relations arising from these two different unions are themselves very different.

We may then ask whether the division of labor plays the same role in more extended groups; whether, in contemporary societies where it has had a development with which we are familiar it functions in such a way as to integrate the social body and to assure its unity. It is reasonable to assume that the facts already observed will reproduce themselves there on a larger scale. We may assume that large social groups, like small ones, maintain themselves in equilibrium because of the specialization of tasks. The division of labor here again is the chief source of social stability. Comte early accepted this point of view. He is the first sociologist, as far as we know, who pointed out in the division of labor anything other than a purely economic phenomenon. He saw there "the most essential condition of social life," if one conceives it "in all its rational extent, that is to say, that one applies the conception to the ensemble of all our diverse operations whatsoever, instead of limiting it, as we so often do, to the simple material usages." Considered under this aspect, he says:

"It immediately leads us to regard not only individuals and classes but also, in many respects, the different peoples as constantly participating, in their own characteristic ways, and in their own proper degree, in an immense and common work whose inevitable development gradually unites the actual co-operators in a series with their predecessors and at the same time in a series with their successors. It is, then, the continuous redivision of our diverse human labors which mainly constitutes social solidarity and which becomes the elementary cause of the extension and increasing complexity of the social organism."

If this hypothesis is demonstrated, then division of labor plays a much more prominent role than has ordinarily been attributed to it. It is not to be regarded as a mere luxury, desirable but not indispensable to society; instead, it is necessary to the very existence of society. It is division of labor that assures the stability of social groups. It determines the chief characteristics of their constitution. Although we cannot yet solve the problem permanently, we can foresee that if this is really the function of the division of labor, it must have a moral character, since the needs of order, harmony, and social stability are understood as moral.

Social life derives from a double source: (a) from a similarity of minds, and (b) from the division of labor. In the first case, the individual is socialized because having no individuality of his own, he is confused with his fellows in the bosom of the same collective type; in the second case, because although he possesses a physiognomy and a temperament that distinguishes him from his fellows, he is dependent upon them to the same extent that he is distinguished from them. The result of this union is society.

Like-mindedness gives rise to judicial regulations which, under the menace of measures of repression, impose upon everybody uniform beliefs and practices. The more pronounced this like-mindedness, the more thoroughly the social life is fused with the religious life, the more nearly do economic institutions approach communism.

The division of labor, on the other hand, gives rise to regulations and laws which determine the nature and the relations of the divided functions; the violations of these regulations entails punitive measures but not of an expiatory character.

Every code of laws is accompanied by a body of regulations that are purely moral. Where the penal law is voluminous, moral consensus is quite extended; that is, a multitude of collective activities is under the guardianship of public opinion. Wherever the right of reparation is well developed, there each profession adheres to a code of professional ethics. In a group of workers there invariably exists a body of opinion, diffused throughout the extent of the group, which although not fortified by legal sanctions, still enforces its decrees.

There are manners and customs accepted by all members of the profession, no one of which could be infringed without incurring the opprobrium of society. This code of morals is distinguished from the preceding by differences similar to those which separate the two corresponding kinds of laws. In fact, it is a code localized in a limited section of society. Furthermore, the sanctions of the code are much less repressive in character. Professional offenses arouse much less antagonism than offenses against the mores of the larger society.

Nevertheless, the customs and code of the professions are

important. They require the individual to act in accordance with ends which are not personal, to make concessions, to accept compromises, to consider interests superior to his own. The result is that, even where the society is based most completely on the division of labor, it does not disintegrate into atoms between which there can exist only external and temporary contacts. Every function exercised by one individual is invariably dependent upon functions exercised by others and with them forms a system of interdependent parts. It follows that there are corresponding duties for every task one chooses. Because we fill this or that domestic or social function, we are imprisoned in a net of obligations from which we have not the right to free ourselves. Toward the institution of the state, our duties and obligations constantly increase. The points at which we are in contact with it steadily multiply. So are the occasions on which it endeavours to remind us of our common solidarity.

In social life there are two great currents, collectivism and individualism. Of these two currents, the one which has its origin in like-mindedness is alone and unrivaled. At present, it is identified with the very life of society; little by little it finds its separate channels, and decreases, while the second constantly increases. In similar fashion, the segmentary structure of society is more and more overlaid by the other; however, it never disappears completely.

SELECTIONS FROM *THE OUTLINES OF SOCIOLOGY*

By LUDWIG GUMPLOWICZ

Modern natural science has successfully demonstrated that even the "human mind" is subject to physical laws; that the phenomena of the individual mind are emanations from matter. But in the domain of social phenomena unchangeable natural laws have not been completely demonstrated. Between "mental" phenomena subject to the laws of matter, and the social world strode the conception of human freedom to distract and confuse. It seemed to order and control social relations according to its own choice. In the domain of mental phenomena, in the narrower sense of the word, monistic natural science has in part demonstrated the unconditional sway of natural laws and in part shown the presence of other factors to be impossible. Dualism, driven from this domain, has retired to the domain of social phenomena, whence it must be dislodged. To this task the distinction which we have drawn between mental and social phenomena is essential; for it is an old rule of strategy to divide the enemy and grapple with the scattered sections separately. The critical question concerning monism is the existence of universal laws valid for social as well as for physical and mental phenomena. If such laws exist, the monistic theory is true; if such laws cannot be discovered, monism is an unproven hypothesis, like dualism.

As we have seen, their existence is hotly denied; and doubtless the earliest defenders of monism in the domain of social phenomena gave occasion for the denial. For with great zeal and less discretion some thought it simply necessary to transfer to the domain of social phenomena the laws that had been discovered in the domain of physical phenomena, the laws of attraction and repulsion, of gravitation and the like. Others seemed to see in the shapes which social phenomena assumed structures similar to animal organisms and they thought that the laws valid for the latter might be accepted as valid for the former also. We have already pointed out the impropriety of these assumptions and we shall criticise them more in detail hereafter.

But in spite of such errors, there are universal laws which prevail alike in the physical, the mental and the social domain; and the existence of the science of sociology can be justified only by proving their existence and validity.

Before calling attention to some of them, we must answer another question: How far, in general, can we expect to find laws common to phenomena so unlike as physical, mental and social phenomena are? Plainly we ought not to go too deeply into the characteristics of the species; for where the peculiarities begin the common traits end. Where the physical nature commences the laws common to the mental and social domain cease to apply.

Of course it may be objected that the universal laws will be taken from such a high sphere of abstraction that every idea beyond the concept of mere existence will have been sacrificed. Such laws, though easily found, would lack significance; and we shall try to find our universal laws close to where the three classes of phenomena become differentiated, in the sphere of the modalities of existence. Having found them here, we shall consider our task complete. It was the great error of our predecessors that they sought universal laws in the lowest sphere of one class alone, even among the differentiated physical phenomena. We ought not to commit the same error; we must not seek to generalize the physical laws of organic life and extend them to the domains of psychic and social phenomena as they did. But we may and indeed must discover the universal laws of the modalities of existence of all being. We must be satisfied to possess in them the keys which, to use Bastian's expression, "unlock in all directions."

Let us now proceed to give examples of such universal laws.

(a) *The Law of Causation*.

The law of causation is just as true of social as it is of physical and mental phenomena. Every social phenomenon is the necessary effect of another causes. No social phenomenon, originates in the nothingness of individual whims. The principle of sufficient cause is true also. Every social phenomenon whether political, juridicial or economic, must have a sufficient cause in one or more social agencies. The effects must also be equal or at least proportional to the energy of the causes alike in the social, the physical and the mental domain. The deed of an individual will never create a social condition nor change it, however much appearances may deceive us. One social condition is produced by another. The task which falls to the writer of pragmatic history is to point out the true connection in each case.

(b) *The Law of Development*.

Parallel with and perhaps emanating from the law of causation is the law of development. Each social phenomenon is a momentary phase in a period of development; though often the end of the period may be beyond the reach of calculation. Every political organization, all rights, every economic relation suffers change. We can distinguish the beginning, the process of growth and often the decline and decay.

But of course manifestations of the law in the social and in the physical domain must not be confounded. Cells, germs, stalks and fruit; or eggs, embryo, lungs, and digestive organs can not be found in social formations. Such analogies lead away from the truth; they becloud scientific vision and give incorrect results. The order of development in the social domain is from one social phenomenon to another.

If we would obtain reliable scientific results in sociology, this distinction must be observed rigorously. No digression to manifestations of the law in other domains can be allowed.

(c) *Regularity of Development*.

Development does not in and of itself involve the idea of regularity, the sequence of like or similar phases might or might not be uniform in all cases. But actually progress is regular; it conforms to law everywhere. We admire the regularity of development in the whole compass of physical nature. It dominates mental phenomena. It is found to be true of the state, of rights, of political economy, and of language which must also be included with the social sciences since, according to the definition given above, language is a social phenomenon. The great honor of discovering it in the domain of social phenomena is shared by the historical schools in the several departments.

(d) *The Law of Periodicity*.

In all domains of phenomena, regularity of development passes into periodicity. Wherever we can watch the whole process, we find a period of existence extending from the origin through the phases of growth and perfection to decline and fall. Of course the manifestation is different for each class of phenomena. Sap flows, the trunk grows strong, the organs develop, etc.; or, thought arises, is confirmed, is spread abroad and gains consideration—then loses influence and is recognized as nothing; or, a social relation arises in small proportions, is extended over larger aggregates, procures ever greater recognition, exercises decisive influence on great masses, is then broken up and supplanted by other relations and disappears leaving no trace. It is one law valid everywhere and universal.

(e) *The Law of Complexity*.

In physical nature we always find the elements in combination, never single. Likewise in the mental domain we meet with combinations only. Our conceptions, our thoughts and our mental powers, too, are complex. So also are all the social phenomena about us. They are structures composed of simpler parts. Every state, every people, every tribe is complex in a great many respects. Every principle of right is a composite of views, conceptions, ideas and principles. Every common economic interest is made up of conditions, activities, relations. In every language there is an endless variety of philological elements.

But further, what is complex may be analyzed. Analysis of physical phenomena will give the elements of matter. Analysis of mental phenomena will disclose ultimate concepts and the simplest mental functions. In the social domain it leads to the simplest social structures thinkable, from state and people to primitive horde; from developed institutional rights to the beginning of actual relations; from the most complex economic interests of the community to the satisfaction of the simplest needs; from a literature in the fullness of bloom to the simplest expression of thought by sound and gesture.

(f) *Reciprocal Action of Foreign (heterogen) Elements.*

Another result of complexity is that phenomena of every class show the reciprocal action of foreign *(heterogen)* reacting elements. Although there is an endless variety of cases in each particular domain, yet the law seems to express the first and most important impulse to development in each and every one of them. The significance of this force in social processes was surmised long ago, but it was erroneously interpreted by individualists and atomists as the reaction of man upon man and was designated as love or hate, as sociability or mutual hostility *(bellum omnium contra omnes)*. The error in this conception will appear as we proceed. Specific reciprocal influence of man upon man cannot be affirmed in a universal law. What holds true between man and man in one group is not necessarily true in another group. Here it may be love and sociability and there hate and thirst for strife. First one and then the other relation was assumed to be normal according as attention was confined to one group or directed to the deportment of group toward group; but neither assumption was correct, because neither was universal. To find a law valid in all times and places for the reciprocal forces inherent in social phenomena we must take, not the individuals, but the social groups as the elements. Thus the law of the reciprocal action of foreign (*heterogen*) elements will be found universal. Social groups exhibit reciprocal effects which are fundamentally the same always and everywhere; they arise from the same exciting causes and obey the same law, though manifested in various forms and ways according to time, circumstances and the peculiar qualities of each.

A more specific expression for the universal action of foreign (*heterogen*) bodies upon each other might seem desirable, but there would be danger of getting entangled in empty analogies and of falsely generalizing formulas valid only in special domains of phenomena.

Suppose we desired to speak of the "absorption" of foreign (*heterogen*) elements as a general principle. Perhaps the universal law is manifested in this way on much of the physical domain. But it is not so manifested in social phenomena. Applied to them the statement would be an empty analogy. On the other hand, the manifestation of this law on the physical domain, especially in inorganic and vegetable phenomena, has been described as a "struggle for existence." Obviously this is an illustration borrowed from animal and social domain. But it is not so manifested in social phenomena. So if we would have a law common to all domains of phenomena we must modestly be content to speak of the reciprocal action of foreign (*heterogen*) elements. The more precise statement of its manifestation on the respective domains must be left to special formulas.

(g) *Adaptation to an Obvious End.*

One thing might be affirmed to characterize this law more precisely, and that is universal adaptation to an end, —though in a very definite, technical sense. For the universal effect of the reciprocal action of foreign (*heterogen*) bodies is to favor further development of the phenomena concerned; which may be expressed by saying that, universally, phenomena in this state are adapted to the end of further development.

This law has been abundantly demonstrated throughout the physical domain. The botanist knows "to what end" the leaves serve the plant. The zoologist knows "why" the respiratory organs of birds and, in general, "why" all animal organs have their peculiar qualities. Among mental phenomena, also, the adaptation of means to the ends produced has been recognized in many cases. On the social domain, to be sure, the law is much questioned. The more warmly it is defended by conservatives, Manchester men, and optimists, the more violently is it opposed by revolutionists, socialists and pessimists. But on one point, at least, there seems to be no dispute; every social growth, every social entity, serves a definite end, however much its worth and morality may be questioned. For the universal law of adaptation signifies simply that no expenditure of effort, no change of condition, is purposeless on any domain of phenomena. Hence the inherent reasonableness of all social facts and conditions must be conceded.

(h) *Identity of Forces*.

The reciprocal action of foreign (*heterogen*) elements obviously proceeds from forces immanent in them or arising from their contact. These forces never change their character. They are identical, as we wish to say. Those operating in the domain of physical phenomena have always been the same that they are now. So of mental forces; thought, feeling, volition, each has moved man and controlled his actions in the same way always. Likewise the social forces, the causes which we must conclude from the effects that follow on the social domain, have ever been the same. Thus the identity of forces is a universal law. We encounter it in every domain of phenomena.

(i) *Similarity of Events*.

A necessary consequence of the last law is the perpetual similarity of events on all domains of phenomena. It has long been recognized of physical phenomena. Nobody doubts that the sun's warming powers acting on moist ground age after age have produced and always will produce the same effects in vegetation that they produce now. Nobody doubts that ocean waves breaking on a rocky coast have always produced the same effects that we see today. So, too, nobody doubts that man's mental faculties have produced the same effects in all times and climes. Always and everywhere men feel and think and plan; even the sensible products of these mental processes are the same. They differ only in form with changing time and circumstances. The Kamtschatkan sings his native song, and so does the Frenchman; thousands of years ago the Chinese thinker philosophized just as did more recently the sage of Koenigsberg; the architect of the pyramids projected his artistic plans and so do the modern European artists. Thus the perpetual similarity of events in the mental domain is obvious. But people are much less conscious of similarity in the social domain, though it is no less a fact. The identity of social forces could not be discovered because individuals instead of natural social groups were taken to be the true elements of social phenomena. But when the true social forces are recognized, the perpetual similarity of social events must also be apparent. Rights, states, languages, religion, etc., have always and everywhere arisen in ways essentially alike. Economic events are controlled by the same forces; they have always been alike in essence, though often differing in form.

(j) *Law of Parallelism.*

In every domain we find some phenomena which are similar but we do not know the ultimate cause of their similarity. In the physical domain such phenomena are ascribed to identical forces directly. But in the mental domain the tendency is rather to attribute the similarity to some alleged connection between them; and in social phenomena it is considered the result of consanguinity or of some historic relationship. But actually there is something fundamental at the bottom of all these similarities, which we must refer temporarily to a law of parallelism, since we do not know more precisely what it is. By resorting to this law we guard ourselves against obviously false and erroneous explanations.

The reason why parallel physical phenomena are referred without question to identical forces, whereas such an explanation of parallel mental and social phenomena is anxiously avoided as long as possible, is partly found in the widely accepted theory of monogenism. The descent of all men from Adam and Eve afforded a very plausible explanation. But if it is rejected as too absurd, the only course left is to refer the countless mental and social parallels also directly to a law of parallelism common to all domains of phenomena.

The existence of universal laws is one of the most convincing proofs that the whole world of phenomena rests upon a single simple principle. It is a weighty argument for monism, a thorough refutation of dualism. Consideration of these laws shows how untenable it is to refer phenomena to two principles, matter and mind, since the modalities of existence are the same for all and point to one simple principle only. Whether it be called nature, or God, or the great unknown world-moving principle matters not. We have presentiments that it is omnipotent, omnipresent, perhaps even omniscient. But we are not in condition to know its essence. Since, however, there are laws which are universally prevalent and valid, we must conclude that this one principle pursues, so to say, a consequent and self-consistent policy; that it reveals itself always and everywhere in the same form and in the same character for all kinds of phenomena. This necessary conclusion is of unending significance to science

THE TENDENCY OF THE DEVELOPMENT OF THE STATE*

By FRANZ OPPENHEIMER

We have endeavored to discover the development of the state from its most remote past up to present times, following its course like an explorer, from its source down the streams to its effluence in the plains. Broad and powerfully its waves roll by, until it disappears into the mist of the horizon, into unexplored and, for the present-day observer, undiscoverable regions.

Just as broadly and powerfully the stream of history—and until the present day all history has been the history of states—rolls past our view, and the course thereof is covered by the blanketing fogs of the future. Shall we dare to set up hypotheses concerning the future course, until "with unrestrained joy he sinks into the arms of his waiting, expectant father?" (Goethe's Prometheus.) Is it possible to establish a scientifically founded prognosis in regard to the future development of the state?

I believe in this possibility. The tendency of state development unmistakably leads to one point: seen in its essentials the state will cease to be the "developed political means" and will become "a freemen's citizenship." In other words, its outer shell will remain in essentials the form which was developed in the constitutional state, under which the administration will be carried on by an officialdom. But the content of the states heretofore known will have changed its vital element by the disappearance of the economic exploitation of one class by another. And since the state will, by this, come to be without either classes or class interests, the

* From *The State*

bureaucracy of the future will truly have attained that ideal of the impartial guardian of the common interests, which nowadays it laboriously attempts to reach. The "state" of the future will be "society" guided by self-government.

Libraries full of books have been written on the delimitation of the concepts "state" and "society." The problem, however, from our point of view has an easy solution. The "state" is the fully developed political means, society the fully developed economic means. Heretofore state and society were indissolubly intertwined: in the "freeman's citizenship," there will be no "state" but only "society."

This prognosis of the future development of the state contains by inclusion all of those famous formulae, whereby the great philosophical historians have endeavoured to determine the "resulting value" of universal history. It contains the "progress from warlike activity to peaceful labor" of St. Simon, as well as Hegel's "development from slavery to freedom;" the "evolution of humanity" of Herder, as well as "the penetration of reason through nature" of Schleiermacher.

Our times have lost the glad optimism of the classical and of the humanist writers; sociologic pessimism rules the spirit of these latter days. The prognosis here stated can not as yet claim to have many adherents. Not only do the persons obtaining the profits of dominion, thanks to their obsession by their class spirit, regard it as an incredible concept; those belonging to the subjugated class as well regard it with the utmost skepticism. It is true that the proletarian theory, as a matter of principle, predicts identically the same results. But the adherents of that theory do not believe it possible by the path of evolution but only through revolution. It is then thought of as a picture of a "society" varying in all respects from that evolved by the progress of history; in other words, as an organization of the economic means, as a system of economics without competition and market, as collectivism. The anarchistic theory makes form and content of the "state" as inseparable as heads and tails of the coin; no "government" without exploitation! It would therefore smash both the form and the content of the state, and thus bring on a condition of anarchy, even if thereby all the economic advantages of a division of labor should have to be sacrificed. Even so great a thinker as the late Ludwig Gumplowicz, who first laid the foundation on which the present theory of the state has been developed, is a sociological pessimist; and from the same reasons as are the anarchists, whom he combated so violently. He too regards as eternally inseparable form and content, government and class-exploitation; since he however, and I think correctly, does not consider it possible that many people may live together without some coercive force vested in some government, he declares the class-state to be an "immanent" and not only an historical category.

Only a small fraction of social liberals, or of liberal socialists, believe in the evolution of a society without class dominion and class exploitation which shall guarantee to the individual, besides political, also economic liberty of movement, within of course the limitations of the economic means. That was the credo of the old social liberalism, of pre-Manchester days, enunciated by Quesnay and especially by Adam Smith, and again taken up in modern times by Henry George and Theodore Hertzka.

This prognosis may be substantiated in two ways, one through history and philosophy, the other by political economy, as a tendency of the development of the state, and as a tendency of the evolution of economcis, both clearly tending toward one point.

The tendency of the development of the state was shown in the preceding discussion as a steady and victorious combat of economic means against political means. We saw that, in the beginning, the right to the economic means, the right to equality and to peace, was restricted to the tiny circle of the horde bound together by ties of blood, an endowment from pre-human conditions of society; while without the limits of this isle of peace raged the typhoon of the political means. But we saw expanding more and more the circles from which the laws of peace crowded out their adversary, and everywhere we saw their advance connected with the advance of the economic means, of the barter of groups for equivalents, amongst one another. The first exchange may have been the exchange of fire, then the barter of women, and finally the exchange of goods, the domain of peace constantly extending its borders. It protected the market places, then the streets leading to them, and finally it protected the merchants traveling on these streets.

In the course of this discussion it was shown how the "state" absorbed and developed these organizations making for peace, and how in consequence these drive back ever further right based on mere might. Merchants' law becomes city law; the industrial city, the developed economic means, undermines the feudal state, the developed political means; and finally the civic population, in open fight, annihilates the political remnants of the feudal state, and re-conquers for the entire population of the state freedom and right to equality; urban law becomes public law and finally international law.

Furthermore, on no horizon can be seen any force now capable of resisting effectively this heretofore efficient tendency. On the contrary, the interference of the past, which temporarily blocked the process, is obviously becoming weaker and weaker. The international relations of commerce and trade acquired among the nations a preponderating importance over the diminishing warlike and political relations; and in the intra-national sphere, by reason of the same process of economic development, movable capital, the creation of the right to peace, preponderates in ever increasing measure over landed property rights, the creation of the right of war. At the same time superstition more and more loses its influence. And therefore one is justified in concluding that the tendency so marked will work out to its logical end, excluding the political means and all its works, until the complete victory of the economic means is attained.

But it may be objected that in the modern constitutional state all the more prominent remnants of the antique law of war have already been chiseled out.

On the contrary, there survives a considerable remnant of these institutions, masked it is true in economic garb, and apparently no longer a legal privilege but only economic right, the ownership of large estates—the first creation and the last stronghold of the political means. Its mask has preserved it from undergoing the fate of all other feudal creations. And yet this last remnant of the right of war is doubtless the last unique obstacle in the pathway of humanity; and doubtless the development of economics is on its way to destroy it.

To substantiate these remarks I must refer the reader to other books, wherein I have given the detailed evidence of the above and can not in the space allotted here repeat it at large. I can only restate the principal points made in these books.

There is no difference in principle between the distribution of the total products of the economic means among the separate classes of a constitutional state, the so-called "capitalistic distribution," from that prevailing in the feudal state.

All the more important economic schools coincide in finding the cause in this, that the supply of "free" laborers (i.e., according to Karl Marx politically free and economically without capital) perpetually exceeds the demand, and that hence there exists "the social relation of capital." There "are constantly two laborers running after one master for work, and lowering, for one another, the wages"; and therefore the "surplus value" remains with the capitalist class, while the laborer never gets a chance to form capital for himself and to become an employer.

Whence comes this surplus supply of free laborers?

The explanation of the "bourgeois" theory, according to which this surplus supply is caused by the overproduction of children by proletarian parents, is based on a logical fallacy, and is contradicted by all known facts.

The explanation of the proletarian theory according to which the capitalistic process of production itself produces the "free laborers," by setting up again and again new labor-saving machines, is also based on a logical fallacy and is likewise contradicted by all known facts.

The evidence of all facts shows rather, and the conclusion may be deduced without fear of contradiction, that the oversupply of "free laborers" is descended from the right of holding landed property in large estates; and that emigration into towns and oversea from these landed properties are the causes of the capitalistic distribution.

Doubtless there is a growing tendency in economic development whereby the ruin of vast landed estates will be accomplished. The system is their bleeding to death, without hope of salvation, caused by the freedom of the former serfs—the necessary consequence of the development of the cities. As soon as the peasants had obtained the right of moving about without their landlords' passport (German Freizuegigkeit), there developed the chance of escape from the countries which formerly oppressed them. The system of emigration created "the competition from oversea," together with the fall, on the Continent, of prices for farm products, and made necessary perpetually rising wages. By these two factors ground rent is reduced from two sides, and must gradually sink to the zero point, since here too no counter-force is to be recognized whereby the process might be diverted. Thus the system of vast territorial estates falls apart. When, however, it has disappeared, there can be no oversupply of "free laborers." On the contrary "two masters will run after one laborer and must raise the price on themselves." There will be no "surplus value" for the capitalist class, because the laborer himself can form capital and himself become an employer. By this the last remaining vestige of the political means will have been destroyed, and economic means alone will exercise sway. The content of such a society is the "pure economics" of the equivalent exchange of commodities against commodities, or of labor force against commodities, and the political form of this society will be the "freemen's citizenship."

This theoretical deduction is moreover confirmed by the experience of history. Wherever there existed a society in which vast estates did not exist to draw an increasing rental, there "pure economics" existed, and society approximated the form of the state to that of the "freemen's citizenship."

Such a community was found in the Germany of the four centuries from A. D. 1000, when the primitive system of vast estates was developed into the socially harmless dominion over vast territories, until about the year 1400, when the newly arisen great properties, created by the political means, the robber wars in the countries formerly Slavic, shut the settlers from the westward out of lands eastward of the Ellie. Such a community was the Mormon state of Utah, which has not been greatly changed in this respect, where a wise land legislation permitted only small and moderate sized farm holdings. Such a community was to be found in the city and county of Vineland, Iowa, U. S. A. as long as every settler could obtain land, without increment of rent. Such a commonwealth is, beyond all others, New Zealand, whose government favors with all its power the possession of small and middle-sized holdings of land, while at the same time it narrows and dissolves, by all means at its command the great landed properties, which by the way, owing to lack of surplus laborers, are almost incapable of producing rentals.

In all these cases there is an astoundingly equalized well-being, not perhaps mechanically equal; but there is no wealth. Because well-being is the control over articles of consumption, while wealth is the dominion over mankind. In no such cases are the means of production, "capital," "producing any surplus values;" there are no "free laborers" and no capitalism, and the political form of these communities approximates very closely to a "freemen's citizenship," and tends to approximate it more and more, so far as the pressure of the surrounding states, organized from and based on the laws of war, permit its development. The "state" decomposes, or else in new countries such as Utah or New Zealand, it returns to a rudimentary stage of development; while the free self-determination of free men, scarcely acquainted with a class fight, constantly tends to pierce through ever more thoroughly. Thus in the German Empire there was a parallel development between the political rise of the unions of the imperial free cities, the decline of the feudal states, the emancipation of the crafts, then still comprising the entire "plebs" of the cities, and the decay of the patrician control of the city government. This beneficent development was stopped by the erection of new primitive feudal states on the easterly border of the former German Empire, and thus the economic blossom of German culture was ruined. Whoever believes in a conscious purpose in history may say that the human race was again required to pass through another school of suffering before it could be redeemed. The Middle Ages had discovered the system of free labor, but had not developed it to its full capacity or efficiency. It was reserved for the new slavery of capitalism to discover and develop the incomparably more efficient system of cooperating labor, the division of labor in the workshops, in order to crown man as the ruler of natural forces, as king of the planet. Slavery of antiquity and of modern capitalism was once necessary; now it has become superfluous. According to the story, every free citizen of Athens disposed of five human slaves; but we have supplied to our fellow citizens of modern society a vast mass of enslaved power, slaves of steel, that do not suffer in creating values. Since then we have ripened toward a civilization as much higher than the civilization of the time of Pericles, as the population, power and riches of the modern communities exceeds those of the tiny state of Athens.

Athens was doomed to dissolution—by reason of slavery as an economic institution, by reason of the political means.

Having once entered that pathway, there was no outlet except death to the population. Our path will lead to life.

The same conclusion is found by either the historical-philosophical view, which took into account the tendency of the development of the state, or the study of political economy, which regards the tendency of economic development; viz., that the economic means wins along the whole line, while the political means disappears from the life of society, in that one of its creations, which is most ancient and most tenacious of life; capitalism decays with large landed estates and ground rentals.

This has been the path of suffering and of salvation of humanity, its Golgotha and its resurrection into an eternal kingdom—from war to peace, from the hostile splitting up of the hordes to the peaceful unity of mankind, from brutality to humanity, from the exploiting State of robbery to the Freemen's Citizenship.

CLASS SOCIETY AND THE STATE*

1. THE STATE AS THE PRODUCT OF THE IRRECONCILABILITY OF CLASS ANTAGONISMS

By NICOLAI LENIN

WHAT is now happening to Marx's doctrine has, in the course of history, often happened to the doctrines of other revolutionary thinkers and leaders of oppressed classes struggling for emancipation. During the lifetime of great revolutionaries, the oppressing classes have visited relentless persecution on them and received their teaching with the most savage hostility, the most furious hatred, the most ruthless campaign of lies and slanders. After their death, attempts are made to turn them into harmless icons, canonise them, and surround their *names* with a certain halo for the "consolation" of the oppressed classes and with the object of duping them, while at the same time emasculating and vulgarising the *real essence* of their revolutionary theories and blunting their revolutionary edge. At the present time, the bourgeoisie and the opportunists within the labour movement are co-operating in this work of adulterating Marxism. They omit, obliterate, and distort the revolutionary side of its teaching, its revolutionary soul. They push to the foreground and extol what is, or seems, acceptable to the bourgeoisie. All the social-chauvinists are now "Marxists"—joking aside! And more and more do German bourgeois professors, erstwhile specialists in the demolition of Marx, speak now of the "national-German" Marx, who, they aver, has educated the labour unions which are so splendidly organised for conducting the present predatory war!

* From *State and Revolution*
Copyright International Publishers.

In such circumstances, the distortion of Marxism being so wide-spread, it is our first task to *resuscitate* the real teachings of Marx on the state. For this purpose it will be necessary to quote at length from the works of Marx and Engels themselves. Of course, long quotations will make the text cumbersome and in no way help to make it popular reading, but we cannot possibly avoid them. All, or at any rate, all the most essential passages in the works of Marx and Engels on the subject of the state must necessarily be given as fully as possible, in order that the reader may form an independent opinion of all the views of the founders of scientific socialism and of the development of those views, and in order that their distortions by the present predominant "Kautskyism" may be proved in black and white and rendered plain to all.

Let us begin with the most popular of Engels' works, *Der Ursprung der Familie, des Privateigentums und des Staats,** the sixth edition of which was published in Stuttgart as far back as 1894. We must translate the quotations from the German originals, as the Russian translations, although very numerous, are for the most part either incomplete or very unsatisfactory.

Summarising his historical analysis Engels says:

The state is therefore by no means a power imposed on society from the outside; just as little is it "the reality of the moral idea," "the image and reality of reason," as Hegel asserted. Rather, it is a product of society at a certain stage of development; it is the admission that this society has become entangled in an insoluble contradiction with itself, that it is cleft into irreconcilable antagonisms which it is powerless to dispel. But in order that these antagonisms, classes with conflicting economic interests, may not consume themselves and society in sterile struggle, a power apparently standing above society becomes necessary, whose purpose is to moderate the conflict and keep it within the bounds of "order"; and this power arising out of society, but placing itself above it, and increasingly separating itself from it, is the state.**

Here we have, expressed in all its clearness, the basic idea of Marxism on the question of the historical rôle and mean-

---

* Friedrich Engels, *The Origin of the Family, Private Property, and the State,* London and New York, 1933.—*Ed.*

** *Ibid.*—*Ed.*

ing of the state. The state is the product and the manifestation of the *irreconcilability* of class antagonisms. The state arises when, where, and to the extent that the class antagonisms *cannot* be objectively reconciled. And, conversely, the existence of the state proves that the class antagonisms *are* irreconcilable.

It is precisely on this most important and fundamental point that distortions of Marxism arise along two main lines.

On the one hand, the bourgeois, and particularly the petty-bourgeois, ideologists, compelled under the pressure of indisputable historical facts to admit that the state only exists where there are class antagonisms and the class struggle, "correct" Marx in such a way as to make it appear that the state is an organ for *reconciling* the classes. According to Marx, the state could neither arise nor maintain itself if a reconciliation of classes were possible. But with the petty-bourgeois and philistine professors and publicists, the state —and this frequently on the strength of benevolent references to Marx!—becomes a conciliator of the classes. According to Marx, the state is an organ of class *domination,* an organ of *oppression* of one class by another; its aim is the creation of "order" which legalises and perpetuates this oppression by moderating the collisions between the classes. But in the opinion of the petty-bourgeois politicians, order means reconciliation of the classes, and not oppression of one class by another; to moderate collisions does not mean, they say, to deprive the oppressed classes of certain definite means and methods of struggle for overthrowing the oppressors, but to practice reconciliation.

For instance, when, in the Revolution of 1917, the question of the real meaning and rôle of the state arose in all its vastness as a practical question demanding immediate action on a wide mass scale, all the Socialist-Revolutionaries and Mensheviks suddenly and completely sank to the petty-bourgeois theory of "reconciliation" of the classes by the "state." Innumerable resolutions and articles by politicians of both these parties are saturated through and through with this purely petty-bourgeois and philistine theory of "reconcilia-tion." That the state is an organ of domination of a definite class which *cannot* be reconciled with its antipode (the class opposed to it)—this petty-bourgeois democracy is never able to understand. Its attitude towards the state is one of the most telling proofs that our Socialist-Revolutionaries and Mensheviks are not Socialists at all (which we Bolsheviks have always maintained), but petty-bourgeois democrats with a near-socialist phraseology.

On the other hand, the "Kautskyist" distortion of Marx is far more subtle. "Theoretically," there is no denying that the state is the organ of class domination, or that class antag-onisms are irreconcilable. But what is forgotten or glossed over is this: if the state is the product of the irreconcilable character of class antagonisms, if it is a force standing *above* society and "increasingly separating itself from it," then it is clear that the liberation of the oppressed class is impossible not only without a violent revolution, *but also without the destruction* of the apparatus of state power, which was creat-ed by the ruling class and in which this "separation" is em-bodied. As we shall see later, Marx drew this theoretically self-evident conclusion from a concrete historical analysis of the problems of revolution. And it is exactly this conclusion which Kautsky—as we shall show fully in our subsequent remarks—has "forgotten" and distorted.

2. SPECIAL BODIES OF ARMED MEN, PRISONS, ETC.

Engels continues:

In contrast with the ancient organisation of the *gens*, the first distin-guishing characteristic of the state is the grouping of the subjects of the state *on a territorial basis*. . . .

Such a grouping seems "natural" to us, but it came after a prolonged and costly struggle against the old form of tribal or gentilic society.

. . . The second is the establishment of a *public force*, which is no longer absolutely identical with the population organising itself as an armed power. This special public force is necessary, because a self-acting armed organisation of the population has become impossible since the cleavage of society into classes. . . . This public force exists in every state; it consists not merely of armed men, but of material appendages, prisons and repressive institutions of all kinds, of which gentilic society knew nothing. . . .*

Engels develops the conception of that "power" which is termed the state—a power arising from society, but placing itself above it and becoming more and more separated from it. What does this power mainly consist of? It consists of special bodies of armed men who have at their disposal prisons, etc.

We are justified in speaking of special bodies of armed men, because the public power peculiar to every state is not "absolutely identical" with the armed population, with its "self-acting armed organisation."

Like all the great revolutionary thinkers, Engels tries to draw the attention of the class-conscious workers to that very fact which to prevailing philistinism appears least of all worthy of attention, most common and sanctified by solid, indeed, one might say, petrified prejudices. A standing army and police are the chief instruments of state power. But can this be otherwise?

From the point of view of the vast majority of Europeans at the end of the nineteenth century whom Engels was addressing, and who had neither lived through nor closely observed a single great revolution, this cannot be otherwise. They cannot understand at all what this "self-acting armed organisation of the population" means. To the question, whence arose the need for special bodies of armed men, standing above society and becoming separated from it (police and standing army), the Western European and Russian philistines are inclined to answer with a few phrases borrowed from Spencer or Mikhailovsky, by reference to the complexity of social life, the differentiation of functions, and so forth.

Such a reference seems "scientific" and effectively dulls

* Ibid.—Ed.

the senses of the average man, obscuring the most important and basic fact, namely, the break-up of society into irreconcilably antagonistic classes.

Without such a break-up, the "self-acting armed organisation of the population" might have differed from the primitive organisation of a herd of monkeys grasping sticks, or of primitive men, or men united in a tribal form of society, by its complexity, its high technique, and so forth, but would still have been possible.

It is impossible now, because society, in the period of civilisation, is broken up into antagonistic and, indeed, irreconcilably antagonistic classes, which, if armed in a "self-acting" manner, would come into armed struggle with each other. A state is formed, a special power is created in the form of special bodies of armed men, and every revolution, by shattering the state apparatus, demonstrates to us how the ruling class aims at the restoration of the special bodies of armed men at *its* service, and how the oppressed class tries to create a new organisation of this kind, capable of serving not the exploiters, but the exploited.

In the above observation, Engels raises theoretically the very same question which every great revolution raises practically, palpably, and on a mass scale of action, namely, the question of the relation between special bodies of armed men and the "self-acting armed organisation of the population." We shall see how this is concretely illustrated by the experience of the European and Russian revolutions.

But let us return to Engels' discourse.

He points out that sometimes, for instance, here and there in North America, this public power is weak (he has in mind an exception that is rare in capitalist society, and he speaks about parts of North America in its pre-imperialist days, where the free colonist predominated), but that in general it tends to become stronger:

It [the public power] grows stronger, however, in proportion as the class antagonisms within the state grow sharper, and with the growth in size and population of the adjacent states. We have only to look at our present-day Europe, where class struggle and rivalry in conquest have screwed up the public power to such a pitch that it threatens to devour the whole of society and even the state itself.*

This was written as early as the beginning of the 'nineties of last century, Engels' last preface being dated June 16, 1891. The turn towards imperialism, understood to mean complete domination of the trusts, full sway of the large banks, and a colonial policy on a grand scale, and so forth, was only just beginning in France, and was even weaker in North America and in Germany. Since then the "rivalry in conquest" has made gigantic progress—especially as, by the beginning of the second decade of the twentieth century, the whole world had been finally divided up between these "rivals in conquest," *i. e.*, between the great predatory powers. Military and naval armaments since then have grown to monstrous proportions, and the predatory war of 1914-1917 for the domination of the world by England or Germany, for the division of the spoils has brought the "swallowing up" of all the forces of society by the rapacious state power nearer to a complete catastrophe.

As early as 1891 Engles was able to point to "rivalry in conquest," as one of the most important features of the foreign policy of the great powers, but in 1914-1917, when this rivalry, many times intensified, has given birth to an imperialist war, the rascally social-chauvinists cover up their defence of the predatory policy of "their" capitalist classes by phrases about the "defence of the fatherland," or the "defence of the republic and the revolution," etc.!

3. THE STATE AS AN INSTRUMENT FOR THE EXPLOITATION OF THE OPPRESSED CLASS

For the maintenance of a special public force standing above society, taxes and state loans are needed.

Having at their disposal the public force and the right to exact taxes, the officials now stand as organs of society *above* society. The free, voluntary

* *Ibid.—Ed.*

respect which was accorded to the organs of the gentilic form of government does not satisfy them, even if they could have it. . . .

Special laws are enacted regarding the sanctity and the in-
violability of the officials. "The shabbiest police servant . . .
has more authority" than the representative of the clan, but
even the head of the military power of a civilised state "may
well envy the least among the chiefs of the clan the uncon-
strained and uncontested respect which is paid to him."*

Here the question regarding the privileged position of the
officials as organs of state power is clearly stated. The main
point is indicated as follows: what is it that places them
above society? We shall see how this theoretical problem was
solved in practice by the Paris Commune in 1871 and how
it was slurred over in a reactionary manner by Kautsky in
1912.

As the state arose out of the need to hold class antagonisms in check;
but as it, at the same time, arose in the midst of the conflict of these classes,
it is, as a rule, the state of the most powerful, economically dominant
class, which by virtue thereof becomes also the dominant class politically,
and thus acquires new means of holding down and exploiting the oppressed class. . . .

Not only the ancient and feudal states were organs of
exploitation of the slaves and serfs, but

the modern representative state is the instrument of the exploitation of
wage-labour by capital. By way of exception, however, there are periods
when the warring classes so nearly attain equilibrium that the state power,
ostensibly appearing as a mediator, assumes for the moment a certain independence in relation to both. . . .**

Such were, for instance, the absolute monarchies of the
seventeenth and eighteenth centuries, the Bonapartism of
the First and Second Empires in France, and the Bismarck
régime in Germany.

Such, we may add, is now the Kerensky government in
republican Russia after its shift to persecuting the revolutionary proletariat, at a moment when the Soviets, thanks to
the leadership of the petty-bourgeois democrats, have *already*

* *Ibid.*—*Ed.*
** *Ibid.*—*Ed.*

become impotent, while the bourgeoisie is *not yet* strong enough to disperse them outright.

In a democratic republic, Engels continues, "wealth wields its power indirectly, but all the more effectively," first, by means of "direct corruption of the officials" (America); second, by means of "the alliance of the government with the stock exchange" (France and America).

At the present time, imperialism and the domination of the banks have "developed" to an unusually fine art both these methods of defending and asserting the omnipotence of wealth in democratic republics of all descriptions. If, for instance, in the very first months of the Russian democratic republic, one might say during the honeymoon of the union of the "Socialists"—Socialist-Revolutionaries and Mensheviks—with the bourgeoisie, Mr. Palchinsky obstructed every measure in the coalition cabinet, restraining the capitalists and their war profiteering, their plundering of the public treasury by means of army contracts; and if, after his resignation, Mr. Palchinsky (replaced, of course, by an exactly similar Palchinsky) was "rewarded" by the capitalists with a "soft" job carrying a salary of 120,000 rubles per annum, what was this? Direct or indirect bribery? A league of the government with the capitalist syndicates, or "only" friendly relations? What is the rôle played by the Chernovs, Tseretelis, Avksentyevs and Skobelevs? Are they the "direct" or only the indirect allies of the millionaire treasury looters?

The omnipotence of "wealth" is thus more *secure* in a democratic republic, since it does not depend on the poor political shell of capitalism. A democratic republic is the best possible political shell for capitalism, and therefore, once capital has gained control (through the Palchinskys, Chernovs, Tseretelis and Co.) of this very best shell, it establishes its power so securely, so firmly that *no* change, either of persons, or institutions, or parties in the bourgeois republic can shake it.

We must also note that Engels quite definitely regards universal suffrage as a means of bourgeois domination. Universal suffrage, he says, obviously summing up the long experience of German Social-Democracy, is "an index of the maturity of the working class; it cannot, and never will, be anything else but that in the modern state."

The petty-bourgeois democrats, such as our Socialist-Revolutionaries and Mensheviks, and also their twin brothers, the social-chauvinists and opportunists of Western Europe, all expect "more" from universal suffrage. They themselves share, and instil into the minds of the people, the wrong idea that universal suffrage "in the *modern* state" is really capable of expressing the will of the majority of the toilers and of assuring its realisation.

We can here only note this wrong idea, only point out that this perfectly clear, exact and concrete statement by Engels is distorted at every step in the propaganda and agitation of the "official" (i. e., opportunist) Socialist parties. A detailed analysis of all the falseness of this idea, which Engels brushes aside, is given in our further account of the views of Marx and Engels on the "modern" state.

A general summary of his views is given by Engels in the most popular of his works in the following words:

The state, therefore, has not existed from all eternity. There have been societies which managed without it, which had no conception of the state and state power. At a certain stage of economic development, which was necessarily bound up with the cleavage of society into classes, the state became a necessity owing to this cleavage. We are now rapidly approaching a stage in the development of production at which the existence of these classes has not only ceased to be a necessity, but is becoming a positive hindrance to production. They will disappear as inevitably as they arose at an earlier stage. Along with them, the state will inevitably disappear. The society that organises production anew on the basis of a free and equal association of the producers will put the whole state machine where it will then belong: in the museum of antiquities, side by side with the spinning wheel and the bronze ax.*

It is not often that we find this passage quoted in the propaganda and agitation literature of contemporary Social-Democracy. But even when we do come across it, it is generally quoted in the same manner as one bows before an

*Ibid.—Ed.

icon, *i. e.,* it is done merely to show official respect for Engels, without any attempt to gauge the breadth and depth of revolutionary action presupposed by this relegating of "the whole state machine . . . to the museum of antiquities." In most cases we do not even find an understanding of what Engels calls the state machine.

4. THE "WITHERING AWAY" OF THE STATE AND VIOLENT REVOLUTION

Engels' words regarding the "withering away" of the state enjoy such popularity, they are so often quoted, and they show so clearly the essence of the usual adulteration by means of which Marxism is made to look like opportunism, that we must dwell on them in detail. Let us quote the whole passage from which they are taken.

The proletariat seizes state power, and then transforms the means of production into state property. But in doing this, it puts an end to itself as the proletariat, it puts an end to all class differences and class antagonisms, it puts an end also to the state as the state. Former society, moving in class antagonisms, had need of the state, that is, an organisation of the exploiting class at each period for the maintenance of its external conditions of production; therefore, in particular, for the forcible holding down of the exploited class in the conditions of oppression (slavery, bondage or serfdom, wage-labour) determined by the existing mode of production. The state was the official representative of society as a whole, its embodiment in a visible corporate body; but it was this only in so far as it was the state of that class which itself, in its epoch, represented society as a whole: in ancient times, the state of the slave-owning citizens; in the Middle Ages, of the feudal nobility; in our epoch, of the bourgeoisie. When ultimately it becomes really representative of society as a whole, it makes itself superfluous. As soon as there is no longer any class of society to be held in subjection; as soon as, along with class domination and the struggle for individual existence based on the former anarchy of production, the collisions and excesses arising from these have also been abolished, there is nothing more to be repressed, and a special repressive force, a state, is no longer necessary. The first act in which the state really comes forward as the representative of society as a whole—the seizure of the means of production in the name of society—is at the same time its last independent act as a state. The interference of a state power in social relations becomes superfluous in one sphere after another, and then becomes dormant of itself. Government over persons is replaced by the administration of things and the direction of the processes of production. The state is not "abolished," *it withers away.* It is from this standpoint that we must appraise the phrase "people's free state"—both its justification at times for agitational purposes, and its ultimate scientific inadequacy—and also the demand of the so-called Anarchists that the state should be abolished overnight.*

Without fear of committing an error, it may be said that of this argument by Engels so singularly rich in ideas, only one point has become an integral part of Socialist thought among modern Socialist parties, namely, that, unlike the Anarchist doctrine of the "abolition" of the state, according to Marx the state "withers away." To emasculate Marxism in such a manner is to reduce it to opportunism, for such an "interpretation" only leaves the hazy conception of a slow, even, gradual change, free from leaps and storms, free from revolution. The current popular conception, if one may say so, of the "withering away" of the state undoubtedly means a slurring over, if not a negation, of revolution.

Yet, such an "interpretation" is the crudest distortion of Marxism, which is advantageous only to the bourgeoisie; in point of theory, it is based on a disregard for the most important circumstances and considerations pointed out in the very passage summarising Engels' ideas, which we have just quoted in full.

In the first place, Engels at the very outset of his argument says that, in assuming state power, the proletariat by that very act "puts an end to the state as the state." One is "not accustomed" to reflect on what this really means. Generally, it is either ignored altogether, or it is considered as a piece of "Hegelian weakness" on Engels' part. As a matter of fact, however, these words express succinctly the experience of one of the greatest proletarian revolutions—the Paris Commune of 1871, of which we shall speak in greater detail in its proper place. As a matter of fact, Engels speaks here of the destruction of the bourgeois state by the proletarian revolution, while the words about its withering away refer to the remains of *proletarian* statehood *after* the Socialist revolution. The bourgeois state does not "wither away," according

* Friedrich Engels, *Anti-Dühring*, London and New York, 1933.—*Ed.*

to Engels, but is "put an end to" by the proletariat in the course of the revolution. What withers away after the revolution is the proletarian state or semi-state.

Secondly, the state is a "special repressive force." This splendid and extremely profound definition of Engels' is given by him here with complete lucidity. It follows from this that the "special repressive force" of the bourgeoisie for the suppression of the proletariat, of the millions of workers by a handful of the rich, must be replaced by a "special repressive force" of the proletariat for the suppression of the bourgeoisie (the dictatorship of the proletariat). It is just this that constitutes the destruction of "the state as the state." It is just this that constitutes the "act" of "the seizure of the means of production in the name of society." And it is obvious that such a substitution of one (proletarian) "special repressive force" for another (bourgeois) "special repressive force" can in no way take place in the form of a "withering away."

Thirdly, as to the "withering away" or, more expressively and colourfully, as to the state "becoming dormant," Engels refers quite clearly and definitely to the period *after* "the seizure of the means of production [by the state] in the name of society," that is, *after* the Socialist revolution. We all know that the political form of the "state" at the time is complete democracy. But it never enters the head of any of the opportunists who shamelessly distort Marx that when Engels speaks here of the state "withering away," or "becoming dormant," he speaks of *democracy*. At first sight this seems very strange. But it is "unintelligible" only to one who has not reflected on the fact that democracy is *also* a state and that, consequently, democracy will *also* disappear when the state disappears. The bourgeois state can only be "put an end to" by a revolution. The state in general, *i. e.,* most complete democracy, can only "wither away."

Fourthly, having formulated his famous proposition that "the state withers away," Engels at once explains concretely that this proposition is directed equally against the opportunists and the Anarchists. In doing this, however, Engels puts in the first place that conclusion from this proposition about the "withering away" of the state which is directed against the opportunists.

One can wager that out of every 10,000 persons who have read or heard about the "withering away" of the state, 9,990 do not know at all, or do not remember, that Engels did not direct his conclusions from this proposition against the Anarchists *alone*. And out of the remaining ten, probably nine do not know the meaning of a "people's free state" nor the reason why an attack on this watchword contains an attack on the opportunists. This is how history is written! This is how a great revolutionary doctrine is imperceptibly adulterated and adapted to current philistinism! The conclusion drawn against the Anarchists has been repeated thousands of times, vulgarised, harangued about in the crudest fashion possible until it has acquired the strength of a prejudice, whereas the conclusion drawn against the opportunists has been hushed up and "forgotten"!

The "people's free state" was a demand in the programme of the German Social-Democrats and their current slogan in the 'seventies. There is no political substance in this slogan other than a pompous middle-class circumlocution of the idea of democracy. In so far as it referred in a lawful manner to a democratic republic, Engels was prepared to "justify" its use "at times" from a propaganda point of view. But this slogan was opportunist, for it not only expressed an exaggerated view of the attractiveness of bourgeois democracy, but also a lack of understanding of the Socialist criticism of every state in general. We are in favour of a democratic republic as the best form of the state for the proletariat under capitalism, but we have no right to forget that wage slavery is the lot of the people even in the most democratic bourgeois republic. Furthermore, every state is a "special repressive force" for the suppression of the oppressed class. Consequently, *no* state is either "free" or a "people's state." Marx and Engels explained this repeatedly to their party comrades in the 'seventies.

Fifthly, in the same work of Engels, from which every one remembers his argument on the "withering away" of the state, there is also a disquisition on the significance of a violent revolution. The historical analysis of its rôle becomes, with Engels, a veritable panegyric on violent revolution. This, of course, "no one remembers"; to talk or even to think of the importance of this idea is not considered good form by contemporary Socialist parties, and in the daily propaganda and agitation among the masses it plays no part whatever. Yet it is indissolubly bound up with the "withering away" of the state in one harmonious whole.

Here is Engels' argument:

> . . . That force, however, plays another rôle (other than that of a diabolical power) in history, a revolutionary rôle; that, in the words of Marx, it is the midwife of every old society which is pregnant with the new; that it is the instrument with whose aid social movement forces its way through and shatters the dead, fossilised political forms—of this there is not a word in Herr Dühring. It is only with sighs and groans that he admits the possibility that force will perhaps be necessary for the overthrow of the economic system of exploitation—unfortunately! because all use of force, forsooth, demoralises the person who uses it. And this in spite of the immense moral and spiritual impetus which has resulted from every victorious revolution! And this in Germany, where a violent collision —which indeed may be forced on the people—would at least have the advantage of wiping out the servility which has permeated the national consciousness as a result of the humiliation of the Thirty Years' War.[2] And this parson's mode of thought—lifeless, insipid and impotent—claims to impose itself on the most revolutionary party which history has known? *

How can this panegyric on violent revolution, which Engels insistently brought to the attention of the German Social-Democrats between 1878 and 1894, *i. e.*, right to the time of his death, be combined with the theory of the "withering away" of the state to form one doctrine?

Usually the two views are combined by means of eclecticism, by an unprincipled, sophistic, arbitrary selection (to oblige the powers that be) of either one or the other argument, and in ninety-nine cases out of a hundred (if not more often), it is the idea of the "withering away" that is specially emphasised. Eclecticism is substituted for dialectics—this is the most usual, the most widespread phenomenon to be met with in the official Social-Democratic literature of our day in relation to Marxism. Such a substitution is, of course, nothing new; it may be observed even in the history of classic Greek philosophy. When Marxism is adulterated to become opportunism, the substitution of eclecticism for dialectics is the best method of deceiving the masses; it gives an illusory satisfaction; it seems to take into account all sides of the process, all the tendencies of development, all the contradictory factors and so forth, whereas in reality it offers no consistent and revolutionary view of the process of social development at all.

We have already said above and shall show more fully later that the teaching of Marx and Engels regarding the inevitability of a violent revolution refers to the bourgeois state. It *cannot* be replaced by the proletarian state (the dictatorship of the proletariat) through "withering away," but, as a general rule, only through a violent revolution. The panegyric sung in its honour by Engels and fully corresponding to the repeated declarations of Marx (remember the concluding passages of the *Poverty of Philosophy* and the *Communist Manifesto,* with its proud and open declaration of the inevitability of a violent revolution; remember Marx's *Critique of the Gotha Programme* of 1875 in which, almost thirty years later, he mercilessly castigates the opportunist character of that programme)—this praise is by no means a mere "impulse," a mere declamation, or a polemical sally. The necessity of systematically fostering among the masses *this* and just this point of view about violent revolution lies at the root of the *whole* of Marx's and Engels' teaching. The neglect of such propaganda and agitation by both the present predominant social-chauvinist and the Kautskyist currents brings their betrayal of Marx's and Engels' teaching into prominent relief.

The replacement of the bourgeois by the proletarian state is impossible without a violent revolution. The abolition of the proletarian state, *i. e.,* of all states, is only possible through "withering away."

Marx and Engels gave a full and concrete exposition of these views in studying each revolutionary situation separately, in analysing the lessons of the experience of each individual revolution.

THE MAKING OF SOCIETY

WHAT IS THE PERMANENT REVOLUTION?*

By LEON TROTSKY

1. The theory of the permanent revolution now demands the greatest attention of every Marxist, for the course of the ideological and class struggle has finally and conclusively raised this question from the realm of reminiscences over the old differences of opinion among Russian Marxists and converted it into a question of the character, the inner coherence and the methods of the international revolution in general.

2. With regard to the countries with a belated bourgeois development, especially the colonial and semi-colonial countries, the theory of the permanent revolution signifies that the complete and genuine solution of their tasks, *democratic and national emancipation,* is conceivable only through the dictatorship of the proletariat as the leader of the subjugated nation, above all of its peasant masses.

3. Not only the agrarian, but also the national question, assigns to the peasantry, the overwhelming majority of the population of the backward countries, an important place in the democratic revolution. Without an alliance of the proletariat with the peasantry, the tasks of the democratic revolution cannot be solved, nor even seriously posed. But the alliance of these two classes can be realized in no other way than through an intransigeant struggle against the influence of the national liberal bourgeoisie.

4. No matter how the first episodic stages of the revolution may be in the individual countries, the realization of the revolutionary alliance between the proletariat and the peasantry is conceivable only under the political direction of the proletarian vanguard, organized in the Communist party. This in turn means that the victory of the democratic

---

* From *The Permanent Revolution*

revolution is conceivable only through the dictatorship of the proletariat which bases itself upon the alliance with the peasantry and first solves the problems of the democratic revolution.

5. The old slogan of Bolshevism—"the democratic dictatorship of the proletariat and peasantry" expresses precisely the above characterized relationship of the proletariat, the peasantry and the liberal bourgeoisie. This has been confirmed by the experience of October. But the old formula of Lenin does not settle in advance the problem of what the mutual relations between the proletariat and the peasantry inside of the revolutionary bloc will be. In other words, the formula has unknown algebraic quantities which have to make way for precise arithmetical quantities in the process of historical experience. The latter showed, and under circumstances that exclude every other interpretation, that no matter how great the revolutionary rôle of the peasantry may be, it can nevertheless not be an independent rôle and even less a leading one. The peasant follows either the worker or the bourgeois. This means that the "democratic dictatorship of the proletariat and peasantry" is only conceivable as a *dictatorship of the proletariat that leads the peasant masses behind it.*

6. A democratic dictatorship of the proletariat and peasantry, as a régime that is distinguished from the dictatorship of the proletariat by its class content, might be realized only in case an *independent* revolutionary party could be constituted which expresses the interests of the peasants and in general of petty-bourgeois democracy—a party that is capable of conquering power with this or that aid of the proletariat and of determining its revolutionary program. As modern history teaches—especially the history of Russia in the last twenty-five years—an insurmountable obstacle on the road to the creation of a peasants' party is the economic and political dependence of the petty bourgeoisie and its deep internal differentiation, thanks to which the upper sections of the

petty bourgeoisie (the peasantry) go with the big bourgeoisie in all decisive cases, especially in war and in revolution, and the lower sections—with the proletariat, while the intermediate section has the choice between the two extreme poles. Between the Kerenskiad and the Bolshevik power, between the Kuo Min Tang and the dictatorship of the proletariat there cannot and does not lie any intermediate stage, that is, no democratic dictatorship of the workers and peasants.

7. The endeavour of the Comintern to foist upon the Eastern countries the slogan of the democratic dictatorship of the proletariat and peasantry, finally and long ago exhausted by history, can have only a reactionary effect. In so far as this slogan is counterposed to the slogan of the dictatorship of the proletariat, it contributes to the dissolution of the proletariat into the petty bourgeois masses and in this manner creates better conditions for the hegemony of the national bourgeoisie and consequently for the collapse of the democratic revolution. The introduction of this slogan into the program of the Comintern is a direct betrayal of Marxism and of the October traditions of Bolshevism.

8. The dictatorship of the proletariat which has risen to power as the leader of the democratic revolution is inevitably and very quickly placed before tasks that are bound up with deep inroads into the rights of bourgeois property. The democratic revolution grows over immediately into the socialist, and thereby becomes a *permanent* revolution.

9. *The conquest of power by the proletariat does not terminate the revolution, but only opens it.* Socialist construction is conceivable only on the foundation of the class struggle, on a national and international scale. This struggle, under the conditions of an overwhelming predominance of capitalist relationships on the world arena, will inevitably lead to explosions, that is, internally to civil wars, and externally to revolutionary wars. Therein lies the permanent character of the socialist revolution as such, regardless of whether it is a backward country that is involved, which

only yesterday accomplished its democratic revolution, or an old capitalist country, which already has behind it a long epoch of democracy and parliamentarism.

10. The completion of the socialist revolution within national limits is unthinkable. One of the basic reasons for the crisis in bourgeois society is the fact that the productive forces created by it conflict with the framework of the national state. From this follow, on the one hand, imperialist wars, and on the other, the utopia of the bourgeois United States of Europe. The socialist revolution commences on the national arena, is developed further on the inter-state and finally on the world arena. Thus, the socialist revolution becomes a permanent revolution in a newer and broader sense of the word; it attains completion only in the final victory of the new society on our entire planet.

11. The above outlined schema of the development of the world revolution eliminates the question of the countries that are "mature" or "immature" for socialism in the spirit of that pedantic, lifeless classification given by the present program of the Comintern. In so far as capitalism has created the world market, the division of labor and productive forces throughout the world, it has also prepared world economy for socialist transformation.

The various countries will go through this process at different tempos. *Backward countries, under certain conditions, can arrive at the dictatorship of the proletariat sooner than the advanced countries, but they come later than the latter to socialism.*

A backward colonial or semi-colonial country, whose proletariat is insufficiently prepared to unite the peasantry and seize power, is thereby incapable of bringing the democratic revolution to its conclusion. On the contrary, in a country where the proletariat has power in its hands as the result of the democratic revolution, the subsequent fate of the dictatorship and socialism is not only and not so much dependent in the final analysis upon the national productive forces, as it is upon the development of the international socialist revolution.

12. The theory of socialism in one country which rose on the yeast of the reaction against October is the only theory that consistently, and to the very end, opposes the theory of the permanent revolution.

The attempt of the epigones, under the blows of our criticism, to confine the application of the theory of socialism in one country exclusively to Russia, because of its specific characteristics (its extensiveness and its natural resources) does not improve matters but only makes them worse. The break with the international position always leads to a national messianism, that is, to attribute special prerogatives and peculiarities to one's own country, which would permit it to play a rôle that other countries cannot attain.

The world division of labor, the dependence of Soviet industry upon foreign technique, the dependence of the productive forces of the advanced countries of Europe upon Asiatic raw materials, etc., etc., make the construction of a socialist society in any single country impossible.

13. The theory of Stalin-Bucharin not only contrasts the democratic revolution quite mechanically to the socialist revolution, but also tears the national revolution from the international path.

This theory sets the revolution in the backward countries the task of establishing an unrealizable régime of the democratic dictatorship, it contrasts this régime to the dictatorship of the proletariat, thus introducing illusion and fiction into politics, paralyzing the struggle for power of the proletariat in the East, and hampering the victory of the colonial revolution.

The very seizure of power by the proletariat signifies, from the standpoint of the theory of the epigones, the completion of the revolution (to "nine-tenths," according to Stalin's formula) and the opening of the epoch of national reform. The theory of the kulak growing into socialism and the theory of the "neutralization" of the world bourgeoisie are consequently inseparable from the theory of socialism in one country. They stand and fall together.

By the theory of national socialism, the communist international is degraded to a weapon useful only for the struggle against military intervention. The present policy of the Comintern, its régime, and the selection of its leading personnel, correspond entirely to the debasement of the communist international to an auxiliary corps which is not destined to solve independent tasks.

14. The program of the Comintern created by Bucharin is thoroughly eclectic. It makes the hopeless attempt to reconcile the theory of socialism in one country with Marxian internationalism, which is, however, inseparable from the permanent character of the world revolution. The struggle of the communist Left Opposition for a correct policy and a healthy régime in the communist international is inseparably combined with a struggle for a Marxian program. The question of the program in turn is inseparable from the question of the two mutually exclusive theories: the theory of permanent revolution and the theory of socialism in one country. The problem of the permanent revolution has long ago outgrown the episodic differences of opinion between Lenin and Trotsky, which were completely exhausted by history. The struggle is between the basic ideas of Marx and Lenin on the one side and the eclectics of the centrists on the other.

The publishers take this opportunity to express their thanks, for the translator, to comrades MORRIS LEWITT and SAM GORDON for their valuable assistance; to comrade CORNELIA DAVIS, who read and revised the proofs; and to comrades JACK BERLIN, NATHAN BERMAN, MAX ENGEL, ALBERT GLOTZER, HERBERT CAPELIS and MAX STERLING, whose generous contributions made the popular publication of this work possible.

ON THE EXPROPRIATION OF THE CAPITALISTS*

By WACLAW MACHAJSKI

NINETEENTH century socialism—regardless of the convictions of its followers—is not an attack upon the basis of the system of slavery that has been in existence throughout the centuries in the form of the various civilized societies. It attacks only *one* of the forms of this slavery—the rule of the *capitalist class.* Even in the case of its victory it does not abolish the age-long exploitation; it destroys only the *private property of the material means of production,* viz., land and factories; it destroys only *capitalist* exploitation.

The abolition of capitalist property, i.e., of the private ownership of the means of production, implies by no means the abolition of *family* property in general. It is this institution which has made for exploitation throughout the ages, which has secured for the well-to-do minority and for its offspring the exclusive ownership of all riches, the entire heritage of mankind, all its culture and civilization. It is this institution which has doomed the majority of the human race to be born in poverty, as slaves condemned to perform manual labor throughout their lives.

The expropriation of the capitalist class by no means signifies the expropriation of the entire bourgeois society. By the mere elimination of the private employers the modern working class, the modern slaves, do not cease to be slaves condemned to livelong manual labor. The national surplus value produced by them does not disappear, but passes into the hands of the State, as the fund for the parasitic existence of all exploiters, of the entire bourgeois society.[1] The latter,

---

[1] In Machajski's terminology "bourgeois society" stands for both property-holders (capitalists) and the non-capitalist owners of education—the so-called "new middle class" or "intellectual workers."

* From: *Socialist Science as a New Religion.* Geneva, 1904. p. 3. (being Section II of Part III of *The Intellectual Worker*)

after the elimination of the capitalists, remains the same ruling society as it was before, the educated master, the world of the "white-hands." [2] It remains the owner of the national surplus value which is distributed in the form of high salaries paid to the intellectual workers. Due to the institute of family property and to the family form of life that fund is maintained and reproduced in their offspring.

Socialization of the means of production means only the abolition of the right of private ownership and control of factories and land.

By attacking the factory-owner the socialist does not touch in the slightest the salary of his manager and engineer. The socialism of the past century leaves inviolate all the incomes of the "white-hands," as the "labor wage of the intellectual worker," and, in the words of Kautsky, it declares that "the intellectuals are not interested in exploitation and are not taking part in it."

Modern socialism is unable and unwilling to abolish the age-long exploitation and slavery.

. . . .

ON THE CLASS STRUGGLE AND THE REVOLUTION OF THE MANUAL WORKERS

Whatever the further development of the events now unrolling in Russia (this was written in April, 1905, during the first months of the First Russian Revolution) the *cause of the workers* consists in that economic struggle [for higher wages] which is being waged by the masses themselves in spite of all democratic and socialist formulas and programs; in that struggle which by all the active socialist parties is looked upon as a necessary evil, as a means of enticing the workers into the bourgeois revolution and of keeping them there; in that economic struggle which is concerned *exclu-*

[2] The equivalent of "white-hand" is often used in Russian to designate all those who are *not* engaged in manual ("black") labor.

sively with the conditions of manual wage labor—of the labor of the slaves of modern society.

Whatever the further developments of the events now unrolling in Russia the cause of the workers demands *that all the revolutionary strength of the masses should be concentrated upon the increase of the economic demands and upon the extension of the strike movement;* upon the liberation of that struggle from the socialist traps placed against it; traps which, more successfully than the liberal and democratic preachers, ensnare the mind of the workers with fairy-tales about the rule of the people in and the liberties of, the democratic states.

The cause of the workers can find its adequate expression only in a movement aiming at an economic general strike that would embrace all of Russia; in a movement which would transform that strike into a workers' revolution, into a united attack upon bourgeois society and its government power with concrete demands to be granted immediately; a movement whose militant forces are united in a secret, underground organization.

A movement of this kind will unite the workers striking for higher wages with the unemployed struggling for their immediate protection against hunger; and for this purpose it will be able to attract to the big cities all the starving masses of the Russian towns and villages.

On a higher phase of its development, at a moment of vast uprisings, fruitful in tangible gains for the working class, a movement of this kind will find a response among, and stir up, the Western European workers who have been lulled to sleep by peaceful socialist sermons. It will thus mark the beginning of the workers' revolution in the civilized world.

From *The Intellectual Worker. Part I. The Evolution of Social Democracy.* Preface pp. XXIII-XXIV.—Geneva, 1905

Contrary to the theories of 19th century socialism, contrary to both the social-democratic and anarchist theories, the working class stands before a new era of struggles, an era of *world-wide workers' conspiracies, dictating the laws to the governments by means of world-wide strikes.*

During this new era of struggles, waged exclusively in the interests of the *manual workers,* that is, for purely economic demands, and in proportion as their secret organization extends and their uprisings gather momentum, the workers will carry out the expropriation not only of the capitalists, but of all the educated classes [3] as well, of all consumers of incomes exceeding those of the manual workers.

They will do away with the present-day family property, and will win the opportunity for every human being to *share, from the day of his birth, on equal terms with everybody else, in the benefits of the earth and of civilization; to acquire by virtue of his birth the right and the material means for spending his childhood and youth in the same manner as everyone else, the right to the same upbringing and education.*

Only with the expropriation of all propertied and educated classes will the age-long exploitation and slavery crumble.

From *The Intellectual Worker. Part I. The Evolution of Social-Democracy.*
Preface p. VIII.—Geneva, 1905.

* * *

ON THE INTELLECTUALS AND SOCIALISM

" 'The intellectual workers', as a privileged layer of population, are antagonistic to the proletariat which, as the lowest class, wishes to make an end of all privileges. . . . During the feudal period military service and the Church represented a means of providing for those members of the nobility who could not become direct owners. Under the capitalist system of production the intellectual occupations serve the same purpose. The intelligentsia is the mental aristocracy, and its interests under the existing system compel it to maintain its aristocratic apartness at any price. Hence its anti-Semitism, its anti-feminism, and so on. The insistence of the

[3] Machajski uses his specific term "educated society" under which he understands the sum total of all capitalists and all members of the "new middle class."

social-democratic party upon equal opportunity for all in the matter of acquiring education and its endeavor to remove the obstacles which *at present* prevent women and workers from rising into the ranks of the intellectual professions may affect the intelligentsia more than anything else—by bringing about an *overproduction of the educated*. In this respect the interests of the proletariat and those of the intelligentsia are *diametrically opposed to each other.*"

In the above passage Kautsky apparently understands something about the parasitism of the existence of the intelligentsia as a class in bourgeois society, which endeavors to maintain its monopoly by every means, and whose interests are "diametrically opposed" to the interests of the proletatariat. Now, in Russian Poland this privilege of the intelligentsia "suffers most from the Russian government." Kautsky is aware of this fact, yet it does not occur to him to draw the only conclusion that could be drawn from it in accordance with the socialist theory; namely that "the sufferings of the Polish intelligentsia" are giving birth to a definite, very strong class interest of the Polish bourgeois society which is impelled to use the labor movement as an instrument for reducing these "sufferings" of the privileged, for the full development of the parasitic life of the intelligentsia. . . .

This opportunist attitude of Kautsky with regard to Polish patriotism is an inevitable consequence of his ability to refrain, in time, from "alluring" investigations in order not to infringe upon some social-democratic formula or other. The new phenomenon of capitalist evolution compels him to point out that the intelligentsia is a definitely growing privileged class, that it is aristocratic in character and that it is closely related to the bourgeoisie. However, his social-democratic principles do not permit him under any circumstances to call it directly a bourgeois class, that is, an enemy of the proletariat, because, as everybody knows, the bourgeoisie—the enemy of the proletariat—is only "a relatively small number of capitalists and big landowners." True, the intelligentsia "is a privileged layer of the bourgeois society," "a means for providing for the offspring of the bourgeoisie"—

yet nevertheless it consists of "workers," even though they may be privileged, because the "non-workers" in the capitalist system are "only the capitalists and the big landowners" (Section 5 of the Erfurt Program).

Thus the infallible social-democratic principles have decided once for all that the "new strong and growing middle layer," the "intelligentsia," is an element that stands outside of the classes of a class-system, and that, according to these principles, it is destined to remain so, no matter how much it will expand and gain in strength. No matter how its privileges multiply, how its parasitic life grows, how the "diametrical opposition" between its interests and those of the proletariat manifests itself, it is destined "not to take part, as a class, in the class struggle of the bourgeoisie" against the proletariat; and consequently, in accordance with the social-democratic theory, it is for all eternity endowed with the ability, to a larger or smaller degree, to "rise above the narrow class horizon." It was shown before that according to these social-democratic principles "the sale of the special knowledge and abilities" by the intelligentsia as a class, is essentially not connected with "capitalist exploitation" and altogether at variance with it. The social-democratic principles do not even suspect that *the ability of the intelligentsia, as a class, from generation to generation, to sell its "special knowledge and abilities," presupposes a "special" hereditary property in the possession of this class, and that consequently, this sale is directly connected with exploitation and directly interested in its existence.*

The social-democratic principles, in their "pure" form, reject the possibility of any increase of the middle layers of society, and declare that "all the benefits of the capitalist development are monopolized by a relatively small number of capitalists and big landowners." In reality, however, capitalist evolution shows an indubitable growth of bourgeois society. Even if the small enterprises are inevitably doomed to disappear, the middle classes, as represented by the ever increasing number of privileged employees of capitalism, are growing nevertheless, and thus "all the benefits of the gigantic growth of the productive forces are monopolized" *not merely by "a handful" of plutocrats, but by the growing bourgeois society.*[4]

The evolution of the social-democratic party, from its subversive intentions to its modern efforts to direct the proletarian movement into reformist channels, does not reflect merely the changed situation of the proletariat. The contradictions of the capitalist system are, of course, not weaker at present than they were half a century ago. True, the revolutionary struggle of the Western European proletariat has enabled some of its layers to improve their situations; but the position of the unemployed whose numbers are growing continually is all the more miserable and hopeless, and the situation of the entire proletariat in such countries as Italy and Hungary, not to speak of the starving masses of Russia, is of course not better than that of the English and German paupers of the forties. Consequently the social-democratic evolution reflects something else as well: *the evolution which is going on within the bourgeois society itself*.

Time was when a rapidly advancing capitalism, an impetuous concentration of wealth and the development of the machine industry not only pauperized peasants and handicraftsmen, but even represented a threat to the privileged classes as a whole. "The middle class is bound to disappear gradually, until the world will be divided into millionaires and paupers, into big landowners and poor laborers" Engels wrote in the forties (Deutsch-Französische Jahrbücher). This was a threat directed against privileged society itself, against the savants and other intellectuals whom the millionaire is ready to treat as if they were ordinary laborers.

That period was reflected by a more or less *revolutionary* mood of the social-democratic party. Under its pressure the growing sum total of the national surplus value which is appropriated by the capitalists provides an ever increasing share for the maintenance of all privileged layers. Bourgeois

[4] See Note 1.

society, "the new middle class which is numerically very strong," expands. The privileged employees of capital are more and more admitted to the task of ruling the country. Science is given an honorary place and proper emoluments, and the bourgeoisie controls the minds of the proletarians with the help of science. The situation thus created found its expression in the determined endeavor of the social-democracy of the nineties to become "the only party of order." [5]

The "new middle class," "numerically strong and growing incessantly," is a class of employees of capital. Consequently, from the point of view of the social-democratic principles, it is, for all that, a class of workers, even though it be privileged. For, according to the Erfurt Program, only the capitalists and the big landowners are non-workers. Thus this class, due to its monopoly of education, acquires merely the ability, as was stated before [by Karl Kautsky] to have no part in capitalist exploitation. . . .

Marx's analysis of the bourgeois system lays bare only the antagonism between the capitalists and the workers and altogether disregards the antagonism between the proletariat and bourgeois society. [6] Consequently [according to Marx] the entire national surplus value consists only of the products of consumption of the capitalist class and of the fund for "the additional means of production" which is "saved by them." . . .

It apparently results from Marx's analysis that the intellectual workers get their maintenance not from the unpaid product of the proletarian's labor, but as a reward for their skilled labor power. Thus the entire parasitic character of

[5] In an article written in 1895 for the Vienna "Zeit", published by progressive middle class elements of Austria, Wilhelm Liebknecht (father of Karl), one of the founders of the German Social-Democratic Party, emphasized the law-abiding character of his party, concluding one section of the article with the words: "we are the only party of order in Germany."

[6] See Note 1.

bourgeois society is concealed behind the following economic relation:

"All labor of a higher or more complicated character than average labor is expenditure of labor-power of a more costly kind, labor power whose production has cost more time and labor, and which therefore has a higher value, than unskilled or simple labor-power. This power being of higher value, its consumption is labor of a higher class, labor that creates in equal times proportionately higher values than unskilled labor does". (*Capital*, Vol. I, p. 220)

At a certain point complicated labor ceases to be labor of mechanical performance, in a broad sense, and becomes labor engaged in directing, managing, superintending the entire labor process of society. This is the labor of the privileged employees of the capitalist system, the labor of the intellectuals, of the army of mental workers. It has a "higher value" because in its value there are contained "higher expenditures for education," [7] that is, for the remuneration of the educators and for the maintenance of the pupils.

For the preparation of the intelligent forces needed for the capitalist system the latter uses a special fund, the sum total of the national surplus value. Every generation of privileged employees, that is, of the intellectuals, during the period of its training, swallows a certain amount of the national surplus value. Thus they become highly skilled labor power, a power of "higher character," of "higher value." This means: *for the very reason that they swallowed a certain amount of surplus value, they acquire, under the logic of the system of exploitation, the right to keep on exacting—as payment for their training—the unpaid product of other people's labor, the labor of the proletarian*. Yet, it is supposed to be the payment for their *individual* abilities! The surplus value which bourgeois society has appropriated as remuneration for labor of a "higher character" is transmitted by that society to its offspring, and knowledge, science, mankind's great-

---

[7] While the English version of *Capital* speaks merely of "labor power of a more costly kind", the German original speaks of labor power "in which higher expenditures for education are included". The Russian text used by Machajski was a literal translation of the German original.

est patrimony, becomes the hereditary monopoly of a privileged minority. *Only members of this hereditary, privileged
minority can become labor power of a "higher character,"
while all the remaining millions are in possession of the hereditary monopoly of manual slave-labor.*

The social-democratic principles have no compunctions in
tolerating within the proletarian movement the presence of a
social force which, due to its very nature, could not possibly
aim at the abolition of the class system. That social force is
the class interest of the intellectual workers. This element
keeps the proletariat from striving towards an immediate
overthrow of the existing system, by telling the workers that
the final emancipation is unthinkable for the time being, and
that a long period of political education of the working class
is still necessary for that purpose.

From *The Intellectual Worker. Part I. The Evolution of Social-Democracy.*
Conclusion. pp. 70-83 (Selected passages).

THE COLLECTIVIST WAGES SYSTEM*

By P. KROPOTKIN

I

In their plans for the reconstruction of society the collectivists commit, in our opinion, a two-fold error. While speaking of abolishing capitalist rule, they intend nevertheless to retain two institutions which are at the very basis of this rule—Representative Government and the Wages' System.

As regards so-called representative government, we have often spoken about it. It is absolutely incomprehensible to us that intelligent men—and such are not wanting in the collectivist party—can remain partisans of national or municipal parliaments after all the lessons history has given them —in France, in England, in Germany, or in the United States.

While we see parliamentary rule breaking up, and from all sides criticism of this rule growing louder—not only of its results, but also of *its principles*—how is it that the revolutionary socialists defend a system already condemned to die?

Built up by the middle classes to hold their own against royalty, sanctioning, and, at the same time strengthening, their sway over the workers, parliamentary rule is pre-eminently a middle-class rule. The upholders of this system have never seriously maintained that a parliament or a municipal council represent a nation or a city. The most intelligent among them know that this is impossible. The middle classes have simply used the parliamentary system to raise a protecting barrier against the pretensions of royalty, without giving the people liberty. But gradually, as the people become conscious of their real interests, and the variety of their

* From *The Conquest of Bread*

interests is growing, the system can no longer work. Therefore democrats of all countries vainly imagine various palli-
atives. The *Referendum* is tried and found to be a failure;
proportional representation is spoken of, the representation
of minorities, and other parliamentary Utopias. In a word,
they strive to find what is not to be found, and after each
new experiment they are bound to recognize that it was a
failure; so that confidence in Representative Government
vanishes more and more.

It is the same with the Wages' system; because, once the
abolition of private property is proclaimed, and the possession in common of all means of production is introduced,—
how can the wages' system be maintained in any form? This
is, nevertheless, what collectivists are doing when they recommend the use of the labour-cheques as a mode of remuneration for labour accomplished for the great collectivist employer—the State.

It is easy to understand why the early English socialists,
since the time of Robert Owen, came to the system of
labour-cheques. They simply tried to make capital and
labour agree. They repudiated the idea of laying hands on
capitalist property by means of revolutionary measures.

It is also easy to understand why Proudhon took up later
on the same idea. In his mutualist system he tried to make
capital less offensive, notwithstanding the retaining of private property, which he detested from the bottom of his
heart, but which he believed to be necessary to guarantee individuals against the State.

Neither is it astonishing that certain economists, more
or less bourgeois, admit labour-cheques. They care little
whether the worker is paid in labour-notes or in coin
stamped with the effigy of the Republic or the Empire. They
only care to save from destruction the individual ownership
of dwelling-houses, of land, of factories; in any case—that,
at least, of dwelling-houses and the capital that is necessary
for manufacturing. And labour-notes would just answer the
purpose of upholding this private property.

As long as labour-notes can be exchanged for jewels or carriages, the owner of the house will willingly accept them for rent. And as long as dwelling-houses, fields, and factories belong to isolated owners, men will have to pay these owners, in one way or another, for being allowed to work in the fields or factories, or for living in the houses. The owners will agree to be paid by the workers in gold, in paper-money, or in cheques exchangeable for all sorts of commodities, once that toll upon labour is maintained, and the right to levy it is left with them. But how can we defend labour-notes, this new form of wagedom, when we admit that the houses, the fields, and the factories will no longer be private property,—that they will belong to the commune or the nation?

II

Let us closely examine this system of remuneration for work done, preached by the French, German, English, and Italian collectivists (the Spanish anarchists, who still call themselves collectivists, imply by collectivism the possession in common of all instruments of production, and the "liberty of each group to divide the produce, as they think fit, according to communist or any other principles").

It amounts to this: Everybody works in field, factory, school, hospital, etc. The working-day is fixed by the State, which owns the land, the factories, the roads, etc. Every work-day is paid for with a labour-note, which is inscribed with these words: *Eight hours' work*. With this cheque the worker can procure all sorts of merchandise in the stores owned by the State or by divers corporations. The cheque is divisible, so that you can buy an hour's-work worth of meat, ten minutes' worth of matches, or half an hour of tobacco. After the collectivist Revolution, instead of saying "twopence worth of soap," we shall say "five minutes' worth of soap."

Most collectivists, true to the distinction laid down by

middle-class economists (and by Marx as well) between qualified work and simple work, tell us, moreover, that qualified or professional work must be paid a certain quantity more than simple work. Thus one hour's work of a doctor will have to be considered as equivalent to two or three hours' work of a hospital nurse, or to three or five hours' work of a navvy. "Professional, or qualified work, will be a multiple of simple work," says the collectivist Gronlund, "because this kind of work needs a more or less long apprenticeship."

Some other collectivists, such as the French Marxist, Guesde, do not make this distinction. They proclaim the "Equality of Wages." The doctor, the schoolmaster, and the professor will be paid (in labour-cheques) at the same rate as the navvy. Eight hours visiting the sick in a hospital will be worth the same as eight hours spent in earthworks or else in mines or factories.

Some make a greater concession; they admit that disagreeable or unhealthy work—such as sewerage—could be paid for at a higher rate than agreeable work. One hour's work of a sewerman would be worth, they say, two hours of a professor's work.

Let us add that certain collectivists admit of corporations being paid a lump sum for work done. Thus a corporation would say: "Here are a hundred tons of steel. A hundred workmen were required to produce them, and it took them ten days. Their work-day being an eight-hours day, it has taken them eight thousand working hours to produce a hundred tons of steel—eight hours a ton." For this the State would pay them eight thousand labour-notes of one hour each, and these eight thousand cheques would be divided among the members of the iron-works as they themselves thought proper.

On the other hand, a hundred miners having taken twenty days to extract eight thousand tons of coal, coal would be worth two hours a ton, and the sixteen thousand cheques of one hour each, received by the Guild of Miners, would be divided among their members according to their own appreciation.

If the miners protested and said that a ton of steel should only cost six hours' work instead of eight; if the professor wished to have his day paid four times more than the nurse, then the State would interfere and would settle their differences.

Such is, in a few words, the organization the collectivists wish to see arise out of the Social Revolution. As we see, their principles are: Collective property of the instruments of production, and remuneration to each according to the time spent in producing, while taking into account the productivity of his labour. As to the political system, it would be the parliamentary system, modified by positive instructions given to those elected, and by the Referendum—a vote, taken by noes and ayes by the nation.

Let us own that this system appears to us simply unrealizable.

Collectivists begin by proclaiming a revolutionary principle—the abolition of private property—and then they deny it, no sooner than proclaimed, by upholding an organization of production and consumption which originated in private property.

They proclaim a revolutionary principle, and ignore the consequences that this principle will inevitably bring about. They forget that the very fact of abolishing individual property in the instruments of work—land, factories, road, capital—must launch society into absolutely new channels; must completely overthrow the present system of production, both in its aim as well as in its means; must modify daily relations between individuals, as soon as land, machinery, and all other instruments of production are considered common property.

They say, "No private property," and immediately after strive to maintain private property in its daily manifestations. "You shall be a commune as far as regards production: fields, tools, machinery, all that has been invented up ɩill now—factories, railways, harbours, mines, etc., all are yours. Not the slightest distinction will be made concerning the share of each in this collective property.

"But from to-morrow you will minutely debate the share you are going to take in the creation of new machinery, in the digging of new mines. You will carefully weigh what part of the new produce belongs to you. You will count your minutes of work, and you will take care that a minute of your neighbours should not buy more than yours.

"And as an hour measures nothing, as in some factories a worker can see to six power-looms at a time, while in another he only tends two, you will weigh the muscular force, the brain energy, and the nervous energy you have expended. You will accurately calculate the years of apprenticeship in order to appraise the amount each will contribute to future production. And this—after having declared that you do not take into account his share in past production."

Well, for us it is evident that a society cannot be based on two absolutely opposed principles, two principles that contradict one another continually. And a nation or a commune which would have such an organization would be compelled to revert to private property in the instruments of production, or to transform itself into a communist society.

III

We have said that certain collectivist writers desire that a distinction should be made between qualified or professional work and simple work. They pretend that an hour's work of an engineer, an architect, or a doctor, must be considered as two or three hours' work of a blacksmith, a mason, or a hospital nurse. And the same distinction must be made between all sorts of trades necessitating apprenticeship, and the simple toil of day labourers.

Well, to establish this distinction would be to maintain all the inequalities of present society. It would mean fixing a dividing line, from the beginning, between the workers and those who pretend to govern them. It would mean dividing society into two very distinct classes—the aristocracy of knowledge placed above the horny-handed lower orders—the one doomed to serve the other; the one working with its hands to feed and clothe those who, profiting by their leisure, study how to govern their fosterers.

It would mean reviving one of the distinct peculiarities of present society and giving it the sanction of the Social Revolution. It would mean setting up as a principle an abuse already condemned in our ancient crumbling society.

We know the answer we shall get. They will speak of "Scientific Socialism"; they will quote bourgeois economists, and Marx too, to prove that a scale of wages has its raison d'être, as "the labour-force" of the engineer will have cost more to society than the "labour-force" of the navvy. In fact —have not economists tried to prove to us that if an engineer is paid twenty times more than a navvy it is because the "necessary" outlay to make an engineer is greater than that necessary to make a navvy? And has not Marx asserted that the same distinction is equally logical between two branches of manual labour? He could not conclude otherwise, having taken up on his own account Ricardo's theory of value, and upheld that goods are exchanged in proportion to the quantity of work socially necessary for their production.

But we know what to think of this. We know that if engineers, scientists, or doctors are paid ten or a hundred times more than a labourer, and if a weaver earns three times more than an agricultural labourer, and ten times more than a girl in a match factory, it is not by reason of their "cost of production," but by reason of a monopoly of education, or a monopoly of industry. Engineers, scientists, and doctors merely exploit their capital—their diplomas—as middle-class employers exploit a factory, or as nobles used to exploit their titles of nobility.

As to the employer who pays an engineer twenty times more than a labourer, it is simply due to personal interest; if the engineer can economize $4,000 a year on the cost of production, the employer pays him $800. And if the employer has a foreman who saves $400 on the work by cleverly sweating workmen, he gladly gives him $80 or $120 a year. He parts with an extra $40 when he expects to gain $400 by it; and this is the essence of the capitalist system. The same dif-. ferences obtain among different manual trades.

Let them, therefore, not talk to us of "the cost of production" which raises the cost of skilled labour, and tell us that a student who has gaily spent his youth in a university has a *right* to a wage ten times greater than the son of a miner who has grown pale in a mine since the age of eleven; or that a weaver has a *right* to a wage three or four times greater than that of an agricultural labourer. The cost of teaching a weaver his work is not four times greater than the cost of teaching a peasant his. The weaver simply benefits by the advantages his industry reaps in international trade, from countries that have as yet no industries, and in consequence of the privileges accorded by all states to industries in preference to the tilling of the soil.

Nobody has ever calculated the *cost of production* of a producer: and if a noble loafer costs far more to society than a worker, it remains to be seen whether a robust day-labourer does not cost more to society than a skilled artisan, when we have taken into account infant-mortality among the poor, the ravages of anaemia, and premature deaths.

Could they, for example, make us believe that the 1s. 3d. paid to a Paris workwoman, the 3d. paid to an Auvergne peasant girl who grows blind at lace-making, or the 1s. 8d. paid to the peasant represent their "cost of production." We know full well that people work for less, but we also know that they do so exclusively because, thanks to our wonderful organization, they would die of hunger did they not accept these mock wages.

For us the scale of remuneration is a complex result of taxes, of governmental tutelage, of capitalist monopoly. In a word, of State and Capital. Therefore, we say that all wages' theories have been invented after the event to justify injustices at present existing, and that we need not take them into consideration.

Neither will they fail to tell us that the collectivist scale of wages would be an improvement. "It would be better," so they say, "to see certain artisans receiving a wage two or three times higher than common labourers, than to see a minister receiving in a day what a workman cannot earn in a year. It would be a great step towards equality."

For us this step would be the reverse of progress. To make a distinction between simple and professional work in a new society would result in the Revolution sanctioning and recognizing as a principle a brutal fact we submit to nowadays, but that we nevertheless find unjust. It would mean imitating those gentlemen of the French Assembly who proclaimed on August 4th, 1789, the abolition of feudal rights, but who on August 8th sanctioned these same rights by imposing dues on the peasants to compensate the noblemen, placing these dues under the protection of the Revolution. It would mean imitating the Russian Government, which proclaimed, at the time of the emancipation of the serfs, that certain lands should henceforth belong to the nobility, while formerly these lands were considered as belonging to the serfs.

Or else, to take a better known example, when the commune of 1871 decided to pay members of the Commune Council 12s. 6d. a day, while the federates on the ramparts received only 1s. 3d., this decision was hailed as an act of superior democratic equality. In reality, the Commune only ratified the former inequality between functionary and soldier, Government and governed. Coming from an opportunist Chamber of Deputies, such a decision would have appeared admirable, but the Commune doomed her own revolutionary principles when she failed to put them into practice.

Under our existing social system, when a minister gets paid $5,000 a year, while a workman must content himself with $40 or less; when a foreman is paid two or three times more than a workman, and among workmen there is every gradation, from 8s. a day down to the peasant girl's 3d., we disapprove of the high salary of the minister as well as of the difference between the 8s. of the workman and the 3d. of the poor woman. And we say, "Down with the privileges of education, as well as with those of birth!" We are anarchists precisely because these privileges revolt us.

They revolt us already in this authoritarian society. Could we endure them in a society that began by proclaiming equality?

This is why some collectivists, understanding the impossibility of maintaining a scale of wages in a society inspired by the breath of the Revolution, hasten to proclaim equality of wage. But they meet with new difficulties, and their equality of wages becomes the same unrealizable Utopia as the scale of wages of other collectivists.

A society having taken possession of all social wealth, having boldly proclaimed the right of all to this wealth—whatever share they may have taken in producing it—will be compelled to abandon any system of wages, whether in currency or labour-notes.

IV

The collectivists say, "To each according to his deeds"; or, in other terms, according to his share of services rendered to society. They think it expedient to put this principle into practice, as soon as the Social Revolution will have made all instruments of production common property. But we think that if the Social Revolution had the misfortune of proclaiming such a principle, it would mean its necessary failure; it would mean leaving the social problem, which past centuries have burdened us with, unsolved.

Of course, in society like ours, in which the more a man works the less he is remunerated, this principle, at first sight, may appear to be a yearning for justice. But in reality it is only the perpetuation of injustice. It was by proclaiming this principle that wagedom began, to end in the glaring inequalities and all the abominations of present society; because, from the moment work done began to be appraised in currency, or in any other form of wage, the day it was agreed upon that man would only receive the wage he should be able to secure to himself, the whole history of a State-aided capitalist society was as good as written; it was contained in germ in this principle.

Shall we, then, return to our starting-point, and go through the same evolution again? Our theorists desire it, but fortunately it is impossible. The Revolution, we maintain, must be communist; if not, it will be drowned in blood, and have to be begun over again.

Services rendered to society, be they work in factory or field, or mental services, cannot be valued in money. There can be no exact measure of value (of what has been wrongly termed exchange value), nor of use value, in terms of production. If two individuals work for the community five hours a day, year in year out, at different work which is equally agreeable to them, we may say that on the whole their labour is approximately equivalent. But we cannot divide their work, and say that the result of any particular day, hour, or minute of work of the one is worth the result of one day, one hour, or one minute of the other.

We may roughly say that the man, who during his lifetime has deprived himself of leisure during ten hours a day has given far more to society than the one who has only deprived himself of leisure during five hours a day, or who has not deprived himself at all. But we cannot take what he has done during two hours, and say that the yield of his two hours' work is worth twice as much as the yield of another individual, who has worked only one hour, and remunerate the two in proportion. It would be disregarding all that is complex in industry, in agriculture, in the whole life of present society; it would be ignoring to what extent all individual work is the result of the past and the present labour of society as a whole. It would mean believing ourselves to be living in the Stone Age, whereas we are living in an age of steel.

If you enter a modern coal-mine you will see a man in charge of a huge machine that raises and lowers a cage. In his hand he holds a lever that stops and reverses the course of the machine; he lowers it and the cage reverses its course in the twinkling of an eye; he sends it upwards or downwards into the depths of the shaft with a giddy swiftness. All attention, he follows with his eyes fixed on an indicator which shows him, on a small scale, at which point of the shaft the cage is at each second of its progress; and as soon as the indicator has reached a certain level, he suddenly stops the course of the cage, not a yard higher nor lower than the required spot. And no sooner have the colliers unloaded their coal-wagonettes, and pushed empty ones instead, than he reverses the lever and again sends the cage back into space.

During eight or ten consecutive hours every day he must keep the same strain of attention. Should his brain relax for a moment, the cage would inevitably strike against the gear, break its wheels, snap the rope, crush men, and put a stop to all work in the mine. Should he waste three seconds at each touch of the lever,—the extraction, in our modern perfected mines, would be reduced from twenty to fifteen tons a day.

Is it he who is the most necessary man in the mine? Or, is it perhaps the boy who signals to him from below to raise the cage? Is it the miner at the bottom of the shaft, who risks his life every instant, and who will some day be killed by fire-damp? Or is it the engineer, who would lose the layer of coal, and would cause the miners to dig on rock by a simple mistake in his calculations? Or, is it the mine owner who has put his capital into the mine, and who has perhaps, contrary to expert advice, asserted that excellent coal would be found there?

All those who are engaged in the mine contribute to the extraction of coal in proportion to their strength, their energy, their knowledge, their intelligence, and their skill. And we may say that all have the right to live, to satisfy their needs, and even their whims, when the necessaries of life have been secured for all. But how can we appraise the work of each one of them?

And, moreover, Is the coal they have extracted entirely *their* work? Is it not also the work of the men who have built the railway leading to the mine and the roads that radiate from all the railway stations? Is it not also the work of those that have tilled and sown the fields, extracted iron, cut wood in the forests, built the machines that burn coal, slowly developed the mining industry altogether, and so on?

It is utterly impossible to draw a distinction between the work of each of those men. To measure the work by its results leads us to an absurdity; to divide the total work, and to measure its fractions by the number of hours spent on the work also leads us to absurdity. One thing remains: to put the *needs* above the *works,* and first of all to recognize *the right to live,* and later on *the right to well-being* for all those who took their share in production.

But take any other branch of human activity—take the manifestations of life as a whole. Which one of us can claim the higher remuneration for his work? Is it the doctor who has found out the illness, or the nurse who has brought about recovery by her hygienic care? Is it the inventor of the first steam-engine, or the boy, who, one day getting tired of pulling the rope that formerly opened the valve to let steam enter the piston, tied the rope to the lever of the machine, without suspecting that he had invented the essential mechanical part of all modern machinery—the automatic valve.

Is it the inventor of the locomotive, or the workman of Newcastle, who suggested replacing the stones formerly laid under the rails by wooden sleepers, as the stones, for want of elasticity, caused the trains to derail? Is it the engineer on the locomotive? The signalman who stops the trains, or lets them pass by? The switchman who transfers a train from one line to another?

Again, to whom do we owe the transatlantic cable? Is it

to the electrical engineer who obstinately affirmed that the cable would transmit messages while learned men of science declared it to be impossible? Is it to Maury, the learned physical geographer, who advised that thick cables should be set aside for others as thin as a walking cane? Or else to those volunteers, come from nobody knows where, who spent their days and nights on deck minutely examining every yard of the cable, and removed the nails that the shareholders of steamship companies stupidly caused to be driven into the non-conducting wrapper of the cable, so as to make it unserviceable?

And in a wider sphere, the true sphere of life, with its joys, its sufferings, and its accidents, cannot each one of us recall someone who has rendered him so great a service that we should be indignant if its equivalent in coin were mentioned? The service may have been but a word, nothing but a word spoken at the right time, or else it may have been months and years of devotion, and are we going to appraise these "incalculable" services in "labour-notes?"

"The works of each!" But human society would not exist for more than two consecutive generations if everyone did not give infinitely more than that for which he is paid in coin, in "cheques," or in civil rewards. The race would soon become extinct if mothers did not sacrifice their lives to take care of their children, if men did not give continually, without demanding an equivalent reward, if men did not give most precisely when they expect no reward.

If middle-class society is decaying, if we have got into a blind alley from which we cannot emerge without attacking past institutions with torch and hatchet, it is precisely because we have given too much to counting. It is because we have let ourselves be influenced into *giving* only to *receive*. It is because we have aimed at turning society into a commercial company based on *debit* and *credit*.

After all, the Collectivists know this themselves. They vaguely understand that a society could not exist if it carried out the principle of "Each according to his deeds." They have a notion that *necessaries*—we do not speak of whims—the needs of the individual, do not always correspond to his *works*. Thus De Paepe tells us: "The principle—the eminently Individualist principle—would, however, be tempered by social intervention for the education of children and young persons (including maintenance and lodging), and by the social organization for assisting the infirm and the sick, for retreats for aged workers, etc." They understand that a man of forty, father of three children, has other needs than a young man of twenty. They know that the woman who suckles her infant and spends sleepless nights at its bedside, cannot do as much *work* as the man who has slept peace-fully. They seem to take in that men and women, worn out maybe by dint of overwork for society, may be incapable of doing as much *work* as those who have spent their time leisurely and pocketed their "labour-notes" in the privileged career of State functionaries.

They are eager to temper their principle. They say: "Society will not fail to maintain and bring up its children; to help both aged and infirm. Without doubt *needs* will be the measure of the cost that society will burden itself with, to temper the principle of deeds."

Charity, charity, always Christian charity, organized by the State this time. They believe in improving the asylums for foundlings, in effecting old-age and sick insurances—so as to *temper* their principle. But they cannot yet throw aside the idea of "wounding first and healing afterwards"!

Thus, after having denied communism, after having laughed at their ease at the formula—"To each according to his needs"—these great economists discover that they have forgotten something, the needs of the producers, which they now admit. Only it is for the State to estimate them, for the State to verify if the needs are not disproportionate to the work.

The State will dole out charity. Thence to the English poor-law and the workhouse is but a step.

There is but a slight difference, because even this step

mother of a society against whom we are in revolt has also been compelled to temper her individualist principles; she, too, has had to make concessions in a communist direction and under the same form of charity.

She, too, distributes halfpenny dinners to prevent the pillaging of her shops; builds hospitals—often very bad ones, but sometimes splendid ones—to prevent the ravages of contagious diseases. She, too, after having paid the hours of labour, shelters the children of those she has wrecked. She takes their needs into consideration and doles out charity.

Poverty, we have said elsewhere, was the primary cause of wealth. It was poverty that created the first capitalist; because before accumulating "surplus value," of which we hear so much, men had to be sufficiently destitute to consent to sell their labour, so as not to die of hunger. It was poverty that made capitalists. And if the number of the poor increased so rapidly during the Middle Ages, it was due to the invasions and wars that followed the founding of States, and to the increase of riches resulting from the exploitation of the East. These two causes tore asunder the bonds that kept men together in the agrarian and urban communities, and taught them to proclaim the principle of *wages,* so dear to the exploiters, instead of the solidarity they formerly practised in their tribal life.

And it is this principle that is to spring from a revolution which men dare to call by the name of Social Revolution,—a name so dear to the starved, the oppressed, and the sufferers!

It can never be. For the day on which old institutions will fall under the proletarian axe, voices will cry out: "Bread, shelter, ease for all!" And those voices will be listened to; the people will say: "Let us begin by allaying our thirst for life, for happiness, for liberty, that we have never quenched. And when we shall have tasted of this joy, we will set to work to demolish the last vestiges of middle-class rule: its morality drawn from account-books, its 'debit and credit' philosophy, its 'mine and yours' institutions. 'In demolishing we shall build,' as Proudhon said; and we shall build in the name of communism and anarchy."

philosophy, its 'mine and yours' institutions. 'In demolishing we shall build,' as Proudhon said, and we shall build

PERSONALITY AND THE CONCEPTION OF THE NATIONAL STATE*

By ADOLF HITLER

To attempt to judge a person's worth by his race and to declare war on the Marxian axiom "One man is like another" would be folly unless we were ready to carry it to its logical conclusion.

A person who holds that it is possible for a National Socialist state to transform itself into something new and different from other states by the mere process of greater equalization of wealth, better control of economic development—that is, by the mechanical method of reconstruction of its economic life—will find himself at an impasse. Such a person has no understanding of what we mean by a world view. The method of economic reconstruction gives no guarantee of permanency and makes no promise of a bright future. A nation trusting in such superficial reforms has no guarantee of victory in the conflict of nations. A movement basing its efforts on such compromises as these will find itself unable to initiate important, profound, and lasting reforms because its efforts will never reach beyond the surface of things.

To understand this clearly it may be wise to examine the real foundation and cause of the development of civilization. The first step which led man away from the animal world was the step toward invention. In the general struggle with other animals man first showed his skill in his ability to control creatures of special capabilities. Even so early, it was clearly personality that produced the decisions and achievements that were later accepted as a matter of course by all humanity. Man's understanding of his own ability, which I

* Selection from *Mein Kampf*

regard even now as the basis of all strategy, was due originally to a determined brain, and it was not until perhaps
thousands of years had passed that it was accepted everywhere as a perfectly natural phenomenon.

Man crowned this first discovery with a second: he
learned, among other things, how to live while occupied in
this struggle for existence. In this way began the inventive
activity characteristic of mankind, the results of which we
see everywhere around us. And it is the result of the creative
power and ability of the individual. It was profoundly effective in causing the man of power continually to rise higher.
But what were once simple devices, helping hunters in the
forest in their struggle for existence, are not the brilliant
scientific inventions of today; these help man in the struggle
for existence today and are forging weapons for struggle in
the future.

The work of evolving pure theory, incapable of measurement, but the requisite preliminary for further material invention, is also seen to be the exclusive achievement of the
individual. The masses do not invent, majorities do not
organize or think. It is only the one man, the Individual.

A human community is well organized only when it furthers in every possible way the work of these creative forces
and uses them for the good of the community. Organization
must be manifestation of the effort to place brains over the
masses and to enslave the masses to the brains. Organization,
therefore, must not prevent the brains from emerging from
the masses; it must, on the contrary, by its own conscious
action encourage it and make it in every way possible. The
severe struggle for existence itself causes brains to emerge.

State administration and the strength of the nations incorporated in the defensive forces are dominated by the idea of
personality, by its authority, and by responsibility towards
the highly placed individual. It is only in the political world
that this principle of nature is persistently ignored. Although
all civilization is the outcome of the creative power of personality, in the community as a whole and particularly

among its leaders, the principle of the dignity of the majority makes a pretence of being the deciding authority; it is beginning to poison all life below it, and, in fact, to destroy it. The destructive machinations of Judaism within other nations can at bottom be ascribed only to the constant effort to lower the importance of personality in all nations who receive them, and to substitute for it the will of the masses.

It is now clear that Marxism is the expressison of the Jewish effort to abolish the importance of personality in all departments of life and to substitute for it the mass of numbers. In politics the parliamentary form of government is its expression. This is what is causing such mischief from the smallest parish council to the power controlling the entire Reich.

Marxism has never been able itself to establish a culture or to create an economic system; further, it has never really been in a position to support an existing system in accordance with its own beliefs. Always, after a brief time, it is forced to retrace its steps and to make concessions to the theory of the principle of personality. Even within its own organization it is unable to deny this principle.

The national theory of the world must be completely differentiated from the Marxist. It must place its faith in race and also on the importance of personality, making them the pillars supporting its whole structure. These are the fundamental factors of its view of the world.

The National State must concentrate its effort on ensuring all government, especially the highest—the political leadership—freedom from the principle of control by majorities—the masses—in order to achieve the undisputed authority of the Individual.

The best form of State and constitution is that which with a deft hand elevates the best brains of the community to a position of leadership and dominance. There must be no majority making decisions, but merely a group of responsible persons. The word "council" will revert to its ancient meaning. Every man shall have counsellors at his side, but the decision must be made by the one man.

The national State will not permit that men whose education and occupation have given no special knowledge shall be invited to advise or judge of subjects of a special nature, such as economics. The State will subdivide its representative body into political committees and committees representative of professions and trades. In order to get helpful cooperation between the two, there will be over them a special senate. But neither the Senate nor Chamber will have the power to make decisions; they are appointed to work and not to make decisions. Individual members may advise, but never decide. That, for the time being, is the exclusive prerogative of the responsible President.

As to the possibility of carrying out our knowledge in practice, I may remind my readers that the parliamentary principle of decision by majorities has not always governed the human race. On the contrary, it appears only during very short periods of history, and those have always been periods of decadence.

In any case, it is not to be imagined that purely theoretical measures from above will effect such a change, as logically it cannot stop at the constitution of a State. All legislation, and, in fact, the citizen's whole life has to be saturated with it. Such a revolution can come about only by means of a movement, itself created in the spirit of that idea, and itself therefore, the begetter of the coming State.

It is clear, then, that the National Socialist movement must today identify itself with that idea, practising it within its own organization so that it may be able not only to conduct the State in the right path, but also that it may have the perfected body of the State ready to be occupied.

THE FASCIST STATE AND THE FUTURE*

By BENITO MUSSOLINI

AMID the innovations and experiments of the new Fascist civilization, there is one which is of interest to the whole world; it is the corporative organization of the state.

Let me assert at once that before we reached this form of state organization, one which I now consider rounded out, the steps we took were long, and our research, analysis and discussion have been exhaustive. Both the experience and the tests have been full of lessons.

Practical reality itself has been the navigator. First of all, we must remember that the corporative organization was not born from a desire to create mere juridical institutions; in my opinion, it grew out of the special necessities of the Italian situation in particular, and out of those necessities which would be general in any situation where there is economic restriction, and where traditions of work and production have not yet been developed by experience and time. Italy, in its first half-century of united political renaissance, has seen classes armed one against the other in political control but also because of the struggle for the limited resources that our surface soil and what was beneath it might be put at the disposition of those who were interested in work and production.

Opposed to the directing middle class, there was another class which I will call, for more easy reference, proletarian. It was influenced by Socialists and anarchists, in an eternal and never-ending struggle with the directing class.

Every year there was a general strike; every year the fertile Po Valley, for instance was subjected to recurring agita-

* From *My Autobiography*

tions which imperiled crops and all production. Opposed to that humane sense of harmony which should be a duty upon citizens of the same Fatherland, there was a chronic struggle of interests, egged on by the professional Socialists, the syndicalist organizers, a struggle against a middle class which, in turn, persisted in its position of negation and of expectation of a messiah. Civil life did not move a decisive step forward on the way toward betterment.

A country like ours, which has no rich resources in the earth, which has mountains for half of its area, cannot have great economic possibilities. If, then, the citizens become naturally quarrelsome, if classes have a tendency to strive to annihilate each other, civil life can have none of that rhythm necessary for developing a modern people. The Liberal and Democratic state, in spite of upheavals, recurrent every year, and even at every season, held to a noncommittal stand, selecting a characteristic slogan: "Neither reaction, nor revolution,"—as if that phrase had a precise or, indeed, any meaning whatsoever!

It was necessary to emerge from the base, clannish habit of class competition and to put aside hates, and enmities. After the war, especially following the subversive propaganda of Lenin, ill-will had reached perilous proportions. Agitations and strikes usually were accompanied by fights, with dead and wounded men as the result. The people went back to work with souls full of hate against the class of the masters, which, rightly or wrongly, was considered so idiotically lacking in vision as to surpass in this regard any other middle class in the world. Between the peasants and the rising industry of the urban centers there were also the phenomena of unmistakable misunderstanding. All our life was dominated by demagogy. Every one was disposed to tolerate, to pretend to understand, to make concessions to the violence of the crowd. But after every incident of disorder, some new situation promised another and even more difficult problem of conflict.

It was necessary, in my opinion, to create a political atmosphere which would allow men in government to have some degree of courage, to speak harsh truths, to affirm rights, only after having exacted duties, and, if necessary, imposing these duties. Liberalism and Democracy were only attempted remedies of milk-and-water character; they exhausted their energies in the halls of parliament. Leading that agitation were employees of the state, railroad men and postmen and troublesome elements. The authority of the state was a kitten handled to death. In such a situation, mere pity and tolerance would have been criminal. Liberalism and Democracy, which had abdicated their duty at every turn, failed utterly to appraise and adjust the rights and duties of the various classes in Italian life. Fascism has done it!

The fact is that five years of harmonious work have transformed in its very essentials the economic life and, in consequence, the political and moral life of Italy. Let me add that the discipline that I have imposed is not a forced discipline; it is not born from perconceived ideas, does not obey the selfish interests of groups and of classes. Our discipline has one vision and one end—the welfare and the good name of the Italian nation.

The discipline that I have imposed is enlightened discipline. The humble classes, because they are more numerous and perhaps more deserving of solicitude, are nearest to my heart as a responsible leader. I have seen the men from the countryside in the trenches, and I have understood how much the nation owes to the healthy people of calloused hands. On the other hand, our industrial workers have qualities of sobriety, geniality, stamina, which feed the pride of one who must rule and lead a people. The middle Italian class, too, including the rural class, is much better than its reputation. Our problems arise from a variety and diversity among the various economic interests, which makes difficult the formation of great national groups of producers. None of the Italian producing groups, however, can be rated as "vampires," as they were rated in the superficial terminology of the old Socialist demagogy. The state is no longer ignorant when it confronts facts and the interests of the various classes. Not only does it obviate strife—it tries to find out the origins of clashes and conflicts. By statistics and the help of studious men, we now are able to define what will be the great issues of to-morrow. In the meantime, with the aid not only of the government, but of the bodies locally organized for consultation, we can know precisely what are to be the outlines of the productive programmes of to-morrow.

I have wanted the Fascist government, above all, to give great care to the social legislation needed to carry out our part of agreed international programmes for industry and for those who bear the future of industry. I think that Italy is advanced beyond all the European nations; in fact, it has ratified the laws for the eight-hour day, for obligatory insurance, for regulation of the work of women and children, for assistance and benefit, for after-work diversion and adult education, and finally for obligatory insurance against tuberculosis. All this shows how, in every detail in the field of labor, I stand by the Italian working classes. All that it was possible to do without working an injury to the principle of solidity in our economy I have set out to do, from the minimum wage to the continuity of employment, from insurance against accidents to indemnity against illness, from old age pensions to the proper regulation of military service. There is little which social welfare research has adjudged practical to national economy or wise for social happiness which has not already been advanced by me. I want to give to every man and woman so generous an opportunity that work will be not a painful necessity but a joy of life. But even such a complex programme cannot be said to equal the creation of the corporative system. Nor can the latter equal something even larger. Beyond the corporative system, beyond the state's labors, is fascism, harmonizer and dominator of Italian life, standing ever as its inspiration.

In 1923, some months after the march on Rome, I insisted on the ratification of the law for an eight-hour day. All the masses which had seen a friend in the legislative policy of fascism gave their approval to national syndicalism. Instead of the old professional syndicates we substituted Fascist corporations. In a meeting of December 19, 1923, I had occasion to affirm that: "Peace within is primarily a task of government. The government has a clear outline of conduct. Public order must never be troubled for any reason whatsoever. That is the political side. But there is also the economic side; it is one of collaboration. There are other problems, such as that of exportation. I remind Italian industry of these principles. Until now it has been too individualistic. The old system and old ways must be abandoned."

A little further on I said: "Over all conflicts of human and legitimate interests, there is the authority of the government; the government alone is in the right position to see things from the point of view of the general welfare. This government is not at the disposition of this man or that man; it is over everybody, because it takes to itself not only the juridical conscience of the nation in the present, but also all that the nation represents for the future. The government has shown that it values at the highest the productive strength of the nation. A government which follows these principles has the right to be listened to by every one. It has a task to fulfill. It will do it. It will do it inexorably for the defence of the moral and material interests of the nation."

Little by little, the old labor structure and associations were abandoned. We were directed more and more toward the corporative conception of the state. I did not want to take away from labor one of its holidays, and so, instead of the first of May, which had foreign origins and the imprint of Socialist internationalism, I fixed on a gay and glorious date in Italian life, April 21st, the birthday of Rome. Rome is the city which has given legislation to the world. The Roman law is still the text which governs the relations of civil life. To celebrate a Labor Day, I could not have selected a more suggestive and worthy date.

To bring into being, in a precise co-ordination, all the

measures that I had undertaken and that fascism and the corporations had brought about, in all their complexity, I had the Grand Council approve a document. I do not hesitate to declare it to be of historical character: it is the Labor Charter.

It is composed of thirty paragraphs, each of which contains a fundamental truth. From the paramount necessity for production arises the need of an equitable sharing of products, the need of the judgment of tribunals in case of discord, and, finally, the need of protective legislation.

That document has been welcomed by all the classes of Italy. The labor magistracy represents, in its consecration to duty, something worthy of a strong state, in contrast to the cloudy aspirations in the misty realms of high-sounding liberalism, Democracy and communistic fantasy. The framing and realization were the tasks of fascism. Old men of the socialist and syndicalist poses and postures were amazed and perplexed at the daring new reform.. Another legend fell: fascism was not the protector of any one class, but a supreme regulator of the relations between all citizens of a state. The Labor Charter found interpreters and attracted the attention of the studious in every part of the world. It became a formidable pillar of the new constitution of the Fascist State.

As a logical consequence of the Charter of Labor and of all the social legislation and of the magistracy of labor, came the necessity of instituting the Corporations. In this institution are concentrated all the branches of national production. Work in all its complex manifestations and in all its breadth, whether of manual or of intellectual nature, requires equally protection and nourishment. The citizen in the Fascist State is no longer a selfish individual who has the anti-social right of rebelling against any law of the Collectivity. The Fascist State with its corporative conception puts men and their possibilities into productive work and interprets for them the duties they have to fulfill.

In this new conception, which has found its logical expression in our representative forms, the citizen is valuable because of his productivity, his work and his thought, and not merely because he is twenty-one years old and has the right to vote!

In the corporative state all national activities are reflected. It was logical that syndicalistic organizations should become a part also of the new representative institutions. From this need, imposed by a new political ideal the directorate select its candidates with regard for their capabilities and for the number of citizens represented, but it is complemented by the work of selection and valuation devoted by the Grand Fascist Council to the task of creating the best, the most stable, the most truly representative and the most expert national board of directors.

We have solved a series of problems of no little extent and importance; we have abolished all those perennial troubles and disorders and doubts that poisoned our national soul. We have given rhythm, law, and protection to Work: we have found in the co-operation of classes the evidence of our possibilities, of our future power. We do not waste time in brawls and strikes, which, while they vex the spirit, imperil our strength and the solidity of our economy. We regard strife as a luxury for the rich. We must conserve our strength. We have exalted work as productive strength; therefore we have the majority of these elements represented in the legislative body, and this body is a more worthy and a stronger helmsman for Italian life.

And Capital is not exiled, as in the Russian communistic dream; we consider it an increasingly important actor in the drama of production.

In this, my Autobiography, I have emphasized more than once the fact that I have always tried to weave an organic and coherent character into all the fabric of my political work. I have not confined myself to giving merely an outward veneer or contour to Italian life; I wished to influence the very depths of its spirit. I founded my work on facts and on the real conditions of the Italian people; from such realistic activity I drew valuable lessons. I have been able to bring about useful, immediate results looking toward a new future for our country.

One of the reforms which I have promoted and have closely followed in all its successive developments is the reorganization of the schools. This has been called the Gentile Reform, after the name of the Minister of Public Instruction, whom I appointed immediately following the March on Rome. The gravity and importance of school problems cannot escape the attention of any modern statesman mindful of the destiny of his people. The School must be considered in all its complete expression. Public schools, Intermediate schools, University institutions, all exercise a profound influence on the trend—both moral and economic—of the life of any nation. From the beginning this has been ever in my mind. Perhaps my early experience as a school teacher increased an unvarying interest in youth and its development. In Italy there were traditions of higher culture, but the public schools had become degraded because of lack of means and, above all, because of lack of spiritual vision.

Although the percentage of illiteracy tended to diminish and even to disappear in certain regions, particularly in Piedmont, the citizens nevertheless were not getting from the school world those broad educational foundations—physical, intellectual and moral—that are possible and humane. The intermediate schools were too crowded because everybody was admitted, even those without merit, through endless sessions of examinations which were reduced often to a spiritless formality. We lacked intelligent systems of selection and vocational and educational valuation of individuals. The mill ground on and on, turning out stock patterns of human beings who ended for the most part by taking tasks in bureaucracy. They lowered the function of the public service by dead and not living personnel. Universities created other puppets in the so-called "free arts," such as law and medicine.

It was time that the delicate machinery which was of such

consequence in the spiritual life of the nation be renewed in a precise, definite, organic form. We had to crowd out from the intermediate schools the negative and supercilious elements. We were determined to infuse into the public schools those broad humanistic currents in which our history and our traditions are so rich. Finally, it was indispensable to impose a new discipline in education—a discipline to which every one must submit, the teachers themselves first of all!

To be sure, teachers draw a very modest wage in Italy, and this is a problem that I am resolved to face and solve as soon as the condition of the budget will allow. Nevertheless, I cannot permit a limited, pinch-penny treatment of education. The niggardly policy is of old and typically Liberal and Democratic origin. It furnished teachers with a good pretext for performing their duties indifferently and for abandoning themselves to subversive thought, even against the state itself. This condition reached its climax in the humiliating fact that many teachers deserted their posts. We had had clamorous examples of such a tendency, not only in the elementary schools, but also in some of the universities.

Fascism put a stop to all this by making discipline supreme, discipline both for the high and for the low, particularly for those who had the high duty of teaching order and discipline and maintaining the highest concepts of human service in the various schools of the regime.

We had an old school law which took its name from Minister Casati, a law that had been enacted in 1859 and had remained the fundamental law even after the successive retouching of Ministers Coppino, Daneo, and Credaro. We had to renew and refashion it, through the ardent will of our Party; we had to give it a broad didactic and moral vision; we had to infuse into it a spirit of vital rebirth which would appeal to the new Italy. Great ideas and great revolutions always create the right hour for the solution of many problems. The school problem, which had dragged on for many decades, has finally found its solution in the Gentile Reform. This is not the place to explain the reform in detail. I want to indicate, however, those fundamental principles which I myself discussed and settled in a few compact discussions with the Minister of Public Instruction. They can be summarized by the following points:

1st—The state provides schooling only for those who deserve it because of their merits and leaves to other initiatives students who are not entitled to a place in the state's schools.

This throws on the scrap heap the democratic concept which considered a state school as an institution for every one—a basket into which treasure and waste were piled together. The middle class had regarded the school as at its service and therefore did not respect it. They demanded only the greatest possible indulgence in order to achieve as quickly as they could their purely utilitarian aims, such as a degree or a perfunctory passing to promotions.

2nd—The students of the state schools and of the independent schools find themselves under equal conditions when taking the state examinations, before committees appointed by the government.

Thus is encouraged the regime of independent schools analogous to those of England. This regime is advantageous for the Catholics, owners of many schools, but displeases the anti-clericals of the old style. It allows me a free development of scholastic initiative outside of the conventional lines.

3rd—The state watches over the independent schools and promotes a rivalry between independent and state schools which raises the cultural level and the general atmosphere of all schools.

The state does not see its jurisdiction diminished because of the independent schools; on the contrary, it extends its watchfulness over all schools.

4th—Admission to the intermediate schools is now possible only through examinations. The schools are directed toward a broad humanistic culture, but with a standard of scholarship which has eliminated forever the disorder and the easygoing ways of the old democratic schools.

By means of these and other reforms the elementary school

comes to have two distinct but co-ordinated purposes. One is that of preparation for the intermediate schools, and the other is a high type of broad popular education complete in itself.

The intermediate schools were broadened by means of the following institutions:

(a) Complementary schools. The abolished technical school, complete in itself, was revived along new lines.

(b) Technical institutes of higher specialization.

(c) Scientific Lyceum, still higher, taking the place of the abolished "Modern Lyceum" and of the Physico-Mathematical departments of the Technical Institute, and preparing the students for the scientific branches of the University.

(d) Teachers' Institute, a purely humanistic and philosophical school taking the place of the abolished complementary and normal schools.

(e) Women's Lyceum, a general culture school, complete in itself.

(f) Classical Lyceum, unchanged in its essential lines, but augmented by the humanistic character of the studies; to it the task of preparing for most university branches has been assigned. To enter the universities, entrance examinations have been instituted. The final examinations of the intermediate schools, of the Classical and the Scientific Lyceum, have been termed Maturity Examinations; all the curricula have been renewed, fitting them for a more modern culture. Latin has been restored in all schools except in the Complementary and Religious Departments of the elementary and intermediate schools.

For all these different types of institutions, one essential rule has been put into practice, that is, every school must be a unit organism, with a set number of classes and students; the candidates may enter through a graduated classification, based on the examinations; those who are not admitted must go to independent schools.

The application of this reform, which overthrew the old interests, the old ideas and especially the utilitarian spirit of the population, aroused an unavoidable spirit of ill-feeling. It was used by the opposition press, especially by the Carricere della Sera, for controversial purposes; but the reform has been put through with energy under direction and has marked the beginning of a real rebirth of the Italian schools and of the Italian culture.

The reform of the universities has been co-ordinated with the reforms in the primary and intermediate schools. Its purpose is to divide the university students into different organic institutions, without useless over-lapping. The rule of state examinations is imposed also for the universities, to which both the students of the state and independent schools can be admitted. The Institute of "Libera Docenza," authorities independently attached to certain faculties of the universities, has also been reformed, appointment no longer being made by the individual departments but by central committees in Rome.

On the occasion of a visit by the delegations of the Fascist university groups, I had the opportunity of declaring that the Gentile Reform "is the most revolutionary of all the reforms which we have voted on, because it has completely transformed a state of affairs which had lasted since 1859."

I was the son of a school-mistress; I myself was taught in the elementary and secondary schools. I knew, therefore, the school problem. Because of that, I had wanted to bring it to a concrete conclusion. The Italian school again will take its deserved place in the world. From our university chairs, true scientists and poets will again illuminate Italian thought, while the secondary schools will provide technical and executive elements for our population, and the public schools will create a background of civic education and collective virtue in the masses.

I have willed that, in collaboration with the universities, departments of Fascist economics, of corporative law, and a whole series of fruitful institutes of Fascist culture, should be created. Thus a purely scholastic and academic world is being permeated by fascism, which is creating a new culture through the fervid and complex activity of real, of theoretical and of spiritual experiences.

But, even closer to my heart than the Institutes of Fascist universities, is a new institution which has all the original marks of the Fascist revolution. It is the National Organization of Balilla. Under the name of a legendary little Genoese hero the new generation of children and of youth was organized. These no longer depend, as in the past, upon various playground associations, scattered political schools and accessory institutions, but are trained through rigid but gay discipline in gymnastic exercises and in the general rules of a well-ordered national life. They are accustomed to obedience and they are made to see a sure vision of the future.

To show the importance that educational revival has in my mind, I myself gave a lecture at the University of Perugia. It has been pronounced by scholars as a broadening of the world's concept of its duty to youth.

Finally, to pay a tribute to culture and to higher culture, and to every one who, in the field of science, art, and letters, has held high the name of Italy, I have created an Italian Academy, with a membership of "immortals."

The armed forces of the state had fallen into degradation in the years 1919, 1920, 1921. The flower of one race had been spurned and humiliated.

Conditions even reached a point where the Minister of War in those "liberal" days had a circular distributed advising officers not to appear in uniform in public and to refrain from carrying arms, in order not to be subjected to the challenges of gangsters and hoodlums.

This aberration, which it is better to pass over quickly for the sake of one's country, was destined to find its avenger in fascism. It was one of the factors which created an atmosphere passionately eager for change. To-day, the spirit of the country is much different; to-day the armed forces of the state are justly considered the secure and worthy and honored defense of the nation.

I had a very clear and decisive programme, when, in 1922,

at the moment of the March on Rome, I selected as my collaborators the best leaders of the Victory of 1918. General Armando Diaz, who after Vittorio Veneto had remained aloof in silence, overwhelmed by the difficulty of the moment, and who had issued and had been able to voice an indignant protest in the Senate against the policies of Nitti's Cabinet, had been selected by me as Minister of War. I appointed Admiral Thaon de Revel, the greatest leader of our war on the sea, as Minister of the Navy. On January 5, 1923, General Diaz presented a complete programme of reform for the army to the Council of Ministers. That was an historic meeting; fundamental decisions for the renewal of the armed forces were taken; and we were able to announce to the country in solemn and explicit fashion that, with that meeting, the army had been given new life, to "accomplish the high mission that had been intrusted to it, in the supreme interests of the nation."

I had fulfilled the first promise I had made to myself and to the Italian people. Immediately after that I dedicated myself to a reorganization of aviation, which had been abandoned to utter decay by the former administrations. The task was not easy; everything had to be done again. The landing fields, the machines, the pilots, the organizers and the technicians all were restored. A feeling of abandonment, of dejection and mistrust had been diffused in Italy by the enemies of aviation; this new type of armed force, many people thought, should be developed only as a sport. Into this situation I put my energy—I gave it personal attention, personal devotion. I have succeeded in my purpose: the successes of De Pinedo, of Maddalena, the flights in squadrons, the great manoeuvers, have demonstrated that Italian aviation has recently acquired great expertness and prestige, not only in Italy, but wherever there is air to fly in.

The same can be said of the navy, which has reordered its formation, bettered its units, completed its fleet, and made its discipline efficient. Fourth, but not least, because of its spirit of emulation and daring, comes the Voluntary Militia for the Safety of the Nation, divided into 160 Legions, commanded by distinguished officers and by enthusiastic Fascists. These are magnificent shock troops.

Finally our barracks and our ships can be said to be, in the true sense of the word, refuges of peace and strength; the officers devote their activities to the physical and educational betterment of the men; the training conforms to the modern technic of war. The army is no longer distracted from its functions, as happened too often under the old governments, in order to assume ordinary duties of public order which were exhausting and humiliating, and to which entire Divisions were assigned. I changed all this. For the last five years, the army has left its barracks for its tactical manoeuvers and for no other reason.

After some time, General Diaz had been obliged to resign on account of the condition of his health. General Di Giorgio commanded ad interim. But later I saw clearly the necessity of gathering all the armed forces of the state under one direction. I assumed the portfolios of War, Navy and Aeronautics. Thanks to this programme, I have created a commander-in-chief of all general staffs, who has the task of shaping, with a complete vision of ensemble, all the plans of the various branches of our forces toward one end: Victory. Our military spirit is lively; it is not aggressive, but it will not be taken by surprise. It is a peaceful spirit, but it is watchful.

To complete the Fascist revival, it was necessary to keep in mind also several lesser problems which, for the sake of the dignity and strength of the life of the nation, were in need of an immediate solution.

The retired employees of the government, who received very small pensions before the war, had seen with alarm the value of their already meager resources diminish because of the successive depreciations of the currency. I had to make a provision of some exceptional nature for their protection, by making their pensions adequate to the necessities of the day and to the current value of money. I made a provision favoring the clergy also; it was a question of a just and necessary disposition. This would have been inconceivable in the days of the Masonic demagogy and social democracy, which was dominated by a superficial and wrathful anti-clericalism. Our clergy number about 60,000 in Italy. They are extraneous to the controversy, which I may call historical, between State and Church. They accomplish a wise task and assist the Italian people in all their religious practices, without meddling with political questions, especially since the rise of fascism. They are reluctant to debase the spiritual character of their mission. The intriguing priest, of course, has to be fought. Instead, the priest who accomplishes his task according to the wise rules of the Gospel and shows the people the great humane and divine truths, will be helped and assisted. Because many of them were living in poverty, we took general measures to better the conditions of their existence.

The policy in regard to public works in Italy had always had an electoral tinge; public works to be done were decided upon here and there, not according to an organic plan or to any plain necessity, but to give sporadic satsifaction to this or that group of voters. I stopped this legalized favoritism. I instituted Bureaus of Public Works, intrusting them to persons in whom I have complete confidence, who obey only the central power of the state, and are immune from pressure by local interests. In this way I was able to better appreciably the conditions of the roads of the South; I mapped out a programme for aqueducts, railroads and ports. All that is just finds in the Italian bureaucracy an immediate comprehension. All the offices of governmental character have received a new impulse and new prestige. The great public utilities of the state, railroads, mails, telegraph, telephone, the monopolies, function again. Certain persons are even sarcastic about the new regularity. And this is easily explained: we should not forget that the Italian people has been for many years rebellious against any discipline; it was accustomed to use its easy-to-hand and clamorous complaints against the work and activity of the government.

Some vestiges of the mental attitudes of bygone days still come to the surface. There is even whining because there is efficiency and order in the world. Certain individualistic ambitions would like to slap at our strong achievements of discipline and regularity. But to-day the state is not an abstract and unknowing entity; the government is present everywhere, every day. He who lives in the ambit of the state or outside the state feels in every way the majesty of law. It is not a thing of small moment that all public utilities are conducted with an efficiency which I might call American, and that the Italian bureaucracy, proverbially slow, has become eager and agile.

I have given particular attention to the Capital. Rome is a universal city, dear to the heart of Italians and of the whole world. It was great in the time of the Roman Empire and has conserved a universal light. It was the historical seat and the centre of diffusion of Christianity. Rome is first of all a city with the aura of destiny and history. It is the Capital of the New Italy. It is the seat of Christianity. It has taught and will continue to teach law and art to the whole world.

I could not refuse the resources necessary to make this magnificent capital a city aesthetically beautiful, politically ordered, and disciplined by a governor. With its natural port of Ostia, with its new roads, it will become one of the most orderly and clean cities of Europe. By isolating the monuments of ancient Rome, the relation between the ancient Romans and the Italians is made more beautiful and suggestive. This work of revaluation—almost recreation—of the capital was not carried on to the detriment of other Italian cities. Each one of them has the typical character of an ancient capital. They are cities like Perugia, Milan, Naples, Florence, Palermo, Bologna, Turin, Genoa, which have had a sovereign history worthy of high respect; but none of them thinks now to contest with Rome and its eternal glory.

Some writers who, as keen observers, have followed point

by point the vicissitudes of our political life at a certain moment raised an interesting question. Why did not the National Fascist Party decree its own disbandment or slip into disorganization after the revolutionary victory of October, 1922?

In order to answer this question it is necessary to bring into relief certain essential points. History teaches us that, normally, a revolutionary movement can be channelled into legality only by means of forceful provisions, directed, if necessary, against even the personnel of the movement. Every revolution assumes unforeseen and complex aspects; in certain historical hours, the sacrifice of those who were the well-deserving lieutenants of yesterday might become indispensable for the supreme interest of to-morrow. Nevertheless, in my own life I have never deliberately desired the sacrifice of any one; therefore I have made use of the high influence which I have always had over my followers to stop stagnation or heresies, personal interests and contentions; I have preferred to prevent rather than to repress.

But, when it has been necessary, I have shown myself to be inexorable. In fact, I had to keep in mind that, when one party has shouldered the responsibility of entire power, it has to know how to perform surgery—and major operations, too—against secession. Because of my personal situation, having created the Party, I have always dominated it. The sporadic cases of secession, due not to differences of method but to personal temperament, usually withered under the general loss of esteem and interest, and after the disclosure of selfish ends.

This consciousness of my incontestable domination has given me the ability to make the Party live on. But other considerations also were opposed to the disbandment of the Party. First of all, a sentimental motif had stamped itself upon my soul and upon the grateful spirit of the nation. The Fascisti, particularly the young, had followed me with blind, absolute, and profound devotion. I had led them through the most dramatic vicissitudes, taking them away from universities, from jobs, from factories. The young men had not hesitated when confronted by danger. They had known how to risk their future positions together with their lives and fortunes. I owed and still owe to the militiamen of previous days my strongest gratitude; to disband the Party and retire would have been first of all an act of utter ingratitude.

There was in the end a much more important reason. I considered the formulation of a new Italian method of government as one of the principal duties of fascism. It was to be created by the vigor of labor, through a well-tested process of selection, without the risky creation of too many improvised military leaders. It was the Party's right to offer me men of our own regime to assume positions of responsibility. In that sense the Party was side by side with the government in the ruling of the new regime. It had to abandon the programme of violent struggle and yet preserve intact its character of proud political intransigentism. Many obvious signs made me understand that it was not possible to patch the old with the new world. I had therefore need of reserves of men for the future. The Chief of the government could very well be the Chief of the Party, just as in every country of the world a representative chief is always the exponent of an aristocracy of wills.

In the meantime, to mark a point fundamental for the public order, my government, in December, 1922, issued an admonition to the Fascists themselves. It was in the following terms:

"Every Fascist must be a guardian of order. Every disturber is an enemy even if he carries in his pocket the identification card of the Party."

Thus, in a few words, were the position and the duty of the Party in the life of the Fascist regime indicated.

We encountered plenty of pitfalls and snares in 1922. The Party had reached a peculiar sensitiveness, through its intense experience. In the moment of its hardest test, it had shown itself to be equipped to guide the interests of the country as a whole. The revolution had not had long, bloody consequences, as in other revolutions, except for the moment of battle. Violence, as I have said before, had been controlled by my will.

Nevertheless, the position of some opposing newspapers was strange indeed. Those of the Carriere della Sera, of Liberal-Democratic coloring, and that of the Avanti, Socialist, agreed—strange bed-fellows!—in harshly criticising the simultaneous and violent action of fascism, while they were wishing in their hearts and writing that the Fascist experiment would soon be finished. According to these political diagnosticians, it was a matter of an experiment of short duration, in which fascism would be destroyed either on the parliamentary rocks or by an obvious inadequacy to direct the complexities of Italian life. We saw later the wretched end of these prophets; but to attain results it had been necessary for me, particularly in the first year, continually to watch the Party. It had always to remain in perfect efficiency, superior to opposing critics and to snares, ready for orders and commands.

One grave danger was threatening the Party: it was the too free admission of new elements. Our small handfuls in the warlike beginnings were now growing to excess, so much so that it was necessary to put a padlock on the door to prevent influx of further membership. Once the solidity of fascism had been proved, all the old world wanted to rush into its ranks. If this had happened, we would have come back to the old mentality, the old defects, by overhasty adulteration instead of keeping our growth selective through education and devotion. Otherwise the Party, augmented by all the opportunists of the eleventh hour, would have lost its vibrating and original soul. A check had to be placed upon the old world. It could go and wait with its bed-slippers on, without spoiling a movement of young people for Italian rebirth.

After I had closed, in 1926, the registration in the Party, I used all my force, care and means for the selection and the education of Youth. The Avanguardia was then created, together with the Opera Nazionale Balilla, the organization for boys and girls which, because of its numerous merits and the high value of its educational activities, I have chosen even recently to term "The invaluable pupil of the Fascist Regime."

This programme brought forth unparalleled results; as a result of it the Party has never encountered a really serious crisis. I believe that I can count among my qualities the ability to act in good season and to strike at the right moment without false sentimentality where the shadow of a weakness or of a trap is hidden.

In this watchful work of prevention, I have always had at my side good secretaries of the Party who have helped me immeasurably. Michele Bianchi had already ably led the Party until the March on Rome. He had been able to balance the particularly violent character of the movement against the demands of political situations which had reality and which must be handled with wisdom. Michele Bianchi has been an excellent political secretary because of this very reason, and to-day he is still with the government, as my greatly appreciated collaborator in internal politics. He has a political mind of the first order, a reflective mind; he is faithful at every hour. The regime can count on him every time.

The Honorable Sansanelli, a courageous participant in the late war, and to-day president of the International Federation of World War Veterans, took his place. The Hon. Sansanelli has been able to face vague secessionist movements, which revealed an origin undoubtedly in the peculiar, pre-Fascist, Italian political Masonry.

There was in that period a reprisal by anti-Fascist forces. The old Liberal world, defeated, but tolerated by the generosity of the regime, was not exactly aware of the new order of things. It regained its wonted haughtiness; Italian Masonry was still developing, with its infinite and uncontrollable tentacles, its practices of corruption and of dissolution.

These forces of negation even armed the Communist remnants in the obscurity of ambushes and cellars. A new "direttorio," presided over by the Secretary Hon. Giunta until September, 1924, was formed after the elections. I have already spoken of the Fascist activity of the Hon. Giunta. In the second half of that year, the anti-Fascist movement, aroused by obscure national and international forces, showed itself in growing intensity on all fronts. I threw it down on its nose with my speech of January 3, 1925. But also, following that, I determined that a line of more combatively intransigent nature should be imposed by our party: and with this duty in mind, on February 12, 1925, I appointed the Hon. Roberto Farinacci General Secretary of the Party.

Farinacci knew how to show himself worthy of the task with which I had intrusted him. His accomplishments, considered in their entirety and in the light of the results attained, were those of a well-deserving Secretary. He broke up the residues of the "aventinismo" which had remained here and there in the country; he gave a tone of high and cutting intransigentism, not only political but also moral, to the whole Party, invoked against offenders and plotters those exceptional laws which I had promulgated after four attempted assassinations had demonstrated the criminality of anti-fascism. I was closely following this movement of vigorous reprisal by the Party and had prepared in time the necessary provisions. The Hon. Farinacci is one of the founders of Italian fascism. He has followed me faithfully since 1914.

After his task had been accomplished, the Hon. Farinacci left the position of General Secretary to the Hon. Augusto Turati, a courageous veteran of the World War, a man of clear mind and aristocratic temperament, who has been able to give the Party the style of the new times and the consciousness of the new needs. The Hon. Turati has accomplished a great and indispensable work of educational improvement with the Fascist masses. Besides these precious elements in the high positions of the Party of to-day, I must mention the Hon. Renato Ricci for the organization of the "Balilla," Melchiorri for the Militia, Marinelli, a courageous administrative secretary, Starrace, a valorous veteran, and Arpinati, a faithful Black Shirt since March, 1919, and a founder of fascism in Bologna.

The Party has yielded me new prefects for Fascist Italy, elements for syndicalist organization, and consuls, while various deputies have been appointed Ministers and Under-Secretaries. Little by little, proceeding by degrees, I have given an ever more integral and intransigent line to the whole world of government. Almost all positions of command have to-day been intrusted to Fascist elements. Thus after four years of the regime we have given actuality to the formula: "All the Power to all-fascism" which I enunciated in June, 1925, at a Fascist meeting in Rome.

I have controlled my impatience. I have avoided leaps into darkness. I do not sleep my way to conclusions, I have blended the pre-existing needs with the formation of a future. Naturally, giving to the state a completely Fascist character and filling all the ganglia of national life with the vitality and newer force of faithful Black-Shirts, I not only did not detract from, but constantly added to the importance of the National Fascist Party as the force of the regime. This transfer from political organization to the permanent organization of a state guarantees in the most solid manner the future of the regime. I have laid, with my own hands, the corner-stone of representative reform, based on the interests of Italian unity and the Italian cosmos, and I have arranged that the Grand Fascist Council became a definite constitutional organ for the constancy of the state. Thus the Fascist Party, while remaining independent is bound by ties of steel to the very essence of the new Fascist state.

A subject that is always interesting and is often misunderstood both by Italians and foreigners is that of the relations between State and Church in Italy. The Law of the Guarantees in 1870, by which the question was believed to be solved, remains a form of relationship which since the rise of fascism has not caused friction of any great significance. To be sure, the Holy See renews, once in a while, protestations for the supposed rights usurped in Rome by the Italian state, but there are no substantial reasons for apprehension, nor profound differences.

This serenity of relations is a tribute to the Fascist regime. In the past a legend had blossomed around dissensions of historical character tending to foment partisan hatreds; an anti-clerical activity had been developed for a long time in various forms, and it served, through many sections of the so-called "Free thought" groups, to augment the nefarious political influence of our form of Masonry. The idea was diffused that religion was a "private affair," and religion was not admitted in any sort of public act.

If, however, anti-clericalism was superficial and coarse, on the other hand, the Church, with its lack of comprehension of the new Italy, with its tenacity in its intransigent position, had only exasperated its opponents. Anti-Church forces even went so far as to ban every Catholic symbol and even Christian doctrine from the schools. These were periods of Social-ist-Masonic audacity. It was necessary that ideas should be clarified. We had to differentiate and separate the principles of political clericalism from the vital essence of the Catholic faith. The situation as it had stood caused, in Italy, danger-ous deviations, which ranged from the policy of "abstention" between 1870 and 1900, to the Popular party of baleful memory which was destined to degenerate little by little until in 1925 it took a form of clerical bolshevism which I resolutely liquidated and put into political and intellectual bankruptcy.

This troubled atmosphere, so infested by misunderstand-ings and superficialities, has been relieved by fascism. I did not deceive myself as to the seriousness of the crisis which is always opening between State and Church; I had not fooled myself into thinking that I would be able to cure a dissension which involves the highest interests and principles, but I had made a deep study of those lines of set directions and inflex·

ible temperaments which, if softened, were destined to make the principles of religious faith, religious observance, and respect for the forms of worship bloom again, independent of political controversies. They are, in fact, the essential factors of the moral and civic development of a country which is renewing itself.

To be sincere, I must add that high circles of the Vatican have not always been known to appreciate my work, possibly for political reasons, and have not helped me in the steps which appeared wise for all. My labour had not been easy nor light; our Masonry had spun a most intricate net of anti-religious activity; it dominated the currents of thought; it exercised its influence over publishing houses, over teaching, over the administration of justice and even over certain dominant sections of the armed forces.

To give an idea of how far things had gone, this significant example is sufficient. When, in parliament, I delivered my first speech of November 16, 1922, after the Fascist revolution, I concluded by invoking the assistance of God in my difficult task. Well, this sentence of mine seemed to be out of place! In the Italian parliament, a field of action for Italian Masonry, the name of God had been banned for a long time. Not even the Popular party—the so-called Catholic party—had ever thought of speaking of God. In Italy, a political man did not even turn his thoughts to the Divinity. And, even if he had ever thought of doing so, political opportunism and cowardice would have deterred him, particularly in a legislative assembly. It remained for me to make this bold innovation! And in an intense period of revolution! What is the truth! It is that a faith openly professed is a sign of strength.

I have seen the religious spirit bloom again; churches once more are crowded, the ministers of God are themselves invested with new respect. Fascism has done and is doing its duty.

Some ecclesiastical circles have not shown, as I have said,

ability to evaluate and understand in all its importance the political and moral rebirth of new Italy.

One of the first symptoms of such lack of comprehension was exhibited at the beginning of Fascist rule: at first the so-called Catholic party wanted to collaborate by having some members in the government, in the new regime. This collaboration, however, began to lead us through a series of reticences and misunderstandings, and after six months I was forced to show the door to the ministers belonging to that party.

I have seen the Popular party allied with Masonry. But when parties have not clashed on the Italian political scene, the troubles between State and Church have been reflected in international politics. The Roman Question has been once more under discussion. Both historical forces have strengthened their concepts. Journalistic controversies and objective discussions have demonstrated that the problem is not ripe and may be insoluble. Perhaps two mentalities and two worlds are confronting each other in a century-old historic and impracticable opposition. One has its roots in the religion of the fathers and lives by the ethical forces of the Civis Romanus; the other has the universal character of equality of brothers in God.

To-day, with the highest loyalty, fascism understands and values the Church and its strength: such is the duty of every Catholic citizen. But politics, the defense of national interests, the battles over ourselves and others, must be the work of the modern Fascist Italians who want to see the immortal and irreplaceable Church of Saint Peter respected, and do not wish ever to confound themselves with any political force which has no disclosed outline and knows no patriotism. Whatever the errors of its representatives may be, nobody thinks of taking away from the Church its universal character, but everybody is right in complaining about certain disavowals of some Italian Catholics, and may justly resent political approval of certain middle-European currents, upon which Italy places even now her most ample reservations. Faith in Italy has been strengthened. Fascism gives impulse and vigor to the religion of the country. But it will never be able for any reason to renounce the sovereign rights of the state and of the functions of the state.

VII

SOCIOLOGY AND CULTURE

COMMENTARY

Going back a little into the theory of sociology, we find in the works of Herbert Spencer one of the most interesting English versions of what sociology is and what it is not. Spencer belongs predominantly to what may, with some elasticity, be called the English tradition. Marx, Proudhon, and Bakunin have no influence upon his work. They exist in a world apart from the world with which he deals. Their interest is in the proletariat, the underdog, whereas his interest is in the middle class, and the middle class intellectual as its most striking by-product. He is not so much concerned with changing society, as were Marx, Proudhon, and Bakunin, as with analyzing and evaluating the virtues and potentialities of the scientific mentality. He believes that evolution and not revolution will determine the advance of the human species. In The Principles of Sociology, *he lays the groundwork for the development of what has since been described as scientific sociology. Although most of Spencer's propositions and conclusions are outmoded today, the influence which he exercises over British and American social thought is still observable and traceable. His contention that the evolution of society represents the development of the differentiated from the undifferentiated remains as one of the most brilliant testimonies of his genius as a social thinker.*

Max Weber and Sombart, who follow somewhat later, as representatives of German thinkers in the sociological realm, reveal the influence of Marx in their respective approaches to the social process. Weber, in his analysis of religion, utilizes the class factor, stressed so emphatically by Marx, as the key to his analysis of Protestantism. Of course, it should be pointed out that Weber tried to turn Marx's thesis upside

COMMENTARY

487

down by contending that thought and religion determine
economic development rather than the reverse. Sombart,
who ventures to criticize and even condemn the Marxian
analysis, resorts to the same tactic when it comes to his dissection of society. Disagreeing with Marx to the extent he
does, Sombart's sociological approach would have been practically impossible had it not been for the fertilizing influence of Marxian doctrine upon his work.

In the case of Pareto, who is familiarly known as "the official fascist philosopher," there are other factors involved.
There can be little doubt but that Pareto is also influenced
by Marx, although in a more secondary sense. Pareto's theories about society and the social process suffer too much from
an extension and elaboration of the obvious, translated into
needlessly technical terminology. Pareto's work is richly replete with fresh illustrations, analogies, and categories, and
from the point of view of new sociological pigeon-holes is
distinctly stimulating and valuable. It attempts to settle problems, however, by classifying them, which is the great virtue
of Pareto's sociology, but not by solving them. While de-
nouncing "derivations," his own system turns out to be
a gigantic derivation—a rationalization of aristocratic and
fascist biases.

Turning back to England once more, we find in the work
of J. M. Robertson, one of the challenging minds of the late
nineteenth and early twentieth century, a mixture of adulterated Marxism, (although he would have been the first to
deny it), belated Buckleism, and advanced Spencerism. The
composite of opposites dominant in his approach prevents
him from being recognized during his life-time as the fertile thinker he is. In his book on Buckle, he did more to do
justice to Buckle's work than any thinker of his day, and in
his essay on "The Economics of Genius," he carries to a
much more advanced and significant point an early analysis
of the American sociologist, Cooley. Cooley, in a brilliant
essay on the subject, nevertheless, hesitates to come to any
clear-cut conclusion; Robertson, on the other hand, takes the

same matter in hand, and drives forward to a conclusion which is of great consequence.

Lester Ward, Thorstein Veblen, and Giddings are the three best representatives of American sociological thought. All three deserve high place for the originality and challenge of their work in a field in which they had to be intellectual trail-blazers and pathfinders. Ward, in Applied Sociology, does the same job, in a different way, that J. M. Robertson does in his Economics of Genius. In his Dynamic Sociology and Pure Sociology Ward paves the way for Veblen's more radical conclusions. Ward was the great opponent of Spencerian individualism. He expected that legislation, guided by the social sciences, would bring about all needed reforms. Veblen in his Theory of the Leisure Class, as well as in his other books, notably The Theory of Business Enterprise, extends Ward's conclusions, and, adding to his own an admixture of Marxism, works out in his analysis the soundest sociology of any American of his time.

Both men give to American sociology a dignity and a solidity which it never possessed in the past, and to which Giddings, with his theory of "consciousness of kind," makes a healthy and worth-while addition. His theory of social causation and his notions of "pluralistic behavior" represent an exciting aspect of his thought. Giddings' theory of "consciousness of kind" is even more important today, with the development of nationalism as the most important sociological force in the modern world; if Giddings does not envision his theory in such magnitudinous dimensions, the fact remains that, inherent in it, are those dimensions and implications.

THE SOCIOLOGICAL VIEW OF ETHICS *

By HERBERT SPENCER

§ 49. NOT for the human race only, but for every race, there are laws of right living. Given its environment and its structure, and there is for each kind of creature a set of actions adapted in their kinds, amounts, and combinations, to secure the highest conservation its nature permits. The animal, like the man, has needs for food, warmth, activity, rest, and so forth, which must be fulfilled in certain relative degrees to make its life whole. Maintenance of its race implies satisfaction of special desires, sexual and philoprogenitive, in due proportions. Hence there is a supposable formula for the activities of each species, which, could it be drawn out, would constitute a system of morality for that species. But such a system of morality would have little or no reference to the welfare of others than self and offspring. Indifferent to individuals of its own kind, as an inferior creature is, and habitually hostile to individuals of other kinds, the formula for its life could take no cognizance of the lives of those with which it came in contact; or, rather, such formula would imply that maintenance of its life was at variance with maintenance of their lives.

But on ascending from beings of lower kinds to the highest kind of being, man; or, more strictly, on ascending from man in his pre-social stage to man in his social stage, the formula has to include an additional factor. Though not peculiar to human life under its developed form, the presence of this factor is still, in the highest degree, characteristic of it. Though there are inferior species displaying considerable degrees of sociality, and though the formulas for their complete lives would have to take account of the relations arising

* From *The Data of Ethics*

489

from union, yet our own species is, on the whole, to be distinguished as having a formula for complete life which specially recognizes the relations of each individual to others, in presence of whom, and in co-operation with whom, he has to live.

This additional factor in the problem of complete living is, indeed, so important that the necessitated modifications of conduct have come to form a chief part of the code of conduct. Because the inherited desires which directly refer to the maintenance of individual life are fairly adjusted to the requirements, there has been no need to insist on that conformity to them which furthers self-conservation. Conversely, because these desires prompt activities that often conflict with the activities of others; and because the sentiments responding to others' claims are relatively weak, moral codes emphasize those restraints on conduct which the presence of fellow-men entails.

From the sociological point of view, then, Ethics becomes nothing else than a definite account of the forms of conduct that are fitted to the associated state, in such wise that the lives of each and all may be the greatest possible, alike in length and breadth.

§ 50.   But here we are met by a fact which forbids us thus to put in the foreground the welfares of citizens, individually considered, and requires us to put in the foreground the welfare of the society as a whole. The life of the social organism must, as an end, rank above the lives of its units. These two ends are not harmonious at the outset; and, though the tendency is toward harmonization of them, they are still partially conflicting.

As fast as the social state establishes itself, the preservation of the society becomes a means of preserving its units. Living together arose because, on the average, it proved more advantageous to each than living apart; and this implies that maintenance of combination is maintenance of the conditions to more satisfactory living than the combined persons would otherwise have. Hence, social self-preservation becomes a proximate aim taking precedence of the ultimate aim, individual self-preservation.

This subordination of personal to social welfare is, however, contingent: it depends on the presence of antagonistic societies. So long as the existence of a community is endangered by the actions of communities around, it must remain true that the interests of individuals must be sacrificed to the interests of the community, as far as is needful for the community's salvation. But if this is manifest, it is, by implication, manifest, that when social antagonisms cease, this need for sacrifice of private claims to public claims ceases also; or rather, there cease to be any public claims at variance with private claims. All along, furtherance of individual lives has been the ultimate end; and, if this ultimate end has been postponed to the proximate end of preserving the community's life, it has been so only because this proximate end was instrumental to the ultimate end. When the aggregate is no longer in danger, the final object of pursuit, the welfare of the units, no longer needing to be postponed, becomes the immediate object of pursuit.

Consequently, unlike sets of conclusions respecting human conduct emerge, according as we are concerned with a state of habitual or occasional war, or are concerned with a state of permanent and general peace. Let us glance at these alternative states and the alternative implications.

§ 51. At present the individual man has to carry on his life with due regard to the lives of others belonging to the same society; while he is sometimes called on to be regardless of the lives of those belonging to other societies. The same mental constitution, having to fulfil both these requirements,·is necessarily incongruous; and the correlative conduct, adjusted first to the one need and then to the other, cannot be brought within any consistent ethical system.

Hate and destroy your fellow-man, is now the command; and then the command is, Love and aid your fellow-man.

Use every means to deceive, says the one code of conduct; while the other code says, Be truthful in word and deed. Seize what property you can, and burn all you cannot take away, are injunctions which the religion of enmity countenances; while by the religion of amity, theft and arson are condemned as crimes. And as conduct has to be made up of parts thus at variance with one another, the theory of conduct remains confused.

There co-exists a kindred irreconcilability between the sentiments answering to the forms of co-operation required for militancy and industrialism respectively. While social antagonisms are habitual, and while, for efficient action against other societies, there needs great subordination to men who command, the virtue of loyalty and the duty of implicit obedience have to be insisted on; disregard of the ruler's will is punished with death. But when war ceases to be chronic, and growing industrialism habituates men to maintaining their own claims while respecting the claims of others, loyalty becomes less profound, the authority of the ruler is questioned or denied in respect of various private actions and beliefs. State dictation is in many directions successfully defied, and the political independence of the citizen comes to be regarded as a claim which it is virtuous to maintain and vicious to yield up. Necessarily, during the transition, these opposite sentiments are incongruously mingled.

So is it, too, with domestic institutions under the two *régimes*. While the first is dominant, ownership of a slave is honorable, and in the slave submission is praiseworthy; but as the last grows dominant, slave-owning becomes a crime, and servile obedience excites contempt. Nor is it otherwise in the family. The subjection of women to men, complete while war is habitual, but qualified as fast as peaceful occupations replace it, comes eventually to be thought wrong, and equality before the law is asserted. At the same time the opinion concerning paternal power changes. The once unquestioned right of the father to take his children's lives is denied, and the duty of absolute submission to him, long in-

sisted on, is changed into the duty of obedience within reasonable limits.

Were the ratio between the life of antagonism with alien
societies, and the life of peaceful co-operation within each
society, a constant ratio, some permanent compromise between the conflicting rules of conduct appropriate to the two
lives might be reached. But since this ratio is a variable one,
the compromise can never be more than temporary. Ever the
tendency is toward congruity between beliefs and requirements. Either the social arrangements are gradually changed
until they come into harmony with prevailing ideas and
sentiments; or, if surrounding conditions prevent change in
the social arrangements, the necessitated habits of life modify
the prevailing ideas and sentiments to the requisite extent.
Hence, for each kind and degree of social evolution determined by external conflict and internal friendship, there is
an appropriate compromise between the moral code of enmity and the moral code of amity; not, indeed, a definable,
consistent compromise, but a compromise fairly well understood.

This compromise, vague, ambiguous, illogical though it
may be, is nevertheless for the time being authoritative. For
if, as above shown, the welfare of the society must take precedence of the welfares of its component individuals, during
those stages in which the individuals have to preserve themselves by preserving their society, then such temporary compromise between the two codes of conduct as duly regards
external defence, while favoring internal co-operation to the
greatest extent practicable, subserves the maintenance of life
in the highest degree; and thus gains the ultimate sanction.
So that the perplexed and inconsistent moralities of which
each society and each age shows us a more or less different
one, are severally justified as being approximately the best
under the circumstances.

But such moralities are, by their definitions, shown to belong to incomplete conduct; not to conduct that is fully
evolved. We saw that the adjustments of acts to ends which,

while constituting the external manifestations of life, conduce to the continuance of life, have been rising to a certain ideal form now approached by the civilized man. But this form is not reached so long as there continue aggressions of one society upon another. Whether the hinderances to complete living result from the trespasses of fellow-citizens, or from the trespasses of aliens, matters not; if they occur there does not yet exist the state defined. The limit to the evolution of conduct is arrived at by members of each society only when, being arrived at by members of other societies also, the causes of international antagonism end simultaneously with the causes of antagonism between individuals.

And now having from the sociological point of view recognized the need for, and authority of, these changing systems of ethics, proper to changing ratios between warlike activities and peaceful activities, we have, from the same point of view, to consider the system of ethics proper to the state in which peaceful activities are undisturbed.

§ 52. If, excluding all thought of danger or hinderances from causes external to a society, we set ourselves to specify those conditions under which the life of each person, and therefore of the aggregate, may be the greatest possible, we come upon certain simple ones which, as here stated, assume the form of truisms.

For, as we have seen, the definition of that highest life accompanying completely evolved conduct, itself excludes all acts of aggression—not only murder, assault, robbery, and the major offences generally, but minor offences, such as libel, injury to property, and so forth. While directly deducting from individual life, these indirectly cause perturbations of social life. Trespasses against others rouse antagonisms in them; and if these are numerous, the group loses coherence. Hence, whether the integrity of the group itself is considered as the end, or whether the end considered is the benefit ultimately secured to its units by maintaining its integrity, or whether the immediate benefit of its units taken separately is considered the end, the implication is the same: such acts are at variance with achievement of the end. That these inferences are self-evident and trite (as indeed the first inferences drawn from the data of every science that reaches the deductive stage naturally are), must not make us pass lightly over the all-important fact that, from the sociological point of view, the leading moral laws are seen to follow as corollaries from the definition of complete life carried on under social conditions.

Respect for these primary moral laws is not enough, however. Associated men pursuing their several lives without injuring one another but without helping one another, reap no advantages from association beyond those of companionship. If, while there is no co-operation for defensive purposes (which is here excluded by the hypothesis) there is also no co-operation for satisfying wants, the social state loses its *raison d'être*—almost, if not entirely. There are, indeed, people who live in a condition little removed from this: as the Esquimaux. But though these, exhibiting none of the co-operation necessitated by war, which is unknown to them, lead lives such that each family is substantially independent of others, occasional co-operation occurs. And, indeed, that families should live in company without ever yielding mutual aid, is scarcely conceivable.

Nevertheless, whether actually existing or only approached, we must here recognize as hypothetically possible a state in which these primary moral laws are conformed to; for the purpose of observing, in their uncomplicated forms, what are the negative conditions to harmonious social life. Whether the members of a social group do or do not co-operate, certain limitations to their individual activities are necessitated by their association; and, after recognizing these as arising in the absence of co-operation, we shall be the better prepared to understand how conformity to them is effected when co-operation begins.

§ 53. For, whether men live together in quite independent ways, careful only to avoid aggressing; or whether, advancing from passive association to active association, they co-operate, their conduct must be such that the achievement of ends by each shall at least not be hindered. And it becomes obvious that when they co-operate there must not only be no resulting hinderance, but there must be facilitation; since, in the absence of facilitation, there can be no motive to co-operate. What shape, then, must the mutual restraints take when co-operations begins? or rather—What, in addition to the primary mutual restraints already specified, are those secondary mutual restraints required to make co-operation possible?

One who, living in an isolated way, expends effort in pursuit of an end, gets compensation for the effort by securing the end, and so achieves satisfaction. If he expends the effort without achieving the end, there results dissatisfaction. The satisfaction and the dissatisfaction are measures of success and failure in life-sustaining acts; since that which is achieved by effort is something which directly or indirectly furthers life, and so pays for the cost of the effort; while if the effort fails there is nothing to pay for the cost of it, and so much life is wasted. What must result from this when men's efforts are joined? The reply will be made clearer if we take the successive forms of co-operation in the order of ascending complexity. We may distinguish as homogeneous co-operation (1) that in which like efforts are joined for like ends that are simultaneously enjoyed. As co-operation that is not completely homogeneous we may distinguish (2) that in which like efforts are joined for like ends that are not simultaneously enjoyed. A co-operation of which the heterogeneity is more distinct is (3) that in which unlike efforts are joined for like ends. And lastly comes the decidedly heterogeneous co-operation (4), that in which unlike efforts are joined for unlike ends.

The simplest and earliest of these in which men's powers, similar in kind and degree, are united in pursuit of a benefit which, when obtained, they all participate in, is most familiarly exemplified in the catching of game by primitive men: this simplest and earliest form of industrial co-operation being also that which is least differentiated from militant co-operation; for the co-operators are the same, and the processes, both destructive of life, are carried on in analogous ways. The condition under which such co-operation may be successfully carried on is that the co-operators shall share alike in the produce. Each thus being enabled to repay himself in food for the expended effort, and being further enabled to achieve other such desired ends as maintenance of family, obtains satisfaction: there is no aggression of one on another, and the co-operation is harmonious. Of course the divided produce can be but roughly proportioned to the several efforts joined in obtaining it, but there is actually among savages, as we see that for harmonious co-operation there must be, a recognition of the principle that efforts when combined shall severally bring equivalent benefits, as they would do if they were separate. Moreover, beyond the taking equal shares in return for labors that are approximately equal, there is generally an attempt at proportioning benefit to achievement, by assigning something extra, in the shape of the best part of the trophy, to the actual slayer of the game. And obviously, if there is a wide departure from this system of sharing benefits when there has been a sharing of efforts, the co-operation will cease. Individual hunters will prefer to do the best they can for themselves separately.

Passing from this simplest case of co-operation to a case not quite so simple—a case in which the homogeneity is incomplete—let us ask how a member of the group may be led without dissatisfaction to expend effort in achieving a benefit which, when achieved, is enjoyed exclusively by another? Clearly he may do this on condition that the other shall afterward expend a like effort, the beneficial result of which shall be similarly rendered up by him in return. This exchange of equivalents of effort is the form which social co-operation takes while yet there is little or no division of labor, save that between the sexes. For example, the Bodo and

Dhimals "mutually assist each other for the nonce, as well in constructing their houses as in clearing their plots for cultivation." And this principle—I will help you if you will help me—common in simple communities where the occupations are alike in kind, and occasionally acted upon in more advanced communities, is one under which the relation between effort and benefit, no longer directly maintained, is maintained indirectly. For, whereas when men's activities are carried on separately, or are joined in the way exemplified above, effort is immediately paid for by benefit, in this form of co-operation the benefit achieved by effort is exchanged for a like benefit to be afterward received when asked for. And in this case as in the preceding case, co-operation can be maintained only by fulfilment of the tacit agreements. For if they are habitually not fulfilled, there will commonly be refusal to give aid when asked; and each man will be left to do the best he can by himself. All those advantages to be gained by union of efforts in doing things that are beyond the powers of the single individual, will be unachievable. At the outset, then, fulfillment of contracts that are implied, if not expressed, becomes a condition to social co-operation, and therefore to social development.

From these simple forms of co-operation in which the labors men carry on are of like kinds, let us turn to the more complex forms in which they carry on labors of unlike kinds. Where men mutually aid in building huts or felling trees, the number of days' work now given by one to another is readily balanced by an equal number of days' work afterward given by the other to him. And no estimation of the relative values of the labors being required, a definite understanding is little needed. But when division of labor arises— when there come transactions between one who makes weapons and another who dresses skins for clothing, or between a grower of roots and a catcher of fish—neither the relative amounts nor the relative qualities of their labors admit of easy measure; and with the multiplication of businesses, implying numerous kinds of skill and power, there ceases to be anything like manifest equivalence between either the bodily and mental efforts set against one another, or between their products. Hence the arrangement cannot now be taken for granted, as while the things exchanged are like in kind: it has to be stated. If A allows B to appropriate a product of his special skill, on condition that he is allowed to appropriate a different product of B's special skill, it results that as equivalence of the two products cannot be determined by direct comparison of their quantities and qualities, there must be a distinct understanding as to how much of the one may be taken in consideration of so much of the other.

Only under voluntary agreement, then, no longer tacit and vague, but overt and definite, can co-operation be harmoniously carried on when division of labor becomes established. And as in the simplest co-operation, where like efforts are joined to secure a common good, the dissatisfaction caused in those who, having expended their labors, do not get their shares of the good, prompts them to cease co-operating; as in the more advanced co-operation, achieved by exchanging equal labors of like kind expended at different times, aversion to co-operate is generated if the expected equivalent of labor is not rendered; so in this developed co-operation, the failure of either to surrender to the other that which was avowedly recognized as of like value with the labor or product given, tends to prevent co-operation by exciting discontent with its results. And evidently, while antagonisms thus caused impede the lives of the units, the life of the aggregate is endangered by diminished cohesion.

§ 54. Beyond these comparatively direct mischiefs, special and general, there have to be noted indirect mischiefs. As already implied by the reasoning in the last paragraph, not only social integration but also social differentiation is hindered by breach of contract.

In Part II. of the *Principles of Sociology,* it was shown that the fundamental principles of organization are the same for an individual organism and for a social organism; because both consist of mutually dependent parts. In the one case as in the other, the assumption of unlike activities by the component members is possible only on condition that they severally benefit in due degrees by one another's activities. That we may the better see what are the implications in respect of social structures, let us first note the implications in respect of individual structures.

The welfare of a living body implies an approximate equilibrium between waste and repair. If the activities involve an expenditure not made good by nutrition, dwindling follows. If the tissues are enabled to take up from the blood enriched by food, fit substances enough to replace those used up in efforts made, the weight may be maintained. And if the gain exceeds the loss, growth results.

That which is true of the whole in its relations to the external world, is no less true of the parts in their relations to one another. Each organ, like the entire organism, is wasted by performing its function, and has to restore itself from the materials brought to it. If the quantity of materials furnished by the joint agency of the other organs is deficient, the particular organ dwindles. If they are sufficient, it can maintain its integrity. If they are in excess, it is enabled to increase. To say that this arrangement constitutes the physiological contract, is to use a metaphor which, though not true in aspect, is true in essence. For the relations of structures are actually such that, by the help of a central regulative system, each organ is supplied with blood in proportion to the work it does. As was pointed out (*Principles of Sociology,* § 254) well-developed animals are so constituted that each muscle or viscus, when called into action, sends to the vaso-motor centres, through certain nerve-fibres, an impulse caused by its action; whereupon, through other nerve-fibres, there comes an impulse causing dilatation of its blood-vessels. That is to say, all other parts of the organism, when they jointly require it to labor, forthwith begin to pay it in blood. During the ordinary state of physiological equilibrium, the loss and the gain balance, and the organ does not sensibly change. If the amount of its function is increased within such moderate limits that the local blood-vessels can bring adequately-increased supplies, the organ grows: beyond replacing its losses by its gains, it makes a profit on its extra transactions; so being enabled by extra structures to meet extra demands. But if the demands made on it become so great that the supply of materials cannot keep pace with the expenditure, either because the local blood-vessels are not large enough, or for any other reason, then the organ begins to decrease from excess of waste over repair: there sets in what is known as atrophy. Now, since each of the organs has thus to be paid in nutriment for its services by the rest, it follows that the due balancing of their respective claims and payments is requisite, directly for the welfare of each organ, and indirectly for the welfare of the organism. For, in a whole formed of mutually dependent parts, anything which prevents due performance of its duty by one part reacts injuriously on all the parts.

With change of terms these statements and inferences hold of a society. That social division of labor which parallels in so many other respects the physiological division of labor, parallels it in this respect also. As was shown at large in the *Principles of Sociology,* Part II., each order of functionaries and each group of producers, severally performing some action or making some article not for direct satisfaction of their own needs but for satisfaction of the needs of fellow-citizens in general, otherwise occupied, can continue to do this only so long as the expenditures of efforts and returns of profit are approximately equivalent. Social organs, like individual organs, remain stationary if there come to them normal proportions of the commodities produced by the society as a whole. If, because the demands made on an industry or profession are unusually great, those engaged in it make excessive profits, more citizens flock to it, and the social structure constituted by its members grows; while decrease of the demands, and therefore of the profits, either leads its members to choose other careers or stops the accessions needful to replace those who die, and the structure dwindles. Thus is maintained that proportion among the powers of the component parts which is most conducive to the welfare of the whole.

And now mark that the primary condition to achievement of this result is fulfilment of contract. If from the members of any part payment is frequently withheld, or falls short of the promised amount, then, through ruin of some, and abandonment of the occupation by others, the part diminishes; and if it was before not more than competent to its duty, it now becomes incompetent, and the society suffers. Or if social needs throw on some part great increase of function, and the members of it are enabled to get for their services unusually high prices; fulfilment of the agreements to give them these high prices, is the only way of drawing to the part such additional number of members as will make it equal to the augmented demands. For citizens will not come to it if they find the high prices agreed upon are not paid.

Briefly then, the universal basis of co-operation is the proportioning of benefits received to services rendered. Without this there can be no physiological division of labor; without this there can be no sociological division of labor. And since division of labor, physiological or sociological, profits the whole and each part; it results that on maintenance of the arrangements necessary to it, depend both special and general welfare. In a society such arrangements are maintained only if bargains, overt or tacit, are carried out. So that beyond the primary requirement to harmonious co-existence in a society, that its units shall not directly aggress on one another; there comes this secondary requirement, that they shall not indirectly aggress by breaking agreements.

§ 55.   But now we have to recognize the fact that complete fulfilment of these conditions, original and derived, is not enough. Social co-operation may be such that no one is impeded in the obtainment of the normal return for effort, but contrariwise is aided by equitable exchange of services; and yet much may remain to be achieved. There is a theoretically possible form of society, purely industrial in its activities, which, though approaching nearer to the moral ideal in its code of conduct than any society not purely industrial, does not fully reach it.

For while industrialism requires the life of each citizen to be such that it may be carried on without direct or indirect aggressions on other citizens, it does not require his life to be such that it shall directly further the lives of other citizens. It is not a necessary implication of industrialism, as thus far defined, that each, beyond the benefits given and received by exchange of services, shall give and receive other benefits. A society is conceivable formed of men leading perfectly inoffensive lives, scrupulously fulfilling their contracts, and efficiently rearing their offspring, who yet, yielding to one another no advantages beyond those agreed upon, fall short of that highest degree of life which the gratuitous rendering of services makes possible. Daily experiences prove that every one would suffer many evils and lose many goods did none give him unpaid assistance. The life of each would be more or less damaged had he to meet all contingencies single-handed. Further, if no one did for his fellows anything more than was required by strict performance of contract, private interests would suffer from the absence of attention to public interests. The limit of evolution of conduct is consequently not reached, until, beyond avoidance of direct and indirect injuries to others, there are spontaneous efforts to further the welfare of others.

It may be shown that the form of nature which thus to justice adds beneficence, is one which adaption to the social state produces. The social man has not reached that harmonization of constitution with conditions forming the limit of evolution, so long as there remains space for the growth of faculties which, by their exercise, bring positive benefit to others and satisfaction to self. If the presence of fellowmen, while putting certain limits to each man's sphere

of activity, opens certain other spheres of activity in which
feelings, while achieving their gratifications, do not diminish, but add to the gratifications of others, then such spheres
will inevitably be occupied. Recognition of this truth does
not, however, call on us to qualify greatly the conception of
the industrial state above set forth, since sympathy is the root
of both justice and beneficence.

§ 56. Thus the sociological view of Ethics supplements
the physical, the biological, and the psychological views, by
disclosing those conditions under which only associated activities can be so carried on, that the complete living of each
consists with, and conduces to, the complete living of all.

At first the welfare of social groups, habitually in antagonism with other such groups, takes precedence of individual
welfare; and the rules of conduct which are authoritative for
the time being, involve incompleteness of individual life that
the general life may be maintained. At the same time the
rules have to enforce the claims of individual life as far as
may be, since on the welfare of the units the welfare of the
aggregate largely depends.

In proportion as societies endanger one another less, the
need for subordinating individual lives to the general life,
decreases; and with approach to a peaceful state, the general
life, having from the beginning had furtherance of individual lives as its ultimate purpose, comes to have this as its
proximate purpose.

During the transitional stages there are necessitated successive compromises between the moral code which asserts
the claims of the society *versus* those of the individual, and
the moral code which asserts the claims of the individual
versus those of the society. And evidently each such compromise, though for the time being authoritative, admits of no
consistent or definite expression.

But gradually as war declines—gradually as the compulsory co-operation needful in dealing with external enemies
becomes unnecessary, and leaves behind the voluntary co-

operation which effectually achieves internal sustentation, there grows increasingly clear the code of conduct which voluntary co-operation implies. And this final permanent code alone admits of being definitely formulated, and so constituting ethics as a science in contrast with empirical ethics.

The leading traits of a code, under which complete living through voluntary co-operation is secured, may be simply stated. The fundamental requirement is that the life-sustaining actions of each shall severally bring him the amounts and kinds of advantage naturally achieved by them, and this implies firstly that he shall suffer no direct aggressions on his person or property, and, secondly, that he shall suffer no indirect aggressions by breach of contract. Observance of these negative conditions to voluntary co-operation having facilitated life to the greatest extent by exchange of services under agreement, life is to be further facilitated by exchange of services beyond agreement: the highest life being reached only when, besides helping to complete one another's lives by specified reciprocities of aid, men otherwise help to complete one another's lives.

THE SPIRIT OF CAPITALISM*

By MAX WEBER

In the title of this study is used the somewhat pretentious phrase, the spirit of capitalism. What is to be understood by it? The attempt to give anything like a definition of it brings out certain difficulties which are in the very nature of this type of investigation.

If any object can be found to which this term can be applied with any understandable meaning, it can only be an historical individual, i.e., a complex of elements associated in historical reality which we unite into a conceptual whole from the standpoint of their cultural significance.

Such an historical concept, however, since it refers in its content to a phenomenon significant for its unique individuality, cannot be defined according to the formula genus proximum, differentia specifica, but it must be gradually put together out of the individual parts which are taken from historical reality to make it up. Thus the final and definitive concept cannot stand at the beginning of the investigation, but must come at the end. We must, in other words, work out in the course of the discussion, as its most important result, the best conceptual formulation of what we here understand by the spirit of capitalism, that is the best from the point of view which interests us here. This point of view (the one of which we shall speak later) is, further, by no means the only possible one from which the historical phenomena we are investigating can be analysed. Other standpoints would, for this as for every historical phenomenon, yield other characteristics as the essential ones. The result is that it is by no means necessary to understand by the spirit of

* From *The Protestant Ethic*

capitalism only what it will come to mean to us for the purposes of our analysis. This is a necessary result of the nature of historical concepts which attempt for their methodological purposes not to grasp historical reality in abstract general formulae, but in concrete genetic sets of relations which are inevitably of a specifically unique and individual character.

Thus, if we try to determine the object, the analysis and historical explanation of which we are attempting, it cannot be in the form of a conceptual definition, but at least in the beginning only a provisional description of what is here meant by the spirit of capitalism. Such a description is, however, indispensable in order clearly to understand the object of the investigation. For this purpose we turn to a document of that spirit which contains what we are looking for in almost classical purity, and at the same time has the advantage of being free from all direct relationship to religion, being thus, for our purposes, free of preconceptions.

"Remember, that time is money. He that can earn ten shillings a day by his labour, and goes abroad, or sits idle, one half of that day, though he spends but sixpence during his diversion or idleness, ought not to reckon that the only expense; he has really spent, or rather thrown away, five shillings besides.

"Remember, that credit is money. If a man lets his money lie in my hands after it is due, he gives me the interest, or so much as I can make of it during that time. This amounts to a considerable sum where a man has good and large credit, and makes good use of it.

"Remember, that money is of the prolific, generating nature. Money can beget money, and its offspring can beget more, and so on. Five shillings turned is six, turned again it is seven and threepence, and so on, till it becomes a hundred pounds. The more there is of it, the more it produces every turning, so that the profits rise quicker and quicker. He that kills a breeding-sow, destroys all her offspring to the thousandth generation. He that murders a crown, destroys all that it might have produced, even scores of pounds."

"Remember this saying, The good paymaster is Lord of another man's purse. He that is known to pay punctually and exactly to the time he promises, may at any time, and on any occasion, raise all the money his friends can spare. This is sometimes of great use. After industry and frugality, nothing contributes more to the raising of a young man in the world than punctuality and justice in all his dealings; therefore never keep borrowed money an hour beyond the time you promised, lest a disappointment shut up your friend's purse for ever.

"The most trifling actions that affect a man's credit are to be regarded. The sound of your hammer at five in the morning, or at eight at night, heard by a creditor, makes him easy six months longer; but if he sees you at a billiard-table, or hears your voice at a tavern, when you should be at work, he sends for his money the next day; demands it, before he can receive it, in a lump.

"It shows, besides, that you are mindful of what you owe; it makes you appear a careful as well as an honest man, and that still increases your credit.

"Beware of thinking all your own that you possess, and of living accordingly. It is a mistake that many people who have credit fall into. To prevent this, keep an exact account for some time both of your expenses and your income. If you take the pains at first to mention particulars, it will have this good effect: you will discover how wonderfully small, trifling expenses mount up to large sums, and will discern what might have been, and may for the future be saved, without occasioning any great inconvenience."

"For six pounds a year you may have the use of one hundred pounds, provided you are a man of known prudence and honesty.

"He that spends a groat a day idly, spends idly above six pounds a year, which is the price for the use of one hundred pounds.

"He that wastes idly a groat's worth of his time per day, one day with another, wastes the privilege of using one hundred pounds each day.

"He that idly loses five shillings' worth of time, loses five shillings, and might as prudently throw five shillings into the sea.

"He that loses five shillings, not only loses that sum, but all the advantage that might be made by turning it in dealing, which by the time that a young man becomes old, will amount to a considerable sum of money."

It is Benjamin Franklin who preaches to us in these sentences, the same which Ferdinand Kurnberger satirizes in his clever and malicious *Picture of American Culture* as the supposed confession of faith of the Yankee. That it is the spirit of capitalism which here speaks in characteristic fashion, no one will doubt, however little we may wish to claim that everything which could be understood as pertaining to that spirit is contained in it. Let us pause a moment to consider this passage, the philosophy of which Kurnberger sums up in the words, "They make tallow out of cattle and money out of men." The peculiarity of this philosophy of avarice appears to be the ideal of the honest man of recognized credit, and above all the idea of a duty of the individual toward the increase of his capital, which is assumed as an end in itself. Truly what is here preached is not simply a means of making one's way in the world, but a peculiar ethic. The infraction of its rules is treated not as foolishness but as forgetfulness of duty. That is the essence of the matter. It is not mere business astuteness; that sort of thing is common enough, it is an ethos. This is the quality which interests us.

When Jacob Fugger, in speaking to a business associate who had retired and who wanted to persuade him to do the same, since he had made enough money and should let others have a chance, rejected that as pusillanimity and answered that "he (Fugger) thought otherwise, he wanted to make money as long as he could," the spirit of his statement is evidently quite different from that of Franklin. What in the former case was an expression of commercial daring and a personal inclination morally neutral, in the latter takes on the character of an ethically coloured maxim for the conduct of life. The concept *spirit of capitalism* is here used in this specific sense, it is the spirit of modern capitalism. For that we are here dealing only with Western European and American capitalism is obvious from the way in which the problem was stated. Capitalism existed in China, India, Babylon, in the classic world, and in the Middle Ages. But in all these cases, as we shall see, this particular ethos was lacking.

Now, all Franklin's moral attitudes are coloured with utilitarianism. Honesty is useful, because it assures credit; so are punctuality, industry, frugality, and that is the reason they are virtues. A logical deduction from this would be that where, for instance, the appearance of honesty serves the same purpose, that would suffice, and an unnecessary surplus of this virtue would evidently appear to Franklin's eyes as unproductive waste. And as a matter of fact, the story in his autobiography of his conversion to those virtues, or the discussion of the value of a strict maintenance of the appearance of modesty, the assiduous belittlement of one's own deserts in order to gain general recognition later, confirms this impression. According to Franklin, those virtues, like all others, are only in so far virtues as they are actually useful to the individual, and the surrogate of mere appearance is always sufficient when it accomplishes the end in view. It is a conclusion which is inevitable for strict utilitarianism. The impression of many Germans that the virtues professed by Americanism are pure hypocrisy seems to have been confirmed by this striking case. But in fact the matter is not by any means so simple. Benjamin Franklin's own character, as it appears in the really unusual candidness of his autobiography, belies that suspicion. The circumstance that he ascribes his recognition of the utility of virtue to a divine revelation which was intended to lead him in the path of righteousness, shows that something more than mere garnishing for purely egocentric motives is involved.

In fact, the summum bonum of this ethic, the earning of more and more money, combined with the strict avoidance of all spontaneous enjoyment of life, is above all completely devoid of any eudaemonistic, not to say hedonistic, admixture. It is thought of so purely as an end in itself, that from the point of view of the happiness of, or utility to, the single individual, it appears entirely transcendental and absolutely irrational. Man is dominated by the making of money, by acquisition as the ultimate purpose of his life. Economic acquisition is no longer subordinated to man as the means for the satisfaction of his material needs. This reversal of what we should call the natural relationship, so irrational from a naïve point of view, is evidently a definitely leading principle of capitalistic influence. At the same time it expresses a type of feeling which is closely connected with certain religious ideas. If we thus ask, why should "money be made out of men," Benjamin Franklin himself, although he was a colourless deist, answers in his autobiography with a quotation from the Bible, which his strict Calvinistic father drummed into him again and again in his youth: "Seest thou a man diligent in his business? He shall stand before kings" (Prov. xxii. 29). The earning of money within the modern economic order is, so long as it is done legally, the result and the expression of virtue and proficiency in a calling; and this virtue and proficiency are, as it is now not difficult to see, the real Alpha and Omega of Franklin's ethic, as expressed in the passages we have quoted, as well as in all his works without exception.

And in truth this peculiar idea, so familiar to us to-day, but in reality so little a matter of course, of one's duty in a calling, is what is most characteristic of the social ethic of capitalistic culture, and is in a sense the fundamental basis of it. It is an obligation which the individual is supposed to feel and does feel towards the content of his professional activity, no matter in what it consists, in particular no matter whether it appears on the surface as a utilization of his personal powers, or only of his material possessions (as capital).

Of course, this conception has not appeared only under capitalistic conditions. On the contrary, we shall later trace its origins back to a time previous to the advent of capitalism. Still less, naturally, do we maintain that a conscious accept-ance of these ethical maxims on the part of the individuals, entrepreneurs or labourers, in modern capitalistic enter-prises, is a condition of the further existence of present-day capitalism. The capitalistic economy of the present day is an immense cosmos into which the individual is born, and which presents itself to him, at least as an individual, as an unalterable order of things in which he must live. It forces the individual, in so far as he is involved in the system of market relationships, to conform to capitalistic rules of ac-tion. The manufacturer who in the long run acts counter to these norms, will just as inevitably be eliminated from the economic scene as the worker who cannot or will not adapt himself to them will be thrown into the streets without a job.

Thus the capitalism of to-day, which has come to domin-ate economic life, educates and selects the economic subjects which it needs through a process of economic survival of the fittest. But here one can easily see the limits of the concept of selection as a means of historical explanation. In order that a manner of life so well adapted to the peculiarities of capitalism could be selected at all, i. e. should come to dom-inate others, it had to originate somewhere, and not in isolat-ed individuals alone, but as a way of life common to whole groups of men. This origin is what really needs explanation. Concerning the doctrine of the more naive historical mate-rialism, that such ideas originate as a reflection or superstruc-ture of economic situations, we shall speak more in detail be-low. At this point it will suffice for our purpose to call at-

tention to the fact that without doubt, in the country of
Benjamin Franklin's birth (Massachusetts), the spirit of
capitalism (in the sense we have attached to it) was present
before the capitalistic order. There were complaints of a
peculiarly calculating sort of profit-seeking in New England,
as distinguished from other parts of America, as early as
1632. It is further undoubted that capitalism remained far
less developed in some of the neighbouring colonies, the
later Southern States of the United States of America, in
spite of the fact that these latter were founded by large capitalists for business motives, while the New England colonies were founded by preachers and seminary graduates
with the help of small bourgeois, craftsmen and yeomen, for
religious reasons. In this case the causal relations is certainly
the reverse of that suggested by the materialistic standpoint.

But the origin and history of such ideas is much more complex than the theorists of the superstructure suppose. The
spirit of capitalism, in the sense in which we are using the
term, had to fight its way to supremacy against a whole
world of hostile forces. A state of mind such as that expressed in the passages we have quoted from Franklin, and
which called forth the applause of a whole people, would
both in ancient times and in the Middle Ages have been pro-
scribed as the lowest sort of avarice and as an attitude entirely lacking in self-respect. It is, in fact, still regularly thus
looked upon by all those social groups which are least involved in or adapted to modern capitalistic conditions. This
is not wholly because the instinct of acquisition was in those
times unknown or undeveloped, as had often been said. Nor
because the *auri sacra fames,* the greed for gold, was then, or
now, less powerful outside of bourgeois capitalism than
within its peculiar sphere, as the illusions of modern romanticists are wont to believe. The difference between the capitalistic and pre-capitalistic spirits is not to be found at this
point. The greed of the Chinese Mandarin, the old Roman
aristocrat, or the modern peasant, can stand up to any com-
praison. And the *auri sacra fames* of a Neapolitan cab-driver

or *barcaiuolo,* and certainly of Asiatic representatives of similar trades, as well as of the craftsmen of southern European or Asiatic countries, is, as anyone can find out for himself, very much more intense, and especially more unscrupulous than that of, say, an Englishman in similar circumstances.

The universal reign of absolute unscrupulousness in the pursuit of selfish interests by the making of money has been a specific characteristic of precisely those countries whose bourgeois-capitalistic development, measured according to Occidental standards, has remained backward. As every employer knows, the lack of *coscienziosita* of the labourers of such countries, for instance Italy as compared with Germany, has been, and to a certain extent still is, one of the principal obstacles to their capitalistic development. Capitalism cannot make use of the labour of those who practise the doctrine of undisciplined *liberum arbitrium,* any more than it can make use of the business man who seems absolutely unscrupulous in his dealings with others, as we can learn from Franklin. Hence the difference does not lie in the degree of development of any impulse to make money. The *auri sacra fames* is as old as the history of man. But we shall see that those who submitted to it without reserve as an uncontrolled impulse, such as the Dutch sea-captain who "would go through hell for gain, even though he scorched his sails", were by no means the representatives of that attitude of mind from which the specifically modern capitalistic spirit as a mass phenomenon is derived, and that is what matters. At all periods of history, wherever it was possible, there has been ruthless acquisition, bound to no ethical norms whatever. Like war and piracy, trade has often been unrestrained in its relations with foreigners and those outside the group. The double ethic has permitted here what was forbidden in dealings among brothers.

Capitalistic acquisition as an adventure has been at home in all types of economic society which have known trade with the use of money and which have offered it opportunities, through *comenda,* farming of taxes, State loans, financing of wars, ducal courts and office-holders. Likewise the inner attitude of the adventurer, which laughs at all ethical limitations, has been universal. Absolute and conscious ruthlessness in acquisition has often stood in the closest connection with the strictest conformity to tradition. Moreover, with the breakdown of tradition and the more or less complete extension of free economic enterprise, even to within the social group, the new thing has not generally been ethically justified and encouraged, but only tolerated as a fact. And this fact has been treated either as ethically indifferent or as reprehensible, but unfortunately unavoidable. This has not only been the normal attitude of all ethical teachings, but, what is more important, also that expressed in the practical action of the average man of precapitalistic times, pre-capitalistic in the sense that the rational utilization of capital in a permanent enterprise and the rational capitalistic organization of labour had not yet become dominant forces in the determination of economic activity. Now just this attitude was one of the strongest inner obstacles which the adaptation of men to the conditions of an ordered bourgeois-capitalistic economy has encountered everywhere.

The most important opponent with which the spirit of capitalism, in the sense of a definite standard of life claiming ethical sanction, has had to struggle, was that type of attitude and reaction to new situations which we may designate as traditionalism. In this case also every attempt at a final definition must be held in abeyance. On the other hand, we must try to make the provisional meaning clear by citing a few cases. We will begin from below, with the labourers.

One of the technical means which the modern employer uses in order to secure the greatest possible amount of work from his men is the device of piece-rates. In agriculture, for instance, the gathering of the harvest is a case where the greatest possible intensity of labour is called for, since the weather being uncertain, the difference between high profit and heavy loss may depend on the speed with which the harvesting can be done. Hence a system of piece-rates is al-most universal in this case. And since the interest of the em-ployer in a speeding-up of harvesting increases with the in-crease of the results and the intensity of the work, the at-tempt has again and again been made, by increasing the piece-rates of the workmen, thereby giving them an oppor-tunity to earn what is for them a very high wage, to interest them in increasing their own efficiency. But a peculiar diffi-culty has been met with surprising frequency: raising the piece-rates has often had the result that not more but less has been accomplished in the same time, because the worker re-acted to the increase not by increasing but by decreasing the amount of his work. A man, for instance, who at the rate of 1 mark per acre moved 2½ acres per day and earned 2½ marks, when the rate was raised to 1·25 marks per acre moved, not 3 acres, as he might easily have done, thus earn-ing 3·75 marks, but only 2 acres, so that he could still earn the 2½ marks to which he was accustomed. The opportunity of earning more was less attractive than that of working less. He did not ask: how much can I earn in a day if I do as much work as possible? but: how much must I work in order to earn the wage, 2½ marks, which I earned before and which takes care of my traditional needs? This is an example of what is here meant by traditionalism. A man does not "by nature" wish to earn more and more money, but simply to live as he is accustomed to live and to earn as much as is necessary for that purpose. Wherever modern capitalism has begun its work of increasing the productivity of human labour by increasing its intensity, it has encount-ered the immensely stubborn resistance of this leading trait of pre-capitalistic labour. And to-day it encounters it the more, the more backward (from a capitalistic point of view) the labouring forces are with which it has to deal.

Another obvious possibility, to return to our example, since the appeal to the acquisitive instinct through higher wage-rates failed, would have been to try the opposite policy, to force the worker by reduction of his wage-rates to work harder to earn the same amount than he did before. Low wages and high profits seem even to-day to a superficial observer to stand in correlation; everything which is paid out in wages seems to involve a corresponding reduction of profits. That road capitalism has taken again and again since its beginning. For centuries it was an article of faith, that low wages were productive, i. e. that they increased the material results of labour so that, as Pieter de la Cour, on this point, as we shall see, quite in the spirit of the old Calvinism, said long ago, the people only work because and so long as they are poor.

But the effectiveness of this apparently so efficient method has its limits. Of course the presence of a surplus population which it can hire cheaply in the labour market is a necessity for the development of capitalism. But though too large a reserve army may in certain cases favour its quantitative expansion, it checks its qualitative development, especially the transition to types of enterprise which make more intensive use of labour. Low wages are by no means identical with cheap labour. From a purely quantitative point of view the efficiency of labour decreases with a wage which is physiologically insufficient, which may in the long run even mean a survival of the unfit. The present-day average Silesian mows, when he exerts himself to the full, little more than two-thirds as much land as the better paid and nourished Pomeranian or Mecklenburger, and the Pole, the further East he comes from, accomplishes progressively less than the German. Low wages fail even from a purely business point of view wherever it is a question of producing goods which require any sort of skilled labour, or the use of expensive machinery which is easily damaged, or in general wherever any great amount of sharp attention or of initiative is required. Here low wages do not pay, and their effect is the opposite of what was intended. For not only is a developed sense of responsibility absolutely indispensable, but in general also an attitude which, as least during working hours, is freed from continual calculations of how the customary wage may be earned with a maximum of comfort and a minimum of exertion. Labour must, on the contrary, be performed as if it were an absolute end in itself, a calling. But such an attitude is by no means a product of nature. It cannot be evoked by low wages or high ones alone, but can only be the product of a long and arduous process of education. To-day, capitalism, once in the saddle, can recruit its labouring force in all industrial countries with comparative ease. In the past this was in every case an extremely difficult problem. And even to-day it could probably not get along without the support of a powerful ally along the way, which, as we shall see below, was at hand at the time of its development.

What is meant can again best be explained by means of an example. The type of backward traditional form of labour is to-day very often exemplified by women workers, especially unmarried ones. An almost universal complaint of employers of girls, for instance German girls, is that they are almost entirely unable and unwilling to give up methods of work inherited or once learned in favour of more efficient ones, to adapt themselves to new methods, to learn and to concentrate their intelligence, or even to use it at all. Explanations of the possibility of making work easier, above all more profitable to themselves, generally encounter a complete lack of understanding. Increases of piece-rates are without avail against the stone wall of habit. In general it is otherwise, and that is a point of no little importance from our view-point, only with girls having a specifically religious, especially a Pietistic, background. One often hears, and statistical investigation confirms it, that by far the best chances of economic education are found among this group. The ability of mental concentration, as well as the absolutely essential feeling of obligation to one's job, are here most often combined with a strict economy which calculates the possibility of high earnings, and a cool self-control and frugality which enormously increase performance. This provides the most favourable foundation for the conception of labour as an end in itself, as a calling which is necessary to capitalism: the chances of overcoming traditionalism are greatest on account of the religious upbringing. This observation of present-day capitalism in itself suggests that it is worth while to ask how this connection of adaptability to capitalism with religious factors may have come about in the days of the early development of capitalism. For that they were even then present in much the same form can be inferred from numerous facts. For instance, the dislike and the persecution which Methodist workmen in the eighteenth century met at the hands of their comrades were not solely nor even principally the result of their religious eccentricities; England had seen many of those and more striking ones. It rested rather, as the destruction of their tools, repeatedly mentioned in the reports, suggests, upon their specific willingness to work as we should say to-day.

However, let us again return to the present, and this time to the entrepreneur, in order to clarify the meaning of traditionalism in his case.

Sombart, in his discussions of the genesis of capitalism, has distinguished between the satisfaction of needs and acquisition as the two great leading principles in economic history. In the former case the attainment of the goods necessary to meet personal needs, in the latter a struggle for profit free from the limits set by needs, have been the ends controlling the form and direction of economic activity. What he calls the economy of needs seems at first glance to be identical with what is here described as economic traditionalism. That may be the case if the concepts of needs is limited to traditional needs. But if that is not done, a number of economic types which must be considered capitalistic according to the definition of capital which Sombart gives in another part of his work, would be excluded from the category of acquisitive economy and put into that of needs economy. Enterprises, namely, which are carried on by private entrepreneurs by utilizing capital (money or goods with a money value) to make a profit, purchasing the means of production and selling the product, i. e. undoubted capitalistic enterprises, may at the same time have a traditionalistic character. This has, in the course even of modern economic history, not been merely an occasional case, but rather the rule, with continual interruptions from repeated and increasingly powerful conquests of the capitalistic spirit. To be sure the capitalistic form of an enterprise and the spirit in which it is run generally stand in some sort of adequate relationship to each other, but not in one of necessary interdependence. Nevertheless, we provisionally use the expression spirit of (modern) capitalism to describe that attitude which seeks profit rationally and systematically in the manner which we have illustrated by the example of Benjamin Franklin. This, however, is justified by the historical fact that that attitude of mind has on the one hand found its most suitable expression in capitalistic enterprise, while on the other the enterprise has derived its most suitable motive force from the spirit of capitalism.

But the two may very well occur separately. Benjamin Franklin was filled with the spirit of capitalism at a time when his printing business did not differ in form from any handicraft enterprise. And we shall see that at the beginning of modern times it was by no means the capitalistic entrepreneurs of the commercial aristocracy, who were either the sole or the predominant bearers of the attitude we have here called the spirit of capitalism. It was much more the rising strata of the lower industrial middle classes. Even in the nineteenth century its classical representatives were not the elegant gentlemen of Liverpool and Hamburg, with their commercial fortunes handed down for generations, but the self-made parvenus of Manchester and Westphalia, who often rose from very modest circumstances. As early as the sixteenth century the situation was similar; the industries which arose at that time were mostly created by parvenus.

The management, for instance, of a bank, a wholesale export business, a large retail establishment, or of a large putting-out enterprise dealing with goods produced in homes, is certainly only possible in the form of a capitalistic enterprise. Nevertheless, they may all be carried on in a traditionalistic spirit. In fact, the business of a large bank of issue cannot be carried on in any other way. The foreign trade of whole epochs has rested on the basis of monopolies and legal privileges of strictly traditional character. In retail trade—and we are not here talking of the small men without capital who are continually crying out for Government aid—the revolution which is making an end of the old traditionalism is still in full swing. It is the same development which broke up the old putting-out system, to which modern domestic labour is related only in form. How this revolution takes place and what is its significance may, in spite of the fact these things are so familiar, be again brought out by a concrete example.

Until about the middle of the past century the life of a putter-out was, at least in many of the branches of the Continental textile industry, what we should to-day consider very comfortable. We may imagine its routine somewhat as follows: The peasants came with their cloth, often (in the case of linen) principally or entirely made from raw material which the peasant himself had produced, to the town in which the putter-out lived, and after a careful, often official, appraisal of the quality, received the customary price for it. The putter-out's customers, for markets any appreciable distance away, were middlemen, who also came to him, generally not yet following samples, but seeking traditional qualities, and bought from his warehouse, or, long before delivery, placed orders which were probably in turn passed on to the peasants. Personal canvassing of customers took place, if at all, only at long intervals. Otherwise correspondence sufficed, though the sending of samples slowly gained ground. The number of business hours was very moderate, perhaps five to six a day, sometimes considerably less; in the rush season, where there was one, more. Earnings were moderate; enough to lead a respectable life and in good times to put away a little. On the whole, relations among competitors were relatively good, with a large degree of agreement on the fundamentals of business. A long daily visit to the tavern, with often plenty to drink, and a congenial circle of friends, made life comfortable and leisurely.

The form of organization was in every respect capitalistic; the entrepreneur's activity was of a purely business character; the use of capital, turned over in the business, was indispensable; and finally, the objective aspect of the economic process, the book-keeping, was rational. But it was traditionalistic business, if one considers the spirit which animated the entrepreneur: the traditional manner of life, the traditional rate of profit, the traditional amount of work, the traditional manner of regulating the relationships with labour, and the essentially traditional circle of customers and the manner of attracting new ones. All these dominated the conduct of the business, were at the basis, one may say, of the ethos of this group of business men.

Now at some time this leisureliness was suddenly destroyed, and often entirely without any essential change in the form of organization, such as the transition to a unified factory, to mechanical weaving, etc. What happened was, on the contrary, often no more than this: some young man from one of the putting-out families went out into the country, carefully chose weavers for his employ, greatly increased the rigour of his supervision of their work, and thus turned them from peasants into labourers. On the other hand, he would begin to change his marketing methods by so far as possible going directly to the final consumer, would take the details into his own hands, would personally solicit customers, visiting them every year, and above all would adapt the quality of the product directly to their needs and wishes. At the same time he began to introduce the principle of low prices and large turnovers. There was repeated what everywhere and always is the result of such a process of rationalization: those who would not follow suit had to go out of business. The idyllic state collapsed under the pressure of a bitter competitive struggle, respectable fortunes were made, and not lent out at interest, but always reinvested in the business. The old leisurely and comfortable attitude toward life gave way to a hard frugality in which some participated and came to the top, because they did not wish to consume but to earn, while others who wished to keep on with the old ways were forced to curtail their consumption.

And, what is most important in this connection, it was not generally in such cases a stream of new money invested in the industry which brought about this revolution—in several cases known to me the whole revolutionary process was set in motion with a few thousands of capital borrowed from relations—but the new spirit, the spirit of modern capitalism, had set to work. The question of the motive forces in the expansion of modern capitalism, is not in the first instance a question of the origin of the capital sums which were available for capitalistic uses, but, above all, of the development of the spirit of capitalism. Where it appears and is able to work itself out, it produces its own capital and monetary supplies as the means to its ends, but the reverse is not true. Its entry on the scene was not generally peaceful. A flood of mistrust, sometimes of hatred, above all of moral indignation, regularly opposed itself to the first innovator. Often—I know of several cases of the sort—regular legends of mysterious shady spots in his previous life have been produced. It is very easy not to recognize that only an unusually strong character could save an entrepreneur of this new type from the loss of his temperate self-control and from both moral and economic shipwreck. Furthermore, along with charity of vision and ability to act, it is only by virtue of very definite and highly developed ethical qualities that it has been possible for him to command the absolutely indispensable confidence of his customers and workmen. Nothing else could have given him the strength to overcome the innumerable obstacles, above all the infinitely more intensive work which is demanded of the modern entrepeneur. But these are ethical qualities of quite a different sort from those adapted to the tradition-alism of the past.

And, as a rule, it has been neither dare-devil and unscrupulous speculators, economic adventurers such as we meet at all periods of economic history, nor simply great financiers who have carried through this change, outwardly so inconspicuous, but nevertheless so decisive for the penetration of economic life with the new spirit. On the contrary, they were men who had grown up in the hard school of life, calculating and daring at the same time, above all temperate and reliable, shrewd and completely devoted to their business, with strictly bourgeois opinions and principles.

One is tempted to think that these personal moral qualities have not the slightest relation to any ethical maxims, to say nothing of religious ideas, but that the essential relation between them is negative. The ability to free oneself from the common tradition, a sort of liberal enlightenment, seems likely to be the most suitable basis for such a business man's success. And to-day that is generally precisely the case. Any relationship between religious beliefs and conduct is generally absent, and where any exists, at least in Germany, it tends to be of the negative sort. The people filled with the spirit of capitalism to-day tend to be indifferent, if not hostile, to the Church. The thought of the pious boredom of paradise has little attraction for their active natures; religion appears to them as a means of drawing people away from labour in this world. If you ask them what is the meaning of their restless activity, why they are never satisfied with what they have, thus appearing so senseless to any purely worldly view of life, they would perhaps give the answer, if they know any at all: "to provide for my children and grandchildren". But more often and, since that motive is not peculiar to them, but was just as effective for the traditionalist, more correctly, simply: that business with its continuous work has become a necessary part of their lives. That is in fact the only possible motivation, but it at the same time expresses what is, seen from the view-point of personal happiness, so irrational about this sort of life, where a man exists for the sake of his business, instead of the reverse.

Of course, the desire for the power and recognition which the mere fact of wealth brings plays its part. When the imagination of a whole people has once been turned toward purely quantitative bigness, as in the United States, this romanticism of numbers exercises an irresistible appeal to the poets among business men. Otherwise it is in general not the real leaders, and especially not the permanently successful entrepreneurs, who are taken in by it. In particular, the resort to entailed estates and nobility, with sons whose conduct at the university and in the officers' corps tries to cover up their social origin, as has been the typical history of German capitalistic parvenu families, is a product of later decadence. The ideal type of the capitalistic entrepreneur, as it has been represented even in Germany by occasional outstanding examples, has no relation to such more or less refined climbers. He avoids ostentation and unnecessary expenditure, as well as conscious enjoyment of his power, and is embarrassed by the outward signs of the social recognition which he receives. His manner of life is, in other words, often, and we shall have to investigate the historical significance of just this important fact, distinguished by a certain ascetic tendency, as appears clearly enough in the sermon of Franklin which we have quoted. It is, namely, by no means exceptional, but rather the rule, for him to have a sort of modesty which is essentially more honest than the reserve which Franklin so shrewdly recommends. He gets nothing out of his wealth for himself, except the irrational sense of having done his job well.

But it is just that which seems to the pre-capitalistic man so incomprehensible and mysterious, so unworthy and contemptible. That anyone should be able to make it the sole purpose of his life-work, to sink into the grave weighed down with a great material load of money and goods, seems to him explicable only as the product of a perverse instinct, the *auri sacra fames*.

At present under our individualistic political, legal, and economic institutions, with the forms of organization and general structure which are peculiar to our economic order, this spirit of capitalism might be understandable, as has been said, purely as a result of adaptation. The capitalistic system so needs this devotion to the calling of making money, it is an attitude toward material goods which is so well suited to that system, so intimately bound up with the conditions of survival in the economic struggle for existence, that there can to-day no longer be any question of a necessary connection of that acquisitive manner of life with any single Weltanschauung. In fact, it no longer needs the support of any religious forces, and feels the attempts of religion to influence economic life, in so far as they can still be felt at all, to be as much an unjustified interference as its regulation by the State. In such circumstances men's commercial and social interests do tend to determine their opinions and attitudes. Whoever does not adapt his manner of life to the conditions of capitalistic success must go under, or at least cannot rise. But these are phenomena of a time in which modern capitalism has become dominant and has become emancipated from its old supports. But as it could at one time destroy the old forms of mediaeval regulation of economic life only in alliance with the growing power of the modern State, the same, we may say provisionally, may have been the case in its relations with religious forces. Whether and in what sense that was the case, it is our task to investigate. For that the conception of money-making as an end in itself to which people were bound, as a calling, was contrary to the ethical feelings of whole epochs, it is hardly necessary to prove. The dogma *Deo placere vix potest* which was incorporated into the canon law and applied to the activities of the merchant, and which at that time (like the passage in the gospel about interest) was considered genuine, as well as St. Thomas's characterization of the desire for gain as *turpitudo* (which term even included unavoidable and hence ethically justified profit-making), already contained a high degree of concession on the part of the Catholic doctrine to the financial powers with which the Church had such intimate political relations in the Italian cities, as compared with the much more radically anti-chrematistic views of comparatively wide circles. But even where the doctrine was still better accommodated to the facts, as for instance with Anthony of Florence, the feeling was never quite overcome, that activity directed to acquisition for its own sake was at bottom a *pudendum* which was to be tolerated only because of the unalterable necessities of life in this world.

Some moralists of that time, especially of the nominalistic school, accepted developed capitalistic business forms as inevitable, and attempted to justify them, especially commerce, as necessary. The industria developed in it they were able to regard, though not without contradictions, as a legitimate source of profit, and hence ethically unobjectionable. But the dominant doctrine rejected the spirit of capitalistic acquisition as turpitudo, or at least could not give it a positive ethical sanction. An ethical attitude like that of Benjamin Franklin would have been simply unthinkable. This was, above all, the attitude of capitalistic circles themselves. Their life-work was, so long as they clung to the tradition of the Church, at best something morally indifferent. It was tolerated, but was still, even if only on account of the continual danger of collision with the Church's doctrine on usury, somewhat dangerous to salvation. Quite considerable sums, as the sources show, went at the death of rich people to religious institutions as conscience money, at times even back to former debtors as *usura* which had been unjustly taken from them. It was otherwise, along with heretical and other tendencies looked upon with disapproval, only in those parts of the commercial aristocracy which were already emancipated from the tradition. But even sceptics and people indifferent to the Church often reconciled themselves with it by gifts, because it was a sort of insurance against the uncertainties of what might come after death, or because (at least according to the very widely held latter view) an external obedience to the commands of the Church was sufficient to insure salvation. Here the either non-moral or immoral character of their action in the opinion of the participants themselves comes clearly to light.

Now, how could activity, which was at best ethically tolerated turn into a calling in the sense of Benjamin Franklin? The fact to be explained historically is that in the most highly capitalistic centre of that time, in Florence of the fourteenth and fifteenth centuries, the money and capital market of all the great political Powers, this attitude was considered ethically unjustifiable, or at best to be tolerated. But in the backwoods small bourgeois circumstances of Pennsylvania in the eighteenth century, where business threatened for simple lack of money to fall back into barter, where there was hardly a sign of large enterprise, where only the earliest beginnings of banking were to be found, the same thing was considered the essence of moral conduct, even commanded in the name of duty. To speak here of a reflection of material conditions in the ideal superstructure would be patent nonsense. What was the background of ideas which could account for the sort of activity apparently directed toward profit alone as a calling toward which the individual feels himself to have an ethical obligation? For it was this idea which gave the way of life of the new entrepreneur its ethical foundation and justification.

The attempt has been made, particularly by Sombart, in what are often judicious and effective observations, to depict economic rationalism as the salient feature of modern economic life as a whole. Undoubtedly with justification, if by that is meant the extension of the productivity of labour which has, through the subordination of the process of production to scientific points of view, relieved it from its dependence upon the natural organic limitations of the human individual. Now this process of rationalization in the field of technique and economic organization undoubtedly determines an important part of the ideals of life of modern bourgeois society. Labour in the service of a rational organization for the provision of humanity with material goods has without doubt always appeared to representatives of the capitalistic spirit as one of the most important purposes of their life-work. It is only necessary, for instance, to read Franklin's account of his efforts in the service of civic improvements in Philadelphia clearly to apprehend this obvious truth. And the joy and pride of having given employment to numerous people, of having had a part in the economic progress of his home town in the sense referring to figures of population and volume of trade which capitalism associated with the word, all these things obviously are part of the specific and undoubtedly idealistic satisfactions in life to modern men of business. Similarly it is one of the fundamental characteristics of an individualistic capitalistic economy that it is rationalized on the basis of rigorous calculation, directed with foresight and caution toward the economic success which is sought in sharp contrast to the hand-to-mouth existence of the peasant, and to the privileged traditionalism of the guild craftsman and of the adventurers' capitalism, oriented to the exploitation of political opportunities and irrational speculation.

It might thus seem that the development of the spirit of capitalism is best understood as part of the development of rationalism as a whole, and could be deduced from the fundamental position of rationalism on the basic problems of life. In the process Protestantism would only have to be considered in so far as it had formed a stage prior to the development of a purely rationalistic philosophy. But any serious attempt to carry this thesis through makes it evident that such a simple way of putting the question will not work, simply because of the fact that the history of rationalism shows a development which by no means follows parallel lines in the various departments of life. The rationalization of private law, for instance, if it is thought of as a logical simplification and rearrangement of the content of the law, was achieved in the highest hitherto known degree in the Roman law of late antiquity. But it remained most backward in some of the countries with the highest degree of economic rationalization, notably in England, where the Renaissance of Roman Law was overcome by the power of the great legal corporations, while it has always retained its supremacy in the Catholic countries of Southern Europe. The worldly rational philosophy of the eighteenth century did not find favour alone or even principally in the countries of highest capitalistic development. The doctrines of Voltaire are even to-day the common property of broad upper, and what is practically more important, middle-class groups in the Roman Catholic countries. Finally, if under practical rationalism is understood the type of attitude which sees and judges the world consciously in terms of the worldly interests of the individual ego, then this view of life was and is the special peculiarity of the peoples of the *liberum arbitrium*, such as the Italians and the French are in very flesh and blood. But we have already convinced ourselves that this is by no means the soil in which that relationship of a man to his calling as a task, which is necessary to capitalism, has pre-eminently grown. In fact, one may—this simple proposition, which is often forgotten, should be placed at the beginning of every study which essays to deal with rationalism—rationalize life from fundamentally different basic points of view and in very different directions. Rationalism is an historical concept which covers a whole world of different things. It will be our task to find out whose intellectual child the particular concrete form of rational thought was, from which the idea of a calling and the devotion to labour in the calling has grown, which is, as we have seen, so irrational from the standpoint of purely eudaemonistic self-

interest, but which has been and still is one of the most characteristic elements of our capitalistic culture. We are here
particularly interested in the origin of precisely the irrational element which lies in this, as in every conception of a
calling.

PROLETARIAT AND RELIGION AND NATIONALISM*

By WERNER SOMBART

OF far-reaching importance, and at this moment of pressing interest, are two points which I would present in conclusion. I mean the attitude of the social movement towards religion and towards nationality. Because here personal feeling and temperament may easily interfere with the clear vision of the observer, it is doubly necessary to divest oneself of all passion and to deal with these problems objectively. Let us make the attempt. Leaving out of consideration the English working-man, who to-day, as a generation ago, seems to oscillate between pietism and positivism, and who on this point cannot be considered typical because of the well-known peculiar conditions of his development, the proletarian movement doubtless is strongly anti-religious. How comes this?

So far as I see, the opposition to religion comes from two different sources; it has a "theoretical" and a "practical" origin. Theoretically the proletariat and its leaders have become heirs of the liberal "age of illumination." Out of a superficial study of natural sciences have sprung all these anti-religious writings of the years 1860-1880 which in an intoxication of joy announced the first recognition of the atheistic dogma to the world. These writers never rose above the level of "itinerant preachers of materialism," and they have never reached to the level of the Marx-Engels conception of life. The platform of this dogmatic atheism may be considered to-day as entirely something of the past. There is no earnest representative of science anywhere who to-day dares to assert that science means atheism and excludes re-

* From *Socialism and the Social Movement in the 19th Century*

ligion. Thus the attitude of the proletariat towards religion would be entirely free and independent if the ground of its irreligion were merely a theoretic and misleading incursion into the dogmatism of natural science. But the enmity to religion has much deeper grounds. Not only has an enthusiasm for scientific materialism taken hold of the proletariat with special force; but also the enthusiasm for unbelief has been helped greatly in its development by the instinctive feeling, or the clear consciousness, that in the materialistic conception of the world lies the germ of a mighty revolutionary force, well suited to drive authority from all spheres of life. What wonder that the proletariat took hold of it as a useful weapon for the strife; for, as we know, one of the conditions of the very existence of the proletariat lies in a tearing asunder of all the old points of faith. Thus the predilection for materialism and atheism is well explained.

And now consider that the acceptance of this dogma betokens a protest against the Christian system of thought, which the working man must look upon as inimical because represented by the ruling classes and used in their interests. For there can be no doubt that, in an overwhelming majority of cases, official Christianity has been used by the ruling classes against the movement for the emancipation of the proletariat. The fate that falls upon heretical Christians is the best proof of this. So long as men try to support monarchy and capitalism as a necessary and Divine institution, using the Christian Church for this purpose, the social movement must become anti-ecclesiastical and thus anti-religious. Thus a mistrust as to the position, in the social struggle, of the official representatives of the Church estranges the proletariat from this Church and thus from religion. In the moment that this mistrust is removed—and you all know that the new Christian-socialists, especially in Germany, have taken this as their task,—in the moment when Christianity is presented either as unpartisan in its social influence, as Goehre preaches it, or as directly social-democratic, as Naumann presents it,—in that moment, so far as I see, there will be no reason why the proletariat should maintain an anti-religious character.

In saying this, of course, I assume that religion is adapted to the needs of the proletariat. Whether or not Christianity possesses this adaptability, I do not dare to say. But that it is thus adapted would seem to be indicated by the fact that it became the religion of Rome in its decadence and of the German tribes in the youthful freshness of their civilization, of feudalism as well as of those stages of civilisation in which the free cities and later the bourgeoisie have had predominance. Then why may it not also be the religion of the proletariat? But it must be presented to the lower classes with all of the joy of life of which Christianity is capable. For the element of asceticism in Christianity pleases little these classes, which press towards air and light and which do not show any inclination to allow the good things of life to be taken from them.

As if overhung with thick clouds of passion, appears now the question as to the attitude of the social movement towards nationality. A great part of the heated discussion on this point, as it seems to me, is due to lack of clearness in thought. It is not so much our German language, as it is our German instinct, that distinguishes between two ideas, rightly but not always sharply separated; we are accustomed to specify them as patriotism and nationalism.

Patriotism, the love of the Fatherland, is indeed a feeling that unconsciously and without effort is held fast in our hearts, and exists therein like love of home and of family. It is an aggregation of impressions, of memories, over which we have no control. It is that indefinable power exercised upon our souls by the sound of the mother tongue, by the harmony of the national song, by many peculiar customs and usages, by the whole history and poetry of the home land. It is that feeling which comes to its fulness only in a strange land, and presses as truly upon the soul of the exiled revolutionist as upon that of the peaceful citizen. I cannot see why this should be the heritage of a particular class.

It is a foolish idea that such a feeling may, or can, die out in the great masses of men, so long as there are lands and peoples with their own languages and songs.

Quite different is nationalism—the intelligent presentation, if I may so express it, of national opinion, especially in opposition and enmity to other nations. The modern proletariat does not simply refuse to share this feeling; it actually fights against it.

Here again we meet the same fact that we observed before in connection with the attitude of the proletariat towards religion; they identify the idea of "nationalism" with the ruling classes, and as enemies of the representatives of the idea they turn their hatred against the idea itself. Especially is this so because, in many lands, it is not made easy for the rising working-men's movement to identify itself with the official representatives of the nation; hate, persecution, repression, are not suitable means to arouse pride in that national structure in which the working men must live together with those from whom all this evil proceeds. At the same time a friendly hand is reached over the national boundary-line by the proletariat of a strange and unfriendly land, by companions in suffering, with similar interests and efforts. Truly it is no wonder that the modern proletariat generally becomes imbued with an anti-national, an international, tendency.

But I hold it to be quite wrong to justify an anti-national theory by this impulsive anti-nationalism. I see in the essence of modern socialism no reason for such an idea. I have explicitly pointed out to you the tendency towards an international understanding and unity on the part of the proletariat. But that is only an artificial abolition of national barriers. Only one who chases after the phantom of a world republic will be able to imagine a social development outside of national limitations. A man will hardly venture to prophesy with certainty, even for only a short time, as to when the social contradictions within a nation shall rival those points of difference at present existing between nations. But it must be clear even to the short-sighted that, so far as we can see, an energetic upholding of national interests can never be entirely unnecessary.

Even if in Western Europe the differences between nations should be so far obviated that only social questions remain in the field, I believe that we could never assume that this Western European civilisation can pursue its course undisturbed and without the admixture of other elements. We must never forget that, as a result of a modern means of communication, not only Russian civilisation threatens that of Western Europe, but even the Asiatic more and more strongly presses upon us. The development in Asia which we have seen in the course of the last decade, the rapid advancement of Japan, and now the attempt of China to enter civilisation in order to nibble at the fruits of commerce and to grow out of its narrow circle—this development will doubtless take a course which must of necessity lead to new international complications. I believe that the moment will come when European society as a whole will say to itself: All our mutual differences are of no importance as compared with that which threatens us from this enemy. As an indication of this see the attitude of America towards Asiatic development. There is a case in which the "internationalism" of the proletariat is simply thrown aside; and this would be the case also among the proletariat of Western Europe, if the coolies should begin to swarm over us like rats. An artificial sympathy with the most down-trodden people would prove too weak to restrain a sound national self-interest. So soon as a common enemy threatens the existence of a society it becomes again conscious of its economic interests and rallies to their support; and in the meantime its internal differences are forgotten.

Thus there can be no talk of an essential repudiation of nationalism on the part of the proletariat throughout the world. Discussion of the question concerns only a circle of kindred nations to which one does not want to see the principle of anti-nationalism applied. How such national groups are constituted is a question which it is not necessary for us here to determine, as I desire only to present the essential point in the national problem. You see that, with this discussion, I complete the circle of my thought, and return to that with which I began—the idea that there is, and apparently always will be, an antithesis around which, as around poles, human history circles, the social and the national. That is something which the proletariat should never forget.

SOCIOLOGY AS A SCIENCE*

By VILFREDO PARETO

A LOGICO-EXPERIMENTAL study merely relates facts with facts. If that is done directly, merely describing facts that are observable simultaneously, we get pure empiricism. Empiricism may serve to discover uniformities if, by observation or experiment, one succeeds in distinguishing not more than two categories of facts that stand in correlation. Once the categories multiply and effects become involved, it proves to be very difficult, and more often impossible, to find uniformities with the tool of pure empiricism. The sum of effects has somehow to be unsnarled. In certain cases that can be done materially by experiment. In others, experiment is out of the question or else fails to unravel the complication. Then one can only resort to hypothetical abstractions, now to one, now to another, testing each in turn with the idea of solving ideally what cannot be solved materially, accepting finally that hypothesis among the many which yields results that accord with experience. The manner in which the hypothesis has been reached may be absurd. That is of little if any importance; for the value of the hypothesis is tested not by the manner in which it has been conceived, but by the verifications that can be made of it.

But if the hypothesis has been inferred in the first place from certain facts, A, B....P, that circumstance in itself is a first step towards verification; for since the hypothesis has been inferred from those facts, they certainly will appear among the results it will yield. What remains to be seen is whether it will also yield the facts Q, R....V, which have not yet been taken into the reckoning.

In these volumes, therefore, we might have followed a de-

* From *The Mind and Society.*

ductive method, positing our residues and derivations at the very outset as mere hypotheses, without explaining how we came by them, thence going on to show that they yielded results which accorded with the facts. Instead we elected to follow the inductive method, deriving our residues and derivations from facts in very large numbers. So, as far as those facts were concerned, the verification was made then and there, and all that remained was to extend the verification to other facts not as yet considered. That verification we proceeded to make and are still making. In a word, then, what we have been doing, and are still doing, is to establish relations between facts.

There is nothing peculiar about such a method. It is the method general in all the sciences. Oftentimes in the sciences a hypothesis serves for a certain length of time and promotes progress in a particular science; then it is replaced by another, which performs the same function until, in its turn, it gives way to still a third; and so on. Sometimes a hypothesis may hold its ground for a long time, as was the case with the hypothesis of universal gravitation.

The logico-experimental sciences are made up of a sum of theories that are like living creatures, in that they are born, live, and die, the young replacing the old, the group alone enduring. As is the case with living beings, the lifetimes of theories vary in length and not always are the long-lived ones the ones that contribute most to the advancement of knowledge. Faith and metaphysics aspire to an ultimate, eternal resting place. Science knows that it can attain only provisory, transitory positions. Every theory fulfils its function, and nothing more can be asked of it.

If such succession in doctrines is in great part determined by a single force, the successive stages may constantly approach a certain limit; their curve may have an asymptote. That is what is happening in the logico-experimental sciences. The force, and if not the only one at least the chief one, that is now influencing those sciences is the investigation of correspondences between theories and experience.

Theories therefore are constantly getting closer to experimental reality; whereas in a day gone by other forces were at work and prevented attainment of that result. Economic and social doctrines are still subject to such forces, and for that reason they continue to be at variance with experimental reality, sometimes to very considerable degrees, and it is doubtful whether there be any asymptote for their oscillations.

If the succession of doctrines is determined by a large number of forces of approximately equal intensities, the movement revealed in the succession may be so complicated as to make it impossible to find any general expression for it. But if such forces, without being so few as one, are at least not many, there are cases in which we can discover such an expression. We may, for instance, recognize movements as oscillating about a given point, whether tending towards an equilibrium in that position or continuing on indefinitely without any tendency of the kind. We have seen movements of that sort taking place under the pressure of two forces in the main: correspondences with experimental reality and social utility.

Only in a first approximation can the numberless forces operating in a concrete case be reduced to two. If, to carry an investigation farther, new forces are brought into consideration as an addition to the two main ones, we get movements that grow increasingly complicated and are harder and harder to manage. In these volumes we have succeeded in taking a few steps along that road, but it bristles with obstacles, and they are too numerous to permit us to go as far as we should have liked.

Kepler's discovery that the orbit of Mars was an ellipse with one of its foci coinciding with the centre of the Sun was purely empirical, providing a summary description of the situation. In that case, owing to the imperfect observations available, it was possible to distinguish the movement of one planet with respect to the Sun from the movements of the other planets. Had the observations been more nearly exact, no such distinction could have been made, Kepler would have found no ellipse, and that would have been a serious obstacle to the advancement of astronomy.

Two cases have to be considered in this connexion:

1. As regards our solar system, the obstacle might have been overcome without great difficulty. Some scientists would have observed that if the curve traversed by Mars was not an ellipse, it was in any case not far from an ellipse; and he could have suggested the *hypothesis* that if Mars and the Sun were considered apart from the other planets, the curve had to be an ellipse, and that if that was not the case, it was because the Sun and Mars were not considered apart from the other planets.

2. The obstacle would have been much greater and perhaps insuperable if instead of our solar system, where the central body has an enormously greater mass than any of its planets, a system of stars and planets of no very appreciable differences in mass had been in question.

Sometimes, though unfortunately very rarely, the facts correlated by statistics may be brought under the first case just mentioned: that is to say, by interpolation, a certain hypothetical curve can be found from which the real curve can be inferred by assuming perturbations. But much more often the facts of economics, and to a still greater extent of sociology, are to be brought under the second case.

Newton advanced a hypothesis, known as the theory of universal gravitation, whereby if the Sun is assumed to be stationary with a planet revolving around it, one gets a curve something like the curve discovered by Kepler—an ellipse.

That hypothesis has one peculiar merit that is rarely met with in other hypotheses of the kind. The relation between the hypothesis and the facts can be inverted. If it be assumed that a planet is moving in an ellipse about a stationary Sun, a law of gravitation results that is Newton's law exactly. Generally, in economics and sociology, a hypothesis may indeed imply the existence of certain facts, but those facts may lend themselves to many other hypotheses.

Newton's hypothesis has also another very great merit, that so far at least (1914), taking the Sun and its planets as a whole, it has been adequate for explaining all the perturbations that have been observed in the movements of the celestial bodies. If that has not been the case, Newton's hypothesis might have stood, but it would have had to be supplemented with other hypotheses, the hypothesis, for instance, that the attraction exerted by the planets upon one another is different from the attraction between the planets and the Sun.

Needless to say, neither economics nor sociology possess simple hypotheses as widely applicable as Newton's.

In political economy and sociology, therefore, it is indispensable to consider many different elements in the complex phenomena that are directly recorded by observation. The simplest thing one can say in economics is that the economic equilibrium results from the conflict between tastes and obstacles; but the simplicity is only apparent, since one then has to go on and take account of an intricate variety of tastes and obstacles. The complications in sociology are greater still and by far. There, in addition to logical conduct, which is alone envisaged in economics, one has to deal with non-logical conduct, and then again, in addition to logical thinking, with derivations.

The laws, so called, of supply and demand cannot be deduced from statistics as to the quantities and prices of a commodity produced or brought to market. When economists said that an increase in supply brings a drop in price, they stated the law of an ideal situation that is rarely observable in the concrete. In working out theories in economics it is an illusion to believe that we get any closer to the concrete by starting with the laws of supply and demand than we do by starting with the "utility" of the early economists, or with the "marginal utility," the "rarity," or the "ophelimity," of more recent economists. Whatever we do, we are resorting to abstraction, and we cannot do otherwise. Theoretically one may start with any one of those considerations or indeed with any others; but however we start, we must use certain cautions that are overlooked by many writers who talk political economy without knowing the first thing about it. From the theoretical standpoint, again, one must not forget that consumptions of commodities are not independent, as not a few of the founders of pure economics assumed them to be. Nor can the undulatory movements of economic phenomena be disregarded, nor a great many other circumstances, such as speculation, which change the simpler form of the phenomena that, for purposes of convenience, was the one considered first.

All that has just been said applies *a fortiori* to sociology. Little or nothing can be inferred directly from the mere description, and in that sense the apothegm that "history never repeats itself" is very true. Concrete phenomena have to be broken up into ideal phenomena that are simpler, that we may so arrive at something more nearly constant than the complex and ever shifting thing we have before us in the concrete. In these volumes we have sought these less variable, these more constant, elements in residues and derivations. They might very well be sought in other directions. That is not so important as to be careful that wherever one goes looking for them, elements and forms that lead away from objective reality are not introduced. That "history never repeats itself" identically is just as certain as it is that history is "always repeating itself" in certain respects that we may call the main respects. It would be inconceivably absurd to imagine that history could produce an event identically repeating the Peloponnesian War, in the sense of being an exact copy of it. But then again, history shows that that war, which arose in the rivalry between Athens and Sparta, is only one item in an endless series of similar wars that have been brought on by similar causes, that in that sense there are numberless copies of it that are likenesses, to some extent at least, from the wars that arose in the rivalries between Carthage and Rome down to all the other wars that have been fought in all periods of history between then and now. In his *Politica,* V, 3, 7 (Rackham, p. 305) Aristotle says: "Finally, it must be evident that those who have been the cause of power (to a city), whether they be private citizens, magistrates, clans, or in short, any part of a people, are responsible for insurrections." In those words he was describing one of the main elements in the great many facts that were known to him, and he was foreseeing a great many other facts that were to come true after his time, the cases of Cromwell and Napoleon, to mention examples closer to our own times.

The main element in such happenings is in fact supplied by sentiments (residues), which have varied but slightly between Aristotle's time and our own. The same may be said of many maxims of Machiavelli, which hold as true today as they were in his time. Classes of residues vary but slightly and but slowly, and they may therefore be counted among the elements that determine the constant, virtually constant, or at least not very variable element in historical phenomena. The separate genera in a class of residues vary to a far greater degree and much more rapidly than the class as a whole, and we must therefore be cautious in giving them any such position. Derivations vary widely and very rapidly; and they are generally to be counted, therefore, only among the subordinate elements that determine secondary, variable, and for the most part negligible phases in a phenomenon. What we have just been saying furnishes the key also to a fact to which we have had frequent occasion to allude—that in a quest for sociological uniformities, too many facts, details too minute, may be a hindrance rather than a help; for if one dwells on all the petty circumstances that figure in a situation, one can easily lose one's way, like a person traveling in a thick underbrush; one is prevented from assigning proper indices to the various elements, mistaking what is secondary for what is principal, what is very variable for what is quasi-constant, and so one ends by writing a piece of literature that is devoid of the slightest scientific value.

In the practice of the social sciences one must especially be on one's guard against intrusions of personal sentiments; for a writer is inclined to look not for what is and nothing else, but for what *ought* to be in order to fit in with his religious, moral, patriotic, humanitarian or other sentiments. The quest for uniformities is an end in itself. Once they have been found, they may be made to serve other purposes. But to mix the two researches is harmful to both, and is in any case a serious and oftentimes insuperable obstacle to the discovery of experimental uniformities. As long as the natural sciences had to deal with such obstacles, they made little or no progress, and only as the obstacles became fewer in number and finally disappeared did they make the marvellous progress they show today. If, accordingly, one would remould the social sciences on the model of the natural sciences, one must proceed in them as in the natural sciences, reducing highly complicated concrete phenomena to simpler theoretical phenomena, being exclusively guided all the while by the intent to discover experimental uniformities, and judging the efficacy of what one has done only by the experimental verifications that may be made of it.

INTELLECTUAL EGALITARIANISM*

By LESTER WARD

THE proposition that the lower classes of society are the intellectual equals of the upper classes will probably shock most minds. At least it will be almost unanimously rejected as altogether false. Yet I do not hesitate to maintain and defend it as an abstract proposition. But of course we must understand what is meant by intellectual equality. I have taken some pains to show that the difference in the intelligence of the two classes is immense. What I insist upon is that this difference in intelligence is not due to any difference in intellect. It is due entirely to difference in mental equipment. It is chiefly due to difference in knowledge, if we include in knowledge a familiarity with the tools of the mind and an acquired ability to utilize the products of human achievement, as I have defined this term in *Pure Sociology* (Chapter III). It was there shown that each age of the world's history stands on a platform erected by all past ages. It is true that all the members of society have the use to a certain extent of the products of past achievement, but in no other sense do those members stand on the elevated platform who do not actually possess the heritage of the past. Now, as a matter of fact, it is only what I have called the intelligent class who really possess this heritage. They of course possess it in varying degrees, but most of them possess enough of it to give them dominion over those who do not possess it.

I have shown in the same work (p. 573) that social heredity is not a process of organic transmission, that no part of the social germ-plasm passes from one individual to another, but that all knowledge must be separately acquired

---

* From *Applied Sociology*.

by every individual. The social organization must be such as to infuse it into the members of society as fast as they are capable of receiving it. This infusion of it is social transmission, and unless it is infused it is not transmitted. The only way in which products of past achievement have been preserved has been through such a degree of social organization as is sufficient to infuse them into a certain number of the members of society. This number has always, in the historical races, been large enough to prevent their being lost, and most or all human achievement has been preserved. But it is easy to imagine this great social duty to be neglected and all human achievement lost. There are parts of the world in which this has virtually happened, and this is the way in which races degenerate.

But society has never and nowhere been so organized as to transmit the products of achievement to more than a small fraction of its members. These constitute the intelligent class. The rest are all intellectually disinherited, and while the intellectually disinherited always include and are nearly coextensive with the materially disinherited, the former is much the more serious condition. For the intellectual inheritance would bring with it the material inheritance and all the other advantages that are enjoyed by the intelligent class. Of all the problems of applied sociology that which towers above all others is the problem of the organization of society so that the heritage of the past shall be transmitted to all its members alike. Until this problem is solved there is scarcely any use in trying to solve other problems. Not only are most of them otherwise incapable of solution, but this primary problem once solved all others will solve themselves.

But here we encounter the great sullen, stubborn error, so universal and ingrained as to constitute a world view, that the difference between the upper and lower classes of society is due to a difference in their intellectual capacity, something existing in the nature of things, something preordained and inherently inevitable. Every form of sophistry is employed to uphold this view. We are told that there must be social classes, that they are a necessary part of the social order. There must be laborers and unskilled workmen to do the drudgery work of the world. There must be menial servants to wait upon us. What would society do without the scavenger. All of which, while clearly showing that the persons who thus argue not only fear but believe that the lower classes are capable of being raised to their own level, reveals a lack of reflection and an incapacity for logical reasoning scarcely to be met with elsewhere. It recalls the remark of the Scotch engineer whom some fortune transported to the plains of Kansas before the days of Pacific railroads, that there could be no railroads in that country, for "where are the hills to put the tunnels through?"

As just remarked, only one man among all the thinkers of the world has ever thought or dared to combat this universal error. His position was stated and briefly discussed in *Pure Sociology,* and certain qualifications of it were made, to which I would still adhere; but with these qualifications the doctrine of the equal intellectual capacity of all men is a perfectly sound doctrine, and is the doctrine upon which the applied sociologist must stand. It is true that this view has appearances against it, but, as I have often shown, there is no great truth in any department of science that did not at first have appearances against it. The whole march of truth has consisted in substituting the hidden and obscure reality for the falsely apparent. With this uniform trend of history before us, we ought by this time to have learned to suspect everything that seems on the face of it to be true. Let us glance at some of the evidence in favor of the Helvetian doctrine and against the current belief.

Rise of the Proletariat.—The history of social classes furnishes to the philosophical student of society the most convincing proof that the lower grades of mankind have never occupied those positions on account of any inherent incapacity to occupy higher ones. Throughout antiquity and well down through the Middle Ages the great mass of mankind were slaves. A little later they were serfs bound to the soil. Finally, with the abolition of slavery, the fall of the feudal system, and the establishment of the industrial system, this great mass took the form of a proletariat, the fourth estate, considered of so little consequence that they are seldom mentioned by the great historians of Europe. Even at the close of the eighteenth century, when the greatest of all political revolutions occurred, it was only the third estate that was at all in evidence—the business class, bourgeoisie, or social mesoderm. This class had been looked down upon and considered inferior, and only the lords spiritual and temporal were regarded as capable of controlling social and national affairs. This class is now at the top. It has furnished the world's brains for two centuries, and if there is any intellectual inferiority it is to be found in the poor remnant that still calls itself the nobility in some countries.

The movement that is now agitating society is different from any of the previous movements, but it differs from them only as they differed from one another. It is nothing less than the coming to consciousness of the proletariat. The class who for ages were slaves or serfs are now voters in enlightened states. They have risen to where they can begin to see out, and they are arising still higher. When a new truth begins to dawn and replace an old error it is always found that the weightiest facts in support of the truth have been furnished by the defenders of the error. The best arguments for organic evolution were supplied by such anti-evolutionists as Baer, Agassiz, and Virchow. Nearly all the facts needed to establish the gynaecocentric theory were drawn from writings specially designed to support the androcentric theory. And now we find one of the strongest believers in the essential distinction between social classes unconsciously arguing for intellectual egalitarianism. Says Mr. Benjamin Kidd:

"One of the most striking and significant signs of the times is the spectacle of Demos, with these new battle-cries ringing in his ears, gradually emerging from the long silence of social and political serfdom. Not now does he come with the violence of revolution foredoomed to failure, but with the slow and majestic progress which marks a natural evolution. He is no longer unwashed and illiterate, for we have universal education. He is no longer muzzled and without political power, for we have universal suffrage. . . . The advance towards more equal conditions of life has been so great, that amongst the more progressive nations such terms as lower orders, common people, and working classes are losing much of their old meaning, the masses of the people are being slowly raised, and the barriers of birth, class, and privilege are everywhere being broken through. But, on the other hand, the pulses of life have not slackened amongst us; the rivalry is keener, the stress severer, and the pace quicker than ever before. . . . The power-holding classes are in full conscious retreat before the incoming people."

All this is true, though somewhat overdrawn, but Kidd is so blinded by the current world view that he will not attribute it to the slowly growing intelligence of the masses. He attributes it to the rise and spread of humanitarianism, which by an obvious bid for the applause of the religious world he falsely calls religion, and repeats Comte's saying that man is becoming more and more religious. He dimly perceives the fact that there has been emotional development as well as brain development, and properly enough emphasizes the truth that this growth of sympathy on the part of the upper classes has greatly accelerated the rise of the lower classes. But he attributes it all to such agencies and strangely confounds the ethical with the religious and supernatural, virtually arguing that the less rational the people are the faster they will rise, and ascribing all human progress to the influence of "ultra-rational sanctions," i. e., to superstition. He flatly denies that intelligence has anything to do with the matter, saying:

"Another explanation, currently offered, is that the result is caused by the growing strength and intelligence of the people's party which render the attack irresistible. But we may readily perceive that the increasing strength and intelligence of the lower classes of the community is the result of the change which is in progress, and that it cannot, therefore, be by itself the cause."

I ought perhaps to apologize for giving so prominent a place to a book which is so obviously written for applause; but Mr. Kidd has a really keen insight into social questions and has contributed much to their elucidation, still, by trimming his sails to catch every breeze, he has made his book a tissue of inconsistencies. It has had a wide influence for both good and evil, and it is doing much to prop up and perpetuate the error we are here combating and to postpone the acceptance of the truth that is destined ultimately to replace it. But he has not himself been able to shut his eyes entirely to the native capacity of the lower classes for education, and in at least one passage he practically admits their substantial equality with the upper classes in this respect:

"It is not yet clearly perceived by the people that there is not any more natural and lasting distinction between the educated and the uneducated classes of which we hear so much nowadays, than there has been between the other classes in the past. Citizen and slave, patrician and plebeian, feudal lord and serf, privileged classes and common people, leisured classes and working masses, have been steps in a process of development."

What has actually taken place in the history of the world has been a gradual upward movement of the mass from the condition of mere slaves to that of more or less skilled laborers with some general ideas about the land they live in and the world at large, until from a state in which at least nine tenths were submerged there is now in enlightened countries only a completely "submerged tenth." But there nevertheless exists in fact only a completely emerged tenth. The essential fact, however, is that there is no valid reason why not only the other partially emerged eight tenths but the completely submerged tenth should not all completely emerge. They are all equally capable of it. This does not at all imply that all men are equal intellectually. It only insists that intellectual inequality is common to all classes, and is as great among the members of the completely emerged tenth as it is between that class and the completely submerged tenth. Or, to state it more clearly, if the same individuals who constitute the intelligent class at any time or place had been surrounded from their birth by exactly the same conditions that have surrounded the lowest stratum of society, they would have inevitably found themselves in that stratum; and if an equal number taken at random of the lowest stratum of society had been surrounded from their birth by exactly the same conditions by which the intelligent class have been surrounded, they would in fact have constituted the intelligent class instead of the particular individuals who happen actually to constitute it. In other words, class distinctions in society are wholly artificial, depend entirely on environing conditions, and are in no sense due to differences in native capacity. Differences in native capacity exist and are as great as they have ever been pictured, but they exist in all classes alike.

Capacity for Truth.—This brings us to the most important of all the considerations involved in this problem, viz, the fact that the difference in the native capacity of individuals is never sufficient to exclude any person from the highest social class. Nothing short of congenital mental imbecility, feeble-mindedness, or idiocy can take an individual out of the social class to which his conditions of existence have assigned him, and this, as we all know, does not remand him to a lower social class, but only to the class of dependents or wards of society; all of which proves that it does not require any great or towering native abilities to enable an individual to maintain his place in the vanguard of society. The minimum natural abilities above the stage of pathological imbecility suffice for this. Herein lies the hope of the world, because it shows that the social heritage is no such burden as to require an Atlas to hold it up, but is readily adjusted to the feeblest shoulders and easily borne by all. It consists simply in the possession of the truth that has been brought into the world through the prolonged labors of thousands of zealous investigators, and which when possessed necessarily drives out the error which it replaces. The truth is no harder to carry than was the error; in many ways it is the lighter load.

This has been perceived, dimly for the most part, sometimes clearly, but never in such a broad and vital connection as to indicate that its utterers at all grasped its momentous import. A few of these adumbrations may not be out of place. Bacon saw it, at least for his own peculiar method. Speaking of positive ideas as contrasted with theological and metaphysical ideas, which is almost the same as the contrast between truth and error, Comte said:

"At any given point in this slow, spontaneous preparation, if a happy external circumstance succeeds in introducing positive conceptions before their time, the eager haste with which they are everywhere welcomed sufficiently shows that the primitive attachment of our intelligence to theological and metaphysical explanations was due solely to the evident impossibility of any better nourishment, and had not at all changed the inherent character of our true cerebral appetites, as daily experience both individual and collective shows."

THE POWER OF CIRCUMSTANCES

That man is a creature of circumstance is an oft-repeated phrase, and while it is usually uttered without much reflection, it nevertheless represents a thought that has been crystallized from untold ages of experience. That it is true of the mind as well as of the life and fortunes of men is a much more modern conception, and one that is by no means universally accepted. After biology began to be scientifically studied the tendency was to class psychic along with vital phenomena, and to assume that what was true of the body must also be true of the mind. And as it was obvious that the circumstances surrounding an animal or a human being during life have no power to modify the body, when such influences are compared with those of heredity in shaping its form and determining its character, it was concluded that the same must be true of the mind. This was and still is looked upon as the scientific view par excellence, and the opposite view, that circumstances determine the character of the mind to any considerable degree, is considered a mere popular notion, devoid of scientific basis. Galton clearly expresses this supposed scientific view when he says:

"I have no patience with the hypothesis occasionally expressed, and often implied, especially in tales written to teach children to be good, that babies are born pretty much alike, and that the sole agencies in creating differences between boy and boy, and man and man, are steady application and moral effort. It is in the most unqualified manner that I object to pretensions of natural equality."

Now the fallacy here is in supposing that the mind is nothing but the brain. It would be all true of the brain, for the brain is simply a part of the body, and whatever is true of the whole body is true of its parts. But it is not true of the mind, because the mind is something besides the brain. It is also something more than intellect. I have defined intelligence as intellect plus knowledge. The mind, as we have been treating it, is the whole of intelligence with all the moral (affective) attributes added. It is the working force of society. The intellect, or the brain, if any one prefers, is a sort of receptacle, and knowledge is its contents.

Let us suppose there to exist hundreds of thousands of boxes, made after a sort of common pattern as regards size and shape, but differing enormously both in the materials of which they are made and the workmanship displayed in making them. Some of them are made of the finest mahogany or rosewood, and are beautifully polished, paneled, and veneered, or exquisitely carved without and inlaid with gold or precious stones. Others are made of very coarse material and not even dressed. Some may even be made of straw paper, incapable of resisting any strain whatever. Between these extremes there are all conceivable degrees of difference in both respects, but all except the very poorest are constructed of substantial materials and firmly put together. Let us next suppose all these boxes to be filled with something—filled with every thinkable kind of objects—the contents to differ in value far more than do the boxes themselves. Some are filled with silver or gold, or with pearls of great price, or large diamonds of the first water. Others are filled with common pebbles gathered on the beach, or with rough angular stones of the gravel-pit, with impure sand, or even with sawdust. And between these extremes again there are all conceivable degrees in the value of the contents of the boxes.

Now the boxes typify the brain, or the intellect, the "preefficients" of intelligence or of mind. The contents, on the contrary, typify the acquired qualities, experience, education, training, study, and meditation, in a word, knowledge—the possessions of the mind—everything that has been added to the original substratum. All except the very poorest strawboard intellects (idiots) are capable, like the boxes, however rudely made, of holding any of the things that are put into them and of preserving them securely. Just as the coarse boxes, made of undressed lumber, will hold the pearls and diamonds as well and safely as the most highly wrought rosewood boxes, so the common intellects of all but the congenitally feeble-minded will hold the greatest truths that have ever been discovered, and just as the rough boxes are capable of being smoothed off, and, when made of firm and fine-grained lumber, may even take a high polish, so the cruder intellects may be cultivated, refined, and polished.

According to this figure the mind is represented by both the boxes and their contents, and it can be readily seen that the contents may be of vastly greater value than the box. One can put sawdust into mahogany boxes and diamonds into those of rude oak. In fact, this is what is constantly happening with the minds of men. It is only when pearls find their way into rosewood boxes that true genius comes forth. The so-called scientific view above mentioned, that no external influences have any power to affect the mind, relates entirely to the boxes and ignores their contents altogether. We may suppose the boxes to be some sort of conventional thing that cannot be changed, but it is always possible to put anything whatever into any box. Over the contents society has a complete control, however fixed may be the receptacle. Why is it not just as scientific to deal with the contents as to deal with the receptacle? It certainly is not scientific to pretend to be dealing with the mind and to ignore the contents of the mind. As a matter of fact, there is not such an essential difference between intellects as to prevent most sane persons from storing their minds with useful knowledge and making good use of such stores when possessed, and almost all the differences that exist among minds are due to differences in their contents. This in turn is due to differences in the experience that different persons have.

The desirable thing would of course be to find a case of a human mind of normal capacity which had had no experience. This is obviously impossible, and the next thing to it would be to find a normal human being who had been so sequestrated during all his early life as never to have come into contact with other human beings. There is quite an array of alleged cases of this kind, but when we investigate them we find them of little value. The oft-repeated story of Psammetichus who secluded twenty new-born children so that they should never hear any one speak, in order to ascertain what natural language would be, is too poorly authenticated and too imperfectly told to have any scientific value. We know still less of Hai ben Yokthan, and he is probably a myth. The wild girl of Champagne had a rudimentary moral sense at least, but apparently no intelligence. Kaspar Hauser was a real character, and we know something of him after he revealed himself, but nothing of his seclusion. It seems not to have been so complete as to prevent him from learning to talk. Rauber has shown that persons belonging to civilized races condemned to complete isolation acquire no trace of a language. Doubtless a sufficient number of such thrown together for a long period would learn to communicate. The children thus isolated by Psammetichus are said to have learned to bleat in imitation of the goat that suckled them, and in other cases persons thus secluded are reported to have uttered sounds resembling the cries of wild animals with which they had associated; all of which shows, as I have stated, that the language of animals is confined to one part of speech, the interjection, and also that the interjection, which constitutes the language of feeling, was the part of speech earliest to be developed.

Father Xavier when a missionary in India was told by the emperor Akbar that an experiment had been made there to determine the origin of language. It consisted in raising thirty children together in an inclosed space, guarded and supplied with food and nurses condemned to silence under pain of death. The children were said to have grown up mute and stupid, having for their language only a few gestures relating to their animal wants.

But why should all the stress be laid, as has been the case in all discussions of this question, on the subject of language? Language is important and its origin interesting, but it is not all. The real question is, What kind of minds would persons thus isolated have? It is only too obvious that their minds would be almost completely blank. No amount of native mental capacity could prevent this. A Bacon or a Descartes, if made the subject of such an experiment, would get no farther than one of moderate powers. He would appear to ordinary persons a fool. Locke was right. Mind without experience is a blank sheet of paper or an empty cabinet. The substratum of mind is nothing until it is supplied with something to exercise itself upon. The real character of the human mind depends upon its contents, and men's minds differ mainly according to what they contain. Henry George has expressed this admirably:

"Take a number of infants born of the most civilized parents and transport them to an uninhabited country. Suppose them in some miraculous way to be sustained until they come of age to take care of themselves, and what would you have? More helpless savages than any we know of. They would have fire to discover; the rudest tools and weapons to invent; language to construct. They would, in short, have to stumble their way to the simplest knowledge which the lowest races now possess, just as a child learns to walk. That they would in time do all these things I have not the slightest doubt, for all these possibilities are latent in the human frame, but I do not believe they would do them any better or worse, any slower or quicker, than the children of barbarian parents placed in the same conditions. Given the very highest mental powers that exceptional individuals have ever displayed, and what could mankind be if one generation were separated from the next by an interval of time, as are the seventeen year locusts? One such interval would reduce mankind, not to savagery, but to a condition compared with which savagery, as we know it, would seem civilization."

Even this falls short of the whole truth embodied in social continuity.

If we reflect a moment it is easy to see that the differences in men's experiences are infinite. No two persons can or ever do have the same experience. Even between Siamese twins there must be some difference. Nor is it desirable that many persons should have the same experiences. What we call a "community" is a number of persons occupying the same area, governed by the same laws, acquainted with the same facts, having largely the same opinions and even the same sentiments. A long continuance of these conditions leads to degeneracy. Certain kinds of knowledge even, such as that furnished by village gossip, may deteriorate the mind.

But it is worthless knowledge. No useful knowledge can do any harm by being shared by a whole community. If most useful knowledge could be shared by all it would so far equalize men's minds that all the now current theories of the essential differences between them would be abandoned. There would certainly remain qualitative differences, and this is as it should be, but the present aristocracy of brains would be shown to have been nothing but monopoly of privilege.

It is circumstances that determine the contents of the mind, and therefore the principal differences in the minds of men are due to circumstances. This explains the power of circumstances. This was seen even by Confucius, who said: "By nature we nearly resemble one another; condition separates us very far." Adam Smith says:

"The difference of natural talent in different men is, in reality, much less than we are aware of; and the very different genius which appears to distinguish men of different professions, when grown up to maturity, is not, upon many occasions, so much the cause, as the effect of the division of labour. The difference between the most dissimilar characters, between a philosopher and a common street porter, for example, seems to arise not so much from nature as from habit, custom, and education. When they came into the world, and for the first six or eight years of their existence, they were, perhaps, very much alike, and neither their parents nor playfellows could perceive any remarkable difference. About that age, or soon after, they come to be employed in very different occupations. The difference of talents comes then to be taken notice of, and widens by degrees, till at last the vanity of the philosopher is willing to acknowledge scarce any resemblance."

Helvetius remarks:

"We may apply to simple citizens what I have said of empires. We see in the same way that their elevation or their decline, their good fortune or their misfortune, are the products of a certain combination of circumstances and of an infinity of accidents, unforeseen and sterile in appearance."

De Condolle, as we have seen, ascribes far more to circumstances than to heredity. The rise of great men to eminence and the principal external causes favorable to their success have been enumerated in a previous chapter. We need here, therefore, cite only a few passages that we find scattered through his book:

"Celebrity is still less hereditary than speciality. It is never anything but an exception, determined by various causes rarely combined. For a man to become celebrated it is not necessary that he be endowed with a great capacity. There must be circumstances favorable to him, and especially the will to act, and to show himself or to be useful. . . . The adaptation to external circumstances becomes then the principal thing in determining his success. . . . The way of conducting himself and of working, the absence of certain causes of distraction, a more habitual surveillance on the part of his father, in a word, moral and family influences, are more effective than a purely hereditary transmission of faculties appropriate to science. . . . Physiological laws are the same for all men. Therefore education in each family, example and advice given, must have exerted a more marked influence than heredity upon the special career of young scientists."

John Stuart Mill, speaking entirely from the economic standpoint and not at all from that of achievement, still very well says:

"It is true that the lot of individuals is not wholly independent of their virtue and intelligence; these do really tell in their favor, but far less than many other things in which there is no merit at all. The most powerful of all the determining circumstances is birth. The great majority are what they were born to be. Some are born rich without work, others are born to a position in which they can become rich by work, the great majority are born to hard work and poverty throughout life, numbers to indigence. Next to birth the chief cause of success in life is accident and opportunity. When a person not born to riches succeeds in acquiring them, his own industry and dexterity would not have sufficed unless there had been also a concurrence of occasions and chances which falls to the lot of only a small number."

Henry George was an egalitarian, and his little book on *Progress and Poverty* contains many true sayings. One of these is in line with the thought of this chapter:

"That the current philosophy, which attributes social progress to changes wrought in the nature of man, does not accord with historical facts, we have already seen. And we may also see, if we consider them, that the differences between communities in different stages of civilisation cannot be ascribed to innate differences in the individuals who compose these communities. That there are natural differences is true, and that there is such a thing as hereditary transmission of peculiarities is undoubtedly true; but the great differences between men in different states of society cannot be explained, in this way. The influence of heredity, which it is now the fashion to rate so highly, is as nothing compared with the influences which mold the man after he comes into the world.

Mr. George Gunton is quite an apostle of opportunity, though, like most of his class, his standpoint is economic. It is, however, true, as he says, that "all religious, educational, and reformatory institutions are based upon the idea that the environment is more powerful than heredity as a factor in determining the wants and habits of man. Indeed, it is only on the condition that the general environment remains unchanged, that it is claimed that the internal or hereditary qualities govern the tendency of character."

There is a great deal of literature on the subject of the relative intellectual capacity of moderns versus ancients, and many foolish things have been said, but all seem to agree that the historic period has not added much to the native brain power of mankind. Very few, however, have perceived the important corollary that grows out of this conclusion. Buckle was one of the few to see it, and he expressed it in these words:

"Whatever, therefore, the moral and intellectual progress of men may be, it resolves itself not into a progress of natural capacity, but into a progress, if I may so say, of opportunity; that is, an improvement in the circumstances under which that capacity after birth comes into play. Here then lies the gist of the whole matter. The progress is one, not of internal power, but of external advantage."

The Mother of Circumstances.—As the reader probably knows, I discussed the general subject of opportunity and advantageous circumstances in the concluding chapter of *Dynamic Sociology* and specified circumstances as fundamental, saying:

"There is one such fundamental circumstance which may, from this point of view, be regarded as the mother of circumstances. This consists in an initial acquaintance with the given field of labor—knowledge that such a field exists. There has been no discoverer so great in this world as to owe nothing to this circumstance, none who might not have lived and died in the profoundest obscurity had not some external force first lifted him to that height, however humble, from which he was able, more or less clearly to overlook the field of his future labors; none, who, had he chanced to live in another land or a prior age, could have achieved results which he was enabled to achieve under the actual circumstances. The number of Newtons who may really be said never to have had an opportunity to watch an apple fall to the ground, may be great; for to the sons of toil and want and circumscribed existence, reflection even is forbidden. It is just this initial circumstance, this vision of the promised land, that education is specially adapted to furnish to those naturally bright minds whom fortune has restricted to dark and narrow regions."

Buckle says:

"The child born in a civilized land is not likely, as such, to be superior to one born among barbarians; and the difference which ensues between the acts of the two children will be caused, so far as we know, solely by the pressure of external circumstances; by which I mean the surrounding opinions, knowledge, associations; in a word, the entire mental atmosphere in which the two children are respectively nurtured."

Suppose the child born among barbarians to be one who, if born among civilized people, would have become a great author, philosopher, scientific discoverer, or inventor. It is clear that owing to his circumstances he can never become any of these. All that the hereditarians can say is that, having superior genius, he may distinguish himself among the barbarians with whom his lot is cast; may invent better weapons, show superior cunning in outwitting enemies, and may possibly be made the ruler of a tribe. Such things have happened. But with his superior mental powers, capable if properly placed of working in the highest field, he must, in consequence of his circumstances alone, labor in a very low field. And yet he is wholly unconscious of his true powers and imagines that he is at his proper level.

But we need not contrast civilized with uncivilized races. There is ample room for contrast between persons living under different circumstances in civilized countries. None of the great men of letters or of science could have attained to the place they occupy if they had been cut off permanently from all knowledge of the field they finally entered. Something must happen to each and every one of them that gives him some glimpse of his future life and arouses his ambition to strive for it. The local environment often performs this serveice. Goethe, speaking of Beranger, who, though poor, was born in the metropolis and lived in the midst of its throbbing, quickening pulsations, is reported by Eckermann to have said:

"But imagine this same Beranger—instead of being born in Paris, and brought up in this metropolis of the world— the son of a poor tailor in Jena or Weimar, and let him commence his career, in an equally miserable manner, in such small places, and ask yourself what fruit would have been produced by this same tree, grown in such soil and in such an atmosphere."

As Professor Cooley says: "A man can hardly fix his ambition upon a literary career when he is perfectly unaware, as millions are, that such a thing as a literary career exists. It is the same with a scientific career. I know this from my own experience. Roaming wildly over the boundless prairies of northern Iowa in the fifties, interested in every animal, bird, insect, and flower I saw, but not knowing what science was, scarcely having ever heard of zoology, ornithology, entomology, or botany, without a single book on any of these subjects, and not knowing a person in the world who could give me the slightest information with regard to them, what chance was there of my becoming a naturalist? It was twenty years before I found my opportunity, and then it was almost too late. A clear view of a congenial field is the one fundamental circumstance in any one's career."

EQUALIZATION OF OPPORTUNITY

There are differences not only in the talents of men but also in their tastes. It is in these latter rather than in the former that they differ by nature. Almost any one has sufficient talent to cultivate almost any field, but there is little hope of success unless the field coincides with his tastes or preferences. True, there is great adaptability, and if one must work in a particular field one can reconcile one's self to it and plod through after a fashion. It is even possible and somewhat common for any one to arouse a certain interest in whatever he is obliged to do. It is fortunate that this is so. But I believe it applies mainly to routine work. I have several times found myself taking quite a strong interest in some kind of routine work that I was compelled to do, which, after I finally left it and engaged in higher work suited to my tastes, I looked back upon and wondered how I could have been interested in it. My experience is probably that of many similarly circumstanced. But there are kinds of high-grade work, even scientific, that are strongly distasteful to me, and which I do not think I could bring myself ever to enjoy. This is also, in all probability, a common occurrence. It is a truism that any one can do more and better work in a field of his own choosing. It may be compared to rowing with the tide or current, while working in an uncongenial field is like stemming the tide or the current. The result in either case is the algebraic sum of personal effort and a natural force, but in the first case both have the plus sign, while in the second one has the minus sign.

Difficult or impossible as it may be to forecast the talent of an untried mind, it is far more difficult and more certainly impossible to forecast its tastes and preferences. If we cannot select in advance the "exceptional man," much less can we pick out for him his career. The only thing that can be done is to equalize opportunities, so as not only to enable the really exceptional man to demonstrate the fact, but to make the open avenues so numerous and so easy to travel that he will be sure to find the one to which he is best adapted by nature. In this way the negative terms of the equation are eliminated and the entire energy of society is set free. There would then be no square pegs in round holes, and the right man would always be in the right place. It may be said that in view of the small number of progressive minds it is not economical to extend opportunities to all the dolts and dunces merely in the hope that a few bright minds may take advantage of them. This is the oligocentric argument. We have seen how false is the assumption that genius is rare. But even admitting that it is rare, and that mediocrity predominates, there are all gradations in that mediocrity, and the social value of even the lowest types of mind, above pathological feeble-mindedness, would be increased by giving them a chance to work up to the full measure of their powers.

The economic aspect is of course the final test. It is the end. But we are here dealing with the means to the end, viz, achievement. In considering the equalization of opportunities we now more especially mean the opportunity to achieve. The whole difficulty with the discussion of social questions has always been this haste to deal with the end, this impatience with everything that relates to the means. This is why so little progress has been made with the questions. The fact is, that the end can only be attained through means. All attempts to reach the end directly are destined to fail. I apprehend that most of the disappointment with this book will be due to my inability to deal with ends, and to the necessity of clinging to the means as the only way by which ends can be attained. But it will be remembered that this was also the method pursued in *Dynamic Sociology*. I there showed that the means constitute a series growing more and more remote from the end, that this series consists of five terms, that not only the end itself but no less than four of the terms of the series are practically beyond the reach of social action, and that not until the fifth term of the series is reached do we find anything tangible, anything upon which society can directly lay hold and exert its power to change, modify, and improve. But it was also found that the entire series of means are so related and dependent, each upon the immediately antecedent one, that whatever affects any one affects all above it, so that it is not necessary to apply force to any of the intermediate terms, as the force applied to the most remote term is communicated automatically through the entire series and ultimately expends itself without loss in transmission upon the end itself. The rude comparison made of a row of bricks stood on end, of which it is only necessary to touch the first one to see them all fall in succession, is a perfect illustration of the process and one within the comprehension of all. The entire second volume of that work is devoted to the logical discussion of the relation of the end to these several means, and to the proof that society need concern itself only with the most remote term of the series, over which it has complete control. All the other terms may be safely left to take care of themselves, and whatever effects can be wrought in this remote term, there called the "initial means," will certainly reach and correspondingly affect the end.

We are now again confronted with practically the same problem. The economic conditions constitute the end, and it is not different from the end described in the earlier treatise. The equalization of opportunity is the tangible, realizable means, and it is the same means as before. The difference in both the end and the means is only a difference in the names. I was simply more strictly philosophical then, and reduced the economic conditions to the bed-rock of human happiness, to which complexion they must come at last; and I called the equalization of opportunity education, but surely the whole trend, drift, and logic of this and the preceding chapter have been to pile up the evidence that all influences, all environments, and all opportunities converge to this one focal point, resolve themselves into and constitute education.

There is no use in talking about the equalization of wealth. Much of the discussion about "equal rights" is utterly hollow. All the ado made over the system of contract is surcharged with fallacy. There can be no equality and no justice, not to speak of equity, so long as society is composed of members, equally endowed by nature, a few of whom only possess the social heritage of truth and ideas resulting from the laborious investigation and profound meditations of all past ages, while the great mass are shut out from all the light that human achievement has shed upon the world. The equalization of opportunity means the equalization of intelligence, and not until this is attained is there any virtue or any hope in schemes for the equalization of the material resources of society.

SELECTIONS FROM *FOLKWAYS*

By WILLIAM GRAHAM SUMNER

Definition and mode of origin of the Folkways. If we put together all that we have learned from anthropology and ethnography about primitive men and primitive society, we perceive that the first task of life is to live. Men begin with acts, not with thoughts. Every moment brings necessities which must be satisfied at once. Need was the first experience, and it was followed at once by a blundering effort to satisfy it. It is generally taken for granted that men inherited some guiding instincts from their beast ancestry, and it may be true, although it has never been proved. If there were such inheritances, they controlled and aided the first efforts to satisfy needs. Analogy makes it easy to assume that the ways of beasts had produced channels of habit and predisposition along which dexterities and other psychophysical activities would run easily. Experiments with newborn animals show that in the absence of any experience of the relation of means to ends, efforts to satisfy needs are clumsy and blundering. The method is that of trial and failure, which produces repeated pain, loss, and disappointments. Nevertheless, it is a method of rude experiment and selection. The earliest efforts of men were of this kind. Need was the impelling force. Pleasure and pain, on the one side and the other, were the rude constraints which defined the line on which efforts must proceed. The ability to distinguish between pleasure and pain is the only physical power which is to be assumed. Thus ways of doing things were selected, which were expedient. They answered the purpose better than other ways, or with less toil and pain. Along the course in which efforts were compelled to go, habit, routine, and skill were developed. The struggle to maintain existence was carried on, not individually, but in groups. Each profited by the other's experience; hence there was concurrence towards that which proved to be most expedient. All at last adopted the same way for the same purpose; hence the ways turned into customs and became mass phenomena. Instincts were developed in connection with them. In this way folkways arise. The young learn them by tradition, imitation, and authority. The folkways, at a time, provide for all the needs of life then and there. They are uniform, universal in the group, imperative, and invariable. As time goes on, the folkways become more and more arbitrary, positive, and imperative. If asked why they act in a certain way in certain cases, primitive people always answer that it is because they and their ancestors always have done so. A sanction also arises from ghost fear. The ghosts of ancestors would be angry if the living should change the ancient folkways.

The folkways are a societal force. The operation by which folkways are produced consists in the frequent repetition of petty acts, often by great numbers acting in concert or, at least, acting in the same way when face to face with the same need. The immediate motive is interest. It produces habit in the individual and custom in the group. It is, therefore, in the highest degree original and primitive. By habit and custom it exerts a strain on every individual within its range; therefore it rises to a societal force to which great classes of societal phenomena are due. Its earliest stages, its course, and laws may be studied; also its influence on individuals and their reaction on it. It is our present purpose so to study it. We have to recognize it as one of the chief forces by which a society is made to be what it is. Out of the unconscious experiment which every repetition of the ways includes, there issues pleasure or pain, and then, so far as the men are capable of reflection, convictions that the ways are conductive to societal welfare. These two experiences are not the same. The most uncivilized men, both in the food quest and in war, do things which are painful, but which have been found to be expedient. Perhaps these cases teach the sense of social welfare better than those which are pleasurable and favorable to welfare. The former cases call for some intelligent reflection on experience. When this conviction as to the relation to welfare is added to the folkways they are converted into mores, and, by virtue of the philosophical and ethical element added to them, they win utility and importance and become the source of the science and the art of living.

Folkways are made unconsciously. It is of the first importance to notice that, from the first acts by which men try to satisfy needs, each act stands by itself, and looks no further than the immediate satisfaction. From recurrent needs arise habits for the individual and customs for the group, but these results are consequences which were never conscious, and never foreseen or intended. They are not noticed until they have long existed, and it is still longer before they are appreciated. Another long time must pass, and a higher stage of mental development must be reached, before they can be used as a basis from which pressure can be foreseen. The folkways, therefore are not creations of human purpose and wit. They are like products of natural forces which men unconsciously set in operation, or they are like the instinctive ways of animals, which are developed out of experience, which reach a final form of maximum adaptation to an interest, which are handed down by tradition and admit of no exception or variation, yet change to meet new conditions, still within the same limited methods, and without rational reflection or purpose. From this it results that all the life of human beings, in all ages and stages of culture, is primarily controlled by a vast mass of folkways handed down from the earliest existence of the race, having the nature of the ways of other animals, only the top-most layers of which are subject to change and control, and have been somewhat modified by human philosophy, ethics, and religion, or by other acts of intelligent reflection. We are told of savages that "It is difficult to exhaust the customs and small ceremonial usages of a savage people. Custom regulates the whole of a man's actions,—his bathing, washing, cutting his hair, eating, drinking, and fasting. From his cradle to his grave he is the slave of ancient usage. In his life there is nothing free, nothing original, nothing spontaneous, no progress towards a higher and better life, and no attempt to improve his condition, mentally, morally, or spiritually." All men act in this way with only a little wider margin of voluntary variation.

The aleatory interest. If we should try to find a specimen society in which expedient ways of satisfying needs and interests were found by trial and failure, and by long selection from experience, as broadly described above, it might be impossible to find one. Such a practical and utilitarian mode of procedure, even when mixed with ghost sanction, is rationalistic. It would not be suited to the ways and temper of primitive men. There was an element in the most elementary experience which was irrational and defied all expedient methods. One might use the best known means with the greatest care, yet fail of the result. On the other hand, one might get a great result with no effort at all. One might also incur a calamity without any fault of his own. This was the aleatory element in life, the element of risk and loss, good or bad fortune. This element is never absent from the affairs of men. It has greatly influenced their life philosophy and policy. On one side, good luck may mean something for nothing, the extreme case of prosperity and felicity. On the other side, ill luck may mean failure, loss, calamity, and disappointment, in spite of the most earnest and well-planned endeavor. The minds of men always dwell more on bad luck. They accept ordinary prosperity as a matter of course. Misfortunes arrest their attention and remain in their memory. Hence the ills of life are the mode of manifestation of the aleatory element which has most affected life policy. Primitive men ascribed all incidents to the agency of men or of ghosts and spirits. Good and ill luck were attributed to the superior powers, and were supposed to be due to their pleasure or displeasure at the conduct of men. This group of notions constitutes goblinism. It furnishes a complete world philosophy. The element of luck is always present in the struggle for existence. That is why primitive men never could carry on the struggle for existence, disregarding the aleatory element and employing a utilitarian method only. The aleatory element has always been the connecting link between the struggle for existence and religion. It was only by religious rites that the aleatory element in the struggle for existence could be controlled. The notions of ghosts, demons, another world, etc., were all fantastic. They lacked all connection with facts, and were arbitrary constructions put upon experience. They were poetic and developed by poetic construction and imaginative deduction. The nexus between them and events was not cause and effect, but magic. They therefore led to delusive deductions in regard to life and its meaning, which entered into subsequent action as guiding faiths, and imperative notions about the conditions of success. The authority of religion and that of custom coalesced into one indivisible obligation. Therefore the simple statement of experiment and expediency in the first paragraph above is not derived directly from actual cases, but is a product of analysis and inference. It must also be added that vanity and ghost fear produced needs which man was as eager to satisfy as those of hunger or the family. Folkways resulted for the former as well as for the latter.

THE MORES CAN MAKE ANYTHING RIGHT AND PREVENT CONDEMNATION OF ANYTHING

Mores define the limits which make anything right. At every turn we find new evidence that the mores can make anything right. What they do is that they cover a usage in dress, language, behavior, manners, etc., with the mantle of current custom, and give it regulation and limits within which it becomes unquestionable. The limit is generally a limit of toleration. Literature, pictures, exhibitions, celebrations, and festivals are controlled by some undefined, and probably undefinable, standard of decency and propriety, which sets a limit of toleration on the appeals to fun, sensuality, and various prejudices. In regard to all social customs, the mores sanction them by defining them and giving them form. Such regulated customs are etiquette. The regulation by the mores always gives order and form, and thus surrounds life with limits within which we may and beyond which we may not pursue our interests (e. g. property and marriage). Horseplay and practical jokes have been tolerated, at various times and places, at weddings. They require good-natured toleration, but soon run to excess and may become unendurable. The mores set the limits or define the disapproval. The wedding journey was invented to escape the "jokes." The rice and old shoes will soon be tabooed. The mores fluctuate in their prescriptions. If the limits are too narrow, there is an overflow into vice and abuse, as was proved by seventeenth-century puritanism in England. If the limit is too remote, there is no discipline, and the regulation fails of its purpose. Then a corruption of manners ensues. In the cases now to be given we shall see the power of the mores to give validity to various customs. The cases are all such that we may see in them sanction and currency given to things which seem to us contrary to simple and self-evident rules of right; that is, they are contrary to the views now inculcated in us by our own moves as axiomatic and beyond the need of proof.

Punishments for crime. Mediaeval punishments for criminals, leaving out of account heretics and witches, bore witness to the grossness, obscenity, inhumanity, and ferocity of the mores of that age. The punishments were not thought wrong or questionable. There was no revolt against them in any one's mind. They were judged right, wise, and necessary, by full public opinion. They were not on the outer boundary of the mores, but in the core of them. Schultz says that the romancers have not exaggerated the horrors of mediaeval dungeons. Many of them still remain and are shown to horrified tourists. There was no arrangement for having them cleaned by anybody, so that in time they were sure to become horribly dangerous to health. They were small, dark, damp, cold and infested by vermin, rats, snakes, etc. Several dungeons in the Bastille were so constructed that the prisoners could neither sit, stand, nor lie, in comfort. Fiendish ingenuity was expended on the invention of refinements of suffering, and executions offered public exhibitions in which the worst vices in the mores of the time were fed and strengthened. Many punishments were not only cruel, but obscene, the cruelty and obscenity being destitute of moral or civil motive and only serving to gratify malignant passion. A case is mentioned of a law in which it was provided that if a criminal had no property, his wife should be violated by a public official as a penalty. In the later Middle Ages, after torture was introduced into civil proceedings, ingenuity and "artistic skill' were manifested in inventing instruments of torture. A case is given of extravagant cruelty and tyranny on the part of a man of rank towards a cook who had displeased him. It was impossible to obtain protection or redress. The standpoint of the ages was that a man of rank must be allowed full discretion in dealing with a cook. In many cases details were added to punishments, which were intended to reach the affections, mental states, faiths, etc., of the accused, and add mental agony to physical pain. "Use and wont" exercised their influence on people who saw or heard of these acts of the authorities until cruelties and horrors became commonplace and familiar, and the lust of cruelty was a characteristic of the age.

Prisons in England in the time of Queen Anne. The prisons of England, in Queen Anne's time were sinks of misery, disease, cruelty, and extortions, from which debtors suffered most, on account of their poverty. Women contributed to the total loathsomeness and suffered from it. The Marshalsea prison was "an infected pest house all the year long." There

SELECTIONS FROM FOLKWAYS 575

were customs by which jailers and chaplains extorted fees from the miserable prisoners. In the country the prisons were worse than in London. Pictures are said to exist in which debtor prisoners are shown catching mice for food, dying of starvation and malaria, covered with boils and blains, assaulted by jailers, imprisoned in underground dungeons, living with hogs, with clogs on their legs, tortured with thumbscrews, etc. "Nobody ever seems to have bothered their heads about it. It was not their business." In 1702 the House of Commons ordered a bill to be brought in for regulating the king's bench and fleet prisons, "but nobody took sufficient interest in it, and it never became an act." If the grade and kind of humanity which the case required did not exist in the mores of the time, there would be no response. It was on the humanitarian wave of the latter half of the century that Howard succeeded in bringing about a reform. The prisons in the American colonies were of the same kind as those in the old country. The Tories, in the revolution, suffered most from their badness. It is not known that personal abuse was perpetrated in them.

Wars of factions. Penalties of defeat. Political factions and religious sects have always far surpassed the criminal law in the ferocity of their penalties against each other. Neither the offenses nor the penalties are defined in advance. As Lea says, the treatment of Alberico, brother of Ezzelino da Romano, and his family (1259) shows the ferocity of the age. Ezzelino showed the same in many cases, and the hatred heaped up against him is easily understood, but the gratification of it was beastly and demonic. Great persons, after winning positions of power, used all their resources to crush old rivals or opponents (Clement V, John XXII) and to exult over the suffering they could inflict. In the case of Wullenweber, at Lubeck, burgesses of cities manifested the same ferocity in faction fights. The history of city after city contains similar episodes. At Ghent, in 1530, the handi-craftsmen got the upper hand for a time and used it like savages. All parties fought out social antagonisms without reserve on the doctrine: To the victors the spoils; to the vanquished the woe! If two parties got into a controversy about such a question as whether Christ and his apostles lived by beggary, they understood that the victorious party in the controversy would burn the defeated party. That was the rule of the game and they went into it on that understanding.

In all these matters the mores of the time set the notions of what was right, or those limits within which conduct must always be kept. No one blamed the conduct on general grounds of wrong and excess, or of broad social inexpediency. The mores of the time were absolutely imperative as to some matters (e. g. duties of church ritual), but did not give any guidance as to the matters here mentioned. In fact, the mores prevented any unfavorable criticism of those matters or any independent judgment about them.

Bundling. One of the most extraordinary instances of what the mores can do to legitimize a custom which, when rationally judged, seems inconsistent with the most elementary requirements of the sex taboo, is bundling. In Latin Europe generally, especially amongst the upper classes, it is not allowed that a young man and a young woman shall be alone together even by day, and the freer usage in England, and still more in the United States, is regarded as improper and contrary to good manners. In the latter countries two young people, if alone together, do not think of transgressing the rules of propriety as set by custom in the society. Such was the case also with night visits. Although the custom was free, and although better taste and judgment have abolished it, yet it was defined and regulated, and was never a proof of licentious manners. It is found amongst uncivilized people, but is hardly to be regarded as a survival in higher civilization. Christians, in the third and fourth centuries, practiced it, even without the limiting conditions which were set in the Middle Ages. Having determined to renounce sex as an evil, they sought to test themselves by extreme temptation. It was a test or proof of the power of moral rule over natural impulse. "It was a widely spread custom in both the east and the west of the Roman empire to live with virgins. Distinguished persons, including one of the greatest bishops of the empire, who was also one of the greatest theologians, joined in the custom. Public opinion in the church judged them lightly, although unfavorably." "After the church took on the episcopal constitution, it persecuted and drove out the subintroductae. They were regarded as a survival from the old church which was disapproved. The custom that virgins dwelt in the house with men arose in the oldest period of the Christian church." "They did not think of any evil as to be apprehended." "In fact, we have only a little clear evidence that the living together did not correspond in the long run to the assumptions on which it was based." The custom was abolished in the sixth century. "Spiritual marriage" was connected with the monastic profession and both were due to the ascetic tendency of the time. "From the time when we can clearly find monastic associations in existence, we find hermits living in comradeship with nuns." We are led back to Jewish association. The custom is older than Christianity. The custom at Corinth was but imitation of Jewish "God worshipers" or "Praying women." The Therapeuts had such companions. Their houses of worship were arranged to separate the sexes. Their dances sometimes lasted all night. In the Middle Ages several sects who renounced marriage introduced tests of great temptation. Individuals also, believing that they were carrying on the war between "the flesh" and "the spirit" subjected themselves to similar tests. These are not properly cases in the mores, but they illustrate the intervention of sectarian doctrines or views to traverse the efforts to satisfy interests, and so to disturb the mores.

Two forms of bundling. Two cases are to be distinguished: (1) night visits as a mode of wooing, (2) extreme intimacy between two persons who are under the sex taboo (one or both being married, or one or both vowed to celibacy), and who nevertheless observe the taboo.

Mediaeval bundling. The custom in the second form be-came common in the woman cult of the twelfth century and it spread all over Europe. As the vassal attended his lord to his bedchamber, so the knight his lady. The woman cult was an aggregation of poses and pretenses to enact a comedy of love, but not to satisfy erotic passion. The custom spread to the peasant classes in later centuries, and it extended to the Netherlands, Scandinavia, Switzerland, England, Scot-land, and Wales, but it took rather the first form in the lower classes and in the process of time. In building houses in Holland the windows were built conveniently for this custom. "In 1666-1667 every house on the island of Texel had an opening under the window where the lover could enter so as to sit on the bed and spend the night making love to the daughter of the house." The custom was called queesten. Parents encouraged it. A girl who had no quester was not esteemed. Rarely did any harm occur. If so, the man was mobbed and wounded or killed. The custom can be traced in North Holland down to the eighteenth century. This was the customary mode of wooing in the low countries and Scandinavia. In spite of the disapproval of both civil and ecclesiastical authorities, the custom continued just as round dances continue now, in spite of the disapproval of many parents, because a girl who should refuse to conform to current usage would be left out of the social movement. The lover was always one who would be accepted as a husband. If he exceeded the limits set by custom he was very hardly dealt with by the people of the village. The custom is re-ported from the Schwarzwald as late as 1780. It was there the regular method of wooing for classes who had to work all day. The lover was required to enter by the dormer window. Even still the custom is said to exist amongst the peasants of Germany, but it is restricted to one night in the month or in the year. Krasinski describes kissing games customary amongst the Unitarians of the Ukraine. He says that they are a Greek custom and he connects them with bundling.

Poverty and wooing. Amongst peasants there was little opportunity for the young people to become acquainted. When the cold season came they could not woo out of doors. The young women could not be protected by careful rules which would prevent wooing. They had to take risks and to take care of themselves. Poverty was the explanation of this custom in all civilized countries, although there was always in it an element of frolic and fun.

Night wooing in North American colonies. All the emigrants to North America were familiar with the custom. In the seventeenth century, in the colonies, the houses were small, poorly warmed, and inconvenient, allowing little privacy. No doubt this is the reason why the custom took new life in the colonies. Burnaby says that it was the custom amongst the lower classes of Massachusetts that a pair who contemplated marriage spent the night together in bed partly dressed. If they did not like each other they might not marry, unless the woman became pregnant. The custom was called "tarrying." It was due to poverty again. Modern inhabitants of tenement houses are constrained in their customs by the same limitation, and the effect is seen in their folkways. The custom of bundling had a wide range of variety. Two people sitting side by side might cover themselves with the same robe, or lie on the bed together for warmth. Peters defended the custom, which, he said, "prevails amongst all classes to the great honor of the country, its religion, and ladies." The older women resented the attempts of the ministers to preach against the custom. Sofas were introduced as an alternative. The country people thought the sofa less proper. In the middle of the eighteenth century the decline in social manners, which was attributed to the wars, caused the custom to produce more evil results. Also the greater wealth, larger houses, and better social arrangements changed the conditions and there was less need for the custom. It fell under social disapproval and was thrown out of the folkways. Stiles says that "it died hard" after the revolution. In 1788 a ballad in an almanac brought

the custom into popular ridicule. Stiles quotes the case of
Seger vs. Slingerland, in which the judge, in a case of seduc-
tion, held that parents who allowed bundling, although it
was the custom, could not recover.

Reasons for bundling. A witness before the Royal Commission on the Marriage Laws, 1868, testified that night
visiting was still common amongst the laboring classes in
some parts of Scotland. "They have no other means of intercourse." It was against custom for a lover to visit his sweet-
heart by day. As to the parents, "Their daughters must
have husbands and there is no other way of courting." This
statement sums up the reasons for this custom which, not
being a public custom, must have varied very much according to the character of individuals who used it. Attempts
were always made to control it by sanctions in public
opinion.

Public lupanars. Perhaps the most incredible case to illustrate the power of the mores to extend toleration and sanction to an evil thing remains to be mentioned,—the lupanars
which were supported by the mediaeval cities. Athenaeus
says that Solon caused female slaves to be bought by the
city and exposed in order to save other women from assaults
on their virtue. In later times prostitution was accepted as
inevitable, but it was not organized by the city. Salvianus
(fifth century, A. D.) represents the brothels as tolerated by
the Roman law in order to prevent adultery. Lupanars continued to exist from Roman times until the Middle Ages.
Those in southern Europe were recruited from the female
pilgrims from the north who set out for Rome or Palestine
and whose means failed them. It is another social phenomenon due to poverty and to a specious argument of protection to women in good position. This argument came
down by tradition with the institution. The city council of
Nuremberg stated, as a reason for establishing a lupanar,
that the church allowed harlots in order to prevent greater
evils. This statement, no doubt, refers to a passage in Augustine, De Ordine: "What is more base, empty of worth, and

full of vileness than harlots and other such pests? Take away harlots from human society and you will have tainted everything with lust. Let them be with the matrons and you will produce contamination and disgrace. So this class of persons, on account of their morals, of a most shameless life, fills a most vile function under the laws of order." The bishop had laid down the proposition that evil things in human society, under the great orderly scheme of things which he was trying to expound, are overruled to produce good. He then sought illustrations to prove this. The passage quoted is one of his illustrations. Everywhere else in his writings where he mentions harlots he expresses the greatest abomination of them. His general proposition is fallacious and extravagant, and he had to strain the cases which he alleged as illustrations, but he was a church father, and five hundred years later no one dared criticise or dissent from anything which he had said. It went far beyond the incidental use of an illustration made by him, to cite the passage, with his authority, for a doctrine that cities might wisely establish lupanars in order to prevent sex vice, especially in the interest of virtuous women. Such houses were maintained without secrecy or shame. Queen Joanna of Naples made ordinances for a lupanar at Avignon, in 1347, when it was the papal residence. Generally the house was rented to a "host" under stipulations as to the food, dress, and treatment of the inmates, and regulations as to order, gambling, etc. The inmates, like the public executioners, were required to wear a distinctive dress. Frequenters did not need to practice secrecy. The houses were free to persons of rank, and were especially prepared by the city when it had to entertain great persons. Women who were natives of the city were not admitted. This is the only feature which is not entirely cynical and shameless. In 1501 a rich citizen of Frankfurt-am Main bequeathed to the city a sum of money with which to build a large house into which all the great number of harlots could be collected, for the number increased greatly. They appeared at all great concourses of men, and were sent out to the Hansa stations. In fact, the people of the time accepted certain social phenomena as "natural" and inevitable, and they made their arrangements accordingly, uninterfered with by "moral sense." In Wyckliffe's time the bishop of Winchester obtained a handsome rent from the stews of Southwark. Probably he and his contemporaries thought no harm. Never until the nineteenth century was it in the mores of any society to feel that the sacrifice of the mortal welfare of one human being to the happiness of another was a thing which civil institutions could not tolerate. It could not enter into the minds of men of the fifteenth century that harlots, serfs, and other miserable classes had personal rights which were outraged by the customs and institutions of that time.

The end of the lupanars. All the authorities agree that the thing which put an end to the city lupanars was syphilis. It was not due to any moral or religious revolt, although there had been individuals who had criticised the institution of harlots, and some pious persons had founded convents, in the thirteenth and fourteenth centuries, for repentant harlots. Protestants and Catholics tried, to some extent, to throw the blame of the lupanars on each other. Luther urged the abolition of them in 1520. They reached their greatest development in the fifteenth century. The mere existence of an article so degrading to both husband and wife as the girdle is significant of the mores of the period, and shows how far the mores can go to make anything "right," or properly customary.

Judgement is beclouded by the atmosphere formed by the mores. Education. Witch persecutions are another case of the extent to which familiarity with the customs prevents any rational judgement of phenomena of experience and observation. How was it possible that men did not see the baseness and folly of their acts? The answer is that the idea of demonism were a part of the mental outfit of the period. The laws were traditions from generations which had drawn deductions from the doctrines of demonism and had applied them in criminal practice. The legal procedure was familiar and corresponded to the horror of crimes and criminals, of which witchcraft and witches were the worst. The mores formed a moral and civil atmosphere through which everything was seen, and rational judgment was made impossible. It cannot be doubted that, at any time, all ethical judgments are made through the atmosphere of the mores of the time. It is they which tell us what is right. It is only by high mental discipline that we can be trained to be above that atmosphere and form rational judgments on current cases. This mental independence and ethical power are the highest products of education. They are also perilous. Our worst cranks are those who get the independence and power, but cannot stand alone and form correct judgments outside of the mores of the time and place. It must be remembered that the mores sometimes becloud the judgment, but they more often guide it.

CONSPICUOUS CONSUMPTION*

By THORSTEIN VEBLEN

In what has been said of the evolution of the vicarious leisure class and its differentiation from the general body of the working classes, reference has been made to a further division of labour,—that between different servant classes. One portion of the servant class, chiefly those persons whose occupation is vicarious leisure, come to undertake a new, subsidiary range of duties—the vicarious consumption of goods. The most obvious form in which this consumption occurs is seen in the wearing of liveries and the occupation of spacious servants' quarters. Another, scarcely less obtrusive or less effective form of vicarious consumption, and a much more widely prevalent one, is the consumption of food, clothing, dwelling, and furniture by the lady and the rest of the domestic establishment.

But already at a point in economic evolution far antedating the emergence of the lady, specialised consumption of goods as an evidence of pecuniary strength had begun to work out in a more or less elaborate system. The beginning of a differentiation in consumption even antedates the appearance of anything that can fairly be called pecuniary strength. It is traceable back to the initial phase of predatory culture, and there is even a suggestion that an incipient differentiation in this respect lies back of the beginnings of the predatory life. This most primitive differentiation in the consumption of goods is like the later differentiation with which we are all so intimately familiar, in that it is largely of a ceremonial character, but unlike the latter it does not rest on a difference in accumulated wealth. The utility of consumption as an evidence of wealth is to be

* From *The Theory of the Leisure Class*

classed as a derivative growth. It is an adaptation to a new end, by a selective process, of a distinction previously existing and well established in men's habits of thought.

In the earlier phases of the predatory culture the only economic differentiation is a broad distinction between an honourable superior class made up of the able-bodied men on the one side, and a base inferior class of labouring women on the other. According to the ideal scheme of life in force at that time it is the office of the men to consume what the women produce. Such consumption as falls to the women is merely incidental to their work; it is a means to their continued labour, and not a consumption directed to their own comfort and fulness of life. Unproductive consumption of goods is honourable, primarily as a mark of prowess and a perquisite of human dignity; secondarily it becomes substantially honourable in itself, especially the consumption of the more desirable things. The consumption of choice articles of food, and frequently also of rare articles of adornment, becomes tabu to the women and children and if there is a base (servile) class of men, the tabu holds also for them. With a further advance in culture this tabu may change into simple custom of a more or less rigorous character; but whatever be the theoretical basis of the distinction which is maintained, whether it be a tabu or a larger conventionality, the features of the conventional scheme of consumption do not change easily. When the quasi-peaceable stage of industry is reached, with its fundamental institution of chattel slavery, the general principle, more or less rigorously applied, is that the base, industrious class should consume only what may be necessary to their subsistence. In the nature of things, luxuries and the comforts of life belong to the leisure class. Under the tabu, certain victuals, and more particularly certain beverages, are strictly reserved for the use of the superior class.

The ceremonial differentiation of the dietary is best seen in the use of intoxicating beverages and narcotics. If these articles of consumption are costly, they are felt to be noble and honorific. Therefore the base classes, primarily the women, practise an enforced continence with respect to these stimulants, except in countries where they are obtainable at a very low cost. From archaic times down through all the length of the patriarchal regime it has been the office of the women to prepare and administer these luxuries, and it has been the perquisite of the men of gentle birth and breeding to consume them. Drunkenness and the other pathological consequences of the free use of stimulants therefore tend in their turn to become honorific, as being a mark, at the second remove, of the superior status of those who are able to afford the indulgence. Infirmities induced by over-indulgence are among some peoples freely recognised as manly attributes. It has even happened that the name for certain diseased conditions of the body arising from such an origin has passed into everyday speech as a synonym for "noble" or "gentle." It is only at a relatively early stage of culture that the symptoms of expensive vice are conventionally accepted as marks of a superior status, and so tend to become virtues and command the deference of the community; but the reputability that attaches to certain expensive vices long retains so much of its force as to appreciably lessen the disapprobation visited upon the men of the wealthy or noble class for any excessive indulgence. The same invidious distinction adds force to the current disapproval of any indulgence of this kind on the part of women, minors, and inferiors. This invidious traditional distinction has not lost its force even among the more advanced peoples of to-day. Where the example set by the leisure class retains its imperative force in the regulation of the conventionalities, it is observable that the women still in great measure practise the same traditional continence with regard to stimulants.

This characterisation of the greater continence in the use of stimulants practised by the women of the reputable classes may seem an excessive refinement of logic at the expense of common sense. But facts within easy reach of any one who cares to know them go to say that the greater abstinence of women is in some part due to an imperative conventionality; and this conventionality is, in a general way, strongest where the patriarchal tradition—the tradition that the woman is a chattel—has retained its hold in greatest vigour. In a sense which has been greatly qualified in scope and rigour, but which has by no means lost its meaning even yet, this tradition says that the woman, being a chattel, should consume only what is necessary to her sustenance,— except so far as her further consumption contributes to the comfort or the good repute of her master. The consumption of luxuries, in the true sense, is a consumption directed to the comfort of the consumer himself, and is, therefore, a mark of the master. Any such consumption by others can take place only on a basis of sufferance. In communities where the popular habits of thought have been profoundly shaped by the patriarchal tradition we may accordingly look for survivals of the tabu on luxuries at least to the extent of a conventional deprecation of their use by the unfree and dependent class. This is more particularly true as regards certain luxuries, the use of which by the dependent class would detract sensibly from the comfort or pleasure of their masters, or which are held to be of doubtful legitimacy on other grounds. In the apprehension of the great conservative middle class of Western civilisation the use of these various stimulants is obnoxious to at least one, if not both, of these objections; and it is a fact too significant to be passed over that it is precisely among these middle classes of the Germanic culture, with their strong surviving sense of the patriarchal proprieties, that the women are to the greatest extent subject to a qualified tabu on narcotics and alcoholic beverages. With many qualifications—with more qualifications as the patriarchal tradition has gradually weakened— the general rule is felt to be right and binding that women should consume only for the benefit of their masters. The objection of course presents itself that expenditure on women's dress and household paraphernalia is an obvious exception to this rule; but it will appear in the sequel that this exception is much more obvious than substantial.

During the earlier stages of economic development, consumption of goods without stint, especially consumption of the better grades of goods,—ideally all consumption in excess of the subsistence minimum, pertains normally to the leisure class. This restriction tends to disappear, at least formally, after the later peaceable stage has been reached, with private ownership of goods and in an industrial system based on wage labour or on the petty household economy. But during the earlier quasi-peaceable stage, when so many of the traditions through which the institution of a leisure class has affected the economic life of later times were taking form and consistency, this principle has had the force of a conventional law. It has served as the norm to which consumption has tended to conform, and any appreciable departure from it is to be regarded as an aberrant form, sure to be eliminated sooner or later in the further course of development.

The quasi-peaceable gentleman of leisure, then, not only consumes of the staff of life beyond the minimum required for subsistence and physical efficiency, but his consumption also undergoes a specialisation as regards the quality of the goods consumed. He consumes freely and of the best, in food, drink, narcotics, shelter, services, ornaments, apparel, weapons and accoutrements, amusements, amulets, and idols or divinities. In the process of gradual amelioration which takes place in the articles of his consumption the motive principle and the proximate aim of innovation is no doubt the higher efficiency of the improved and more elaborate products for personal comfort and well-being. But that does not remain the sole purpose of their consumption. The canon of reputability is at hand and seizes upon such innovations as are, according to its standard, fit to survive. Since the consumption of these more excellent goods is an evidence of wealth, it becomes honorific; and conversely, the failure to consume in due quantity and quality becomes a mark of inferiority and demerit.

This growth of punctilious discrimination as to qualitative excellence in eating, drinking, etc., presently affects not only the manner of life, but also the training and intellectual activity of the gentleman of leisure. He is no longer simply the successful, aggressive male,—the man of strength, resource, and intrepidity. In order to avoid stultification he must also cultivate his tastes, for it now becomes incumbent on him to discriminate with some nicety between the noble and the ignoble in consumable goods. He becomes a connoisseur in creditable viands of various degrees of merit, in manly beverages and trinkets, in seemly apparel and architecture, in weapons, games, dancers, and the narcotics. This cultivation of the aesthetic faculty requires time and application, and the demands made upon the gentleman in this direction therefore tend to change his life of leisure into a more or less arduous application to the business of learning how to live a life of ostensible leisure in a becoming way. Closely related to the requirement that the gentleman must consume freely and of the right kind of goods, there is the requirement that he must know how to consume them in a seemly manner. His life of leisure must be conducted in due form. Hence arise good manners in the way pointed out in an earlier chapter. High-bred manners and ways of living are items of conformity to the norm of conspicuous leisure and conspicuous consumption.

Conspicuous consumption of valuable goods is a means of reputability to the gentleman of leisure. As wealth accumulates on his hands, his own unaided effort will not avail to sufficiently put his opulence in evidence by this method. The aid of friends and competitors is therefore brought in by resorting to the giving of valuable presents and expensive feasts and entertainments. Presents and feasts had probably another origin than that of naive ostentation, but they acquired their utility for this purpose very early, and they have retained that character to the present; so that their utility in this respect has now long been the substantial ground on which these usages rest. Costly entertainments, such as the potlatch or the ball, are peculiarly adapted to serve this end. The competitor with whom the entertainer wishes to institute a comparison is, by this method, made to serve as a means to the end. He consumes vicariously for his host at the same time that he is a witness to the consumption of that excess of good things which his host is unable to dispose of single-handed, and he is also made to witness his host's facility in etiquette.

In the giving of costly entertainments other motives, of a more genial kind, are of course also present. The custom of festive gatherings probably originated in motives of conviviality and religion; these motives are also present in the later development, but they do not continue to be the sole motives. The latter-day leisure-class festivities and entertainments may continue in some slight degree to serve the religious need and in a higher degree the needs of recreation and conviviality, but they also serve an invidious purpose; and they serve it none the less effectually for having a colourable non-invidious ground in these more avowable motives. But the economic effect of these social amenities is not therefore lessened, either in the vicarious consumption of goods or in the exhibition of difficult and costly achievements in etiquette.

As wealth accumulates, the leisure class develops further in function and structures, and there arises a differentiation within the class. There is a more or less elaborate system of rank and grades. This differentiation is furthered by the inheritance of wealth and the consequent inheritance of gentility. With the inheritance of gentility goes the inheritance of obligatory leisure; and gentility of a sufficient potency to entail a life of leisure may be inherited without the complement of wealth required to maintain a dignified leisure. Gentle blood may be transmitted without goods enough to afford a reputably free consumption at one's ease. Hence results a class of impecunious gentlemen of leisure, incidentally referred to already. These half-caste gentlemen of leisure fall into a system of hierarchical gradations. Those who stand near the higher and the highest grades of the wealthy leisure class, in point of birth, or in point of wealth, or both, outrank the remoter-born and the pecuniarily weaker. These lower grades, especially the impecunious, or marginal, gentlemen of leisure, affiliate themselves by a system of dependence or fealty to the great ones; by so doing they gain an increment of repute, or of the means with which to lead a life of leisure, from their patron. They become his courtiers or retainers, servants; and being fed and countenanced by their patron they are indices of his rank and vicarious consumers of his superfluous wealth. Many of these affiliated gentlemen of leisure are at the same time lesser men of substance in their own right; so that some of them are scarcely at all, others only partially, to be rated as vicarious consumers. So many of them, however, as make up the retainers and hangers-on of the patron may be classed as vicarious consumers without qualification. Many of these again, and also many of the other aristocracy of less degree, have in turn attached to their persons a more or less comprehensive group of vicarious consumers in the persons of their wives and children, their servants, retainers, etc.

Throughout this graduated scheme of vicarious leisure and vicarious consumption the rule holds that these offices must be performed in some such manner, or under some such circumstance or insigna, as shall point plainly to the master to whom this leisure or consumption pertains, and to whom therefore the resulting increment of good repute of right inures. The consumption and leisure executed by these persons for their master or patron represents an investment on his part with a view to an increase of good fame As regards feasts and largesses this is obvious enough, and the imputation of repute to the host or patron here takes place immediately, on the ground of common notoriety. Where leisure and consumption is performed vicariously

by henchmen and retainers, imputation of the resulting repute to the patron is effected by their residing near his person so that it may be plain to all men from what source they
draw. As the group whose good esteem is to be secured in
this way grows larger, more patent means are required to
indicate the imputation of merit for the leisure performed,
and to this end uniforms, badges, and liveries come into
vogue. The wearing of uniforms or liveries implies a considerable degree of dependence, and may even be said to be
a mark of servitude, real or ostensible. The wearers of uniforms and liveries may be roughly divided into two classes
—the free and the servile, or the noble and the ignoble. The
services performed by them are likewise divisible into noble
and ignoble. Of course the distinction is not observed with
strict consistency in practice; the less debasing of the base
services and the less honorific of the noble functions are
not infrequently merged in the same person. But the general
distinction is not on that account to be overlooked. What
may add some perplexity is the fact that this fundamental
distinction between noble and ignoble, which rests on the
nature of the ostensible service performed, is traversed by a
secondary distinction into honorific and humiliating, resting
on the rank of the person for whom the service is performed
or whose livery is worn. So, those offices which are by right
the proper employment of the leisure class are noble; such
are government, and the like,—in short, those which may
be classed as ostensibly predatory employments. On the
other hand, those employments which properly fall to the
industrious class are ignoble; such as handicraft or other
productive labour, menial services, and the like. But a base
service performed for a person of very high degree may become a very honorific office; as for instance the office of a
Maid of Honour or of a Lady in Waiting to the Queen, or
the King's Master of the Horse or his Keeper of the Hounds.
The two offices last named suggest a principle of some general bearing. Whenever, as in these cases, the menial service in question has to do directly with the primary leisure

employments of fighting and hunting, it easily acquires a reflected honorific character. In this way great honour may come to attach to an employment which in its own nature belongs to the baser sort.

In the later development of peaceable industry, the usage of employing an idle corps of uniformed men-at-arms gradually lapses. Vicarious consumption by dependents bearing the insignia of their patron or master narrows down to a corps of liveried menials. In a heightened degree, therefore, the livery comes to be a badge of servitude, or rather of servility. Something of a honorific character is always attached to the livery of the armed retainer, but this honorific character disappears when the livery becomes the exclusive badge of the menial. The livery becomes obnoxious to nearly all who are required to wear it. We are yet so little removed from a state of effective slavery as still to be fully sensitive to the sting of any imputation of servility. This antipathy asserts itself even in the case of the liveries or uniforms which some corporations prescribe as the distinctive dress of their employees. In this country the aversion even goes the length of discrediting—in a mild and uncertain way—those government employments, military and civil, which require the wearing of a livery or uniform.

With the disappearance of servitude, the number of vicarious consumers attached to any one gentleman tends, on the whole, to decrease. The like is of course true, and perhaps in a still higher degree, of the number of dependents who perform vicarious leisure for him. In a general way, though not wholly nor consistently, these two groups coincide. The dependent who was first delegated for these duties was the wife, or the chief wife; and, as would be expected, in the later development of the institution, when the number of persons by whom these duties are customarily performed gradually narrows, the wife remains the last. In the higher grades of society a large volume of both these kinds of service is required; and here the wife is of course still assisted in the work by a more or less numerous corps of menials.

But as we descend the social scale, the point is presently reached where the duties of vicarious leisure and consumption devolve upon the wife alone. In the communities of the Western culture, this point is at present found among the lower middle class.

And here occurs a curious inversion. It is a fact of common observation that in this lower middle class there is no pretence of leisure on the part of the head of the household. Through force of circumstances it has fallen into disuse. But the middle-class wife still carries on the business of vicarious leisure, for the good name of the household and its master. In descending the social scale in any modern industrial community, the primary fact—the conspicuous leisure of the master of the household—disappears at a relatively high point. The head of the middle-class household has been reduced by economic circumstances to turn his hand to gaining a livelihood by occupations which often partake largely of the character of industry, as in the case of the ordinary business man of to-day. But the derivative fact—the vicarious leisure and consumption rendered by the wife, and the auxiliary vicarious performance of leisure by menials—remains in vogue as a conventionality which the demands of reputability will not suffer to be slighted. It is by no means an uncommon spectacle to find a man applying himself to work with the utmost assiduity, in order that his wife may in due form render for him that degree of vicarious leisure which the common sense of the time demands.

The leisure rendered by the wife in such cases is, of course, not a simple manifestation of idleness or indolence. It almost invariably occurs disguised under some form of work or household duties or social amenities, which prove on analysis to serve little or no ulterior end beyond showing that she does not and need not occupy herself with anything that is gainful or that is of substantial use. As has already been noticed under the head of manners, the greater part of the customary round of domestic cares to which the middle-class house-wife gives her time and effort is of this character. Not that the results of her attention to household matters, of a decorative and mundificatory character, are not pleasing to the sense of men trained in middle-class proprieties; but the taste to which these effects of household adornment and tidiness appeal is a taste which has been formed under the selective guidance of a canon of propriety that demands just these evidences of wasted effort. The effects are pleasing to us chiefly because we have been taught to find them pleasing. There goes into these domestic duties much solicitude for a proper combination of form and colour, and for other ends that are to be classed as aesthetic in the proper sense of the term; and it is not denied that effects having some substantial aesthetic value are sometimes attained. Pretty much all that is here insisted on is that, as regards these amenities of life, the housewife's efforts are under the guidance of traditions that have been shaped by the law of conspicuously wasteful expenditure of time and substance. If beauty or comfort is achieved,—and it is a more or less fortuitous circumstance if they are,—they must be achieved by means and methods that commend themselves to the great economic law of wasted effort. The more reputable, "presentable" portion of middle-class household paraphernalia are, on the one hand, items of conspicuous consumption, and on the other hand, apparatus for putting in evidence the vicarious leisure rendered by the housewife.

The requirement of vicarious consumption at the hands of the wife continues in force even at a lower point in the pecuniary scale than the requirement of vicarious leisure. At a point below which little if any pretence of wasted effort, in ceremonial cleanness and the like, is observable, and where there is assuredly no conscious attempt at ostensible leisure, decency still requires the wife to consume some goods conspicuously for the reputability of the household and its head. So that, as the latter-day outcome of this evolution of an archaic institution, the wife, who was at the outset the drudge and chattel of the man, both in fact and in theory,—the producer of goods for him to consume,—has become the ceremonial consumer of goods which he produces. But still quite unmistakably remains his chattel in theory; for the habitual rendering of vicarious leisure and consumption is the abiding mark of the unfree servant.

This vicarious consumption practised by the household of the middle and lower classes can not be counted as a direct expression of the leisure-class scheme of life, since the household of this pecuniary grade does not belong within the leisure class. It is rather that the leisure-class scheme of life here comes to an expression at the second remove. The leisure class stands at the head of the social structure in point of reputability; and its manner of life and its standards of worth therefore afford the norm of reputability for the community. The observance of these standards in some degree of approximation, becomes incumbent upon all classes lower in the scale. In modern civilized communities the lines of demarcation between social classes have grown vague and transient, and wherever this happens the norm of reputability imposed by the upper class extends its coercive influence with but slight hindrance down through the social structure to the lowest strata. The result is that the members of each stratum accept as their ideal of decency the scheme of life in vogue in the next higher stratum, and bend their energies to live up to that ideal. On pain of forfeiting their good name and their self-respect in case of failure, they must conform to the accepted code, at least in appearance.

The basis on which good repute in any highly organised industrial community ultimately rests is pecuniary strength; and the means of showing pecuniary strength, and so of gaining or retaining a good name, are leisure and a conspicuous consumption of goods. Accordingly, both of these methods are in vogue as far down the scale as it remains possible; and in the lower strata in which the two methods are employed, both offices are in great part delegated to the wife and children of the household. Lower still, where any degree of leisure, even ostensible, has become impracticable for the wife, the conspicuous consumption of goods remains and is carried on by the wife and children. The man of the household also can do something in this direction, and, indeed, he commonly does; but with a still lower descent into the levels of indigence—along, the margin of the slums—the man, and presently also the children, virtually cease to consume valuable goods for appearances, and the woman remains virtually the sole exponent of the household's pecuniary decency. No class of society, not even the most abjectly poor, foregoes all customary conspicuous consumption. The last items of this category of consumption are not given up except under stress of the direst necessity. Very much of squalor and discomfort will be endured before the last trinket or the last pretence of pecuniary decency is put away. There is no class and no country that has yielded so abjectly before the pressure of physical want as to deny themselves all gratification of this higher or spiritual need.

From the foregoing survey of the growth of conspicuous leisure and consumption, it appears that the utility of both alike for the purposes of reputability lies in the element of waste that is common to both. In the one case it is a waste of time and effort, in the other it is a waste of goods. Both are methods of demonstrating the possession of wealth, and the two are conventionally accepted as equivalents. The choice between them is a question of advertising expediency simply, except so far as it may be affected by other standards of propriety, springing from a different source. On grounds of expediency the preference may be given to the one or the other at different stages of the economic development. The question is, which of the two methods will most effectively reach the persons whose convictions it is desired to affect. Usage has answered this question in different ways under different circumstances.

So long as the community or social group is small enough and compact enough to be effectually reached by common notoriety alone,—that is to say, so long as the human environment to which the individual is required to adapt himself in respect of reputability is comprised within his sphere of personal acquaintance and neighbourhood gossip,—so long the one method is about as effective as the other. Each will therefore serve about equally well during the earlier stages of social growth. But when the differentiation has gone farther and it becomes necessary to reach a wider human environment, consumption begins to hold over leisure as an ordinary means of decency. This is especially true during the later, peaceable economic stage. The means of communication and the nobility of the population now expose the individual to the observation of many persons who have no other means of judging of his reputability than the display of goods (and perhaps of breeding) which he is able to make while he is under their direct observation.

The modern organisation of industry works in the same direction also by another line. The exigencies of the modern industrial system frequently place individuals and households in juxtaposition between whom there is little contact in any other sense than that of juxtaposition. One's neighbours, mechanically speaking, often are socially not one's neighbours, or even acquaintances; and still their transient good opinion has a high degree of utility. The only practicable means of impressing one's pecuniary ability on these unsympathetic observers of one's everyday life is an unremitting demonstration of ability to pay. In the modern community there is also a more frequent attendance at large gatherings of people to whom one's everyday life is unknown; in such places as churches, theatres, ballrooms, parks, shops, and the like. In order to impress these transient observers, and to retain one's self-complacency under their observation, the signature of one's pecuniary strength should be written in characters which he who runs may read. It is evident, therefore, that the present trend of the development is in the direction of heightening the utility of conspicuous consumption as compared with leisure.

It is also noticeable that the serviceability of consumption as a means of repute, as well as the insistence on it as an element of decency, is at its best in those portions of the community where the human contact of the individual is widest and the mobility of the population is greatest. Conspicuous consumption claims a relatively larger portion of the income of the urban than of the rural population, and the claim is also more imperative. The result is that, in order to keep up a decent appearance, the former habitually live hand-to-mouth to a greater extent than the latter. So it comes, for instance, that the American farmer and his wife and daughters are notoriously less modish in their dress, as well as less urbane in their manners, than the city artisan's family with an equal income. It is not that the city population is by nature much more eager for the peculiar complacency that comes of a conspicuous consumption, nor has the rural population less regard for pecuniary decency. But the provocation to this line of evidence, as well as its transient effectiveness, are more decided in the city. This method is therefore more readily resorted to, and in the struggle to outdo one another the city population push their normal standard of conspicuous consumption to a higher point, with the result that a relatively greater expenditure in this direction is required to indicate a given degree of pecuniary decency in the city. The requirement of conformity to this higher conventional standard becomes mandatory. The standard of decency is higher, class for class, and this requirement of decent appearance must be lived up to on pain of losing caste.

Consumption becomes a larger element in the standard of living in the city than in the country. Among the country population its place is to some extent taken by savings and home comforts known through the medium of neighbourhood gossip sufficiently to serve the like general purpose of pecuniary repute. These home comforts and the leisure indulged in—where the indulgence is found—are of course also in great part to be classed as items of conspicuous consumption; and much the same is to be said of the savings.

The smaller amount of the savings laid by by the artisan class
is no doubt due, in some measure, to the fact that in the
case of the artisan the savings are a less effective means of
advertisement, relative to the environment in which he is
placed, than are the savings of the people living on farms
and in the small villages. Among the latter, everybody's
affairs, especially everybody's pecuniary status, are known
to everybody else. Considered by itself simply—taken in the
first degree—this added provocation to which the artisan
and the urban labouring classes are exposed may not very
seriously decrease the amount of savings; but in its cumulative action, through raising the standard of decent expenditure, its deterrent effect on the tendency to save cannot but be very great.

A felicitous illustration of the manner in which this canon
of reputability works out its results is seen in the practice
of dram-drinking, "treating," and smoking in public places,
which is customary among the labourers and handicraftsmen of the towns, and among the lower middle class of
the urban population generally. Journeymen printers may
be named as a class among whom this form of conspicuous
consumption has a great vogue, and among whom it carries
with it certain well-marked consequences that are often
deprecated. The peculiar habits of the class in this respect
are commonly set down to some kind of an ill-defined moral
deficiency with which this class is credited, or to a morally
deleterious influence which their occupation is supposed to
exert, in some unascertainable way, upon the men employed in it. The state of the case for the men who work in
the composition and press rooms of the common run of
printing-houses may be summed up as follows. Skill acquired in any printing-house or any city is easily turned to
account in almost any other house or city; that is to say, the
inertia due to special training is slight. Also, this occupation
requires more than the average of intelligence and general
information, and the men employed in it are therefore ordinarily more ready than many others to take advantage of

any slight variation in the demand for their labour from one place to another. The inertia due to the home feeling is consequently also slight. At the same time the wages in the trade are high enough to make movement from place to place relatively easy. The result is a great mobility of the labour employed in printing; perhaps greater than in any other equally well-defined and considerable body of work-men. These men are constantly thrown in contact with new groups of acquaintances, with whom the relations estab-lished are transient or ephemeral, but whose good opinion is valued none the less for the time being. The human pro-clivity to ostentation, reenforced by sentiments of good-fellowship, leads them to spend freely in those directions which will best serve these needs. Here as elsewhere pre-scription seizes upon the customs as soon as it gains a vogue, and incorporates it in the accredited standard of decency. The next step is to make this standard of decency the point of departure for a new move in advance in the same direc-tion,—for there is no merit in simple spiritless conformity to a standard of dissipation that is lived up to as a matter of course by every one in the trade.

The greater prevalence of dissipation among printers than among the average of workmen is accordingly attri-butable, at least in some measure, to the greater ease of movement and the more transient character of acquaintance and human contact in this trade. But the substantial ground of this high requirement in dissipation is in the last analysis no other than that same propensity for a manifestation of dominance and pecuniary decency which makes the French peasant-proprietor parsimonious and frugal, and induces the American millionaire to found colleges, hospitals and museums. If the canon of conspicuous consumption were not offset to a considerable extent by other features of human nature, alien to it, any saving should logically be impossible for a population situated as the artisan and labouring classes of the cities are at present, however high their wages or their income might be.

But there are other standards of repute and other, more or less imperative, canons of conduct, besides wealth and its manifestation, and some of these come in to accentuate or to qualify the broad, fundamental canon of conspicuous waste. Under the simple test of effectiveness for advertising, we should expect to find leisure and the conspicuous consumption of goods dividing the field of pecuniary emulation pretty evenly between them at the outset. Leisure might then be expected gradually to yield ground and tend to obsolescence as the economic development goes forward, and the community increases in size; while the conspicuous consumption of goods should gradually gain in importance, both absolutely and relatively, until it had absorbed all the available product, leaving nothing over beyond a bare livelihood. But the actual course of development has been somewhat different from this ideal scheme. Leisure held the first place at the start, and came to hold a rank very much above wasteful consumption of goods, both as a direct exponent of wealth and as an element in the standard of decency, during the quasi-peaceable culture. From that point onward, consumption has gained ground, until, at present, it unquestionably holds the primacy, though it is still far from absorbing the entire margin of production above the subsistence minimum.

The early ascendency of leisure as a means of reputability is traceable to the archaic distinction between noble and ignoble employments. Leisure is honourable and becomes imperative partly because it shows exemption from ignoble labour. The archaic differentiation into noble and ignoble classes is based on an invidious distinction between employments as honorific or debasing; and this traditional distinction grows into an imperative canon of decency during the early quasi-peaceable stage. Its ascendency is furthered by the fact that leisure is still fully as effective an evidence of wealth as consumption. Indeed, so effective is it in the relatively small and stable human environment to which the individual is exposed at that cultural stage, that, with the aid of the archaic tradition which deprecates all productive labour, it gives rise to a large impecunious leisure class, and it even tends to limit the production of the community's industry to the subsistence minimum. This extreme inhibition of industry is avoided because slave labour, working under a compulsion more rigorous than that of reputability, is forced to turn out a product in excess of the subsistence minimum of the working class. The subsequent relative decline in the use of conspicuous leisure as a basis of repute is due partly to an increasing relative effectiveness of consumption as an evidence of wealth; but in part it is traceable to another force, alien, and in some degree antagonistic, to the usage of conspicuous waste.

This alien factor is the instinct of workmanship. Other circumstances permitting, that instinct disposes men to look with favour upon the productive efficiency and on whatever is of human use. It disposes them to deprecate waste of substance or effort. The instinct of workmanship is present in all men, and asserts itself even under very adverse circumstances. So that however wasteful a given expenditure may be in reality, it must at least have some colourable excuse in the way of an ostensible purpose. The manner in which, under special circumstances, the instinct eventuates in a taste for exploit and an invidious discrimination between noble and ignoble classes has been indicated in an earlier chapter. In so far as it comes into conflict with the law of conspicuous waste, the instinct of workmanship expresses itself not so much in insistence on substantial usefulness as in an abiding sense of the odiousness and aesthetic impossibility of what is obviously futile. Being of the nature of an instinctive affection, its guidance touches chiefly and immediately the obvious and apparent violations of its requirements. It is only less promptly and with less constraining force that it reaches such substantial violations of its requirements as are appreciated only upon reflection.

So long as all labour continues to be performed exclusively or usually by slaves, the baseness of all productive effort is too constantly and deterrently present in the mind of men to allow the instinct of workmanship seriously to take effect in the direction of industrial usefulness; but when the quasi-peaceable stage (with slavery and status) passes into the peaceable stage of industry (with wage labour and cash payment), the instinct comes more effectively into play. It then begins aggressively to shape men's views of what is meritorious, and asserts itself at least as an auxiliary canon of self-complacency. All extraneous considerations apart, those persons (adults) are but a vanishing minority today who harbour no inclination to the accomplishment of some end, or who are not impelled of their own motion to shape some object or fact or relation for human use. The propensity may in large measure be overborne by the more immediately constraining incentive to a reputable leisure and an avoidance of indecorous usefulness, and it may therefore work itself out in make-believe only; as for instance in "social duties," and in quasi-artistic or quasi-scholarly accomplishments, in the care and decoration of the house, in sewing-circle activity or dress reform, in proficiency at dress, cards, yachting, golf, and various sports. But the fact that it may under stress of circumstance eventuate in inanities no more disproves the presence of the instinct than the reality of the brooding instinct is disproved by inducing a hen to sit on a nestful of china eggs.

This latter-day uneasy reaching-out for some form of purposeful activity that shall at the same time not be indecorously productive of either individual or collective gain marks a difference of attitude between the modern leisure class and that of the quasi-peaceable stage. At the earlier stage, as was said above, the all-dominating institution of slavery and status acted resistlessly to discountenance exertion directed to other than naively predatory ends. It was still possible to find some habitual employment for the inclination to action in the way of forcible aggression or repression directed against hostile groups or against the subject classes within the group; and this served to relieve the pressure and draw off the energy of the leisure class without a resort to actually useful, or even ostensibly useful employments. The practice of hunting also served the same purpose in some degree. When the community developed into a peaceful industrial organisation, and when fuller occupation of the land had reduced the opportunities for the hunt to an inconsiderable residue, the pressure of energy seeking purposeful employment was left to find an outlet in some other direction. The ignominy which attaches to useful effort also entered upon a less acute phase with the disappearance of compulsory labour; and the instinct of workmanship then came to assert itself with more persistence and consistency.

The line of least resistance has changed in some measure, and the energy which formerly found a vent in predatory activity, now in part takes the direction of some ostensibly useful end. Ostensibly purposeless leisure has come to be deprecated, especially among that large portion of the leisure class whose plebeian origin acts to set them at variance with the tradition of the *otium cum dignitate*. But that canon of reputability which discountenances all employment that is of the nature of productive effort is still at hand, and will permit nothing beyond the most transient vogue to any employment that is substantially useful or productive. The consequence is that a change has been wrought in the conspicuous leisure practised by the leisure class; not so much in substance as in form. A reconciliation between the two conflicting requirements is effected by a resort to make-believe. Many and intricate polite observances and social duties of a ceremonial nature are developed; many organisations are founded, with some specious object of amelioration embodied in their official style and title; there is much coming and going, and a deal of talk, to the end that the talkers may not have occasion to reflect on what is the effectual economic value of their traffic. And along with the make-believe of purposeful employment, and woven inextricably into its texture, there is commonly, if not invariably, a more or less appreciable element of purposeful effort directed to some serious end.

In the narrower sphere of vicarious leisure a similar change has gone forward. Instead of simply passing her time in visible idleness, as in the best days of the patriarchal regime, the housewife of the advanced peaceable stage applies herself assiduously to household cares. The salient features of this development of domestic service have already been indicated.

Throughout the entire evolution of conspicuous expenditure, whether of goods or of services or human life, runs the obvious implication that in order to effectually mend the consumer's good fame it must be an expenditure of superfluities. In order to be reputable it must be wasteful. No merit would accrue from the consumption of the bare necessaries of life, except by comparison with the abjectly poor who fall short even of the subsistence minimum; and no standard of expenditure could result from such a comparison, except the most prosaic and unattractive level of decency. A standard of life would still be possible which should admit of individious comparison in other respects than that of opulence; as, for instance, a comparison in various directions in the manifestation of moral, physical, intellectual, or aesthetic force. Comparison in all these directions is in vogue to-day; and the comparison made in these respects is commonly so inextricably bound up with the pecuniary comparison as to be scarcely distinguishable from the latter. This is especially true as regards the current rating of expressions of intellectual and aesthetic force or proficiency; so that we frequently interpret as aesthetic or intellectual a difference which in substance is pecuniary only.

The use of the term "waste" is in one respect an unfortunate one. As used in the speech of everyday life the word carries an undertone of deprecation. It is here used for want of a better term that will adequately describe the same range of motives and of phenomena, and it is not to be taken in an odious sense, as implying an illegitimate expenditure of human products or of human life. In the view of economic theory the expenditure in question is no more and no less legitimate than any other expenditure. It is here called "waste" because this expenditure does not serve human life or human well-being on the whole, not because it is waste or misdirection of effort or expenditure as viewed from the standpoint of the individual consumer who chooses it. If he chooses it, that disposes of the question of its relative utility to him, as compared with other forms of consumption that would not be deprecated on account of their wastefulness. Whatever form of expenditure the consumer chooses, or whatever end he seeks in making his choice, has utility to him by virtue of his preference. As seen from the point of view of the individual consumer, the question of wastefulness does not arise within the scope of economic theory proper. The use of the word "waste" as a technical term, therefore, implies no deprecation of the motives or of the ends sought by the consumer under this canon of conspicuous waste.

But it is, on other grounds, worth noting that the term "waste" in the language of everyday life implies deprecation of what is characterised as wasteful. This common-sense implication is itself an outcropping of the instinct of workmanship. The popular reprobation of waste goes to say that in order to be at peace with himself the common man must be able to see in any and all human effort and human enjoyment an enhancement of life and well-being on the whole. In order to meet with unqualified approval, any economic fact must approve itself under the test of impersonal usefulness—usefulness as seen from the point of view of the generically human. Relative or competitive advantage of one individual in comparison with another does not satisfy the economic conscience, and therefore competitive expenditure has not the approval of this conscience.

In strict accuracy nothing should be included under the head of conspicuous waste but such expenditure as is incurred on the ground of an invidious pecuniary comparison.

But in order to bring any given item or element in under this head it is not necessary that it should be recognized as waste in this sense by the person incurring the expenditure. It frequently happens that an element of the standard of living which set out with being primarily wasteful, ends with becoming, in the apprehension of the consumer, a necessary of life; and it may in this way become as indispensable as any other item of the consumer's habitual expenditure. As items which sometimes fall under this head, and are therefore available as illustrations of the manner in which this principle applies, may be cited carpets and tapestries, silver table service, waiter's services, silk hats, starched linen, many articles of jewellery and of dress. The indispensability of these things after the habit and the convention have been formed, however, has little to say in the classification of expenditures as waste or not waste in the technical meaning of the word. The test to which all expenditure must be brought in an attempt to decide that point is the question whether it serves directly to enhance human life on the whole—whether it furthers the life process taken impersonally. For this is the basis of award of the instinct of workmanship, and that instinct is the court of final appeal in any question of economic truth or adequacy. It is a question as to the award rendered by a dispassionate common sense. The question is, therefore, not whether, under the existing circumstances of individual habit and social custom, a given expenditure conduces to the particular consumer's gratification or peace of mind; but whether, aside from acquired tastes and from the canons of usage and conventional decency, its result is a net gain in comfort or in the fulness of life. Customary expenditure must be classed under the head of waste in so far as the custom on which it rests is traceable to the habit of making an invidious pecuniary comparison—in so far as it is conceived that it could not have become customary and prescriptive without the backing of this principle of pecuniary reputability of relative economic success.

It is obviously not necessary that a given object of expenditure should be exclusively wasteful in order to come in under the category of conspicuous waste. An article may be useful and wasteful both, and its utility to the consumer may be made up of use and waste in the most varying proportions. Consumable goods, and even productive goods, generally show the two elements in combination, as constituents of their utility; although, in a general way, the element of waste tends to predominate in articles of consumption, while the contrary is true of articles designed for productive use. Even in articles which appear at first glance to serve for pure ostentation only, it is always possible to detect the presence of some, at least ostensible, useful purpose; and on the other hand, even in special machinery and tools contrived for some particular industrial process, as well as in the rudest appliances of human industry, the traces of conspicuous waste, or at least of the habit of ostentation, usually become evident on a close scrutiny. It would be hazardous to assert that a useful purpose is ever absent from the utility of any article or of any service, however obviously its prime purpose and chief element is conspicuous waste; and it would be only less hazardous to assert of any primarily useful product that the element of waste is in no way concerned in its value, immediately or remotely.

THE SCIENTIFIC SCRUTINY OF
SOCIETAL FACTS *

By F. H. GIDDINGS

For practical reasons even more than for merely intellectual ones, we need rigorously scientific studies of human
society and of our individual relations to it. In particular we
need such studies of the societal interests that are labeled
"public policy," "education," "missions" and "social work."
I am aware that this proposition is resented by men and
women who suffer from an anti-"academic" complex and
worry lest "the human touch," "the ways of the neighbourhood" and the naïve thinking of "plain people" shall have
spontaneity squeezed out of them by theory. This is an unfortunate misapprehension of what science is and of what
it does for us. It ought not to be necessary at this late day,
but it is necessary, to tell the general public that science is
nothing more nor less than getting at facts, and trying to
understand them, and that what science does for us is
nothing more nor less than helping us to face facts. Facing
the facts that the physical and biological sciences have made
known to us has enabled us to live more comfortably and
longer than men once did. Facing the facts that the social
sciences are making known to us, and will make better
known, should enable us to diminish human misery and
to live more wisely than the human race has lived hitherto.
In particular it should enable us to take the kinks out of our
imperfect codes of conduct. It will be discovered one day
that the chief value of social science, far from being academic, is moral.

Let me sharpen the point by illustrations. I have on my
desk the latest report of an organization which purports to

* From *Scientific Study of Human Society*

ameliorate prison life and to reform convicts. Little exact information is given. Instead, the pages are filled with auto-biographical tales by "reformed" felons. These tell us that neglected childhood, evil communications, unemployment (for which the narrators were not to blame) or other hard luck, drove these unhappy persons into careers of crime which they would have followed to the end of their days if the beneficent organization had not discovered their inherent goodness and obtained for them, by parole or otherwise, "another chance." Conceivably one or two of the tales may be true, but no proof is offered that any of them is. If verification of any sort has been attempted there is no mention of the fact in this self-glorifying report. Therefore, in all human probability, the organization has experimentally satisfied itself that there are enough rich morons in the world to sustain its merciful activities without asking embarrassing questions.

An active worker in an organization of wide reach, which devotes itself to the religious and moral guardianship of young men, read a seminar paper on the "program" which the association attempts to carry out. It appeared that four great lines of work had been projected and are being followed. Young men are being made physically "fit"; they are being intellectually "developed"; their religious life is being "deepened"; and they are being trained to be of "service." I asked the reader to describe the methods of checking up which the association employs to satisfy itself that these admirable objects are being attained. He was unable to enlighten us, and I therefore made my questions specific. Are the young men physically examined and rated from time to time by medical or other experts? No. Is their intellectual progress tested from time to time, as the progress of public school pupils is, or in any other way? No. Is the "depth" of religious life now and then sounded, or otherwise measured? No. Are tangible evidences of "service" obtained and recorded? No.

Another seminar paper, read on another occasion, set forth

the well-advertised social work of an "influential" metro-
politan church. A chief item was the relief and "oversight"
of more than one hundred indigent families. The writer of
the paper (an unfeeling wretch) had asked the almoner
what procedure was followed to ascertain that the families
were deserving. Not satisfied with the answer received he
had gone to the records of a charity organization society
and had learned that more than ninety per cent of the
families in question were "notorious" cases of professional
mendicancy, each of them "working" from two or three to
eight to ten sources of income.

My readers may object that these illustrations of irresponsible social work are not representative, presuming that they
are discreditable survivals of traditions and practices now
passing. Up to date social work, they may insist, is both more
intelligently and more responsibly conducted.

I want to believe that it is, but then, *is it,* always or generally? Does anybody *know* that it usually is, or is everybody just *saying* that it is? If anybody does know he is more
wicked than the servant who hid his lord's treasure in a
napkin, if he keeps the information much longer to himself.
Frankly, I doubt if the information is obtainable. I have
made more attempts to get it than I can count, and without
success. One thing is certain. Our social workers and our
uplift organizations do not know what results they are
getting, and by what methods they are getting them, in the
same rigourous sense in which a well-managed business
corporation knows what it is getting out of its personnel, its
machines, and its methods.

This brings us back to my main contention, that the major
value of a scientific study of society is moral. It is only by
the methods of making sure (which constitute scientific
study) that we ever can know what our public policies, our
educational procedures, our religious endeavours and our
social work are accomplishing. Therefore nothing but the
scientific study of society can save us from the sin, the scandal and the humiliation of obtaining money under false

pretenses, for the attainment of righteous ends which, like enough, we are not in fact attaining.

The scientific study of any subject is a substitution of businesslike ways of "making sure" about it for the lazy habit of "taking it for granted" and the worse habit of making irresponsible assertions about it. To make sure, it is necessary to have done with a careless "looking into it" and to undertake precise observations, many times repeated. It is necessary to make measurements and accountings, to substitute realistic thinking (an honest dealing with facts as they are) for wishful or fanciful or other self deceiving thinking and to carry on a systematic "checking up." At every step we must make sure that the methods which we use and rely on have been accredited by exhaustive criticism and trial, and are applicable to the investigation in hand.

Inasmuch then, as science, as was said, "is nothing more nor less than getting at facts, and trying to understand them" the discovery of facts *which prove to be facts* is initial scientific activity. In the nature of things it continues more or less fortuitously, however systematic we try to make it. The *scrutiny* of alleged facts to determine whether or not they *are* facts, is the fundamental *systematic* work of science.

We make acquaintance with a fact as an individual instance of something or other which arrests attention. A hundred other things, quite as obvious, quite as important, and possibly more significant, we may not see at all. If we reflect for a moment on this circumstance we discover that the assortment of facts which we carry in our heads and build into the structure of knowledge must be smaller than the assortment which makes up the world of actuality, and differently arranged. So, right at the beginning of inquiry, we are warned to watch our steps. Relativity, it seems, is a factor in reality.

The particular instance of something or other which has arrested our attention looks like a unit or item, detached or detachable, and so we think of it for the moment. Then we make further discoveries. Our instance is a unit as far as its relations with other instances like itself or different happen to go, but if we leave them out of our field of vision and forget them, and look intently at our particular instance we see it resolve into a multitude of lesser items, arranged perhaps in clusters or patterns, and, like enough, moving about. Each of these items in turn, we presently ascertain, is composite, and so on, without end.

Human society abounds in examples and the social worker encounters them. He may be interested chiefly in a mill town, or chiefly in a neighbourhood, or chiefly in certain families. At one time he will be most concerned about what the mill town or the neighbourhood or a family *does*. At another time he will be most concerned about what it *is*. As long as he is attending to what the mill town does he thinks of it as a whole. It is a community. He compares it with other communities as wholes. He observes similarities and differences of activity and achievement. These observations may lead him to ask why such similarities and differences exist, how they are to be accounted for. Trying to answer this question, he finds himself inquiring what his mill town is, and from that moment he is resolving it into components. He is discovering that it is made up of corporations, trade unions, churches, schools, shops and markets, professional men and business men, skilled mechanics and unskilled labourers, native born folk and foreign born folk of various nationalities; in fine, of inhabitants arranged in bewildering clusters and patterns. If he is interested chiefly in a neighbourhood or in a family he has a like experience. He thinks of it as a unit while he is learning what it does. He necessarily thinks of it as a composite when he tries to learn what it is.

A particular instance, then, is a unit or not as we happen, or have occasion, to see it. and we have occasion to see it in the one or the other way according to the nature of the investigation that we attempt to make. If it is our purpose to learn how our particular instance is related to other instances like itself, or behaves toward them or with them, or enters into combination with them to make up a bigger whole; or how it is related to things (that is to say instances) unlike itself, and behaves toward them or with them, or enters into combination with them—our instance is a unit, and we deal with it as such. But if our purpose is to learn what it *is,* if we are attempting to account for it, and to understand it, our unit of investigation must obviously be an item of lower order. Practically it must be an item of the next lower order. In accounting for things we must go back step by step.

Here it is important to understand that in so viewing the particular instance, and in so choosing a unit of investigation, we are not acting arbitrarily. In books on scientific method, and most often, perhaps, in books on statistical method, we encounter the statement that we do take our unit arbitrarily, or pragmatically. This is a shorthand expression, a talk saving device, and harmless enough if we do not take it too literally. Speaking strictly, our choice is determined by a logical necessity. We take the particular instance as a unit if we are investigating what it does. We do not take it as a unit, but resolve it into units of the next lower order if we are investigating what it is.

What is the practical value of all this for the social worker, or for the investigator? It is the same for both, and it lies in an admonition. Don't mix up things that should be discriminated, and don't take your knowledge for something that it is not. Do not deceive yourself with the notion that you can understand what your nation, or your town, or your neighbourhood, or your family, *does,* or why it does it, until you have had the patience to learn what it *is,* or with the notion that you can learn what it is in any other way than by painstakingly resolving it into component units and scrutinizing them. Short cuts to a knowledge of society and to proficiency in helping it through tribulations will yield you nothing, and get you nowhere.

When we have determined whether the particular instance of something or other which has arrested our attention, and in which we have become interested, shall be regarded for our further purposes as doing something, or as being or becoming something, and thereby have chosen our unit subject, it is good scientific practice to ascertain next, as accurately as may be necessary for our further purposes, its position in time and in space. To place a thing roughly in its time and space relations to other things is usually not difficult. To place it accurately is another matter. This operation takes patience, energy, time and money. Unfortunately, in the study of societal variables these costs are often almost prohibitive. It is therefore highly important that the investigator should bring good practical judgment to the task of deciding how precise he ought to be; in other words, how much precision is worth while. He is likely to find that this depends upon the shifting, that is to say, the variability, of the position which he is observing. If the variability is negligible—as it is, for example, in the case of a town as old as London or even as San Francisco; or as it is in the case of one of those French peasant families that have lived continuously on the same piece of land for more than five hundred years—the problem is relatively simple. But it is not at all simple in the case of one of those colonies of Italians or of Jews that are moving continuously from one end of one side of Manhattan Island to the other, or of a migrating church, or school, or shopping district. It is least of all simple in the case of a migrating wage-earning family, or dependent family, or criminal family. Yet it is precisely in these cases that accurate determination of position in space and in time is imperative for purposes of identification.

Similar requirements of scientific scrutiny apply to our determination of other categorical matters, including the conditions attaching to persistence in one or another place or in one or another succession of events; the identifying marks and attributes of the thing, individual, or group in which we are interested; its form or changing forms; its magnitudes, or varying magnitudes, and its reactions, that is to say, its behaviour. Here should be noted certain important differences between the task of the physicist or of the biologist, on the one hand, and that of the sociologist, on the other. Form and magnitude are, in general, of more immediate and continuing concern to the physicist and the biologist than they are to the sociologist, although they never can be neglected by the latter. Again, the forms which the physical and biological sciences have to do with are relatively definite and constant patterns, while those that sociology has to do with are somewhat less definite and more variable patterns. Magnitudes also offer striking contrasts. The magnitudes with which physics and chemistry have to do are inconceivably minute, and can be measured only with instruments of the utmost precision. Those with which astronomy has to do are inconceivably vast, but their calculation is made possible by means of the fine measurements of physics. The magnitudes with which sociology has to do lie within the ranges of every day observation, and they are measured by commonplace counting, and by subsequent statistical operations. Accurate counting, however, is not always as easy as it looks, and costly investigations are too often invalidated by untrustworthy enumerations. And statistical methods are fine-edged tools. The sociologist and the social worker should acquire expertness in counting, under varying circumstances, including the coming and going of not too large crowds, and they must get a sound, if not necessarily extensive, knowledge of statistics.

When it comes to the scrutiny of qualities and reactions, as much painstaking and precision are necessary in sociology as in the physical sciences or in biology. Carelessness and error are fatal. It is above all important to discriminate between those relatively unvarying ways in which things, individuals and groups impinge upon our consciousness,— and which we call their traits, properties, characters or characteristics, or, collectively, their qualities—and those relatively variable ways of impinging which we call their changes, activities, reactions, or behaviour. Among qualities it is necessary to discriminate between those which are usually, but not always, associated with their subjects, and those which, always inseparable from them, we call their attributes. In human beings inherited qualities only are attributes.

The behaviour in which the social psychologist is interested is the reaction of an individual or of an intimate group to a fellow individual or to another intimate group. It may take the form of indifference or of interest; of fear or of trust; of liking or of disliking; of anger or of sympathy; of envy, jealousy, malice or hate, or of rejoicing in another's good fortune; of respect, reverence or affection. It may be aloofness or coöperation. The social worker is every moment dealing with social or unsocial behaviour. He should thoroughly know his social psychology.

The behaviour in which the sociologist is interested, as was shown in our first chapter, is the approximately simultaneous reaction of a considerable number of individuals that happen to be in the same situation or circumstance. Their reactions may be alike or different; equally or unequally alert and persistent. This behaviour we called multiindividual or pluralistic. It develops into group ways, class ways, and folk ways, and into organization. The social worker is at all times in contact with it and dealing with it. He should thoroughly know his sociology.

Pluralistic behaviour can be seen or heard, or both seen and heard, and no further acquaintance with it is necessary to satisfy us of its occurrence, but to check up our knowledge of a particular instance of occurrence, so that it shall be reasonably complete and accurate, it is necessary to do more or less counting. Only by counting can we know how much more effective in provoking pluralistic reaction a given stimulus is at one time than at another, or in one place than in another. Counting for this purpose has become an important factor in determining the relative attractiveness of residential areas, of occupations, recreations, styles, and a hundred other interests of every day life. Business and professional men make or lose money by their attention or indifference to it. To determine the relative efficacy of alternative stimuli in calling forth pluralistic response, for example in shop work, or in school work, the counting must be accurate. So, also, it must be to determine alertness and persistence of response to varying stimuli. By no other means can we certainly know, for example, whether the percentage of workers at their places within three minutes after the whistle blows in the morning is equal to the percentage outside the door within three minutes after it blows at noon, or the effect upon these ratios of such devices as fines and bonuses. Persisting reaction and its extent can be ascertained in no other way than by counting, which is always resorted to for measuring the effectiveness of religious and of political activity, but too often stops short of satisfying completeness. I have before me an account of the revival meetings which Dwight L. Moody conducted in one of the larger American cities. It says: "A careful computation puts the total attendance at 900,000 and the converts at 4,000." We are not told how many of the 4,000 converts (they were less than three tenths of one per cent of the attendance) *continued* to live a "sober, righteous, and godly life."

The *consciousness of kind* is obvious enough as a state of mind which continually obtrudes itself into our relations with other persons, but our notion of it may be vague. A simple counting of a few items will clarify and define. Write down the names of twenty-five acquaintances of your own sex and colour race whom you like and associate with, and twenty-five names of persons who annoy you so that you dislike them and, whenever possible, avoid them. Go over each list and note in which one you find more persons who are like yourself in colouring (blondness or brunetness); in which one you find more who are like yourself in being conventional or unconventional in dress and in manners; in which one you find more whose notions about right and wrong are like your own; in which one you find more whose tastes and interests are yours. Now get a considerable number of careful persons to make similar lists and comparisons. The more lists you can get the better, but fifty is a good number. Assemble the results, and you will make interesting discoveries. Similarity or contrast of colouring within the same colour race is a negligible factor in your likings and dislikings. You may have been told or taught otherwise. Similar or dissimilar notions of right and wrong have a good deal of influence, but the big factors are similarities or dissimilarities of manners, tastes and interests.

We observe concerted volition of a spontaneous, or at least unorganized, kind whenever we see a mob bent on mischief, or watch the proceedings of a public meeting which adopts resolutions, or participates in a referendum election. These casual observations, however, tell us only that people actually do these things. By counting certain combinations of items we make further discoveries. For example, not everybody participates who might; the number of qualified voters answering to a roll call varies from question to question, from resolution to resolution, and you do not have to make an impossible number of countings to learn that the constant factor affecting the number of votes is the degree of mental equipment [1] required, not to *understand* the question, but to be *interested* in it. It will not be long before the data made available in states which have referendum voting on questions will afford a convincing confirmation of other hotly discussed results of mentality tests.

Pluralistic behaviour, complicated by the *consciousness of kind,* and becoming concerted volition, is over and over repeated. Through repetition it acquires form or mode. It is subject to fault-finding and disapproval. Forms or modes that are usually approved survive. They become conventions or customs, that is to say, group ways, class ways and folk ways. That each of these is followed more or less, and disregarded more or less, is familiar knowledge; but in order

---

[1] I use here the term "mental equipment" instead of "intelligence" because as yet we are unable to test intelligence unmixed with habit, knowledge, and familiarity, irrespective of native intelligence. Mental equipment includes the factor intelligence, the factors familiarity and practice, and the factor knowledge.

to know which ones are most followed and which ones most disregarded, in particular to know to what extent each one is followed and each one disregarded, it is necessary to do a good deal of counting. This proposition will not be disputed, and I need not say more about it now.

The particular instance of something or other in which one is interested may be amenable to experimental control, which is the best of all the ways of scientific scrutiny, or it may not be. It has generally been held that the phenomena of human society are too complicated for a strictly scientific experimental investigation. It is true, of course, that we are all the time making social and societal experiments. In no other field do we make so many, but these are not usually of the scientific sort. In scientific experimentation we control everything that happens. We determine when it shall occur and where. We arrange circumstances and surroundings; atmospheres and temperatures; possible ways of getting in and possible ways of getting out. We take out something that has been in, or put in something that has been out, and see what happens. At every step we describe what we do and the things that we deal with, with accurate specifications. We count, measure and weigh, and make records. To manage all this in societal experimentation cannot be easy. Is it at all possible?

Among unnecessary ways of being mistaken none is more unnecessary or more discredited by experience than to assume that something or other can not be done.

As far as I know there is no record of a strictly scientific societal experiment completely carried through on a large scale, but there have been many tentative and partial experiments (experiments in experimenting, if one may call them that) and they are multiplying. The more promising ones have been and are being made in workshops and in schools and by a few intelligently managed corporations, industrial or philanthropic. The more disappointing, although often sincerely attempted ones, have been made by neighbourhood houses and by churches. The cause of failure, in many instances, has been a commendable aversion to anything that has looked like prying into private affairs and keeping tab on them. This aversion I share and unqualifiedly approve; but in the environment of every settlement and of every church there are opportunities for social and societal experimentation that would not require intrusiveness or meddling. That these have not been more successfully exploited must be explained, I am afraid, by aversion to the tedium of counting and recording, to note books and statistics.

Among small but insignificant societal experiments which, without question, could be conducted in a strictly scientific manner and carried through to indisputable results, are a few rigourous and crucial ones to determine what are the best ways and means of awakening group, class, or neighbourhood interest, and of holding it. Settlements and churches are continually trying out these ways and means, practical ones and fantastic ones, sane ones and crazy ones, but their results are astonishingly meagre. Their reports, with commendable exceptions, are a flotsam of unverified assertions, uncritical impressions, and optimistic forecasts, made, not to establish a fact, but to wheedle money for more loose work of the same kind. It is possible to do this work in a scientific and convincing way, and it ought to be so done. A good many schools and a good many employers of wage-earners are making carefully conducted experiments in the formation of group and class habits. The results are of great and increasing value. Year by year they are being checked up and extended. Big corporations managed by men of vision are making experiments in organization. These, too, are of increasing value.

The final verification of an alleged fact (its conclusive establishment as a fact) is attained only through much repeating of observations and measurements. Not until we can safely challenge anybody to go over our work and discover errors in it can we be quite sure that we *know* anything. As I have heretofore insisted a fact in the scientific sense of the word "is the close agreement of many observations or measurements of the same phenomenon." Error creeps into observation in unaccountable ways, and different observers make different mistakes. Precise measurement by one person at one time and in one place is next to impossible. The nearest approximation to accuracy is made by taking the average of many measurements made by many measurers and calculating its probable error. Physicists and chemists, astronomers and geologists, biologists and psychologists, are tirelessly repeating their observations and their measurements of presumptive fact. Social psychologists and sociologists must get this habit.

THE ECONOMICS OF GENIUS *

By JOHN M. ROBERTSON

Haud facile emergunt.—JUVENAL

In the *Annals of the American Academy of Political and Social Science* for May, 1897, Prof. C. H. Cooley, of the University of Michigan, works out an able and successful refutation of a prevalent theory—of which the typical exponent is Mr. Francis Galton—concerning the distribution and emergence of genius in human affairs. Theory is perhaps too strong a name for what is really the statement of a common empirical assumption; but, as Galton supports his view of the matter by a certain process of statistics, it may fitly be allowed the status of a scientific contention. *Briefly, this theory is that, although conditions count for something, genius in general is sure to work its way to the front;* that fame, or the consensus of educated opinion, is a sufficiently sure test of genius; and that a prevailing preponderance of genius *per capita* in any society is to be taken as proving *pro tanto* a superiority in the race. These positions Mr. Cooley examines, in his essay on 'Genius, Fame, and the Comparison of Races,' with great candor and acumen; exposing their collective unsoundness, in my judgment, with convincing clearness.

So far as my reading goes, Mr. Cooley is entitled to claim that, while his position is not new,* no one has so fully maintained it in this particular connection; although the research of M. de Candolle in his *Histoire des Sciences et des Savants* handles the general problem perhaps more comprehensively.

---

* From *Essays in Sociology.*

* See, for instance, the discussion in Prof. William James's essay on 'Great Men, Great Thoughts and the Environment,' reprinted in his recent volume, 'The Will to Believe'.

It is with some diffidence, therefore, that I venture to suggest that the argument may be carried further, not only as against Galton, but as against more circumspect attacks from Galton's point of view. The practical importance of the question, however, may excuse an attempt—made in entire sympathy with Mr. Cooley—thus to develop the discussion.

What Mr. Cooley has shown, as against the optimistic assumption that genius will always work its way to the front, is that, in view of the relatively very large number of cases in which admitted genius is found to have had distinctly favoring conditions, and of the number in which it could not conceivably have developed without either special stimulus, *we are bound to conclude that much genius normally runs to waste*—fame giving no account of it— and that race has practically nothing to do with the explanation. It is true that Galton has in a measure safeguarded his theory by the question-begging definition of genius† as "those qualities of intellect and disposition which *urge* and *qualify* a man to perform acts that lead to reputation. . . . I mean a nature which, when left to itself, *will*, urged by an inherent stimulus, climb the path that leads to eminence, *and has strength to reach the summit.*" As he justly observes, "it is almost a contradiction in terms to doubt that such men will generally become eminent." A man who "will climb", and "has strength to reach the summit", seems pretty sure to get there; and if such men only are to be credited with the highest "natural ability", why, then, those who do not reach the summit are defined as deficient.

But the rest of the exposition shows that Galton's doctrine must be susceptible of a more courageous definition. He recognises as geniuses a number of celebrities of the past who would be generally so classed without dispute; and he

---

† In the current edition of 'Hereditary Genius' (1892, p. 33) Galton uses the term "natural ability", instead of "genius", in this connection; but the use of "genius", which is so much more convenient, does not in any way pervert his argument. Reputation he defines of "the opinion of contemporaries, revised by posterity". This will do equally well for fame.

implies that these would under any circumstances have succeeded. Noting, too, that "culture is far more widely spread in America than with us [in England], and the education of their middle and lower classes far more advanced," without producing a proportionate amount of first-class intellectual work, he argues that "if the hindrances to the rise of genius were removed from English society as completely as they have been removed from that of America, we should not become materially richer in highly eminent men." The hindrances here assumed are, by implication, those set up by lack of elementary schooling and of facilities for acquiring ordinary culture. But, if the argument holds good to that extent, it should follow that any other social hindrance to the development of genius is equally ineffective, *and that society at all times gets the benefit of practically all the genius there is.*

The disproof of this opinion, as put by Mr. Cooley, may be condensed in two lines of statement. First, on an examination of the list of names classed as pre-eminent in European literature in Prof. Nichol's synoptical 'Tables'—a manual compiled for strictly historical purposes—it is found that out of seventy-one specified in a period of six hundred years (1265-1865) *only two are those of sons of poor men;* while forty-five may be classed as born in the upper or upper-middle class, and twenty-four in the lower middle. Allowing some re-adjustment of the latter two classifications, the fact remains *that two only of the seventy-one men of genius in question were sons of poor men; to wit, Bunyan and Burns.*‡ Now, the parents of Bunyan, though very poor, were at the then unusual pains to have him taught reading and writing; so that he was thus put on the same average level of intellectual opportunity with the lower-middle class of his day. In the case of *Burns,* again, though

‡ Luther might perhaps be taken from the category of the lower-middle class, in which Mr. Cooley places him, and included in that of the poor. But his parents, like those of Bunyan and Burns, were able to send him to school, and he had his further education gratis; so that, in any view, his case strongly supports the principle contended for.

boys of his class in Scotland were usually taught reading and writing, *we find special conditions set up by the un-common devotion of the father to the education of his children.*

I have compared Mr. Cooley's list of seventy-one cele-brities with Prof. Nichol's 'Tables', and noted its omissions. He has dealt with the great majority of the most famous writers; but in addition to his list, the following thirty-nine names are by analogy entitled to be included:—Bayle, Beau-mont, Berkeley, Björnson, Bolingbroke, Buffon, Butler, Calvin, Chateaubriand, Comines, Diderot, Emerson, Flau-bert, Fletcher, Franklin, Hawthorne, Herder, Herrick, Hood, Ibsen, Joubert, Lamb, Le Sage, Marmontel, Marvell, Meredith, More, Poe, Sachs, Schopenhauer, Smollett, Sterne, Jeremy Taylor, De Tocqueville, Turgéneff, Vauvenargues, Villon, Webster, and Wieland. Not a single name in the list, however, can fairly be added to the category of poor men's sons; *nor can I find in all the 'Tables' a single literary man of eminence who made his way from unschooled poverty by force of genius.*

Thus far, then, it is ascertained that the only two (or three) poor men's sons who, out of one hundred and ten celebrities during six centuries, attained the highest degree of fame in European literature, really had advantages quite abnormal in their class. Yet we are implicitly asked to be-lieve that, had the cultural advantages been the same for all classes, the division which is broadly marked as "poor", and which has at all times been at least thrice as numerous as the remainder, would have yielded no larger proportion of eminent intellectual achievement than it has done. A propo-sition so unreasonable can have been advanced only through lack of due reflection. In order to justify it, it would be nec-essary to show, by critical tests, that the composite masses classed as "poor" are actually deficient, number for number, in congenital brain-power, as compared with those born in better circumstances; and that, say, a given million of poor children, educated in the same conditions with a given million of the upper and middle classes, would yield less than one-hundredth part of the number of cases of first-rate literary ability supplied by the latter. *No such evidence exists.* The assumption under notice is an uncritical, empirical inference from statistics, the very nature of which suggests another explanation.

II

The strongest argument for any part of the Galtonian view seems to be that based on the relative infrequency of ostensible genius in the population of the United States as compared with that of England, where the elementary schooling is still less complete, and was for a long time much more scanty. It is at this point that the argument from the presence or absence of such conditions in the case of British men of letters must be followed up by an examination of the conditions of intellectual success in a community where the poorer masses are secured a measure of schooling, and where mere class prejudice puts little or no hindrance in the way of a poor youth's reaching intellectual eminence.

Galton argues, by implication, that if genius be socially suppressible by adverse conditions, and if favorable conditions be capable of developing a larger proportion of genius, the population of the United States ought to yield more great writers, thinkers, poets, artists, and men of science than the British. At the first glance, this assumption is plausible; especially when we have been arguing that the illiteracy of the mass of the English population in past ages is the explanation of there being only two poor men's sons among the literary men of genius of six centuries. But it is only at a first glance that the plausibility subsists. A little reflection makes it clear that *the emergence of high literary capacity is the outcome of the totality of intellectual and economic conditions,* and that Galton has given no thought to this totality, which varies greatly from age to age, and which differs widely as between England and the United States. Let us first note a few of the differences in the latter case.

(1) *To this day England has a much larger leisured class,* in the sense of a class living on inherited incomes, than the United States. This class has, in the past hundred and fifty years, supplied the following writers:—Bentham, Browning, Buckle, Byron, Cowper, Darwin, Disraeli, Finlay, Fitzgerald, the author of "Supernatural Religion", Freeman, Francis Galton, Gibbon, Hallam, P. G. Hamerton, Hamilton, Hume, Keats, Kinglake, Landor, Lecky, Cornewall Lewis, Long, Lytton, Mitford, William Morris, Napier, Palgrave, De Quincey, Ruskin, Senior, Shelley, Stanhope, Swinburne, Symonds, Tennyson (also pensioned), Thackeray (lost income before thirty), Tylor, and Wordsworth. In our own day this class appears to yield a decreasing supply of eminent men—a fact to be dealt with later.

(2) *Until quite recently there was in Britain a much larger provision for intellectual life than in the United States in the way of University and other endowments* and ecclesiastical semi-sinecures. To such provision may be attributed much of the output of such writers as Austin, Bain, Cairnes, Clifford, Colenso, Gardiner, Gray, T. H. Green, Huxley, Jevons, Maine, Malthus, Mansel, Merivale, Milman, Newman, Owen, Pater, Pattison, Reid, Robertson, Thorold Rogers, Sayce, Seeley, Sidwick, Stanley, Stubbs, Thirlwall, Warton, Whewell, and others. Now that American University endowments are multiplying, the competent output of serious treatises is seen to be increasing much more rapidly in the United States than in England.

(3) Public appointments which are (*a*) semi-sinecures, or (*b*) so well salaried as to permit of the speedy accumulation of a fortune, or (*c*) so easy as to permit of a great deal of leisure, have always been far more numerous in England than in the States. To the help of such appointments may be attributed much of the production of the following writers:

—Matthew Arnold, Hill Burton, Charles Lamb, Macaulay, James Mill, John Stuart Mill, Patmore, Scott (whose sheriff-alty was an easy post), and Trollope.

(4) Certain business positions a generation or more ago, if not to-day, permitted a much larger amount of leisure in England than was usually possible in similar positions in the United States. In such positions were: Bagehot (banker), Grote (banker), Lubbock (banker), Hugh Miller (well-schooled quarryman, afterwards bank accountant), Ricardo (stockbroker), and Samuel Sharp (banker).

The foregoing heads have reference to the superior directly protective conditions in England. But with these there have concurred certain favorable conditions which may be termed indirectly protective, either absolutely or relatively to the conditions in the States. Such have been:

(5) *The presence, in the past, of what may be described as an old and relatively rich literary soil and a literary atmosphere.* These were jointly supplied by the leisured, the scholarly, and the educated official classes, all built up on old protective foundations. Among the English idle class in particular, despite much frivolity, the conditions of political life for two hundred years have tended to stimulate certain kinds of study. The State clergy, too, by reason of the secure character of the incomes of the better paid and of the social status accorded them for over a century back, have till recently been more liberally educated than those of most of the sects in America. There has thus been generated all round an atmosphere much more favorable to specialised culture than that which prevailed in the greater part of the United States till twenty or thirty years ago, when Galton first wrote, and this despite the greater diffusion in the States of elementary education.

(6) Partly by reason of the conditions just specified, American writers were for a long time handicapped as compared with English. Not only did a certain prestige attach, for competent American readers, to English work, but the law as to copyright permitted, till recently, the sale of re-

printed English books at prices which often left nothing for the author, and with which native writers could not possibly compete. *The United States, indeed, may be said to have protected every native activity that incurred foreign competition save literature.* In consequence, Americans who sought to live by the higher or more laborious sorts of literature had an almost hopeless struggle before them. Washington Irving, after producing his first book, took to business for a while; and after he had returned to authorship as a profession, was glad to have the secretaryship of the American Embassy in London. Poe's life was one of constant and at times desperate hardships, and would have been so even if he had been a teetotaller. *Hawthorne could hardly have subsisted but for his political appointments*— appointments which, since his time, are more and more seldom given to men who, like him, can render their party little political service. *Cooper had to work to excess, forcing his vein, to support himself.* Emerson's adoption of serious literature as a vocation was the result of his being left, through change of religious opinion, unfitted for any other income-earning pursuit. Lowell had private means apart from his professorship. *Bryant made his income as a banker.* Longfellow had a good unearned income. Whitman lived as a poor man all his life, and finally had to be supported by donations. On Galton's theory of genius these were all, or nearly all, the men of high potential literary genius in the States during fifty years. Reason would seem to force us to the conclusion that, on the contrary, there were among the mass of the population at least some hundreds of brains which, with due fostering and opportunity, could have produced first-class intellectual work, whether in the way of *belles lettres,* or science, or philosophy, or historical research. The American historians, like those of England, have one and all either possessed private means or public appointments, or else have had to add to their incomes by lecturing or impermanent literary work.

Galton himself has affirmed that such commanders as

Alexander, Scipio, Hannibal, Cæsar, Cromwell, Marlborough, the Princes of Nassau, Wellington, and Napoleon
"would have distinguished themselves under any circumstances." While noting the difficulty of conceiving of Scipio,
Marlborough, and Wellington distinguishing themselves as
thinkers or writers, we may fairly take this proposition to
mean that the men named could have succeeded greatly
either as politicians or as men of business in a non-military
society. If, then, that be conceivable, it is equally arguable
that men who have succeeded greatly in politics or business in a non-military society might have succeeded no less
in the intellectual life had their circumstances been sufficiently favorable to that vocation.

The most pressing necessity for most men being the earning of a livelihood, it stands to reason that some men with
the capacity for great things in thought or expression, finding it nearly impossible to earn a fair income by such activity, will turn from that path to one of those where earning is incomparably easier. In many cases, men are forced
so to choose by the need to support those dear to or dependent upon them: in other cases, they may rationally so choose
for their own sakes.

On Galton's principle, the much larger number of culture-
specialists in Germany than in England is a proof of a proportionally greater capacity for such things in the German
people. A more considerate induction will show that it is
merely the special provision made for such activities by the
German university system, concurrently with the contrary
influence of the commercial development long ago imposed
on England by her natural resources and her political system, that sets up the difference.

Mr. Cooley has well shown, further, the breakdown of
the Galtonian principle when applied to such a case as the
rise, florescence, and fall of the art of painting in Italy between the thirteenth and seventeenth centuries. On the
theory of special national faculties, that process is inexplic-

able. *On the theory of the potency of economic and social conditions, it is perfectly intelligible.*

III

As with nations, so with classes. The researches of M. de Candolle have shown that the proportion of successful men of science drawn from the working-class has varied, as between France and other countries, in a way that can be explained only by special evocative influences. Studying the lists of the members and foreign associates of the French Academy of Sciences between 1666 and 1870, he finds that out of ninety of the ninety-two foreign associates whose careers he can trace, six only, or 7 per cent., belong to the rich or aristocratic families, and forty-seven, or 52 per cent., to the middle class. Making up a list of sixty first-rate French *savants* of the same period, forty of whom had been associates of both the French Academy of Sciences and the Royal Society of London, he finds that, of this number, fourteen, or 23 per cent., belonged to the multitude, twenty-one, or 35 per cent., to the rich or noble class, and twenty-five, or 42 per cent., to the middle class. In the list of forty eminent Frenchmen honored at London and Berlin, he has traced thirty-six careers; and of these no fewer than nine, or 25 per cent., spring from the working class.

M. de Candolle does not attempt to explain the difference thus indicated between France and other countries; but, in view of what has gone before, we may provisionally do so by attributing it to the special educative machinery set up in France in the eighteenth century by the Jesuit schools,* and, since the Revolution, by the republican and Napoleonic provision of a similar kind. When all is said, however,

* M. de Candolle notes that while the Catholic Church has produced no great naturalists, and few of any grade, she can claim so large a number of astronomers, physicists, and mathematicians, that *"one would say the Church has wished to repel the reproach made against her on the score of Galileo, by cultivating precisely his sciences"*.

the researches of M. de Candolle yield the outstanding result that, of all social grades, the numerically small upper class has in the past yielded the largest proportion of eminent men of science, from the days when, in Britain, Napier and Bacon, Newton and Boyle, were contemporaries, till at least the last generation; *the middle class yielding proportionally fewer, and the poor class by far the least of all.* And as the principle of heredity entirely fails to explain the facts,† we are driven back once more to the conclusion *that potential genius is probably about as frequent in one class as in another, and that it emerges in the ratio of its total opportunities.*

That view, it may be pointed out, is in full harmony with the summing-up of M. de Candolle, who thus states the conditions which he finally finds to be favorable to the emergence of high *scientific* capacity:—

† Galton admits ('Hereditary Genius,' p. 213) that "Newton's ancestry appears to have been in no way remarkable for intellectual ability". Boyle is the only case of scientific genius in *his* numerous stock. The fact that Napier's father was Master of the Scottish Mint at sixteen, when it is alleged his son was born, proves only court favor. *And Galton freely admits that "the fathers of the ablest men in science have frequently been unscientific"* (p. 190).

"1. A considerable proportion of persons belonging to the rich or well-to-do classes of the population, relatively to those who are obliged to work constantly for their living, especially by hand labor.

"2. An important proportion, among the rich or well-to-do classes, of persons content with their incomes, having a fortune easy to administer, and consequently content to occupy themselves with intellectual matters which 'do not pay'.

"3. An old intellectual culture, directed for several generations back toward real things and true ideas.

"4. Immigration of cultured foreign families, with a taste for non-lucrative intellectual tasks.

"5. The existence of a number of families with traditions favorable to the sciences and to intellectual occupations of all kinds.

"6. Primary and, above all, secondary and superior education, well organised, independent of political and religious parties, tending to stimulate research and to encourage young men and specialists devoted to science.

"7. Abundant and well-organised material means for scientific pursuits (libraries, observatories, laboratories, collections).

"8. A public interested in things real and true rather than in things imaginary or fictitious.

"9. The liberty to announce and publish every opinion, at least on sci-

Comprehensive as is this estimate, it is perhaps too specially directed to the case of Switzerland, that being the country where, as M. de Candolle's statistics amply prove, *scientific capacity has been developed in the largest proportion relatively to population.* But any additions made to his explanation would leave its essentials untouched; and it would need no great readjustment to make it cover the cases of literary, philosophic, and artistic ability. The principal addenda which suggest themselves to me are:—

(*a*) That the special cultivation of the sciences in Switzerland within the past century and a half is in a measure due to the conditions left by the old Calvinistic *régime,* which there deliberately crushed all the imaginative arts, as it did in Scotland. Intellectual curiosity played where it could.

(*b*) That the lack of important philosophers in Switzerland, at a time when such were arising in Britain, France, and Germany, was a result of the strong hold of the orthodox tradition even at a time when men were freely studying the physical sciences. Philosophy in the other countries was developed by the stimulus of scepticism.

(*c*) That smallness of a State is not essential to the abundant development of either science, art, or literature. It was not the smallness of Athens, compared with, say, Rome and Egypt, that determined Attic development. *What is important is abundance of culture-contacts,* which certainly have

entific subjects, without suffering inconveniences of any gravity.

"10. A public opinion favorable to the sciences and to those who cultivate them.

"11. Liberty to follow any profession, to avoid any, to travel, to avoid all personal service other than what is voluntarily undertaken.

"12. A religion laying little stress on the principle of authority.

"13. A clergy friendly to instruction for its own members and for the public.

"14. A clergy not restricted to celibacy.

"15. The habitual use of one of the three principal languages, English, German, or French. A well-diffused knowledge of these languages in the educated class.

"16. A small independent State or union of small independent States.

"17. Geographical position in a temperate or northerly climate.

"18. Nearness of civilised countries."

abounded in the case of Switzerland, in touch at once with France, Germany, and Italy. Holland, again, is a small State; but it has latterly done proportionally less than France in the sciences, the arts, and in fine literature.

(d) Relative *lack of opportunity* for commercial expansion, *i.e.*, inducement to seek wealth rather than knowledge, is an important factor in the intellectual differentiation of, say, Switzerland and England. In Newton's day, England was scientifically far ahead of Switzerland. The later enormous expansion of English industry, through abundant coal and iron, made England pre-eminently a commercial country, where large incomes were the ideal for the middle and upper classes. The narrower industrial conditions in Switzerland‡ counted for more than mere family tradition in maintaining plain living and disinterested study. The conditions in Scotland last century closely resembled those of Switzerland; but commercial development has modified culture-history in Scotland as in England.

Taking these considerations with those adduced by Mr. Cooley and M. de Candolle, we get a pretty general view of the conditions of emergence for some of the most important forms of abnormal intellectual ability, and a pretty general refutation of Galton's teaching.

IV

There remains, however, the criterion of individual cases, as against Galton's assumption that genius is a self-securing force. Mr. Cooley has pointed to two—Darwin and Thackeray. In the former, there was clearly needed the condition of a private income to permit of due leisure, and, further, the strictest economy of strength. In the latter, it seems to have needed the condition of pecuniary necessity to spur

‡ About 1790, the Swiss population was 1,700,000; in 1836 it was 2,177,420; and in 1888 it had only increased to 2,933,334. This is a much slower rate of increase than that seen in Scotland, where the population in 1801 was 1,608,420, and in 1891 had increased to 4,025,647.

the artistic faculty into strenuous play. *In all probability we should have had few or none of Thackeray's novels had his private fortune remained intact.* Then in the case of Thackeray we have, in terms of Galton's formulas, capacity without zeal, and in the case of Darwin zeal without due physical strength. *Darwin could never have done his work without his inherited means;* and as a poor man's son, without help, he would certainly have remained obscure.

At this rate, then, we should have to strike off the list of geniuses an indefinite number of those who realise for us our notion of the species. Above all, we should be compelled to strike off the name of *Shakspere.* Few who have closely studied the life of the latter, the typical man of genius, will dispute the proposition that, *had he been able to make a good livelihood in his father's business, he would never have turned actor or playwright.* He happened to combine with a temperament and literary faculty of extraordinary plasticity, a thoroughly business-like attitude toward the main chance; securing his gains and his dues with scrupulous exactitude; writing nothing, save his sonnets, without a clear pecuniary motive; *and curtailing his literary career as soon as he had made a comfortable fortune.* On the other hand, as his sonnets distinctly tell, he suffered enough in his life as an actor to *make it impossible that he should have sought the stage had he not been driven by need;* and had he not turned actor he would never have become a dramatist. In brief, Shakspere untaught, unschooled, and living where players never came, would probably never have written a line; and Shakspere well-to-do in Stratford would have felt no compelling necessity for self-expression, save perchance in forms even more factitious than "Venus and Adonis".

V

It thus begins to appear that the aggressive and inevitable impulse to action or utterance, which Galton identifies with genius, is merely an occasional concomitant thereof. Some such impulse does appear, at the first glance, in the cases of Bacon, Newton, Pope, and many others. But in these cases, in turn, there is not the least reason to suppose that, with an obscure birth, illiterate childhood, and a toilsome youth, the congenital faculty could ever have come to any such develment as it actually chanced to attain under favorable conditions. On the contrary, a wide survey of literary biography entitles us to surmise that there have lived and died in toilsome poverty some potential Bacons and a few Shaksperes, several "mute, inglorious" Miltons, and many a Cromwell "guiltless of his country's blood".

Putting aside Homer as an unsolved problem, we are led to note, first *that a large part of Greek literature is the chance outcome of the possession of private means* and literary gifts by the same persons. Herodotus, Thucydides, Aristotle, Plato, and Xenophon are cases in point. Aristotle and Plato might indeed have supported themselves by their lectures, given the necessary maintenance during their training time; but none of the others could conceivably have made a living by the sale of his writings. *Demosthenes had a heritage to begin with. Socrates,* if he is to be reckoned an author, proves the same point, *having had to work as a statuary till he was helped by Crito,* and put in the way of maintaining himself humbly as a teacher. Epicurus in turn had a good schooling, and either inherited some means or was early able to earn a good livelihood as a philosophic teacher—a mode of life exceptionally favorable to literary production in the ancient world. Lucian is a somewhat obscure case; but at least he was apprenticed to a well-to-do uncle who was a sculptor, and was later enabled to become a lawyer. In that capacity he practised, and he clearly could not have lived on his book sales.

The *drama, again, is a matter of civic evocation, and could not otherwise have existed.* Dramatic genius would have remained merely potential in Æschylus, Sophocles, and Euripides but for the public institution and support of the theatre; and comedy likewise was an outcome of special

local institutions. *Had any, or all, of the great Greek dramatists chanced to be kidnapped and sold into Persian slavery
in early youth, their genius could no more have come to
light than could that of Mozart and Beethoven had they
been born and bred in Constantinople.* Reflection on such
obvious truths would have precluded the formation of a
great many generalisations as to "racial genius." *Greek
genius could emerge only when it was provided for.*

In Rome the rule was the same. *Lucretius had inherited
means, as had Cicero,* whose later wealth seems to have
come mainly from legacies, and whose writings, apart from
his orations, can have brought him no gains. *Catullus,* the
most lyrically inspired of all the Latins, was *of a landed
family,* and wrote wholly for his own pleasure. Indeed, we
gather from Martial that books—that is, manuscript rolls—
sold in Rome for a few pence, a price that could barely pay
for the labor of copying.* It is thus clear that we owe the
works of Virgil to the fact of his inheriting the small patrimony which Augustus restored to him when it had been
confiscated. The *Æneid* cannot be even considered as having
been published in his lifetime. Of *Horace,* who on the confiscation of his father's estate *contrived to buy a post as a
Government clerk,* it may be said that by his early verses he
earned the estate which was presented to him by Mæcenas;
but the fact remains that first the office and later the estate
were his sources of subsistence during his life as an author.
Ovid, again, was rich; and Juvenal—who put as clearly as
any man ever did the economic conditions essential to the
manifestations of literary genius—*was fairly so.* Concerning
Martial, it is not clear whether he was often paid for a
panegyrical epigram as such, or whether he depended on
the general donations of his admirers. On either view he
may be regarded as having earned his living by his pen;
but whether the transaction was a great gain to literature is
a matter for energetic doubt.

* There is a good research on this subject in W. A. Schmidt's *Geschichte
der Denk- und Glaubensfreiheit im ersten Jahrhundert,* 1847, Kap. 5.

Of the historians it is hardly necessary to speak. In the nature of things neither Sallust nor Livy, neither Tacitus nor Polybius, could have looked to historical study and composition as sources of income. In short, it holds good of the great mass of Roman literature that its existence is to be attributed to the coincidence in a certain number of cases, of private means or acquired fortune for men who had literary gift or industry. Gift without fortune had almost no chance of earning subsistence: ninety-nine per cent of the talent of the moneyless men must have come to nothing in such conditions. Plautus and Terence, indeed, did earn freely by their plays: here again the drama constituted an exception to the rule that held good in the literature written for reading—a fact arising out of the nature of the dramatic art, which can be practised from hand to mouth by its cultivators, was originally State-supported, and can generally count on a certain amount of gate-money. *The world, broadly speaking, really paid for its scenic entertainment,* if not for the best of its book-culture as such; and as the entertainment has included the products of Æschylus and Aristophanes, Sophocles and Shakspere, Molière and Ibsen, the *contra* is not to be made light of. But as regards the problem in hand the inference is the same: *unless special social economic conditions are set up, potential dramatic genius comes to nothing.*

VI

In the mediæval period, printing being not yet invented, the economic conditions of literary production were very much the same as in ancient Rome. Thus *the writings of Dante, Boccaccio, and Petrarch could not have been sources of income to them.* In that age, and later, large prices were paid by rich amateurs for classic manuscripts, whence arose a great industry of forgery, which reached its high-water mark, perhaps under the auspices of Annius of Viterbo, a Dominican monk, master of the Palace under Alexander VI.

In 1498 Annius published a whole library of alleged ex-
humed classics, all forgeries, with forged commentaries
superadded, the whole having been palmed off upon the
trusting editor by unscrupulous or at least impecunious
scholars. In that way probably a good many incomes, or
fortunes, were earned during some centuries. But manuscripts of new books can have had no selling value: the
best that could happen to an author was that his work
should recommend him to the patronage and bounty of a
prince or prelate or other wealthy amateur, as happened to
Politian when he won the favor of Lorenzo de' Medici by
his elaborate poem on a tournament in which Julian de'
Medici distinguished himself in 1468. The Troubadours,
again, figured as ministers of entertainment; and those of
them who had need of pay would receive it on the same
footing as minstrels and actors; *so that not genius but birth
on the one hand and economic demand on the other determined their performance.* Dante, in turn, belonged to
the monied class, and, though of all men of genius he had
perhaps the strongest impulse to utterance, he owed to his
social status the culture which made the utterance possible,
and even the bitter bread of dependence which sustained
him while he wrought his masterpiece. *Born poor, he could
never have been the Dante we know.* Nor did the more
fortunate Petrarch and Boccaccio, on the other hand, live
by authorship, though their writings—the Latin compositions of Petrarch, that is, and the Italian tales of Boccaccio—
doubtless helped them to their diplomatic employments and
won them acclamation.

When we come down to Ariosto, whose *Orlando Furioso*
was printed in 1516, and went through four editions in sixteen years, we naturally look for signs that the author's
work enabled him to live. Inheriting little from his father,
he had entered the service of a rich Cardinal as secretary,
and while in that employ he had worked at his epic for
eleven years. But it does not appear that his book sales counted for much of his income; for after quarreling with his

Cardinal he entered the political service of Alphonso I, Duke of Ferrara, passing from that department in his last years to that of controller of the Court Theatre. The duke's patronage may be regarded as the reward for the poem, but not otherwise did it maintain the poet. Nor was the case otherwise with Tasso, who, like Ariosto and Boccaccio and so many another, had to resist his father's desire to make a lawyer of him. Fathers in the past as in the present had abundant reason to regard literature as a poor profession; and Tasso's father, a poet himself, was doubly entitled to his opinion. And though the son did on the score of his youthful poem *Rinaldo* obtain from Alfonso II of Ferrara a home and a revenue, in virtue of which he produced his drama of *Amyntas* and his epic of "Jerusalem Delivered," the well-known troubles of his life in the palace leave the paternal view well justified. In any case, *Tasso's epic brought him no lucre*. It was published during his confinement, without his consent; and when he at length recovered his liberty it was to live out his life in perpetual embarrassment, despite the hospitality of many admirers. It is part of literary history that in 1573, while he had his stipend from the Duke of Ferrara, his wardrobe was pawned; and in later life he had many opportunities of renewing that experience. The book trade of that day was not on such a footing that he could raise money on copyrights; and his career was not such as to lure to the lyre later men of genius who heard of it.

It is barely necessary again to establish the fact *that the leading prose writers did not make literature pay any better than did the poets*. Machiavelli wrote his comedies and his novel *Belphegor* for his own pleasure during the period of his employ as State Secretary; and his *Prince* and his treatise on Livy were written in his latter years, not for sale, though he may have counted on their bringing him new political preferment. In short, in Italian as in Latin literature, the best products are found to be as a rule social windfalls, princely patronage serving in only a few cases to reward and sustain authors as such. It is not till we come to Metastasio, who produced opera librettos on a commercial footing, that we find anything like economic reciprocity between the writer and his audience; and in that case the literary product is of no permanent value.

VII

In French literature of the modern or printing period, we early meet with prospects or possibilities of commercial stimulus and reward for authors; *but here again it turns out that save in drama the chance of payment counts for nothing in production until we arrive at the age of the novel.* Villon, Rabelais, and Montaigne, in their different ways, represent literary gratuities to society. The "sad, bad, glad, mad" lad, the first finely inspired poet who wrote in French, may at times have made a little money by the manuscript of his ballads, but never enough to keep him long from the necessity of thieving. On the other hand, it was the chance of his clerkly training that alone made his gift demonstrable. Rabelais, also indebted to his good schooling for his chance of self-revelation, might conceivably have made a good deal of money by the sale of his books, which went quickly and far, but he never for a moment depended on them. As doctor, as professor, as curé, he had his professional earning or his regular stipend. Montaigne was a country gentleman of good estate, else had we never had his immortal essays, the fruit of comfortable and bookish leisure.

Corneille and Racine, ministering to their day by way of scenic entertainment, could in part live by the returns from the theatre; but even they were glad of regular pensions from the Crown. Molière, like Shakspere, had a direct share of the profits of the theatre—a far steadier source of income than the fees of a mere author.

Aside from the drama, the best French literature of the classic period continues to depend mainly on coincidences of capacity with unearned income or official provision. Bossuet,

placed and paid as a bishop, chanced to have uncommon
literary gift, whence his published orations and treatises;
Pascal, belonging to a well-to-do family, could not otherwise
have found strength at once to maintain and to reveal himself. As already noted, it is with the rise of the novel that
there emerges the beginning of a class who really live by
literature as apart from drama, Le Sage being the most
famous type; and the mass of high-class fiction, in proportion
to the total output, seems from the first to have been relatively small. *Montesquieu, being a man of means and
official position, belongs to the class of the gratuitous
authors.* Even Voltaire, who might have made large sums by
his works despite constant piracy, and who could probably
have lived by play-writing alone, relied mainly on non-
literary sources of income after the English subscription for
his *Henriade,* and wrote for influence, not for profit. With
a less fortunate start in life, he would indeed have figured,
in all likelihood, as a man of uncommon ability, since he
had in rare combination the gifts of making money and of
brilliant speech, but had he been born poor he would probably have been made a priest, or become a man of business—
anything but the Voltaire we know. *Diderot is the first distinguished French man of letters who earned a living as did
Goldsmith and De Foe in England by a general literary
activity*; and much of his work is impermanent, while
much was mere translation. The steadiest source of his income, too, was the *Encyclopédie,* on which he worked as
editor, sub-editor, adaptor, and proof-reader, as well as contributor; and his earlier earnings from other sources were
sufficiently precarious.

Mr. John Morley, who as a self-supporting man of
letters has had occasion to think on these matters, has
noted in a passage of his "Diderot" the difficulty of existence
for the great majority of writers of the middle decades
of last century. The second sentence is an exaggeration, as
it overlooks Montesquieu, Hume, Helvétius, Burke, Middle-
ton, and some others; but it is substantially just:—

"The man of letters shortly before the middle of the century was as much of an outcast and a beggar in Paris as he was in London. *Voltaire, Gray, and Richardson were perhaps the only three conspicuous writers of the time who had never known what it was to want a meal or go without a shirt*. But then none of the three depended on his pen for his livelihood. Every other man of that day whose writings have delighted and instructed the world since, had begun his career, and more than one of them continued and ended it, as a drudge and a vagabond. Fielding and Collins, Goldsmith and Johnson in England; Goldoni in Italy; Vauvenargues, Marmontel, Rousseau in France; Winckelmann and Lessing in Germany, had all alike been doubtful of dinner, and trembled about a night's lodging. They all knew the life of mean hazard, sorry shift, and petty expedient again and again renewed. It is sorrowful to think how many of the compositions of that time that do most to soothe and elevate some of the best hours of our lives, were written by men with aching hearts in the midst of haggard perplexities. The man of letters, as distinguished alike from the old-fashioned scholar and the systematic thinker, now first became a distinctly marked type."

The last quoted sentence unconsciously emphasises the point. *Literature as a profession,* save in the department of systematic novel-writing and play-making, *is typically impecunious*. Adam Smith in his day spoke of "that unprosperous race of men commonly called men of letters", going on to account for their poverty by an explanation which proves merely his own determination to recognise no economic principle save *laissez-faire. Smith's theory was that men of letters were poor because there were too many of them,* and that there were too many of them because they had generally been educated "at the public expense" to be clergymen—a twofold fallacy. Men of letters were and are as a rule educated not otherwise than lawyers and doctors and multitudes of men of business; and their frequent difficulty in finding a market is not a matter of their competing to supply a given article in excess of the demand, but of their rising above or falling below the grade of article wanted. And as Mr. Morley's list suggests, the cause of lack of demand is as often the temporary superiority as the inferiority of the product. Of course the men who succeed, even in fiction, often begin faultily, and learn mastery through failure. But the trouble is that the original literature which instead of amusing instructs, unless it be made for use in schools and colleges, ·is in the nature of things likely to pay ill or at best to pay slowly. Diderot got a French bookseller to pay Condillac a hundred crowns for the MS. of his book on Sensation; but even that exceptional windfall would hardly support Condillac during the time needed to think out such a treatise.

French literature since Diderot's day, while it does not reverse the generalisations above arrived at, exhibits the play of new social tendencies, since the "gratuitous" element tends to come from new sources, and the earning power of serious literature has certainly increased. The higher journalism, to begin with, offered gradually enlarging financial opportunities to men of letters; *and La Harpe's success showed that criticism and lecturing could be profitably combined*. Sainte-Beuve later earned a sufficient income by steady hard work as a critic on a high class journal; and he was only the most famous of a considerable tribe. Hugo from his youth up must have had a considerable revenue from his books, the poetry as well as the prose. Chateaubriand and Madame de Staël, though not depending on literature for a living, gained a good deal by it, as did Lamartine and De Musset; while Balzac and George Sand, the former with difficulties of his own making, lived entirely by the writing of fiction. And since that group passed away, whether it be that the competition of specially trained men has tended to drive the men of cultured leisure out of the field, or that the mere increase in the variety of pleasure now open to men of means and education draws the leisured class away from the literary work, it appears that it contributes progressively less of permanently valuable matter to literature.

Guizot, for instance, after working hard as a journalist, and translating Gibbon, became a professor of history, and later held a series of political offices. Cousin was successively a Sorbonne professor, a Councillor of State, and a Minister of Public Instruction. Thiers supported himself as a journalist while writing his histories. Michelet, after holding minor teaching posts, received a Government office and a professorship. Duruy was successively an inspector, a Normal College lecturer, a professor of history, and a Minister of Public Instruction. Henri Martin, who inherited a great library as well as private means, is the only eminent French historian of his day who does not seem to have needed to earn a salary; and he received a prize of 20,000 francs from the Institute. *Taine does not seem to have been at any time indigent.* Renan, who latterly earned large sums from a number of his books, had at first to be helped by his sister, then won money prizes, and later held a series of official positions apart from his professorship of Hebrew, without which he could hardly have done his work. Of all *the famous French publicists* of the century, *only Proudhon seems to have lived long by his pen alone;* and he, always poor, did much journalism, besides taking to business at one period for five years. It thus appears that while the rewards for serious book-writing have increased, they are still quite insufficient to yield a maintenance, save after a number of years of great cumulative success. *Such literature then remains in the main a result of special economic conditions,* though it latterly comes more often from professors and officials and journalists than from men of inherited fortune

VIII

It remains only to take a rapid view of our own literature, by way of checking the generalisations reached in the survey of others. Taking Chaucer as our starting point, we at once recognise the accidental conditions of his performance, which was accomplished in the leisure of a life either salaried in court service or sustained, albeit poorly, by court patronage. There was no other payment worth speaking of for the 'Canterbury Tales', and but for the support in question they would never have been written. In the early part of the printing period, too, the important author is always either possessed of means, however small, or supported otherwise than by the sale of his books. Spenser throughout his life was in one or the other case. Bacon, with all his literary and scientific enthusiasm, could never have produced his works but for private means and the income which came to him as a result of his legal training. By the drama, indeed, in England as elsewhere, educated men could live, but not well; Shakspere being, in virtue if his partnership in a theatre company, the one Elizabethan dramatist who made a fortune, or even a good livelihood. Ben Jonson was impecunious to the end: the others were chronically in want. Away from the drama, no income accrued to authorship. Hobbes was throughout his life maintained otherwise than by his books, his place in the Devonshire family giving him his leisure and his security during many years. Concerning *Milton, we have the significant record that for the first edition of 'Paradise Lost' the publisher paid him £5.* Locke, again, must have received a good deal more for his writings; but he, too, always had other sources of income, without which he could not possibly have done his work.

In the eighteenth century, however, we find arising in England, earlier than in France, incomes earned in the way of higher journalism and *belles lettres* apart from fiction and drama; and now the theory of the self-assertive omnipotence of genius becomes more plausible. Still, the thesis remains a fallacy. Swift, the greatest of the literary tribe in his day, had his professional income behind him; but De Foe, Addison, Steele, as later Goldsmith and Johnson, made more or less regular gains by essay-writing and hack-work. Pope, on the other hand, though like Dryden he made a good deal of money by his verse-translations as well as by his poetry, had private means, which took the place of Dryden's pension. Thomson had a pension and a sinecure, though he too earned money by poems and plays. The philosophic work, of course, continued to depend on special economic provision. Berkeley and Butler subsisted as bishops; Hume had various non-literary sources of income; Smith and Reid were university professors, and Smith was, further, privately pensioned. And though *Robertson and Gibbon earned large sums by their histories,* as did Hume, they could never have written them had they not had, the one a private fortune and the other an academic post. It is still in fiction and drama and hack-work and the higher jornalism that incomes are earned, and these not large or steady, as in the case of Goldsmith, Johnson, and Fielding, of whom the first was always embarrassed; while the second, after all his toils, was glad of a pension; and the third was glad of a magistracy. The prosperous Richardson, on the other hand, had a printing business behind him; and Sterne, though very successful as a writer, held one or more church-livings from the time of his leaving college till his death.

Broadly speaking, we may say that in English as in other literatures, poetry, philosophy, history, and science have been given to the world not for bread and butter, but by way of disinterested contribution from men who were enabled to live, well or ill, on other bases than those of book sales. Even Burns had done the bulk of his best work before he printed any, though he got £500 from his first edition; and he was able to refuse payment for the scores of songs he contributed to a publisher's collection, though at the end he had to cancel this refusal. As regards Burns's opportunities, be it repeated, it is a great mistake to regard him as uncultured. His father, though poor, was a man of strong literary tastes and intellectual capacity, who gave his children not only an exceptionally good schooling for their station, but a lead to literature such as few children receive in any class. And Burns suffered both as poet and man for his lack of financial advantages, as compared with contemporary poets. Chatterton's life and death tell a similar tale. Cowper never supported himself. Crabbe was provided for by a benefice.

The lives of men of science from Boyle and Newton onwards exhibit the same law. Dalton was first a schoolmaster, later a professor in a dissenting college, then again a tutor in mathematics, before he became secretary of the Manchester

Philosophical Society. Davy was successively a lecturer and a professor; and married a woman of fortune. Banks inherited private means. Black and Cullen were university professors; Hunter supported himself by medical instruction and practice. Burke seems to have been in large part supported by his aristocratic patrons till in his last years he received a pension, and withal he was always embarrassed. Sir William Hamilton, like Hume, had private means; and for the last twenty years of his life was a university professor.

The literary biography of the present century accumulates the proof to any desired extent. All of the distinguished poets, to begin with, were so provided for that they had a leisurely youth, and a good schooling. Wordsworth, Coleridge, Keats, Shelley, and Byron were one and all enabled to write their poetry by the chance of their having unearned incomes—Wordsworth from a legacy and a Government sinecure; Coleridge during many years from a private pension; Keats from his small inheritance; Shelley and Byron from their family fortunes. Even Southey, the most industrious writer of his day, had private help in his youth, and had poet laureate's pay during most of his literary life; Charles Lamb lived by his fairly easy clerkship in the India House; and De Quincey's private means supported him till he was nearly forty. Similarly Tennyson, who in the latter half of his life had a large income from his books, was in the first half poor on private means and a pension; Browning never needed to earn a shilling; Arnold, after starting with educational advantages, was able to secure a measure of leisure, though all too little, as a school inspector; while William Morris had inherited means, and added to them in business. Even Scott, though he latterly earned great sums by his books, began life in an easy fashion as a practising advocate and a law court official, and held his sheriffship while he wrote his novels; and Jane Austen and the Brontës were able to try novel-writing from the shelter of their homes. In fiction Thackeray and Dickens and George Eliot certainly succeeded financially from the first; but with the serious writers, as in previous ages, the case was otherwise. Bentham and Hallam had private means; James Mill, after hard times, secured a good post in the India office, held after him by his son John; Carlyle, after saving a little money as a schoolmaster, and meeting luck in getting good pay for long essays in the quarterlies, had his wife's little heritage to help him till his books brought him a steady income; Ruskin, whose private works latterly yielded him a large revenue, had his private fortune to proceed upon, as had Buckle; and Macaulay had his official posts in England and India before he wrote his history. Clinton had inherited means; Ricardo was a lucky stockbroker; *Grote a leisured banker;* Thirlwall a bishop; Milman a dean. It is needless to swell the list. We know that Mr. Spencer's performance was made possible only by his small private means, and, at a critical time, by help from America. *Darwin could never have done his scientific work had he been obliged to earn his living;* and Huxley and Tyndall like Kelvin and Jevons, subsisted long by their salaries as instructors. How letters have fared in the United States we have already seen.

To sum up, when we look at literature in any of the leading nations we find it self-supporting only in the departments of fiction and drama, and, let us add, the higher journalism, the lower journalism being of course outside the line of definition. Thus it comes about that in England to-day the word "author", as a special designation, means "novelist" far more often than anything else, since the writers of other books must in most cases be officials or professors or professional or business men, or possessors of private means. The few who, holding no offices, live by literature other than fiction and drama, usually eke out their incomes, it is believed, by journalism or lecturing, or by acting as advisers to publishers; that is to say, by happening to combine with "genius" faculties of another order, depending upon the chance of a good educational start. So that still, as of old, we owe our output in history, in philosophy, in social and natural science, and partly in criticism, to the chance combination of zeal and productive capacity by men who either earn their living in other ways or have no need to earn it at all. Even the successful Stevenson was past thirty, with domestic responsibilities, before he could support himself, and had he been less fortunately born might never have been heard of. It is true that latterly some of the leading younger poets—as Mr. Watson, Mr. Le Gallienne, Mr. Davidson, Mr. Yeats, Mr. Henley, and Mr. Bliss Carman—have lived by their pens, thus contrasting rather remarkably with their predecessors. But none of these, probably, makes by his mere poetry the income of an average middle-class shopkeeper; so that for them too, as for their fore-runners, poetry must have been a passion and not a pot-boiler.

IX

In fine, the individualistic society of the past, so often credited with creating conditions favoring the "survival of the fittest", in the intellectual as in the physical life, is seen rather to have fixed conditions which theoretically are almost the least favorable to a maximum (numerical) *development of potential mental faculty*. It has set up circumstances under which from a small minority only of the total population at any given moment could its best intellectual workers be drawn; and its methods have tended, in a degree that seems to be progressive in each civilisation after a certain stage, to keep latent even a large part of the capacity of this small minority. Hereditary opportunity of doing well in business keeps dumb, presumptively, the middle-class Shakspers, no matter how few: the inheritance of fortunes keeps free of due pressure the upper-class Thackerays, perhaps a less rare variety.

I have said that, *as time goes on, the class with inherited incomes appears to be yielding proportionally less and less intellectual service to society*. This seems to hold good in

England and the United States alike, since in both cases, especially the latter, the idle class has increased in number during the past fifty years, while its intellectual output has decreased, at least as regards the higher grades. I do not confidently undertake to explain this in terms of social conditions. M. de Candolle's specification of "family traditions" here suggests itself; the "new rich" being so often differently situated in this respect from the former rich, whose scions in many cases have had to revert to commerce. Again, some allowance ought perhaps to be made for the fact that an enormous amount of knowledge, scientific and historical, has been amassed within the past hundred and fifty years, and that a mind which fifty years ago might have been moved to write would to-day decide that enough had been written. But on the whole I strongly lean to the conclusion that the main factor at work is the growing power of civilised society, as a sphere of entertainment and enjoyment, to absorb the interests of leisured men. Since railways have so immeasurably facilitated travel; since European peace has so enormously encouraged it; since the opening up of North America, much of Asia, and much of Africa to the ordinary rich traveller has so vastly increased his field; since amusement of every description and physical comfort in every direction have been so remarkably developed; and since the literature of enjoyment, from the superior newspaper with its short tale and poem and its anecdotal biography to the masterly social novel and the entertaining history, has been so bewilderingly multiplied, the man of private means has been subjected to an incalculable amount of invitation—not to say temptation—to rest content with enjoying the good things of life. Such a process took place in the society of ancient Rome, from 100 B.C. till the end of the Empire; and the modern development of wealth and luxury has far exceeded anything in antiquity. In the Dark and Middle Ages, men turned to war through sheer need of excitement. After the height of the feudal period, in the north as previously in the south, we find the men of the

class which of old had been idle or military turning to literature and science—witness More, Montaigne, Bacon, Worces-
ter, and Napier. When the middle military period of civil
wars had led to that of quietude and standing armies, we
find aristocrats taking to literature anew—witness the titled
authors of the Restoration, and the generations of De Retz
and Saint Simon, Shaftesbury and Bolingbroke, followed
by those of Montesquieu and Condorcet, Hume and Gibbon, the Humboldts and Alfieri, Chénier and Shelley, De
Maistre, De Tocqueville, De Belloguet, Mahon, Von Ense,
and Fustel de Coulanges. *But the literary aristocrat promises
to disappear,* as do the divers tyes of Bacon, Goethe, Grote,
Guizot, Humboldt, and Buckle, and, for different reasons,
those of Milman, Thirlwall, and Stubbs. Of all which the
moral is that, if society in the strictly industrial period does
not deliberately construct an evocative machinery to do well
and systematically what the institution of inherited wealth
sometimes did imperfectly and at random, it will forfeit its
birthright in an even larger degree than did the military and
semi-military societies of the past.

Genius is conditioned economically, morally and socially.
Conditions which are partly favorable to it are seen to disappear by economic evolution even in an age of moral progress; and unless to the achieved moral and scientific progress be added a social science which takes intelligent heed
of such changes, there may follow manifold retrogression.

POSTSCRIPT.—Since the preceding pages went to press there
has been published the Autobiography of Mr. Herbert
Spencer, from which it appears that the statement on p. 651
is partly inaccurate. He had been enabled by the funds
which came to him on the death of his father to resume his
work while the American fund was being collected; and he
had further had generous offers of help in England, notably
from Mill. *But the Autobiography now makes it clear that*

his work as a whole could never have been accomplished save for the successive legacies which came to him from his uncles, and his inheritance from his father. That is to say, *the 'Synthetic Philosophy' was socially a windfall, turning on a set of economic accidents.* There could be no better confutation of his own social prescription, which would leave literary, scientific and artistic production wholly to the play of such chances, thus virtually restricting it to the small minority of the middle and upper classes.

his work as a whole could never have been accomplished
once for the successive legacies which came to him from his
uncles, and his inheritance from his father. That is to say
the Synthetic Philosophy was socially a windfall, turning
on a set of economic accidents. There could be no better
confirmation of his own social prescription, which would
leave literary, scientific and artistic production wholly to the
play of such chances, thus virtually restricting it to the small
minority of the middle and upper classes.

VIII
CONTEMPORARY SOCIOLOGICAL REFLECTIONS

COMMENTARY

When we come to contemporary sociology, we find it divided into different categories, conditioned by the tempo and interests of the times. In Europe, sociology deserts its quest for the objective, and orients itself in considerable part about the new concerns of the era. In Nazi Germany, sociology becomes Nazified; in Fascist Italy, it becomes Mussolini-ized; in Soviet Russia, it becomes Marxianized. In other countries, it assumes, in each case, the character of the culture of which it is a part.

In the United States, where such concerns are not yet urgent, sociology does not develop such marked differences and divisions. For the time being at least, because the United States is not confronted with economic or political crises of an imperative character, sociology is still free from the immediate claims and clamors of national doctrine. In all democratic countries sociology continues to maintain its independence and integrity as a science. Nevertheless, even in those countries, tendencies and trends are beginning to crop forth, especially in France and England, which represent danger-signs for the future. The United States in that respect is the only country in which no such danger-signs have appeared as yet on the horizon. Sociology in this country, although it is not so advanced in many respects as in a number of European countries, is still freer of state dictation and coercion than in any other country in the world.

The sociological doctrines that have developed here in recent years and decades are doctrines conditioned and qualified, to be sure, by the nature of the American social and economic environment; nevertheless, the nature of that environment has made and continues to make it possible for whatever doctrines that do develop to do so without restrictions or constrictions of state pressure. How long this

COMMENTARY 659

will continue, of course, is a matter of conjecture. If the conflict between classes does not intensify here as it has done in Europe such a condition may continue to prevail indefinitely, If, on the other hand, economic classes should develop the same conflicts here which they have done in European countries, it is plausible to assume that our sociological thought will begin to assume a European pattern.

For the time being, however, the only development suggestive of the European pattern is the emergence of Marxism in the work of various American social thinkers. This emergence to date is episodic and tangential. Notwithstanding, it is important as a possible foreshadowing of what may prove to be a full-fledged tendency within the next decade. At all events, it cannot be dismissed. Those whose contributions have been most outstanding in this field are Max Eastman, Sidney Hook, Max Nomad, and the editor of this volume. It is interesting to note, that all four are heterodox rather than orthodox Marxists. John Strachey, who, to be sure, is English, but whose influence has been mainly American, is the leading orthodox Marxian. Close to that school and yet not part of it is Stuart Chase, who in his essay on "Technocracy" expresses a point of view which ultimately may prove to be an Americanization of Marxism.

Major Douglas represents a financial solution to the world's sociological and economic ills which is making great headway in England and is making, largely through the agencies of Gorham Munson, some slight headway in America.

Among the more academic, liberal sociologists, who are far more typical than the radical sociologists of American sociology of today, there is a growing vision of society as a whole, which is represented most arrestingly and effectively by the work of Barnes, Maciver, Herskovits, Willey, Ross, Ogburn, Cairns, and Dewey, who, although a philosopher rather than a sociologist, has so successfully converted philosophy into sociology that he can be considered either with equal convenience and accuracy. These men along with a

number of others evidence the increasing interest which
academic sociologists reveal in the social process as a whole.
The close specialized emphasis so conspicuous in American
sociology a short while ago is giving way to larger interests
and wider perspectives.

THE DEVELOPMENT OF SOCIOLOGY

By HARRY ELMER BARNES

I. THE MOVEMENT FOR SOCIAL BETTERMENT AND THE ORIGINS OF SOCIOLOGY

WHILE the problems with which sociology concerns itself have been discussed by philosophers since the days of Oriental antiquity, sociology first definitely appeared, properly christened as a specific department of social science, about the middle of the nineteenth century. A large number of factors contributed to its origins, among them the growing interest in man and society and an increasing knowledge of the nature of man and his physical environment. Probably the most important influence creating sociology was, however, that general groping for social betterment which was produced by the misery that came in the wake of the industrial revolution and the factory system.

In the writings of certain early sociologists, this impulse to social betterment emerged in concrete utopian plans for a more happy and perfect system of social and industrial relations. With certain other writers, like Saint-Simon and Auguste Comte, it made its influence felt by suggesting that sociology should be a science of social progress. Such writers opposed sociology, thus conceived, to the well-meant but often naïve contemporary programs for social improvement.

On the other hand, such sociologists as Herbert Spencer, Ludwig Gumplowicz and William Graham Sumner were chiefly interested in developing the science of sociology to furnish irrefutable proof of man's inability to improve his social surroundings through any conscious effort at an artificial redirection of the trend of social evolution. It is apparent, therefore, that with both the enemies and friends of social reform it was this urge to social reconstruction which gave rise to the science of sociology.

II. THE FIRST PERIOD OF SOCIOLOGY: ANALOGY, DEFINITION, FIRST PRINCIPLES AND SYSTEMATIZATION

The first half century or more of sociology was given over chiefly to the effort to bring about a transition from social philosophy to social science. During most of this period writers approached the subject of social origins and social processes primarily from the standpoint of dogmatic *a priori* assumptions, sweeping generalizations and heroic efforts at systematization and at a synthesis of sociological information.

The first generation of sociologists after Auguste Comte were influenced chiefly by the effect of Darwinism upon social science. One school devoted itself mainly to an elaboration of the analogy between the individual organism and human society. These writers endeavored to show that human society exhibited in its organization systems of organs possessed by the individual biological organism. While often grotesque in matters of detail, this body of doctrine was of significance for social science in the way of emphasizing the necessity of a proper coordination and harmony between the various constituent groups of human society.

The other group of early biological sociologists devoted their attention primarily to illustrating the alleged analogies between biological evolution and social evolution, laying stress chiefly upon the similarity between the struggle for existence in biological evolution and the function of war in social evolution. This school of so-called "Social Darwinists" contended that in the same way that the struggle for existence had been the dynamic factor in the evolution of organisms, so war had been the chief constructive process in the evolution of humanity. It must be pointed out, however, that Darwin himself never sanctioned any such sociological interpretation of his evolutionary theories, and the title "Social Darwinism" was appropriated by this group without the approval of Darwin himself.

While enormously overemphasizing the importance of a single process, this school made an important contribution by pointing out the very great services of war in bringing an end to tribal society and in creating the origins of the political or territorial states which were to give to society that order and security essential to the further progress of civilization.

A large group of writers were dissatisfied with this tendency to be absorbed either in elaborating the analogies between the organism and society or in emphasizing the social significance of human warfare. They turned to: (1) a discussion of the scope and methods of sociology and of its relationships with the natural sciences and the other social sciences; (2) definitions of its chief concepts; and (3) the clarification of its province.

The so-called methodological discussions which this trend in sociology produced gave rise to much heated altercation between the exponents of these diverse interpretations of the nature, purpose and methods of sociology. It absorbed a great deal of energy in the somewhat sterile and unproductive task of definition, classification and demarcation, but there is no doubt that the net result was a clarification of the sociological atmosphere and a more general agreement as to the subject-matter and objectives of sociology. In other words, this sort of work represented the inevitable and essential preliminary period of definition and classification which marks the early stages of all science, natural or social. Certain writers, such as Georg Simmel and Albion W. Small, devoted their lives chiefly to these problems and methodology.

Paralleling these battles over definitions and methods was a comparable conflict among the sociologists as to the basic factor in the social process and the key to the development of a system of sociology. For example, Gabriel Tarde contended that the elementary social facts were to be located in the process of imitation; Emile Durkheim maintained, on the contrary, that the key to society lay in the impression of the group mind upon the individual psyche; Alexander Sutherland, Prince Kropotkin and others defended the assertion that the vital fact in the social life of man was to be found in sympathy and mutual aid; Gumplowicz and his disciples expounded the opposite thesis that it was in war and social conflict that one was to look for the core of the social process; Franklin H. Giddings asserted that in the consciousness of kind and differential reaction to stimulation one could discover the only valid basis for the construction of the principles of sociology; Gustav Ratzenhofer and Albion W. Small found in human interests the only rational clue to an understanding of social activity and organization; and Guillaume De Greef and Alfred Fouillée defended the contention that contractual relationships between individuals and societies constituted the *rationale* of society.

The debates thus generated gave rise to a large amount of acrimony and personal recrimination, but they stimulated each writer to the most effective defense of his particular thesis, with the resulting enrichment of our knowledge of the nature and potency of all these very important social influences and processes. The discriminating sociologist of the present day takes little stock in the all-sufficiency of any one of these unilateral views of society, but they each helped to create that body of subject-matter out of which a reliable synthesis can now be constructed. The growing recognition of the inadequacy of single-track interpretations of the social process has likewise produced that salutary and desirable tolerance among sociologists which was so notably lacking a generation ago.

The fourth significant characteristic of this earlier stage of sociological science was the effort of the leading writers to achieve a comprehensive systematization of sociological theory. Auguste Comte's system was given over chiefly to a comprehensive philosophy of history and an elaborate plan for the future reorganization of society along the lines of what he believed to be scientific principles. Herbert Spencer devoted himself to an attempt to interpret the origins and organization of society in terms of his particular formulae of cosmic evolution, incidentally giving some attention to the analogy between the organism and society and demonstrating to his own satisfaction the futility of social unlift. Lester F. Ward, taking his departure from Comte, exploited the terminology of natural science, particularly that of botany, to prove the original supremacy of the female sex and to demonstrate the possibility and desirability of conscious social reform guided by an ever-improving body of sociological knowledge.

Giddings, more eclectic and less dogmatic than these earlier writers, exploited and synthesized the great majority of sociological writings prior to his time in what was the most impressive and comprehensive system of sociology formulated prior to the opening of the present century. His particularistic emphasis upon the consciousness of kind was worked in as the primary item in a broad view of the origins and processes of society. Ratzenhofer and Small constructed a system of sociology about a classification and schedule of those vital human interests which give rise alike to individual activity and the organization and struggles of human groups. Hobhouse salvaged from the wreckage of the organic analogy the basic fact of the desirability of a harmonious coordination of social groups and classes and argued for a growing control by human knowledge and the human mind over the processes of social evolution. A similar point of view was elaborated by Ludwig Stein in Germany. One of the latest efforts at a system of sociology, that by Professor Franz Oppenheimer, is constructed upon an exploitation of the history of human society and the economic elements in the conflict of social classes. The most elaborate recent system of sociology is that of Dr. Leopold von Weise. He regards sociology as a study of the social process, conceived of mainly as "interhuman" relationships and behavior.

It is now very generally conceded that most of these efforts to produce comprehensive and finished systems of sociology were premature. The knowledge upon which a fairly secure synthesis could be built was not available when most of these writers formulated their concepts. Further, it is doubtful if the energy or mentality of any individual is adequate to a thorough mastery of the vast range of facts essential to sociological synthesis. Nevertheless, these early systems of sociology were in no sense a total loss. They called attention to the general nature of sociological material and vindicated for all time the importance of the sociological type of analysis. They also provided the point of departure for subsequent discussion and criticism.

III. CONTEMPORARY SOCIOLOGY AND THE TREND OF SPECIALIZATION

In the place of ambitious efforts at an all-embracing synthesis of sociology in the form of closed systems, the dominant trend in sociological science since about the opening of the twentieth century has been toward the splitting up of sociological endeavor among various groups of scientific men interested in one or another phase of the social process. Some have given their attention to a consideration of the problems of an adequate sociological methodology. Others have become interested in the relation between the physical environment and social processes. Another group has devoted itself to a consideration of the bearing of the facts of modern biology and genetics upon the origins, organization and future of human society. A large number of writers have surveyed and analyzed the wide range of psychological factors affecting the groupings and activities of men.

Another school has applied its efforts to a reconstruction of the course of cultural and social evolution. They have traced out the various stages in the development of the present-day forms of social organization and cultural expression, indicating as far as possible the various factors which have brought about the transition from the cave-dweller to the modern urban tenant, with all the social and cultural implications involved in this transformation. Then, the problems of social organization have attracted the attention of a large and active corps of workers in the sociological field. Finally, perhaps the most diverse and enthusiastic contribution to the literature of sociology is to be found on the part of those who are attempting to use the facts assembled by social science in the last century as the basis of more reliable and convincing plans for social and economic reconstruction than could be offered by the Utopian Socialists of the age of Robert Owen.

The progress of scientific method and specialization in the field of sociology can be well illustrated by the advances within each of these divers fields of approach to sociological analysis. In the first place, there has been an enormous improvement in the last twenty-five years with respect to both the exactness of method and the depth of knowledge possessed by the so-called specialists in particular fields of sociological study. In the second place, the process of specialization has been carried on so as to embody specialization within specialisms. For example, few social scientists would to-day contend that it is possible for them to master all the geographical factors affecting human society or all the biological processes which are of significance to the sociologists. It has become necessary, in other words, for the anthropogeographer or the social biologist to specialize upon a certain restricted range of problems and interests within his particular field.

In the cultivation of sociological methodology the first generations of students was absorbed chiefly with problems of definition, classification and the demarcation of the province of sociology. At the present time, this sort of work has been almost entirely abandoned, and we find those interested in methodology concerned with such problems as the application of statistical measurement to social processes, the analysis of the methods and limitations of the cultural approach to social origins and social organization and the consideration of the methodology essential for the study and comparison of the intelligence and social interests of definite human groups and cultures.

In other words, the generalized study of methodology has been supplanted by an examination of the utility and limitations of particular and relatively exact methodologies. The important fact is that all of them insist upon an ever greater utilization of the exact quantitative methods of natural science and a relative abandonment of the *a priori* and deductive technique of social philosophy. There is a general agreement that sociology can become a true science of society only in the degree to which it is able to appropriate and apply those exact methods of measurement and analysis which constitute the indispensable attributes of science in general. William F. Ogburn and his sympathizers and followers have been especially earnest in emphasizing this point.

In studying the absorbing and stimulating problem of the effect of the multifarious influences of the physical or geographical environment upon man in human society we find a corresponding progress away from sweeping and dogmatic generalizations and towards concrete study of the influence of particular geographical factors upon specific groups of men dwelling in well-defined geographical regions. The older anthropogeographers, from Ritter and Peschel to Ratzel, Reclus, Kirchhoff and Semple, attempted to present a systematic and comprehensive survey of the operation of all the so-called geographical "influences" upon man and society. With the progress of knowledge in this field, it became more and more difficult, however, for a single student to master all the facts involved in the various phases of the incidence of the environment upon man. Hence, we discover a growing tendency towards the specialization of writers upon some single type of geographic factor, such as climate, topography, routes of travel, waterways and routes of water communication, meteorological factors and alteration of geographic influences by the progress of the material culture of man.

But this is not all. Following the suggestions of the great French geographer, Paul Vidal de la Blache, and his disciples in other countries, the most advanced school of anthropogeographers have even come to doubt the feasibility of a generalized study of any one of these special geographic factors or influences. They contend that anthropogeography can become truly scientific only through an exclusive concentration upon the study of the effects of specific geographic factors upon a group of men inhabiting some very definite geographic region. In other words, regional physical geography has been followed by recognition of the inevitability and necessity of regional anthropogeography.

Further, the modern scientific anthropogeographer no longer proceeds from the naïve assumption of geographical determinism, but adopts the cultural point of view of the modern critical anthropologist and cultural historian. He recognizes that human culture is the dynamic element in society and civilization, and simply endeavors to discover the particular ways in which culture is conditioned by the geographical factors operating upon the inhabitants of the particular region studied. When one compares such a summary of the contemporary point of view as Lucien Febvre's "Geographical Introduction to History" with one of the best syntheses of the older generalizing anthropogeography, such as Miss Semple's English adaptation of Ratzel, he realizes the extent of the progress made in this field in the last generation with respect to both the degree of specialization and the precision of methodology.

The same advances toward detailed specialization and greater exactness of scientific method is to be observed among the biological sociologists. We have already pointed out that the first generation of biological sociologists concerned themselves primarily with an elaboration of such hypothetical analogies as the theory of the social organism and the doctrine of Social Darwinism. There was little effort to study in a scientific fashion well-founded biological processes and to discover through detailed observation their bearing upon the problems of human society. Such interests and activities as characterized biological sociologists thirty years ago have now become thorough anachronisms in the field.

In the first place, we have the demographers, represented by such men as Willcox, Thompson and Kuczynski, who are interested in gathering and classifying the facts descriptive of the social population, thus collecting the raw material for theoretical students of the problem. Along with these we have the students of the theory of population. They take their cue from Malthus and are known in general as Neo-Malthusians, primarily because of their reliance upon birth control, which Malthus had refused to sanction. These writers, well represented by Professor East, author of "Mankind at the Crossroads," are concerned with the quantitative aspect of population, namely, (1) the relation between the increase of population and the means of subsistence, and (2) the bearing of this situation upon the prosperity and progress of human society. They are, in general, sympathetic with the birth control movement as led by Mrs. Sanger and others, holding that the chief avenue to social well-being is to be found mainly through some practicable method of maintaining the population at the level which will insure a relatively high standard of living, assuming the existence of an adequate technology and an efficient economic system. Certain members of this school have endeavored to formulate laws of population, qualifying or supplementing the original generalizations of Malthus.

Another important group of writers concentrate their attention upon the qualitative aspects of the population problem. They are concerned with the biological evolution of man, the question as to whether civilization has had a disastrous effect upon the biological quality of the human race, and the whole issue of eugenics, involving the problem of the possibility of the artificial improvement of the physical quality of the human stock. Writers like Otto Ammon, Karl Pearson, Edwin Grant Conklin and Samuel J. Holmes represent discriminating scientific exponents of this point of view, which has been set forth in a more popular and exuberant fashion in the writings of Mr. A. E. Wiggam.

Finally, there should be noted the physical anthropologists and the scientific students of race and racial characteristics. Such scientific men devote themselves to the ascertainment of the physical criteria of race and to the accumulation of exact facts with respect to the physical traits of the major races of mankind. In carrying their researches beyond physical investigations to an analysis of the mental traits of the various races, they link hands with the differential psychologists. The work of the physical anthropologists, admirably represented by men like Arthur Keith, Rudolph Martin and Aleš Hrdlička, together with that of the differential psychologists and the cultural historians, offers the best possible antidote to the vagaries of Madison Grant and his disciples who have been busy in recent years disseminating the Nordic rehabilitation of the old Aryan myth.

These various groups of scientific students of the biological foundations of society are at last making available the relevant facts and processes of biology, so that they may be appropriated in an intelligent fashion by the alert legislator and discriminating social worker. Only superstition and bigotry prevent us today from undertaking a speedy adoption and application of their more significant and demonstrably valid recommendations.

Psychological sociology likewise had its origins in the last quarter of the nineteenth century with writers who dealt in broad and sweeping dogmatisms concerning such complex and general psychological factors as custom, imitation, fashion, impression, emulation, sympathy, etc. At this time there was little or no reliable technical psychology to be learned, and these writers possessed but a slight familiarity with even such psychology as existed. While some progress took place in the interval between 1890 and 1910, as exemplified by the sociological interests of psychologists like Baldwin or the better mastery of psychological principles by a sociologist like Cooley, it may safely be said that the first treatise on psychological sociology which demonstrated the author's comprehensive familiarity with the facts of reliable psychology was C. A. Ellwood's "Sociology in its Psychological Aspects," published in 1912. W. I. Thomas's mastery of social psychology had been demonstrated mainly by a number of erudite articles and monographs.

Yet this ambitious attempt at synthesis to be found in Professor Ellwood's useful book did not set the pattern for the development of psychological sociology in the next decade. Rather, we find an altogether commendable tendency toward further specialization and a more thorough cultivation of technical psychology. The popularity of the instinct hypothesis, launched by the appearance of Professor McDougall's book in 1908, has provoked a vast amount of controversy and has resulted in a general clarification of this problem, the best synthesis now existing in the field being Professor Bernard's monograph on "Instinct." The behavioristic impulse emanating from Watson and Max Myer, has been exploited for social psycholology by Allport, Burnham and a number of others who are interested in the important social applications of the theory of the conditioned-reflex.

The social significance and applications of Freudianism have been examined and exploited in a discriminating fashion by Martin, Groves, Ogburn, Holt and Thomas. An extremely promising effort has been made to work out the all-important synthesis of behaviorism and Freudianism by Allport, Martin, Hamilton, Young and others, a development which has been hampered by the vigorous rhetorical, but somewhat illusory, opposition of Watson to Freudianism. The psychology of the crowd is now beginning to be studied in a scientific fashion by Martin and others. The significance of habit-forming complexes for psychological sociology has been indicated in detail by Ellwood, Dewey and Gault. Wundt, Hall, Lévy-Bruhl, Paul Radin, Golden-weiser, James Harvey Robinson and others have devoted themselves to a study of the psychological history of the race, clarifying the similarities and contrasts between the thinking of primitive and modern man.

The provision of scientific and practicable methods of mental testing by Binet, Simon, Goddard, Yerkes, Terman, Otis and others has made possible the development of differential psychology, a technique of the greatest significance for the further analysis of the problems of eugenics, mental hygiene, criminology, immigration and democracy. Finally, the necessity of abandoning a theory of psychological determinism and adapting the psychological theories of society to the notion of cultural conditioning has been recognized by nearly every group now interested in psychological sociology. The most ardent exponents of this point of view have been the critical anthropologists of the Boas school, and Graham Wallas, F. C. Bartlett, W. I. Thomas, C. A. Ellwood, W. F. Ogburn and F. Znaniecki.

The net result of these labors has been to put at our disposal a vast body of relevant psychological information of the greatest practical significance for human betterment and a more adequate and penetrating conception of social processes. Nothing could more effectively illustrate the progress in psychological sociology in the last generation than a comparison of such books as Gustave Le Bon's "The Crowd," or Gabriel Tarde's "Laws of Imitation," with Allport's or Young's "Social Psychology."

In the study of the history of human society there has been notable progress away from the *a priori* philosophy of history characteristic of the early stages of historical sociology. Building upon the firm foundation of the laws of cultural development established by the critical anthropologists and upon the vast array of facts concerning social and cultural evolution gathered by the conventional historians, the students of social and cultural history have been able to work out a most impressive survey of the history of human culture from the Old Stone Age to the Hoover prosperity. There has been an escape both from the inaccuracies of the old philosophy of history and from the irrelevancies of the episodical and anecdotal historians of the conventional academic school of history-writing. In this field, as in others, specialization has been necessary, as no single student of social evolution could personally master the technical equipment or the body of facts involved in a survey of the totality of human cultural development.

The study of the facts and problems of social organization has attracted a varied group of authorities. The forms of social organization have been discussed in great theoretical detail by Georg Simmel. Simmel's conclusions have been made intelligible, as well as accessible, to English readers by his disciple, Dr. N. J. Spykman. The biological basis of social organization has been analyzed by writers such as Gini, Pearson, Carr-Saunders, Ammon, West, Holmes, Kelsey and Hankins. Tarde, Durkheim, Wallas, Cooley, Ross, Ellwood, Bernard, Bogardus, Young, Williams and others have devoted their attention to the psychological factors involved in the organization of society. The economic aspects of the question have been investigated by Loria, Sombart, Weber, Schmoller, Webb, Hobson, Hammond and Cole, by Veblen and the institutional economists, and by Professors Seba Eldridge, Charles Austin Beard and others interested in the economic basis of politics. The political foundations of social organization have received especial attention from Gustav Ratzenhofer, Robert Michels, Graham Wallas, Harold Laski, Albion W. Small, A. F. Bentley and F. H. Giddings.

The most significant fact about all these modes of approach as specialized forms of analysis of social organization is that the old obsession with definition and classification has been superseded by a concern with the vital and dynamic processes involved in the origins of social groups and their mutual conflicts and adjustments. Much of the credit for this wholesome change is due to Ratzenhofer and Small.

The reaction of these various phases of progress in scientific sociology upon social work and social reform has forwarded the ultimate realization of the ambitions of the founders of sociology to create a scientific guide for the betterment of mankind. On the whole, social work has abandoned the ideal of amelioration and has adopted the slogan of prevention, the key to which is to be derived from a mastery of the scientific facts of sociology.

Sociology, properly understood, does not discourage "uplift." Indeed, it would seem that the chief vindication of sociology is its real potential service to the cause of increasing the happiness and prosperity of human society. What sociology does insist is that uplift shall cease to be governed by theological and sentimental motives and shall found its objectives and methods upon the indisputable facts wrought out by sociology in the last quarter of a century.

The extensive advances in the subject-matter of sociology, as well as the increasing tendency towards specialization, which have been all too briefly summarized in the preceding paragraphs, make it obvious that the future of sociology must decisively be a cooperative matter. Any synthesis of the field by a single individual is doomed to result in either grotesque inaccuracies or in the superficialities compatible only with a brief text-book survey of the field.

IV. THE INFLUENCE OF SOCIOLOGY UPON THE SPECIAL SOCIAL SCIENCES

We should at least make passing mention of the influence of sociology upon the other social sciences. Its effect upon the study of history has been chiefly to emphasize the fact that man does not function as an individual but as a member of a group; to aid the progressive historian in his analysis of the various forms of institutional life in which man participates; and to emphasize the conception of civilization as a genetic and dynamic process. Sociology has been particularly useful in promoting a broad and synthetic view of the processes of historical causation.

Sociology has been able to offer a number of helpful suggestions to open-minded economists, for example: emphasis upon the group basis of custom and fashion which determine to so large a degree the nature of economic demand; an indication of the interrelation of the economic with the other factors in the social process; and a clarification of the nature of the social institutions which condition the operation of the economic factors in society.

On no other special social science has the influence of sociology been more significant than with regard to political science. Sociology has furnished indispensable information as to the nature and foundations of political control and has cleared up many obscure problems related to the origins of the state. It has also given a real *rationale* to politics by indicating the social process which goes on within the state and by making it clear that the real function of the state is to act as an umpire of this social process. The influence of sociology upon jurisprudence is comparable to that upon the science of government. Sociology has emphasized the social origins and function of law; has indicated the fundamental social basis of all valid legal principles and has emphasized the function of progressive jurisprudence in the way of social engineering and the guidance of social change.

The sociological influence upon ethics has been revolutionary in theory, however little it may have affected conduct in practice. It has made clear the group basis of all ethical guides and criteria, however dogmatic a social group may be with respect to the allegation of the divinely revealed nature of its ethical concepts and practices. Sociology has also emphasized the necessity of adopting a secular basis for the judgment of commendable conduct. It insists that the object of ethics should be to produce an ever greater number of happy and efficient human beings here upon the earth, and not to save a vast throng·of souls eagerly quitting their earthly misery.

The relationships between sociology and esthetics have not been adequately cultivated thus far, but the group foundation of esthetic judgments is readily apparent, and enough has already been done to indicate the real importance of art as a form of social expression and a mode of social control. With the gradual secularization of human interests we may predict that esthetics will ultimately come to occupy the position held by theology in the interest and affections of the early sociologists.

The most important general effect which sociology has had upon all the special social sciences is to emphasize continually the unity of the social process and to promote a synthetic point of view on the part of all types of social scientists. This guards against the narrowness and superficiality which invariably accompany a partial view of the processes and institutions of society.

V. OBSTACLES TO THE DEVELOPMENT OF SOCIOLOGY

In spite of the remarkable strides which sociology has made in volume of subject-matter and increasing exactness of its methods, it has made relatively slow progress in achieving academic recognition, in receiving adequate consideration from legislators and public officials, and in securing the good-will and confidence of the general reading public.

There are a number of causes of this situation. The first might be called the "euphonistic" obstacle, namely, the confusion of sociology with socialism because of the similarity in the pronunciation of the two words. This may seem preposterous, but the writer believes it to have been more important than any other influence in prejudicing the average timid and conservative citizen against sociology. Even the librarian of one of our foremost graduate schools in this country fiercely opposed sociology and sociological books for a generation because of his firm belief that a socialist and a sociologist were one and the same person in each and every case.

In the second place, we must consider the opposition of pure and pious folk, who look upon sociology as a subject which undermines morality and leads to atheism. When properly taught, sociology must of necessity provide the foundation for any valid body of morality or any social religion. It is true, however, that sociology analyzes with frankness and candor the anachronisms in the present moral code and Fundamentalist religion. Hence the alarm with which half-educated people view the teachings of sociologists.

At the same time, these "vile" sociologists, as they appear to the late Mr. Bryan and not a few college professors, are viewed with a mixture of amusement and pity by those in real touch with life and its problems. There is no doubt that three fourths of our American academic sociologists would read such an innocuous if illuminating book as Miss Kirchwey's "Our Changing Morality" or Professor Joad's "Thrasymachus" with unmitigated horror and disgust. Over half of them would gladly lock arms with the late Wayne Wheeler and John S. Sumner. Likewise, most of them are thoroughly "sold" to the capitalistic system and the "theories of the leisure class," a fact which removes them from active contact with the campaign for social and economic reconstruction.

Hence, those on the "firing line" of cultural, social, economic and ethical advance will have nothing to do with the majority of the sociologists. What appears to the pious and respectable as unmistakable proof of depravity and revolutionary radicalism on the part of sociologists seems to the realists and reformers to be nothing less than pedantry, ignorance, prudery, hypocrisy or infantile timidity.

Another recent form of opposition to sociology arises from progressives who fear the alleged pernicious influence of foundations and endowments. Much current sociological research is subsidized by the great foundations which have been endowed by very wealthy men interested in preserving the existing social, economic and political order. Naturally, most subsidized research must carefully avoid projects likely to result in unsettling discoveries, or, if such results do emerge, they must be obscured. Such considerations, as Benjamin Stolberg has amply indicated, hamstring both scientific candor and the practical value of sociological research.

Again, we must list among the powerful sources of opposition to the progress of sociology the jealousy of the other social sciences. History, economics and political science were established as academic subjects from a half century to a century earlier than sociology. This has given them a stronger hold upon the faculties and administrative boards of the colleges and universities. The opposition of these older vested interests to sociology has been intensified by the fact that the vivd human appeal of sociology has attracted to sociology courses large numbers of students who would otherwise have been swelling the class registers and enhancing the local prestige of solemn and respectable teachers of history, political science or economics. Therefore, in certain institutions, such as Princeton, Harvard, California, Cornell and Johns Hopkins, together with most of the aristocratic New England colleges, sociology has been excluded altogether or has been offered in an inadequate and misleading fashion by professors of economics. In many institutions, such as Wisconsin, while courses in sociology are tolerated, the instructors in sociology have been kept under the general control of the department of economics or government.

To the opposition of the vested interests of the older social sciences must also be added the even more vigorous antipathy of the departments of mathematics, science, literature and other even older and more respectable departments and vested curricular interests.

The future of sociology is a matter for prophecy and not for history, and we are only concerned in this article with history. The place that sociology will occupy in the future of human thought and action will depend upon a multitude of factors, some connected with sociology itself and others with general trends in the public mind.

Before sociology can command the unqualified respect and support of intelligent and thoughtful persons it must divest itself of a sentimental adherence to indiscriminate efforts at uplift; it must reject whole-heartedly the impurity-complex which it has inherited from its Puritan and ministerial ancestry; and it must reduce the paralyzing influence of discipleship and dogmatism to which all the social sciences are in differing degrees susceptible. The degree to which it will influence social thought and action will also depend upon how far society surrenders its contemporary submission to rhetoric, convention, tradition and propaganda, and demands competent technical and scientific guidance.

If it be objected by many that sociology has not yet secured a sufficiently high level of agreement among its various schools, and that it has not yet perfected its methodology with adequate scientific precision, it may safely be answered that it will probably remedy these defects long before society will be willing to accept its constructive assistance.

I

CLASSES OF SOCIAL INTEREST

By R. M. MACIVER

THERE are . . . two great classes of interests, as also of the forms of thinking and willing which correspond to these, which must at all hazards be kept distinct in our thought. The confusion of them has vastly retarded sociological reasoning, and it is part of the nemesis attaching to uncritical discussion that, however we now distinguish them, our terms can only with difficulty be kept free from wrong associations. When each of a number of beings pursues an interest like or identical *in type* to that which every other pursues, say a livelihood, or reputation, or wealth, or any other interest which is for each discrete and personal, we may call the interests they severally pursue *like* interests. Such interests do not necessarily involve any community, any social relationship, between the beings who will them, however like the interests are. The interests of all the beasts of the field when they seek their food create no unity, and were there food enough for all, would create no conflict. The interests of all are identical in type, but there is no common interest. When, on the other hand, a number of people all pursue one single comprehensive interest of them all, say the welfare or reputation of town or country or family, or again the success of some business in which they are all concerned, we may call that interest a *common* interest. The pursuit of the common welfare of many remains a common interest, no matter what ulterior interest may inspire that pursuit. The consideration of motives may lead us into a further sphere of like interests, as when men seek the welfare of their community for the sake of some direct or reflected glory it brings themselves; but the interest itself remains common. Often the attainment of like interests is sought through the establishment of a common interest, as when men form a trading company. Here the common interest, that in the welfare of the company as such, as a single indivisible organization, is secondary, the like interests being prior. In other cases the common interest is primary. The common interest is always a directly social interest; the like interests are always egoistic. And the two form the inextricably entwined motives of the greater part of our activity. But it is for that very reason we must keep them distinct in our analysis. Otherwise we shall find in social phenomena a simplicity they do not possess.

By secondary common interest I mean that interest in associational or communal welfare which is itself dependent on a further exclusive interest, as when men seek the good of others because of the advantage or glory it brings themselves. Primary common interest is that which is dependent on no such further interest. Primary and secondary common interests are the mingled sources of all our social activity. The love of an association or community is very often like the love of many parents for their children, whom they love as a kind of extension of their own individuality, as a kind of property. Even when the primary interest is predominant, the secondary interest supports it. The two are not so much kinds of common interest as its factors. In all our relations with others, it is difficult to evade the promptings of the intrusive self-interest. The psychologist finds in his sympathy with the sorrows of others an element of reflected sympathy with himself conceived as in a like situation, in his efforts to relieve the sufferings of others a desire to attain also a certain self-satisfaction and to banish a cause of self-pain; he finds his sympathy with the happiness of others crossed by pangs of envy if the same happiness has passed him by, and his efforts to bring happiness to others stimulated by the reflected happiness the endeavor brings to himself. The mind of man is infinitely too complex to admit of "single-mindedness"; it has been shaped by infinite experiences that reach out of all imaginable time. It is only a lunatic, a man whose past has suffered violent dissociation from his present, whose motives are ever simple. To have *absolutely* simple motives *is* to be a lunatic, for not even genius can ever attain to such simplicity.

We can now make some further distinctions. Like interests fall within the wider class of discrete interests, *i.e.,* interests as pursued by each for his own personal or individual fulfillment. It is better to call these interests "discrete" than "individual," since of course all interests are individual in one sense, *i.e.,* that they are all interests of individuals. When several persons pursue discrete interests which yet are like or identical in type, we have *like* interests; when they pursue discrete interests which differ in type, we have *unlike* interests. Unlike interests are interests which, so far as those who pursue them are concerned, lie in unrelated spheres of activity and so do not involve or create any direct social relations. For example, the interests of philately and astronomy need never bring the philatelist and the astronomer into social relations. But such isolation of interests is always relative. Again, intermediate between like and unlike interests are the very significant class of *complementary* interests, partly like, partly unlike. When the interests of two or more persons, while not wholly alike, are yet interdependent, involving reciprocal service, we may call them complementary. The most obvious example are sexual interests, but others of very great importance are revealed in the division of labor within community and in the whole fabric of reciprocal rights and obligations. It is obvious that complementary interests do most easily and immediately create common interest.

A further distinction within like interests has already been implied. Men may pursue their like interests in social isolation; their interests may run *parallel,* involving, for the individuals in question, no contact whatever. Or again their pursuit of like interests may bring them into relationships either of conflict or of harmony. When two or more persons pursue an object of such a character that the attainment of it by one involves in so far the failure of the others to attain it, we have *conflicting* interests. In the simultaneous pursuit of such an exclusive object, there results, as Kant said, the kind of "harmony" involved in the pledge of Francis I to the Emperor Charles V, "What my brother wants [*i.e.,* Milan], that I want too." But on the other hand many objects which men seek, each for himself, are yet either expansive through coöperation, or at any rate such as to be more easily attainable by each through the coöperation of all, and under these conditions the like interests are *concordant*. Coöperation increases, conflict diminishes the objects to which the like interests of men are directed. This fact that like interests may lead either to harmony or to conflict, that these attitudes are in some measure alternatives, has vast significance for the evolution of community. . . .

We may now map out the whole field of interests, from the standpoint of social relationship, as follows:

INTERESTS

Discrete — Common

Unlike Complementary Like   Secondary Primary

Conflicting   Parallel Concordant

The Kinds of Common Interest.—We have next to enumerate and classify the various types of interests which create and sustain community and its associations. The task has often been attempted in recent years, and various helpful classifications have been made.* If we do not adopt any of

* Perhaps the best of these classifications is that of Lester Ward, *Pure Sociology,* 2nd ed., p. 261.

those, it is because none of them is made from the point of view set out in the introduction of this work. A completer classification than any yet offered is necessary for our purpose. Interests are the springs of community, and a comprehensive classification of them is a necessary preliminary to the study of it.

Our concern here is with interests as common and not as discrete, for it is common interests which are the sources of community. All like interests are potential common interests; in so far as that potentiality is realized community exists.

Like interests pass by endless transitions from the most universal, shared by all men, down to the most particular and intimate. All men are alike in respect of certain fundamental interests. We all have like organic needs, needs of food and drink, air and light, clothing and shelter. As these are needs of all living beings, they create like interests for all living beings. But every like interest, as we shall see more clearly at a later stage, is best secured for all when all whom its pursuit brings into contact pursue it in common under regulated social conditions. The universality of like organic needs is thus in the long run a mighty socializing force.

Some psychical interests seem equally as universal as are organic needs. For example, justice and liberty (properly defined) are interests of all men, demanding and creating social unity, though not yet in the measure of universality. But on the whole, the more specific psychical interests are not so universal as the specific organic interests. If we adopt Aristotle's distinction of "life" from "good life," we may say that universal like interests are those on which "life" depends, while the particular like interests of men reveal their varying conceptions of "good life." Men seek power, distinction, adornment, knowledge, and endless forms of spiritual satisfaction, but not with unanimity of their pursuit of organic necessities.

The like interests of likes become in part the common interests of likes. In so far as men realize that likeness of nature or of interest means potential common interest, in so far as they realize the value of community, they create associations for its furtherance. In the classification which follows, interests are viewed in relation to the associations which they create. These associations answer to (a) the whole complex of communal interests, or (b) some less extensive group of interests, or (c) single specific interests.

(a) A community is a social unity whose members recognize as common a sufficiency of interests to allow of the interactivities of common life. We have already seen that community is a matter of degree and that it is most readily determined by territorial boundaries. For local contiguity not only permits the conversion of preëxistent like interests into common interests, but itself ensures the operation of biological and psychical laws which constantly weave new common interests.

The completest type of community is the nation; and when a nation is allowed free expression it creates an autonomous state. Within the state there are established, corresponding to the narrower communities within the nation, the local governments of district and town. The state and its subdivisions are associations, organized *forms* of society. Communities must create associations in order to uphold communal interests, associations which pursue these interests in specific ways. And the state is the greatest of associations because it upholds, in its specific political way, the greatest recognized complex of common interests, those of a determinate community.

(b) When a group is held together by a complex of interests, but itself is constituted as a portion and not the whole of any community, it is usually called a class. A class may have some one predominant interest round which the others cluster and which gives its name to the class. Thus we speak of governing classes, in terms of a predominant political interest, of leisured classes, working classes, professional classes, agricultural classes, aind so on, in terms of their respective economic interests. Or again we distinguish classes as upper, middle, and lower, in terms of social status. To constitute a class, a group must have a complex of common interests, and these common interests must distinguish them from other groups of the community possessing other, and it may be antagonistic, common interests. The extreme of this opposition is revealed when classes constitute castes.

A class in turn pursues its complex of interests through associations. Being only an element in a community its members cannot constitute a state, but they create associations, of which the type is the political party, which seek to control the policy of the state. We may include here also those associations which foster and are held together by group sympathies or "class spirit," that general sociality which exists between members of any group.

(c) Men are not content to pursue common interests merely in so far as these form complexes of greater or less completeness. They come more and more to establish associations for every interest in its specificity. Only by the help of such associations can the endless degrees and varieties of likeness (and thus of community) in interests be adeqately recognized and furthered. Wherever men discover that they have any common interest the ground is prepared for the corresponding association. It is in line of evolution that these associations should grow continually in extent, in number, and in singleness of aim. Already they present a vast and bewildering array.

It is exceedingly difficult to classify, completely and without cross-division, these specific interests and the associations which they create. One obstacle to classification is the lack of definite names for the various groupings of social phenomena. A more serious obstacle is that interests lie behind interests in the most perplexing ways. We have, for instance, an interest in wealth; but it is in general for the sake of further interests which wealth may serve. Or we have an interest in knowledge, but it may be for the sake of the wealth which that knowledge may bring, and thus ultimately for the sake of the further satisfactions which wealth may acquire—or it may be for the sake of knowledge itself. Or again, we may have a political interest which is determined by an economic interest, and so on.

Reflection on this difficulty leads to the first division of specific interests, that into ultimate and derivative. For, although any specific interest whatever *may* be derivative, *i.e.*, may exist as an interest because it is a means to some ultimate interest; yet some are essentially derivative and others are in their proper nature ultimate.

Of derivative interests the two great classes are the political and the economic. The political interest is directed towards the character of that great organization of society which upholds liberty in order, the condition of the fulfillment of all other interests and whose policy and direction is of vital significance for these other interests. It is for the sake of these that the political interest, in all its degrees and forms, exists. The economic interest is in like manner derivative. This interest is so universal simply because it too is a means of all ultimate interests. It is in no way limited to the field of industrial and commercial activity; but it is bound up, in one way or another, with the pursuit of *every* interest. If men paint or preach or philosophize, they usually expect to derive from that work, besides the satisfaction it may bring, the means of satisfying their other interests, just as certainly as if they cultivated the land or manufactured goods or bought and sold. Man has many ultimate interests, and he can satisfy them only if he adds these derivative interests to the rest.

Of ultimate interests the two main classes are those based on organic needs and those based on psychical needs. We may, for the sake of conciseness, call these, respectively, organic and psychical interests; but we must in so doing remember that all interests are psychical, the interests of minds. But some interests are created by organic needs and some by non-organic needs. There is no line of demarcation between the two; they pass by subtle transitions into one another. They are interdependent and are indeed meaningless apart. Again, interests of the one type may be made the means to interests of the other; we have derivative organic interests, dependent on ultimate psychical interests, and we have the reverse order of dependence. But both types may be pursued, and usually are pursued, though not in equal degrees, as underivative.

Organic interests are best divided, for our purpose, into sexual and non-sexual. The former have a social significance and a character of complementariness which distinguish them sharply from all other organic interests. The term "sexual" is here used in a wide sense, to include all those interests which we ascribe to sexual love, family affection, and the spirit of kinship. Non-sexual interests comprise our interests in food and drink, in exercise and recreation, in clothing and shelter, in whatever fulfills all the other organic needs.

From these we pass to psychical interests. These are both difficult to distinguish at the border line from organic interests, and are themselves so interwoven and complex as to render classification difficult. The following line of distinction seems the simplest and may be adequate for our purpose. We adopt the psychological distinction between knowing, feeling, and willing as *aspects* of mental activity, and distinguish interests according to the predominant aspect in each case. (1) There are interests in which the intellectual aspect predominates, the scientific, philosophic, and educational interests in the discovery, systematization, and communication of knowledge. To discover, to systematize, and to communicate, these are interdependent activities and form a unity of interests. They create the multitude of scientific associations, whose labors have both widened the horizons of our knowledge and are in especial the source of those technical utilities which are constantly transforming our social world. We must add to these the specifically educational associations, which, however diverse and comprehensive their aims, can pursue them in one way only, by imparting knowledge. (2) There are interests in which the emotional aspect dominates, the artistic and religious interests. The former creates a multitude of associations, artistic (in the narrower sense), musical, dramatic, literary; and the latter creates that most significant association, the church. (3) We may add to these the interests in which the aspect of will predominates, the interests in power, prestige, and self-assertion. These do not directly create specific associations, owing to their lack of content or definition, but they are always actively at work shaping associations, determining both their internal structure and their modes of operation. They are especially important as determinants of the derivative interests, for government and wealth are in a peculiar way at once the forms and the sources of power.

All specific common interests of men fall within the scheme we have outlined above. Every one of those interests, it must be noted, may be pursued either as primary or as secondary, either for the sake of the common good involved or for the sake of the private advantages it may bring to the pursuer; and usually the two motives are inextricably blended. It is therefore a mistake of analysis to add the "egotic" as a kind of interest comparable with, say, the organic interests. Egoism and altruism are not kinds of interests at all, but rather ways in which we relate ourselves to our interests. Even the interests in power and prestige may not be "egotic." The power sought after may be that of family, class, or nation; and even when we seek power for ourselves, it may be for the sake of any of these. Again, it is a mistake to place the "ethical interest" alongside, say, the scientific or artistic. If we speak of an ethical interest at all, we must count it as general and not specific, for ethical activity works in and through all interests, their universal and final determinant.

As we have said, it is only in later stages of social evolution that specific interests are demarcated and create specific associations. In primitive community they exist only as complexes of interests. This does not mean, of course, that in civilization these complexes are broken up; on the contrary, they become greater and completer. Differentiation never means the dissolution of unity, but only the revelation of its character.

THE CULTURAL APPROACH TO SOCIOLOGY

By MELVILLE J. HERSKOVITS and MALCOLM M. WILLEY

As a general summary of the importance of the cultural approach to the study of sociology, the following remarks may prove useful. Since the days when Man first began to think about society, there have been evolved numerous systems to account for the motives and mechanisms of human association. Race, psychology, environment—each has in turn been utilized to furnish the universal key to their solution. And each in turn has been found to contain a modicum of truth. And each, in the end, has been found too rigid, or too locally conceived, to fit the seeming chaos that comes when mankind at large is brought within the range of vision. The usual consequence is that, when an attempt is made to explain all social phenomena in the light of one of these theories, so many exceptions become at once apparent that the numerous applications attempted are seen to be not at all comprehensive, and the theory is thereby vitiated. The difficulty seems to have been that the earlier sociologists have been more philosophers than scientists. Each imbued with his idea has sought those instances which would support his *a priori* premises and has quite neglected to take into account historical relationships in the working of his principle in concrete instances. No fault can be found with the logic of the systems as such, once the premises are granted. The concentration has thus far, however, been so on concept that method has been neglected. It would seem that more emphasis has been laid upon the collection of data to support these preconceived systems than upon the collection of data which must be antecedent to an hypothesis truly *a fortiori*.

This objection has been sensed by others who have been

dissatisfied with the insufficiency of sociological theorizing. Especially is this the case with a group of American anthropologists, who by their detailed investigations of exotic peoples, have come to see and realize more and more clearly that no theory of society yet advanced has a universal applicability. Thus far there has been a notable hesitancy upon the part of sociologists in general to regard the objects that their fellow workers in anthropology have been advancing. However, such a mass of anthropological material has been accumulated within the past few years, particularly in connection with the study of our own North American Indians, that the facts and their sociological implications can no longer be ignored. The disregard of this treasury of material has continued so long that the anthropologists have taken matters into their own hands, and have not only demonstrated conclusively the essential philosophical content of social theories hitherto developed, but are in a fair way to present a strong theory of their own. Thus we find Kroeber disposing of the universality of the theories of Le-Bon, Ward, and the entire eugenics school as insufficient.

Neither environment nor race is sufficient in itself to account for the bewildering variety of human societal behavior, as Boas has so conclusively demonstrated. This does not imply that any of these theories are to be rejected in their entirety. That physiological and psychological peculiarities are inherited is obvious. The Inca suture, no less than the hereditary mental deficiences of the members of the Kallikak family, are the results of inbreeding. Neither can it be denied that the environmentalist is correct when he notices that Negroes of the tropics do not build snow houses; environment obviously is a limiting factor, but this is far from justifying the assumption that environment can account for all behavior. We must regard society as composed of a number of elements, which are variable, and to single out any one of these for treatment as a constant is to fall into the methodological fallacy of which the sociological writers have been guilty.

If we take a theory of society based upon the concept of conflict, it is interesting to observe that among the Indians of southern California the conception of war is extremely weak. Or if we consider a theory based upon the assumption that all human behavior is a direct outcome of the stimulation of the primal instincts, what is to prevent us from becoming disconcerted when we find among the Australians, often termed the most primitive of the human family, that a personal quarrel is not followed by immediate pugnacious behavior? The elemental Australians settle their disputes in a manner more difficult to sustain than our modern court procedure. With but one club between them, they take turns at knocking each other on the head, and the man who remains standing under the blows is the winner. The formality of this practice indicates that the instinct of pugnacity in this case, at least, has ceased to operate with the promptness which is regarded as essential to instinctive behavior. It is obvious that an inhibiting factor is present.

If it be true, then, that these bewildering aberrations from expected behavior can be so readily pointed out and each fails to fit into the universal systems constructed by sociological writers, is there anything which will account for the diversified customs and manners of peoples the world over? The anthropological group would seem to believe that, as is so often the case, the most obvious factor in human social behavior has been overlooked in the search for a principle to explain behavior. They maintain that "neither mental nor biological attributes are of the least avail in explaining the origin of specific cultural traits, and that it is only when we know the *history* of a case that we can give anything like an adequate account of its origin."

Culture, as we have already stressed, is "the mode of life" of a people.

It must not be assumed, of course, that culture is a metaphysical entity which operates of itself. It is rather a generic term that covers an amazing number of types of behavior, each incomprehensible unless explained in terms of relation to other customs in the civilization in which it is found and to its historic background. Wissler has perhaps gone farthest toward a systematic presentation of this phenomenon, culture, which is manifest not only in primitive societies, but in our own as well. Under the "universal pattern" that he presents, we can subsume our civilization as well as that of the Patagonian, the Blackfoot, the Chuckchee, or the Bushman. Granted that we all live in social groups, it is at once apparent that we all manifest speech, that none of us is without material traits of culture; that we all possess a craving for æsthetic values; and a *Weltanschauung*. There is further no people without religious practices, or a family and social system, or some kind of property, or government. The exact form which a weapon or a relationship group may take is aside from the point. The fact remains that all people have these and the other elements in some form or other. That we are living in an age of intense development of the material side of civilization is no reason for assuming that this development is generally different from that of the material culture of any other people. On the other hand, our religious development is conspicuously weak, while that of many other people is as exuberant as is our own machine complex. The outstanding differences between our civilization and that of any other people lie in historical backgrounds.

In this insistence upon the explanation of social phenomena in terms strictly historical we see one of the outstanding characteristics of the method of approach of the anthropological group. Thus Boas maintains that "each cultural group has its own unique history, dependent partly on the peculiar inner development of the social group and partly upon the foreign influences to which it has been subjected." The method is stated by Goldenweiser: "On the one hand primitive cultures are examined in the totality of their present interrelations, each tribe being considered both as a unit and in its relation to other tribes. On the other hand cultural changes which are to be interpreted historically are referred to cultural antecedents, not to racial, environmental, or general psychological ones." The significance of this point of view for sociology has been most succinctly stated by Ogburn, who feels that "the historical method is particularly fruitful in the study of society, and is also valuable in the analysis of social phenomena when we are trying to ascertain the cultural, psychological, biological, and climatic factors. The historical method is usually not only the best first procedure in such analysis, but is a remarkable safeguard against mistakes in diagnosing for the other factors. The historical method in its extreme simplification means getting the cultural facts."

The most elementary form which culture takes, according to Wissler, is the culture trait. Every culture is composed of a large number of traits; and although these differ from one people to another, "the history of anthropology shows clearly that progress in the study of culture has been substantiated only in so far as the enumeration of tribal traits has approximated completeness." This lesson in method may well be comprehended by our sociologists who have too often disregarded the complete lists of cultural traits in our own civilization which are theirs for the taking. We next find that although there are traits which may travel alone there is a tendency for them to group themselves, to adhere in a complex. The existence of such complexes is universal. The business complex, the sport complex, the religious complex, the education complex of our own society, need only be mentioned to be recognized. The essential point for the sociologist to grasp is that there is no difference in kind between one of these complexes and the horse complex of the Plains Indians of North America, the hunting complex of the eastern Algonquins, or the cattle complex of the East African Negroes.

If the distribution of traits be plotted on a map, it will be found that certain objectively associated traits will tend to fall in well-defined *areas*. The concept is descriptive, and the boundaries which it envisages are not rigid. We find that there is a shading from the culture of one area to that of the next and that geographical conditions often impose their limitations on the spread of a culture complex in a given direction. This clustering of cultural traits in definite areas is a fact which has either been completely overlooked by sociological writers or unduly stressed. It is interesting to observe that in a series of articles in the *Nation* called "These United States," (more recently issued in book form under this same title) each state was treated as an entity. A more complete understanding of culture processes would have, perhaps, made obvious to the writers the fallacy of attempting to treat each of our states as a cultural unit; for culture is no respecter of political boundaries, and every characteristic emphasized in one state can be found in lessening degrees in adjacent ones. For it is found that cultural traits tend to center in definite spots, and thus it might be that a given characteristic was only centered in the state in which it was stressed and exerted a weakening influence in proportion to the distance from the center. It is true that the objection may be brought to the above statement that the culture of the United States as a whole is a unit; but if the map of the spread of Euro-American culture be consulted in *Man and Culture*, it will be found that the culture area holds for our civilization no less than for any other. That the area is larger is of no moment. It is simply that our whole society is more complex.

When we consider the mechanisms of culture, we find that they are, in the main, two in number. The first of these consists of the workings of what Boas terms the inner forces of society. Although this is by far the most difficult to comprehend, we may go so far as to state that it is this which accounts for inventions and discoveries. Differences in the abilities of individuals in a society, combined with different cultural backgrounds, must be looked to for the origination of new ways of dealing with specific situations. The earlier anthropologists and sociologists, swayed by the biological theories of evolution, posited parallel development in every people, following upon innate psychological tendencies. Complete systems, with stages of development culminating in our own particular type of civilization, were posited by such early writers as Morgan, Spencer, Tylor, and others. However, it has been found that the other cultural mechanism, that of diffusion, constituted a grave stumbling block to this *a priori* scheme of stage development. It is now known that independent origins of inventions are infinitely more rare than was believed, and that inventions are conditioned not by innate psychological tendencies, but by the cultural *milieu* in which they occur. The diffusion of culture, which we know occurs to no small extent, would of necessity make parallel development of neighboring peoples impossible. Indeed, the pendulum has swung to the other extreme; and in the writings of the German school headed by F. Graebner and of the English group centering about G. Elliot Smith and W. H. R. Rivers, we find an assumption of stability of traits under diffusion and over long periods of time, which constitute a *reductio ad absurdum* of their theory of the singleness of origin of cultural traits. Whatever may be said as to the extent to which traits of culture may or may not owe their origin to a single or a plural source, the importance of the phenomena of diffusion for the student of society cannot be overlooked. That it has not been taken into consideration is shown by the fact that it rarely receives mention in our sociological treatises. Yet, if we consider the vastness of the operation of this tendency on the part of one culture to borrow from another and its significance in these days of the intentional spread of culture, its importance to the student of societal behavior must at once become evident.

It is interesting to note that recognition of the importance of culture has been foreshadowed in the writings of Benjamin Kidd, Thomas Buckle, and the adherents of the conflict school of social origins, to whom cross-fertilization of cultures has been of importance. These writers, however, have not in any discernible way influenced the writers of the American group; in fact, their approach has been based upon assumption and keen intuition rather than upon accumulated field data. Graham Wallas, *The Social Heritage,* has also stressed the importance of culture in society, but his approach has not been exactly that of the anthropologists whom we have been discussing.

It is not surprising that the sociologist, immersed in the culture of his own group, should have missed quite completely the importance of that culture itself as the element by which he might explain the problems which puzzle him. It is perhaps one of the most confusing characteristics of culture that we are quite unconscious of it, almost as much so as we are of the air we breathe. We have been born into it, and our responses have been completely conditioned by it. It is only when we consider cultures as different from our own as are those of primitive people that we begin to see the working of culture. And we begin to recognize that the actions of human beings fall into definite patterns no less than do the actions of social groups. While we must agree with Wissler that there is a universal pattern in which all cultures fall, it could be wished that he had selected a different term for his concept, for it would seem that the pattern of any given civilization includes just those elements in which that civilization differs from others. Further, each trait gained from a foreign group is absorbed so as to conform to the general pattern of the society taking it; and if the trait goes contrary to the pattern, it will be rejected.

That this concept of pattern, in the sense in which it has been used here, is important to the sociologist is evidence by a slight consideration of the problems of Americanization, for example. The immigrant who comes to this country is acculturated to a pattern different from the one which he finds here, and the process of "becoming American" is a bewildering one. If those who insist on registration laws and Fourth of July orations as measures of Americanization were more conversant with the workings of the culture pattern and the relation of the individual to it, there might be more efficiency and less heartburning in this process. The concepts of "good' and "bad" which we apply in cultural judgments fade before the broadness of vision which is consequent upon an application of the workings of the cultural pattern. Comprehension that cultural patterns arise through historical processes, that they are unconscious in their development, and capricious in the extreme, is essential to the one who would undertake the difficult problem of social control or amelioration.

It has been suggested, further, that this problem of social control is not to be approached as lightly as some sociologists are wont to approach it. The earnest attempts, for example, of the Esperantists, to make for change in a huge cultural, imponderable language, gives a text for a lesson on the difficulties which strew the path of him who would direct the march of culture. Some students of society seem to be convinced of the impossibility of conscious social change. Kroeber, for example, holds that ". . . it can well be argued on theoretical grounds that the greater or less innate capacity of this or that individual, or of any limited number of individuals, is of negligible consequence" in the development of a culture. Others, including Wissler, feel that conscious change, though difficult, is not an impossibility. Whichever hypothesis one accept, it is certain that culture is vastly less amenable to change than he had imagined. That directed change may not be utterly impossible would seem to be indicated by the vast changes in the position of women brought about by conscious agitation in the past fifty years. Although this may be an inevitable development from historical antecedents, the question is yet an open one; and we can only be sure of the fact that much effort must be exerted by any one who would direct change.

It is also to be noticed, further, that changes are not uniform. There is the element which Ogburn calls "lag."

Thus we see that the older and more philosophical systems of sociology have failed under the test of applicability to the vast amount of concrete material from societies other than our own. Conceived by men so thoroughly acculturated that they could not be expected to see over the top of the culture in which they lived, these systems have failed because, though it was intended that their applicability be universal, they were based on data derived from one civilization alone. It has been for the anthropologist to realize that man is above all a culture-building animal and to point the way theoretically and methodologically to a system of social thought which, inductively conceived, may be termed truly scientific.

THE MITIGATION OF CLASS STRUGGLE *

By EDWARD ALSWORTH ROSS

In most societies there is a cleavage between families possessing permanent sources of large income which relieve them forever from the necessity of working for a living—the leisure class—and the rest of the population. The never-works strive to brand the active producing people as inferior to themselves. In Europe feudal traditions and the aftermath of ancient conquests have left on manual labor a deep stigma which is only slowly being bleached out. Even down into this age of mechanical warfare, the nobility retain something of glamour from the time when they were warriors and inheritors of the baton of military command. The new rich whose wealth rests on modern industrial bases do their utmost to assimilate themselves to the old nobility and thereby enter into its heritage of social prestige.

In the United States the stigma on labor has come to be fainter than it has ever been in any rich society. Among the manly and intelligent, whatever their lot in life, there is level speech and a readiness to fraternize in all save conventional situations. In our laws and institutions no class is awarded any recognition or privilege. In access to appointive offices and in immunity from prosecution for law-breaking, there are very real privileges to be enjoyed by the shrewd exercise of the power of wealth; but the American people have never countenanced or ratified them, nor is there prospect of their doing so.

Nevertheless, sections of the wealthy leisure class scheme and plot continually to get themselves looked up to as social superiors and brand with inferiority the rest of society, par-

* From *Roads to Social Peace.*

ticularly the workers. For supporting their claim to be superior they have a whole arsenal of tactics. Thanks to their deep purses, they avail themselves of everything clothes can do to hide commonness and transfigure the wearer. With the aid of architects and artists and decorators they provide themselves with noble and splendid backgrounds which deeply impress simple folk. They try to eliminate their not-rich competitors for social prestige by setting up certain reputable expenditures as sure touchstones of social worth. Thanks to their ownership of or influence in the newspapers they obtain much glorifying publicity for their doings, poses, and diversions. Seeking to shine by reflected light, they snuggle close to all who have social prestige in their own right, such as captains of industry, lofty prelates, high officials, the head men in the professions, renowned scientists, writers, artists, and explorers. They maneuver themselves into ornamental and ceremonial posts, such as those of the diplomatic service. They have their children educated in snobbish and exclusive schools, where conviction of the superiority of their class will become a second nature. They marry their daughters to the scions of impoverished European noble families. So far as possible they create about themselves the atmosphere of the aristocracies of other times—the French noblesse, the English lords, the German junkers, the southern slave-holding planters.

Nevertheless, for all their tricks and shifts to get themselves taken seriously as were the earlier leisure classes, theirs is an uphill fight. The tide of the times is against them. The spirit of democracy is their poison gas. They have no special place in the social constitution as the feudal lords did. They have no monopoly of the higher and more dignified places, as a European country gentleman had. Politically they are so weak that often they are mortified to see their cause or their candidate voted down with loud guffaws by the horny-handed. The army, navy, and diplomatic service have not been set aside as their sacred preserve as used to be the case in Europe. We have no state church in which their sons may rise to be dignitaries, no dependencies in which the ambitious sons of the rich may have a proconsular career. The widening application of mental tests to the young discloses that the sons and daughters of the wealthy, despite their imposing background and costly tutoring, include about the normal contingent of blockheads. Moreover, the "literature of exposure" has exhibited to the gaze of all the oozy foundations of fraud, chicane, and crime on which rest not a few lordly fortunes.

On the other hand, with the majestic inevitability of the advance of a glacier, the manual laboring class is gaining self-respect and social weight. More and more the workers are schooled, read, learn, think, discuss, arrive at worthwhile opinions. They know too much about Dives and how he got his millions to take him always at his own valuation. With the dissemination of soap, underclothing, bathtubs, safety razors, nail scissors, toothbrushes, dentistry, and self respect among the wage earners, the age-old association of manual labor with sweat, grime, bad odors, ill-kept teeth, unshaven faces, and dirty clothes is dissolved and there emerge types like the well-groomed young electrician which the casual eye cannot distinguish from the polo player. The universal diffusion of civil rights, the ballot, and access to office raises the social prestige of the workers. Veblen's demonstration that many of the current accepted standards of truth, rightness, propriety, and beauty are of never-work origin and intended to discredit the useful people by consecrating conspicuous waste, punctures leisure class pretensions. Finally, for a century most of the writers of genius—Carlyle, Ruskin, Kingsley, Dickens, Thackeray, Hardy, Shaw, Galsworthy, Wells, Hugo, Zola, Anatole France, Ibsen, Hauptmann, Tolstoy—have riddled the legend of leisure class superiority and idealized the laboring people.

There is no reason, then, to anticipate that heavy spenders who have rid themselves of all responsibility for production will be conceded their coveted place of superiority. The scepter of society is, in fact, passing to a very different element, viz., those charged with the direction of large enterprises. The merely rich are visibly losing in power to inspire awe and capture prestige by sheer lavishness of expenditure. While there will always be pelf-struck circles in which their claims are conceded, it is likely that the functional people will more and more go their way and recognize their own hierarchy of merit without paying much heed to the pretensions of snobs.

Another struggle to be noted is that between business men and the farmer-labor people. It is a strange and arresting fact that with us the fortune in the making is more potent socially than the fortune made. Never before have the men of big affairs so held the spotlight and thrust the merely rich out of the scene as in the United States to-day. There could be no question that active business men, the heads of large enterprises, are far more looked up to and deferred to than those who have converted their wealth into forms needing little attention and retired to lead the life of a country gentleman.

This is wholesome, no doubt, but why should it occur? The cause seems to be the tone of the newspapers and the magazines. More and more these live by their receipts from advertising and hence they habitually laud and glorify the active business man who is a possible buyer of advertising space. On the other hand, not being venal, they have no motive for showing a special tenderness toward those who have retired with a bushel of bonds.

Continually pictured as a superman, a being of tremendous intellectual grasp, beside whom the proletarians are pigmies and the professional men weaklings, the business man at last comes to believe it and takes himself with tremendous seriousness. While it has come to be quite the common thing for the business man to give his boy a college education, so that the college bred in the ranks of business are more frequent every year, there is no reason to suppose that the gap has been much narrowed which separates them from the members of the learned professions. Nevertheless, professional men enjoy no such undisputed community leadership as they did two generations ago. Emboldened by the rush of newspaper flattery to the head, the business men have brushed them aside, seized the reins, and "sold" themselves to the public. In Rotary or Kiwanis Club, it is amusing to watch the growing disposition of hardware dealers and haberdashers to show the professional men their place.

In the *Saturday Evening Post,* which in the last dozen years has degenerated from a national weekly into a sycophant of business, one notices quite telling onslaughts on lawyers, physicians, and professors. Since none of these provide any advertising for the costly pages of the *Post,* they are fair game. Likewise, there are innumerable articles and cartoons aimed at the economic vagaries and the political follies of working men and farmers. The one element which is never censored, exposed, belittled, or ridiculed is the business man. On the contrary, they are fed taffy of a thousand flavors in disguises and made to feel themselves a tortoise upon whom the whole visible scheme of things exists. Is it any wonder that the regular consumers of this adulation throw out their chests and assume a supermanly air? In the last dozen years there has been an extraordinary association among business men. There is hardly a sizable town that has not, besides its chamber of commerce or merchants and manufacturers association, its Rotary, Kiwanis, Lions, Gyro, and Optimist Clubs. From them, no doubt, flow many excellent results. They promote good fellowship and check the growth of petty grudges among trade competitors. They stage addresses and discussions which broaden the outlook of their members. Thanks to association, the grasping, clutching, penny-pinching curmudgeon type of shopkeeper is nearly a being of the past. These clubs do not fail to remind the member that a man owes his community something, and the wholesome note of service is often struck.

On the other hand, working men and farmers never figure appreciably in these organizations, and rarely are their views aired. The members hear, too, much laudation of their class, too much consecration of their prejudices. They listen to too many fulsome obsequious speeches. They come to feel so sure of themselves that they have no tolerance for views which clash with their ingrained conviction of superiority and infallibility. Toward the speaker who deals ruthlessly with their pet delusions they show instant animus. Even upon one another they impose an iron yoke of orthodoxy. For a while they playfully "josh" one of their number who gives other than the standard business man reaction to labor unionism, price-fixing, excess-profits taxes, government regulation of business, and the Non-Partisan League. But, if he is not amenable to this benign treatment, he becomes a pariah unless he is a financial whale whose eccentricities must be tolerated.

We have no reason to suppose that the men of business are either more selfish or less selfish than other people. On an issue which comes up between a section of the business class and the body of consumers or mill hands or policy holders, some will unhesitatingly side with their own class, while others lean to a public point of view and inquire what justice or truth calls for in the given premises. Now this latter type is rapidly being eliminated by the power of propaganda. The way things are going, the broad disinterested view of public questions will become only a memory among business men. The speakers and organs which are circulated among these clubs and mold their minds are intended to line them up solidly for a class view of every issue which comes up. The ramifying interests and the key men who secretly pull the wires of these organizations aim to marshal them in hearty support of everything the dominating business groups want, whether or not it is in the public interest that they should have it, and against everything consumers or wage-earners or farmers or school patrons want which is disadvantageous to these dominant business groups, no matter how much they may be entitled to it. No system could be devised more efficacious in killing in the individual merchant the impulse to react to a question as an American, a patriot, a citizen, a parent, or a Christian, and to establish in him the habit of reacting always as a member of a self-confident superior class whose opinions and claims, he is constantly assured, should take precedence over all other opinions and claims.

In these groups, lunching together once a week, suggestioned and indoctrinated constantly by higher-ups from outside, the conviction of the wonderful thought-power, will-force, and social value of the business class becomes so intense that they see nothing out of the way in taking into their hands decisions about matters which pertain to the community as a whole, such as parks, police, taxes, bond issues, poor relief, and schools. That union men, householders, classroom teachers, or other groups should object to the business man self-sacrificingly making these decisions for them seems to them monstrous and intolerable. Any one who raises a voice against their dictation to city officials or public schools or private charities is a "bolshevik" and must forthwith be deprived of his means of livelihood *pour encourager les autres*. When one observes how a knot of smug bankers and merchants will cause to be pursued with the most tireless malignancy the preacher, teacher, or employee who ventures to arraign their sordid local domination, one wonders whether the world has ever known poorer sportsmen than the typical organized business men.

It is certain that the egoism and aggressiveness which this element is frequently seduced into by their astute leaders will not go on forever without being challenged. If business men do not make their organizations express their public spirit and good will rather than the greed and intolerance of a self-conscious dominant class, they will find the rest of the community united to checkmate their every demand. Non-business elements, obliged in self-defense to learn the lesson of standing together, will narrow the gap in organizedness between themselves and the business element. Community councils will be set up, giving fair representation to all the elements of the community, and the local chamber of commerce will be politely requested to content itself henceforth with looking after the legitimate interests of business.

Finally we come to consider what the socialists regard as the real "class struggle," that is, the conflicts between employers and employees, or between "labor" and "capital," as popular parlance runs. This is, of course, a by-product of extension of the market and of machine production. It has developed in the course of a century and a half, because the giant rôle of capital, both mercantile and industrial, has raised up in the industrial field groups whose interests sharply clash.

Mark how the going over from handicraft to machine production affects human relationships. In the little stalls which lined the streets of an oriental city, each occupied by a worker in ivory or blockwood or lacquer or silk or brass, the worker owns the shop, the tools, and the materials. So naturally he owns the product. Here there is no room for strife between labor and capital. But in modern industry the worker works in another man's factory under another man's supervision, with another man's machinery, on another man's material; and the product belongs to the other man, all the worker's claim being liquidated in the wage he receives. Here is the root of the vast issue which has grown up in modern society.

As the invested capital per worker grows there is a larger stake between employees and employers. A century ago a striker cost the mill owner the use of, say, two hundred dollars, so long as the strike was in force. Now the striker costs him the use of $2000 and there are industries in which a tie-up sterilizes $35,000 per striker. Naturally, the faster a man is losing money, the more he is tempted to resort to desperate measures. The capitalist of to-day goes further in hiring labor spies and gunmen, in secretly controlling the local government or the state government, in order to be able to inject police or militia into the situation, than the capitalist of two generations ago. Not that he is a worse man than his predecessors. Generally he is a broader, better man, but he is in a more trying situation. On the other hand, working-men understand quite well that capitalists resort to drastic measures in order to head off or break a strike; so they, too, go to the limit to prevent their strike being broken. The result is that both parties are more willing to trample upon morality and violate the law in order to avoid defeat.

Here is the reason why strikes in such branches as railroads, shipping, docks, telegraphs, telephones, and steel, in which the average striker sterilizes from $10,000 to $30,000, are generally attended with much more law-breaking than mill strikes, in which the average striker sterilizes from $2000 to $7000. It is significant, too, that the strike is being wielded more freely. Before 1835 we know of only twenty-four strikes in American industry. From 1835 to 1880 there is a record of three hundred. In the twenty-five years from 1880 to 1905 there were 38,303 strikes, lasting more than a day. About the same number occurred in the next fifteen years. The combatants seem to be in the grasp of relentless forces which oblige them to behave as they do.

Again consider the continual growth in the size of the producing unit. One hundred years ago the average wagon shop in this country employed ten men; now it employs a hundred. In the old days if a worker in one of these shops had a grievance, he got a sympathetic hearing; for if he quit, he took with him ten per cent of the producing capacity of that shop. Hence, the boss was willing to listen to him and to give him satisfaction if he could. Now the disgruntled worker who quits takes with him only one per cent of the producing capacity of the concern. He is only one-tenth as important as he used to be. The individual protesting worker has become a pigmy in the eyes of the employer.

On the other hand, in the olden days the workman who quit might walk around the block and find another job just as good. Now, with shops so much bigger, there are fewer of them, and he may have to look for weeks or remove his family to another town before he can get a job at his specialty.

So that while the individual workman has shrunken to a pigmy in the eyes of the boss, the boss has become a giant in the eyes of the workman.

Here is the motive of the immense movement all over the modern industrial world toward the organization of labor and the substitution of collective bargaining for individual bargaining. Now such organizations may assume either of two forms. Suppose that the capitalist makes with the committee of his organized employees a single bargain for all of them for the coming year. This in a measure equalizes them with him. He can cut off their income if they balk at his demands, but they can cut off his income if he balks at their demands. However, notice this. If the capitalist owns his plant, he can borrow money on it even if it is idle, so that it will be a long time before his family comes into want; whereas the workmen, not being capitalists, are sure to come into acute distress after a few weeks of idleness. The workers try to overcome this handicap by forming comprehensive unions. If those in this establishment are in a union with those in forty other establishments, then if this union approves their strike, they may be supported during the strike by contributions from the workers in the forty other establishments. In this way the holding-out-power of workmen comes to equal approximately that of their employer. The employers realize this, and hence men who accept the principle of collective bargaining with their own organized employees absolutely refuse to deal with the representative of a wide union. Their motive is camouflaged by some such high-sounding phrase as "open shop," the "American plan," "freedom of industry," or "I refuse to allow any walking delegate to come between me and my employees."

On the other hand, a development has been going on which makes for peace between capital and labor. Forty years ago in the heyday of cut-throat competition, when the profits of even the successful manufacturing concern were likely to be precarious, it was natural for the hard-pressed manufacturer to save business by slashing his prices, hoping to pass on the cut to labor in the form of a reduction of wages. When the workers found themselves with their backs against the wall defending their standard of living, they hit back with bitter, hard-fought strikes attended with rough treatment of the "scab" and the strike breaker. Since then ruthless price cutting among producers of the same thing has become the exception.

The claws of competitors have been pretty well trimmed. Combination, good understandings, quiet price fixing, "live and let live" have become the order of the day. Production is carried on in bigger concerns enjoying greater control over the market. The practice of cutting prices expecting to take it out of the worker's hide has been largely abandoned. Prices are better sustained, profits are ampler and surer, and a large number of concerns have made it their policy to do anything within reason to live at peace with their employees.

In their primitive form, labor disputes are not class struggle at all, for the parties are a group of working men and a group of capitalists together with salaried employees, not self-conscious social classes. The stakes are definite things such as the removal of a concrete abuse, the curtailment of the length of the working day or ten cents more pay per hour, not the sharing of power or prestige as you would expect in a true class struggle.

Nevertheless, there is a marked tendency for the struggle in the individual shop to reach out and draw in more persons until you have something like a class line-up. Just as after the First Battle of the Marne, the Germans and the Allies, each fearful of being outflanked by the other, extended their lines laterally until they reached to the Channel on the one side and to Switzerland on the other; so there is a tendency on the part of labor unions to extend their organization into the unorganized plants and fields. When this has occurred, the "independent" employer becomes conscious of being at a disadvantage. In knowledge of wages and labor supply and demand the union officials are his superiors. In handling a strike he is a novice, whereas his opponents are experts; for they spend all their time on such matters, whereas he has to wrestle with many problems of other types. If a hard-fought strike results in a nation-wide boycott of his product, he faces ruin or the alternative of a long and costly litigation. Accordingly, there is a tendency for employers within a certain field to unite in an employers' association, such as the National Founders' Association, the National Erectors' Association, or the National Metal Trades Association with its thousand employer members. So organization on both sides expands until nation-wide blocks of labor confront nation-wide blocks of capital. The soft coal operators in West Virginia are in sharp competition with the soft coal operators of Illinois. The clothing manufacturers of New York are competing with the clothing manufacturers of Rochester and Chicago. If the soft coal miners of Illinois win something from the operators, the latter will profess that they cannot compete with the operators of West Virginia or Kansas unless the miners there organize and secure like terms. The workers of one garment-making center cannot feel sure of gain unless the garment workers of other centers can be roused to exact like terms of *their* bosses.

But the product of coal miners does not compete with the product of iron miners or silver miners, so we perceive no tendency for the line-up in industrial battle to cross the frontiers between industries. The workers in one industry do not combine for economic action with workers in another industry, nor do employers in one industry make common cause in an industrial contest with employers in other industries.

A brimstone smell is in the air when a local citizens' alliance or merchants' and manufacturers' association confronts a central labor union or the I. W. W., or when a national centralized belligerent propaganda association of manufacturers dedicates itself to opposing any legislation which is sought by the American Federation of Labor. Nor can we doubt the presence of class struggle when would-be neutrals are intimidated and obliged to come into the fray on one side or the other.

In view of the forms ever more extreme and startling which industrial strife has assumed in recent decades, in view of the increasing difficulty of the position of those who do not wish to identify themselves with either side, but wish to investigate and consider, until it becomes clear what economic policy is best for society as a whole, one may well wonder whether the process for consolidation will go on until every one has been obliged to choose his side. Then there would be no neutrals left to mediate between the infuriated classes, and society would be wrecked by real social war.

An analysis of the grounds of the propositions between labor and capital does not warrant so gloomy a prophesy. The field of battle is being widened, to be sure, and with increasing frequency consolidated labor faces consolidated employers. But there is ground for hoping that means may be found of making the struggle less ruthless and desperate. A century hence it will be recognized that our troubles to-day arise from the necessity of adjusting human relations to a new type of industry: viz., machine production. The progressively capitalistic character of production and the greater size of production units are translating industry from the sphere of the individual to the sphere of society. The autocratic control of the representatives of capital over the lives of thousands of workers with their families, over the degree of risk, the menace to health, the pace of labor, the length of the working day, factory discipline, pay, housing, and other features of existence is a relic from an earlier stage of industry. To-day such control is an anachronism and a misfit. Its support in the moral and legal conceptions which grew up in the era of petty production is crumbling. Great industry will be, in some degree, institutionalized. Every considerable establishment bids fair to be treated as a "public utility." Power without responsibility for its exercise will not be conceded to the captain of industry. In the words of President Hadley: "Property owners and their counsel must accept the idea that private property is in the large sense a public trust and that the rights of the property owner depend on the extent to which the perpetuation of the trust contributes to the purposes for which it was created."

By enforcing safety measures and the obligation to compensate for industrial accidents, by outlawing working conditions inimical to health and morals, by limiting the hours and fixing a legal minimum wage for working women, by protecting the workers from the competition of immigrants with a lower standard of living and a more abject attitude toward the employer, by providing for the amicable adjustment of industrial disputes which threaten the continuou- operation of public utilities and by other remedial measures, organized society is, here and there, projecting its rational will into the relations between labor and capital. The larger the number of successful interventions of society to remove some abuse which exasperates labor, the fewer will be the stakes of industrial conflict and the greater will be the realized well-being working men jeopardize by engaging in an ill-considered or ill-fought battle with capital. Moreover, the less often the wage-earners have been goaded to desperation by suffering unredressed wrongs, the more willing they should be to keep their quarrels within the limits laid down by law and public opinion.

The wage-earners ought to be able to achieve in time the necessary enlargement of their legal rights in industry, for they are no longer a hopeless minority as they were in an earlier stage of our industrial development. Between 1870 and 1920 the industrial wage earners from being 26.6 per cent of the gainfully employed, became 42.4 per cent. In these fifty years the industrial workers, servants, and lower salaried from being 37 per cent of the gainfully employed became 55 per cent. As layer after layer from being independent or self-employed come to sell their services, more ability and income is comprised within the wage-earning body and it includes more persons fit to lead it. Every success in modifying their status to their advantage heightens their confidence in the political remedy and renders them less disposed to attempt to correct their ills by a resort to the economic weapon.

There is good cheer, too, in the spread among employers of the conviction that the inherited structure of industry cannot continue unmodified and that somehow the workers must be more completely incorporated into the enterprise than they have been. It seems clear that the one-sided determination of everything in industry by the will of the agents of capital is bound to be the exception rather than the rule and that means will be found for giving the organized workers a voice in those decisions which affect their welfare. It is a good sign that the number of works councils which have sprung up in American industry in the last half-dozen years is not now far from a thousand.

The greatest difficulty in keeping American society from drifting over the brink into the abyss of class war is that so many persons in the ranks of capital deem class war inevitable and rush to meet it in utter ignorance of what horrors they would unloose. Since the Civil War every intelligent American has an intense fear of sectionalism and uses the greatest prudence in avoiding it. Mindful of the frightful religious wars of the sixteenth and seventeenth centuries, he is also haunted by the dread of sectarian strife and will make almost any concession to keep the religious issue from being injected into politics. But the same citizen who has learned these wholesome lessons from the bloody past shows in labor-capital disputes the same reckless spirit which prompted the northern anti-slavery men to denounce the American Constitution as "a covenant with Death and an agreement with Hell," and the southern secessionists to promise to mop up all the blood that would be shed with a pocket handkerchief and to pay the cost of the Civil War with a ten-cent piece. These madmen brought on the cataclysm of 1861-1865, and the same type of madmen to-day are doing their utmost to bring on a social war which would be unspeakably worse than the Civil War. Shall we have to suffer so dreadful a tragedy before we learn that the alteration in relations between employers and working men to suit the new age is not something in which fools and hotheads should be listened to? The I. W. W. with its war cry, "The working class and the employing class have nothing in common" and "Labor is entitled to all it produces," and the hard-shell employers with their slogans, "Nothing to arbitrate" and "I propose to run my business in my own way," are madmen and should be thrust aside in order to let sober-minded judicial men tackle the question.

MEANS OF AVERTING CLASS WAR

1. Free speech, free press, and free assemblage should be protected with a religious scrupulousness. The unhindered ventilation of wrongs and grievances not only affords emotional relief but also calls into operation healing and corrective agencies. To throttle free communications is to tie down a safety valve.

2. The establishment of the essential facts in all disputed matters by impartial authorities trusted by both sides may be expected to narrow the distance between the contentions of opponents.

3. If teachers of the social sciences be assured of immunity from molestation on account of their utterances, they will exercise a most beneficial influence by giving an unbiased judgment on issues which arise between classes and guiding the inclinations of the disinterested public. By throwing their support, now to one party, now to the other, they will make both wary of taking up extreme and indefensible positions.

4. Every removal of evils suffered by some group of wage-earners contributes in some measure to lessen the scope

or intensity of class animosity. On the other hand the accumulation of unredressed abuses drives the workers toward despair and desperation.

5. The assuagement of the labor-capital strife calls for the acquisition by labor of reward, a security, and a degree of self-determination which hitherto it has not generally had. But these gains should not be made in such a way as to lower the morale of industry or to impair the motives upon which the proper functioning of private capitalism depends.

6. Every effort should be made by the improvement of publication, the multiplication of scholarships, vocational guidance, and access to credit to provide staircases for ascent from one economic level to another and to prevent the wielding of industrial power from becoming a matter of inheritance.

THE HYPOTHESIS OF CULTURAL LAG*

By WILLIAM FIELDING OGBURN

THIS rapidity of change in modern times raises the very important question of social adjustment. Problems of social adjustment are of two sorts. One concerns the adaptation of man to culture or perhaps preferably the adapting of culture to man. The other problem is the question of adjustments, occasioned as a result of these rapid social changes, between the different parts of culture, which no doubt means ultimately the adaptation of culture to man. This second problem of adjustment between the different parts of culture is the immediate subject of our inquiry.

The thesis is that the various parts of modern culture are not changing at the same rate, some parts are changing much more rapidly than others; and since there is a correlation and interdependence of parts, a rapid change in one part of our culture requires readjustments through other changes in the various correlated parts of culture. For instance, industry and education are correlated, hence a change in industry makes adjustments necessary through changes in the educational system. Industry and education are two variables, and if the change in industry occurs first and the adjustment through education follows, industry may be referred to as the independent variable and education as the dependent variable. Where one part of culture changes first, through some discovery or invention, and occasions changes in some part of culture dependent upon it, there frequently is a delay in the changes occasioned in the dependent part of culture. The extent of this lag will vary according to the nature of the cultural material, but may exist for a considerable number of years, during which

* From *Social Change*

time there may be said to be a maladjustment. It is desirable to reduce the period of maladjustment, to make the cultural adjustments as quickly as possible.

The foregoing account sets forth a problem that occurs when there is a rapid change in a culture of interdependent parts and when the rates of change in the parts are unequal. The discussion will be presented according to the following outlines. First the hypothesis will be presented, then examined and tested by a rather full consideration of the facts of a single instance, to be followed by several illustrations. Next the nature and cause of the phenomenon of cultural maladjustment in general will be analyzed. The extent of such cultural lags will be estimated, and finally the significance for society will be set forth.

A first simple statement of the hypothesis we wish to investigate now follows. A large part of our environment consists of the material conditions of life and a large part of our social heritage is our material culture. These material things consist of houses, factories, machines, raw materials, manufactured products, foodstuffs and other material objects. In using these material things we employ certain methods. Some of these methods are as simple as the technique of handling a tool. But a good many of the ways of using the material objects of culture involve rather larger usages and adjustments, such as customs, beliefs, philosophies, laws, governments. One important function of government, for instance, is the adjustment of the population to the material conditions of life, although there are other governmental functions. Sumner has called many of these processes of adjustments, mores. The cultural adjustments to material conditions, however, include a larger body of processes than the mores; certainly they include the folk ways and social institutions. These ways of adjustment may be called, for purposes of this particular analysis, the adaptive culture. The adaptive culture is therefore that portion of the non-material culture which is adjusted or adapted to the material conditions. Some parts of the non-material culture are thoroughly adaptive culture such as certain rules involved in handling technical appliances, and some parts are only indirectly or partially so, as for instance, religion. The family makes some adjustments to fit changed material conditions, while some of its functions remain constant. The family therefore, under the terminology used here is a part of the non-material culture that is only partly adaptive. When the material conditions change, changes are occasioned in the adaptive culture. But these changes in the adaptive culture do not synchronize exactly with the change in the material culture. There is a lag which may last for varying lengths of time, sometimes indeed, for many years.

An illustration will serve to make the hypothesis more clearly understood. One class of material objects to which we adjust ourselves is the forests. The material conditions of forestry have changed a good deal in the United States during the past century. At one time the forests were quite plentiful for the needs of the small population. There was plenty of wood easily accessible for fuel, building and manufacture. The forests were sufficiently extensive to prevent in many large areas the washing of the soil, and the streams were clear. In fact, at one time, the forests seemed to be too plentiful, from the point of view of the needs of the people. Food and agricultural products were at one time the first need of the people and the clearing of land of trees and stumps was a common undertaking of the community in the days of the early settlers. In some places, the quickest procedure was to kill and burn the trees and plant between the stumps. When the material conditions were like these, the method of adjustment to the forests was characterized by a policy which has been called exploitation. Exploitation in regard to the forests was indeed a part of the mores of the time, and describes a part of the adaptive culture in relation to forests.

As time went on, however, the population grew, manufacturing became highly developed, and the need for forests increased. But the forests were being destroyed. This was particularly true in the Appalachian, Great Lakes and Gulf regions. The policy of exploitation continued. Then rather suddenly it began to be realized in certain centres of thought that if the policy of cutting timber continued at the same rate and in the same manner the forests would in a short time be gone and very soon indeed they would be inadequate to supply the needs of the population. It was realized that the custom in regard to using the forests must be changed and a policy of conservation was advocated. The new policy of conservation means not only a restriction in the amount of cutting down of trees, but it means a more scientific method of cutting, and also reforestation. Forests may be cut in such a way, by selecting trees according to their size, age and location, as to yield a large quantity of timber and yet not diminish the forest area. Also by the proper distribution of cutting plots in a particular area, the cutting can be so timed that by the time the last plot is cut the young trees on the plot first cut will be grown. Some areas when cut leave a land which is well adapted to farming, whereas such sections as mountainous regions when denuded of forests are poorly suited to agriculture. There of course are many other methods of conservation of forests. The science of forestry is, indeed, fairly highly developed in principle, though not in practice in the United States. A new adaptive culture, one of conservation, is therefore suited to the changed material conditions.

That the conservation of forests in the United States should have been earlier is quite generally admitted. We may say, therefore, that the old policy of exploitation has hung over longer than it should before the institution of the new policy. In other words, the material conditions in regard to our forests have changed but the old customs of the use of forests which once fitted the material conditions very well have hung over into a period of changed conditions. These old customs are not only not satisfactorily adapted, but are really socially harmful. These customs of course have a utility, since they meet certain human needs; but methods of greater utility are needed. There seems to be a lag in the mores in regard to forestry after the material conditions have changed.

The foregoing discussion of forestry illustrates the hypothesis which it is proposed to discuss. It is desirable to state more clearly and fully the points involved in the analysis. The first point concerns the degree of adjustment or correlation between the material conditions and the adaptive nonmaterial culture. The degree of this adjustment may be only more or less perfect or satisfactory; but we do adjust ourselves to the material conditions through some form of culture; that is, we live, we get along, through this adjustment. The particular culture which is adjusted to the material conditions may be very complex, and, indeed, quite a number of widely different parts of culture may be adjusted to a fairly homogeneous material condition. Of a particular cultural form, such as the family or government, relationship to a particular material culture is only one of its purposes or functions. Not all functions of family organization, as, for instance, the affectional function, are primarily adaptive to material conditions.

Another point to observe is that the changes in the material culture precede changes in the adaptive culture. This statement is not in the form of a universal dictum. Conceivably, forms of adaptation might be worked out prior to a change in the material situation and the adaptation might be applied practically at the same time as the change in the material conditions. But such a situation presumes a very high degree of planning, prediction and control. The collection of data, it is thought, will show that at the present time there are a very large number of cases where the material conditions change and the changes in the adaptive culture follow later. There are certain general theoretical reasons why this is so; but it is not desirable to discuss these until later. For the present, the analysis will only concern those cases where changes in the adaptive culture do not precede changes in the material culture. Furthermore, it is not implied that changes may not occur in non-material culture while the material culture remains the same. Art or education, for instance, may undergo many changes with a constant material culture. Still another point in the analysis is that the old, unchanged, adaptive culture is not adjusted to the new, changed, material conditions. It may be true that the old adaptive culture is never wholly unadjusted to the new conditions. There may be some degree of adjustment. But the thesis is that the unchanged adaptive culture was more harmoniously related to the old than to the new material conditions and that a new adaptive culture will be better suited to the new material conditions than was the old adaptive culture. Adjustment is therefore a relative term, and perhaps only in a few cases would there be a situation which might be called perfect adjustment or perfect lack of adjustment.

It is desirable, however, not to make the analysis too general until there has been a more careful consideration of particular instances. We now propose, therefore, to test the hypothesis by the facts in a definite case of social change. In attempting to verify the hypothesis in a particular case by measurement, the following series of steps will be followed. The old material conditions will be described, that part of the adaptive culture under consideration will be described, and the degree of adjustment between these two parts of culture shown. Then the changed material conditions and the changed adaptive culture will be defined and the degree of adaptation shown. It is necessary also to show that the unchanged adaptive culture is not as harmoniously adjusted to the new conditions as to the old and not as harmoniously adjusted to the new conditions as is a changed adaptive culture.

ART, SCIENCE, AND SOCIOLOGY *

By C. H. COOLEY

AN ART OF SOCIETY?

IF language is subject matter for art, and manners, why not the social order itself, of which these are aspects? Is not the creation of a fair society the supreme and inclusive art?

Our democracy might be a work of art, a joyous whole, rich in form and color, free but chastened, tumultuously harmonious, unfolding strange beauty year by year. Each of us would be spontaneously functional, like the detail in great architecture.

ART AND SCIENCE

The idea of a gulf between art and science, as things different in kind, seems to be recent. Leonardo da Vinci, with his attainments in mathematics and physics, and being a great painter withal, reveals no sense of it, but looks upon all his studies as *scienze* or branches of knowledge. The basis for our view seems to be that the sciences are cumulative, an imperishable and ever-increasing structure, while the arts bloom and die like flowers. This notion perhaps arose as science was observed to develop a technique of its own, quite different from that of art.

It is a sound distinction, because practical, but not so sharp as is commonly supposed. In general our branches of study, judged by this test, are both sciences and arts, and the name you call them by will depend upon which aspect you consider the more essential. There is a science of natural appearances and of technique connected with painting, but we re-

* From *Life and the Student*

gard this as subsidiary to the art; there is an art of description and of conjecture connected with geology, but we regard this as subsidiary to the science. The worker almost always practices both, and the worker in science and the worker in art are more like each other than either is like any one else.

Indeed as processes of mind in the worker science and art are much the same; both occupy themselves with a precise study of facts; in both man seeks to interpret and reconstruct nature after patterns of his own; both, in the pursuit of truth, rise above the tumult of the hour to serene and lasting aims.

Any one whose need it is to strive for something perfect, something noble in itself without regard to any transient utility, one whose thoughts are bent on truth or beauty and not on the market, may be said to be of the artist type, whether he be called artist, scientist, poet, scholar, craftsman or teacher.

Science steps more assuredly than art, but its path is narrower; it cannot deal with life in its fulness. And so the humanistic studies—history, literature, psychology, sociology—can be sciences only as to detail; when they interpret life largely they are arts.

But indeed all science becomes art when it passes to the construction of truth.

That part of the progress of knowledge that interests most minds and affords the main field for discussion is not science, properly speaking, not the discovery of facts as such (about which there is very little to be said), but the art which is based on the facts, the theories and arguments by which it is endeavored to build up a system of ideal truth. Take a work on primitive man; how meager, when you sift it out, is the knowledge—a few tools, drawings and fragments of bone— how ample the structure imagination has built upon it!

To arrive at abstract formulas is indeed one aim of science, but surely not the only one. To illuminate the concrete object is an equal need. "All theory is gray," especially if you separate it from the bright detail. Science, then, is not in this regard so very far from art, which is not all bright detail, but abstracts in a way of its own.

While science seeks to discover a fact or relation which can be shown to all by experiment, art aims to express a personal vision of truth which can be shared by sympathy. One minimizes personality, the other exalts it. Yet they overlap in dealing with human life, for here the facts themselves are personal and experience becomes sympathy. Are the maxims of La Rochefoucauld science or art? And how about William James's psychology?

The man of science, like the artist, may easily have more facts than he can use. Both seek the one fact out of a million that will illuminate their idea. Both find that it is rarely to be had without research.

The test of truth in art is authenticity, that is, something in the work itself by which we judge that it expresses faithfully a real vision of the artist, very much as we judge of the truth of a witness by his face and bearing. A portrait by Holbein, a novel by W. D. Howells, a poem by Robert Frost, is authentic. And in science this test is by no means absent, since the sciences of life, especially, including the social, consist largely of description, the guaranty of which is the credibility of the observer.

Science, because it is more separable from personality, tends to be more anonymous, and can never be as prolific in fames as art is. Compare Newton with Shakespeare, Galileo with Dante or Michelangelo. Newton and Galileo are only names, familiar enough because they are on the lists of great men, but without rich meaning; what they contributed we have absorbed in another way. But the poets and painters and sculptors are alive still, in a unique and personal body of work which we can know only by knowing them. The world of literature and art has hundreds of names, each of which, to people of some culture, is an indispensable key to life.

Philosophy may be either science or art, or both, or neither. There is a sort that is impersonal, verifiable and cumulative, a large view of science, good to build on but not otherwise of much interest; another that is personal and of a speculative beauty, a third that is perhaps neither enduring nor beautiful, but influential for a particular state of thought.

Art colors science in unsuspected ways. There are formulas, like "trial and error" which gain vogue not because they are precise (this one is not) but because of an attractive sound and flow, a suggestiveness faintly poetic.

THE FALLIBILITY OF SCIENTIFIC GROUPS

SCIENCE is knowledge that is verifiable and cumulative, that can be established to the satisfaction of an expert group and endure as the basis of new acquisitions. But it is not easy to test this, since much that seems to an expert group verified and enduring may in the end prove transitory.

It is with science as elsewhere; the premises of thought, being common to a group, escape scrutiny, and so, by the most rigorous methods, the common error may be propagated indefinitely. No group is a trustworthy critic of its own premises. The men of the past thought they proved a world of things we regard as nonsense, and we cannot know how much of our own science will turn out to be of the same sort. Some results are permanent, but only time reveals which they are.

It is perhaps not sufficiently understood that nineteen twentieths of what men of science write, and what the public takes for science, is not such but an overflow of speculative discussion not necessarily less biased or more grounded than any other matter of the kind. No doubt this has a scientific value in that from the flood of conjecture fruitful hypotheses may emerge, but in the meantime all men should know that it *is* conjecture.

Scientific men are almost as eager to believe as the religious. Their doctrine differs from that of the church mainly in having a confessed obligation to show, sooner or later, that it consists with verifiable fact.

"Our facts will endure," you say, "though our theory is tentative." True; but is there any test of what is a fact except that it endures? What we have taken for granted or striven to prove appears to us to be a fact; unfamiliar or unwelcome facts seem theoretical.

Verification is the assent of competent minds, not of the public. When you get beyond precise and easily repeated experiment it involves interpretation and is never unquestionable. A. R. Wallace got into serious trouble by attempting to prove, on a bet, that the surface of the earth was curved. The referee gave him the money, I believe, but the other man was never convinced. It all comes back to the verdict of the expert group, which is the best guide we have, but not infallible.

No wonder the plain people distrust "science" and cling in spite of it to cherished beliefs. It shows their good sense. What honest and thoughtful student expects that more than a small part of the contemporary speculation that reputable men proclaim as truth will be believed a century hence?

But evolution, you say, is no longer a speculation. It has proved the key to a hundred tangles, and is solving more every day. Yes, but you cannot expect the plain man to know all that. He judges by what he can see and by the credibility of the witnesses, of which he may have a poor opinion. He sees that many professed men of science are no less partisans, propagandists and followers of fads than other people, and draws his own conclusions.

The group disciplines its members, but who will discipline the group?

MENTAL PATTERNS IN RELATION TO CULTURE *

By WILSON D. WALLIS

A DESCRIPTION of the behavior pattern of the group, its related action and reaction, gives detail and objectivity to the data of social psychology which is an urgent need of that science. It demonstrates that the psychology of the group is no more the sum of the psychology of its component individuals than the psychology of an individual is the sum of his mental states; it gives the tonal value and the *nuances* of group psychology.

The various culture areas illustrate mental patterns, and the mental pattern is as real as the cultural. There is in each culture area a type of mind reflecting and reflected in the various phases of the culture, responsible for it and responsive to it. The contours of the mental pattern are almost coterminous with the contours of the culture and the content of one is reflected in that of the other.

Thus, among the Dakota there is an interrelated system of beliefs, attitudes, values, presuppositions, and inductions, which gives unity to the psychic life in this area and at the same time marks it off from psychic life in other areas. In no other area is there the same system of reactions toward the world of nature, the animals in the environment, neighbors or fellow-tribesmen. Dakota philosophy regarding stone is closely interwoven with the cosmogony and is based on inductions from the use of stone in medicine bags and by medicine-men. The mythology is rationalized and the rationalization is mythologized. The virtues of water have similar confirmation. Spider is powerful, because one of the first of the animals to be created, as shown by its ability to walk on

* From the *Journal of Abnormal Psychology and Social Psychology*

water, to climb in the air (on his "rope"), to walk on land. Low visibility adds to the evidence regarding ubiquity, and his ingenuity in making "nets," as they call his webs, indicates more than mere animal intelligence. Accounts of contests with other animals confirm the correctness of the cosmogony and the indications of mysterious power. We call the process "rationalization"; but whatever we call it, the fact is that it indicates an interconnected scheme of thought in which the parts are intertwined in such manner that you cannot destroy a part without endangering the whole. A change in one portion of the mental pattern will be felt throughout the psychic organism. You cannot destroy a part without affecting the whole; for the parts are interdigitated, the influence of each part permeates the whole, a part being responsive to change in any other part.

So if we take other phases of their psychic life, we find that the beliefs which the Dakota have about stone, water, and spider are interdigitated with beliefs regarding spirits, ceremonies, folklore, tradition, activities in war. The complex of their life falls into an organization of thought, partly rational, partly non-rational, interwoven into a functioning unified complex which constitutes Dakota mind. You cannot eliminate part of the pattern without affecting the whole.

In another culture area, such as that of the Micmac of the Canadian maritime provinces, we encounter another mental pattern. It is not merely Algonkian, it is Micmac, and in almost every phase Micmacish. Here, too, one finds traditions, but of a different sort; they give the psychic life different roots in a different past. Magic is an important feature of culture life, but it is a different magic than that which is practiced by and receives credence among the Dakota. It starts with different premises and accomplishes different results. The *késkAmzit,* the magical good luck which the Micmac craves, operates in different medium and with different instrumentalities than the *wakan,* the sacred, mysterious, pervading power which the Dakota strives to control or appease. The Micmac obtains *késkAmzit* in different manner and uses it to different purpose. Animals enter into the psychic life in a way consonant with the mythology and the magic, and this is not as they enter into the mental pattern of the Dakota. The culture background is different and the difference is recorded in Micmac psychic life. The culture pattern is reflected in an analogous mental pattern, peculiar to those who share the culture and have confidence in its values. Historical contacts have been different, friendships and enmities are different, not merely in the identity of outside peoples but in the emotional and rationalistic attitudes toward the different peoples with whom the Micmac have come into willing or unwilling contact. Here, too, is an interfunctioning complex which is also a unity, a pattern of mind in which no part can be understood without reference to the whole.

Not only is it true that whenever we go to new culture areas in savagery we find new culture patterns; the story of civilization itself is in part a story of changes in mental pattern.

There is, indeed, a medieval mind. Medieval mind is a complex of ideas, interrelated and interfunctioning, which pertain to a certain period of the development of thought. Medieval mind cannot be understood without reference to the cultural and historical background, the science, religion, magic, ethics then prevalent.

These enter vitally into its composition, so that a part influences the whole. That this interrelation was unconsciously realized even in the times is illustrated by the concern of religion when science found new interpretation of the solar system. The material world could not be changed by Copernicus without that change being reflected in the world of religious concepts—with consequences that bore hardly on the supporters of the new science. One might give other illustrations, but all would be illustrations of the interconnectedness of medieval mind and of the reality of its pattern.

And if only by way of comparison, there is a "contemporary mind." But perhaps no mind is completely "contemporary." Any mind has in it, it is true, elements relatively, if not absolutely, medieval. The patterns overlap, and the texture of a given mind is, of course, an empirical issue. This, however, does not detract from the truth of the statement that contemporary mind functions as a unity, with a different complex than that of previous centuries or even previous decades.

How closely the parts are interrelated is shown by the readjustments in many other phases of mind following upon a doctrine of evolution introduced into biology, a doctrine of dreams introduced into neurology, a doctrine of economics introduced into political life, and so on.

Within our modern social order there are a number of class or culture patterns. The pattern of the worker seldom is that of the employer, the pattern of each national group has its own cast. The mental patterns of groups are the problem of the social psychologist, as the patterns of individual minds are the problems of the conventional psychologist. But if we are correct in pointing to the existence of patterns and of interconnected parts, the ramifications and the interdependences, the surety that change in one part will be reflected by change in other parts, then the part is understood only when the whole is envisaged. As the physiologist cannot arrive at an understanding of organism by studying leg, arm, heart, nose, as so many independent and disconnected parts, proceeding then to synthesize the organism, but rather must first see organism and then proceed to the parts, so the student of the psychology of individual mind must see it in its wholeness before he can see it intelligently in its parts, a fact which psychoanalysis has helped to bring home. No knowledge of parts which are summed up will give the mental pattern; and without the pattern the psychologist will not be able to understand the part, for its significance depends upon its place in the complex. Such a pattern psychology of both individual and group tells us more about the fundamental type of behavior than does any analytical study of an atomistic sort. Mental life, if not a unity, is in large part a group of unities. Now and then the patterns are woven into a comprehensive pattern of unified design expressing the rationale of a well-ordered mental life.

RENASCENT LIBERALISM *

By JOHN DEWEY

THE argument drawn from past history that radical change must be effected by means of class struggle, culminating in open war, fails to discriminate between the two forces, one active, the other resistant and deflecting, that have produced the social scene in which we live. The active force is, as I have said, scientific method and technological application. The opposite force is that of older institutions and the habits that have grown up around them. Instead of discrimination between forces and distribution of their consequences, we find the two things lumped together. The compound is labeled the capitalistic or the bourgeois class, and to this class as a class is imputed all the important features of present industrialized society—much as the defenders of the regime of economic liberty exercised for private property are accustomed to attribute every improvement made in the last century and a half to the same capitalistic regime. Thus in orthodox communist literature, from the communist manifesto of 1848 to the present day, we are told that the bourgeoisie, the name for a distinctive class, has done this and that. It has, so it is said, given a cosmopolitan character to production and consumption; has destroyed the national basis of industry; has agglomerated population in urban centers; has transferred power from the country to the city, in the process of creating colossal productive force, its chief achievement. In addition, it has created crises of ever renewed intensity; has created imperialism of a new type in frantic effort to control raw materials and markets. Finally, it has created a new class, the proletariat, and has created it as a class having a common interest opposed to that of the

* From *From Liberalism and Social Action*

735

bourgeoisie, and is giving an irresistible stimulus to its organization, first as a class and then as a political power. According to the economic version of the Hegelian dialectic, the bourgeois class is thus creating its own complete and polar opposite, and this in time will end the old power and rule. The class struggle of veiled civil war will finally burst into open revolution and the result will be either the common ruin of the contending parties or a revolutionary reconstitution of society at large through a transfer of power from one class to another.

The position thus sketched unites vast sweep with great simplicity. I am concerned with it here only as far as it emphasizes the idea of a struggle between classes, culminating in open and violent warfare as being the method for production of radical social change. For, be it noted, the issue is not whether some amount of violence will accompany the effectuation of radical change of institutions. The question is whether force or intelligence is to be the method upon which we consistently rely and to whose promotion we devote our energies. Insistence that the use of violent force is inevitable limits the use of available intelligence, for wherever the inevitable reigns intelligence cannot be used. Commitment to inevitability is always the fruit of dogma; intelligence does not pretend to know save as a result of experimentation, the opposite of preconceived dogma. Moreover, acceptance in advance of the inevitability of violence tends to produce the use of violence in cases where peaceful methods might otherwise avail. The curious fact is that while it is generally admitted that this and that particular social problem, say of the family, or railroads or banking, must be solved, if at all, by the method of intelligence, yet there is supposed to be some one all inclusive social problem which can be solved only by the use of violence. This fact would be inexplicable were it not a conclusion from dogma as its premise.

It is frequently asserted that the method of experimental intelligence can be applied to physical facts because physical nature does not present conflicts of class interests, while it is inapplicable to society because the latter is so deeply marked by incompatible interests. It is then assumed that the "experimentalist" is one who has chosen to ignore the uncomfortable fact of conflicting interests. Of course, there are conflicting interests; otherwise there would be no social problems. The problem under discussion is precisely how conflicting claims are to be settled in the interest of the widest possible contribution to the interests of all—or at least of the great majority. The method of democracy—inasfar as it is that of organized intelligence—is to bring these conflicts out into the open where their special claims can be seen and appraised, where they can be discussed and judged in the light of more inclusive interests than are represented by either of them separately. There is, for example, a clash of interests between munition manufacturers and most of the rest of the population. The more the respective claims of the two are publicly and scientifically weighed, the more likely it is that the public interest will be disclosed and be made effective. There is an undoubted objective clash of interests between finance-capitalism that controls the means of production and whose profit is served by maintaining relative scarcity, and idle workers and hungry consumers. But what generates violent strife is failure to bring the conflict into the light of intelligence where the conflicting interests can be adjudicated in behalf of the interest of the great majority. Those most committed to the dogma of inevitable force recognize the need for intelligently discovering and expressing the dominant social interest up to a certain point and then draw back. The "experimentalist" is one who would see to it that the method depended upon by all in some degree in every democratic community be followed through to completion.

In spite of the existence of class conflicts, amounting at times to veiled civil war, any one habituated to the use of the method of science will view with considerable suspicion the erection of actual human beings into fixed entities called classes, having no overlapping interests and so internally unified and externally separated that they are made the protagonists of history—itself hypothetical. Such an idea of classes is a survival of a rigid logic that once prevailed in the sciences of nature, but that no longer has any place there. This conversion of abstractions into entities smells more of a dialectic of concepts than of a realistic examination of facts, even though it makes more of an emotional appeal to many than do the results of the latter. To say that all past historic social progress has been the result of cooperation and not of conflict would be also an exaggeration. But exaggeration against exaggeration, it is the more reasonable of the two. And it is no exaggeration to say that the measure of civilization is the degree in which the method of cooperative intelligence replaces the method of brute conflict.

But the point I am especially concerned with just here is the indiscriminate lumping together as a single force of two different things—the results of scientific technology and of a legal system of property relations. It is science and technology that have had the revolutionary social effect while the legal system has been the relatively static element. According to the Marxians themselves, the economic foundations of society consist of two things, the forces of production on one side and on the other side, the social relations of production, that is, the legal property system under which the former operates. The latter lags behind, and "revolutions" are produced by the power of the forces of production to change the system of institutional relations. But what are the modern forces of production save those of scientific technology? And what is scientific technology save a large-scale demonstration of organized intelligence in action?

It is quite true that what is happening socially is the result of the combination of the two factors, one dynamic, the other relatively static. If we choose to call the combination by the name of capitalism, then it is true, or a truism, that capitalism is the "case" of all the important social changes that have occurred—an argument that the representatives of capitalism are eager to put forward whenever the increase of productivity is in question. But if we want to understand, and not just to paste labels, unfavorable or favorable as the case may be, we shall certainly begin and end with discrimination. Colossal increase in productivity, the bringing of men together in cities and large factories, the elimination of distance, the accumulation of capital, fixed and liquid—these things would have come about, at a certain stage, no matter what the established institutional system. They are the consequence of the new means of technological production. Certain other things have happened because of inherited institutions and the habits of belief and character that accompany and support them. If we begin at this point, we shall see that the release of productivity is the product of cooperatively organized intelligence, and shall also see that the institutional framework is precisely that which is not subjected as yet, in any considerable measure, to the impact of inventive and constructive intelligence. That coercion and oppression on a large scale exist, no honest person can deny. But these things are not the product of science and technology but of the perpetuation of old institutions and patterns untouched by scientific method. The inference to be drawn is clear.

The argument, drawn from history, that great social changes have been effected only by violent means, needs considerable qualification, in view of the vast scope of changes that are taking place without the use of violence. But even if it be admitted to hold of the past, the conclusion that violence is the method now to be depended upon does not follow—unless one is committed to a dogmatic philosophy of history. The radical who insists that the future method of change must be like that of the past has much in common with the hide-bound reactionary who holds to the past as an ultimate fact. Both overlook the fact that history in being a process of change generates change not only in details but also in the method of directing social change. I recur to what I said at the beginning of this chapter. It is true that the social order is largely conditioned by the use of coercive force, bursting at times into open violence. But what is also true is that mankind now has in its possession a new method, that of cooperative and experimental science which expresses the method of intelligence. I should be meeting dogmatism with dogmatism if I asserted that the existence of this historically new factor completely invalidates all arguments drawn from the effect of force in the past. But it is within the bounds of reason to assert that the presence of this social factor demands that the present situation be analyzed on its own terms, and not be rigidly subsumed under fixed conceptions drawn from the past.

Any analysis made in terms of the present situation will not fail to note one fact that militates powerfully against arguments drawn from past use of violence. Modern warfare is destructive beyond anything known in older times. This increased destructiveness is due primarily, of course, to the fact that science has raised to a new pitch of destructive power all the agencies of armed hostility. But it is also due to the much greater interdependence of all the elements of society. The bonds that hold modern communities and states together are as delicate as they are numerous. The self-sufficiency and independence of a local community, characteristic of more primitive societies, have disappeared in every highly industrialized country. The gulf that once separated the civilian population from the military has virtually gone. War involves paralysis of all normal social activities, and not merely the meeting of armed forces in the field. The communist manifesto presented two alternatives: either the revolutionary change and transfer of power to the proletariat, or the common ruin of the contending parties. Today, the civil war that would be adequate to effect transfer of power and a reconstitution of society at large, as understood by official communists, would seem to present but one possible consequence: the ruin of all parties and the destruction of civilized life. This fact alone is enough to lead us to consider the potentialities of the method of intelligence.

The argument for putting chief dependence upon violence

as the method of effecting change is, moreover, usually put in a way that proves altogether too much for its own case. It is said that the dominant economic class has all the agencies of power in its hands, directly the army, militia and police; indirectly, the courts, schools, press and radio. I shall not stop to analyze this statement. But if one admits it to be valid, the conclusion to be drawn is surely the folly of resorting to a use of force against force that is so well intrenched. The positive conclusion that emerges is that conditions that would promise success in the case of use of force are such as to make possible great change without any great recourse to such a method.

Those who uphold the necessity of dependence upon violence usually much oversimplify the case by setting up a disjunction they regard as self-evident. They say that the sole alternative is putting our trust in parliamentary procedures as they now exist. This isolation of law-making from other social forces and agencies that are constantly operative is wholly unrealistic. Legislatures and congresses do not exist in a vacuum—not even the judges on the bench live in completely secluded sound-proof chambers. The assumption that it is possible for the constitution and activities of law-making bodies to persist unchanged while society itself is undergoing great change is an exercise in verbal formal logic.

It is true that in this country, because of the interpretations made by courts of a written constitution, our political institutions are unusually inflexible. It is also true, as well as even more important (because it is a factor in causing this rigidity) that our institutions, democratic in form, tend to favor in substance a privileged plutocracy. Nevertheless, it is sheer defeatism to assume in advance of actual trial that democratic political institutions are incapable either of further development or of constructive social application. Even as they now exist, the forms of representative government are potentially capable of expressing the public will when that assumes anything like unification. And there is nothing inherent in them that forbids their supplementation by political agencies that represent definitely economic social interests, like those of producers and consumers.

The final argument in behalf of the use of intelligence is that as are the means used so are the actual ends achieved— that is, the consequences. I know of no greater fallacy than the claim of those who hold to the dogma of the necessity of brute force that this use will be the method of calling genuine democracy into existence—of which they profess themselves the simon-pure adherents. It requires an unusually credulous faith in the Hegelian dialectic of opposites to think that all of a sudden the use of force by a class will be transmuted into a democratic classless society. Force breeds counter-force; the Newtonian law of action and reaction still holds in physics, and violence is physical. To profess democracy as an ultimate ideal and the suppression of democracy as a means to the ideal may be possible in a country that has never known even rudimentary democracy, but when professed in a country that has anything of a genuine democratic spirit in its traditions, it signifies desire for possession and retention of power by a class, whether that class be called fascist or proletarian. In the light of what happens in non-democratic countries, it is pertinent to ask whether the rule of a class signifies the dictatorship of the majority, or dictatorship over the chosen class by a minority party; whether dissenters are allowed even within the class the party claims to represent; and whether the development of literature and the other arts proceeds according to a formula prescribed by a party in conformity with a doctrinaire dogma of history and of infallible leadership, or whether artists are free from regimentation? Until these questions are satisfactorily answered, it is permissible to look with considerable suspicion upon those who assert that suppression of democracy is the road to the adequate establishment of genuine democracy. The one exception—and that apparent rather than real—to dependence upon organized intelligence as the method for directing social change is found when society through an authorized majority has entered upon the path of social experimentation leading to great social change, and a minority refuses by force to permit the method of intelligent action to go into effect. Then force may be intelligently employed to subdue and disarm the recalcitrant minority.

There may be some who think I am unduly dignifying a position held by a comparatively small group by taking their arguments as seriously as I have done. But their position serves to bring into strong relief the alternatives before us. It makes clear the meaning of renascent liberalism. The alternatives are continuation of drift with attendant improvisations to meet special emergencies; dependence upon violence; dependence upon socially organized intelligence. The first two alternatives, however, are not mutually exclusive, for if things are allowed to drift the result may be some sort of social change effected by the use of force, whether so planned or not. Upon the whole, the recent policy of liberalism has been to further "social legislation"; that is, measures which add performance of social services to the older functions of government. The value of this addition is not to be despised. It marks a decided move away from laissez faire liberalism, and has considerable importance in educating the public mind to a realization of the possibilities of organized social control. It has helped to develop some of the techniques that in any case will be needed in a socialized economy. But the cause of liberalism will be lost for a considerable period if it is not prepared to go further and socialize the forces of production, now at hand, so that the liberty of individuals will be supported by the very structure of economic organization.

The ultimate place of economic organization in human life is to assure the secure basis for an ordered expression of individual capacity and for the satisfaction of the needs of man in non-economic directions. The effort of mankind in connection with material production belongs, as I said earlier, among interests and activities that are, relatively speaking, routine in character, "routine" being defined as that which, without absorbing attention and energy, provides a constant basis for liberation of the values of intellectual, aesthetic and companionship life. Every significant religious and moral teacher and prophet has asserted that the material is instrumental to the good life. Nominally at least, this idea is accepted by every civilized community. The transfer of the burden of material production from human muscles and brain to steam, electricity and chemical processes now makes possible the effective actualization of this ideal. Needs, wants and desires are always the moving force in generating creative action. When these wants are compelled by force of conditions to be directed for the most part, among the mass of mankind, into obtaining the means of subsistence, what should be a means becomes perforce an end in itself. Up to the present the new mechanical forces of production, which are the means of emancipation from this state of affairs, have been employed to intensify and exaggerate the reversal of the true relation between means and ends. Humanly speaking I do not see how it would have been possible to avoid an epoch having this character. But its perpetuation is the cause of the continually growing social chaos and strife. Its termination cannot be effected by preaching to individuals that they should place spiritual ends above material means. It can be brought about by organized social reconstruction that puts the results of the mechanism of abundance at the free disposal of individuals. The actual corrosive "materialism" of our times does not proceed from science. It springs from the notion, sedulously cultivated by the class in power, that the creative capacities of individuals can be evoked and developed only in a struggle for material possessions and material gain. We either should surrender our professed belief in the supremacy of ideal and spiritual values and accommodate our beliefs to the predominant material orientation, or we should through organized endeavor institute the socialized economy of material security and plenty that will release human energy for pursuit of higher values.

Since liberation of the capacities of individuals for free, self-initiated expression is an essential part of the creed of liberalism, liberalism that is sincere must will the means that condition the achieving of its ends. Regimentation of material and mechanical forces is the only way by which the mass of individuals can be released from regimentation and consequent suppression of their cultural possibilities. The eclipse of liberalism is due to the fact that it has not faced the alternatives and adopted the means upon which realization of its professed aims depends. Liberalism can be true to its ideals only as it takes the course that leads to their attainment. The notion that organized social control of economic forces lies outside the historic path of liberalism shows that liberalism is still impeded by remnants of its earlier laissez faire phase, with its opposition of society and the individual. The thing which now dampens liberal ardor and paralyzes its efforts is the conception that liberty and development of individuality as ends exclude the use of organized social effort as means. Earlier liberalism regarded the separate and competing economic action of individuals as the means to social well-being. We must reverse the perspective and see that socialized economy is the means of free individual development as the end.

That liberals are divided in outlook and endeavor while reactionaries are held together by community of interest and the ties of custom is well nigh a common-place. Organization of standpoint and belief among liberals can be achieved only in and by unity of endeavor. Organized unity of action attended by consensus of beliefs will come about in the degree in which social control of economic forces is made the goal of liberal action. The greatest educational power, the greatest force in shaping the dispositions and attitudes of individuals is the social medium in which they live. The medium that now lies closest to us is that of unified action for the inclusive end of a socialized economy. The attainment of a state of society in which a basis of material security will release the powers of individuals for cultural expression is not the work of a day. But by concentrating upon the task of securing a socialized economy as the ground and medium for release of the impulses and capacities men agree to call ideal, the now scattered and often conflicting activities of liberals can be brought to effective unity.

It is no part of my task to outline in detail a program for renascent liberalism. But the question of "what is to be done" cannot be ignored. Ideas must be organized, and this organization implies an organization of individuals who hold these ideas and whose faith is ready to translate itself into action. Translation into action signifies that the general creed of liberalism be formulated as a concrete program of action. It is in organization for action that liberals are weak, and without this organization there is danger that democratic ideals may go by default. Democracy has been a fighting faith. When its ideals are reenforced by those of scientific method and experimental intelligence, it cannot be that it is incapable of evoking discipline, ardor and organization. To narrow the issue for the future to a struggle between Fascism and Communism is to invite a castastrophe that may carry civilization down in the struggle. Vital and courageous democratic liberalism is the one force that can surely avoid such a disastrous narrowing of the issue. I for one do not believe that Americans living in the tradition of Jefferson and Lincoln will weaken and give up without a whole-hearted effort to make democracy a living reality. This, I repeat, involves organization.

The question cannot be answered by argument. Experimental method means experiment, and the question can be answered only by trying, by organized effort. The reasons for making the trial are not abstract or recondite. They are found in the confusion, uncertainty and conflict that mark the modern world. The reasons for thinking that the effort if made will be successful are also not abstract and remote.

They lie in what the method of experimental and cooperative intelligence has already accomplished in subduing to potential human use the energies of physical nature. In material production, the method of intelligence is now the established rule; to abandon it would be to revert to savagery. The task is to go on, and not backward, until the method of intelligence and experimental control is the rule in social relations and social direction. Either we take this road or we admit that the problem of social organization in behalf of human liberty and the flowering of human capacities is insoluble.

It would be fantastic folly to ignore or to belittle the obstacles that stand in the way. But what has taken place, also against great odds, in the scientific and industrial revolutions, is an accomplished fact; the way is marked out. It may be that the way will remain untrodden. If so, the future holds the menace of confusion moving into chaos, a chaos that will be externally masked for a time by an organization of force, coercive and violent, in which the liberties of men will all but disappear. Even so, the cause of the liberty of the human spirit, the cause of opportunity of human beings for full development of their powers, the cause for which liberalism enduringly stands, is too precious and too ingrained in the human constitution to be forever obscured. Intelligence after millions of years of errancy has found itself as a method, and it will not be lost forever in the blackness of night. The business of liberalism is to bend every energy and exhibit every courage so that these precious gods may not even be temporarily lost but be intensified and expanded here and now.

LAW AS A SOCIAL SCIENCE

By HUNTINGTON CAIRNS

IT IS the contemporary belief, in American legal circles at all events, that law or jurisprudence, whatever it may have been in the past, has now the status of a social science. This is an assumption easier to make than to substantiate, and in view of the increasing insistence upon this point, it is now appropriate to inquire whether or not it possesses a tangible· foundation. This requires a consideration of the distinctive characteristics of social science, the determination whether or not jurisprudence exhibits these characteristics, and, if not, if it is possible for it to assume them. It will be convenient to begin, briefly and concisely, with an examination of the characteristics of modern legal thought.

Legal thinking is no exception to the general rule that the distinctive characteristics, even the choice of subject matter, of many domains of thought, are determined by their first assumptions. Maine's [1] conviction that civilization is a rare exception in world history, and that Rousseau's doctrine of natural rights was inimical to its continued existence fixed the general character of his theory of law and government and influenced the selection of the problems he chose to in-vestigate. Brooks Adams' [2] materialist conception of history led him inevitably to the conclusion that the law's content is the product of the self-interest of successive dominant classes. So it is with other legal thinkers and with other schools of legal thought. Fundamental opinions in law and the social sciences, however the case may be with some at least of the natural sciences, possess a special importance and it is well to pause from time to time to take stock of them.

Underlying the investigations of modern legal research is the conviction that such research can be made beneficial to the administration of justice. It is equally an assumption of the sociological jurists,[3] the realists[4] and the new born experimental jurists.[5] Perhaps this conviction came into legal thought partly as a result of the contempt in which jurisprudence was held by the legal profession of the nineteenth century. "Jurisprudence," said Dicey in an often quoted remark, "stinks in the nostrils of the practising barrister." It would be an adequate answer to the practising barrister, however, and one which would effectively silence him, if it were pointed out that legal research—not in the sense of mere historical investigation, but in the sense of a complete analysis of "law in action"—was being undertaken for the purposes of law reform and not with the aim of inventing another game similar to the entertaining one with which the analytical jurists amused themselves a generation or two ago. Perhaps also the conviction became a part of legal thought as the outcome of the endless stream of criticism directed by social scientists at the actual administration of justice. There seemed indeed to be a prevalent opinion that law could never become a social science unless something were done with respect to the improvement of the administration of justice, although it never occurred to anyone to suggest that economics could never attain the status of a social science unless it corrected the much worse state of affairs obtaining in its field. Perhaps this underlying assumption can also be accounted for by the simple fact that legal students here recognized a profitable field of research. Whatever may be its explanation, it is indubitably an essential part of contemporary legal thinking and it has had an unequivocal effect upon the aims and methods of contemporary legal research.

It has had its deepest influence in the selection of the subject matter for investigation. This subject matter in its broadest terms may be denominated "law in action." Each school approaches this field from the standpoint of its own special conceptions but its program rarely exceeds the limits marked out by the subject matter "law in action." The programme of the sociological school, formulated by Pound,[6] insists upon eight points: (1) Study of the actual social effects of legal institutions, legal precepts, and legal doctrines; (2) Sociological study in preparation for law-making; (3) Study of the means of making legal precepts effective in action; (4) Study of juridical action; (5) A sociological legal history; (6) Recognition of the importance of individualized application of legal precepts—of reasonable and just solutions of individual cases; (7) In English-speaking countries, a Ministry of Justice; and (8) That the end of juristic study, toward which the foregoing are but some of the means, is to make effort more effective in achieving the purposes of law. Llewellyn [7] has similarly, but less systematically, marked out for the realists their domain of study. He thinks that the immediate aim of legal research ought to be, and probably for the next ten years will be, the "checking up on the effects of the law in life. . . . first, for the purpose of discovering what the rules really are and mean; second, for the purpose of utilizing them and planning their utilization; third, for the purpose of criticizing them and preparing a way for law reform; and, lastly, as the indispensable basis of any pure legal science which deserves the name." An ambitious programme for the so-called experimental jurists has been stated recently by Beutel.[8] This school's primary object is to discover, with the assistance of an instrument—the experimental method— which they hope will yield more precise results than those obtained in the past, the extent to which law reform is necessary and how it should be accomplished. The programmes of all these schools have in common fundamentally the same subject matter—law in action; and it is apparent that the selection of that subject matter in the first instance was determined in large part by the initial assumption that legal research might be profitable for the administration of justice. Such are the two distinctive characteristics of contemporary legal thought.

A rationalization and defense of these characteristics has recently been put forward by Professor Yntema,[9] who declares that the objective analysis of the legal system for the purpose of reform constitutes the "Copernican discovery of modern legal science." His purpose is to show the scientific legitimacy of the subject matter, the necessity for such an objective investigation, and the probability of the realization of fruitful results. He concludes "that such a study of law in action is an essential, if not under present conditions the most essential, object of a legal science which is not to remain esoteric."

It requires little reflection, however, to realize that the characteristics exhibited by modern legal study are not characteristics of the principal social sciences. Contemporary legal study is a technology; but the social sciences are not technologies. Their ideal, like the ideal of those departments of knowledge commonly denominated the "natural sciences," is the discovery of general laws which unite a number of particular facts. We may pass over the circumstance that the successes of the social sciences in formulating laws have been relatively few in number. The ideal remains warranted in the absence of a demonstration—which is still to be offered— that its realization is impossible. Moreover, the fact that the social sciences have put forward some "general laws" which appear to be "true" with respect to the subject matter for which they were framed, is a positive indication that the ideal is permissible. The ideals of the technologies are, however, entirely different and vary from one technology to another. In the case of modern legal study, it is, as we have seen, law reform. It seems scarcely necessary to point out that this difference in ideals is a crucial one. Each ideal determines in large part the subject matter to be selected for examination, the methods to be adopted, even the facts which will be chosen for study. The possibility of legal study as a technology, moreover, raises a special question, one not peculiar to the other studies we know as technologies. It is the characteristic of a technology that it is indebted to many sciences, although it has in many cases its own contribution to make of matter and method. Mechanical engineering, which is beholden to a score or more of sources, is such a subject. This, however, although characteristic, is not always the case; psychology, which until recently was principally concerned with the gathering of facts as a basis for the formulation of general principles or "laws," has now felt that enough of such principles have been formulated to permit it to become an "applied" science or technology. In its case, psychology is the principal source upon which psychologists draw in making their application. The important point with respect to every technology is, however, that it involves to an exclusive or considerable degree the application of principles or laws formulated by a "pure" science. But this is not the situation in which modern legal study finds itself. It is attempting to be an applied science, although there has been as yet no pure science of law in the sense of a study of the principles governing the relations of law and society. In the absence of such a previous study, the applications of modern legal research must necessarily be of a crude order. They would seem to be confined largely to such problems as the discovery of the manner in which legal procedure should be altered so as to make possible a more expeditious, and at the same time equitable, trial of issues. By its emphasis upon law reform, modern legal study overlooks the fact that it is limiting itself to a circumscribed field of study, and that no matter how successful its accomplishments in this field, it is not a social science nor will it, so long as it maintains its present ideal, ever become one. More important than these considerations, however, is the fact that modern legal study, by reason of its technological ideal, is overlooking a field of investigation which must be tilled before we can ever have a really fruitful applied legal science. It is the domain which legal research would necessarily explore if it were properly a social science.

The concept of law as a social science implies, for the present at any rate, at least three propositions: (1) That its ideal will be the ideal of the other social sciences, namely, the formulation of statements asserting invariant, or almost invariant, relationships among the facts in its specific field and, in its special case, the organization of such principles into a coherent pattern in conjunction with a rational system of ethics; (2) that its subject matter will be the subject matter of the other social sciences, namely, culture in the sense in which it is understood by anthropologists and the influences which work upon culture;[10] (3) that its methods in general will be the methods commonly employed in the other social sciences.

It should be said at once that legal research so conceived holds out no prospect of ultimate usefulness. Its justification, if it stands in need of one, is not different from that of the other sciences; it gratifies our intellectual appetites. It is not impossible that such research will lead to fruitful ends, but it should be made abundantly clear that no such claims are advanced on its behalf. In this attitude it is no more than assuming the position of the more successful sciences. "Social science," Professor Cohen[11] has written, "can . . . in the long run best attain its goal only when those who cultivate it care more for the scientific game itself and for the meticulous adherence to its rules of evidence than for any of the uses to which their discoveries can be put." It is, indeed, as Titchener[12] observed more than a score of years ago, a distinctive feature of science that it is more rigorous than technology in its observation of the established laws and approved method of logic; "not," as he was careful to add, "through any superior virtue in the man of science, but simply because the technologist, in the nature of the case, is a logical opportunist, working for results and towards a practical end, and therefore content to work in a logical twilight so long as results are forthcoming and progress can be reported."

Culture as the subject matter of legal research raises a set of problems entirely different from those encountered if the subject matter is regarded as "law in action." Law in action, it should be pointed out, is also within the domain of legal research if culture is taken as its subject matter. Law in action is one aspect of culture, and, as such, an element of the social process which must be studied if the relationship of law and society is to be understood in its entirety. Even here, however, the difference in attitude between the investigation of "law in action" as such, and the study of "law in action" in order to relate it to the social process generally, is important. Facts, as Cook [13] has recently emphasized, do not speak for themselves. Their meaning depends to a greater or lesser extent upon the point of view with which we approach them. "The heavens declare the glory of God to one whose mind is kindled with religious zeal," writes Cunningham.[14] "They speak the language of infinite vastness governed by law to the mind fertile in scientific hypotheses; they tell a story of gods and heroes, of loves and antipathies, of births and deaths, to the mind of the romantic poet; they become father, mother, and children, and animals all living a life like our own, to the mind of the myth maker." The facts in the field of "law in action" will speak with one voice to the research student who studies cultural processes generally, and with a different voice to the student whose main concern is law reform. This, however, is a condition which develops as research progresses. At this point it is advisable to consider the nature of some of the typical problems involved in the cultural approach.

Since ancient times it has been noticed that a correlation exists between certain aspects of social life and geographical conditions. Thus Aristotle[15] explained the superiority of the Greeks over other races upon the basis of the middle position which the Greeks occupied between the over-civilized Asiatics and the under-civilized Gaul and Thracian. He argued that the northern races were courageous but stupid and the Orientals intelligent but spiritless, while the Greeks, who dwelt in an intermediate region were high-spirited and also intelligent. Observations of this sort have been put forward in countless numbers until, as Sorokin[16] has observed, there is scarcely "any physical or psychical trait in man, any characteristic in the social organization of a group, any social process or historical event, which has not been accounted for by geographical factors." In recent times a serious attempt has been made to give these hypotheses a more scientific form. Brunhes[17] suggests that there is a more direct correlation between geographical factors and man's first vital necessities—food, sleep, clothing, defense—than between such factors and other social phenomena. He, therefore, attempts a positive classification of the types of social phenomena which are more directly influenced by geographical agencies. These he conceives to be six in number: The shelter or habitation, the road or line of passage, the cultivation of fields and the breeding of animals, the exploitation of minerals and devastation in plant and animal life. Beyond these six essential facts social phenomena exhibit less, if any, correlation with geographical influences; still to the limited extent to which the essential facts explain, or serve to explain, the social facts by their localization and their particular forms, we have the right to connect the social facts with human geography.[18] He utters one final word of caution: "Between the facts of the physical order there are sometimes relations of causality; between facts of human geography there are usually only relations of connection. To force, so to speak, the bond which connects phenomena with each other is scientifically false; and there will be great need of the spirit of criticism which will enable one to see clearly the many cases where connection is accidental and not causal." [19] Brunhes' approach to the problem of relationship of social phenomena and geographical factors is typical of the reformed spirit of investigation which now marks the whole subject.[20]

Is there a connection between legal phenomena and geography? Montesquieu[21] and Buckle[22] thought that in some respects there was a direct connection, although their chief emphasis was on the factor of climate. Randall,[23] in what appears to be the only existing systematic study of the subject, offers a number of interesting suggestions for further investigation, and he concludes that it can be fairly claimed on behalf of the geographic method that it is likely to throw considerable light upon the phases of culture that are embodied

in legal rules. Certain obvious and direct relationships between law and geography have long been noted. It is clear, as
Randall says, that the maritime law of Peru and Switzerland
will be rudimentary; that the law of a pastoral community
will differ from that of an agricultural; that of one based on
tree cultivation from one based on corn raising; and that of
industrial and trading communities from all others. Black-
stone[24] pointed out that "in the Isle of Man, to take away a
horse or ox was no felony, but a trespass, because of the difficulty in that little territory to conceal them or to carry them
off; but to steal a pig or a fowl, which is easily done, was a
capital misdemeanor, and the offender punished with death."
The influence of the sea in this island of fishermen is apparent in the customary form of oath. The judges or deemsters
swear to execute the laws as impartially "as the herring's
backbone doth lie in the middle of the fish." Manifestly, a
multitude of such relationships exist between law and geography. The task remains, however, to collect enough of such
instances to decide whether or not any general principle can
be deduced from them. In addition, the concept itself may be
extended in at least three directions. First, we may endeavor
to understand the more subtle influences of geography upon
the law, although, of course, here the need for care cannot be
too over-stressed. An instance of an attempt in this direction
is Pound's[25] hypothesis of the pioneer influence of American
jurisprudence. Pound has shown that the two great generic
forms of human habitation, urban and rural life, have had a
direct effect upon the development of American law. Our
American common-law polity reflects the spirit of the pioneer; "it presupposes," he writes, "an American farming
community of the first half of the nineteenth century; a situation as far apart as the poles from what our legal system has
had to meet in the endeavor to administer justice to great
urban communities at the end of the nineteenth and in the
twentieth century." Second, we may think of the relationship
of law and geography not merely as the connection of law
with its physical surroundings, but in the broader sense of

the relationship of law and the environment. Under this classification we may subsume the physical surroundings and what Graham Wallas[26] has termed the "social heritage" and Briffault[27] "traditional heredity." By the term "social heritage" is meant the habits, knowledge and expedients which are handed down from one generation to another by the social process of teaching and learning. All those mental characters which are specifically human, as Briffault has shown, are the products of traditional heredity. "Every step," he writes, "in human thought and feeling is strictly determined by what went before. The boldest speculation of the thinker is bound within narrow limits by the thought of his predecessors, and is the direct outcome of an evolution which goes back in unbroken continuity to the first flickerings of the human mind. Here, as elsewhere, evolution is gradual modification, not creation. No human sentiment, no idea, no institution has ever been created and made its appearance suddenly and 'de novo.' " All the social techniques and arts, all the folkways and institutions, which are manifested in society are also a part of the social heritage. "If the earth were struck by one of Mr. Wells' comets," Wallas writes, "and if, in consequence, every human being now alive were to lose all the knowledge and habits which he had acquired from preceding generations (though retaining unchanged all his own powers of invention, and memory, and habitation), nine-tenths of the inhabitants of London or New York would be dead in a month, and 99 per cent. of the remaining tenth would be dead in six months. They would have no language to express their thoughts, and no thoughts but vague reverie. They could not read notices, or drive motors or horses. They would wander about, led by the inarticulate voices of a few naturally dominant individuals, drowning themselves, as thirst came on, in hundreds at the riverside landing places, looting those shops where the smell of decaying food attracted them, and perhaps at the end stumbling on the expedient of cannibalism." Law is both a part and a product of the social heritage. This is a relationship which today is explored only incidentally and unconsciously as an aspect of historical research; it still remains, so far as its importance to the law is concerned, to be brought within the realm of social theory and related to social process generally. Finally, we should remember that the problem of the relationship of law and the environment is but a phase of the problem of social causation; it is one of the many doors which open on this still relatively undeveloped field.

A characteristic of American, as distinguished from European, social thought is its antipathy to philosophical analysis; nevertheless, it is difficult to see how the metaphysical questions connected with the problem of social causation can be safely ignored. At the very threshold we must determine whether the cause and effect concept has any meaning. Russell [28] once took the position that "the word 'cause' is so inextricably bound up with misleading associations as to make its complete extrusion from the philosophical vocabulary desirable." He argued that the idea of "cause" broke down under philosophical analysis, and that, in fact, laws of probable sequence of the type contemplated by Mill, though useful in the infancy of science, were displaced by laws, the constancy of which consist in a "sameness of relations" or a "sameness of differential equations." This position had the historic support of Galileo in the *Discorsi,* who in discussing the law of falling bodies said: "It does not seem to me advantageous now to examine what the cause of acceleration is." [29] Similarly, Newton remarked: "I have not yet been able to determine from the phenomena the cause of these properties of gravitation, and I do not invent hypotheses (*Hypotheses non fingo*). It is sufficient that gravitation exists, that it acts according to the laws we have formulated, and that it is capable of explaining all motions of heavenly bodies and of the sea." [30] It may be said of this position that it is an admirably cautious one; but it is nevertheless a position which can be taken only by those advanced sciences which have been successful in the discovery and establishment of laws asserting invariant relations. Furthermore, it ignores, rather than solves, the question whether or not the statement "A causes B" can be interpreted so as to possess satisfactory meaning. On this latter point, philosophers are still hopelessly at odds. The influence of Hume[31] has persisted, but the present dispute oscillates around Russell's[32] recent assertion that causal laws express nothing but regularities of sequence. This view has much to recommend it, but it appears to lead to certain paradoxical conclusions. Thus night will be the cause of day and day the cause of night. Similarly, the blowing of the factory whistle is the cause of the position of the hands of the clock when the men begin to leave the factory for dinner and the blowing of the whistle in a New York factory causes both the departure of the men from that factory and also the departure of the men from factories in Philadelphia and in Baltimore, and conversely.[33] These difficulties seem to arise because of the present inability to isolate a causal characteristic. However, it does not follow that the statement "A causes B" is without meaning or that social scientists should abandon the concept of cause. It means only that the social scientist should formulate as precisely as may be what *he* means by causation. It may not be possible for him to isolate the causal characterisitc, but he may be able to discover sequences entitled to be called "causal."

If the social scientist is to continue to employ the notion of cause—and no valid reasons suggest themselves why he should not—it seems advisable to use it in the sense suggested by Keynes: "We wish to know," he writes,[34] "whether knowledge of one fact throws light *of any kind* upon the likelihood of another. The theory of causality is only important because it is thought that by means of its assumptions light can be thrown by the experience of one phenomenon upon the expectation of another." This appears to be the most general statement of the problem confronting the social scientist. It is in this sense that Weber[35] sought to ascertain the extent to which Protestantism took part in the qualitative formation and the quantitative expansion of capitalism throughout the world. The concept also indicates the importance of focusing the inquiry, in the first stages at any rate, upon specific institutions or patterns. To state that technological adaptation or economic pressure is the cause of social change is too vague to have any meaning, unless the particular institution which is the subject of change is pointed out. It is perhaps of greater importance, as Cohen[36] has suggested "to recognize that social science is for the most part concerned not like physics with laws expressing the invariant repetition of elements, nor with laws of individual psychic events, but with laws about the relation of very complex patterns to one another." Undoubtedly this is one of the ideal goals of the social scientist; it represents also perhaps the only possible achievement in this field. We may look at social change in two ways: (a) We may consider the relation of one complex pattern to another, and from this position hope to formulate laws expressing social causation; (b) but social change is not solely the result of the relation of one complex pattern to another: it may be the product of a simple event, such as the invention of the cotton gin. Since we can never foretell when events of this latter class will occur, causation in this sense must always be historical; it can not be the basis, until the event has occurred, for prediction as to the future.

The intimate connections between this problem and law are too obvious to dwell upon. Law is subject to incessant change, and in turn itself exercises a determining influence upon most or all of the major patterns of society. There is here a real task for both the legal student and the social scientist in isolating the major determiners of legal change, and in evaluating the status of law itself as a causative social factor.

As a final example of the kind of problems suggested by the cultural approach, it is enough to mention the question of the nature and function of the regulative principles by which society is sustained.[37] Here are raised the general problems of the place in society of law and custom, fashion, habit, religion and morals; the nature of sanctions; the basis of authority; the character of primitive law; and the application of the social codes to individual conduct. These and similar questions are as properly within the scope of legal theory as within that of sociology. All of them must be answered before we can hope to have a satisfactory science of law; but they are in grave danger of being overlooked entirely by the legal theorist unless the present emphasis upon legal reform is qualified so as to stimulate the study of the cultural aspects of law, irrespective of the question of its possible benefit to the administration of justice.

The view advocated in this paper is the simple one that a science of law must be founded on an adequate theory of human society, and that the construction of that theory is in part a task within the domain of the legal theorist. Today, as I have attempted to show, legal study does not exhibit the characteristics of a social science; it is a technology. By its emphasis upon technological ideals it is overlooking a set of problems which must be solved before we can ever have a fruitful theory of law or a sound applied legal science. I have said nothing here with respect to the question of method, as it has seemed to me that no exclusive position is warranted by our present knowledge. We cannot rule out as inherently imperfect the comparative, the statistical or any other method; neither can we say that a particular method shall be employed to the exclusion of all others. The general method, until more satisfactory tools are developed, will be that of hypothesis and verification, with such assistance as the more individualized methods can render.

¹ Ancient Law (World's Classics ed. 1931) 18; Popular Government (1886) 75, 134, 143, 152-54, and passim.
² Centralization and the Law (1906) 63-4; The Modern Conception of Animus (1907) 19 Green Bag 12.
³ Pound, Interpretations of Legal History (1923) 151-165; idem, Criminal Justice in America (1930) 211-12; idem, The Spirit of the Common Law (1921) 212-16; idem, art. Jurisprudence in Gee (ed) Research in the Social Sciences (1929) 181.
⁴ Llewellyn, The Conditions for and the Aims and Methods of Legal Research, American Law School Review, March, 1930, 672.
⁵ Beutel, Some Implications of Experimental Jurisprudence (1934) 48 Harv. L. R. 169.

[6] Outlines of Lectures on Jurisprudence (4th ed. 1928) 16-18.

[7] Op. cit. supra note 4 at 674; cf. idem, *A Realistic Jurisprudence—The Next Step* (1930) 30 Col. Law Rev. 431.

[8] Op. cit. supra note 5. Cf. Robinson, Law—*An Unscientific Science* (1934) 44 Yale Law Journal 235, for a statement by an eminent psychologist of a legal programme from a psychological point of view.

[9] *Legal Science and Reform* (1934) 34 Col. L. R. 207.

[10] Culture was defined by Tylor as "that complex whole which includes knowledge, belief, art, morals, law, custom, and any other capabilities and habits acquired by man as a member of society." 1 Primitive Culture (1903) 1. A modern definition has been put forward by Malinowski which stresses the fact that artifacts are a part of culture, a point not emphasized by Tylor: "Culture comprises inherited artifacts, goods, technical processes, ideas, habits and values." 4 Ency. Social Sciences, s. v. *Culture* 621 (1931).

[11] Reason and Nature (1931) 349.

[12] *Psychology: Science or Technology* (1914) 84 The Popular Science Monthly 39.

[13] *The Possibilities of Social Study as a Science* (1931) in Essays on Research in the Social Sciences (1931) 27.

[14] Textbook of Logic (1924) 247. Quoted Cook op. cit. supra note 13 at 32.

[15] Politics, vii, 7. (Jowett's Translation 1885).

[16] Contemporary Sociological Theories (1927) 100.

[17] Human Geography (1920) 46-51.

[18] Op. cit. supra note 17 at c. viii.

[19] Op. cit. supra note 17 at 593.

[20] It is interesting to note that in geography as well as in law there has been a separation of "pure" and "applied" science. "For centuries two conceptions of geography have been opposed to each other," Brunhes writes (op. cit. supra note 17 at 29); " by generalizing and perhaps stretching the facts a bit, one might be called the Greek conception, the other the Roman conception. The Greek conception was loftier and truer. The Greek geographers, Thales of Miletus, Eratosthenes, Hippocrates, and Aristotle, were philosophers. They had a general, philosophic conception of the physical universe and they sought *before everything else* to work out the natural succession of phenomena and how these phenomena were subordinated to each other. Then came the Romans with their utilitarian spirit; their geograpy was *practical*. They established itineraries, and composed topographical dictionaries; they were especially dominated by commercial interests, by administrative problems, or by ambitions of conquest. From that time general and speculative geography was neglected; the spirit of geographical science and the taste for it were lost. Only a few men, as rare as they were farseeing, strove to preserve the scientific point of view in geography. (Author's italics.)

[21] The Spirit of Laws (Bohn. ed., 1909) Bk, I, c. iii.

[22] 1 History of Civilization (World's classics ed. 1925) ci. ii.

[23] Law and Geography (1918) 3 Evolution of Law 198. See also Wigmore 3 A Panorama of the World's Legal Systems (1928) 1133; idem, *A Map of the World's Law*, 19 Geographical Review (1929) 114; Dubbs,

The Unfolding of Law in the Mountain Region (1926) 3 Colorado Magazine 113.

[24] Quoted Semple, Influences of Geographic Environment (1927) 40.

[25] The Spirit of the Common Law (1921) c. v.

[26] Our Social Heritage (1921) 14 et seq.

[27] 1 The Mothers (1927) 23 et seq.

[28] Mysticism and Logic (1925) 180.

[29] Quoted Weyl, The Open World (1932) 36.

[30] Ibid.

[31] A Treatise of Human Nature (1920) Pt. III.

[32] The Analysis of Mind (1921) c. v. A valuable discussion of the present difficulties is contained in Stebbing, A Modern Introduction to Logic (1930) c. xv.

[33] Stebbing op. cit. supra note 32 at 283; Broad, The Mind and its Place in Nature (1925) 455.

[34] A Treatise on Probability (1921) 277.

[35] The Protestant Ethic and the Spirit of Capitalism (1930).

[36] Op. cit. supra note 11 at 361.

[37] The most satisfactory discussion of this question from the sociological position is contained in MacIver, Society, Its Structure and Changes (1931) 248, et seq.

THE IDOL OF THE LABORATORY *

By GRAHAM WALLAS

"Natural" or "physical" science, since Bentham and Mill urged that its methods should be applied to the social sciences, has become a world-wide discipline, whose elastic but effective organization and success in discovering and co-ordinating hitherto unknown relations of causes and effects surpass the dreams of the most enthusiastic thinkers of a hundred years ago.

In the natural sciences we no longer rely on the occasional appearance of a genius who, like Faraday, forces his own way into recognition, or on a monarch or noble who is ready to patronize genius, or on the mutual stimulation of intellectual curiosity in some group of friends, or in a short-lived local academy. No civilized State, however impoverished, now neglects to subsidize the development of natural science. The scientist who follows "whithersoever the argument leads him" no longer has to face the fear and hatred which met Anaxagoras or Bruno or Galileo, or even the milder social disapproval which was roused in my boyhood by the name of Darwin. A young scientist may, and too often does, waste some of the best years of his early manhood in mechanical academic "research," whose only result will be the saving of a little trouble to his professor. But he knows and feels that the purpose of his work is discovery, and any important discovery which he makes or helps to make is published in a few weeks throughout the civilized world and its methods are tested and its implications sought for in a thousand laboratories.

Those emotions which are stimulated in a modern natural scientist by his daily work are comparatively simple and

* From *Social Judgment*

do not hinder each other. The instinctive curiosity and aesthetic delight in the ordered pattern of the universe which guided the earliest discoveries of our stone-age ancestors have developed without inner contradiction into the scientific passion of the modern student, just as man's primitive delight in ordered sound has developed into the creative passion of Beethoven. And if the scientist's passion flags, his official post, his salary, and the needs of his family combine with habit and the expectation of his fellows to carry him over the "dead points" of his intellectual life. He may suffer weariness and disappointment, or be diverted from his course by loyalty to a teacher or school, or by jealousy of a colleague, or by the desire for fame or wealth; but he knows, and everyone else knows, that the man who accepts the name of scientist pledges himself to resist those things as the professional soldier pledges himself to resist panic. Within this world-discipline the natural sciences themselves are profoundly changing. All of them are drawing together. The distinction between chemistry and physics has disappeared. Matter is no longer distinguishable from energy; atoms have become universes; and the behaviour of the atom is studied by observation of stars and nebulae. The biologist no longer draws a sharp line between man and other animals, or between animal and vegetable life. And the biochemist tells us that when dealing with viruses and ferments he can no longer distinguish between chemical and vital activity.

Scientific inquiry is therefore penetrating into every region of human activity, and the methods of the laboratory are acquiring a constantly growing prestige.

But the world events of the last twenty years show that those methods have not yet enabled us to attain the art of judgment which would enable us to use our scientific knowledge for the general human good. We still, as Shelley said in 1821, "want the creative faculty to imagine that which we know," and still, as Shelley said, "the accumulation of the materials of external life exceed the quantity of the power of assimilating them to the internal laws of human nature." [1]

Civilization is still reeling from the effects of a war in which the whole organization of natural science was devoted to the destruction of human life and health and welfare.

Everyone, indeed, now admits our own urgent need of creative imagination. We must invent new patterns of living, and social invention requires as intimate a co-operation of emotion and reason as does poetry.

But it is not enough to know that we need creative imagination; we must, if we are to escape disaster, acquire the art of producing it in ourselves and our fellows. At present we seem to be slowly groping towards that art, too often by realizing when it is too late that we might have used it. Mr. Harold Nicolson was, during the weeks before August 4, 1914, a young official in the British Foreign Office under Lord Grey as Secretary of State, and his father (Sir Arthur Nicolson, afterwards Lord Carnock) and Sir Eyre Crowe were Grey's chief professional officials. The officials had "thought out" all the logical corollaries of British and German foreign policy and were ready with "scientific" plans for a defensive alliance with France and Russia. Grey was less consciously trying also to "feel out" the human significance of the whole position. "Grey," says Mr. H. Nicolson in his admirable *Life of Lord Carnock,* "stumbled and fumbled at places where Nicolson and Crowe saw clearly and incisively: their aim was to clear a way through the immediate thicket: his aim was to reach to something wider. But if he stumbled, it was because his eyes—those sad eagle eyes—were fixed upon an ultimate and distant ideal." [2]

Mr. Nicolson here describes the contrast as being between two processes of calculation, one seeking a solution to a nearer, and the other a more distant problem. He would, I believe, have given a truer psychological picture if he had used Shelley's contrast between the "Reason" which is "the enumeration of quantities already known" and the "Imagination," which is "the perception of the value of those quantities, both separately and as a whole." [3]

And if ever statesmen learn the art of consciously harmonizing emotion and reason, it may be no longer necessary that those who seek for values as well as for causal relationships—for ends as well as for means—should "stumble and fumble."

During the writing of this book I have been conscious of a growing conviction that the formulation and practice of such an art of harmonization, with a hitherto unknown degree of sucess, is not an impossible ideal. Before the end of the twentieth century, perhaps after more dreadful experiences than those of 1914 to 1932, there may begin to emerge signs of a "Wisdom," more difficult perhaps at first than the Wisdoms of Egypt and China and Greece and Palestine and Galileo and Newton, but more suited to our needs. And the essential element in that Wisdom may be the "due balance among the faculties" which John Stuart Mill strove to find.

The main obstacles to the creation and diffusion of such a Wisdom are, as I have said, the mental attitudes which hinder the co-operation of reason and emotion; and one of those mental attitudes is a habit of mind which often claims a monopoly of the word "science." Twelve years ago, in *Our Social Heritage,* I tried to describe what seemed to me a dangerous tendency among the thinkers in Russia and America who called themselves Materialist or Behaviourist and claimed to be supported by the authority of "science." These men took the measurable movements of human muscles and the chemical and physical processes which resulted in such movements as a complete account of human behaviour. In practice, I said, they tended to treat those motives, like anger and sex and greed, whose muscular results were most obvious, as being the only legitimate subject-matter of science, and to ignore as unscientific more complex motives such as pity and kindness or even the scientific curiosity which they took for granted in themselves. The present tendency among writers of this school seems to be to treat the facts and tendencies disclosed by physical measurement as alone "objective" and "real," and all conscious emotional preferences of any kind as unreal "epiphenomena."

Professor P. A. Sorokin, for instance, of the University of Minnesota, published in 1927 an essay (accompanied by a useful bibliography) on *Sociology and Ethics* in which he says, "As poetry represents a kind of social thought quite different from science, judgments of valuation represent a kind of social thought quite different from the scientific judgments."

The particular type of emotional preference of which Sorokin was writing is the traditional sense of moral obligation. " 'Love thy neighbour,' " he says, " 'kill thy enemy,' and other similar expressions are neither true nor non-true. . . . Natural science and other real sciences study the reality as it is, irrespective of whether it is 'good' or 'bad.' " [4]

Some of the writers of this school use the word "public" for easily measurable and therefore easily communicable and repeatable physical events, and the word "private" for those less easily measurable and less communicable events which are states of consciousness described by those who experience them. Professor L. Hogben, for instance, defines "the public world of science" as "the external world of physics enlarged to take in the subject-matter of biology." "The private component," he says, "offers no profitable basis for discussion," and he adds that "to the private worlds belong values." [5] "This distinction," he tells us, "is not abolished by the fact that the temperaments of some philosophers lead them to apply the term *real* to the private, and *imaginary* to the public component." [6] Between the introspective psychologist and the behaviourist "there is," he says, "a great gulf fixed, as old as that which separates the philosophy of Plato from that of Democritus." [7] ". . . Science can supply us with aviation, broadcasting, and twilight sleep. Transcendental philosophy can only offer us the good life." [8]

Under the influence of his enthusiasm Professor Hogben even makes statements about the relation between his "private" and his "public" worlds, which are capable of rigidly materialist verification or refutation. "Our expectation of living," he says, "has increased as we have learned to worry less about the good life and more about the good drain." [9] The "expectation of life" among European men of military age during the years 1914-20 would undoubtedly have been increased instead of diminished, if the statesmen of Europe had "worried" rather more than they did in the preceding ten years about that pattern of thinking and feeling the adoption of which might have brought them somewhat nearer to Nietzsche's ideal of a "good European."

In a review in the *New Republic* of November 5, 1930, of a *History of Experimental Psychology*, by Dr. E. G. Boring, the reviewer (Mr. Leonard Carmichael) prophesies a rapid growth of the science of psychology, and adds: "This development, however, must be in the hands of scientists who are almost harshly empirical and who, like Dr. Boring himself, yield to no emotional desire to leave the laboratory in order to save society."

It is easy to sympathize with the rage with which young American psychologists react against the edifying psychological generalizations which characterized the nineteenth-century sociological courses in American universities and their insistence upon the evidence for every psychological statement. But psychologists and their students will have to use judgment both as thinkers and as voters in the "saving" of society "outside the laboratory" from its present dangers. A harshly empirical psychology may mean a psychology which deliberately neglects some of the most important elements in its own problems.

Sorokin and Hogben are systematic thinkers determined to argue out the full implications of their position. Those of us who disagree with them may hope to convert them or to be converted by them. But the influence of that conception of "science" which they state in its most extreme form spreads far beyond the laboratories of experimental psychologists and physiologists, and constantly tends to introduce a "harshly empirical" element into the intellectual-emotional process of social judgment.

Not much harm and not much good is likely to result from a verbal controversey as to the exact meaning to be given to the word "science," whether, for instance, the work of a British sociologist is "scientific" or not, when he is trying to form a "judgment of valuation" as to which of two constitutions for India is most desirable, or whether a proposed change in the divorce laws would do good or harm. But a great deal of harm will result if a young thinker, because he is told that such efforts are "unscientific," is discouraged from any attempts to make them.

General Smuts gave, on November 30, 1929, to an audience of students at Newnham College, Cambridge, an eloquent address in which he said: "The mature sober impartial spirit of science . . . may yet become the governing factor in our human organization, whether that organization will take the form of government or something better than government which may evolve in course of time. As justice is said to be blind, so science is deaf and blind to illusion and passion; it deals with facts on their merit. . . . The application of the true scientific spirit to human affairs, if it were humanly possible, would mean such a reign of justice and fair play on earth as only poets have dreamt of." [10]

General Smuts is obviously right in believing that the conception of science can be made a powerful political force in a modern industrial community. Every voter who has passed through an elementary school or has used modern appliances in his work has now some conception of the method of experimental science and has profited by its results. The twentieth-century artisan and machine-tender has learnt something at school, and more at the bench, about scientific principles. He is often grateful for the system that preserves his children's health and increases the national output of wealth, however unfair he may believe the distribution of that wealth to be. Even the English country labourers, the descendants of the men who in the Middle Ages were frightened by stories of Friar Bacon and Friar Bungay, are now discovering that science can improve the seed they sow and protect their wheat from rust.

But though scientists may be wise, science as at present studied is not co-extensive with wisdom, and a conception of science as "deaf and blind to passion" does not offer to the voter or statesman a sufficient guide towards what General Smuts calls "justice and fair play," or to the merits of the "facts" to which he refers.

The "merits" of social facts include their value and significance in the realm of feeling. General Smuts is himself a member of the white minority in South Africa who are committed, it seems, irrevocably to a policy of "scientific" government, based on the indefinite continuance of serfdom for the Kaffir majority. And future historians may record that that minority would have been more successful in producing "a reign of justice and fair play" if they had been less "deaf and blind" to any emotion of sympathy with their coloured fellow-men.

The social effects of the "laboratory" attitude may be not unlike the effect of the Laws of Political Economy on English manufacturing policy a hundred years ago, or of the Marxist dialectic on Russian social administration today. But when American and British Behaviourists discuss social policy one often feels that they are substituting a metaphysical idea of determinism for the confident working generalizations of Ricardo or Marx or Spencer. The nineteenth-century economists and sociologists believed that social laws had already been discovered, and took the risk of predicting their results. Herbert Spencer was only exaggerating the mental attitude of his school when he wrote in 1851, "The ultimate development of the ideal man is logically certain— as certain as any conclusion in which we place the most implicit faith; for instance that all men will die." [11]

The laws of political economy have gone and with them the sense of "scientific certainty" in social prediction. Professor M. R. Cohen wrote in 1927: "If . . . social phenom-

ena depend upon more factors than we can readily manip-
ulate, the doctrine of universal determinism will not guarantee an attainable expression of laws governing the specific
phenomena of social life." [12]

The growing complexity of social organization has already
brought the fully industrialized nations of the world into
Professor Cohen's hypothetical position. Even if the doctrine
of universal determinism is true, we cannot now deduce
from it reliable predictions as to the future course of social
events. But the determinist mental attitude may remain as
a vague background for the ideas associated with the word
"science"; and may result in a half-conscious and half-hearted acceptance of the doctrine of the book of Ecclesiastes or
the Taoist literature, that everything which has happened in
the past had to happen, and that nothing which any of us can
do will greatly alter that which will happen in the future.
In America this half-hearted fatalism often presents itself in
a strange form as a plea for political democracy against political leadership. A reader of American sociological literature
soon gets bored with the pun which contrasts the scientific
reality of the corporate action of the "great many" with the
romantic dream of the influence of "Great Men." [13] And
the "anti-great-man" attitude unfortunately supports and is
supported by the deep-rooted American tradition that democracy must be based on equality and that the conception of
equality must assume, however contrary that assumption
may be to obvious facts, that in intellectual power and force
of will every citizen is or ought to be equivalent to every
other citizen. [14] I can never forget a conversation to which I
listened in a New England summer camp a few years ago
between the clever mothers of two exceptionally clever boys.
They both regretfully agreed that in an American high
school supernormal ability or knowledge or keenness was an
almost certain cause of unhappiness, and that they, as wise
mothers, ought to restrain their sons from knowing more or
working harder than the average of the school.

The change in American philosophy which has helped to

produce this mental attitude may be illustrated from Mr. J. Truslow Adams's admirable history of the Adams family. On December 3, 1845, John Quincy Adams, at the age of seventy-eight, carried through the House of Representatives a motion (restoring the right of petitioning Congress) for which, during the preceding nine years, he had struggled almost unaided against an overwhelming majority.[15] In 1907 his grandson, Henry Adams, who had come strongly under the influence of what Sorokin calls the "real sciences," printed privately *The Education of Henry Adams,* in which, as his biographer sums up his argument, he expressed the opinion that history "was clearly and emphatically not a science unless its phenomena could be made to fall into patterns that would permit of establishing mathematical formulae that would allow of a fairly definite predictableness."[16] Henry Adams may have influenced American history in the future by his insistence, fantastic as it sometimes was, on certain relations of cause and effect. But he did not leave behind him, like his grandfather, an example of that vital co-ordination of reason and emotion on the attainment of which the future of American civilization depends.[17]

The dogma of determinism does not, of course, always create a submissive acquiescence in things as they are. The Calvinist dogma of predestination helped to produce the ferocity of the Fifth Monarchy men. And Stalin has shown that as ruthless an energy may be inspired by the determinism of the Marxian theory of history as by the Moslem belief that every action of the elect is willed by God. But fanaticism may distort the balance of wise judgment as dangerously as fatalism.

In British political thought the doctrine that mass-psychology is guided either by the "voice of God" or by "manifest destiny" has never had the same power as in America. But in August 1931 I seemed to observe among some non-Marxian as well as Marxian members of the British Labour Party a tendency to ascribe the dislocation of our national economic system to inevitable and impersonal "world-causes."

And the ascription seemed half-consciously to blunt the edge
of their own readiness to undertake the agony of social invention.

[1] Shelley, *Defence of Poetry, Works* (H. B. Forman, 1880) vol. iii, pp.
135-6. (See Wallas, *Art of Thought,* Chap. V, 1926.)

[2] H. Nicolson, *Lord Carnock,* p. 333, 1930.

[3] H. B. Forman, Shelley's *Works,* vol. iii, p. 100.

[4] In the volume on *The Social Sciences and their Interrelations,* edited
by Ogburn and Goldenweiser, p. 311.

[5] L. Hogben, *Nature of Living Matter,* p. 301, 1930.

[6] Ibid., p. 247.

[7] Inaugural Address, *Economica,* p. 14, 1931.

[8] *Nature of Living Matter,* p. 221.

[9] Ibid., p. 236.

[10] *Africa and some World Problems,* pp. 167-9, 1930.

[11] *Social Statics,* Chap. II, quoted in Bury, *Idea of Progress,* p. 338.

[12] See Ogburn and Goldenweiser, p. 461.

[13] See, e.g., A. M. Schlesinger, in W. Gee, *Research in the Social Sciences,*
p. 219.

[14] See Dr. Abraham Flexner's admirable book, *Universities, American,
English, German* (Oxford University Press, 1930).

[15] James Truslow Adams, *The Adams Family,* pp. 215-33, 1930.

[16] Ibid., p. 346.

[17] In the same chapter Mr. J. T. Adams says of Brooks Adams (Henry's
brother) that he "became convinced that conscious thought had played a
negligible part in the historic process, and sought to link the latter up to
the physical universe" (ibid., p. 339).

ANGLO-SAXONISM AND NORDICISM IN AMERICA

By F. H. HANKINS

THE American people have been nearly as completely committed to the doctrine of Anglo-Saxon superiority, not only as regards political institutions but also as regards all the other features of an advancing civilization, as were the German people committed to doctrines of Teutonic superiority. The validity of such a point of view can be tested through an examination of the present form of Anglo-Saxonism, namely: the current theories of the special and unexampled endowment of the so-called Nordics or tall, blond long-heads presumably originating in northwestern Europe.

The most systematic disposition of these doctrines is contained in Madison Grant's *The Passing of the Great Race, or the Racial Basis of European History,* Scribner's, 1916, revised edition, 1918. This work has proven to be a veritable fountainhead from which has poured an avalanche of Nordic mythologizing, race mysticism, and sociological dogmatizing of a sort remarkably similar to the writings of Gobineau and Chamberlain. This similarity extends not merely to the tone and manner of expositions, to the infusion of the whole with poetical imagination and literary power, to the assembling of an impressive array of historical, anthropological, and archæological fact and rumor mixed with striking hypotheses and emotionally charged dogmas, but also to the fundamental biological assumptions as well.

The primary races of Europe are described in terms with which the reader of Lapouge is familiar. Certain concessions, however, are made to the inferior races. Thus, "The earlier Alpines made a very large contribution to the civilization of the world." Similarly the Mediterraneans were responsible for the civilizations of Egypt, Crete, Venetia, Etruria, and Mycenean Greece; and after being invigorated by the Nordic infusion it produced the civilizations of Greece and Rome. Most astonishingly it is even asserted that the Mediterranean race excels others in intellectual achievements, while its superiority in the field of art is declared to be unquestioned. We are not, however, left in any doubt that the Nordics are the true gods and heroes of the Grantian cosmogony. While the Alpines are "always and everywhere a race of peasants," the Nordics are "all over the world a race of soldiers, sailors, adventurers, and explorers; and above all of rulers, organizers, and aristocrats."

As we read on we behold Gobineau, Lapouge, and Woltmann pass before us in review. The geniuses of the western world are claimed for the chosen race. The ascendancy of a nation is measured in terms of its proportion of Nordic blood; the decline of nations is due to the absorption of this competent racial stock by the mongrel blood which it was created to rule. The United States seems destined to follow a downward course similar to that of Spain, France, and England before it; for while its white population was, until the Civil War, "purely Nordic," indeed, "not only purely Nordic but also purely Teutonic, a very large majority being Anglo-Saxon in the most limited meaning of that term," nevertheless, it is in obvious danger of ruin through the submergence of this super-caste among the Nordic peoples in the less well-endowed Alpine and Mediterranean elements that have flocked to our shores. All of this may strike one as a bit curious if he notes that the Nordic, "the big fighting man," is also characterized as "rather stupid but honest." One is therefore a bit puzzled to understand why a race that is given to reckless fighting, and at the same time is simple-minded even to stupidity, should be the sole possessor of the open sesame to the grandeurs of a high and complex civilization when it is admitted that the Alpines were mainly responsible for raising western Europe out of the savagery of the paleolithic age to the culture of the bronze age, while the Mediterraneans are admitted to be the intellectual superiors of all other races of men and to excel also in artistic appreciation and creative power.

But with this work as with its predecessors, contradictions and inconsistencies are overlooked, while preference is given to those doctrines which strike a deeply responsive chord in popular tradition and race egotism. It may, therefore, be worth while to examine some of its assumptions more critically. In the first place, the informed reader will be much impressed with Grant's easy and dogmatic solution of all the primary questions regarding the racial history of Europe. Not only does he adopt the view of Penka, Lapouge, and others, which places the origin of the original blond Aryans near the Baltic, but in a paragraph or a page he settles the vexed and as yet unsolved questions of the origins of the Prussians and the Finns, while his adoption of an antiquated view regarding the Celts and the Celtic invasions evidences the spirit of the propagandist rather than that of the scientist. Inevitably he involves himself in contradictions and finds facts too stubborn for his hypotheses. Contending that all pure Nordics were blonds and all pure blonds are Nordics, he fails to mention the fact that among the Finns, the Esths, and the Lithuanians are thousands of round-heads with hair as blond and eyes as blue as those we are accustomed to expect in the idealized Nordic strain. Moreover, after contending that mixed traits such as dark hair and light eyes or vice versa represent "disharmonious combinations," he finds himself impelled to pay his respects not only to the beauty of such combinations, but also to the genius of some of their possessors.

The fundamental historical error of Grant and his numerous imitators is that they have credited to the Nordic stock all those advances in civilization which have occurred among populations possessing a Nordic element. But civilizations have arisen only in areas of heterogeneous population. In all such areas, race mixture has gone on for many centuries before civilization has reached a high level of advancement. Even the populations which have moved into the areas where civilizations develop were doubtless heterogeneous during the periods of their migration. It is now no longer a matter of doubt that the various types of man rendered more or less distinct through periods of geographical isolation have been infusing their blood one with another throughout the European continent for thousands of years. So much is this so that Ripley found it necessary to idealize the fundamental racial types because in thousands of actual persons the pure type was so rarely found.

The fundamental anthropological error of this school has been its neglect of the fact of variation or individual differences. Even when it be admitted that the Nordic type may excel other types in the spirit of adventure and migratoriness, it must be admitted that this is not a specific difference but represents a difference of greater or less degree only. Many individuals, in fact, the vast majority of the purest Nordics, would consequently possess a spirit of adventure in very moderate degree.

A similar fundamental error is the assumption that superiorities of many and varied kinds may be found in the same racial element. As above indicated, this is a source of hopeless confusion to the reader of Madison Grant. The Nietzschian "blond beast," however invincible in war and conquest, can only by a violent stretch of the imagination be assumed to excel also in the arts of peace, the development of coöperation, the creation of art and poetry, and those sustained intellectual activities necessary for the progress of science.

Similar criticisms apply to Grant's nearly numberless imitators among the recent American writers. It seems probable that the Great War with its emotional excitement was in part responsible for the great vogue of Grantian hypotheses. Eight years earlier, Mr. Alfred P. Schultz had published similar doctrines in his *Race or Mongrel,* 1908. This work was avowedly based upon the works of Gobineau, Chamberlain, and Woltmann. Its subtitle ran as follows: "A brief history of the rise and fall of the ancient races of the world; a theory that the fall of nations is due to the intermarriage with alien stocks; a demonstration that a nation's strength is due to racial purity; a prophecy that America will sink to early decay unless emigration is rigorously restricted." How fortunate for Madison Grant that this work was published before popular fancy was aroused to a profound interest in doctrines of race!

To Grant, however, must be given the distinction of placing vividly before the American public the almost forgotten doctrines of the race dogmatists. No doubt he will not wish to accept responsibility for all his disciples, for example, William S. Sadler. This author in his *Long Heads and Round Heads, or What's the Matter With Germany,* 1918, has given about the most puerile, unscholarly, and offensive presentation of the combined effects of race mania and war phobia which has thus far been palmed off on the American public. Not much better are some of the effusions of that honored and distinguished historian, William Roscoe Thayer, *Out of Their Own Mouths,* "Introduction," 1917. While his authority in other fields might lead him to be taken seriously in the field of racial interpretations of history also, the reader soon becomes aware that he here has drawn heavily on violent emotions and excited fancy.

Much more typical of the traditional note is Charles W. Gould's *America, A Family Matter,* 1922. Nothing could be more untrue of the character or contents of this book than the publisher's advertisement to this effect: "A remarkable study of the present racial problems in the United States. It is based on a careful study of biological principles." This advertisement is itself most remarkable in view of the contents of the book; for one finds in the volume no examination of biological principles, and nothing in the way of a careful study of present racial problems in this country. The chief contents of the work constitute an astonishingly cheap reiteration of Gobineau-Chamberlain historical fact, myth and rumor, and interpretation. One illustration of historical naïveté and racial mysticism must suffice. In the opening pages he gives an imaginative picture of the simultaneous outburst of civilization in India, Persia, Greece, and Rome, in the years 530-510 B.C. How is this remarkable phenomenon explained? It was due to the fact that these four great civilizations were all based on the genius of a great "White Race" which had moved out from a mythical homeland into these four areas at about the same time and in consequence of "the varying but rhythmical pulsation of race life whose throb was that of the life of the united people before they knew parting and division" had carried forward their inherent need of creating culture in all four areas at once. When after this the author tells us that in this interpretation of history in terms of the "throbs" of "race life" "there is nothing mystical," one does not hesitate to place him beyond the pale of serious students of historical phenomena.

But wonders never cease. The amazement of the student who knows something of the history of the doctrines we are tracing and of the work of critical anthropology is almost beyond expression when he finds this book of Gould's the inspiration of another of quite different character, Carl C. Brigham's *A Study of American Intelligence,* 1923. Not the least amazing thing about this work is the "Foreword" by Robert M. Yerkes. He says, "It appears that Mr. Charles W. Gould, a clear, vigorous, fearless thinker on problems of race characteristics, amalgamation of peoples and immigration, raised perplexing questions which drove Mr. Brigham to his careful and critical re-examination, analysis, and discussion of army data concerning the relations of intelligence to nativity and length of residence in the United States. In a recently published book, *America, A Family Matter,* to which this little book is a companion volume, Mr. Gould has pointed the lesson of history for our nation and has argued strongly for pure-bred races."

This quotation indicates the problem set in this book. This question of the reason why there has been a decline in the intelligence of immigrants during the last twenty years as shown by the army mental examinations was raised by the army examiners themselves. Numerous other tests leave little, if any, room for doubt as to the fact. (See especially Kimball Young, "Mental Differences in Certain Immigrant Groups," *University of Oregon Publications,* 1922.) There are two possible answers: either the nations from which these immigrants have come in increasing numbers are of lower natural intelligence than those from which earlier immigrants were mostly derived, or we have been receiving immigrants from lower levels of intelligence and capacity from Europe than was formerly the case. In one case we would say that the lower intelligence of recent immigrants is due to the fact that they are Italians and Greeks rather than Germans and Swedes; in the other case, we would say that it is due to the fact that the cheapening of the cost of immigration and similar factors have resulted in bringing us larger proportions of those who were unsuccessful in their own countries.

Brigham is intent on proving the former hypothesis. Needless to say, he does not succeed in spite of an elaborate make-believe of classifying the nations of Europe on the basis of the proportions of "Nordic" blood which they contain. But all this and some pages of consequent statistics add nothing to the facts already known, namely: that we recently were receiving a smaller proportion of immigrants from northwestern Europe than we formerly did and that the intelligence of immigrants as revealed in the army scores has declined. Nor do the numerous quotations from Grant, Lapouge, and McDougall add to the explanation, though they do reveal the author's predilections for the Nordic mythology, his slight esteem for the Jews, and his conviction that the Irish are a degenerate mob. When the scientific spirit meets the warm blasts of race prejudices it withers like the green corn before the hot winds of a western Kansas summer.

In view of the elaborate character of the scientific gesture which Professor Brigham makes, it is quite humorous to find that he is not a little mystified to find that by his method the round-headed Alpines prove somewhat higher in intelligence than the Mediterraneans. All the great authorities on race characterization had placed them lower, while, as we have seen, Madison Grant, the great Nestor of race sophists, had made even the Mediterraneans superior to the Nordics. The "apparent contradictions" he easily explains as due to the degeneration of the Italians in recent times. Suffice it to say that, if Professor Brigham had contented himself with making clear to the American public that recent immigration was of lower quality, so far as could now be determined by methods known to mental testing, he would have rendered a real service to the advancement of what is doubtless one of the very greatest problems before the American people. But to muddle up the whole issue with the long since out-worn and threadbare doctrines of a mythical, Aryan, once Teutonic, now Nordic, race endowed with semi-divine powers for the creation of culture is to cause all informed readers to close his book with a wry face.

Space does not permit more than mention of several other much discussed books of recent date dealing with similar matters. Clinton Stoddard Burr in *America's Race Heritage*, 1922, makes an effort to substantiate the thesis of the racial purists that we are still about eighty-six per cent Nordic in this country, but he succeeds in this only by mixing all earlier stocks together, from Welsh to Swedes, as Nordics. He tops this with another doctrine dear to the heart of the race purists: namely, that many of the warped brains now menacing our domestic political life and the politics of the world are a result of the mixing of racial types. He seems never to have read any of those numerous studies of the Jukes, the Kallikak family, the Hill folk, the Ishmaelites, the Nam family, and a host of eugenic investigations from Oneida County to Topeka which have revealed every sort of degeneracy known to the combined calendars of crime and mental deficiency in the pure native American stock.

Nor shall we omit reference to the immensely stirring works of Professor William McDougall, *Is America Safe for Democracy?* 1922, and Theodore Lothrop Stoddard, *The*

Revolt Against Civilization, 1922. Both of these repeat more or less of the dogmatisms of the racialists, but mix them indiscriminatingly with the facts of individual differences. At opposite poles are certain of the American anthropologists who would deny all distinctions in racial capacities and who have fallen into the equally dreadful and deluding modification of eighteenth-century egalitarianism, that the races are all equal. This is just as contrary to facts and just as dogmatic, and just as mystical, in last analysis, as the doctrine of a definite hierarchy of races.

The fact would seem to be that there is some truth in both viewpoints, and that an extreme view held in a partisan manner leads to a distortion of the true situation. The European races, so-called, are all very much mixed. Indeed, we are as yet only in an early stage of anthropological determination of the racial history of that continent. The three races of La-pouge and Ripley are only first approximations. One need not accept either the method or the conclusions of Professor Dixon in his very valuable study of *The Racial History of Man,* 1923, to realize that he has demonstrated that the racial history of our ancestors from whatever country was much more complex than we had yet dreamed it to be. Pure races at any time during the historical epoch become matters of fiction rather than fact when one glimpses the long period of time man has dwelt in Europe and the constant mingling of racial types.

There is thus to-day no convincing demonstration of the innate superiority of one European nation over another. As between white and Negro in this country or north European and south European in this country, there can, on the other hand, be no longer doubt of differences in average mental capacity. But the average differences are slight in contrast with the wide variation of abilities in each group. Even the group with the lowest average shows a greater or less proportion of its members above the average of the highest group. Moreover, while some groups reach higher levels than those attained by any members of other groups, the lower limits in all cases reach down through imbecility to idiocy. Thus throughout most of the range of variation there is overlapping. In consequence, the fundamental questions become less those of race than of the relative rates at which the different levels in each race or nationality group are adding to the next generation. The proof of the low average level of recent immigration need not, indeed, be taken as a final argument against the restriction of immigration to smaller numbers, but as a convincing proof of the necessity of a more vigorous selection of higher types of individuals regardless of race for our immigrant quotas. Even reproduction of the population from the proud native Nordics will not save the country, provided the lower levels of Nordic intelligences multiply at a rate faster than the more gifted. Moreover, the country might be saved from its being swamped by its degenerate Nordics provided it could import enough of highly endowed Europeans of whatever nationality.

We are thus inclined to make this slight concession to the race dogmatists, that there is doubtless some difference between races in special powers and aptitudes in different directions. Just what and how extensive these differences are is largely a matter for future determination. As regards the European races these differences, for the races as wholes, are small in terms of averages, and if they exist at all, are less than the differences between certain nationality groups in this country. But vastly more important than any possible differences between the average capacities of the European races, are the individual differences among the members of the same race. An ounce of eugenics is worth a pound of race dogmatism so far as the future political security of the country is concerned.

A PLANNED SOCIETY—COMMUNIST VERSION *

By JOHN STRACHEY

THE economic and social system under which the British and American people now live is commonly called capitalism. By this word capitalism we mean an economic system under which the fields, factories and mines are owned by individuals and groups of individuals. These means of production, as they are called, are worked by those who do not own them for the profit of those who do. Under capitalism it is profit-making, not love, that makes the world go round. For it is the expectation of profit which induces those who own the above means of production to permit them to be used.

But profit-making is not only the incentive, it is also the regulator of capitalist production. Under capitalism it is not only the object, it is the very *condition* of production that a profit should result. Those things, that is to say, which will yield a profit can and will be produced, *but those things alone*. For anybody who produces things which do not, either directly or indirectly, yield a profit will sooner or later go bankrupt, lose his ownership of the means of production, and so cease to be an independent producer. Capitalism, in other words, uses profitability as the criterion, or test, of whether any given thing should or should not be produced, and, if so, how much of it should be produced.

Now the test of profitability ensures that those things, and only those things, for which there is demand shall be produced. Profit is, as it were, a magnet which draws production after demand. For it is profitable to produce those things for which there is a demand, and unprofitable to produce those things for which there is no demand. [1]

* From *The Theory and Practice of Socialism*

But things are not either in demand or not in demand. The demand for them varies in strength. Under capitalism it will be profitable to produce more and more of those things for which there is an increasing demand, and less and less of those things for which there is a decreasing demand. Thus our productive resources are continually being pulled by the magnet of profit towards the production of those things for which there is an increasing demand, and away from the production of those things for which there is a diminishing demand.

This is how the capitalist system works. The question is, does it work well or badly? You would certainly suppose, would you not, that such a system as this would work exceedingly well? It seems to contain in this ingenious device of drawing production after demand by the magnet of profit a method of ensuring that all our productive resources should be used to the very best possible advantage. And this is just what admirers of the capitalist system claim for it. They claim that under it just those goods and services which most people most want, and no others, are bound to get produced. And they claim that no other economic system could possibly produce a more desirable result than this.

Why, then, do communists and socialists wish to abolish capitalism? We wish to do so because we have been unable to avoid noticing that capitalism does not give the above admirable result. The goods which most people most want are not produced. In contemporary Britain and America goods and services, for the lack of which many millions of persons slowly perish, are not produced, and instead goods which only a few people want, and which they want only a little, are produced. For example, it is today unprofitable to produce the additional bread, meat, milk, clothes and houses which millions of British and American citizens desperately need. But it is profitable to produce the foolish luxuries desired by a handful of the very rich. Inevitably, then, so long as we continue to regulate our production by the principle of profitability, the luxuries are, and the necessaries are not produced.

We say that there must be something wrong with an economic system which gives results like this. We call this result of contemporary capitalism a gigantic, and very wicked, *misdirection* of production.

Moreover, capitalism now from time to time produces substantial quantities of things which the rich do not want and the poor cannot pay for, and which consequently have to be destroyed. This is a more extreme example of the misdirection of production. Such abominable absurdities as the deliberate destruction of food, when very many people are under-nourished, to which it periodically leads, strike people very forcibly and have been responsible for making many people feel that something must be wrong with capitalism.

But, as a matter of fact, this dramatic type of breakdown is a less serious matter than is capitalism's now chronic inability to allow many of us to produce anything at all. The extent to which the British and American people are now unable to use their productive resources varies greatly from year to year and from place to place. In 1929, for example, the American people probably used their productive resources to the fullest extent that any people have ever been able to do under the capitalist system. But a careful survey [2] has since been made, by a number of conservatively minded American economists and statisticians, of what was the actual capacity of the American people to produce, both in that year and subsequently. They estimate that in 1929 the American people used their productive resources to 81% of their capacity. *And in the immediately following years they used them to under 50% of their capacity.* Now in these latter years (1930-31-32-33) the American capitalist system was working about as abnormally badly as it was working abnormally well in 1929. So we may say that the American people are nowadays never able to use somewhere between 19 and 50% of their productive resources.

I do not know of any comparable figures for Britain. But the level of British unemployment gives us some ideas of the extent of Britain's unused productive resources. Judging by this, and by some other indications, we may guess that the British people have never since the war been able to use as much (81%) of their productive resources as the American people used in 1929, and have never been reduced to using so little of them (50%) as the Americans used in 1931-32. Probably the average proportion of available productive resources actually used, calculated over a number of years, would not work out very differently for the two countries.

In any case, what is the exact percentage of our productive resources which we cannot at present use at all is not the important question. The point is that this proportion has long been, and is now, substantial. For this means that we now lack all the goods and services which these idle resources could and would have produced, if we had used them. The British and American men and machines which have stood idle, and which now stand idle, could have produced those houses, that food, those clothes, those educational facilities, those medical services, etc. etc. for the lack of which either we, or, if we are fortunate, the people whom we see around us, are at this moment suffering so bitterly.

Thus waste is today the most striking of all the characteristics of capitalism. The waste which has resulted from our failure to use at all many of our resources of production is cumulative and has now become almost immeasurable in both Britain and America. We are accustomed to think of it chiefly in terms of the waste of our available supply of labour, and to call it the problem of unemployment. And, truly, the waste which results from keeping between ten and twenty million British and American workers, many of them capable and industrious, in enforced idleness is the very worst part of the business. For this waste results not only in the loss of the goods which the unemployed would have produced had they been permitted to work; it also results in their own slow torture by destitution, frustration and social humiliation.

These are the reasons why we say that although the British and American capitalist systems of production still work, yet they work in a way intolerable alike for its injustice and its waste. For under them not only do many hundreds of thousands of us British and American citizens work hard all day and every day to satisfy the foolish whims of the rich, while no one is allowed to work at producing the additional food, clothes, houses and the like which by far the greater number of us urgently need; but, worse still, some ten to twenty millions of us are prevented from working and producing at all.

It is this degree of failure in our economic system, and this alone, which keeps by far the larger number of us very poor.

The extent of poverty varies greatly, it is true, between different capitalist states. The present destitution of the inhabitants of many of the capitalist states of the world, such as Poland, Italy, Austria, and many more, can hardly be exaggerated. A famous capitalist economist, John Stuart Mill, suggested that the capitalist use of the marvelous inventions of science had not lightened the toil of a single labourer by a single hour. In the case of most contemporary states we may add that neither has it put another yard of cloth on to the backs, nor a piece of bread into the mouths, of the greater part of the population. Moreover, even in Britain and America, the two richest capitalist countries of the world, the mass of the population is much poorer than we are accustomed to suppose. In Great Britain, which is at the moment (1936) probably the richer and more prosperous of the two, two-thirds of the population have incomes averaging £25 per head per year.[3]

It will always remain impossible for those of us whose incomes are of a different order of magnitude to imagine what this degree of poverty means in terms of the restriction, embitterment and stunting of the possibilities of human life. But at any rate, we can all grasp this essential fact: *the ocean of human suffering involved in such poverty is now totally unnecessary*. It is a result, not of an inability to produce an adequate supply of goods and services, but of the failure of our existing economic system. For that system does not allow us to use one part of our productive resources at all, and so misdirects the use of the other part that it largely fails to satisfy human needs.

The simple truth is that general plenty and security are now possible in both Britain and America. It is not, I think possible to foretell with scientific accuracy exactly what standard of life the British and American people could provide themselves with if they used their productive resources continuously for the purpose of the satisfaction of their needs in the order of their urgency. We do now possess, however, in the case of America, an interesting estimate on just this point. In the year 1934 the government of the United States of America appointed a committee to enquire into the capacity of American industry and agriculture to produce goods and services. In February 1935 this committee issued its report. [4] *It found that every family of four persons* could provide itself with an income of $4,400 (about £915) a year, at 1929 prices, if America's productive resources were used to the full and their product equally divided among all families.[5]

In the next chapter we shall discuss the extent to which this estimate is true, or rather, we shall discuss the conditions under which it is alone true. Speaking very broadly, however, this estimate is true. All sorts of circumstances, foreseeable and unforeseeable, might effect in one way or another the exact level of the standard of life with which the British and American people could provide themselves. [6] But what we are concerned with is not the exact figure arrived at —£915, or £1,000, or £700 a year—as the income now possible for all American families of four persons. What we are concerned with is the broad fact that the people of such highly developed countries as Britain and America could unquestionably now provide themselves with secure incomes now enjoyed by the middle sections of the professional classes. We are concerned with the fact that this conclusion cannot now be denied by anyone who takes the trouble to investigate the extent and nature of our available productive resources.

Let us pause a moment upon this conclusion. General plenty, an average level of income for all families, of the order of magnitude of from £700 to £1000 a year, instead of from £75 to £200 a year, as at present, is now possible in all highly developed countries. We cannot know what would be the exact effect of this total abolition of poverty. But we do know that it would transform human life.

The loss of a man's livelihood, although it does not in contemporary Britain and America usually involve his family in actual starvation, does usually render it destitute. In Britain and America the millions of the destitute are fed, and to some extent clothed. But its amount, the uncertainty of its receipt and the onerous restrictions which it carries with it, prevent the relief which is given them from effectively mitigating the face of those who lose their opportunity to work and earn. They do not, for the most part, quickly die; but their lives become so miserable that the dread of this fate is today the haunting companion of almost everyone outside the small class of the securely rich.

Our psychologists should, but do not, inform us of what is the effect upon the psychological stability of our communities of thus keeping the greater part of the population in anxiety for their very livelihoods. The larger part of mankind is thereby reduced to a condition of terrible, childish helplessness. Contemporary man fears, and has good reason to fear, social forces which he does not comprehend, far less control. The mediaeval peasant, the savage huntsman even, knew no such helpless insecurity. They had to contend with the drought, the flood and the storm; but the forces of nature were kinder than the forces of man.

Whichever of the other ills of men are inevitable this extraordinary economic insecurity is needless. The proposition that we could all now provide ourselves with plenty is disputable (it is, at any rate, sometimes disputed). Or, to put the matter more precisely, the particular standard of life which our existing means of production would make it possible for us all to enjoy, if we used them to the full, is disputable. But what is not disputable is that we could use our existing means of production to give us all *some* definite, stable and secure standard of life. There *can* be no necessity for the sickening oscillations of our present economic system. There *can* be no necessity suddenly to leave great parts of our productive apparatus idle, and many millions of ourselves unemployed and destitute.

It is true, however, that the inability of capitalism to realise the dazzling possibilities of plenty and security which are now open to the British and American people is not, and never will be, an efficient cause for their abandonment of that economic system. We live in poverty and fear when we could live in plenty and security. But this is not in itself enough to make us act.

The true alternative which faces us, however, is not one of continuing in our present conditions, or achieving much superior ones. The truth is that we must attain security and plenty or suffer the rapid growth of every form of that fear and destitution which already ruin the lives of so many of us. For the existing evils of our societies are the result of certain features of the capitalist system which cannot be eradicated, but which must, on the contrary, grow more and more pronounced. Moreover, it is in the nature of capitalism to produce, not only unnecessary poverty and insecurity, but also certain other and far more rapidly disastrous consequences. It is of the nature of capitalism to produce civil conflict and international war. Communists and socialists propose, then, that we should rid ourselves of capitalism, not merely because it denies us a now plainly attainable plenty and security, but more especially because it is now visibly about to destroy us in the social and international violence which it generates.

We cannot reject capitalism unless we have some effective substitute to put in its place. Unless it can be shown that a workable alternative exists, denunciations of the evils of capitalism are vain and empty.

For every society must possess some way of organising its

economic life. If there were no practicable alternative, we should have to put up with the existing way, no matter how unjust, how wasteful and how finally catastrophic were its results. Hence before we go on to discuss the political and social systems, and the cultural and ethical values, associated respectively with capitalism and socialism, we must give a clear account of the economic ground plan of a socialist society. For "human beings must first of all eat, drink, shelter and clothe themselves before they can turn their attention to politics, science, art and religion."[7] Thus we shall have to plunge at once into questions of economics. For not until these questions have been given satisfactory and convincing answers can we go on to a description of the whole structure of socialist society.

The essential economic problem of socialism is this: If we are not to settle the question of what goods, and what quantities of goods, are to be produced, by producing only those which yield a profit, how are we to settle it? For settled it must be.

If we reject the self-acting mechanism of profitability, as too unjust and too wasteful, we must find some other mechanism of regulation. The sole alternative method by which complex, highly developed, economic systems as those of Britain and America can be regulated is by means of the deliberate decisions of some central body as to what goods, and how many of each of them, shall be produced. The organization of production by means of such conscious decisions is called a system of "planned production for use." This is the type of economic system now being built up in the Soviet Union. It is socialism.

The best way to define the principle upon which a socialist economic system works is not to discuss socialism in the abstract, but to describe a particular system of planned production for use, worked out for Britain or America, or some other such highly industrialized community. In Britain and America we still organize our economic life on the basis of the capitalist system of production for profit. But this does not make it impossible to prepare a survey, or catalogue, of the productive resources of either country and to estimate what results, in terms of quantities of goods and services, these resources would give us if they were used on the basis of planned production for use. And in the case of America such a draft economic plan has actually been made, *although unintentionally*. It was made by the aforementioned authors of the "National Survey of Potential Product Capacity," who came to the conclusion that every American family of four might have an income of $4,400 a year.

This group of American statisticians and economists set out with the limited purpose of discovering what was the real productive capacity of American industry and agriculture, without reference to any particular economic system. Their enquiry was to be, they imagined, strictly technical and statistical. Nothing, surely, was farther from their thoughts, or from those of the American government when it appointed and financed them, than any idea of demonstrating how a planned economic system—how, in other words, socialism—would work in the United States of America. And yet this is just what they did demonstrate. It will be worth our while to enquire how this misadventure occurred; to observe how the N. S. P. P. C. investigators were led on, by one problem raising another, to elaborate the ground plan of a socialist America. For by so doing we shall stumble, as they did, upon one after another of the economic problems involved in the establishment of a socialist economic system. Moreover, we shall not only raise these problems, but we shall see how they can be solved in practice.

The authors of the N. S. P. P. C. report had been appointed by the American government in order to discover, we repeat, what was America's total productive capacity. They interpreted these terms of reference to mean what was the capacity of the American productive system to satisfy the needs of the American people. This naturally involved ascertaining what the needs of the American people were. But that did not seem difficult. In 1933, when the investigation was started, the American people seemed to be short of a great many prime necessaries, such as food, clothes and shelter.

Let us take the example of shelter. Fifteen and a half million new dwellings were needed, it was estimated, to satisfy the American people's need for shelter. The building of this number of dwellings would, to be more precise, enable every American family of four to have a home of from five to six rooms equipped with modern conveniences. It would be reasonable to build them, the report estimated, under a ten-year building programme (involving the erection of 1,550,000 dwellings a year). But did there, or did there not, exist the productive resources necessary to enable the American people to build 1,550,000 dwellings a year? Was there enough labour, enough bricks, enough steel, enough power, enough of everything needed? This question clearly involved another. Of course there was enough of these productive resources, if none of them was used for any other purpose. Clearly, however, some resources had to be used for other purposes. You cannot divert the whole of a community's available labour, for example, to building dwellings. You will starve if you do. Sufficient labour, sufficient steel, sufficient power, and sufficient everything else, has to be left to satisfy all the community's other equally urgent needs—such as the need for food and clothes—and for that matter, in practice, for transport, education, amusement and many other things as well.

So the question had to be re-stated thus: Would there be enough productive resources left over, *after the other equally urgent needs of the American people had been satisfied,* to enable them to build 1,550,000 dwellings a year for ten years? And this question, in its turn, clearly depended on what you meant by "equally urgent" needs. *How, in a word was the question to be decided as to what uses the American people's productive resources were to be put, and who was to decide it?* For when you come to think of it, most productive resources have alternative uses. You can use the labour of a given number of workers either to grow food or to build houses; you can use a given supply of copper either for domestic plumbing or for making locomotives. You can use so many units of electrical energy either to drive the machinery of a steel mill or to light dwellings. *But you cannot use any of these things for both purposes simultaneously.*

Let us take a particular example. One of the productive resources needed for building 1,550,000 dwellings a year is structural steel. Would there be, the N. S. P. P. C. authors enquired, enough structural steel left over from other equally urgent work for the job? At once we are led to ask whether all the uses which actually were made of the available structural steel were as urgent as building dwellings. Now in 1929 a very high proportion of America's output of structural steel was used to build skyscrapers, mainly intended for offices. And the authors of the N. S. P. P. C. report could not help noticing that what the American people seemed to need was not office skyscrapers, but dwellings. A substantial proportion of the American people were (and still are) housed in the most wretched kinds of run-down, tumble-down, unsanitary and overcrowded slums and shacks. And, on the other hand, nothing was more notorious than that nobody needed more office accommodation. For a high proportion of the recently built skyscrapers stood empty; while those that had filled up with tenants had done so by emptying the surrounding office accommodation of theirs. Yet in 1929 most of America's structural steel was being used to build still more office skyscrapers. The authors of the report found this situation very peculiar, because they, like the rest of us, had been brought up to believe that the fact that effective demand in 1929 had been for office skyscrapers, and not for dwellings, was proof that what the ill-housed and over-officed American people truly wanted and needed were office skyscrapers, and not homes. And this they found incredible.

Their next discovery was that even in the book year of 1929 the American people only used their steel plants to some 84% of their capacity (In 1932 they used them to under

20% of their capacity.) If, in 1929, the Americans had chosen
to use their capacity to produce steel to the full, they would
have been able to turn out, amongst other forms of steel, another 8.7 million tons of structural steel. Hence this question arose for the authors of the N. S. P. P. C. report. In calculating how much structural steel could be made available
for building dwellings, would you, or would you not, have
to reckon that the American people would have allotted the
same high proportion of this extra 8.7 million tons of the
stuff, had they produced it, to building office skyscrapers?

If you followed the guidance of demand you would have
to assume just that. But if you did so, not enough structural
steel would be left over to build the 1,550,000 dwellings a year.
The authors of the report found it impossible to believe that
the American people's real needs included a yearly output
of *even more* towers than had been built in 1929. Surely these
had been enough, and too many? Why not, then assume that
if the 8.7 million tons extra of structural steel had been produced they could almost all have gone to building dwelling-
houses? Why not indeed? The authors of the N. S. P. P. C.
report made this assumption. It was one of the assumptions
upon which they based their conclusion that every American family might have enjoyed that standard of life which
was actually enjoyed by those families which had incomes
of $4,400 (£915) in 1929. (For that is another way of put-
ting their main conclusion.)

Now at first sight this action on the part of our ingenious
authors may seem to have been innocent enough. But innocent it was not. For the assumption that almost all the
extra structural steel, which would have been produced by
the capacity working of the American mills, could have
been used for building homes, involved the conscious and
deliberate re-allotment of resources of production between
alternative uses. *And to do this is considered to be economic
original sin. For it means breaking irrevocably with the
capitalist system, the test of profitability, and the self-adjust-
ing mechanism which this test provides.*

For see what our authors have taken upon themselves to do! They have decided that it would be better to use more of the available supply of steel for building dwellings, and less for building office skyscrapers. But the reputedly infallible indicator of demand showed that what the American people wanted were skyscrapers, not dwellings. Who made the authors of the N. S. P. P. C. report, the defenders of the capitalist system may object, into rulers and judges over us, to say how we should or should not use our available supply of structural steel?

Moreover, these authors did not content themselves with reallotting the available supply of structural steel as between skyscrapers and dwellings. *For as soon as the capacity of the American people to provide themselves with food, clothing, motor cars and a hundred other kinds of goods and services was investigated, it became apparent that it was impossible to say to what extent their needs could be satisfied, unless the investigators could decide, not only the productive capacity of America's basic industries, but also what use was going to be made of the products of such basic industries.* Accordingly, they re-allotted all the extra supplies of raw materials and semi-finished goods which the capacity working of America's basic industries would have produced; they allotted these extra supplies, not in proportion to the uses which actually were made of such goods in 1929, but to other uses which the authors of the report thought more desirable.

But how, we ask, at once, did they decide what were the more, and what the less, desirable uses for these supplies? They evidently worked on the assumption that it was more desirable to use available supplies in the way which best satisfied visible and urgent human needs, such as the need for decent dwellings to live in; that it was less desirable to use them in a way that satisfied less urgent human needs, such as the need to have towers to look at. But now we see that the authors of the report took upon themselves no less a task than to decide upon the relative urgency of human needs—in plain language, to decide what people really wanted to have.

Before they had gone very far with their investigation they found themselves working out a comprehensive budget of the needs of an American family. Then they worked back, through the productive system, and enquired whether or not there existed resources of production which could be used to supply the goods and services necessary to meet these needs. They came to the conclusion that such resources did exist. But some of these resources would have to be re-allotted from their existing uses *and used according to a plan. They would have to be used according to a plan which provided that the available raw materials and semi-finished products should be finally fabricated into the particular goods, and no others, which they had laid down in advance when they made out their family budget.*

Now when our intrepid authors compiled this budget of human needs, they did something which almost every economist of almost every British and American university has declared to be impossible. It is quite impossible, say these authorities, to make any estimate of people's real needs. The multiplicity of human needs and the variety of human desires are so great, they continue, that it is quite impossible to *foretell* what people will want, and so consciously to plan production in advance. The only practicable procedure is our present one, namely to allow people to express their wants by making money offers for particular goods and services, and then to allow production to adapt itself, by means of the pull of profit and the push of loss, to this ever-changing demand. If this method results in most of the community's structural steel being used to build useless skyscrapers, so that millions of its citizens must continue to live in slums, if it results in an important proportion of our productive resources not being used at all, so that we starve amidst potential plenty, well, this is unfortunate. But, say the economists, it cannot be helped. To cut across the free play of demand and supply involves attempting to dictate to people what they should buy; it involves forcing them to buy what you think they ought to have, instead of what they really want.

The reader will see that if we apply this argument to our wants in general, and not merely to the question of shelter, it does not lack plausibility. It does seem a rather arbitrary proceeding to draw up a budget of food, clothing, housing and everything else, for everybody, and say that these things, and consequently nothing else, shall be produced.

And yet this is just what the authors of the N. S. P. P. C. report found, greatly to their surprise, no difficulty in doing. Here is their description of how they did it.

"Strange as it may seem, it is easier to determine human needs than it is to determine the ability of society to extract raw materials. On the average, people of a given culture eat only so much food, wear out only so many clothes, live in only so many rooms. If 'scarcity values' (of works of art, etc.) are excluded from consideration—and they naturally fall outside the scope of our study since our concern was with physical quantities—the amount of goods and services the population would like to consume can be calculated with an accuracy far greater than the accuracy with which we can determine the possible output of any industry.

"In the case of food, for example, we employed the budget sponsored by the Department of Agriculture, adopting the preferred schedule, 'the liberal diet,' as a criterion of the desirable individual consumption in various foodstuffs.

"In clothing, we based our budget on the actual expenditures of the professional classes in the San Francisco area.

"In housing, we merely assumed that the American family would like to live in a modern five- or six-room house or its equivalent (apartment, renovated old mansion, or the like), fully equipped with the best labor-saving devices, and that the single individual in the city would continue using smaller apartments.

"For medical care, we took the advice of the medical authorities in regard to what was needed to care properly for the American people.

"In education, our budget was set by authorities at Teachers College, Columbia University; in recreation, we were governed by the existing taste of the people."

And so on through the list of all the main classes of goods and services which human beings consume.

Now there seems nothing arbitrary about this procedure when we see it in practice. It does not seem as if the N. S. P. P. C. authors were ordering us to consume just those particular commodities which they thought we ought to consume, and no others. How has the arbitrary element been avoided then? How were our authors able to make up a budget of needs, the satisfaction of which would certainly mean a very decent, civilised life for any family?

Two considerations made it possible for the authors of the N. S. P. P. C. report to show how the planning of the economic life of a great industrial nation could be accomplished. And these same considerations after the abolition of capitalism, will make it possible for a British or American planning commission actually to do the job.

The first factor which makes possible the estimation in advance of consumers' real needs is the fact that we know what people have consumed up till now. There is little difficulty in discovering how much food, medical attention, education, clothing, etc. etc., the population has consumed in the past year. We know that this standard of consumption was unsatisfactory. Still, it gives us a basis to go on. We shall be able to plan the production of additions to, or alterations of, the quantities of each commodity consumed last year. We shall budget for an increase of so many million tons of meat, and of so many million houses, and a decrease of so many hundred skyscrapers. We shall not, in other words, have to start from scratch and think up what a typical family ought to consume. We know already what they do consume, and we shall have to estimate merely what more they would have liked to have consumed.

The second factor is the existence of a certain number of families who can now buy the things which they need and want. The consumption of the immense majority of families is most unsatisfactory, but there do exist in our modern communities certain classes of people whose consumption is quite satisfactory. We are not thinking of the very rich, whose consumption is of a peculiar and fantastic nature, but of the professional classes in prosperous times. Thus, if we want to know what the mass of the population would consume, by way of food, clothes, transportation, or anything else, if only they were better off, we naturally look at what those families which *are* now better off actually do consume. Thus we notice that the N. S. P. P. C. authors have guessed that if the whole American people could buy all the clothes they need they would in fact buy the same amount and kind of clothes which the professional classes in and around San Francisco did in 1929 actually buy and consume. And we can, surely, agree that this is a reasonable assumption.

With the aid of these two guides it is possible to estimate what people would like to have produced for them, and then to allot the available resources of production in such a way that this quantity of goods and services will be produced. It is undoubtedly possible, that is to say, to meet and satisfy people's needs by this method, instead of by the present method of allowing production to follow the pull of demand.

Let us envisage how the first budget, or plan of production giving what is, in effect, a list of all the goods and services which are to be made available to the population, will be compiled in a socialist Britain or America. This first budget will be based upon the existing output of such goods with the additions indicated by what the better-off classes do now consume, and the realisation of this production programme will be made possible by utilising those productive resources at present grossly misdirected, or unused altogether, by capitalism. But only the first budget need be made up in this way. All subsequent budgets will be merely corrections of the miscalculations discovered in the first. For miscalculations there will certainly be. The planning authority will be sure to provide, say, too many new motor cars and not enough wireless sets, or too many transport facilities and not enough sports clothes, etc. etc. Such errors will show themselves in that at the end of the year some motor cars, for example, will be left over, while the stock of wireless sets will be exhausted before the end of the year. But this error will not be allowed automatically to affect the respective prices of the two goods, raising the price of wireless sets and lowering the price of motor cars. Their respective prices, which will be based upon their respective costs of production, will only be varied by the conscious and deliberate decision of the planning authority.

The following year the planning authority will arrange for the production of more wireless sets and fewer motor cars. In order to do so it will have to turn certain productive resources (in this case metal, skilled labour, assembling plants, etc. etc.) which have been making motor cars on to making wireless sets. Year by year there will have to be corrections of this kind.

Such corrections will have to be made not only in order to remedy errors and miscalculations upon the part of the planning authority, but also in order to meet the development of new methods of production and the changes in public taste which will be associated with these developments. For we must not think of the budget of human needs which the planning authority will draw up as something fixed or permanent. On the contrary, human needs develop *with* the capacity to satisfy them. The planning authority will constantly have to allocate productive resources to new purposes in order either to fulfill some new need (e.g., for the widespread ownership of private aeroplanes) or to fulfill an old need in some new, more efficient and economical way (e.g., the production of one or other of the basic food-stuffs synthetically.)

No planning authority will perfectly perform these func-tions. But it is impossible to believe that even in the very first year, and even if the planning authority is composed of the most fallible of fallible human beings, it can fail to provide for human needs to so gross an extent as does the capitalist principle of regulating production by profitability. However serious were the mistakes of the planning author-ity, it *could* not achieve such grandiose misdirections of production as does capitalism. It could not do anything so insane or so horrible as to produce a plethora of yachts and beauty parlours while millions of men and women lack for food and shelter; it could not succeed, as does our present system, in *simultaneously* torturing the town workers with a lack of bread and ruining the farmers by a glut of wheat.

The authors of the N. S. P. P. C. report provided us with a demonstration of an exceedingly important economic principle. They did so when they decided that, in order to carry out their instructions to estimate America's capa-city to produce wealth, they would have to make out a budget of the real needs of the American people, and to re-allot resources of production to meet these needs. For by doing these two things they, in effect, made an outline One-Year Plan for America. This was their great achievement.

Their detailed demonstration of how a One-Year Plan of production for great industrial communities such as the United States and Britain could be, and will be, com-piled is of unquestionable value. For it shows far better than could many pages of argumentation how socialist eco-nomic planning is done. It shows in particular and con-vincing detail how it will be possible to organise mighty and complex economic systems of production for use, and so establish general plenty and security. It shows what we could put in the place of the now grossly defective test of profitability as the regulating principle of production. We must certainly assume, however, that the N. S. P. P. C.

authors' demonstration of the possibility of planned production for use was accidental. For if it were intentional they could be accused of using the money of the government of the United States in order to demonstrate the practicability, and the extreme desirability, of that system of production favoured by communists and socialists! And I would not dream of bringing this serious allegation against Mr. Doan (the leader of the investigation) and his associates. No, let us assume that when they wrote the sketch of a One-Year Plan of production for America they did not know what they were doing. By the end of their report they had been talking pure socialism for 200 pages. But like M. Jourdain in Moliere's play, they knew not what they did.

This, then, is how a socialist economic system works. This is how a planning authority settles to relative proportions in which consumers' goods (as they are called) shall be produced.

[1] Whence demand comes, and whether it is not largely created by the producers themselves is another matter, and one which the exponents of capitalism have somewhat neglected.

[2] Undertaken by the Brookings Institution and published by that institution under the title of *America's Capacity to Produce*.

[3] According to a calculation made by a well-known statistician and economist, Mr. O. R. Hobson, and published in *Lloyd's Bank Monthly Review* for July 1934. This means, the reader will observe, that a family of four will have an income of £100 a year or just under £2 a week. As Mr Hobson's conclusion is startling, it may be well to quote his calculation in full.

"The National Income of Great Britain and Northern Ireland is estimated at about £3,400,000,000, equivalent to £74 per head of the population, a figure which does not suggest that the danger of inconveniently large production is very imminent. But of this £3,400,000,000 about £2,550,000,000 represents income belonging to income-tax payers—for this is the amount of 'actual income' assessed to income tax in 1932-3, and the 'actual income' figure of the Commissioners of Inland Revenue has been shown by Professor Bowley and Sir Josiah Stamp to be very close to that part of the 'National Income which accrues to the income-tax-paying class'. Thus the aggregate income, of the class below the income-tax exemption limit (£100 assessable income, equivalent to £125 earned income) was, say, £850,000,000. Now the total number of income-taxpayers in 1932-3 was 3,500,000, and if we assume that each of these has, on the average, two-and-a-half dependants, we arrive at the figure of 12,250,000 as the number of persons in the 'income-taxpaying class.' Subtraction from the total population of 46,000,000 therefore gives

the number of persons whose incomes are below the exemption limit as
33,750,000. Dividing this last figure into the residual income of £850,-
000,000 we have a figure of approximately £25 as the average annual
income per capita of the non-income-taxpaying classes."

⁴ This was the preliminary report issued under the title of "The Chart
of Plenty" (Viking Press, New York City), issued by "The National
Survey of Potential Product Capacity."

⁵ And pro-rata for larger and smaller families.

⁶ Unnecessary destitution is not the only disastrous effect produced
upon us by the malfunctioning of capitalism. Almost more than plenty
itself, the people of Britain and America desire security.

Their lives are dominated even more by the fear of want than by want
itself. The people of Britain and America, with the exception of the very
small minority of the securely rich, and of the larger minority of the
actually and presently destitute, live under the more or less imminent,
and always awful, threat of destitution. The way in which we now organise our economic life results in an extraordinary, and now ever-increasing, degree of instability and insecurity for the whole population.
Those who live on the weekly wages paid by industry, the smaller, independent owner-producers, such as the farmers, and the professional
workers of all kinds, have this at least in common: they all live under
the fear of the disappearance of their livelihoods. And substantial numbers of them do continually suffer this terrifying loss. For the violent and
unpredictable fluctuations of trade which now more and more characterise
our economic system fling about and capsise their little enterprises as row-
boats are tossed by the Atlantic.

⁷ Frederick Engels' speech beside the grave of Marx.

TECHNOCRACY: AN INTERPRETATION

By STUART CHASE

IN 1919, Thorstein Veblen, the greatest economist whom America has produced, published a book entitled *The Engineers and the Price System*. His thesis was that the engineer and the technician had made industry "inordinately productive," capable of throwing off a huge and mounting volume of goods. The men who controlled industry, however, the vested interests, the priests of the price system, were not disposed to give this productivity full sway. Seeking maximum profit in terms of dollars, they proceeded to throw dams and barricades across the smooth functioning of the engineer's industrial mechanisms, and they sabotaged production to the level of what the traffic would bear. New inventions were used, but judiciously used; always in the interest of the greatest immediate money profit to be made out of them.

This, said Veblen, is all very well for the captains of industry, but it tends dangerously to irritate the delicate, highly specialized organism of modern machine production. These artificial dams and barricades are likely in the course of time to break down the physical layout of power lines, railroads, factories, mechanized farms, warehouses, stores— which the technical arts have been making ever more productive, efficient and interlocking. The captains of industry are, as it were, defying the laws of physics. They know a good deal about the manipulation of money, credit and high finance, but they do not know a turbine from a bus bar. They think these machines are toys to play with. But the machines are not toys; they are the means, the overwhelming means, by which the people of a continent are fed, housed and clothed; and they operate only by virtue of certain physical laws of energy and dynamics which have a sequence, an integration and a rhythm that cannot be indefinitely outraged.

Furthermore, the one hundred thousand technicians, more or less, who alone are capable of operating these mechanisms, also have a probable saturation point of outrage. Given a free hand to operate at capacity on the principle of the balanced load, they could deluge the nation with sound and durable goods. Yet they are continually forced by the captains of industry to violate their standards of craftsmanship by adulteration, peak loading, the manufacture of trash, by stoppages, excessive selling and advertising costs, cross hauling, patent monopolies, tariffs, overexpansion, waste. And so Veblen suggested, without enthusiasm, delicately, that the engineers—who could bring the whole economic system to complete quiescence in a few days' time—disallow the dams and barricades of the captains of industry, and proceed to vindicate their integrity, and justify their technical training, by taking over the industrial system and operating it on the principles of the laws of physics and of the balanced load; the latter meaning smooth operation at capacity, where the cost per unit of output is at a minimum. Incidentally, their fellow citizens, down to the last family, would enjoy a standard of living hitherto undreamed of.

Here is a sample of his reasoning:

"It has been argued, and it seems not unreasonable to believe, that the established order of business enterprise, vested rights and commercialized nationalism, is due presently to go under in a muddle of shame and confusion, because it is no longer a practicable system of industrial management under the conditions created by the later state of the industrial arts. Twentieth century technology has outgrown the eighteenth-century system of vested rights . . . and all the while it is an open secret that with a reasonably free hand the production experts would today [1919] readily increase the various ordinary output of industry by several fold—variously estimated at some 300 to 1200 per cent. And what stands in the way of so increasing the ordinary output of goods and services is business as usual. . . . So also, to these men who are trained in the stubborn logic of technology, nothing is quite real that cannot be stated in terms of tangible performance; and they are accordingly coming to understand that the whole fabric of credit and corporation finance is a tissue of make-believe."

I read the book and was immensely stimulated by it. But it was too far in advance of its time to make a deep popular impression. The nation, sick of the idealisms of a war for democracy, prepared to return to normalcy with an overwhelming yearning. Shortly after the book was published, there drifted into Washington, where I was living at the time, a tall, gaunt, somewhat mysterious young man by the name of Howard Scott. He announced himself as an engineer but lately engaged at Muscle Shoals. He too had read Veblen, and better, had been talking to him in New York. He had been talking to Charles P. Steinmetz, the "electrical wizard of Schenectady"; he had been talking to Dr. Wesley C. Mitchell; to many people. He announced the organization of a group called the Technical Alliance, to give concrete expression to Veblen's challenge. But Mr. Scott, delivering an amazing flow of technical information and discovery, sidewise, out of a wry mouth, was obviously no man's disciple. He had ideas of his own, some of them far more lofty and far more mathematical than anything Veblen had advanced. His disrespect for economists, with the sole exceptions of Veblen and Mitchell, was profane and profound. They could think only in terms of price; and price, he said, in the last analysis was quantitatively immeasurable and meaningless. He invited those of us in Washington who admired Veblen, and could lift our minds above the pathology of money, to join the Technical Alliance. Some of us did, myself included.

The Alliance as a formal organization did not long survive the upbeat to normalcy. Most of the members went their various ways, sorrowfully perhaps, but inevitably. Howard

Scott, however, with a small residual group about him, kept on. He had a great idea by the tail and he refused to let go of it. Whether it was his idea or Veblen's idea I never knew and never cared. According to Mr. F. L. Ackerman, who knew both men well, each had arrived independently at substantially the same conclusions. The impact of mechanical energy on the financial system is no one man's idea. The laws of that impact, stated in mathematical—even ultra-mathematical—terms, Scott took under his special and personal supervision. While the New Era danced to its destruction, he continued—supporting himself somehow, anyhow—to plot his curves of energy, add to his amazing store of technical information, develop his industrial philosophy.

Veblen died, and no salutes were fired. A monument was raised to the martyred Warren Gamaliel Harding. Two movements developed in industry which, since they were then in the womb of time, had not been discussed at length in *The Engineers and the Price System*. They operated to shift the thesis somewhat, but did not fundamentally damage it. Both of them Scott and his group immediately took into account. They were:

The rapid growth in the automatic factory (where the machine does *all* the physical work), remote control, and the automatic process, leading to what has come to be called technological unemployment. The first automatic factory appeared in 1915, but the movement did not become general until the 'twenties.

The recognition on the part of certain captains of industry of the big-low-price formula, was superseding the good old monopoly-high-price formula. The new formula occasionally encouraged high wages to provide popular purchasing power to take the big volume off the market.

It was found that more money could be made—flying in the face of the principles of a thousand years of money-making—by going into mass production, increasing mechanical power, decreasing manpower, reducing prices and raising wages. More profit by *raising wages*. Shades of Adam

Smith! But even the scepticism of the academic economists melted as they viewed Mr. Henry Ford rolling a golden snowball toward a billion dollars. No monopolist on all-the-traffic-will-bear formula had ever rolled so lustily. It was classically wrong, but it worked. That was enough for pragmatic America. It admired and imitated. The formula gained momentum all through the New Era.

Higher wages, lower costs. It seemed indeed all wrong. So wrong that the dullest should have smelled a nigger in the woodpile. Those four words fairly shouted that something of the utmost importance, something revolutionary, had happened to industry. They meant, if anybody had cared to give them ten minutes of intelligent attention, that human labor was beginning to pass out of the picture as the prime factor in the production of wealth. In an automobile selling for $3,000, the direct labor cost was found to be $180—a beggarly six per cent of the whole price. Not labor, not wages—but *energy,* locked up in coal, petroleum, waterfalls, was what really counted. Wages per man or per hour could be increased because the total wage bill was falling. Fewer and fewer men were required to produce a given quantity of goods.

Scott saw this clearly. A few others saw it. Nor was the other end of the formula less significant. While the prices of mass-produced commodities did not drastically decline in most cases, costs, time and again, went into a regular tailspin. The new automatic and semi-automatic factories, at capacity operation—twenty-four hours a day on a straight line, continuous basis—could make things which once were dear, unbelievably cheap. Safety razors, formerly priced at five dollars, were given away with tubes of shaving cream. Capacity operation, to be sure, could seldom be maintained; prices were loaded with fantastic selling and advertising costs; but the clear potentiality was there.

Direct labor, per unit of output, sliding downhill; costs of production on a long glissade. The laws of physics had captured two critical trenches; one from the worker, one from the captain of industry, and both from the price system. The tension between the engineer and the banker became more acute than ever Veblen had sensed. The balloon of credit inflation which had shadowed this victory for physics finally burst on an October morning in 1929. The Happiness Boys, headed by Mr. Hoover, pinned on badges, gathered in Rotary formation, and assured us that nothing had happened. Now, after three years of acute depression, even the voice of that champion of hog callers, Mr. Charlie Schwab, is stilled.

About a year ago, as the conviction spread that something was very, very wrong indeed, members of the old Technical Alliance began drifting back to find out what Howard Scott thought of it all. He had plenty to tell them. And he had rechristened both his group and his industrial philosophy, Technocracy.

The group began to grow. Presently it was found possible, through the courtesy of Columbia University and the American Institute of Architects, to turn some fifty draftsmen, for the moment unemployed, to work on the Energy Survey of North America, which Scott had projected, but had never been able adequately to finance. To date some three hundred large charts have been completed, and it is primarily the shattering conclusions deduced therefrom which have set the newspaper boys swarming like bees, turned respectable bankers upside down, filled the pages of foreign journals, and made Technocracy a household word.

What is Technocracy? It is Veblen pushed a few steps forward, modified by recent industrial history and Mr. Howard Scott. It is an attempt to measure by means of figures and charts the impact of energy (the machine, if you like the term better) on civilization. It is an expedition into the higher mathematics. It is a prophecy and a challenge. It has hinted at a blue print of a possible new society where economic activity is controlled by the technician, with a sixteen hour work week, but the blue print has not yet been divulged. It is the name of a group said to consist of some 350 engineers and technical men. And, if it is not careful, it may turn into an esoteric cult. . . .

THE ATTACK ON TECHNOCRACY

As I write, every item in the definition, save the last, is under criticism and attack. This was inevitable. What Mr. Scott and his group have said, and particularly what bright journalists with a taste for melodrama have said, is sufficient to stir a hornet's nest anywhere. Mr. Scott has no hestitation in declaring that the impact of energy is shattering the price system. Bankers in the breadline are always big news. "The nation stands at the threshold of what is simultaneously opportunity and disaster. The opportunity is one of social benefit, the disaster is the failure of the price system and neither opportunity nor disaster may be escaped." [1] Retaliation has been swift and reasonably bitter—as why should it not? It is alleged:

1. That Mr. Scott's character and past personal history leave much to be desired.

2. That the facts and figures so far released by the Technocracy group are full of errors.

3. That, *ipso facto*, the conclusions drawn from the figures are wild, irresponsible and untrue.

Well, let us see.

The personal character of Mr. Scott, or of any member of his group, may or may not be subject to criticism, but has nothing whatever to do with a series of quantitative findings, and conclusions drawn therefrom. The question is not whether Scott has lived in Greenwich Village or in Lung Tung Pen, but what his figures show. The first charge may interest you, but it does not interest me, and I shall say no more about it. I personally know that Scott has devoted himself to this subject for nearly fifteen years with unrelenting zeal.

Are the facts and figures sound? Well, what facts and figures have we? Two varieties: the charts of the Energy Survey, now in process at Columbia, and a miscellaneous assortment of data bearing on new inventions, automatic processes, technological unemployment, energy consumption in other countries, and the like.

I have inspected perhaps thirty of the big charts of the Energy Survey and have been informed that they are based on Census material and other accredited sources of data. I have checked one or two of them with such data and found them substantially correct. Furthermore, I believe I possess enough knowledge of the past industrial history of the United States to affirm that the curves, on such charts as I have seen, follow the expected major tendencies.

Here, for instance, is the curve of the production of steel for the last fifty years. Here on the same chart is the curve of horse-power expended in such production. Here is the total number of workers in the steel industry, year by year. Here is the curve showing man hours per unit of output. The first curve, production, rises steadily, until, about 1907, it breaks into a series of violent oscillations. The second, horse-power, climbs rapidly. The third, total employment, rises more slowly, until about 1920 it begins to decline. More production; fewer workers. The last curve, man hours per unit of output, starts far up on the left hand side of the chart and, bisecting the other curves, heads remorselessly for zero on the lower right hand corner. The other charts exhibit much the same tendency; and we know without verifying Technocracy's figures in detail that such *is* the tendency in American industrial history. The charts, however, should be checked by impartial experts in due time. I understand that a series of them are shortly to be made public and the opportunity for careful verification thrown open.

The production and energy curves on chart after chart warrant special attention. Following a reasonably smooth upward trend for a long series of years, they begin to break, some time after the turn of the century, into a fever of increasingly violent oscillations. Take a whip with a long lash. Hold the straight black handle at a rising angle. Agitate the lash in violent vertical zigzags. This is what many of Technocracy's curves look like. It is only too clear that the dams and barricades of the financial system have been throwing the physical system into a series of increasingly wild gyrations. (It should be pointed out, however, that the production of consumer's goods—flour, meat, clothing—show as a group less violent oscillations than in the case of producers' goods—coal, copper, pig iron.) It is clear also from the survey charts that the peak of *employment* in physical production and transportation was reached shortly before 1920, while the peak of production itself was reached in 1929—a decade later.

So much for the Energy Survey. Technocracy has from time to time set forth other facts dealing with new inventions and special processes; dramatic contrasts have been drawn. Mr. Scott for instance says, "If the total one billion installed horse-power of the United States were operated to full capacity, its output would be equivalent to the human labor of over five times the present total world population." [2] Mr. Bassett Jones, another distinguished member of the group, says, "In incandescent lamp manufacture, one man-hour accomplishes as much as 9,000 man-hours accomplished only so short a time past as 1914." [3] Mr. F. L. Ackerman says, "In 1920 the railroads employed 2,160,000 men; in 1930 they employed 1,300,000 men. Yet in 1929 the carriage of freight was 7 percent greater than in 1920." [4] Scores of assertions of this nature have appeared in the various press stories about Technocracy. It is doubtful if the reporters made them up; they must have secured them somewhere, probably from members of the Technocracy group. It is not at all doubtful, however, that in some cases the journalist garbled the figures. In the Wayne Parrish article in the November, 1932, *New Outlook,* two flatly contradictory statements are made about pig iron production. One or the other is wrong.

These dramatic examples are open to more statistical suspicion than the Energy Survey. Many of them need careful checking and rather ampler description than has so far been given. There is, for instance, a statement attributed to Technocracy that a new road machine is capable of laying eight miles of surfaced road a day with two workers on the machine. [5] It is not explained that to feed such a machine, some 35 trucks must be in constant attendance, while a large gang of hand laborers must constantly be employed in constructing feeder roadways. When this qualification is given full weight, the initial dramatic contrast fades. We cannot know to what extent a given machine displaces labor until we know all the surrounding facts. The stories about Technocracy have not always supplied us with the collateral facts. Again, such stories have given us the performance of figures of the most efficient plants—some of them in the blue print stage only—so worded that many readers construe them as the average performance figures of plants or processes in actual operation.

But here also I cannot doubt the *tendency* shown. Machines are displacing men, swiftly, dramatically, terribly. I have enough stored facts in my own files amply to prove Technocracy's general thesis in this connection. Here is a random selection from my store:

From 1912 to 1927, the Buick Motor Company increased its production 1400 percent, and its labor force only 10 percent. Energy made up the difference.

Two men can cut out about six boards in one day's hand sawing. Two men with a power gang saw can cut 60,000 feet of boards a day, and the hardest work they do is to press an electric button. Their output would construct four six-room houses.

In Proctor and Gamble's soap factory, "Furnace, pump, mill and tank apparatus do the work; men watch, control and aid, but the force and rate of production is far outside their power."

In the Ruhr in 1913, 95 per cent of coal was mined by hand; in 1926, only 33 percent. Machines had taken over two-thirds of the job.

In the New York subways, eleven men used to operate a ten-car train. Today, by virtue of automatic controls, two men run it. Meanwhile, due to electric turnstiles, ten ticket choppers have given way to a couple of change makers.

The hod-carrier has almost disappeared in the face of the power hoist.

In the boiler room of the liner *California* three white-uniformed firemen, presiding over valves and guages, replace the usual fireroom crew of 120 men—a 4,000 percent shrinkage.

The photo-electric cell, which never makes a mistake and never knows fatigue, has been introduced to sort vegetables, fruits and eggs, to measure illumination, appraise colors, classify minerals, count bills and throw out counterfeits, time horse races, count people and vehicles, determine thickness of cloth, see through fog, record smoke in tunnels, inspect tin cans, substitute a new process for photo-engraving, direct traffic automatically, open doors at the approach of a waitress, count sheets of paper and measure their thickness, automatically control trains—to name only a few of its uses.

So much for facts and figures. The trend I cannot doubt, even though certain details may be erroneous or incomplete. We will proceed to the conclusions arising from the facts. This is the section of Technocracy's work which interests me most, and to which I shall devote the remainder of this pamphlet.

The industrial philosophy of Technocracy seems to fall under three main headings:

1. An approach to industrial activity which rivets the mind on physical things, rigorously excluding financial things.

2. The conception of energy magnitudes as the condition governing social and political institutions. Men can do only what available energy—human, animal, or mechanical—permits them to do. Energy may or may not circumscribe their thinking; it does circumscribe their economic and social behavior in a very cardinal way.

3. The physical facts of industrial development in the United States in the past century, and particularly the past fifteen years, show a cause-and-result series which may be

written down in the form of a syllogism; a syllogism capable
of projection into the future, with shattering implications for
the price system, the debt structure, the labor movement, the
whole traditional performance of business enterprise.

Let us consider these three elements in turn.

WORLD WITHOUT MONEY

Much of the hostility against Technocracy arises from the
incapacity of the critic to think about economic activity with
dollar signs omitted. His early conditioning has made such
objectivity psychologically impossible. As an economist who
has dealt largely in non-financial phenomena myself, I have
frequently been subject to the same kind of criticism. Those
of us who try to look steadfastly at the movement of men,
materials, and energy, are obviously long-haired theorists
and impractical visionaries. The practical man is he who
asks: "What will it cost? Who is going to pay for it? How
much profit is there in it?" The practical man, in short, is
he who stakes his all on an abstraction, the dollar, which is
immeasurable and undefinable. It may exchange for five
pounds of rubber today and twenty-five tomorrow. Money,
as Mr. J. M. Keynes has pointed out, is anything the state
declares it to be. A solid German citizen, who in 1903 had
taken out a twenty-year endowment policy for 100,000 marks,
paid his premiums on the nail until 1923, when the policy
fell due. He went and got his money, every mark of it, and
the total at the time was just sufficient to purchase a cheap
straw hat. So reliable and no more is the standard unit of the
practical man.

Neither the Technocrats nor any one else concerned with
physical analysis would contend for an instant that money
in its fundamental sense of a medium of exchange, is not
important, or not to be reckoned with. Technocracy indeed
has devoted serious consideration to the debt structure in the
course of its analysis. No. The point of the physical approach
is that it thrusts money back into its proper relative position.

Instead of being the whole of life—as so many Americans pathologically believe—it becomes only one element in the total economic picture, and, on the basis of physical standards, a very crude and unsatisfactory element at the present time. In the nineteenth century it worked rather better.

The dollar is in profound need of modification and modernization. Even bankers are beginning to admit this. And the only sensible way to plan for a new and less chaotic medium of exchange is to look steadfastly for a time at the physical things which lie back of money, and which, in the last analysis, give it whatever meaning it possesses. Money is not wealth, but only a ticket permitting one to take wealth. Wealth is the physical thing taken—the shoes or the fur coat or the necklace. It is exceedingly important to make this distinction, and the physical approach of Technocracy is thus something of which Americans generally stand in bitter need, to restore perspective. (Fortunately or unfortunately some millions of Americans are going to have their perspective restored in 1933 by means of barter exchanges and the creation of local "wooden" money. They will learn that food, shelter and clothing do not come out of banks, but out of their own efforts.)

ENERGY AND CIVILIZATION

Technocracy sets before us three figures which, to the physically-minded if not the money-minded observer, are of commanding importance.

Primitive communities, both ancient and modern, do work primarily by virtue of the energy of the food eaten by their members, converted into the physical power of human muscle. The chief engine is the human being, and not only the standard of living of the community but most of its social institutions are delimited by his available energy. The power of the human engine (incidentally not very efficient as engines go) is measurable. Its intake of food—proteins, starches, and carbohydrates—is equivalent to about 2,000 *kilogram calories per capita per day.* Such is the lowest energy magnitude of *homo sapiens;* our base line. It was in force universally until the first civilization arose in Mesopotamia about 7,000 years ago. It is still in force in backward regions throughout the world. I saw it in full operation in remote mountain villages in Mexico. Hikers on a climbing trip live under its mandates and know what it means. If there is physical work to be done, their muscles must do it. Two thousand kilogram calories per capita per day; this is the first figure.

With the coming of early civilizations, new non-human sources of energy were tapped. Horses were saddled, oxen and bullocks harnessed. More use of fire was made for cooking and heating. A few clumsy waterwheels and windmills were invented. Presently gunpowder was introduced. The donkey and the carrot made their appearance in literature; the donkey's function being to grind corn. By virtue of these devices, animal, mechanical, and chemical, the energy magnitude in favored communities was doubled; *4,000 kilogram calories per capita per day,* according to Professor A. B. Lamb of Harvard. Approximately half of it came from manpower; half from non-human sources. All civilizations, until the invention of a practical steam engine in 1775, were constrained within this energy limit. Standards of living, social institutions, were fixed on a 4,000 kilogram calory base. The common law, the rights and uses of property, the gold standard currency system, the joint stock company, the relationships between debtors and creditors, the law of contracts, the Constitution of the United States, were all developed in this energy magnitude.

Today, in the United States, the energy consumed by virtue of coal, oil, natural gas and waterpower alone, is the equivalent of *154,000 kilogram calories per capita per day!* If we add to this the time-honored 4,000 of earlier civilizations—for men and animals still use their muscles to a degree—and add windmills, tidemills, rotor engines, rocket ships, and other rarer forms, we secure a total of perhaps

160,000 or some forty times the energy limit of all earlier cultures. The machine age has stepped up our capacity to perform work forty-fold,[6] and in doing it, according to Technocracy, has stepped all over the common law, the concepts of property, the gold standard, the price system and the Constitution. With energy operating in such colossal terms, the institutions formed under far lower quotas are increasingly incapable of functioning. They are being shattered under the impact of this stupendous mechanical power. Earlier depressions have indicated a growing tension; the present depression shows that the tension has become almost unendurable. Twentieth-century power and eighteenth-century economic and political institutions, as Veblen said, cannot much longer tolerate each other's company. One of them must go. It will not be power, says Technocracy. Why? Because the technical arts tend to advance by geometrical progression. Every new invention lays the base for several more. Scientific knowledge is cumulative. It cannot be suppressed, reversed, or blunted. Above all it cannot be stopped by refusing to recognize it; by cutting it dead. There the damn thing is. It will not stand indefinite barricading by captains of industry, as this depression proves; it will not tolerate the shackles of outmoded institutions.

So, says Technocracy, if we cannot cut off the power it might be wise to think about altering institutions.

Why did the Spaniards conquer the Aztecs and the Incas? Primarily because of horses and gunpowder. The Spanish lived in a 4,000 kilogram calory civilization, the Americans in a 2,000; the latter had neither the energy of draft animals nor that of guns. They were as brave as the Spaniards and in their way at least as civilized. But they lacked the crucial store of energy. The power of horses and explosives was clearly supernatural to a people that built stone pyramids by manpower. They were conquered. If this is what can happen by virtue of only doubling an energy magnitude, consider calmly the implication when the magnitude is multiplied forty-fold.

The transition from one energy magnitude to another has been quantitatively stated by Mr. Scott in a series of very elaborate and very abstruse mathematical equations. A good working knowledge of Einstein and the quantum theory is said to be necessary to follow them with any facility. They are beyond me; though I can understand, and you can understand, the magnitudes in terms of 2, 4, and 154. Another theory pronounced by Scott is that the amounts of energy necessary to produce commodities are capable of exact measurement. So many ergs for a pair of boots, so many for a razor blade, so many for an automobile. Energy, therefore, constitutes a more dependable base for a medium of exchange than gold or silver. It is an idea worth careful consideration.

We may summarize this section as follows: Here is a horse and here is a stout buggy—say the Deacon's one-hoss shay. The buggy represents social institutions, the horse an expenditure of energy. The horse is hitched to the buggy, and excellent progress is made—considering the state of the roads at the time. The combination works. Presently Dobbin is released from the buggy, the shafts are removed, and a small steam engine is placed under the seat and geared to the rear wheels. The buggy creaks, expostulates, but moves. (I drove such a buggy in 1906. It was called a Stanley Steamer. It was steered with a tiller, and blew up every 40 miles.) This combination leaves something to be desired, true, but it travels faster than a horse, and it *travels*. It represents our economic history to the end of the nineteenth century. Finally we eliminate the small steam engine and sling a Lincoln motor, 100 horsepower beneath the buggy's wheels. Transmission is made and power is thrown on. The buggy lurches, shivers, groans, and after a swift dash forward, flies into a thousand fragments. . . .

THE BASIC FORMULA

We come now to the third and last section of Technocracy's industrial philosophy. Granted a great increase in energy in the last hundred years, how, precisely, does it affect us and our institutions? A friend of mine puts it this way, a querulous note in his voice: "Well, we've got a lot more energy than we used to have, any fool knows that, and we've got a lot more things, and a lot more money and credit. Even if the connection has jammed temporarily, there is no reason why it can't be brought into line again. Why all the hullaballoo? Why should these wild engineers be whipping out slide rules and prophesying a grand smash?"

Let us try to answer my friend.

As I see it the formula may be stated in some such series as this:

1. In the United States we have developed energy resources from coal, oil, natural gas, and water power until the total consumed has grown from 75 trillion British Thermal Units in 1830 to 27,000 trillion B. T. U. in 1930; while population has grown only twelve-fold.

2. We have developed prime movers (engines) to convert this energy into horse-power, mechanical work, until the total now approaches one billion horse-power—capable of performing as much work as 10 billion men, some 250 times the working population.

3. We have developed a bewildering variety of clever machines to direct the brute power of the prime mover into thousands of useful operations, in manufacturing, agriculture, transportation, even in clerical work, merchandising, housework.

4. By virtue of these energy sources, prime movers and machines, the business of growing, manufacturing, and transporting economic goods is enormously accelerated. Due to the irresistible growth in the technical arts all three factors become constantly more efficient and more interlocked. The whole industrial system is approaching the status of one vast machine, the operation of every part of which depends on the operation of every other part. If people in Texas do not consume automobiles, people in Detroit cannot consume as much food, whereupon farmers in Iowa

cannot consume as many radios and harvesting machines, whereupon . . . The self-sufficient local community has gone forever. We are all tied together with chains of power and of steel.

5. The tendency in manufacturing and power production, and to a lesser degree in transportation, agriculture and clerical work, is in the direction of the full automatic process, where the machine does everything, the human muscle nothing. Such labor as is required increasingly takes the form of dial watching, control cabin work, switch throwing, inspection and set up. Even in this domain the photo-electric cell has been found to be a more dependable switch thrower than any human hand or eye.

6. The result of this tendency is drastically to reduce costs —measured in energy or money or labor power. By virtue of standardization, and the extension of physical and chemical research, cost can be further reduced through the factors of durability, high quality, and more accurate design. Scott tells us that a razor blade with a tungsten carbide edge, fabricated with only a 20 percent increase in energy, would last for a generation.

7. Ultimately the costs of certain products—by no means all—become so low that they approach the status of air, water, sticks and stones. Their economic "value" approaches zero. A steel pin or a paper clip was once an article of "value" and was carefully preserved for future use. Today, stamped out by the millions, we treat them as cavalierly as we do the water from the faucet. Many commodities are headed in the same direction. Consider second-hand motor cars today. Even when the cost of a given essential commodity is not susceptible to drastic reduction, there is always the possibility of replacing it with a substitute. Houses of lumber, brick, or stone are difficult to put into mass production. They are threatened today by fabricated steel houses, turned out in sections by the mile in automatic factories. Synthetic foods are a growing menace to the farmer. The whole textile industry, in both its agricultural and its manufacturing divi-

sions, may be undermined by some such fibrous nettle plant as ramie. As science develops, these threats to established industries become increasingly severe.

8. In the last one hundred years, the following tendencies are observable:[7]

> Energy has grown to the curve t^8—where t equals time.
> Debt has grown to the curve t^4.
> Production has grown to the curve t^3.
> Population has grown to the curve t^2.
> Man hours per unit of output to the curve *minus* t^4.

The whole Technocracy analysis is implicit in these five curves.

Debt has been increasing faster than production, or faster than tangible wealth. As debt comes to nothing but a shower of paper without real wealth behind it, these curves indicate a paradox which obviously cannot indefinitely continue.

Here we have a series of eight facts and tendencies. We can immediately draw certain major conclusions.

The decline in direct labor per unit of output as mechanical energy is substituted for human muscle can only lead to more and more technological unemployment.

Technological unemployment, like all unemployment, operates to reduce popular purchasing power. Yet without a tremendous base of popular purchasing power, modern industry cannot function.

The automatic process operates to drive down costs and ultimately prices, and so depress the "valuations" of the price system.

The automatic process, due to its huge output in relatively small space, reduces opportunities for profitable investment. When one or two plants can supply the nation, *they* may be very profitable, but they undermine investment throughout the rest of the industry.

As bulk opportunities for profitable investment decline, the interest rate turns downward toward an ultimate zero.

The burden of debt, based on process rapidly becoming obsolete, becomes increasingly intolerable. We see this happening very clearly in the case of the railroads.

New energy forms have made certain functions of the railroad obsolete over large areas. The Reconstruction Finance Corporation, in trying to keep railroad debts intact, is in the last analysis defying the laws of physics. It is a losing fight. Furthermore, to maintain the debt structure intact, production must increase by t^4, a compound interest rate, which is probably in excess of consumers' wants and certainly in excess of the purchasing power released by current financial methods, and in excess of the technical possibilities of production and natural resources over an extended period.

These conclusions cannot be controverted because they are now in more or less active operation—in boom periods, observe, as well as in depressions. The question is, how far flung and important are the operations to date, and can the price system adjust itself to them? Technocracy says they are dangerously far flung and that the price system cannot adjust itself. Technocracy's critics say the process is nascent only and can be accommodated within the price system. Before, however, we examine this crucial question, there are two important corollaries of the basic formula which should be listed.

The automatic process continually displaces the manual worker. He secures a job, if he is lucky, in one of the "service" trades, usually a white collar trade. He leaves, or is thrown out of, the classic proletariat. What becomes of the class struggle theory; where are the toiling masses, without a worker in the plant? Photo-electric cells can readily identify the color red, but they are difficult to organize. Service trade workers are even more difficult. The official labor movement, it is significant to note, has not progressed in the new mass production industries, and in the next phase, the automatic industry, there will be nobody to organize. When this development proceeds to a certain point, which we may or may not yet have reached, the whole Marxian thesis stands in need of substantial revision. Marx wrote in a time of far lower energy magnitudes. One suspects he would be the first to recognize the changed situation today.

As the proletariat declines in numbers and importance, the technical class grows. The latter point, of course, was cardinal in Veblen's analysis. History may now be in the process of creating a new industrial class, more important than worker, owner, creditor or financial manager—the men who understand and operate energy. Technocracy is the first formal organization of this class. As an organization it may be discredited; may fail. But if the laws of physics are actually throwing up such a class, the idea it stands for cannot fail. A new and stronger organization will take its place.

Perhaps now without undue violence we may state this new industrial philosophy in its simplest terms:

The technical arts cannot be halted. As they march they are exploding employment, money values and vested interests. The price system cannot withstand an indefinite series of such explosions without collapse. At which point, if we can keep our wits about us and see that the collapse is one of paper only, we have the opportunity to institute a more modern system, amenable to the laws of physics, capable of dealing with 154,000 kilogram calory magnitudes and upwards, and perhaps solving the economic problem for all time. It should be operated, says Technocracy with charming modesty, by technicians.

WHAT IS WRONG WITH THIS PICTURE?

Such is my interpretation of the conclusions to be drawn from Technocracy's data. What is wrong with them? Broadly speaking, I can find little wrong with them. They coincide roughly with an industrial philosophy which I have held for a long time—indeed, ever since I read Veblen. I would raise, however, certain collateral questions.

Why cannot the price system continue to stagger along for another decade or two by virtue of inflation or the devaluation of the dollar—either of which operates to reduce the burden of debt? Neither offers any permanent solution, but I strongly suspect that one or the other is going to be tried whenever a collapse—i.e., a wholesale repudiation of debts—becomes sufficiently imminent.

Some authorities believe that the old system can stagger along by stabilization on a low production, low standard of living, low income basis. Articles are already being written in business journals to the effect that mass production has been overdone. Back to nineteenth century frugalities, hard work, and saving pennies. This means falling down an elevator shaft of energy magnitudes. I incline to agree with Technocracy that scientific development is an irreversible process. It might possibly be hammered to pieces by a stupendous war or revolution, but it would hardly tolerate stabilization on an 1890 basis. The automatic process is the best and cheapest way to produce goods. It cannot be closed up and discarded. The only hope lies in social control of its relentless advance.

This raises a further question, however. *How far has the automatic process actually gone?* I have a drawerful of cases similar to those I have cited, and probably Technocracy has more. But my drawerful, while it may account for two or three million men on the street, and threaten millions more, is certainly not powerful enough yet to overturn a system. I have seen one factory, 400 feet long, capable at capacity operation of supplying the whole national demand for automobile frames—10,000 frames a day. If there are several hundred plants like this in actual operation, or ready to be put into operation, each capable of supplying all, or a huge fraction of, the national demand for its product, I can readily visualize the breakdown of the price system in a remarkably short time. I have reason to believe that there are not hundreds of such plants as yet. They are coming, yes, but they are not here. It will take a few more years to get them here. The blueprints are quite possibly ready, but the bankers are not. Indeed we may require another inflationary boom to secure enough automatic factories and processes to make good the threat of imminent breakdown. In brief, I am not nearly so sure of the *time factor* as Technocracy appears to be.

Again, how long can industry maintain, to put it bluntly, the annual model racket? The manufacture of quick replacement goods uses up a lot of energy and employs a lot of labor. It is probably true that if every plant today started to produce the best product of which it was capable, the factor of durability would be so high—things would last so long— that the price system would be water-logged within a year. Most of the factories would have to close for lack of reorders. But the fact remains that the price system has kept afloat on shoddy, wasteful, quick replacement goods (the dams and barricades again), and proposes, so far as I know, to continue to do so. We consumers are becoming somewhat fatigued with it, to be sure, but there is little real revolt in us— yet. We shall continue for a time to buy boots that open to the breezes in six months, when it is perfectly possible, technically, to make boots which would last until we were sick of the sight of them. How much more life is there in the replacement method? Technocracy says very little. I am not so sure.

Again there is the question of new industries—brand new industries. It is painfully obvious that a new industry like ramie, which threatens to capsize the whole standing textile investment, gets the old system nowhere except downhill. There may well be opportunities however for the development of commodities and services hitherto unknown. The automobile was such a development and created 4,000,000 new jobs out of thin air. How about air conditioning, or a fool-proof airplane—to mention two life-savers which have been proposed? It will have to be a very large new industry (or group of industries) capable of absorbing literally millions of workers. It will have to avoid a great output on the automatic process basis, because such a basis provides comparatively few jobs. Frankly, I see no such industry on the horizon. Technocracy appears to discount the idea altogether in the sense that it can really shore up the price system. But such an industry just possibly might arrive.

Slum clearance and housing on a grand scale have been proposed to keep us afloat. In so far as the new houses were mass produced of fabricated steel, the project would be hopeless, in that it would wreck real estate valuations in old housing areas. A banker, shown a model of an $1800 fabricated house, equipped with all modern conveniences, said: "Splendid! But it would ruin my business." In so far as the new housing was of the old type—stone, brick, wood—it is the universal opinion of experts that it can be developed in the grand manner only by state subsidy. Private capital cannot afford to touch it. Socialized housing, observe, would not be shoring up the old system. It would be a radical step towards a new collective system. The vested interests could be counted on to oppose it implacably.

Finally, to return to our collateral questions, is the production of tangible goods all of economic activity? Assuredly not. Economic activity includes many valuable services not susceptible to measurement in terms of energy—the work of teachers, doctors, artists, professional baseball players, traffic officers, research workers. In 1930 roughly half as many people were employed in the "service" trades as in the production and distribution of physical goods. The ratio has been growing rapidly in recent years, especially since 1920. How far can the old system keep afloat on the purchasing power of service workers rather than factory workers? They must fit into the whole economic picture in a large and definite way, and I do not see clearly where Technocracy in its pronouncements to date allows for them. Many essential services seem to lie outside the concept of energy magnitudes altogether.

This brings us to consumers' choices and human nature generally. Whenever a critic desires to refute any body of doctrine in this republic, he says, first, that it is inspired from Moscow; second, that it is against human nature. Technocracy, it appears, is both, and immediately is endeared to me. At the same time I should like to know where the service trades fit in, and how a painting is to be measured in ergs. I can readily comprehend an energy system confining itself to physical things, like a water system confining itself to supplying the people of a given city with water. But as Technocracy's analysis stands, it accounts for only about half, or to be generous, two-thirds, of the present economic total. For all I know, a million men could, by 1950, make and distribute all the essential physical goods which one hundred million people could consume. What arrangements—necessarily economic arrangements—should be made to cover the activities of the rest of the workers?

And what about consumers' choices in the physical budget? I realize that there is considerable nonsense talked about an unlimited ceiling of consumers' wants. Some millions of us in 1929 were beginning to feel that we had too much stuff already to take care of. There is no such unlimited ceiling. But though the total tonnage has a limit, there is a serious question of *variety within that limit*. You like radios and I would not have one in the house. I want to wear rough sports clothes and you like smooth and silky clothes. Furthermore, mass production at best can only approximately fit human individuals, their bodies or their tastes. This makes national budget-making complicated, and requires far more intensive consideration than has yet been devoted to it. It is probably not insoluble.

I cannot, therefore, take my energy economics straight. I require a chaser of psychology and anthropology. It does not follow that either Veblen's or Technocracy's conclusions are shaky, only that they do not go far enough. The total economic problem is not comprehended. As far as they go, however—and in their cardinal domain they plough deep—these conclusions, and the data on which they are based, constitute perhaps the most arresting challenge which the American industrial system has ever faced.

[1] Technology Smashes the Price System. Prepared under the supervision

[2] *The Living Age*, December, 1932. p. 299.
of Howard Scott. Harper's Magazine, January, 1933.
[3] *Electrical Engineering*, November, 1932. p. 813.
[4] Unpublished monograph: *The Technologist Looks at the Depression.*
[5] Wayne W. Parrish: Technocracy's Question. *New Outlook*, December, 1932.
[6] On the basis of non-human energy input alone, we have stepped from 2,000 k.g. cal. in 1775 to 154,000 k.g. cal. in 1930, a 77-fold increase.
[7] Bassett Jones in *Electrical Engineering*, November, 1932.

THE MARXIAN PHILOSOPHY

By MAX EASTMAN

I. THE WORD "DIALECTIC"

FEW people on this side of the planet understand the Marxian system of philosophy. Its whole context and posture of mind are so foreign to the sceptical and empirical temper of our Anglo-Saxon culture that we find it difficult to imagine, or even to believe when we are told, that it is what it is. Thus it is winning a foothold here by mere default. Our leftward intellectuals are beginning to let fall the word *dialectic*—the key word in this system—as lightly as though it meant nothing, and entailed nothing, but a belief in change and the possibility of successful revolutions. They have not the slightest idea what the state of mind is which they are helping to propagate by accepting with this numb acquiescence a word so highly charged with meaning. For my part, I think there is no intellectual question of more importance to the future of American culture than the question whether we are going to conduct our revolutionary efforts in the name of science, or are going to swallow down this romantic German philosophy.

To the Greeks the word dialectic first meant conversation, and when in the time of the sophists argumentative conversation developed into a fashionable parlor game, the rules of this game were also called dialectic. The game consisted of someone's making an assertion, and someone else's trying to lead him into self-contradiction by asking questions to be answered *yes* or *no*. If you have ever played "twenty questions," and played it ardently, you will remember how it leads inevitably to a consideration of the fundamental categories of conception—the ways in which things can be said to "be."

This game, I think, would form an excellent introduction to the study of philosophy. At any rate, that similar game of dialectic did introduce the Greeks to the main body of what became philosophy. And if you will imagine a small leisure-class society, just waking up to the joys of unsuperstitious thinking, "going in for" this slightly bold and improper diversion—improper because it was always leading up to irreverent conclusions about gods—and making a steady fad of it, and then imagine some clever persons coming along and writing "scientific" books on it like Sims on Contract Bridge, you will understand how inevitably this happened. For there were earnest people there, of course, like Socrates and Zeno, who loved truth too well to toss her back and forth quite frivolously. They took the fascinating sport of dialectic seriously, insisting that it is the very essence of the method by which a mind arrives at truth.

And then Plato came, with his mature and calmly smiling equilibrium, and without letting fall the playful humor altogether, converted these parlor games into the greatest of all works of intellectual art, his philosophic dialogues. And when he proposed—not without a hint that perhaps those who believe it are a little crazy—his famous doctrine that the general ideas arrived at and defined in this manner are alone real, and that individual things are a mere shadow, he naturally gave the name of *dialectic* to the science which knows and understands all about these ideas in their pure form. It is a science of intellectual conversation or debate, whether with another or within one's own mind, a taking of contrary positions and then slicing off what is false in each, and so arriving at a higher and better formulation—a mode of progress toward the truth by contradiction and reconciliation.

With Aristotle, who brought those Platonic ideas down into the material world, and made them function as a kind of regulating norm for the growth of actual things, the word dialectic took a drop from its exalted position. Aristotle was interested in observing how things do grow. He had therefore a more complete and scientific view than Plato of the method by which a mind arrives at truth. Dialectic thinking seemed merely critical to him, or "tentative," and not concerned with real or philosophic knowing.

In the Dark or Theological Ages, however, when people again believed that with the help of an initial revelation and of Aristotle's rules for thinking, true knowledge could be spun out of man's head by a thought-process, this word regained its high position. It became in fact a name for all those rules of thinking which had come down from Aristotle. But now, although a sense of the importance of *disputation* still remained, the parlor game was well forgotten. The word no longer called to mind, as with Plato and his predecessors, a definite method of mental progress, a zigzag movement of the mind towards true ideas by setting two views against each other, and letting them resolve their differences in a third. It meant simply logic, and was, as Abelard said, "that *doctrina* . . . whose function is to distinguish between every truth and falsity," and which "as leader in all knowledge . . . holds the primacy and rule of all philosophy."

It was man's gradual understanding that real knowledge —the kind of knowledge you can rely on in action—is neither revealed by God, nor spun out of the head by Aristotle's logic, but is come at by observation and experiment, that made possible our modern world. The development of this "scientific" kind of knowledge throughout the last four hundred years has been perhaps the most momentous thing that ever happened, or could be imagined to happen, in the history of human culture. Do not be deceived about this because from time to time a fad arises to be impatient, or "sceptical," of science. Science itself is sceptical, and the high standard set by scientific knowledge is the very thing that makes us impatient of it.

With this moving up of *investigation* into the place of *disputation,* the word dialectic again dropped low, just as it had with Aristotle. It played no part in the minds of Copernicus, Harvey, Galileo, Newton, and it soon fell out of use entirely except among the churchly and historic-minded. Laplace, Lavoisier, Helmholtz, Maxwell, Mendeliev, Darwin did their work without it. Science never has made use of it in any form. Only once, when Karl Marx came forward with his so-called "scientific socialism," did this word make even an appearance in a position of honor in any significant work laying claim to the title of science. It then turned up, however, in the field of *social science* with a glory round it like that it had possessed in the Middle Ages. In the mind of the orthodox Marxist, dialectic is again the "leader in all knowledge" and "holds the primacy and rule of all philosophy," and of all science too. It is the supreme *organon*, the ultimate height and perfect instrument of understanding, an inherently revolutionary super-science to which all genuinely progressive minds in every field must eventually learn to conform.

How did this peculiar thing happen? And is it really true that a new "method of thinking" has been discovered, better than that upon which all modern science is built, and that this wonderful discovery is now only slowly filtering through the world along with communist propaganda? It is not true, of course. But the fable is believed in by increasing millions, and it is well worth a strenuous mental effort to find out what *is* true, and how this fable came to be mixed up with a socialism which pretends to be, and seems to be, "scientific."

II. THE RELIGIOUS HERITAGE OF SCIENTIFIC SOCIALISM

In order to understand this renewed apotheosis of the word dialectic, it is necessary to realize that the whole momentous growth of matter-of-fact knowledge which we call modern science has had to fight its way every step against resistance from people who were not matter-of-fact, and wanted to go on holding to the old emotional "beliefs" which used to stand firm upon the ground of divine revelation and logical "disputation." These over-soulful people have not wanted to deny science or deprive themselves of its benefits, but neither have they wanted to commit themselves to its methods of acquiring knowledge, and above all to the *limitations* of knowledge which those methods imply. They have wanted to use the faculty of ideation not only in order to change real things in an ideal direction, but also in order to make themselves comfortable among things-as-they-are by thinking up ideal ways of conceiving them. Thus while matter-of-fact men—or men in their matter-of-fact moods—have been building science and trying to clarify its principles, other men or moods of men, less based in matter and less bent on fact, have been inventing a variety of complicated intellectual machinery for keeping up the old wish-fulfilling views of the world as a whole, in spite of the disillusioning discoveries of science about each particular part of it. This wish-fulfilling machinery constitutes about one half, I suppose, of what is called modern philosophy. And it constitutes far more than half of what is called German idealistic philosophy. That may be described almost wholesale as a "disguised theology"—a colossally ingenious speculative wizardry by which the old religious attitudes were maintained in the new scientific world. It was so described by Marx himself. And the most ingenious of all these disguised theologians—the "master wizard" as Marx called him—was George Wilhelm Friedrich Hegel, who dominated German intellectual life when Marx was young.

We need not explore all the intricacies of Hegel's wish-fulfilling machinery. It has two essential elements, or rather two legs upon which it stands, and without which it is nothing. One is an absolute conviction as to the notion put forward somewhat tentatively, I think, by Plato, that the veritable realities of this world are ideas and not things. The other is the brilliant device of conceiving these ideas, not as static entities, but as in a state of fluid logical development. Plato had said, you remember, that these real ideas, conceived as changeless, are to be studied and arrived at by a debating, or dialectic, process, a process of affirmation, contradiction and reconciliation of the opposing views. Hegel declared that the ideas are themselves going through this process. This auto-debating, or dialectic unfolding, of an idea is what every reality in this world consists of. And not only every particular reality, but the world as a whole is a Mind engaged in defining its content by affirmation, self-contradiction and reconciliation of the opposites in a higher unity. It is a Divine Mind evolving with logical necessity and with intense, creative emotion like a deadly serious, soulfully important and noble and inexorable parlor game of dialectic toward the goal of "self-realization."

Now if you are going to believe in God in a scientific age, there are decided advantages in believing in this kind of God. It enables you to be almost as "empirical" and hardheaded and unillusioned as the scientists themselves in describing any particular "phase" that this God may have to go through. It enables you to accept, and even carry forward, the discovery of science that the heavens and the earth and everything on the earth have evolved, that all is change, that nothing we care about is eternal. Next to the discovery that the earth is not the center of the heavens, that has been the most upsetting thought to soulful people. It has been the most difficult for the Eternal Being, the Unchanging, the Ancient of Days, to cope with and survive. And I think it is not too much to say that the essential function of Hegel's philosophy, what has made its ingenuity so significant, is that it saves the face of the Deity when confronted by this modern scientific world of flux and universal evolution. It saves the face of the Deity, and it saves the face of pious, conservative, optimistic morality—not shallowly but deeply optimistic morality—and it re-establishes with a cosmic glamour the virtues of a civil and loyally devout submission to the ordered course of things. If all the world, and human history most especially, is the mind of God moving with logical necessity through a process of affirmation and self-contradiction, and reformulation in a higher unity, toward the truth of His own being—toward that freedom which you feel when you have solved a problem and got all your definitions right—then obviously there is no use rebelling deeply against the world, or making totally disruptive efforts to reform it. The thing is to feel reverent, to feel that you are a part and member of this divine Reasoning Process, this cosmical Debating Society, and go dutifully along with it toward the logically inevitable solution.

It is easy, when you do not believe in any of it at all, to smile at this colossal enterprise of self-deception. But if you leave your smiles outside, and enter into it and see with what staggering sweeps and intricate ingenuities it is bewilderingly constructed, and if you remember too that it flourished a hundred and more years ago when our own great-grandparents were believing in the literal licks of hell's flames up the pants-legs of the sinner, you will not smile too scornfully. Remember, too, that Hegel did not wait for modern science to confront the godhead with this world of flux and universal evolution so well known to us. He got the jump on science. He foresaw this world, and had his mighty and obscure machinery of cosmic casuistics ready for the job of reinstating soulfulness before the scientists themselves quite knew what they were coming to. It is no wonder, then, that Hegel's metaphysics seemed to many Germans ultimate, and had such influence on those who learned it in their youth.

Marx learned this system in his youth, and fervently believed it all. He believed it, of course, with a "leftward" tendency, a tendency to emphasize the temporal and historic character of the divine evolution, and the importance of each forward step in the process, each "negation" of the *status quo* —and particularly the one which he felt to be about due in his own time. It requires only a shift of emphasis in Hegel's system to put God on the side of the rebels. But real rebels in the days of science have no use for God. They do not ask assistance from the cosmos, or any soul-upholding conception of it, in their attempt to overthrow a tyrant class. They ask a scientific method for going at it, and the devil take the cosmos. Indeed they see that all godly cosmic systems tend, in the long run, to reconcile men to oppressive conditions by cherishing illusions about the metaphysical status of those conditions. Marx himself formulated this view of religion in one of his early writings. "The abolition of religion as the illusory happiness of the people," he said, "is a demand for their real happiness"—a thought expressed with greater felicity in the I.W.W. song, "There'll be pie in the sky bye and bye." With this feeling in him, it was inevitable that Marx should throw aside Hegel's scheme for reading soul into the universe, and particularly into the bloody pages of human history, and begin talking about the world as ordinary practical-minded people talk. The world is not made out of ideas, he suddenly discovered, and much less ideas evolving with passionate logic in a benign direction. It is made out of things.

Marx was twenty-five when he arrived at this conviction, which all modern radical-minded people start with. It was then that he denounced Hegel as the "master wizard," denounced his whole system as "drunken speculation," and endorsed the opinion of the German "materialist," Ludwig Feuerbach, that all speculative philosophers are "priests in disguise." Indeed, Marx went further than Feuerbach, who himself softened the hard facts of science with a sort of "anthropological philosophy," or philosophy of human love. Marx renounced all kinds of wish-fulfilling speculation whatsoever, declaring that if you adopt the attitude of a scientific investigator, no philosophy of any kind except a mere "summary" of your findings is either possible or necessary.

"We recognize but one science," he said, "the science of history . . . a history of nature and a history of men. . . . With the presentation of reality, an independent philosophy loses its existence-medium. In its place can appear at the most a summary of the general results abstracted from an investigation of the historical development of men."

Nowhere in literature is there a more wholesale rejection

of the very idea of super-scientific knowledge, a more arrant declaration of independence from metaphysical conceptions of the universe, than in Marx's writings from the age of twenty-five to twenty-seven. Nevertheless, when he came to formulate his own views of what science is—a thing he did very sketchily, and that is why there is so much argument about "understanding Marxism"—it appeared that he had really got rid of but one-half of Hegel's machinery of wish-fulfillment, the notion, namely, that reality is made out of ideas. The notion that reality is "dialectic," which was the very king-pin in the whole soulful-consolatory apparatus of the master-wizard, he never did get rid of. Reality is material, he said emphatically, and even human history can be explained in its grand outlines as an evolution of material things. But nevertheless this evolution is proceeding towards humanly ideal ends. "All successive historic conditions are only transitory steps in the endless evolution of human society from the lower to the higher," as Engels put it. And Marx himself spoke of the "higher life-form toward which the existing society tends irresistibly by its own economic development," and declared on this ground that the workers "have no ideal to realize, they have only to release the elements of the new society which the collapsing bourgeois society carries in its womb." This mysteriously "noble" and ascending movement, moreover, is taking place in the very manner proper to an apotheosis of the parlor game of dialectic. It first asserts something and then this something passes over into its opposite, and then by its own "self-active motion," or in other words by a *logical* necessity, it reconciles or "sublates" these opposites in a higher—that is, a more desirable—unity.

III. WHAT DIALECTIC MEANT TO MARX AND LENIN

Modern Marxists will hasten to assure you that the "triadic" character of the dialectic movement is not essential. And they are quite right. The essential thing is its going "from the lower to the higher"—in the direction, that is, of the Marxist's wish—and its doing this by way of conflict within a self-contradictory "totality." However, it is not difficult to find sufficiently triadic examples in both Marx and Lenin. Wealth, or private property, said Marx, is "the positive side of an antithesis"; "proletariat and wealth are opposites": it lies therefore in the very nature of a dialectic reality that the conflict between these two "opposites" should resolve itself in a successful proletarian revolution in which "the proletariat itself disappears no less than its conditioning opposite, private property."

To declare that "proletariat and wealth are opposites" is such loose thinking that to us it seems obvious the purpose must be other than the definition of fact with a view to verified knowledge. And yet this loose thinking forms the framework into which the mass of empirical information in *Das Kapital* has to be forced in order to make credible the "historic necessity" of a social revolution. This loose thinking is essential to the belief that reality is dialectic. It will be found *whenever and wherever* a downright attempt is made to explain what that belief is. Even Benedetto Croce, who wants to save all that he possibly can of Hegel's philosophy because he likes it, is compelled to remark this. Hegel made an "essential error," he says, in failing clearly to conceive what he meant by "opposite"—failing, indeed, to distinguish things which are opposite from things which are merely "distinct." "Who could ever persuade himself," he exclaims, "that religion is the not-being of art and that art and religion are two abstractions which possess truth only in philosophy, the synthesis of both; or that the practical spirit is the negation of the theoretical, that representation is the negation of intuition, civil society the negation of the family, and morality the negation of rights; and that all these concepts are unthinkable outside their synthesis—free spirit, thought, state, ethicity—in the same way as being and not being, which are true only in becoming?" Obviously nobody could persuade himself of these fantastic propositions unless he had some reason to do so other than the desire to understand the world. Hegel's reason was that he wished to keep up, in spite of scientific understanding, a certain attitude of feeling toward the world. It was an attitude of action rather than of feeling that Marx and Lenin wished to keep up. But the thinking by which they did so was just as loose, and the lists of "opposites" which they composed just as fantastic as those of Hegel. In fact, they merely added the class struggle—the opposition of "wealth," or bourgeoisie, and proletariat—to the old lists.

Here, for instance, is Lenin's conception of the dialectic, written in his note-book after studying Hegel's *Science of Logic:*

"Dialectic is the study of how there can be and are (how there can become) identical opposites—under what circumstances they are identical, converting themselves one into the other—why the mind of man ought not to take these opposites for dead, stagnant, but for living, conditional, moving things converting themselves one into another. . . .

"The doubleness of the single and the understanding of its contradictory parts . . . is the *essence* . . . of the dialectic. . . .

"In ·mathematics: + and —. Differential and integral.

"In mechanics: action and reaction.

"In physics: positive and negative electricity.

"In chemistry: the combining and dissociation of atoms.

"In social science: the class struggle. . . ."

To this list he adds, in some later notes, the distinction in logic between the particular and the general: "A leaf of a tree is green; Ivan is a man; Zhuchka is a dog, etc. Here already (as Hegel's genius observed) is the dialectic; the particular is the general." And in another place, he calls the progress of the mind "from living contemplation to abstract thought and from this to practice" a "dialectic path."

The science of psychology, with all its failings, has done

enough for us so that when a man makes in dead earnest such preposterous assertions as that $+$ and $-$, action and reaction, wealth and proletariat, particular and general, bear the same relation to each other—still more, that wealth and proletariat resolve their opposition in the social revolution with the same "self-active motion" with which a mind resolves in practice the "opposition" between contemplation and abstract thought—we know that he is driven, whether consciously or not, by some motive other than a desire to understand the world. He is not engaged in scientific investigation, but in rationalizing his motives. Just what the motive was, moreover, whose satisfaction gave a color of solid and solemn truth to this loose mixture of remarks, appears in almost every page of Lenin's notes. This, for instance, from the paragraph next following:

"Development is a 'struggle' of opposites. . . . Only [this] conception affords a key to the 'self-movement' of every existent thing; it alone offers a key to 'leaps,' to 'interruptions of continuity,' to 'transformations into the opposite,' to the destruction of the old and the arising of the new."

It is the "leaps," the "interruptions of continuity," the "destruction of the old and the arising of the new"—in short, the social revolution—that Lenin is interested in. And an underlying, always unspoken assumption that the new is going to be what he wants it to be—that the real is in harmony with the human ideal, provided it is *our* ideal—is just as essential to his philosophy as it was to Hegel's. As a philosopher he is using his mind not merely in order to promote the success of his action, but in order to assure himself that his action will succeed.

That this kind of thinking is not science, but is something which the "speculative thinker" *reads into* science was clearly recognized and stated by Hegel. "The speculative science," he said, "does not in the least ignore the empirical facts contained in the several sciences, but recognizes and adopts them. . . . But besides all this, into the categories of science it introduces and gives currency to other categories." Exactly the same thing is true of the Marxian "dialectic philosophy," as you may see in the assertion of Engels, who expounded it, that Marx did not use the dialectic in order to establish any fact, and also that an understanding of the dialectic nature of such a thing as a barley seed does not enable one to raise barley any better than he could if he did not understand it. What makes the Marxian philosophy so much more difficult than the Hegelian to combat, is that while Marx took over from Hegel this conception of a "speculative" or super-scientific mental operation, he thought that he was being purely scientific, and, indeed, *more* purely scientific than anybody else in the field of sociology. All radically thoughtful modern minds well know that this special kind of thinking, lofty and yet loose, which stands above the best efforts of science, and is not used to prove any facts, and gives you a knowledge of the barley seed which has nothing to do with raising barley, is emotional rationalization, and what it introduces into the categories of science and gives currency to, is the wish-fulfillments of the human heart.

Marx—to sum it up—rejected Hegel's divine spiritualization of the world and the historic process; he declared the fundamental reality to be solid, stubborn, unconscious and unconsoling matter. And then he proceeded to read into that matter the very essence of the Divine Spirit as it had been conceived in Hegel's consoling system, its self-active motion by an inherent logical necessity, the necessity with which in a debating mind the conclusion follows from the premise, toward an ideal end. The end was different, and so were the actions and emotions of one who participated in its evolution toward them, but the conception of the universe was essentially the same.

Hegel apotheosized a parlor game, and managed to attach pious emotions and a conservative goal and moral to a God who had nothing better to do than argue with himself about abstract ideas. Marx took the soul out of the whole fabrication, dispelled the pious emotions and replaced the conservative with a revolutionary goal and moral, but left the apotheosis of the parlor game working away just as miraculously, just as super-scientifically, as it had before. Indeed, in his mature reflections, he left it *more* miraculous, for now it is going through the motions of a debating society, obeying all the rules of order and arriving at the logically imposed result, without possessing reason or knowing anything about what it is doing.

"History proceeds in such a way that the end-result always issues from the conflict of many individual wills. . . . We have thus innumerable conflicting forces, an endless group of parallelograms of forces, giving a resultant—the historic event—which may itself again be regarded as the product of a force acting as a whole without consciousness and without will. For that which each individual desires, meets an opposition from every other, and the result is something which nobody desired."

It is in this blind way, according to Engels, that a material world accomplishes that "endless evolutionary progress . . . from the lower to the higher" which is its dialectic essence. And Marx, if you gather the quotations with some care, leaves equally independent of human will or consciousness the "historic necessity" of the dictatorship of the proletariat and its transition to the "society of the free and equal."

"Man makes his own history, but he does not make it out of the whole cloth; he does not make it out of conditions chosen by himself, but out of such as he finds at hand." "It is unnecessary to add that man is not free to choose the forces of production which serve as the foundation of his entire history, for every force of production is an acquired force, the product of former activity. . . . By virtue of the simple fact that every generation finds at hand the forces of production acquired by an earlier generation . . . there arises a connection in human history, and the history of mankind takes form and shape." "I have added as a new contribution the following propositions: 1) that the existence of classes is bound up in certain phases of material production, 2) that the class struggle leads necessarily to the dictatorship of the proletariat, 3) that this dictatorship is but a transition to the abolition of all classes and the creation of a society of the free and equal."

Far from abandoning "all philosophy" for science, Marx did not even abandon Hegel's philosophy. He merely replaced Hegel's World Spirit with a World Robot who performs to a different purpose, and without demanding social attentions, all the work which the World Spirit was employed to perform.

"Scientific" socialism, then, *in its intellectual form,* is anything but scientific. It is "philosophy" in the very sense that Marx himself denounced philosophy. A revolutionary science would study the material world with a view to changing it according to some practical plan. Marx studied the world with a view to making himself believe that it is in process of change according to his plan. Since his plan *is* practical, a revolutionary science is contained in his writings, tangled up in and somewhat distorted by an optimistic system of belief. But the belief is super-scientific, metaphysical—religious in the truest sense of the term. It is a scheme for reading the ideal purpose of the communists and their plan for achieving it into the objective facts, so that their account of the changing world and their plans for changing it become one and the same thing. "It is not a question of putting through some utopian system," they cry, "but of taking a conscious part in the process of social transformation which is going on before our very eyes,"—and therefore,—"All our theories are programs of action." Or, as we find it in the words of Lenin: the dialectic philosophy is "deeper and richer" than "objectivism," because it "includes in itself, so to speak, partisanship, obliging a man in every appraisal of events directly, frankly and openly to take his stand with a definite social group."

IV. SCIENCE AND THE DIALECTIC FAITH

To identify theoretic knowledge-of-fact with the program-of-action of a special social group—to regard partisanship as "deeper" than objective investigation—is so exactly *not* the attitude in which science approaches the world, whether it be pure science or applied, that you would hardly expect to find this thought still living in the minds of educated modern men like Lenin and Trotsky. To hold your wish or purpose in suspense while you define existing facts may be said almost to be the essence of what science is. For a practical revolutionist, however, this complicated mental trick has, or at least has had, advantages entirely apart from its wish-fulfillment function. It has inculcated a flexibility of mind, a freedom from fixed concepts in dealing with social phenomena, a habit of constantly recurring to the facts for new starting-points, new slogans, which—foreshadowed in Marx—became in Lenin the basis for the most brilliant political leadership, perhaps, that this world has seen. It inculcated this free and fluid, and nevertheless inflexibly purposive manner of thinking, before it could have been learned from the evolutionary science of social formations and of the human mind.

It is not true, as Marxians assert, that Marx brought into the social theories of the eighteenth century rationalists the idea of development, and taught them to regard society as a totality and not just a dog-pile of individuals. Both the study of society as an organic whole, and the study of that whole as in a state of evolution, grew up out of the views of the eighteenth-century rationalist, pushed on by the general development of evolutionary science, without the slightest influence from Marx's working-class philosophy of dialectic materialism. It is true, however, that with his metaphysical conception of society and the mind as cooperatively evolving on a dialectic pattern toward the goal he wanted it to reach, Marx anticipated a social engineering attitude, and invented a technique of engineering with class forces, which might have been a very late result of that more purely scientific development. Just as Hegel forestalled the scientists with his conservative metaphysics, so Marx with his revolutionary metaphysics was far ahead of them in the technique of social action. That may give us a tolerant respect for dialectic materialism, and for the whole German romantic movement in philosophy, but it is, of course, no reason for clinging to a system that is unscientific.

There are two other facts, however, which make it hard to escape from Marx's wish-fulfillment system, and yet retain his scientific contribution and hold to his technique of revolution. One is that social science, when it is applied in action on a grand scale, does differ from physical or mechanical or any other kind of engineering in that the scientists themselves are a part of the material they work with, and *what they think about the experiment may affect its result*. That gives to the dialectic myth bound up in scientific socialism a value similar to that at times possessed by the Christian Science myth in the eyes of a neuro-pathologist. True and resolutely practical science does not hesitate on that account, of course, to explode the myth and face the problem that results. It merely finds an obstacle of genuine though limited utility to overcome.

A similar, though still more limited utility, is the emotional ease with which this cosmic objectification of their plans enables the scientific intellectuals, the "professional revolutionists" as Lenin called them, to identify themselves with the spontaneous movement of the working class. The idea that the socialist thinker, who comes almost inevitably from other classes, is merely "bringing the proletariat a consciousness of its own destiny," enables him to avoid a certain appearance of patronizing, or "putting something over on," the proletariat. His theory-program is a mere "mental reflection" of the proletariat's evolutionary position; his own class origin is incidental; the proletariat would, moreover, in the long run evolve its own consciousness and reach its goal without him. He can at best accelerate the inevitable.

This nicety of the dialectic conception inculcates a mood of humble cooperativeness in the *intelligentsia* that can hardly be denied a value on occasions. Nevertheless it is just this nicety that Lenin over-stepped so rudely in his book *What To Do*, which laid the foundations for the Bolshevik triumph.

These subtleties of emotional equilibrium are worth nothing in the long run compared to a clear vision of the facts. And the fact that Marx's dialectic philosophy, with all its wish to be "scientific," and even to out-science the scientists, is a survival of the intellectual machinery with which over-soulful people have kept up in the face of science wish-fulfillment thoughts about the world. It is an elaborate device for reading the plans of the communists into their description of the developing objective facts. The world is on our side, it teaches them. The real and the motion toward our ideal are the same thing. In order to perceive with accuracy, we must conceive with prejudice.

THE SCOPE OF MARXIAN THEORY

By SIDNEY HOOK

In a recent book an English critic refers to Marxism as the opium of the socialist orthodox. If one examines what Marxism means to most socialist and communist parties throughout the world to-day, i.e., to those which *profess* themselves Marxist, it will be found that the characterization is quite apt. For a variety of reasons, "orthodox" Marxists, and particularly communists, have turned Marxism into a philosophy of the universe relevant to every domain of knowledge and every field of human activity. From the movement of planets and electrons in their orbits, to the action of classes and parties no question has ever arisen upon which orthodox Marxists have not felt competent to speak. For after all, are not the laws of dialectic universal? Indeed, the analogy drawn in many quarters between orthodox Marxism and religion is unfair to religion, for most contemporary religions, in their ideology at least, restrict themselves to half-hearted affirmations of ethical ideals. One must go back to the great traditional religions to find anything which matches orthodox Marxism in the pretension of its claims, and in the intensity with which a monistic world-view is asserted.

It is easy to deny that Marxism is a systematic doctrine of the universe, society and man, and not very difficult to show that such interpretations rest upon a neglect of the context and intent of Marx's own writings. It is not so easy, however, to define adequately the scope of Marxian theory and to distinguish it on the one hand, from a cosmic religious opiate, and on the other, from the narrow view that Marxism is nothing but a set of economic doctrines. I shall try to sketch briefly what I regard the legitimate province of

Marxism to be without at this time discussing or evaluating any of Marx's specific doctrines or conclusions.

If a man's life has any connection with his thought, then Marx's revolutionary activity should provide the clue to the central purpose of his thinking. Whatever Marxism may mean to the disciples, there can be no question but that to Marx it meant the theory and practice of the proletarian revolution. Every one of his doctrines was a generalization of an historic experience in the class struggle or a proposed solution of some problem in that struggle. I propose frankly to take the defining purpose of Marx's life and thought as the point of departure for determining the scope of Marxian theory. Without such a point of departure we have no way of determining what is directly relevant, what is peripheral, and what is irrelevant to Marxism and run the danger of talking *ins Blau hinein* or narrowing Marxism to some special doctrine.

If Marxism is the theory and practice of social revolution in capitalist society, then its first consideration must be a persistent and critical survey of all the social and political factors which affect the possibilities of successful political action. Obstacles to the achievement of our ends are always experienced as the most relevant and pressing factors, and the chief obstacle to the realization of the proletarian revolution, it is obvious, is the existence of the state power and apparatus. Consequently one of the prime concerns of Marxism is the theory and practice of the state, its overt and hidden role in the class struggle, the social and economic factors which influence at different times its form, expression and ideology. Historically it is interesting to know that in his critical reaction against Hegel's philosophy of law, it was the Hegelian theory of the state which Marx overthrew first. The initial impulse to question the Hegelian theory was derived from first hand observations of the way in which the state *functioned* in relation to the German problems of freedom of education, freedom of press, provision for the poor, and, later, in the weavers' revolts. (In passing, we must note that the traditional German social-democratic emasculation of Marx—now shared by the Communist Party —lies precisely in its unrealistic approach to the question of state power.) If the state is, as Marx held, the executive committee of the ruling class—and this must always be shown by an analysis of legislative practices, the use of executive power, judicial decisions, etc.—then no working class party can share the existing political power, or once established as a government, tolerate the existence of the old state machinery without abandoning the standpoint of the class struggle, or rather the class struggle from the point of view of proletarian interests and the proletarian revolution.

Now although the nature of the state structure and function is always important, it becomes *focally* important only in a period when the question of the conquest of power is on the order of the day. The precise instrumentalities to be employed, peaceful or not, are functions of the concrete historical situation and depend just as much upon what opponents of Marxism do as upon the intelligence of Marxists. But antecedent to the attempted conquest of power, one must develop a working conception of the social conditions under which such an attempt can be made, and conditions under which such an attempt can *succeed*. It is the failure to do this which distinguished Blanquism from Marxism. For Blanquism a social revolution is a live possibility at any time and place; for Marxism the revolution is the critical point in a social process which must first be understood before the final action which actualizes it can be launched. Here again Marx's own experience is vitally reflected in the development of Marx's thought. After the defeat of the revolution of 1848 Marx devoted himself to the great task of discovering the laws and tendencies of capitalist production in order to determine not only the reasons for the failure of the revolution but the perspectives of future political action. The economic doctrines of Marx in their specific Marxian form were projected as integral parts of the central problems of the coming social revolution and not merely as the formal equations of doom of capitalist society. They indicated the nature and periodic rhythms of capitalist decline, how the objective conditions of the new social order are generated by the imminent processes of the old, and why the working class must be the base of the socialist revolution and not some other class. This knowledge, scorned by the impatient revolutionists of the Blanquist stripe, became essential to realistic political action. Indeed the kind of economics in which the Marxist is interested, why and what he selects out of the infinite complexity of available data, can only be explained in terms of a contemplated *program of action* which he checks and modifies in its light. Whether Marx's economic predictions have been realized, and whether if they have been realized the logical analysis by which he arrived at them is valid, are questions which do not concern us in this context.

But now it must be observed that knowledge of economic tendencies although essential to revolutionary action is not sufficient. If the economic factors were the *only* ones that counted, the social revolution in the western world would have occurred long ago. So long as history is made by men, their sentiments, passions, traditions and religious allegiances—conditioned as they may be by economic causes—have an influence upon social development which cannot be reduced to, or intelligibly explained in, economic terms. The economic analysis may show that some things are impossible: by itself, however, it cannot establish the fact that any thing *must* be. From the point of view of the revolutionary process and the revolutionary act, the Marxist must take into account all those—to use one synoptic term—*"psychological"* factors which bear upon the conquest of political power.

Theoretically and practically, the most serious failures of Marxism have arisen from inability to evaluate properly extra-economic factors which bear upon the problems of political power. Indeed, out of a self-imposed intellectual terror most Marxists have feared to introduce and interpret other factors, for fear of falling into revisionism. Instead they have either denied the efficacy of these factors or have sought to reduce them to economic terms. After all, economic facts are more or less measurable while traditions, national and religious feelings are not. And a mistaken theory of science which has held that only what is measurable can be scientifically treated has been even more confused by a mistaken philosophy which holds that only what can be scientifically treated exists. But nationalism and fascism indicate that it is possible to measure poverty, and yet not be able to measure its political effects; that it is possible to establish statistically the decline of capitalism and yet be unable to predict on that data alone the quality, expression and direction of the resentment which the decline generates.

The view that economic realities *alone* are the guide to understanding and action is not Marxian and leads to a vulgarization of Marx's theory of historical materialism. All ideals are viewed as a form of self-interest and it is presupposed that every one knows what his real interests are. Such a theory of motivation, however, is patently inadequate to the facts of the class-struggle and especially to the activity, heroism and sacrifice of the most revolutionary elements within it. The simple truth which Marx stressed against the Utopians that ideals and values cannot be pursued for long by men who have no bread has been converted into the proposition that all ideals and values are merely the instruments by which bread is secured. An adequate statement of Marxism must reassert those larger ideals which were so much a part of the socialist movement of his time that Marx did not regard it as necessary to make them explicit. It is all the more necessary to do this in view of the newer movements which have arisen which seek to catch men's enthusiasm for causes that threaten the very existence of civilization.

The whole question becomes clearer if we go back to our starting point to complete the definition of Marxism as the theory and practice of proletarian revolution. It is clear that the proletarian revolution or the conquest of power is not an end in itself. It is the use to which political power is to be put which constitutes its justification. It is the conception of a society in which the assurance of material plenty makes possible the greatest realization of those ideal goods which the seers, prophets and philosophers have taught to be the constituents of the good life and the good society—intelligence, courage, humanity and creative activity. Of course these are terms which the Marxian analysis has shown to be differently interpreted in different times by different classes. But they have an unchanging nucleus of meaning to which the nature of man in society, especially in conflict, always responds. There is nothing incompatible with Marxism in coupling together these larger ideals with specific economic interests and motivations, the multitude of short time levers by which the revolutionary movement advances. Without these larger ideals it is unlikely that people will stake their lives and fortunes in struggle; without these ideals the argument that in liberating itself, the working class liberates the whole of society, cannot be plausibly sustained. That is why Marxism is something more than a matter of social engineering, something more than a cut and dried method by which a group of intellectuals calling themselves social-engineers puts the revolution over by using the working class as so much material or so much energy in an engineering construction. Those whose Marxist consciences are uneasy and who ask for the sacred texts on this point can be supplied with them. But it is not a question of texts; it is a question of what is implied in the recognition that a revolution, as Marx understood it, is not an end in itself but a means of achieving Socialism; it is a question of what the Marxists must oppose to the Nazi hosts whose unctuous idealism, compounded of passionate lies, illusions and mythology as it may be, is demogogically effective because it is based on the insight that man cannot live and be moved by negations alone.

Another point which must be stressed today is the essentially democratic character of Socialism as Marx conceived it. By the phrase "dictatorship of the proletariat" (used only twice in print) Marx understood a workers' democracy, administered by representative councils of *all* producers, functioning repressively against minority groups only when the latter are guilty of overt action. Marx emphatically did not mean by the "dictatorship of the proletariat" a dictatorship of a minority political party enjoying a monopoly of political power, and permitting only that degree of freedom to citizen-producers which insures the perpetuation of its own hegemony.

We now come to the problem of Marxism and culture. The Marxian attitude to any given culture complex is twofold. On the one hand, the Marxist seeks evidence for the hypothesis that the fundamental social relations of production influence the character, extent and development of cultural activity: on the other, he seeks to reveal and oppose the manifold ways in which different tendencies in culture create the psychological blockages,—emotional attitudes and intellectual habits—that stand in the way of revolutionizing the masses. His attitude to existing culture is, therefore, essentially critical. He is always asking: whom does this serve? What are the social consequences of this cultural pattern or text? In what way does this method of interpreting life and experience bear upon working class activity? In making inquiries of this kind it is not the function of the Marxist under capitalism to *create* a culture *de novo*. This does not of course deny that the movement produces a characteristic culture of revolt in song, literature and social thought. But this is something quite different from the attitude taken by orthodox dialectical materialists in Russia and the official Communist Parties of the world who try to apply some mythical party line in evaluating the validity of doctrine and technical achievement in all fields. Such an attitude presupposes that every aspect of culture from the theory of numbers to the science of philology is equally relevant to the class-struggle; something which only a cultural barbarian could assert. To be sure, the Marxist critically examines the findings of modern science, not to lay down the mumbo-jumbo formulae or laws of the "yes-no" dialectical logic to the scientist, but merely to expose and oppose the illegitimate excursions of the doctrines of the physical sciences into social affairs. He shows, for example, that, although the biological premises of Conklin, Osborn and other geneticists with reactionary political penchants, may be true, their social views, presumably based upon these premises, are elaborate *non-sequiturs*. He lays bare the peculiar mystical philosophy and obscurantism which leads Eddington and Jeans into claiming that the jump of electrons from one atomic orbit to another establishes the existence of free will: he does not, as some orthodox dialectical materialists have done, maintain that these electronic jumps furnish an additional argument for social *revolution* as against continuous social evolution.

The dangers of trying to determine what the correct point of view in *all* fields of culture must be on the basis of correct political lines are best illustrated in the intellectual debacle of orthodox Marxism in the field of anthropology. Here orthodox Marxists still cling to Morgan's anthropology almost every one of whose leading ideas has been decisively rejected by the scientific field workers. Indeed, had Marxists familiarized themselves with, and disseminated, the critical findings of the American school of anthropologists on the nature of race, with half the zealousness with which they propagated Morgan's outworn views, the Nazi mythology of race would not have taken hold so easily in Germany and elsewhere.

The Marxist tries to show how social conditions under capitalism, whatever the benefits of their initial impulse may have been, *now* exercise a distorting effect upon most cultural activity. He uses as an additional argument for the classless society, the freedom which the physicist, mathematician or musician can enjoy to work out his own problems undisturbed by the impact of irrelevant economic obstacles or difficulties. That is to say, the intellectual and artist can work either in conjunction with those who are active in the organization of production or pursue his own theoretical bent once his competence is established. But in either case voluntarily. From this point of view, the Marxist can contend that he is interested in preserving all genuine culture and in providing the social milieu in which a new culture—class or class-less—so long as it be rich in meaning and diversified in form, can flourish.

It follows from the foregoing that Marxism is not a complete system of sociology and certainly not exclusively an economic doctrine. All of its propositions have a specific historic context and presupposition. That is why both Marx and Engels always insisted upon the historical character of their leading principles, viz: the class struggle, historical materialism and theory of value. Their abstract generalizations once divorced from the concrete situations of social life today are either meaningless or quite definitely false. This account of the meaning of Marxian theory makes intelligible the role which Marx assigned to the political party in educating, organizing and leading the masses, and in supplying a principle of continuity in the vicissitudes of struggle. It also makes intelligible why the Marxian theory itself can function as an historical force. In other words, it recognizes that knowledge and intelligence make a difference—which is indeed no more than a direct, but sadly overlooked implication, of the doctrine of the unity between theory and practice. This is a far cry from the customary fatalism read into Marxist theory by most of its friends and foes. If knowledge and intelligence make a difference, then any form of dogma whether it be expressed as *a priori* rationalism or voluntaristic irrationalism must be ruled out as foreign to the spirit of Marxian theory. And to those who feel that this account lacks the simplicity and assurance of certainty necessary to bring people into motion, it can easily be demonstrated that a recognition of the complexity of the social and historical process and the tentative character of the conclusions reached is not at all incompatible with resolute action in behalf of goals chosen after reflection.

SOCIOLOGICAL CRITICISM OF LITERATURE *

By V. F. CALVERTON

THE time when literature was considered the product of a supernatural afflatus or peculiar impartation of spirit or impulse has disappeared. The passing of this notion has been a very simple and perceptible phenomenon. Explanations and descriptions of it have been legion. The advance of science with its revelations of both sidereal and terrestrial activity, and the consequent decline of other-wordly conceptions, the change from the deductive to the inductive method, created a different attitude toward man and his achievements. This change and progress in thought and science have been an inevitable reflection of the steadily transforming material conditions of present and past centuries. Creative and critical composition, if we must make that division for the moment, have altered both in style and substance with each of the vicissitudes of social evolution. The criteria of excellence have varied with each advancing epoch. Literature of the "impossible" and "improbable" cast, which fascinated one age, suffice but to dull and stupefy another; pictures of court and chivalry, the gilded pageantry of palace and field, the sunny romance of knight and lady, which captivated the imagination of artists and critics of olden centuries, no longer allure. The demand for the inevitable and the real becomes as vital a part of the literary creed as the scientific. The tendencies of art, religion, and science are but the interwoven threads of the social texture.

Theories of scientific criticism urged by Hennequin and James M. Robertson are no more than the necessary extension of sociological development into the critical realm. The idea of Mr. Mencken that the excellency of an author's

* From: *The Newer Spirit*.

writing may depend upon nothing more exalted than the activity of his pylorus, and Mr. W. Huntington Wright's, that literary creation is merely a form of physico-chemical reaction, are likewise similar manifestations of this sociological trend. The application of the biographical method to criticism is but part of this same phase. Taine's progress in the examination of literature as the product of telluric and social environment is no more singular, although more happily significant. All are common, and in no way surprising, expressions of our modern age of industrial and scientific growth. They could be characteristic of no other age.

As we continue to cautiously and minutely study the literature of any race or period, then, we eventually discover that all of the theories and concepts, the dicta and shibboleths, of creative and critical effort are but the outgrowths of the social system in which they have their being, and which in turn is the product of the material conditions of the time. This point we shall illustrate at considerable length. Under feudalism, for instance, we shall show that the literary conceptions which prevailed were in consonance with the social structure and did not change until the latter began to alter. In similar manner we shall picture the changes in social environment that brought with them the different literary concepts and tactics of the eighteenth and nineteenth centuries. And finally we shall consider the complex expansion of science and industry during the latter part of the nineteenth and beginning of the twentieth centuries, and its effects upon the form and substance of contemporary literature.

Social classes develop within one another. There is no fixed line of demarcation to determine the precise moment of their birth and extinction. Caused by newly arising conditions, they spring into existence slowly or swiftly according to the nature of the exigency, and for considerable period are quite overlapping entities. The bourgeois class, for example, was a gradual growth in the very heart of feudal society. Developing primarily as a result of the industrial changes circling about the Renaissance: the inventions of gunpowder, printing with movable type, the compass, the manufacture of paper on a large scale, and the extension of commerce with the Orient, it did not become permanently dominant until the disappearance of feudalism, or cause any enduring changes in literature until the beginning of the eighteenth century. That does not mean, as some might suppose, that previous to the eighteenth century, literature was entirely unaffected by its rise, but that the effects were too scattered and incoherent to create a distinct and lasting change of literary trend. In the seventeenth century, for instance, the bourgeois class in England rose in successful rebellion against the nobility, and for eleven years established a government of their own, which was characterized by all the extensions and restrictions of the puritanic bourgeois conceptions of the period. The progress of theatrics was temporarily interrupted, and the mundane in literature was supplanted by the religious. The romantic poetry of the Elizabethans was succeeded by the sombre metaphysical lyrics of Daniel, Breton, Donne and Herbert. The change, however, though sharp was ephemeral. The Restoration brought with it a swift return to the older conceptions and manners. The recoil, for a time, was virulent and excessive. This bourgeois incursion then, as we shall see, wrought no fundamental and permanent change in esthetic theory or practice. Nevertheless, coming as a consequence of economic difficulties forced upon them by the tyrannic taxation of the king, it furnishes incontestable proof of the rising potency of the bourgeois class at the time. It was not to be until some decades later, however, that its class concepts were to become a steadily ruling element in the social and esthetic consciousness of the time.

The attitude toward tragedy that prevailed throughout the feudal period and continued to persist over much of Europe until the bourgeois revolution of 1789, is interesting and conclusive illustration of this division of class-psychology caused by the existing types of social structure. Since the time of Aristotle, tragedy was considered the loftiest form of literary art, and to its construction have been devoted the highest artistic energies of man. The psychological reasons, reduced to their material motives, why tragedy has been conceived in such exalted fashion need not be discussed in this essay.

Feudal society, dependent upon agricultural production, was the necessary outgrowth of the various systems of slavery that preceded it. Its apex, the nobility, was the class that determined and fostered the leading conceptions of the age; the manners of court, the practice of chivalry, the system of judicature, the pursuance of the arts, the metaphysics of the period—all were products of the peculiar agrarian system of production and distribution that then existed. The religious class, in possession of extensive and fertile lands, came into conflict with the nobility only when the latter threatened usurpation of church territory, and in general worked for the perpetuation of the feudal regime. The burghers of the town, as we mentioned earlier in our discussion, became influential only as feudalism started to decline. And these esthetic and ethical concepts which prevailed, and that were but the patent reflections of the character of the reigning class, were defended with sincere and unremitting zeal and justified as "absolute."

There is perhaps no clearer evidence of precisely how the ideas of a community, those of its artists and critics, statesmen and metaphysicians, are determined by the nature of material conditions, from which arise the structure of society than that afforded by the esthetic concept of tragedy. Until the eighteenth century, when the bourgeois class had acquired sufficient power to exert a permanent influence upon social conceptions, the attitude towards tragedy was uniformly feudal and aristocratic. The distinction between higher and lower drama, tragedy and comedy, throughout the Middle Ages and extending to the decline and decease of feudalism, was considered by critics as being fundamentally a distinction of social status. Tragedy could be concerned only with noble characters—the illustrious—and to conceive it as being written about a bourgeois protagonist would have been literary sacrilege. If, for a moment, we consider the writings of that French classicist, Abbe d'Aubignac (1604-76), we shall discover an explicit statement of this attitude. Tragedy, says d'Aubignac, "inheres not in the nature of the catastrophe but in the rank of persons." W. H. Hudson in *A Quiet Corner of the Library* cites the statements of many writers to similar effect. The other French classicists were equally firm in their position. Pellitier, Ronsard, de Laudun, Vauquelin de la Fresnay, Pelet de la Mesnardière, each supported the aristocratic theory of tragedy, and wrote as if a deviation from it were an impossibility. Voltaire, a radical in so many things, and whose death occurred only eleven years before the bourgeois revolution in France, was certain that tragedy required characters elevated above the common level. Even Joubert, in the memorable *Encyclopedie,* declared that tragedy is "the imitation of the lives and speech of heroes, subject by their elevation to passions and catastrophes as well as to the manifestations of virtues, of the most illustrious kind." It must not be forgotten that at the time, the *Encyclopedie,* under the organization of Diderot, made pretensions to advance to modernism, unrivalled by any other literary or scientific production. The Italian humanists in no case dissented from the aristocratic theory of tragedy. The German pseudo-classicists, Opitz and Gottsched, the dictators of literary taste in Germany during a century and a half, the former during the most of the seventeenth and the latter during the first half of the eighteenth, were in avowed agreement with the classicist attitude. In his *Buch von der Deutschen Poeterey* (1624), Opitz gave the aristocratic interpretation to poetry, and later in *Versuch einer Critische Dichtkunst vor die Deutschen* in 1730, Gottsched continued the same criticism. The following quotation from Opitz, for instance, clearly represents the attitude of these German classicists toward tragedy:

Tragedy . . . seldom permits the introduction of people of humble or common deeds, because it deals with only royal decrees, murders, despairs, slaughters of fathers and children, fires, incests, wars and rebellions, lamentations, outcries, sighs, and the like. Comedy has to do with ordinary matters and persons; it speaks of weddings, banquets, games, tricks and knaveries of serving men, bragging foot-soldiers, love affairs, frivolity of youth, avarice of old age, match-making, and such things which daily occur among the common people.

Gottsched, in his *Critische Dichtkunst,* expresses in terms no less unequivocal the same sentiment:

> If you wish to have a comedy of your subject, the persons must be citizens; for heroes and princes belong in a tragedy. Tragedy is distinguished from comedy only in this, that, instead of laughter, it tries to arouse wonder, terror and pity; therefore it usually concerns itself with men of birth only, who are conspicuous by their rank, name, and appearance. In an epic, which is the masterpiece of all poetry, the persons must be the most impressive in the world, kings, heroes, and great statesmen, and everything in it must sound majestic, strange and wonderful.

The very titles of certain of the romances and tragedies of the period are an interesting and significant index to its social trend: Bucholz's *Pleasant Romance of the Royal Prince Herculiscus and Herculadisla and their Princely Company,* (1659); Ziegler's *The Asiatic Banise, or Bloody but Courageous Pegu, Based on Historic Truth but Covered with the Veil of a Pleasing Story of Heroic Love-Adventure,* (1688); and Lohenstein's *The Magnanimous General Arminus, with his Illustrious Thusnelda, Held up to the German Nobility as an Honourable Example and for Praiseworthy Emulation,* (1689).

But do we discover dissenting voices in England at the time?—England to which so many panegyrics of liberty have been dedicated. The attitude of their artists and critics is clear and inflexible. For tragedy only the great can be characters; the "dignity of persons," to employ the phrase of Ben Jonson used in this reference, is a necessity if tragedy is to possess elements of the sublime. Such was the avowed attitude of Stubbes, Puttenham, Gosson, Webbe, and Harrington, the eminent critics in the era of the romantic drama, and no deviation from it is to be noted in the writings of Ben Jonson, whom we quoted above, or any of the Restorationists. Rymer contended that tragedy "required not only what is natural, but what is great (noble) in nature." Both Congreve and Dryden declared in favor of the aristocratic conception of tragedy; in Dryden's words "tragedy, as we know, is wont to image to us the minds and fortunes of noble persons," and in those of Congreve, tragedy "distinguishes itself for vulgar poetry by the dignity of its characters." Even Oliver Goldsmith, the son of a poor curate, a pale struggling genius acquainted with all of the pain and torture of deprivation, maintained that "the distresses of the mean (the middle and poorer classes) by no means affect us so strongly as the calamities of the great." There is no question, therefore, that the aristocratic conception of tragedy was not an isolated, sporadic phenomenon, but a widespread, generally accepted theory.*

The dramas of Shakespeare can be taken as fitting examples of the application of the feudal concept. There have been many, aside from Tolstoi and Shaw, who have attacked Shakespeare for what they call his narrowness of vision, his bigoted reverence for the aristocracy and blatant contempt for the rabble. We might as well attack Plato for considering soldiers an important class in the state, a class to be studied and promoted, and fighting an art to be developed and practiced—or Aristotle for not condemning slavery, the institution that made it possible for Greece at the time to progress and flourish. These strictures, of course, remain, the environment that produced them notwithstanding. It is the environment however, that makes them explicable—and inevitable. Shakespeare did nothing more than represent the esthetic conceptions of his period. In weaving every tragedy about the struggles of the noble and the illustrious, he violated no concept of his age. Both the commoner and the bourgeois were subjects of humor and satire, the

* For certain data presented in this essay credit must be acknowledged to Kuno Francke's "History of German Literature," and to the literary research of William H. Hudson and Ernest Crosby, all of which authors caught hints of the effects of material conditions but did not attempt to coordinate the facts assembled.

means of affording comedy to the situation and relieving tenseness in the drama. The humbler classes, as they were called, appear often under titles themselves ludicrous enough to indicate the nature of their treatment: Quince, the Carpenter; Snug, the Joiner; Starveling, the Tailor; Smooth, the Silkman; Bottom, the Weaver; and Flute, the Bellows-maker. In *Midsummer Nights Dream,* for instance, most of the trades are ridiculed. In all of Shakespeare's works with but a few exceptions, one in *Richard II,* where we find a loyal servant, another in *Cymbeline,* still another in *King Lear,* several in *Timon of Athens,* one in the *Winter's Tale,* two in *Anthony and Cleopatra*—all servants, shepherds or soldiers, who are pictured as faithful and honest—we find unflattering pictures of both proletarian and tradesman. Of the lower class as a whole, the dramatist is even more satirical. In one place characterized as "hempen-homespuns," another as "the barren sort," in still another as "mechanic slaves, with greasy aprons, rules and hammers"; he goes still further in *Coriolanus* to speak of the "stinking breath of the commoner" and decry them as "the mutable, rank-scented many," "garlic eaters," "multiplying spawn," "worthless peasants," "rude unpolished hinds," all phrases consistent with the aristocratic attitude of the time. In *Hamlet,* Shakespeare laments the seeming rise of the lower strata and declares that "the age has grown so picked, that the toe of the peasant comes so near the heel of the courtier, he galls his kibe." Then in *Henry IV* he sneers at the famous rebellion of Wat Tyler, the "damned commotion," which he describes as coming "in base and abject routs, led on by bloody youth, guarded with rags, and countenanced by beggary." In *Pericles* the dramatist proclaims that "princes are a model, which heaven makes like to itself," and in *Henry VI* he has the Duke of York denounce the "mean-born man," and in *Henry VI,* Joan of Arc is made to speak of her "contemptible estate." This reference to Shakespeare was made only because his works so excellently illustrate how the esthetic and ethical ideas of the feudal period were expressed in literature, and stand out in such sharp and striking contrast to the changing conceptions of later centuries.

And from whence could such a conception arise? The Hegelian idealist with his thesis of the absolute might attempt to explain it as the logical development of the absolute idea. But, to us, this appears ridiculously illogical. We can readily perceive how such a conception, of necessity, must have arisen from the material conditions that created the feudal regime. So long as the nobility remained the ruling class, the administering and not the administered, it would be a sociological solecism to expect ideas to be other than reflections of the aristocratic, courtly attitude. In no instance in history do we discover such a solecism. The aristocratic conception of tragedy, therefore, continued so long as feudalism existed, and when the system of feudalism could no longer function, the declining nobility steadily becoming more and more dependent upon the rising bourgeoisie, and had to recede in favor of another system of more adequate and satisfactory dimensions, the concept faded into a myth. That this process of the decline and disappearance of the aristocratic concept was purely a matter of change of social environment, which at basis was due to the failure of feudalism to adapt itself to the demands of its growing communities, was unquestionably proven by the sequence of "bourgeois" tragedy, concomitant with the ascent of the bourgeois class.

In England feudalism experienced a more rapid retrogression than in any other European country. Due to its peninsular location, which afforded a sense of security and protection, a merchant class was an early historical necessity, and in correspondence with the growth of towns and commerce this class became augmented. In France, for example, where the land was part of the continent, without peninsular advantages or handicaps, the bourgeois class did not revolt until over one hundred and forty years after the bloody revolution of the bourgeoisie in England. As a consequence, we find bourgeois concepts, political and esthetic, developing in

England long before France, and Voltaire's letters, therefore, appear in no way singular. The political and judicial
liberty for which England, in every history, has been so
conspicuously noted, then, was ultimately the result of this
geographic and economic factor.

In England, it follows, if our logic be correct, we should
locate the first deviations from the aristocratic conception.
And so we do. The play that is commonly referred to as
marking the origin of *tragedie bourgeoise* in England is
Lillo's *The London Merchant* which was staged by Theo-
philus Cibber in 1731. The tragedy of this play is concerned
with the moral decay and execution of a merchant's appren-
tice, George Barnwell, whose end was so dismal because he
failed to live a life of sincerity and rectitude. In brief, the
play is an encomium of bourgeois virtues made emphatic by
frequent moral lessons and sharp condemnations of all way-
ward traits. This play received more comment and laudation than perhaps any other play of the century. It was acted before crowded audiences, night after night in the heat
of mid-summer, and drew the patronage and praise of poet
and critic. Within a few years five authorized editions of it
were printed. Pope, amid the clamor of court and forum,
gave the tragedy his commendation. Later the play won the
attention and admiration of Rousseau, Marmontel, Prevost,
Lessing, Goethe, Schiller and the extravagant eulogy of
Diderot. In 1796 its theme was worked into a novel by
Thomas Skinner Surr, and afterwards memoirs of George
Barnwell and a life history were written. It was acted by a
number of famous actors and actresses, among whom were
Charles Kemble, Mrs. Siddons and Sir Henry Irving. Considered by our present dramatic standards, *The London
Merchant* is a fifth-rate production. Its homilies are ludicrous, its characters stilted and unnatural, including the merchant Thorowgood, and its points of dramatic intensity almost laughably unconvincing. From a historical standpoint,
however, as we have noted, the tragedy is significant.

It is necessary to admit, of course, that *The London Mer-*

chant was not the first tragedy in English which was constructed about bourgeois characters. No social movement can be said to have expressed itself in any single moment or episode; the expression is usually gradual and hints of its coming appear long before its arrival. In Heywood's *A Woman Killed With Kindness* we have an early suggestion of the rising trend and in Otway's *Orphan,* Southern's *Fatal Marriage,* and Rowe's *Fair Penitent* we meet with even more marked evidences of the Domestic Tragedy. Yet none of these tragedies possess the thoroughly bourgeois character of *The London Merchant,* or, for that matter, of the two famous plays that followed Lillo's tragedy: *The Gamester* and *The Mysterious Husband,* and cannot be considered as anything more than mild and minor predecessors.

As the bourgeois class, with the steady decline of feudalism, continued to rise in other countries, the aristocratic conception waned. In Germany, for instance, we find Lessing acting the part of the revolutionist. His play *Miss Sarah Simpson,* which appeared in 1755, was the first German tragedy of bourgeois life. His achievement in this drama was very similar to that of George Lillo in *The London Merchant* and Edward Moore in *The Gamester.* This, of course, was a complete departure from the theories of Opitz and Gottsched, and later was explained and justified by Lessing in his critical writings. It is important to observe here that with all of his radical notions as to dramatic theme and technique, and even his attack upon Frederick he still clung to a kind of nationalist sentiment that the internationalist of the twentieth century would ridicule. In *Minna van Barnheim* he devoted himself to a description of "a people beginning to feel itself again as a whole, and to be again conscious of national responsibilities." It would be illogical, from a sociological viewpoint, to expect Lessing to have been otherwise. In *Emilia Galloti* (1772) he fought against the oppression of the bourgeoisie by the aristocracy; from the play, according to Francke, can be traced the beginnings of the battles carried on by the *"Sturm und Drang"* movement. In

France, Nivelle de la Chaussee and Diderot were the inno-
vators of the *tragedie bourgeoise,* and later Saurin, the
author of *Beverly,* an adaptation of Moore's *Gamester,* in the
century following, extended the *tragedie bourgeoise* to include a wider scope.

So long as the supremacy of the bourgeoisie remained unquestioned, which was certainly the case until the appearance
of the modern utopians, Pierre le Roux, Fourier and Saint
Simon, there could be but two kinds of ethical and esthetic
conceptions, one dominant, the bourgeois, the other recessive
or vestigial, the aristocratic. If we take America during the
period immediately following the Revolutionary War, we
shall discover a fruitful illustration of the effects of bourgeois ascendancy. One would scarcely expect, nor does he
find, in a country that has just experienced a triumph of its
bourgeoisie, a literature devoted to the praise either of its
aristocracy or its proletariat. In a nation where Madison
and Pinckney disagreed as to the three classes for which the
Constitution should provide, Madison being in favor of
the landed, the commercial, and the manufacturing, and
Pinckney in favor of the professional, the landed, and the
commercial, neither believing the proletariat worthy of consideration, it would be contrary to social evolution to find
literary themes revolving about the tragic struggles and tribulations of proletarian characters. In no work of the period
do we see the proletarian accepted as fit character for
tragedy, or his adversity pictured in bold but sympathetic
line and color. Irving used him as a source of sport and
satire, Cooper as a frontiersman to combat his fantastic,
rainbow-plumed Indians, and Franklin as suitable object for
bourgeois sermons on thrift and wisdom. Neither can the
verse of Freneau, Barlow, Hopkinson and Drake, nor the
prose of Jefferson, Washington or Brockdon Brown be said
to have treated him in gentler fashion. In England, as we
have described, the proletarian now served as material for
wit and comedy. In France and Germany, where de la
Chaussee and Lessing had emancipated the stage from the

aristocratic conception, the proletarian remained subservient to the bourgeoisie, the ascending class.

In the first stages of capitalism the distinction between the bourgeois and the proletarian is not as wide and definite and not so difficult to bridge, as in its later stages, when, through the increase and concentration of its mass, it steadily dispossesses and enlarges its lower element and fortifies and narrows its upper. As this dispossessing process continues, unless there is some disturbing and deceptive factor, such as the free-land policy, which we found in America during the nineteenth century, the class-consciousness of the dispossessed class grows in ratio with the degree of dispossession. Until this process has developed and intensified there is no significant class-organization, and without organization a class cannot impress itself upon the activity of a society, or function as a determinant of its basic conceptions. During this period, the incipiency of capitalism, for instance, the bourgeoisie exercised supreme and unquestioned authority; the first labor unions did not organize in America until about 1805 or 1810, over forty-five years after the beginning of the Industrial Revolution, and their organization approximated nothing extensive or involved until the sixties or seventies. The Haymarket episode, of course, weakened the purpose and temporarily wrecked much of this later complexity of organization. These labor organizations, distinct products of class-consciousness, came as the inevitable result of the increasing concentration of capital. With this steady rise of the proletarian, his organization into a definite class, with definite class-interests, and with the acquisition of certain educational priviliges necessary to his expression, society was driven into acknowledgment of the reality and importance of his existence, and consequently he became a force in the molding of social conceptions. James Russell Lowell was one of the voices of this trend. In his Birmingham address in 1864, just two years before the Haymarket riot, he revealed how very profoundly the rise of the proletariat had affected his ideas and changed his attitude:

What is really ominous of danger to the existing order of things is not democracy, (which, properly understood, is a conservative force), but the socialism which may find a fulcrum in it. If we cannot equalize conditions and fortunes any more than we can equalize the brains of men— and a very sagacious person has said that "where two men ride of a horse, one must ride behind"—we can yet, perhaps, do something to correct these methods and influences that lead to enormous inequalities, and to prevent their growing more enormous . . . Communism means barbarism, but Socialism means, or wishes to mean, cooperation and community of interests, sympathy, the giving to the hands not so large a share as to the brains, but a larger share than hitherto in the wealth they must combine to produce—means, in short, the practical application of Christianity to life, and has in it the secret of an orderly and benign reconstruction.

Although this is what we should classify as sentimental or utopian socialism, it nevertheless is an interesting reflection of the movement of thought caused by the change in material conditions which brought the proletariat into economical and political significance.

Walt Whitman was a finer product of this trend. Into more genuinely poetic, although more mystical, phraseology did he put its aspirations and dreams. With Whitman we find the proletarian no longer the inferior, the source of sport and travesty, but a being infused with the same elements of power and excellence as the heroic general or statesman, a being capable of the deepest thoughts and feelings, and of the profoundest struggle and tragedy. A little over a century earlier, Whitman—but he would not have been the Walt Whitman we know because he would have been made by different conditions—would have sung of other heroes and embodied in his poetic philosophy nothing of the spirit of the proletarian. Instead of a hymn to *A Common Prostitute* he would have bemoaned the fateful end of a princess, or perhaps the daughter of a Thorowgood, and instead of crying that "no one thing in the universe is inferior to another thing," that "behind each mask was a kindred soul," he would have crooned the songs of a priest or composed madrigals to stupid courtly dames or romantic and prurient maidens.

It is important at this point to note likewise the indisseverable connection between the nature of literary technique and the stage of development of society. Hitherto we have shown how the social conceptions that prevail determine the substance of literature, but not how the form, the technique, the very manner in which the composition is constructed, is determined also by the same material conditions that created the social conceptions. We shall draw only one parallel, which will prove sufficient evidence to establish the premise. This time, to introduce variety, we shall take the novel for our illustration. The first novels, if we exclude such *olla podrida* as Petronius' *Satyricon,* Cervantes' *Don Quixote,* Sidney's *Arcadia,* Mrs. Manley's *The Power of Love, in Seven Novels* (1720), and the like, appeared in England during the heyday of bourgeois supremacy. Exactly nine years after the staging of *The London Merchant,* Richardson's *Pamela* was printed. Although *Pamela* was parodied by Fielding in *Joseph Andrews,* and the general spirit of the Richardson novels for a time was satirized also by Smollett and Sterne, it was succeeded by *David Simple* and Goldsmith's *Vicar of Wakefield,* both novels dedicated to a similar exaltation of bourgeois virtues. But we are not concerned here with an analysis of the substance of the novel, as we were in the case of the drama, but with its form which renders further dissection of content at this point entirely superfluous.

The more carefully we notice the history of fiction, and the novel need only serve as one instance, we are immediately impressed by the evolution from the impossible to the improbable, thence to the probable and finally to the inevitable. To many, even to the American critic, we daresay, who first recorded this feature, this evolution seems a quite unaccountable affair. That the mythical, legendary romances of Arthur and the Round Table should have prevailed in the four or five centuries following the Norman Conquest, and finally been crystallized into the memorable *Morte D'Arthur* in 1485, all "impossible" in content, is nothing strange nor unexpected to the scientific critic. The fierce encounters of knights with the perilous enemies of the forest, giants, dragons, mystical swords that could be drawn only with an enchanting sign or whisper, charms evoked by the wicked sor-

cery of mediaeval magicians, made up the category of fascinating "impossibilities." *The Castle of Otranto, The Champion of Virtue,* Matthew Lewis' *The Monk,* the weird stories
of Mrs Radcliffe, even Godwin's *St. Leon,* can be classified
also in the "impossible" group. The romance of castle and
field, which was carried on in the tragedies of the Elizabethans and all of the seventeenth and early eighteenth century
dramatists, under more realistic and convincing guise,
marked the advance to the improbable and probable stage.
The nineteenth century for instance, was the century for the
"probable" in fiction, although the grotesque tales of Poe and
Hoffman are clear evidence of the survival of the improbable
and even a phase of the impossible trend. Romantic fiction is
all a vestige of these older trends, each produced by different
stages of social structure. That certain of these trends should
persist after the social environment that caused them has declined and disappeared does not mean that a surprising or
confusing element has been introduced into the historical
process. It would be surprising and confusing if such remnants of the old ideology did not from time to time spring
into print. By our very knowledge of the law of cause and
effect we can easily see that the advance of a new social system though it achieved a change in the dominant esthetic
and ethical ideas cannot hope to annihilate at once, or in a
generation or two, all of the remains of those conceptions that
have been forced to recede into the background.

It was not until science advanced into its later stages, when
the reactions of the mind and body as well as those of matter
came to be recognized as following the same inescapable law
of cause and effect, that the idea of the inevitable could assume scientific form. Prediction, the aim of science, now became possible in mental as well as physical things, and the
causal law attained the extensions necessary to undermine
belief in the fortuitous. Without the rise of science, which
was part of the development of the capitalist system, the
idea of the inevitable would never have emerged from its
religious raiment, and esthetic conceptions would have been

but scantily affected by its existence. At the time that prose and poetic fiction possessed the impossible and improbable cast, the human mind, ignorant of natural law and scientific generalization, demanded nothing more of its literary substance; when knowledge advanced, however, and reality began to be sifted from myth, the literary form became modified in accordance with the nature of the advance. In pace with the progress of science, therefore, metamorphosis in literary practice developed. At the present time, the twentieth century, and also during the latter part of the nineteenth, particularly after the appearance of *The History of Civilization in England, The Origin of Species* and *Das Kapital,* realism of the inevitable character developed. The realism of Sterne, Smollett and even Fielding, was not the realism that the nineteenth and twentieth centuries require; the former was more plastic, yielding, without the quality of the inevitable, the undeviating necessity, such as we find exemplified in the novels of Hardy and Conrad. The inflexible criterion of modern realism is "inevitability." Situations must flow inevitably from each other; characters must perform only those actions which, in the nature of their being, it was impossible for them not to perform. There must be no appeal to mere possibility or probability, if the fiction is to convince. Although the large category of so-called popular magazines, of the amorous, snappy and adventurous variety, with which every civilized country is flooded, the Wrightian and Corellian novels, still cling to the improbable and probable types, there is not a single significant literary periodical or author that would dare publish material of such character. This evolution in structure, then, has been but a reflection of the rise of the scientific attitude, itself a product of the capitalist system, which brought with it a fuller understanding of the essence and inevitability of human reaction.

Now let us turn to the literature that followed Whitman, the literature of the late 90's and the twentieth century. The rise of labor organizations, a necessity for the expression of proletarian class-consciousness which was described on a previous page, was and is a constant factor in driving proletarian conceptions to the foreground. Without this rise and the impression of the proletarian upon society, novels and dramas with proletarian protagonists, treated in the serious and a searching manner befitting a tragic study, would never have attained expression. This point cannot be emphasized too strongly for those idealist critics who are so prone to view the changes in literary tendencies as developments of the absolute idea or more whimsical alterations of interest and motive.

A glance at the literature of any country in which the proletariat has become a force in the social organization will reveal how very marked the literature has become by its rise. The literary artist in these lands comes to recognize that there is a soul in the common man, that the proletarian is not without his tragic affections and aspirations. And the study of these affections and aspirations becomes the subject for tragedies as elevated and sublime as those of *Edipus* and *Athalie*. Dramas like *The Weavers, Strife* and *Beyond the Horizon,* built about the sufferings of those of the proletariat, become masterpieces of dramatic art, and novels like *Tess of the D'Urbervilles, Frau Sorge* and *Sons and Lovers,* stories concerned with the misery and anguish of the dispossessed class, are accepted as tragedies of genuine and vital character. It should not be thought that proletarian tragedy, if such we must call it in contradistinction to the aristocratic and bourgeois, began in any particular year or with any special book, but rather that it sprang up gradually as the proletariat became more and more a class demanding social consideration. As early as 1864 in the Naturalist novel, *Germinie Lacerteux,* the Goncourts dealt with the tragic life of a servant girl,* and de Maupassant, although many of his stories

---

* In the preface we find an interesting and illuminating statement of the Goncourts' position: "Living in the nineteenth century, at a time of universal suffrage, and democracy, and liberalism, we asked ourselves whether what are called the "lower orders" had no claim upon the Novel; whether the people—this world beneath a world—were to remain under the literary ban and disdain of authors who have hitherto maintained

are concerned solely with the bourgeoisie, gave tragic significance to the fate of Maitre Hauchecorne, the poor Norman,
in *A Piece of String*. These characters were treated in a different manner from Richardson's seamstress, the difference being the consequence of the different ages in which the
works appeared. Hugo, of course, in many instances gave a
sympathetic though romantic description to the proletarian,
the description, nevertheless, usually interlarded with appeals
to bourgeois virtues and sentimentality. And Zola, with all
his brutality, did not fail to see and depict the strength as
well as oftimes deep-rooted viciousness of proletarian character. All of these men, it should be noted, wrote after the
revolution of 1848.

It is not until contemporary times, however, that we begin
to see a steady and opulent literature growing up about the
proletarian. Pierre Hamp, in France, for example, in that
one collection of his stories entitled *People*, has seen great
and inspiring tragedy in the life of *The Sweet Smeller* and
The Potato Sisters. Joyce in more than one place in *Dublin-
ers*, particularly in *The Little Cloud*, realizes the tragedy of
the drab—and what is so drab as the life of the proletarian?
And if we turn to American literature we meet with a very
striking picture of the new concept, the proletarian concept.
Certainly it would be neither rash nor hasty criticism to say
that among the most important pieces of fiction that have
appeared in America during the last two decades, three
works stand out very distinctly: *Ethan Frome*, by Edith
Wharton; *Winesburg, Ohio*, by Sherwood Anderson, and
Sister Carrie, by Theodore Dreiser. The protagonists in

silence regarding any soul and heart that they might possess. We asked
ourselves whether, in these days of equality, there were still for writer and
reader unworthy classes, misfortunes that were too low, dramas too foul-
mouthed, catastrophies too base in their terror. We became curious to know
whether Tragedy, that conventional form of a forgotten literature and a
vanished society, was finally dead; whether, in a country devoid of caste
and legal aristocracy, the miseries of the lowly and the poor would speak
to interest, to motion, to piety, as loudly as the miseries of the great
and rich; whether, in a word, the tears that are wept below could provoke
weeping like those that are wept above."

these books are underdogs and without exception the histories of their lives are woven into the texture of strange and telling tragedy. To many this fact, if it has been recognized, has not seemed to deserve notice. Yet it is of utmost significance. It mirrors the advance of the proletariat. It is additional proof that literature is the product of sociology, and can only be satisfactorily approached, studied, and criticized by the sociological method.

It is because most of us today believe that the life-experience of the proletarian offers as purifying material for tragedy as that of the bourgeois or aristocrat, that we fail to realize how very brief, in historical duration, has been the existence of this attitude. The mere existence of an idea or conception too often gives the delusion of permanence. What must be realized is the social process that has brought about the conditions necessary for the creation of this conception. In understanding this process, however, we do not mean to conclude that all these artists who, in their work, embody this conception are aware of the sociological factors that have made it a part of civilization. In the greater number of instances, on the contrary, the attitude prevails, in spite of ignorance of its cause. The attitude becomes a social-reflex.

Today, to be sure, the proletarian tendency has taken on all the aspects of a movement. In the United States, this movement has developed with greatest rapidity during the depression years. Today its members are to be found in key positions in the book and magazine field. In half the New York publishing firms today, there are one or more persons of influence who encourage the publication of books which favor the outlook and philosophy of this school. In the magazine and newspaper field, there are editors, associate editors, assistant editors, feature writers, columnists, star reporters, who are in sympathy with the proletarian outlook and encourage its appearance in their publications wherever possible. In novels such as *The Shadow Before* by William Rollins, Jr., *The Death and Birth of David Markand* by Waldo Frank, and Robert Cantwell's *Land of Plenty* there are the vigor and challenge of rediscovered hope, of renewed faith in the future of man—and of America. Like Whitman they envision the future of this country with optimism. In the majority of the novels, poems, and dramas of the proletarian school, the strike has become the center of conflict. Even more striking than the proletarian novels have been the proletarian dramas written by such playwrights as Clifford Odets, whose drama *Awake and Sing* was one of the best plays produced in this country during this decade, Albert Maltz, George Sklar, John Wexley, and Michael Blankfort.

Behind all this change in literary tendency and outlook is the social fact. In the final analysis, revolutions in aesthetics are due to revolutions in ideas, and every revolution in ideas is a consequence of a revolution in the social structure that the prevailing material conditions have produced.

MASTERS—OLD AND NEW

A Social Philosophy Without Myths

By MAX NOMAD

As a saying credited to Machiavelli has it, "nobody has yet killed his own successor." That dictum has often been applied to the coming "final struggle" between the beneficiaries of decaying capitalism and their proletarian successors. Its soothing value to the still waiting inheritors is certainly incontestable.

When feudalism lay in its death throes its enemies predicted the succession of the rule of the people. That "people" turned out to be the modern bourgeoisie. With capitalism in a similar predicament, history seems to be repeating itself and playing the same trick upon the "proletariat."

The beneficiary of that momentous piece of sleight-of-hand is no longer in hiding. Sandwiched between the capitalists and the manual workers there has emerged an ever growing stratum of neo-bourgeois or not-yet-quite-bourgeois engaged in mental or near-mental occupations. "Intellectual workers," "privileged employees of capital," "new middle class"—these are the various terms used interchangeably for this amazing variety of people: office-holders, teachers, professional men, technicians, clergymen, commercial and financial experts, journalists, writers, artists, politicians, professional revolutionists and agitators, trade union organizers and so on. In short, a vast crowd of educated and semi-educated people, all of them "propertyless," who may or may not have a college degree, but can make a livelihood without resorting to manual or lower clerical labor.

Sometimes scions of the prosperous capitalists, of the "privileged employees" or of the lower middle classes, and sometimes self-educated upstart workers, the intellectuals are divided into various income groups, just as the property holders are. Some of them, the "ins," are satisfied with the existing system; others, the "outs," the underpaid or unemployed, are just as strenuously opposed to it. The "ins" devour an enormous part of the national wealth: they enjoy a bourgeois standard of living, and in their large mass are always ready to side with the existing system against the manual workers.

In short, formally "employees," the "ins" are in fact, due to their higher educational qualifications, *minor partners* of the capitalists as a whole: the lesser nobility, as it were, within the great bourgeois aristocracy of the modern age. And in proportion as the *major partner,* the capitalist, becomes a mere consuming parasite, leaving most of the functions of technical and commercial management to his "paid employees"—in the same proportion these "employees" become the potential successors of their employers. But, being satisfied with their social position, they are naturally a conservative element; they are not in a hurry to dispossess their masters (or major partners); for any serious interference with the property relations may disturb the social peace and endanger their own privileged incomes.

Against these defenders of the status quo are arrayed the "outs," the unemployed or underpaid journalists, lecturers, college graduates and undergraduates, "lawyers without clients and doctors without patients" (Marx), educated ex-workers in search of a white-collar position—in short all that motley army of impecunious or starving intellectuals, near-intellectuals and would-be intellectuals, who are dissatisfied with the existing system and are very often militantly active in the various radical or fascist movements. It is the members of this group who have the ambition of eliminating the capitalist class of parasitic consumers and of establishing their own rule in a system based on government control or ownership of industries, and an unequal distribution of incomes.

II

The first case in history when this group came into its own was the Bolshevik revolution and the establishment of the so-called Soviet system. That system has evolved an enormous hierarchy of intellectuals who are bureaucrats at the same time: administrative office-holders, technical managers and engineers, judges, savants, journalists, writers, professors, higher transport and postal employees, Marx-theologians, army officers, actors, singers, scientific spies, bank accountants, trade union and sports organizers—all of them government employees who owe their bourgeois comfort to the labor of the uneducated workers and peasants. Having eliminated the old parasitic strata of feudal lords and capitalist proprietors, these office-holders have become the only consumers of privileged incomes. The badge of admission to this new privileged class is a certain amount of education or training exceeding the average level of the manual workers. That amount of higher education or training guarantees its owner a soft job and a salary which is above the average wage of the manual worker.

It is this class which, being identical with the government, has become the collective owner of the country's socialized economy—its industries and its land. The workers and peasants are merely the nationalized laborers, menials and serfs of the new ruling class which has combined the fiction of the "proletarian dictatorship" with that of "the factories and fields belonging to the workers and peasants."

The bolshevik form of class rule and inequality of incomes is not a distortion of the original equalitarian character of socialism, as some sentimental souls may believe. Stripped of its emotional content and reduced to the simplest economic terms, socialism has always meant merely *government ownership of the means of production.* In other words, socialism means primarily a change in the *form of production,* or in the *ownership of the means of production.* The rest is poetry and propaganda. The question of *distribution* has always been considered a secondary matter by the various socialist schools after the first and most important task of socialization had been carried out. Practically all socialist theorists take it for granted that immediately after the socialist revolution, during "the first phase of communism," to use an expression of Marx, there would be no equality of incomes. It is only under "the higher phase of communism," after God knows how many generations or centuries, that the principle of "from each according to his abilities, to each according to his needs," would be applied. A formula which is as hazy as it is deceitful. For who is to determine a man's needs? None other apparently than the bureaucrats, the same men who in present-day Russia determine that a high class manager "needs," or, let us say, "deserves," several thousand rubles a month, while for an ordinary laborer or other plain worker one hundred or one hundred fifty a month is sufficient. In other words, for the future as for the present the real meaning of that formula is to be conceived as "from the workers according to their abilities, to the bureaucrats according to their needs".

Only the beneficiaries of such glaring inequalities of income can assert that the means of production under the new dispensation are "owned by the workers." They are owned, collectively of course, by those who hire and fire; by those who constitute the government machine, the bureaucrats, the sum total of all educated people who have good apartments in city and countryside, who have the best food, the use of the available automobiles, domestic servants, and all the other comforts from which the enormous majority of manually working "owners" are excluded. Only paid propagandists, or would-be "ins" of such a new system of exploitation, can speak of a "proletarian state" because the maximum proportion of inequality is "merely" one to one hundred, instead of being one to one thousand as in the typically capitalist countries.

III

The Soviet example has proven that *exploitation is just as much possible under socialism as under any other previous social system*. (Granting of course, that any system of planned, socialized economy, historically speaking, represents a great step forward as compared with the productive process under private capitalism with its calamities resulting from the business cycles). If one were to indulge in prophecy one could make a guess that *the coming universal form of exploitation of man by man, as foreshadowed by Russia's system of government ownership and inequality of incomes, will simply be called socialism,* and that in the ears of the underdog this word will, in time, assume the same connotation of master-and-slave-relationship as feudalism and capitalism. Like the previous social systems that relationship will be self-perpetuating. For while the *entire offspring of the new masters is given all the facilities of higher education, only the most gifted children of the lower orders get those opportunities of the higher schooling that will enable them to rise above the level of manual labor.* Whether it is inaugurated by communists or socialists, whether it maintains the strictest political one-party absolutism, Bolshevik style, or is ready to permit democratic competition of various political currents—the *distribution* within the new system is to be based upon the immemorial aristocratic principle of giving the greater share to the "more deserving." "Socialism is not equalization" Otto Bauer, greatest theorist of the socialist wing of Marxism, wrote in his magazine "Kampf" in May 1936. "It levels society by *abolishing the classes,* thus removing the privileges deriving from descent or property. But it differentiates society by rewarding those whose achievements for society are particularly outstanding, and by raising them above the masses in matters of *income* [my emphasis—M.N.] and social prestige." * (The "abolition of classes"

---

* In a lecture delivered in Vienna (*Arbeiter-Zeitung* of September 25, 1932) Paul Goebbels, Hitler's chief propaganda expert, expressed the fol-

under socialism with the higher incomes going to the more
deserving, i.e. to the bureaucracy and occasional "shock
workers," is on a par with the bourgeois theory of the "non-
existence of classes" under a system of capitalist democracy
where every one has the vote and an "equal opportunity" of
acquiring property. Under socialism "every one" owns an
"equal share" in the nation's means of production, and has
an "equal opportunity" of becoming an office-holder, provided he had selected the right parents or was endowed with
those special gifts which in America enable "every" office-
boy to become a high-class executive.)

No wonder then that ever increasing sections of the more
enlightened part of the intelligentsia in non-fascist Europe
and America are flocking now to the various radical parties.
They see in the Russian example the possibility of putting an
end to their economic insecurity, the hope of throwing off the
financial magnates, and the prospect of themselves becoming
masters of the country. They are the pioneers of their class—
opposed not only by the well-paid "ins" who are satisfied
with their present condition, but by a large number of other
educated "outs" and déclassés as well.

IV

If a large part of the intellectuals in various countries, instead of turning socialist or communist, join the fascist ranks,
they do so largely for the same reason for which many workers likewise don the black or brown shirt. No doubt, the influence of reactionary ideology plays a certain part in the
process. But it is largely their impatience, their desire for a
short cut to power, that is responsible for the success of the
new gospel. Many of the fascist intellectuals would join the

lowing opinion: "We say 'to every one his due.' Hence we take the *aristocratic* point of view: not according to property or rank, but according
to ability and achievement." Cynic though he may be, the Fascist Goebbels, by frankly admitting the aristocratic nature of this principle, is more
honest than Socialist or Communist Marxists who defend inequality of rewards as a "proletarian" theory.

communist movement, if they saw that it had any chances, or at least intentions of winning *immediately*. For by now it has become obvious to most observers that the leading communists of the non-fascist countries have altogether ceased to be revolutionaries: that ever since 1923 they have been ordinary Russian patriots abroad, *actually* opposed to any revolutionary steps that might disturb the international status quo in which the U.S.S.R. has been interested for many years. Like the socialists of pre-war times the communists— meaning of course the official leadership—have become a party of "gradualist" anti-capitalist *protest* and *reform,* and *not* of anti-capitalist *revolt.* (It is only the extreme-left fringe of radicalism, as represented by the followers of Trotsky and of various anarchist or syndicalist groups, that now advocates going beyond the mere defense of the bourgeois-democratic status quo.)

The fascists in power, in spite of the reverence they show towards all the taboos of the past, are not just flunkeys of the capitalist class, as most of the socialists and communists believe or pretend to believe. They are their *major partners;* they swallow an ever growing share of the nation's wealth; and while in some countries they are now greatly favoring the munition magnates, their taxes and assessments are impoverishing the bourgeoisie as a whole in order to feed an enormous bureaucratic machine. That machine is both a "protector" of the rich, and their blackmailing parasite at the same time; largely comparable to the Praetorians of the Roman Empire, who, while permitting the property-owners to exist, actually were the masters of the country and lived at the expense of all the other classes of the population.

The fascists' present close association with capitalism does not imply that this association will have to be permanent. History is replete with cases where mercenaries of various sorts, Mamertines, Praetorians, Mamelukes, Condottieri, became the masters of those who hired them. There is an openly anti-capitalist wing within the Italian fascist party which recommends the "road to Moscow," i.e. the expropriation of the capitalists. Mussolini himself, if driven to a corner, will not hesitate to turn Bolshevik if by doing so he can save the rule of his party—the rule of the most determined section of the Italian intelligentsia. His widely publicized threats to do away with capitalism, and the serious character of these threats, contributed their share in preventing capitalist Europe from interfering with his Ethiopian expedition. Similar anti-capitalist tendencies are becoming more and more discernible among certain unorthodox German Nazis, as well as within Japan's officers' caste and its bureaucratic and would-be-bureaucratic hangers-on.

There is no reason why the rank and file as well as the leaders of the job-hungry fascist intellectuals should be opposed to the elimination of the capitalists—*provided they themselves can get the best positions to the exclusion of their leftist competitors*. Socialism, as a new form of class rule, is possible under all forms of philosophical "superstructures." A system embodying the mastery of the office-holders' class is just as compatible with a Paretist-Mussolinian aristocratic nationalism and its glorification of the "élite," as it is with a Marxist-Leninist "proletarian internationalism" with its no less aristocratic "proletarian vanguard," or with Bauer's democratic socialism which takes for granted the higher incomes enjoyed by men of "achievement" and "prestige." Just as private capitalism can gather its profits both under the Voltairian iconoclasm of the French Republic and under its crassest opposite—the medieval Emperor-God worship of a militarist semi-absolutism, Japanese style.

V

Thus the abolition of capitalism, the result of the "final revolution" championed by the various political parties of the underdog, eventually leads to the establishment of a new class rule, of a new exploitation of man by man. That new form of class rule must naturally call forth a violent dissatisfaction both among the down-trodden manual workers and

among the step-brothers or poorer relations of the new bureaucratic masters. There arises the urge towards a new "final
revolution" in which the old process is repeated under the
guise of a changed vocabulary. For whether they call themselves left communists, syndicalists or anarchists, the victorious rebels against the bureaucracy of a socialized form of
exploitation cannot help establishing a new bureaucracy, a
new ruling aristocracy—in other words, follow the example
of the Russian communists. For the process of revolution is
always the same: Seizure of power; organization of a revolutionary government; its defense against the reactionaries
at first; and then its consolidation against the masses as well
in the interest of a better paid aristocracy of office-holders,
technicians, and other members of the educated layers of
society.

Does this all, in its final analysis, amount to the old philosophy of "thus it had been, thus it is, thus it will be?" In other
words, does this conclusion consign the poor to statistics and
to eternal slavery?

No, this "skepticism," if skepticism there be, is the very
opposite of submission to fate. On the contrary, it implies
permanent revolt against any status quo: capitalist exploitation of today, as well as socialist inequality of tomorrow. It
is directed both against the property-owning oppressors of
today and the job-holding "liberators" of tomorrow; against
the middle class of yesterday which used the workers in its
struggle against feudal tyranny; and against the *new middle
class* of today which uses them against the capitalist bourgeoisie; against the college-trained apologists of the coming
form of slavery, and against their competitors from the ranks
of the self-educated ex-workers.

However, that "skepticism" likewise implies the realization of certain phenomena which hitherto have been consistently overlooked or glossed over: The acknowledgment
of the non-proletarian neo-bourgeois character of the educated non-capitalist strata of society roughly comprised under
the designation of "intellectual workers" to whom the dis-

satisfaction and the struggles of the manual workers offer an opportunity for taking the place of the old masters; and the admission of the tragic dualism involved in the composition of the labor movement with its inevitable partnership between mass and leadership. A partnership which, though to a certain extent beneficial to the masses, invariably results in a conflict between the interests of the leading élite and those of the masses constituting the following.

Those leading élites, even if they rise from the working masses themselves, being more educated and consequently better endowed than their following, are essentially aristocratic in character, no matter whether they profess to be democratic, anarchist, socialist-communist, syndicalist or fascist. Like all aristocratic groups they are inevitably Machiavellian or amoral in their policies, keeping up their "morale" with all sorts of philosophical justifications ("rationalizations") and resorting constantly to a conscious or unconscious deception of the masses. For all their activities and endeavors converge in the single purpose of obtaining and maintaining all power and its resulting benefits for their specific revolutionary or counter-revolutionary group. And to strengthen their hold upon the masses they evolve certain religious features within their respective movements—the analogy with the material growth and the spiritual decay of many of the great religions being particularly striking. The intolerance and ruthless suppression of any unorthodox opinion, as well as the divine veneration bestowed upon the Leader are the common characteristics of most of these groups, whether they place themselves at the extreme right or at the extreme left.

The desire to concentrate all the power and the privileges deriving from it within a restricted circle results in an ever recurring competition for power between various groups of educated malcontents leading, or aspiring to leadership of, the dissatisfied masses. Some of these groups may be more crude than the others in their efforts to win the masses; some of them may be in the pay of domestic capitalists or of foreign bureaucrats; but at bottom even the most "honest" and "consistent" group cannot claim to be "really proletarian" in its aims. For every *organization* wants only one thing: power, that is privilege, for itself and for its more active members. That competition for power between the various groups is a guaranty against stagnation and against the perpetuation of the status quo. Under the present conditions of a decaying private capitalism it is bound to hasten the inauguration of some system or other of a socialized economy.

After the elimination or a considerable restriction of the capitalist owners, that competition for power leads to an internecine struggle between various groups of intellectuals and educated ex-workers for predominance within the government machine, that is, the office-holding class, now ruling supreme. It is the ever recurring struggle between the Trotzkys and the Stalins, or the Roehms and the Goerings, caused by the oligarchical tendencies prevailing within each ruling class. *The urge to win forces the rebellious rivals to appeal to the dissatisfaction of the manual workers and of the lower clerical force and to assist them in obtaining a larger share of the national income.* This process is accompanied by the rise of the most educated and most intelligent elements among the manual workers themselves, joining either of the contending groups or making their own bid for power.

Each of the contending parties or groups constituting the opposition is bound to include disinterested idealists or "romanticists" whose sentiments are with the horny-handed underdog and who, consciously at least, care neither for power nor for personal advantage. These quite naturally will push forward any mass struggle for better conditions, as expressed in higher wages, shorter hours and jobs for the unemployed. And they will denounce the leaders who for one reason or another may be suspected of restraining the masses or of selling them out. Yet the very success of his revolutionary opposition may force the disinterested rebel, in a given situation, to accept the responsibilities of leadership and power—and to imitate the example of those whom he had just denounced; when he will in turn be opposed by a new set of fighters who, again, may go through the same cycle. Until that blessed time, when the miracle of all miracles, the "good master" will have made his appearance.

The permanent change of masters and the accompanying striving of the masses in the direction of an ever greater *approach* towards equality in the enjoyment of the good things of life forms the basic content of the historical process. That process knows of no millennium when full harmony has been achieved once for all eternity. There is no "happy ending" just as there is no "final revolution" that will eliminate all further class struggles. For the working masses every "final victory" proclaimed by their victorious leaders, even if it is a real step forward, can be only another starting point in their endless struggle *for more and always more*.

The chasm separating the great toiling majority from the men of "outstanding achievement," from those wielding the most efficient combination of knowledge, intelligence and ruthlessness, from the socialist and communist aristocracy of superior brains and incomes—may never be bridged completely. But the "evil passions" (Bakunin) of the underdog, his legitimate envy of, and hatred for, his luckier "betters," will drive him forward—under ever changing leaders. Those leaders may fall by the side, martyrs in defeat or masters in victory, but the struggle will go on.

That struggle is the *permanent revolution*. Permanent—not as conceived by those who would cut short their "dialectical process" the moment they themselves are enthroned over a socialized world; but in the real meaning of the word.

THE APPLICATION OF ENGINEERING
METHODS TO FINANCE*

By C. H. DOUGLAS

IN defining the profession of engineering as the application of the forces of nature to the uses of man, the Institution
of Civil Engineers no doubt had in mind those forces
which at the present time we are accustomed to call physical forces. There is no reason to limit the definition of such
forces, and it is becoming increasingly recognized that the
province of the engineer and in particular the scope of the
engineering method, can with advantage be extended to
cover forces of a more metaphysical and psychological
character.

Assuming that there is reason to bring the financial system under review, on the ground that it is not operating
satisfactorily, and that, being in essence a combination of an
enlarged Works Order and Distribution System combined
with a metaphysical scheme for the mobilisation of human
activities, it is at any rate interesting to consider the matter
from an engineering point of view, and stripped of the
emotional irrelevances with which it is frequently clothed.

In attacking an engineering problem the first point we
settle, with as much exactness as possible, is our objective. No
engineer observer of the discussions which take place in
political and lay circles on the industrial problems of the present day can fail to be struck with the fact that the problem
itself is rarely stated with any clearness. For instance, the
paramount difficulty of the industrial system is commonly
expressed as that of unemployment. Therefore the suggestion involved is that the industrial system exists to provide

* From *The Monopoly of Credit*

employment, and fails. Those who are engaged in the actual conduct of industry, however, are specifically concerned to obtain a given output with a minimum of employment, and in fact, a decreasing amount of employment. Consequently, those who are talking about industry and those who are conducting industry have in their minds objectives which are diametrically opposed and incompatible. On the other hand, the great majority of those engaged in industry, anyhow, in its lower ranks would claim that what they want from the industrial system is goods. Finally, those whose interest in industry is purely financial, require from industry, simply money.

We have, therefore, to recognise that there are at least three separate and distinct objectives alleged in the industrail system. (1) Employment. (2) Goods and service. (3) Money.

(1) *Employment as the Objective of the Industrial System.* —For a given programme of production and a given standard of development of the industrial arts, output is proportionate to the energy employed in industry. Broadly speaking, the source of this energy is immaterial. So much solar or mechanical energy, so much less human energy. If employment is accepted as the objective of the industrial system, therefore, and output to be a dependent variable of this objective (a) either process and mechanical energy employed must be kept rigidly constant, or (b) output must be completely unfettered by any difficulties of sale.

(2) *Goods and Services as the Objective of the Industrial System.*—There are here two possible cases: (a) A fixed programme of production with unlimited improvement of process and employment of mechanical energy, resulting in a rapidly and constantly decreasing amount of employment in man-hours. (b) an advancing programme of production with unlimited improvement of process and employment of mechanical energy, resulting eventually in a saturated psychological demand, and automatically becoming similar to (a).

(3) *Money as the Objective of the Industrial System.*—It is perhaps only necessary to state this in brief form. Money is not made by making or selling goods, it is made: (1) By digging gold, silver, and copper out of the earth and minting them. This represents perhaps 0.3 of 1 per cent. of money in circulation. (2) By the printing of paper money, representing, perhaps, 10 per cent. of the money in circulation. (3) The creation of credits by banks, representing perhaps, 90 per cent. of the money in circulation. With the exception of the labour employed in mining and working the metals in the first insignificant division, and the labour employed in the elaborate organisation of the banking system, the creation of money has nothing to do with the industrial system, although it represents an effective demand upon the whole product of the industrial system. The making of money as an objective of the industrial system, therefore, bears a close resemblance to Charles Lamb's method of obtaining roast pork by burning down the piggery.

Since money is not made by the industrial system, it is important to understand from whence it originates and to whither it eventually returns. The matter has been epitomised in a short sentence by Mr. McKenna, Chairman of the Midland Bank: "Every loan creates a deposit, and the repayment of every loan destroys a deposit." The following explanation may make this clear to those who are not familiar with the technique, and who imagine that the money which banks loan to their customers is limited by the amount they receive from other customers. Imagine a new bank to be started—its so-called capital is immaterial. Ten depositers each deposit £100 in Treasury Notes with this bank. Its liabilities to the public are now £1,000. These ten depositors have business with each other and find it more convenient in many cases to write notes (checques) to the banker, instructing him to adjust their several accounts in accordance with these business transactions, rather than to draw out cash and pay it over personally. After a little while, the banker notes that only about 10 per cent. of his business is done in cash (in England it is only 0.7 of 1 per cent.), the rest being merely bookkeeping. At this point depositor No. 10, who is a manufacturer, receives a large order for his product. Before he can deliver, he realizes that he will have to pay out, in wages, salaries, and other expenses, considerably more "money" than he has at command. In this difficulty he consults his banker, who, having in mind the situation just outlined, agrees to allow him to draw from his account not merely his own £100, but an "overdraft" of £100, making £200 in all, in consideration of repayment in, say, three months, of £102. This overdraft of £100 is a credit to the account of depositor No. 10, who can now draw £200.

The banker's liabilities to the public are now £1,100, none of the original depositors have had their credits of £100 each reduced by the transaction, nor were they consulted in regard to it, and it is absolutely correct to say that £100 of new money has been created by a stroke of the banker's pen.

Depositor No. 10 having, happily obtained his overdraft, pays it out to his employees in wages and salaries. These wages and salaries, together with the banker's interest, all go into costs. All costs go into the price the public pays for its goods, and consequently, when depositor No. 10 repays his banker with £102 obtained from the public in exchange for his goods, and the banker, after placing £2, created by himself, to his profit and loss account, sets the £100 received against the phantom credit previously created, and cancels both of them, there are £100 worth more goods in the world which are immobilised—of which no one, not even the banker, except potentially, has the money equivalent. A short mathematical proof of this process is as follows:—

$$\text{Let Deposits} = \text{D.}$$
$$\text{Let Loans, etc.} = \text{L.}$$
$$\text{Let Cash in Hand} = \text{C.}$$
$$\text{Let Capital} = \text{K.}$$

Then we have—

$$\text{Assets} = L + C$$
$$\text{Liabilities} = D + K$$
$$\text{So that } L + C = D + K$$

Differentiating with respect to time, we have—

$$\frac{dL}{dT} \frac{dC}{dT} \frac{dD}{dT}; \quad K \text{ being fixed, } \frac{dK}{dT} = 0$$

Assuming that the Cash in Hand is kept constant $\frac{dC}{dT} = 0$

Therefore

$$\frac{dL}{dT} = \frac{dD}{dt}$$

which means of course that the rate of increase, or decrease, of loans is equal to the rate of increase, or decrease, of deposits.

There is, I think, little question that the true objective of the industrial system is the production and distribution of goods and services. Assuming this to be so, an examination of the existing arrangements with a view to discovering the causes of their partial failure, is involved.

The application of engineering methods to the production of goods and services has enabled one human unit to produce considerably more goods and services than are necessary for his own use. The application of mechanical power and improved process and organization can tend only to increase the output per man-hour. It should be obvious, therefore, that a system by which purchasing power is mainly distributed through the agency of wages conflicts sharply with the physical reality involved in the fact that a decreasing number of persons tend to be involved in the production of the necessary amount of goods and services.

Before leaving this portion of the subject, however, it may be desirable to indicate the effect of raising or lowering wages considered as a component in the cost of unit production.

The money distributed in the production of goods consists in wages, and salaries. (Dividends are distributed subsequent to the sale of goods.) Since labour costs are not the only costs of production,

$$\text{Labour costs are} < \text{prices,}$$

$$\frac{\text{costs}}{\text{prices}} \text{ is } < 1$$

If wages, that is to say, labour costs, are reduced by an amount x, the ratio of purchasing power to prices is lessened

$$\frac{\text{costs}-x}{\text{prices}-x} \text{ is } < \frac{\text{costs}}{\text{prices}}$$

We can deduce, therefore, that lessening the item of labour costs in the total factory cost of an article reduces the capacity of the wage-earning portion of the population to buy the total volume of goods produced, although for a total amount of wages distributed the amount of goods produced is obviously greater.

Since it is generally recognised that the average dividend of an industrial undertaking distributed to the shareholders is very small compared to the amount distributed in wages and salaries, probably not averaging more than 3 per cent., we may be led to suspect that the reduction of the ratio of direct labour costs to total costs involves a principle of fundamental importance. This is so. If we take a cross-section of the flow of purchasing power delivered to the buying public in the form of wages, salaries, and dividends, and at the same moment take a cross-section of the flow of prices generated in the industrial system, we shall find that the latter cross-section is always greater than the former. This may be put as follows. All industrial payments may be divided into two Groups.

Group A.—All payments made to individuals (wages, salaries, and dividends).

Group B.—All payments made to other organizations (raw materials, repayment of bank loans, and other non-personal costs).

Now the rate of flow of purchasing power to individuals is represented by A, but since all payments go into prices, the rate of flow of prices cannot be less than A plus B. Since A will not purchase A plus B, a proportion of the product at least equivalent to B must be distributed by a form of purchasing-power which is not comprised in the description grouped under "A."

The explanation of this apparent anomaly is complex, but is in the main due to the fact that the buyer of goods is at one and the same time paying for the goods and repaying to the banking system *via* immediate producers, the money which the industrial system borrowed from it but which the banking system created by means of a book-keeping transaction.

The repayment of bank loans in the industrial system may be considered as included in the balance of the payment made from one business organisation to another, that is to say, in Group B, as explained above.

On the assumption that the delivery of goods and services is the objective of the industrial system, it is obvious that the rate of flow of purchasing power should be equal to the rate of generation of prices. The existing financial arrangements make a crude effort to approximate this condition by issuing purchasing power to manufacturing organizations in the form of loans, which in turn the manufacturing organisations distribute in wages and salaries against future production. In other words, the existing financial system increasingly mortages the future in order to sell the goods existing at present, the most recent and most obvious form of this practice being the installment system of purchase. Since the financial system is in essence merely a book-keeping system, having for its proper objective something not very dissimilar to the "Progress" Department of a large factory, the defect in it which is disclosed by the preceding cursory examination is obviously capable of adjustment.

Bearing in mind the premise that the consumer should collectively have the financial means to exercise the full call on both the sum of actual production and the balance of potential production represented by unused plant and available labour and material, it is easy to see that under existing conditions prices ought to vary inversely as the rate of production. The difficulty involved in this is that producers would lose money, and to avoid this and to stimulate production some modification is necessary.

Reverting to the physical realities of the productive system, it can easily be seen that the true cost of a given programme of production is the consumption of all production over an equivalent period of time, that is to say, if P equals production and C equals consumption, and M equals money distributed for a given programme of production, the true cost of this programme of production is not M,

$$\text{but } Mx \cdot \frac{\int_{T_1}^{T_2} \frac{dC}{dt}\, dt}{\int_{T_1}^{T_2} \frac{dP}{dt}\, dt} = Mx \quad \begin{array}{l}\text{mean consumption rate for selected period} \\[2em] \text{mean production rate for selected period}\end{array}$$

In other words, the true cost of a programme of production is in general not the money cost, but considerably less than the money cost, and a given programme of production can only be distributed to the buying public if sold at its true cost.

Many methods will suggest themselves for putting into operation the foregoing principles. Articles might be sold at cost *plus* profit as at present, and a rebate to the purchaser be made through the banking system, representing the difference between the apparent cost and the true cost. The source from which this rebate would be made would be exactly the same source from which at present the banking system creates money out of nothing, that is to say a book entry based on the security of a country considered as a producing mechanism. No inflation is involved in such a process. Inflation consists in an expansion of the figures of money available accompanied by a corresponding rise in prices. The objective in this case being a fall of prices to bring them collectively within the buying range of the general public, any rise of prices would merely result in the use of a smaller amount of credit.

It will be realized from the foregoing analysis that a considerable increase in the total purchasing power is necessary to obtain a sufficient effective demand upon the possibilities of the modern industrial system. Having obtained this initial increase in effective demand, the problem of the distribution of the increase assumes manageable proportions. Merely to endeavour to reallocate the initially deficient amount of purchasing power by taxation, as at present, can only result in a serious curtailment of production.

BIOGRAPHIES

BIOGRAPHIES

text of his life. The fullest expression of Plato's philosophy
is found in the *Republic*, one of the greatest books of all
time.

BIOGRAPHIES

Confucius (551-478 B. C.), the great Chinese sage, was born in
poverty. While still a young man, Confucius established a
school where boys were to be taught the principles of right
conduct and government. His pupils became his disciples,
their number amounting to 3000. They were devoted to
him and treasured up every word he spoke.

Confucius in his teaching made no claim to divine revelation. His ideas are conservative and have been acceptable, therefore, to successive dynasties. He believed that society was made up of five relationships—ruler and subject,
husband and wife, father and son, elder brothers and younger, and friends. There must be rule on the one side and
submission on the other. Confucius did a great deal to preserve the ancient literature of the Chinese people in his
books *Ancient Poems,* the *Books of Rites and Ceremonies*
and the *Book of Changes.*

Lao-Tse, the great mystic after whom the Taoist religion is
named, was born about 604 B. C. His philosophy is one of
negation and passivity. The three things which he prized
most were compassion, economy, and not presuming
to take precedence in the world. At one place he wrote "It
is the way of Tao not to act from any personal motive, to
conduct affairs without feeling the trouble of them, to taste
without being aware of the flavour, to account the great as
small and the small as great, to recompense injury with
kindness." The Taoist religion did not take form until about
500 years after the death of Lao-Tse, and he is not to be
held responsible for the superstition which is so strong an
element of Taoism.

Plato (c 428 B. C.—c. 348 B. C.) was born of a distinguished
family in Athens. His early ambitions were political but he
was repulsed by the violence and dishonesty he observed and
decided that a man of conscience could not be active in
politics. He traveled widely and when he was about fifty,
founded the Academy, over which he presided during the

rest of his life. The fullest expression of Plato's philosophy is found in the *Republic,* one of the greatest books of all time.

Aristotle (384-322 B. C.), the great Greek philosopher, has influenced the world for 2000 years. From the age of 17 to 37 he studied and worked with Plato, who died in 348 B. C. When Aristotle became associated with Plato, the latter was already 61. At this period Plato was concerned with the problem of "ideas", and Aristotle here got the germ of his logic. Master and pupil were undivided when Plato died. Aristotle set up a school of his own through which he became so well known that Phillip of Macedon invited him to become the teacher of his son Alexander. Aristotle remained in Macedonia seven years, after which he returned to Athens, the intellectual center of Greece. Here Aristotle set up his own school which became known as the Peripatetic. The body of the extant Aristotelian treatises represents the lectures which Aristotle delivered in his school in the evening of his life. It is now that he departs from his master, Plato, in his study of the historical and biological processes rather than in concentration on "the heavenly things".

Aristotle's great work is an encyclopaedia covering vast fields. In human history were accounts of the Pythian and Olympic games, a chronology of the Athenian drama, an account of customs of barbarians, and the treatises on constitutional law. In natural history he planned a treatise on biology, and a history of the sciences, including physics, mathematics, medicine, anatomy and physiology.

Aristotle's work on politics has been a model for generations; he teaches that law is the true sovereign of States, that governments are servants of law; and that there is an inherent right in the people to elect their rulers and to hold them to account.

St. Augustine (354-430) was born in Numidia. Although his mother was a Christian and his father later became a convert Augustine did not embrace Christianity until his thirty-third year. In the year 396 at the age of forty he was made bishop of Hippo, a small seaport town which he made famous. After becoming bishop, he never left Africa, but kept in touch with the world through correspondence. Many of his letters and sermons have been preserved. *His*

Confessions and *De Civitate Dei,* his most influential works, give a comprehensive idea of his life and work.

Giovanni Battista Vico (1668-1744) was born in Naples where years later he became the great professor of jurisprudence at the University. Vico was a profound student, read widely, and was deeply influenced by Plato and Sir Francis Bacon. His philosophy of history is expounded in his great work *Scienza Nuova,* 1725. Although Vico's work has never been translated into English, his ideas have been familiar to all later historians and philosophers and his influence has been profound. (Fortunately Professor Elio Gianturco has just finished an English translation of *Scienza Nuova* which will appear in a few months.)

Niccolo Machiavelli (1469-1527), Italian statesman and writer, was born in Florence of well-to-do middle class parents. From 1498 until 1512 Machiavelli served the rulers of Florence and was exiled with them when the Medicis recaptured the city. He traveled widely in Italy, Germany, and France studying the political and military regimes in each country. His effort to substitute in Florence a national militia for the traditional mercenary troops met with failure and led to his downfall. After 1513 he lived in retirement and spent his restless energy in writing. His most famous book *The Prince,* is an analysis of the methods whereby an ambitious man may rise to sovereign power.

John Locke (1632-1704) was born in Somersetshire. His father was a prosperous Puritan who had fought in the Civil War. Locke was educated at Oxford where he became a lecturer in philosophy. He also studied medicine and for a time was associated with Sydenham. In 1667 Locke became Secretary to the earl of Shaftesbury with whom he lived for the next fifteen years. When political conditions made England an unpleasant place for him, Locke spent three years in France and five in Holland. Here he became known to William of Orange. Locke returned to England immediately after William's accession to the throne. *Two Treatises on Government* was published in 1685, and *Essay Concerning Human Understanding* in 1690. Although Locke was not entirely in sympathy with the government since it fell short of his ideal of toleration and civil liberty, he did accept an appointment to the Board of Trade, on which he served until 1700. His last years were devoted to biblical studies. Locke's works are classics in rational thought and have had wide influence on social economy, politics, education, and philosophy.

Thomas Hobbes (1588-1679) was the son of an English vicar. He was educated at church schools until the age of fifteen, when he entered Oxford. After graduation, he served as tutor to William Cavendish, afterward earl of Devonshire. With his pupil he traveled on the continent, where he became interested in the revolt against scholasticism. On subsequent tours he met Descartes and Galileo and became engrossed in the physical sciences. He determined to embody his ideas in three treatises: *De corpore,* to show that physical phenomena were explicable in terms of motion: *De homine,* to show what specific bodily motions were involved in the phenomena of sensation and knowledge; and *De cive,* discussing social relations and the proper regulation of society. This work was not finally completed until 1658.

His most influential work is *Leviathan,* a statement of his doctrine of sovereignty. Hobbes ran counter to the conformists of his day and was considerably hounded as an atheist, though he was a church member. At the age of eighty he found it necessary to bury all his papers that he thought might compromise him with the powerful Church Party. After 1666 he could never get anything published in England, though he was given protection by the king until his death. His reputation on the continent never suffered and in his last years he was frequently visited by the noble and learned who came to pay their respects to the old philosopher.

Jean Jacques Rousseau (1712-1778) was born at Geneva of French parents. After a desultory education and a series of apprenticeships, be began a career of wandering which ended when he became the lover of Madame de Warens. This estimable lady had him instructed in the classics and in music. In later years Rousseau frequently supported himself by copying music. Diderot admitted him as a contributor to the *Encyclopedie.* Rousseau's fame grew after the publication of *Discourse sur Les Arts et Sciences,* in which he expounded his theory of the superiority of the savage state.

His novels, *La Nouvelle Heloise* and *Emile* are treatises rather than fiction. His *Social Contract* won him the enmity of the aristocracy and Rousseau fled from Paris in 1762. He was given shelter in England by David Hume. As he grew older Rousseau became very irritable and eventually quarrelled with each of his friends. One of the most remarkable books of all times is his *Confessions* written during his troubled last years.

Thomas Paine (1737-1809), the son of a Quaker, was born in Thetford, England. He had a meager grammar school education, which was supplemented by attendance at science lectures in London when a young man. When thirty-seven years old he came to America, on the advice of Benjamin Franklin. For two years he edited the *Pennsylvania Magazine*. The publication of *Common Sense* in 1776 made him famous. Washington said the book "worked a powerful change in the minds of many men." The open revolutionary movement dates from the publication of *Common Sense*. When the war began, Paine continued to inspire the people in a series of tracts, *The Crisis,* the opening words of which were the now familiar—"These are the times that try men's souls."

After the Revolution, Paine was for a time secretary to the Congressional committee of foreign affairs. He received gifts of money from Congress and was given an estate at New Rochelle by the State of New York.

In 1787 he returned to Europe where he took an active part in the French Revolution. His reply to Burke's attack on the Revolution, *The Rights of Man,* had an enormous influence, and was finally suppressed while Paine was indicted for treason. Paine escaped to France where he was regarded with suspicion by Robespierre and narrowly escaped the guillotine.

In 1802 he was back in America, but found himself unpopular. His *Age of Reason* had shocked readers on both sides of the Atlantic. Paine died in New York in 1809. In 1819 his body was removed to England.

Montesquieu (1689-1755) was born near Bordeaux, on the property La Brede. He received a thorough education, and at twenty-seven became president of the parliament of Bor-

deaux. His first literary work was a series of letters satiriz-
ing social, political, ecclesiastical and literary follies of the
day.

Montesquieu travelled widely studying the people and
customs of the places he visited. The first expression of his
philosophy of history is found in his *The Grandeur and the
Decadence of the Romans*. His great book, *Spirit of the
Laws* was the work of several years. It deals with laws in
general and with forms of government, with taxation, with
manners and customs of a people and their dependence on
climatic conditions, with economic matters, and with religion. It is upon this great book that Montesquieu's fame
rests.

Adam Smith (1723-1790) was born in Scotland. He was educated at Glasgow University and at Oxford. In 1751 he became professor of logic at Glasgow. His first important publication was the *Theory of Moral Sentiments, 1759*. Smith
traveled on the continent in 1764-65, and was greatly influenced by the physiocratic school, many of whose leaders became his friends. His interest was now absorbed by economic questions, and his great book, *Wealth of Nations,*
appeared in 1776.

Thomas Robert Malthus (1766-1834) was born in Surrey. He
was educated at Cambridge, became a clergyman, and for
a short while had a pastorate in Surrey. He later turned to
teaching, choosing the fields of modern history and political
economy. His *Essay on Population, 1798*, was one of the
most influential books of the century.

John Stuart Mill (1806-1873) was the son of James Mill, who
was the co-founder with Jeremy Bentham of the Utilitarian
school of economic thought. Mill's education has been the
cause of great wonder. Under the guidance of his father, he
was reading Greek at the age of three, and by the age of
ten had read all the Latin and Greek authors commonly read
in the universities. At twelve he was studying with his
father, Adam Smith and Ricardo. He was very much under
the domination of his father until his marriage at the age of
forty-five. Mill earned his living in the India House where
he had charge of the company's relations with the native
states.

Although Mill was under the strict tutelage of his father,

his clear mind enabled him to advance beyond many of his father's views. He became a liberal, was interested in Socialism, and hoped for a more equal distribution of the products of labor. Mill did not finally accept the socialist position, but he influenced his age by his fresh consideration of the foundations of society. His most characteristic works are the reasoned and liberal essays on *Liberty, Utilitarianism, Thought on Parliamentary Reform,* and *Subjection of Women.* In 1865 Mill was elected to Parliament, where he was able to continue his advocacy of liberal reforms. He retired in 1868 to his cottage at Avignon where he died in 1873.

Auguste Comte (1798-1857) was born at Montpellier, France, where his father was in the government service. He early exhibited the rebellious spirit and intellectual acumen that distinguished him throughout his life time. In 1816 he began teaching in Paris. Here he was greatly influenced by Saint Simon. His great work *Positive Philosophy* was published during the years (1830-1842). After his twelve years' activity on the work, it was not a financial success and Comte continued a long struggle with poverty. At one time he received financial help from John S. Mill and other English scientists interested in his work.

During the revolutionary period of 1848, Comte founded the Positive Society, hoping it would be as powerful over the new revolution as was the Jacobin Club in 1789. In a lecture given in 1851, he explained his system in these words: "In the name of the past and of the future, the servants of humanity—both its philosophical and its practical servants—come forward to claim as their due the general direction of this world. Their object is to constitute at length a real Providence in all departments—moral, intellectual and material. Consequently they exclude once for all from political supremacy all the different servants of God—Catholic, Protestant, or Deist—as being behind hand and a cause of disturbance." Comte died of cancer on September 5, 1857.

Pierre Joseph Proudhon (1809-1865) was born at Besancon where his father earned his living as a cooper. Proudhon as a child revealed his brilliance and was given every opportunity to study. He became a printer and proof-reader and continued to educate himself. In 1838 he won a small pension by an essay on Sabbath observance. He was enabled to go to Paris where he wrote his first revolutionary work, an essay on property. From this time until his death he was a leader in the revolutionary movement. During the revolutionary period of 1848, Proudhon published a daily paper, *Representant du Peuple,* which was repeatedly suppressed and which finally caused his imprisonment for three years. During the reaction following 1848, he continued his revolutionary activity, until finally he had to flee to Brussels to escape further imprisonment. His persecutions undermined his health and he died when only fifty-six. Proudhon was the first to use the word *anarchy* to express the highest perfection of social organization. "Government of man by man in every form is oppression," he writes. "The highest perfection of society is found in the union of order and anarchy."

Mikhail Bakunin (1814-1876) was the leading Russian exponent of anarchism until his death. He early incurred the displeasure of the Czarist government, his estate was confiscated; and he was forced to live in exile. In 1849 he took part in the revolution in Dresden, was captured, and turned over to the Russian government which promptly exiled him to Siberia. After six years he escaped and spent the rest of his life in western Europe, where his influence can be seen today in the Anarchist and anarcho-syndicalist movements.

Charles Darwin (1809-1882) was born in Shrewsbury of wealthy and influential parents. He was educated at Cambridge and was intended for the church or medicine. He soon manifested an intense interest in science, however, and immediately after leaving Cambridge became a member of the expedition on the "Beagle", visiting the islands of the South Sea. It was during his four years on the "Beagle" that he gathered material for his *Origin of Species,* 1859. This epoch-making book was sold out on the first day of publication. Darwin's entire life was devoted to research.

Henry Thomas Buckle (1821-1862), author of the famous *History of Civilization,* was the son of a wealthy London merchant. Because of his delicate health, he was privately educated at home. He traveled extensively in Europe, northern Africa, and Palestine. Buckle planned to write a history of civilization in which he would show the general laws which govern the course of human progress and exemplify these laws through the histories of certain nations. The publication of the first volume of his history in 1857 made Buckle famous. The second appeared in 1861, and the third was in preparation when Buckle died suddenly in Damascus. Buckle's importance as pointed out by Leslie Stephen in his biography, lies in the fact that "he popularized the belief in the possibility of applying scientific treatment to historical problems."

Karl Marx (1818-1883) was born in Prussia. He was educated at the universities of Bonn and Berlin where he excelled in law, history, and philosophy. His study of Hegel combined with his concern for the masses led him to espouse a radical philosophy and he became the founder and greatest exponent of scientific socialism, the classic expression of which is found in *Capital,* 1867. Marx lived in London from 1849 until his death. With his friend Friederich Engels, he wrote the *Communist Manifesto* in 1847. He was also the organizer of the First International with headquarters in London and later in New York. Marx's writings are the great classics of socialist philosophy.

Emile Durkheim (1858———), the French philosopher, was born at Les Vosges. In 1892 Durkheim became professor at the University of Paris, where he has been a great influence on modern thought. The mental life of the individual, says Durkheim, comes principally from his social environment. Among his best known works are the *Method of Sociology,* 1894, and *Sociology and Philosophy,* 1924.

Ludwig Gumplowicz (1838-1909) was born in Poland. His Jewish birth made him acutely aware of the repressive nature of the government and he became active in the national and social struggle for liberation. He was active in the Polish uprising of 1863. In 1875 he became professor of law at the University of Graz where he remained until on realization that he was a victim of cancer he took his own life. He had a great influence on other sociologists. *Race and State,* published in Vienna in 1875, was his first book. This was followed by other studies, among which are *System of Sociology,* 1887, and *Sociology and Politics,* 1892.

Franz Oppenheimer (1864-   ) was born in Berlin. He studied medicine and practiced it for several years. His intense interest in political economy caused him finally to give up medicine however to devote himself to economics. In 1909 he began lecturing at the University of Berlin. He published several works expressing the liberal views which made him suspect among conservative circles. In 1919 he became Professor of Sociology at the University of Frankfort. The publication of *The State,* 1908, brought Oppenheimer international fame.

Nicolai Lenin (Vladimir Ilyitch Ulianov) (1870-1924) was born in Simbirsk, Russia. His early life was in the tradition of the Russian revolutionists; his student days at the University of Kazan were given over to radical activity, and he was soon caught and exiled to Siberia. After his exile, he lived in Western Europe, where he organized the Bolshevik Party and directed the revolutionary work of the party. In 1917 he returned to Russia, took charge of the propaganda of the Bolsheviks, and prepared the way for the November revolution. From the establishment of the dictatorship of the proletariat in November 1917 until his death, Lenin was engrossed with the problems of civil war, counter-revolution, allied intervention, and the economic development of the country.

Lenin is one of the great pamphleteers of history. Among his Marxian works are *The Development of Capitalism in Russia,* 1899; *What is To Be Done,* 1902, and *The State and Revolution,* 1917.

Leon Trotsky (1879-   ) was born in Russia, and was educated at the University of Odessa, where he entered the revolutionary movement. In 1898 he was exiled to Siberia, but escaped and went to England. In 1905 he was again in Russia, taking an active part in the revolution of that year. Again he was exiled and again he escaped. During the next few years Trotsky engaged in revolutionary activity in Switzerland, France, and for a short time in New York City. When the revolution of 1917 broke out, Trotsky returned to Russia where he became next in importance to Lenin in directing the course of the revolution. As People's Commissar of War, he organized the Red army which crushed foreign interventionists and the Whites. After the death of Lenin, Trotsky was gradually eclipsed, and he was finally exiled. He is now living in Mexico.

Like Lenin, Trotsky is a brilliant writer. He is the author of the monumental *History of the Russian Revolution*, 1932; *Literature and Revolution*, 1925, and *My Life*, 1929, besides numerous other books and pamphlets.

Waclaw Machajski was born in Russian Poland in 1866 and died in Moscow in 1926. While still a student he became active in the revolutionary movement. His first arrest was in 1892 when he was caught smuggling literature to revolting Polish workers. As a result he spent five years in the prisons of Warsaw and Moscow and six years in a sub-Arctic corner of northeastern Siberia. In 1903 he escaped and was in Russia during the Revolution of 1905. During the reaction following the revolution he was forced again to leave Russia, but 1917 found him back, engaged in editorial work for the Soviet government.

Machajski's works were published in Geneva in 1905. Most important are *The Intellectual Workers, The Bankruptcy of Nineteenth Century Socialism, The Bourgeois Revolution* and the *Workers' Cause*.

Peter Kropotkin (1842-1921) was born in Moscow of a family of princes. He was a member of the Corps of Pages attached to the Czar's household, but his liberal tendencies and questioning mind led to a study of the conditions of the peasants, and he became convinced that nothing short of revolution would solve the Russian peasant problem. He served as officer in a Cossack regiment, was director of a geographical expedition in Manchuria, and made notable contributions to the science of geography. Kropotkin felt that his real work was with the people, in their struggle to overthrow autocracy. At the age of thirty he gave up all other activities in order to engage in revolutionary work. He was in prison several times and was one of the few political prisoners ever to escape from the Peter and Paul Fortress. From 1874 he was the leader of the Anarchist movement, serving the cause by lecturing and writing. Because of his revolutionary activity he was unwelcome in all European countries. He made his home in England from 1886 until the Russian revolution in 1917, when he returned to Russia, where he lived quietly until his death.

Adolph Hitler (1889-   ) was born in Austria. He was the
son of a petty official. Hitler served in the German army,
achieving the rank of corporal. After the war, Hitler tried
to establish himself as draughtsman, but became absorbed
in the movement in opposition to the social democrats. He
founded the Nationalist Socialist Workers' Party in 1919,
a military force with the avowed purpose of overthrowing
the social democrat government. His first attempt was made
in Munich in November 1923. The revolt was crushed and
Hitler was sent to prison for five years. After eight months,
he was released and continued his activity unmolested. His
party grew in strength and power, drawing to it all disgruntled elements in Germany. In 1933 Hitler came to
power as fascist dictator of Germany.

Benito Mussolini (1883-   ) was the son of a revolutionary
blacksmith of the commune of Predappio. He grew up in a
socialistic community and absorbed the ideas of those about
him. He qualified as a teacher when 18 years old, but gave
up teaching to go to Switzerland apparently for further
study. Here he became active in the Socialist movement.
Later, back in Italy he was editor of the Socialist organ
Avanti. Until the outbreak of the World War, Mussolini
was strongly pacifist. In 1914 he made a complete about-
face, establishing a militaristic paper, *Il Popolo d'Italia*. He
served in the trenches, also, was wounded in 1917, and
thereafter continued to publish his paper. In 1919 he organized the first *Fascio di Combattimento,* the organization
through which he achieved control of the Italian government in 1922. He gathered all discontented elements of
post-war Italy into his civilian army, and, supported by the
reactionary nobles and capitalists, was able to crush all liberal and progressive movements and to launch Italy on her
campaign of aggression.

Herbert Spencer (1820-1903), the great English philosopher, was
born at Derby, the son of a liberal school master. Spencer
was a constant contributor to the *Westminster Review,*
where his ideas first found an audience. Spencer is the
philosopher of the scientific movement of the period. He
was a close friend of Darwin and Huxley. Spencer's work
appeared as follows: *Social Statics,* 1850; *Principles of Psy-*

chology, 1855; *Synthetic Philosophy,* and *Principles of Sociology,* 1896.

Max Weber (1864-1920), a pioneer in the study of the relation between capitalism and Protestantism, was born in Erfurt, Germany. He was educated to the law, but his interests were universal. He was at various times connected with the universities of Freiburg, Heidelberg, and Munich. He took a keen interest in German politics and was with the German delegation at Versailles in 1919. His *Protestant Ethic and the Spirit of Capitalism,* and *The Protestant Sects,* aroused great interest when they were published in Germany in 1904-1906. They were not translated into English until 1930, but Weber's influence had already made itself felt through the English writer, R. H. Tawney.

Werner Sombart (1863-   ) was born in Ermsleben, Germany. He studied at Pisa and Berlin. In 1888 he became secretary of the Chamber of Commerce in Bremen. His teaching career began in 1890 when he became associated with the University of Breslau. In 1917 he was appointed professor at the University of Berlin. His best known work is *Der Moderne Kapitalismus,* which first appeared in 1902 followed by an enlarged edition in 1916. In 1926 further material was added, bringing the history of capitalism down to the present day.

Vilfredo Pareto (1848-1923), the Italian economist, was educated in mathematics and was a practicing engineer for twenty years before turning his attention to economics. In 1893 he was appointed professor of political economy at Lausanne. He has been a strong influence in Italy, and is popularly regarded as the theorist of the fascists. He was introduced to the English speaking world in 1935, when his *Mind and Society* was first translated. He is the author of numerous studies in economics and sociology.

Lester Frank Ward (1841-1913) was born in Joliet, Illinois. He gave up his studies at the George Washington University to serve in the Union army during the Civil War. When war ended, he continued his education, being graduated in law in 1871. His interest in science caused him to associate himself with the United States Geological survey. Subsequently he became professor of botany at George Washing ton. His early works were concerned with plant life, but he soon became absorbed by a study of society. His *Dynamic Sociology,* first published in 1883, was reissued in 1897. There followed many authoritative studies of society; among them are *Psychic Factors of Civilization,* 1897; *Sociology and Economics,* 1899, and *Applied Sociology,* 1906.

William Graham Sumner (1840-1910) was born in Patterson, New Jersey. After graduation from Yale, he studied at Geneva and at Gottingen. He was ordained in the Episcopal Church and served as rector in New York City and at Morristown, New Jersey. From 1872-1909 he was professor of political and social science at Yale. His *Folkways* is a classic in its field.

Thorstein Veblen (1857-1929) is perhaps America's greatest economist. Born in Minnesota of Scandinavian parents, he was educated at Carleton College and later at Johns Hopkins, Yale, and Cornell. He was a teacher at Stanford University and later at the University of Missouri. The restricted life of the campus became unbearable, however, and in 1918, Veblen went to New York where he was associated with the *New School for Social Research.* As a profound and satirical critic of the capitalist system, he found himself always in conflict with authority, and his working life was seldom a happy one. Since 1920 his influence has grown steadily and he is recognized today as a great thinker and theorist. His most widely read book is *The Theory of the Leisure Class* 1899. He is the author of *The Theory of Business Enterprise* 1904; *The Instinct of Workmanship* 1914; *The Engineers and the Price System* 1921, and other works of social and economic interest. Veblen died in California in 1929.

Franklin H. Giddings (1855-1931) was one of the most influential of American sociologists. He began his career as editorial writer in Springfield, but eventually became professor of sociology at Columbia University. Among his best known works are *The Principles of Sociology,* 1896, and *The Scientific Study of Human Society,* 1924.

Rt. Hon. J. M. Robertson (1856-1934) the noted English philosopher was born on the Isle of Arran. At the age of thirteen he left school and when only twenty-two joined the staff of

the Edinburgh Evening News as leader writer. His long
life has been a record of achievement in criticism, rationalism, and liberalism. Among his best known works are
*Modern Humanists, Essays Toward a Critical Method, His-
tory of Free Thought,* and the *Evolution of States.*

Harry Elmer Barnes (1889-   ) was born in Auburn New
York where he still resides. He was educated at Syracuse
University and at Columbia and Harvard. He has had a
varied career as teacher, writer, lecturer. His literary output
is nothing short of stupendous. Beginning with his *Sociology Before Comte,* 1917, it ranges through prison reform,
causes of the world war, politics, and religion. His brilliant and comprehensive *History of Western Civilization,*
1935, is his latest work. He is also the author of more than
200 magazine articles and has contributed to the Encyclopedia of Social Sciences, and to the Encyclopedia Britan-
nica. Of late years he has been actively engaged in editorial
and column work for the Scripps-Howard newspapers.

Robert Morison MacIver (1882-   ) was born in Scotland and
was educated at the University of Edinburgh and at Oxford. He was lecturer on political science and sociology at
the University of Aberdeen until 1915 when he became associated with the University of Toronto. Since 1927 he has
been lecturer on political philosophy and sociology at Columbia. He is the author of several studies of sociology,
notably *The Modern State,* 1926, and *Society—Its Structure
and Changes,* 1931.

Dr. Melville Herskovitz (1895-   ) was born in Ohio. He was
educated at Northwestern University, Chicago and Columbia. Since 1927 he has been on the staff of Northwestern
University. In 1928-29 he carried on his anthropological
studies in Dutch Guiana and in 1931 in West Africa. He
has made notable contributions in the field of race and culture.

Malcolm M. Willey (1897-   ) was born in Portland, Maine.
He studied at Clark University and at Columbia. In 1923
he became instructor in sociology at Dartmouth. Since 1927
he has been associated with the University of Minnesota.
He was one of the co-workers with the President's Research
Committee on Social Trends 1931. He is a contributor to

sociological journals and co-author of several books on sociological subjects, among which his *Readings in Sociology* (with Wilson D. Wallis) is among the best known.

Edward A. Ross (1866-   ), the well-known sociologist, was born in Illinois. He was educated at the Johns Hopkins University and the University of Berlin. He has been lecturer at the Universities of Indiana, Cornell, Stanford, Nebraska, Wisconsin, Harvard, and Chicago. He is the author of numerous books on social problems and is contributor to economic and sociological journals. Among his works are *Social Control*, 1901; *The Foundations of Sociology*, 1905; *Social Psychology*, 1908, and *The Principles of Sociology*, 1920.

William F. Ogburn (1886-   ) was born in Georgia. He studied at Mercer University and at Columbia University. He has been professor of sociology at the University of Chicago since 1927. From 1930-33 he was director of research, President's Research Committee on Social Trends. In 1933 he was appointed a member of the Consumers Advisory Board, N R A. He is the author of *Social Change*, 1922; *The Social Sciences*, 1927, and other studies.

Charles Horton Cooley (1864-1929) was a graduate of the University of Michigan, and later professor of sociology there. He was a quiet, unvigorous writer, but his influence has been extensive. He is the author of *Human Nature and the Social Order*, 1902; *Social Organization*, 1909; *Social Process*, 1918, and *Life and the Student*, 1927.

Wilson D. Wallis (1886-   ) was born in Forest Hill, Maryland. He was Rhodes scholar at Oxford, 1907-1910. Returning to America, he continued his studies at the University of Pennsylvania. He has been professor of anthropology at the University of Minnesota since 1923. He is the author of *Messiahs—Christian and Pagan*, 1918; *Introduction to Anthropology*, 1926; *Culture and Progresss*, 1930, and other well-known scientific works.

John Dewey (1859-   ) was born in Burlington, Vermont, and was educated at the state university and at the Johns Hopkins University. He is one of America's greatest philosophers and has had wide influence on contemporary thought. Since 1904 he has been professor of philosophy at Columbia University, except for a year at the University of Pekin

(1920), and a year at the University of Paris (1930). Among his many books are the influential *School and Society*, 1899; *How We Think*, 1909, and *Human Nature and Conduct*, 1922.

Huntington Cairns was born in Baltimore in 1904 and graduated in law from the University of Maryland where he teaches Taxation. He is the author of *Law and the Social Sciences* published in the *International Library of Psychology, Philosophy and Scientific Method*. For this book he was given the Baltimore Civic award for the year 1935 in recognition of his contribution to the professions and science. He published in 1936 a book on Maryland Taxation; he is now at work on his third book *The Theory of Legal Science*. In 1934 he was appointed Special Legal Adviser to the United States Treasury to advise the government with respect to the importation of foreign books, and objects of art. He is a member of the Baltimore law firm of Piper, Carey and Hall.

Graham Wallas (1858-1932), the English sociologist, was for years one of the leaders of the Fabian society. His *Life of Francis Place*, 1898 was one of the first studies of the English working class movement. Wallas was professor of political science at the University of London. His studies, *Human Nature in Politics*, 1914, and *Our Social Heritage*, 1921 are classics in their field.

Frank Hamilton Hankins (1877-   ) was born in Ohio and was educated at Baker University and at Columbia. He has taught the social sciences at Clark University, Amherst, Columbia and Cornell, and has been professor of sociology at Smith College since 1922. *The Racial Basis of Civilization*, 1926, and *An Introduction to the Study of Society*, 1928, are his best known works.

John Strachey (1901-   ), the son of John St. Loe Strachey, was educated at Eton and at Oxford. He became a member of the Labour Party and was elected to the House of Commons in 1929. In 1931 he resigned from the Labour Party and has since moved steadily left in politics. He has lectured widely and with much success in the United States where the effort to deport him proved excellent publicity. His books are popular in both England and America. His most recent publications are *The Coming Struggle for*

Power, 1932; *The Nature of the Capitalist Crisis,* 1935, and
The Theory and Practice of Socialism, 1936.

Stuart Chase (1888-   ), born in New Hampshire, was graduated from Harvard in 1910. Since 1922 he has been associated with the Labor Bureau, Inc. He is a frequent contributor to magazines and has written many books on the
contemporary state of capitalism in the United States.
Among his most popular and widely discussed books are
The Tragedy of Waste, 1925; *Men and Machines,* 1929, and
A New Deal, 1932.

Max Eastman (1883-   ) was born in Canandaigia, New York.
He was educated at Williams College and Columbia University and served as an assistant in the Philosophy Department at the latter institution. He was one of the founders
and the first editor of *The Masses,* which became *The Liberator* during the World War. He is the author of many
books and translator of the works of Leon Trotsky. Some
of his better-known books are: *Enjoyment of Poetry, Sense
of Humor, Marx and Lenin, The Science of Revolution,
Artists in Uniform* and *Enjoyment of Laughter.*

Sidney Hook (1902-   ) is Chairman of the Department of
Philosophy at New York University. He was educated at
the College of the City of New York and at Columbia
University. During 1928-30 he held the Guggenheim Fellowship in Philosophy for study in Germany and Russia.
He has contributed to various philosophical and Marxian
periodicals and is the author, among several books, of the
much discussed *Toward the Understanding of Karl Marx*
and *From Hegel to Marx.*

V. F. Calverton (1900-   ) was born in Baltimore and educated at the Johns Hopkins University. In 1923 he founded
the Modern Quarterly, later The Modern Monthly, a magazine devoted to a radical revaluation of American culture.
His best known books are *The Newer Spirit* 1925; *The
Liberation of American Literature* 1932, and *The Passing
of the Gods* 1934. He is also the author of two volumes
of fiction, his latest being *The Man Inside,* a sociological
novel. In addition, he is the Editor of several books, and
a contributor to various periodicals.

Max Nomad is the pen-name of a native of Poland who received his education at the University of Vienna. He is now a resident of the United States.

His political philosophy was shaped under the influence of Marx's class-struggle theory; of the French syndicalists; of the Polish-Russian revolutionary thinker, Waclaw Machajski; and of certain concepts of Ludwig Gumplowicz; Vilfredo Pareto ("circulation of elites"); and of Robert Michels' writings about the oligarchical tendencies in human society.

He is the author of *Rebels and Renegades* (Macmillan, 1932) and of various monographs dealing with the history of revolutionary movements and ideas.

Major Clifford Hugh Douglas (1877-   ) is of Scotch ancestry. He was educated at Cambridge University and has carried out engineering contracts in Canada, South America, India, and the British Isles. Soon after the World War Douglas's proposals known as Social Credit were accepted by a number of intellectuals in the National Guilds movement, and an independent movement was launched. Since 1932 Social Credit has been prominent in the British political consciousness. Major Douglas's theories are expounded in several works, among them *Economic Democracy,* 1919; *Social Credit,* 1924, and *Warning Democracy,* 1932.

his education at the University of Vienna. He is now a resident of the United States.

His political philosophy was shaped under the influence of Marx's class-struggle theory; of the French syndicalist; of the Polish-Russian revolutionary thinker, Waclaw Machajski; and of certain concepts of Ludwig Gumplowicz; Vilfredo Pareto ("circulation of elites"); and of Robert Michels' writings about the oligarchical tendencies in human society.

He is the author of Rebels and Renegades (Macmillan, 1933) and of various monographs dealing with the history of revolutionary movements and ideas.

Major Clifford Hugh Douglas (1879-   ) is of Scotch ancestry. He was educated at Cambridge University and has carried out engineering contracts in Canada, South America, India, and the British Isles. Soon after the World War Douglas's proposals known as Social Credit were accepted by a number of intellectuals in the National Guilds movement, and an independent movement was launched. Since 1932 Social Credit has been prominent in the British political consciousness. Major Douglas's theories are expounded in several works, among them Economic Democracy, 1919; Social Credit, 1924, and Warning Democracy, 1934.